39439   HV
     8579

Teeters   T4

"...Hang by the neck..."

Date Due

CHABOT
COLLEGE
LIBRARY

25555 Hesperian Boulevard
Hayward, California 94545

PRINTED IN U.S.A.

"...HANG BY THE NECK..."

"...HANG BY THE NECK..."

The Legal Use of Scaffold and Noose, Gibbet, Stake, and Firing Squad from Colonial Times to the Present

By

NEGLEY K. TEETERS

Professor Emeritus, Temple University
Visiting Professor, Hartwick College
Oneonta, New York

In Collaboration with

JACK H. HEDBLOM

Staff Sociologist, Pennsylvania Prison Society
Philadelphia, Pennsylvania

With a Foreword by

Thomas M. McDade
Scotland Yard
Purchase, New York

CHARLES C THOMAS • PUBLISHER
Springfield • Illinois • U.S.A.

Published and Distributed Throughout the World by
CHARLES C THOMAS • PUBLISHER
BANNERSTONE HOUSE
301-327 East Lawrence Avenue, Springfield, Illinois, U.S.A.
NATCHEZ PLANTATION HOUSE
735 North Atlantic Boulevard, Fort Lauderdale, Florida, U.S.A.

*With THOMAS BOOKS careful attention is given to all details of
manufacturing and design. It is the Publisher's desire to present books
that are satisfactory as to their physical qualities and artistic possibilities
and appropriate for their particular use. THOMAS BOOKS will be true
to those laws of quality that assure a good name and good will.*

Printed in the United States of America
A-2

FOREWORD

W e have long passed the time when history is recounted in a description of wars and battles or the reigns of kings, queens or dictators. To the military, political and economic history, we have added social or cultural history, describing all the minutae of every day life. It is from the social customs of a period that the larger events get a sense of depth; they are thrown into relief by the lights and darks of the times. Classical or conventional historians are indebted to scholars, collectors, even hobbyists who accumulate a vast amount of detail on one small segment of the local, social or informal practices of an earlier day. The books they write or papers they read are special, narrow and detailed, but they cast light into strange corners which are unrevealed by the larger studies. There is often an air of nostalgia in these studies which might relate the story of the rise and decline of the general store, the antics of the patent medicine business or the pseudo-science of phrenology or spiritualism. It may be merely quaint in a study of folk songs, children's games or antique glass. It touches on the macabre, the bizarre and the shameful when it turns to imprisonment, torture and execution.

In this volume Professor Teeters and Mr. Hedblom have explored the customs and practices of our legal executions. From prison records, newspapers, broadsides, pamphlets and ephemera of the period they have dredged us a great amount of information on the dark side of our criminal process when it undertakes to carry out the dread sentence of the community. The authors are opposed to capital punishment, but their book is no polemic against it in the usual sense. More as Charles Duff with *A Handbook for Hanging* they let their recital of cases carry its own conviction; its cause requires no special pleading. The reader will come to his own conclusion when he reads this bloody record.

That record is long, sordid and painful. Though we inherited our judicial customs and mores from our British forebears, we did

v

not always follow nor long continue their practices. The colonial and frontier atmosphere imposed its own special circumstances as well as its own spirit of independence which was soon reflected in our own practices and customs. The bloody practice of quartering never took hold here; pressing to death or *peine forte et dure* claimed but one victim, and burning and gibbeting were infrequent compared with practice in England. We abandoned public executions in many states before Great Britain did and modernized our trial procedure by permitting the accused to testify long before England reluctantly changed its practice.

Little is said of the legal or trial procedures which lead up to the execution; once the sentence has been imposed, however, the authors take us through every step in the painful process, reporting episodes of pain, horror, humor and pathos. The execution of a human being by society is a "social event" as truly as is an inauguration or election. Even when executions no longer were public, the manners, means and customs were an expression of society's feeling about the event. Here we sit up the last night with the condemned, we see him measured for his shroud, inspected by the executioner to judge how long to drop the prisoner through the trap. We hear the hammer of the scaffold going up, the reading of the death warrant, the parade to the execution grounds in a cart with the prisoner sitting on his coffin, the military companies providing both a guard and a festive and colorful air to the proceedings, the mounting tension at the scaffold with the harangues of the preachers speaking to crowds greater than have ever filled their churches; then perhaps a speech by the prisoner himself, sometimes defiant, but more frequently contrite and selfcondemning. The whole mechanism of the fatal drop, from the technique of tying the knot to the invention of the hanging machine which yanked the victim upward, is covered, not omitting the ghastly consequences of ignorance or ineptness of amateur executioners who bungled their job. No matter is too small a detail to be overlooked: the material and construction of the rope, including the preferable number of strands and the required weighting of it to take out all stretch before use, the British preference for a ring instead of a loop, the length of the drop and the anatomizing which became an added terror to the mind of the simple prisoner.

In our great search for our past and our origins we are setting up minature "villages" consisting of an orderly collection of buildings representative of the eighteenth and nineteenth centuries. Fully furnished and staffed with weavers at their looms, blacksmiths at the forge and the inn staff bewigged and buckled in traditional dress, these sterile exhibits give us a faint taste of a vanished age. Spick and span in clean bright "Colonial" colors of pale blue and mulberry, they accent the craft, the cozy and the cute. Here in the East, at least, none has put up a gallows; the furthest they have gone is the stocks and a ducking stool. The writers of this book do not see their history with the same nostalgic eye as the builders of these quaint hamlets. They see and report it with a bluntness that could be mistaken for callousness. But a hanging was not quaint; it was a grim, solemn and sometimes gory event. There is no need to editorialize on what they report; the events speak for themselves. This book recaptures much valuable information which will find its place in the history of our early days.

THOMAS M. McDADE
Scotland Yard
Purchase, New York

INTRODUCTION

The debt we owe to the work of Thomas M. McDade in his *The Annals of Murder: A Bibliography of Books and Pamphlets on American Murders from Colonial Times to 1900* (Norman, University of Oklahoma Press, 1961) is inestimable. It is the great pioneering work in its field and to it every student or casual reader in the field must turn. It is authoritative, well organized, and succinct. Not least of all, it reflects Mr. McDade's admirable insights and sense of humor in grim contexts. It not only can but must be recommended to all who pursue the subject.

We also take this means of expressing to Mr. McDade's publishers, the University of Oklahoma Press, our gratitude for their permission to make use of Mr. McDade's book in the compilation of our own. Without this permission, the character of our book must have been greatly altered.

In fact, our work had its inception after the publication of the McDade compilation and, with the aid of material accumulated by and incorporated in Olive Woolley Burt's companion-piece, *AMERICAN MURDER BALLADS,* (Oxford University Press, 1958), it grew into its own peculiar and unique shape. The above mentioned works called attention to the far-flung crime patterns of earlier days, the first not only by means of pamphlets, but also gallows-side confessions and sermons as well, and the second through the crude, sad, and sometimes bawdy contemporary ballads.

The phrase "man's inhumanity to man" is admittedly hackneyed; yet it can be legitimately used in any discussion of or treatise on capital or corporal punishment. Throughout the centuries of recorded history the casual nature of human brutality, whether as an integral part of tribal sanctions or more deliberately affirmed by legal codes, can scarcely be surveyed without a feeling of repugnance.

Many books, monographs and pamphlets have been written on

capital punishment, but few that are restricted to any specific technique of administering the supreme penalty. One exception, written in this country, is that by August Mencken, *By the Neck* (Hastings House, 1942) which has also been of value to the authors. Several British books deal with the overall subject of the death penalty, and since up to the year 1966, hanging was the sole method employed, we find much on this specific subject in their literature.

Additional sources for such a study as this are varied and, in many instances, difficult of attainment. The nice, neat, and complete original sources which are the scientific delight of the researchers are elusive and sparse. The availability of court dockets and what they do not contain are frustrating. In some jurisdictions and in some county and state archives they are almost non-existent. Those that survive are often musty, torn, ragged, weathered, yellowed and soiled, the inevitable results of neglect. In all too many jurisdictions the records are filled with wide gaps and often discrepancies in the news accounts of crimes and hangings. In a few instances the archives contain a governor's pardon for the victim although a newspaper story describes the hanging, embellished with an account of his funeral.

The many librarians and local historians who have aided in assembling the data that comprise this work deserve special mention. They are identified with local, county and state historical societies as well as colleges and universities. Many went beyond the call of professional duty to furnish photostats from rare documents and newspapers and to run down elusive information that proved of great interest and value. Many public officials such as archivists, sheriffs, and wardens of prisons, were also most helpful. Where possible their names are identified with the various items used.

Some financial assistance for pursuing the research for this work came from the Faculty Research Committee Fund of Temple University and for this assistance the writers wish to express their appreciation.

This work, in reality, is only a beginning. A vast amount of research in this dismal realm awaits those who might, like the writers, find the field exciting, despite its macabre nature. Each state has its legends, folklore and ballads relative to murder, and to hanging. All too often they have not been collected even by local historians. Yet these stories, whether of fact or mingled with fiction, call for serious study and investigation. This book purports to be something of a pioneer in the social practice of hanging and its companion methods of a bygone day. The fact that as this work goes to press, more stories and episodes are being called to the writers' attention from the vast areas of the country, is ample proof that sequels or supplemental works are possible.

Because of the many incidents, widely scattered in time and place, and sometimes not fully substantiated and verified, there can be no doubt that errors have crept into the narrative. We have been cautious and careful to check when this was possible, but many cases have come to our attention by somewhat nebulous routes. Whatever the error, the writers alone assume responsibility. We place no blame on our informants.

Acknowledgement is here recorded to persons who have aided in various ways—suggesting or furnishing material on certain cases, assisting in checking sources in specific instances, and, in general lending encouragement. Among these are Edwin Powers, Deputy Commissioner of Correction of Massachusetts, author of *Crime and Punishment in Early Massachusetts,* (Boston: Beacon Press, 1966); Dr. William S. Barker, Great Falls, Va. for use of his excellent *Bibliotheca Criminalis et Juridica;* and to Charles Zibulka of Spokane, Washington for his assistance in furnishing us many data relative to the subject. These and many others have been credited for their assistance in the various footnotes. It is only hoped that no one who has helped the writers has been overlooked. In such cases, apologies are extended at this point and in this manner.

Finally, we are further indebted to Thomas M. McDade for writing the Foreword.

N.K.T.
J.H.H.

CONTENTS

Page

Foreword—THOMAS M. MCDADE v

Introduction vii

Chapter

I. HANGING AS A SOCIAL PRACTICE 3

     ✧ A Few Introductory Remarks 3

     First Hangings in the Country 7

     Hanging of the Quakers in Massachusetts 10

     The Youngest Victims of the Tree 12

     Hangings in the Streets and Squares 19

     Further Descriptions of Public Hangings 30

     Types of Early Gallows 46

     Attitudes of Victims at the "Tree" 47

     Status of the Hangman 51

     Places of Execution 59

     Superstitions Surrounding the Hanging Tree 63

     Bungling at the Tree 66

     Pardons, Reprieves and Commutations of

         Sentence of Death 71

     Sermons Delivered at the Tree 77

     Confessions and Gallows-side Speeches 82

II. EXCESSIVE RETRIBUTION AND PURITANICAL

     ZEAL IN EARLY DAYS 87

     Gibbeting 87

     Other Frightful Punishments 93

     Pressed to Death (The Case of Giles Corey) 98

     Burning at the Stake 102

     The Last Legal Burning in the United States 109

     Early Hangings for Sex Crimes 110

     Early Mass Hangings—Negro Conspiracies 114

     A Mass Hanging—The Wheelbarrow Men

         of Philadelphia—1789 118

     More Females Hanged in the Early Days 120

     The Mournful Story of Elizabeth Wilson's Betrayal 123

Chapter	Page
III. THE TREATMENT OF WITCHES	126
Hanged Not Burned	126
The Roster of Those Hanged for Witchcraft	132
The Salem Victims of the Tree	136
IV. HANGINGS INSIDE—FAR FROM THE MADDING THRONGS	151
Public Hangings Gradually Outlawed	151
Is Hanging Painful?	153
Improved Gallows in the Private Era	159
Buckshot and Water-trap Scaffolds	164
Hangmen's Ropes	167
The Sad Story of Bungling at the Gallows	173
Gallows Tidbits	181
Last Requests of the Condemned	184
Dress at the Gallows	187
Mass Killers	190
The Infamous Mudgett—Alias H. H. Holmes	192
Edward H. Rulloff—Professor Edward Leurio	195
The Robert McConaghy Case— Huntingdon, Pennsylvania	199
Samuel Mohawk—Cornplanter Indian— Butler, Pennsylvania	200
The Anton Probst Case—Philadelphia	201
Wife-killer James-Lisemba—California	203
Revenge or Spite Murders	203
The Tom Dula Saga of North Carolina	206
V. A WIDE RANGE OF CASES	210
The Role of the Medical Men and the Hanging Practice	210
The Ballad of Julian	218
Fictional Hanging Cases	224
The Gallows—Almost	228
The Classic Case of Will Purvis—Mississippi	228
An English Counterpart—John Lee	231
Strange Cases Not So Fortunate	232
The Stephen Boorn Case—Vermont	234
The Strange Case of Farnsworth	237
William Freeman Comings—New Hampshire	238
Those Who Cheated the Gallows	241

Chapter *Page*

VI. MURDER FOR GREED, ANGER AND LUST................266
    The Smutty Nose Murder Case...................266
    The Nelson E. Wade Case of Pennsylvania.........268
    The Knapp-Crowinshield Case:
        Greed on a High Level......................269
    The Col. George Davenport Murder—Illinois........272
    Insurance Policies and Greed:
        The Hayward-Ging Case—Minnesota...........273
    A Triple Hanging—The Thayer Brothers
        of Buffalo, New York......................275
    The Murder of Thomas Walsh—
        Willow City, North Dakota—1902..............277
    William Udderzook—Pennsylvania.................278
    The Hazardous Plight of Early Peddlers: Jost Folhaber,
        the German Peddler of Mahoney Mountain—
        Pennsylvania 279
    The Plight of Some Other Peddlers...............282
    The Postboy Murder—Ohio—1825...............284
    The Rosensweig-Blank Case—Pennsylvania—1893....285
    Other Cases of Greed..........................285
    Greed and Bank Thefts.........................286
    New Hampshire Murders and Their Ballads.........288
    Josie Langmaid—Pembroke Schoolgirl—1875.......289
    The Daniel Farmer Case—Amherst,
        New Hampshire—1822.....................291
    The Almy-Abbott-Christie Warden Case...........293

VII. A FURTHER POTPOURRI OF CASES...................300
    Frankie Silver—North Carolina—1833............300
    The Roxalana Druse Case—Herkimer, New York.....303
    Bathsheba Spooner, Beautiful, Disgruntled Colonial
        Wife—Worcester, Massachusetts................305
    Bridget Dergan, New Jersey Slavey and Her
        Evil Deed—Hanged 1867....................307
    Ann Carson, Quaker City Coquette...............307
    Professor Webster—Dr. Parkman:
        Harvard University—1849-1850................310

Chapter   *Page*

The Boyington Tragedy—Mobile, Alabama—1835. . . .313
A Strange Civil War Murder and Hanging—
    Dr. David M. Wright—Norfolk, Virginia 317
The Jesse Strang Case—Albany, New York—1827. . . .319
The Talberts of Maryville, Missouri 320
Women of the Street and Murder 321
    The Ellen Jewett Case 321
    Kesiah Stowe—Philadelphia Victim—1823 322
    The John Millian-Julia Bulette Case—
        Virginia City, Nevada—1868 322
    Other Such Cases 323
Murder in Church Belfries 324
Trunk or Barrel Murders that Ended in Hanging 327
A Nun Murder in a Hospital .329
The Kidnaping Scourge 329
The Pearl Bryan Tragedy—Ohio and
    Kentucky—1897 337
The Tragedy of Mountain Meadows and
    the Execution of John D. Lee 339
Some Classic Cases 342

VIII.   THE POISONERS 344
How Murderous are Females? 344
Some Classical Cases 347
Triangle Murder Cases 352
The Ann Simpson (North Carolina) and
    Ann Bilansky (Minnesota) Poison Cases 355
The Harris-Hellum Case—Monroe, Louisiana 359
The Cannon-Nettles Case—Goosecreek,
    South Carolina 361
The Amasa Fuller Case—Indiana—1820 361
The Jereboam O. Beauchamp Case—Kentucky, 1826. .364
The Fisk-Stokes Affair—New York City—1872 365

IX.   HANGINGS IN THE INTEREST OF NATIONAL SECURITY 368
Necessity for National Security 368
John Brown's Body—At Harper's Ferry 373
The Hanging of Thirty-eight Sioux Indians—
    Mankato, Minnesota—December 26, 1862 375

Chapter *Page*

The Fort Sam Houston Hangings—1917. 379
The Hanging of the Lincoln Conspirators in
    Washington, D. C. 381
The Commandant of Andersonville Prison—
    Capt. Henry Wirz. 389
The Hanging of Twenty Mollie Maguires
    in Pennsylvania 390
Charles Julius Guiteau, Presidential Assassin. 393
The Hanging of the Chicago Anarchists—
    November 11, 1887. 396
"Hanging" Judge Isaac C. Parker, Nemesis of the
    Outlaws of the Indian Country. 398
Banditry in Early California. .404
The Great San Francisco Fire and the
    Gaspipe Murders. 408

X. THE TREE EMBELLISHED BY BALLAD AND ALLUSION. 411
The Hanging Ballad. 411
The Green-Wyatt Case. 411
The Ashland, Kentucky Tragedy. 413
The Case of Reuben Dunbar, "The Murderer"—
    New York State—1851. 416
Charles Birger—Prohibition Era Gangster
    and His Ballad. 418
Ballad of the Braswell Brothers—Tennessee. 419
The Ballads of Thomas Duffy, Mollie Maguire
    of the Pennsylvania Coal Fields. 422
Marine James Bird—"Fighter with Perry"—1813. 423
Other Quaint Ballads. 426
The Tree in Prose and Poetry. 432

XI. THE DRIFT AWAY FROM CAPITAL PUNISHMENT. 440
Ancient and Classical Methods of Inflicting
    the Death Penalty. 440
Introduction of Electrocution. 446
How Effective is the Death Penalty?. 455

Index of Selected Names. 463
Index of Subjects. 473

"...HANG BY THE NECK..."

Chapter I

HANGING AS A SOCIAL PRACTICE

And if a man have committed a sin worthy of death, and
he be put to death, and thou hang him on a tree; his body
shall not remain all night upon the tree, but thou shalt
surely bury him the same day; for he that be hanged is
accursed of God. (First mention of hanging in the BIBLE,
DEUTERONOMY, 30: 22-23.)

A FEW INTRODUCTORY REMARKS

THE SOCIAL HISTORIAN has an obligation to investigate the mean,
the tawdry, the tragic and the violent, as well as the heroic, in
the doings of man. Here we examine hangings. As part of the
doings of man, they are deserving of examination. The lessons
in them are a part of the fabric of history and should not be lost.

The hanging, or fatal, tree, or gallows, has been the subject of
story and ballad throughout the ages; from the tale of Sam Hall,
the unrepentent murderer, to Tom Dooley (Tom Dula in reality),
the hypotenuse of the eternal triangle, it may be estimated that
some 16,000 persons have legally been hanged by the neck until
dead. It is their cases that are the subject of our tract—those persons legally executed. We do not include lynchings or vigilante
hangings.

Despite the fact that hanging has been used as a means of
eliminating criminals for over one thousand years, and is even
mentioned in the Old Testament,[1] it would seem to take a ballad
to memorialize a hanging. Certainly most of the executions, by
whatever method, have been forgotten by all but a few social
historians who have relied on ballads, published confessions, or

---

[1]The first person recorded to be hanged—Haman (Esther 7:9-10): . . . Behold also,
the gallows fifty cubits high, which Haman hath made for Mordecai . . . And the
king Ahasueras said, Hang him thereon. So they hanged Haman on the gallows that
he had prepared for Mordecai. Then was the king's wrath pacified.

3

other broadsides, to preserve the events. The general public knows little of the most spectacular hanging orgies that have occurred in the country despite the work of some antiquarians and biblio- philes who have tried to preserve some of the most notorious and famous murders. Some of these have ended in hangings, and so constitute part of the subject dealt with here.

It would be safe to assume that the public is unaware of the hanging of thirty-eight Sioux Indians at Mankato, Minnesota on December 16, 1862. They were hanged to atone for the unholy massacre of hundreds of white settlers. See Chapter IX. Even those hangings that have occurred in relation to events of national tragedy are clouded in myth and misunderstanding. It is well known that the conspirators in the Lincoln assassination were hanged at Washington, D.C., July 7, 1865. What is not generally known is the feeling of national hysteria or the speed of imposed justice that characterized the times and the trial (see page 375-9 for a more complete description).

What percentage of the American public is familiar with the climate of opinion surrounding the trial and subsequent hangings of the Haymarket Anarchists at Chicago, November 11, 1887? Or the Molly Maguires hanged in the anthracite coal regions of Pennsylvania during the 1870's?[2]

Earlier in history, hysteria has played an important part in the practice of hanging. Despite the widespread notion that persons were burned at the stake during the colonial witch trials in the latter part of the seventeenth century, the victims were hanged.[3] In short, hanging has been a part of this country's culture since the founding of the colonies, yet the American people remain quite vague about that era of our social history that is associated with the practice of hanging. Persons have been hanged for burglary, highway robbery, piracy, counterfeiting, arson, infanti- cide, rape, horse stealing, violations of exile and other offenses considered heinous at the time and place, yet nowhere has this story been told in its entirety.

We mentioned 16,000 as an estimate of the number of persons hanged in this country. This is merely an estimate—the figure

[2]For further description of these cases, see Chapter IX.
[3]See Chapter III

may well be hundreds off, or even thousands, one way or the other. No census has been taken of those executed, let alone hanged. Within the State of Pennsylvania, we know that slightly more than 260 persons were publicly hanged from 1682 to 1834, when such public hangings were declared illegal. From 1834 to 1915 (the year when electrocution was introduced), 441 persons were hanged in the county jails. Hangings still exist. From 1930 to 1963, statistics indicate that approximately 100 hangings have occurred in states where the penalty still pertains. The state of Washington alone accounts for half of these, 47 out of 98.

At this time, legalized hanging is the method of administering capital punishment six states: Delaware, Idaho, Kansas, Montana, New Hampshire, and Washington. In some cases, the federal government and armed forces are active participants. The United States Navy has not executed a person since 1849; whereas the army and air force have executed 160 persons since 1942. The period from 1942-50 witnessed 148 of that number, with three each in 1954, 55, 57 and one each in 1958, 59 and 61 (*National Prisoner Statistics. Executions, 1930-1963*. No. 34, May, 1964).

(Through the years, many were not suspended from a tree; they were hanged from a man-made tree: the scaffold.) While the majority of hanging trees were to be found in the area west of the Mississippi, there were several tree hangings in the eastern states. One of the earliest of these tree hangings was the hanging of a so-called Salem witch, Bridget Bishop, hanged on June 10, 1692, "from the branch of a great oak tree" (as reported by Marion L. Starkey: *The Devil in Massachusetts,* New York, Knopf, 1949, p. 154; reprinted by Doubleday, 1961, p. 156). Another, John McFall, hanged at Uniontown, Fayette County, Pennsylvania, met his death on a "sycamore tree" on March 7, 1795.

A news item from Jonesboro, Washington County, Tennessee, states that the early place set aside for hangings was called "Hanging Hollow" and was reputed to be haunted—the victims of the area dangled from a locust tree. It is further stated that this "spooky place" was near the town on "Boones Creek Road" (*Herald Tribune,* June 5, 1963, courtesy Mr. William Shannon, Carbondale, Pennsylvania).

In fact, the first three hangings which took place in Scott County (Georgetown County Seat), Kentucky, were from trees. All three were slaves—they were hanged in a little thicket not far from town.[4]

From the colonization of this country until the mid-nineteenth century, hangings were public affairs. That is, they took place in front of whatever elements of the local populace craved to attend. In many instances, especially in the larger centers of population, a cart would be drawn under the gallows, and a rope thrown around the neck of the condemned, who stood at the back of the cart or sat on his own coffin, which was often carried in the cart also. At the appropriate moment, after the ceremonies were concluded, the cart would be pulled from under the victim, and he would be left to strangle. This was sometimes referred to as "dancing in the air." In time, more workmanlike gallows were devised by "ingenious" inventors. These made the hanging more precise, but no less macabre (some are described in Chapter IV).

With the slowly emerging sensitivity of the American people, unevenly developed though it was, laws were enacted calling for less public or private hangings. They were to occur within the county jails or state prisons—in the county jails, the hangings could take place either in the courtyard or in the building proper, an important provision, as we shall see later.

The last public hanging in England took place on May 26, 1868, outside Newgate Prison, in London.

> The person hanged was Michael Barrett "author of the Fenian explosion at Clerkenwell" as stated by William Andrews in his *Bygone Punishments* (London, 1899, 38). He further states that the first person hanged within a prison was Thomas Wells, murderer of a Mr. Walsh, station-master of Dover on August 13, 1869, at Maidstone.

The last public hanging (legal) in the United States took place in Owensboro, Kentucky, on August 14, 1936, when a twenty-two-year-old Negro named Ramsey Bethea was executed before an estimated crowd of 20,000 for criminally assaulting a seventy-year-old woman. It was in 1938 that Kentucky got around to

---

[4]So stated by S. G. Gaines: *History of Scott County,* Georgetown, 1905, 383 f.; they were Nancy on Sept. 30, 1808, and Martha and Burrell in a double hanging on Oct. 8, 1839.

abolishing public hanging. Despite Kentucky, public hangings were abolished in some states in this country many years before England put an end to them. Pennsylvania was the first when, on April 10, 1834, the law was passed providing that hangings be dispatched in county jails. New Jersey passed similar legislation on March 5, 1835; New York State on May 9 of the same year; Massachusetts on November 4 (further implemented in February, 1836), and New Hampshire on January 13, 1837.

What constitutes a private rather than a public hanging or execution is a moot point. Perhaps the best measure is the legal wordings of procedure and number of persons attending the affair. Fortunately, there are no totally private or "star chamber" legal executions in this country. The term private is relative and as it is understood here, only those may attend who, by law of a specific state, are so entitled. The place of the execution is also specified by law and is away from the prying eyes of the general public. Executions today, whether carried out by electrocution (twenty-one states, including the District of Columbia) by lethal gas (ten states), by hanging (six states), or by shooting (Utah only, and then with the option of hanging by the condemned), may be too public to suit some people. Objections have been lodged against too many witnesses, reporters, spectators invited by the wardens or sheriffs.

> Even in these modern times, executions can scarcely be regarded as strictly "private." When Mrs. Elizabeth Ann ("Ma") Duncan was gassed in the San Quentin death chamber on August 8, 1962, fifty-seven persons clustered around the glass-enclosed capsule to see the woman gasp her way into eternity. She had been convicted of hiring two drifters to kill her daughter-in-law. They, too, were gassed.

FIRST HANGINGS IN THE COUNTRY

It is difficult to determine the first person legally hanged in the United States, due to the dearth of colonial records. We have found the case of Daniell Frank, hanged "in the Colony" of Virginia, on March 1, 1622, for stealing a calf and other chattels from Sir George Yeardley."[5] This was many years after the first

---

[5]*Minutes of the Council and General Court of Colonial Virginia*, 1620-23—1670-76, Richmond, 1924.

settlers arrived at Jamestown, in 1607, and so may not be the first legal hanging.

There must have been hangings for other charges. The first person to be hanged for murder was a John Billington, Plymouth, Massachusetts, on September 30, 1630. Billington came over on the Mayflower, but from the start was "a maverick," a "stranger" rather than a "saint." It is recorded that he defied an order issued by Captain Miles Standish, "with approbrious phrases" during the first year of the "heavenly experiment" of colonizing the Massachusetts coast. As early as 1625, Governor William Bradford wrote a letter to his London agent: "Billington still rails against you and threatens to arrest you, I know not whereof; he is a knave, and so will live and die."[6] Billington lived up to this prophesy—he killed John New-Comen "with a gun whereof he dyed." This victim of the tree, the first to die for murder, left a wife and two sons.

Records indicate that the first female to be hanged in this country was Dorothy Talby, probably of Boston, in the Massachusetts Bay Colony. She was convicted of killing her three-year-old daughter. Curiously, the child was named Difficulty. It was also alleged that earlier she had tried to kill her husband, as well as herself. Her execution took place some time in 1638.[7]

There were other females who suffered at the hands of the hangman in Massachusetts. One was Mary Latham, age eighteen. She and her accomplice, James Britton, were hanged some time in 1655. The case is interesting in that it is the only one in the history of the Colony of a couple being hanged for the offense of adultery. It seems that Mary had been rejected by a young man of her own age and then and there vowed that she would marry the next man that came to her. Accordingly, against the advice of her friends, she "matched with an ancient man who had neither honesty nor ability, and one whom she had no affection unto." From that point on, her conduct became more and more loose— she began abusing her husband and participating in drinking

---

[6]Bradford's *Letter Book*, reprinted in *Massachusetts Historical Collection*, first series III, pp. 27-84.

[7]John Winthrop *History of New England*, Savage Edition, 1, 333 6 Court of Assistants II 78, 1638.

bouts with nondescript men. In time she was intimate with Britton —he was not the only one to enjoy her favors. It was apparently difficult for the authorities to apprehend all who had sinned and equally difficult to condemn all those that were charged. A case was made against Mary and Britton. They were condemned, and made to suffer execution for the good of public morals. It was reported that Mary "proved very penitent and had deep apprehension of the foulness of her sin."[8]

Another case in the early history of the Bay Colony was that of Mary Martin—she was a grandchild of the Mayor of Plymouth, England, but in the new colony she was but a servant girl in the employ of a Mrs. Bourns of Boston. Unable to face the talk of her friends and "the infamy of living in a Puritan community" she killed her bastard child and hid the body. At the trial, according to Cotton Mather, that fire-eating New England Divine, she was asked to touch the body of her dead child. As she did so, the "blood came fresh into it so she confessed the whole truth." She was hanged some time in 1646—Mary was but twenty-two.[9] This superstition was known as the law of the bier, and was widely practiced in colonial times.

> A well-known case in which it was involved is that of Thomas Lutherland, a tranported felon from England hanged at Salem, New Jersey, on February 23, 1691, for the murder of John Clark, a Philadelphia trader who operated from his produce boat at the Delaware River. Lutherland "barbarously" killed Clark and stole his merchandise. At the bier of his victim, he was obliged to touch the corpse, under the belief that if he were guilty, the corpse would bleed. In his confusion and emotional state, he blurted out a confession and was hanged. (A pamphlet regarding the case was published by James Bradford, a Philadelphia printer, under the title "Blood Will Out—an example of justice in the trial, condemnation, confession and execution

---

[8]*Ibid.*, pp. 190-191. See Edwin Powers, *Crime and Punishment in Early Massachusetts,* Boston: Beacon Press, 1966, Chapter 9.

[9]*Pillar of Salt,* Boston, 1699—case cited by Thomas McDade, *The Annals of Murder,* Norman: University of Oklahoma Press, 1961, p. xxi. At the Mary Martin hanging, it is believed that a bungled job was done in "turning her off." This tragic young woman spake and asked "What did they mean to do?" "Then someone stepped up and turned the knot of the rope backward, and she soon died" (Winthrop, *History,* II, pp. 368-70).

of Thomas Lutherland who barbarously murthered the body of
John Clark, etc., Philadelphia, 1692," republished by Joseph S.
Sickler, Woodstown, New Jersey, 1948.)

This ancient law was a companion piece to the better-known
"Benefit of Clergy" also quite venerable and a part of our heritage
from Mother England. It was an instrument of mitigation, as
applied to certain offenses, such as murder. Originally designed
to save members of the clergy from punishment, by temporal
courts, it was soon seized upon as a device to rob the common
law of some of its rigor. The early Colonial test was to read a
verse from the Bible. This verse was referred to by the rabble as
the "Neck Verse." In time, the reading was dispensed with, so
that the illiterate could take advantage of the privilege. With this
modification, it was only necessary to invoke a form of grace to
save oneself from punishment. If grace was granted, the peti-
tioner was usually branded on the thumb, with an "M" for murder,
or a "T" for all other offenses. Generally, this was followed by a
token term of imprisonment. Rules, however, forbade this privilege
being extended more than once, and the branded thumb stood
as mute testimony that the offender had already been awarded
the concession.

HANGING OF THE QUAKERS IN MASSACHUSETTS

It is little wonder that members of the Society of Friends, who
were so persecuted in England should meet the same fate in some
of the American Colonies, West Jersey and Pennsylvania excepted.
There were many cases of vicious treatment of Quakers in Massachusetts. According to Peleg W. Chandler, one who tells us something of the vicissitudes and harassments suffered by the Quakers
from the zealous colonists of the Bay Colony in those early days,
"The colonists . . . had no idea of religious toleration—it was
preached against as a sin in Rulers, which would bring down the
judgment of heaven upon the land."[10] Another rather whimsical
note is mentioned by Chandler. He states that when two Quakers,
Anne Austin and Mary Fisher, arrived in July, 1656, from the
Barbadoes, their trunks were searched and their books were burned
by the official hangman.[11]

---

[10] *American Criminal Trials,* Boston, 1842, Vol. I, p. 34.
[11] *Ibid.,* p. 33.

In those days, the executioner's life was a harried one, and he was responsible for many onerous duties. The following warrant, we are told, was actually carried into effect against the unfortunate members of this Quaker group:

> "To the Marshal General or his Deputy.
>
> Ye are to take with you the *Executioner* (*italics added*) and repair to the House of Correction, and there see him cut off the right ears of John Copeland, Christopher Holder, and John Rouse, Quakers, in execution of the sentence of the Court of Assistants for the breach of the law entitled 'Quakers.' "[12]

On October 19, 1658, a law was introduced that every person of the "cursed sect of the Quakers" who should be found within the colony, "should immediately be imprisoned without fail . . . . and, being convicted to be of the sect of the Quakers, should immediately be banished on pain of death." Indeed, four persons purporting to be Quakers were hanged in the Colony of Massachusetts, not because they were members of that religious sect, but because, being despised by the Puritans for their radical ways, they refused to stay banished from the colony when they were thus penalized. The four who were doomed to be hanged were William Robinson and Marmaduke Stevenson, executed on October 22, 1659; Mary Dyer, on June 1, 1660, and William Leddra, on March 14, 1661, all from Boston. Stevenson and Robinson refused to take umbrage under the cloak of banishment and decided to take the consequences. Mary Dyer's husband took her off to Rhode Island. It is curious that she did not stay there long, and returned to face the consequences, the same as the other two had done. On the afternoon of October 22nd, the three prisoners were taken out of jail to be hanged, surrounded by an armed guard and several horsemen, with guns and drums beating to prevent the crowd from hearing anything the condemned might say; yet, they did speak out, saying: "This is an hour of greatest joy I ever knew"—this from Mary Dyer, with marvelous conviction. The last words murmured by Robinson were "I suffer for Christ in Whom I live and for Whom I die," and Stevenson added, "This day shall we be at rest with the Lord."

Mary Dyer was saved, due to the intercession of her son, but

---

[12]*Op. Cit.,* p. 36.

not until she had witnessed the hanging of her companions for their faith. She returned to Rhode Island under pressure from her family. However, her religious conviction and her personal compulsion would not permit her to remain in that sanctuary. She returned to that "bloody town of Boston" and was immediately picked up and processed for death on the gallows. She heroically answered the questions of the court, rejecting any proposal that might save her life. Accordingly, Mary Dyer, on June 1, 1660, was brought forth and with a band of soldiers led through the town for about a mile to the place of execution, with the drums beating before and behind her the whole distance. Again, on the gallows, she was told that if she would return home she could save herself; and she persistently refused the offer, and she was "turned off." Tradition says that one of the court remarked "She hangs as a flag, for others to take example by." One might wonder who could have best benefited from the example.

William Leddra was no less stubborn, no less compelled than was Mary Dyer. He had been whipped several times, imprisoned, and banished on pain of death, but as Mary Dyer, he stubbornly returned. He was immediately seized and chained to a log in prison, where he suffered much. He was placed on trial in March, 1661, and executed on the 14th of that month. As with the others, the court tried to persuade Leddra to leave the city and thus save himself. Like the others, however, he refused to leave Boston, and he was, accordingly, hanged. His last words on the scaffold were: "Lord Jesus, receive my spirit." The crowd gradually dispersed, but a few friends remained and caught the body when it was cut down, and after the executioners stripped it, they were permitted to pay the last tribute of affection to their friend. It is believed that these hangings took place on Boston Commons, near where the Hollis Street Church later stood. (The foregoing is taken largely from Chandler, *op. cit.,* I, pp. 33-63.)

THE YOUNGEST VICTIMS OF THE TREE

Until the beginning of the twentieth century, and the founding of the juvenile court, children were subject to the same penalties and court procedures as were adults. This is still the case, legally, since minors may always be certified for criminal court action by the prosecutor. When children of "tender years" commit murder today, it always appears to be particularly embarrassing and legally confusing. Generally, they are spirited away for psychiatric examination, and, in time, their cases tend to fade away into the realm of the forgotton, at least by the public and the local press. The *New York Times* conducted a nationwide survey of cases of children who had been found guilty of murder and were liable to execution (see January 7, 1962). While the article stated that children as young as seven could be legally executed in some states, few under sixteen have met that fate. Instances of cases of very young children being hanged come from English sources, and have for many years, that is, prior to fairly modern times, but we have found few cases of children "of tender years" actually being hanged in our colonies or our states. To cite a few English cases, we find Andrew Benning, aged thirteen, publicly hanged for breaking into a house and stealing a spoon—date not given. In 1808, a girl aged seven, publicly hanged at Lynd, and in 1831, a boy of nine met the same fate at Plemscourt for arson.[13]

While it is difficult to find instances of persons under the age of sixteen being executed, cases do exist. The *New York Times* survey lists one of recent years, George Stinney, Jr., a Negro of fourteen years, executed for murder on June 16, 1944, in the South Carolina state prison at Columbia. Despite exceptions, many children under sixteen have been convicted of heinous crimes and have actually been sentenced to death, though these sentences were later commuted to long terms of imprisonment. It is more common that children of tender years (under sixteen) languish in prison until it seems decent enough to execute them, perhaps when they are seventeen or older. One case of a child who was spared being executed deserves more than cursory inspection, since it has become a criminological classic.

> Jesse Harding Pomeroy was a native of Boston during the 1870's, the son of a poor widowed dressmaker residing in the southern part of that town. Pomeroy, at fourteen years of age, was sentenced to be hanged on December 10, 1874. His crim-

---

[13]Cases cited by Arthur Koestler, *Reflections on Hanging,* New York, Macmillan, 1957, p. 15; Koestler documents these cases. He also cites several others "sentenced" to be hanged but does not suggest their disposition.

inal career included a series of sexual assaults on younger boys at least one little girl, and included at least two murders. As early as 1871, and all through the following year, small boys of the area had been sexually and brutally attacked by a young ruffian, and in some cases brutally beaten, tied to poles, and carved with a knife. On December 22, 1871, the small son of Mrs. Payne, of Chelsea, was inveigled to Powder Horn Hill. The child was stripped and tied to a beam and beaten unconscious with a length of rope. On February 21, 1872, little Tracy Hayden was taken to the same place and tortured in a similar manner, and in addition, beaten in the face with a board so that several of his teeth were knocked out. July 4, 1872 witnessed John Balch, similarly attacked at the same locale and in addition taken to a salt creek to "bathe his open wounds." In September of the same year, Robert Gould was taken to a railroad track, tied naked to a telegraph pole, beaten and cut in the face with a knife. A "few days later," George Pratt was enticed into the cabin of a yacht, where he was beaten and stabbed in the groin and the back with a pen knife.

Scarcely a week had elapsed when Joseph Kennedy was taken to Old Colony Road, where he was abused exactly the same as the Pratt boy. The cases inspired public wrath. Suspicion finally came to rest upon young Pomeroy, and so he was arrested and easily identified by his victims. Because of his youth, considered even at that date, he was sent to the reform school at Westborough, where he was to remain until he reached his majority. Procedures at that time made it possible for him to be released on a kind of parole to his mother. This was done on February 6, 1874. Less than five weeks later, the ten-year-old daughter of one John Curran, who lived in the boy's neighborhood, disappeared, but, at that time, Pomeroy was not actually suspected. On April 22nd, however, the body of four-year-old Horace Millen was found in a marsh near Dorchester, mutilated all over his body with thirty-one knife wounds. The public was shocked to a white heat with this young sadist, and his bizarre crimes, and accordingly called for a swift trial and the death penalty. This feeling was compounded later when the body of little Kate Curran was found in the cellar of Pomeroy's home, concealed under piles of trash and ashes. He readily admitted her murder, and her concealment. The trial and pronouncement of the death sentence quickly followed. Due to a series of strange yet naturally human legal phenomena, Pomeroy never hanged. Two governors refused to sign his death warrant, and one governor refused to commute. Finally, on August 31, 1876, two years after pronouncement of the death sentence, this sixteen-year-old boy was resentenced to solitary confinement for life.

It is the novelty of Pomeroy's life sentence to solitary confinement that has made of him, and of his case, a kind of criminologic classic. Aside from his keepers at the Charlestown prison, he had no social contacts with anyone but his mother. During his long enforced seclusion, he gradually became a voracious reader, and learned several languages. In short, he became a self-educated man. For a period of forty-two years, Jesse Pomeroy was kept in solitary, but in 1916, he was permitted, at the age of fifty-six, to mingle with other prisoners. He had apparently suffered this strange ordeal without his mentality becoming noticeably impaired. In 1929, he was transferred to the Bridgewater Prison Farm, against his protests. On September 29th, 1932, he succumbed to senility in his seventy-third year.*

As mentioned previously, there are cases of children of "tender years" hanging for various and sundry offenses. To locate such offenses, however, during the early eras of our country's history, is quite difficult, since there were few records kept, and those that were kept have, in the main, been destroyed. Some years ago, Henry W. Thurston maintained that in 1688, the colony of East Jersey (Anglican) passed a law imposing the penalty of hanging on any child convicted of stubbornness, or of cursing his parents. No case has thus far turned up in New Jersey to indicate that any child was ever hanged for this offense.[14]

New Jersey does produce one of the very few cases in which the hanging of a child resulted. In 1828, a young Negro named James Guild, referred to as "Little Jim" was hanged at Flemington, Hunterdon County, not far from the state capital at Trenton. He was apparently but fourteen years of age—parenthetically, it

---

*McDade, *op. cit.*, 757-9. Note: Unless otherwise specified, all numbers following McDade citations throughout this book, refer to cases or "items" dealt with in his work *The Annals of Murder;* for further details of the Pomeroy case, see A. Warren Stearms, "The Life and Crimes of Jesse Harding Pomeroy," *J. Maine Medical Association, 19*:No. 4 pp. 49 ff, April, 1948.

[14]*Concerning Juvenile Delinquency,* New York, Columbia University Press, 1942, p. 69.

must be stated that we cannot always accept that the age set down in the records is accurate. In those early days there were no vital statistics kept, and often people really did not know their own age. Often, too, if two or more sources tell the same story, we find discrepancies in stating age; this is particularly true of slaves, or of the "little people" who are most likely to stumble into sordid trouble. Nonetheless, Little Jim was known among his contemporaries in Flemington as a "child of tender years."

Jim had been convicted of killing his mistress, a Mrs. Beak, of Hopewell, a small town that was to be poignantly associated with the kidnapping of the little Lindbergh baby a hundred years later.

The New Jersey Law Journal, in 1901, re-examined the case in an editorial and commented on the tragic turn of judicial events in the "Little Jim case." It implies that "cajolery and bad faith was used to extract the confession from the boy." His story was that he became angry with his mistress, hit her, and later returned and killed her with a yoke (October, 1901, XXIV; 681-2; the editorial was signed Green Bag, Boston; see also *The Tradition of Hunterdon,* a history of the county, pp. 75-77).

The youngest child-hanging that has come to our attention was Hannah Ocuish, a half-breed mulatto Indian, who was executed at New London, Connecticut, on December 20, 1786, for killing a six-year-old girl named Eunice Bolles. Hannah's age is given in the court records as twelve years, nine months. The story of this unfortunate occurrence is best recounted in the *History of New London* (pp. 576-7):

> The crime was committed July 21, 1786. The perpetrator was an Indian girl of Pequot parentage. . . . the murdered child was found about ten o'clock in the morning on Norwich Road, about two or three miles from town. She lay under a wall, from which heavy stones had been thrown upon her body. On examination it was shown that her death could not have been the result of an accident, and after a day or two, suspicion having rested on Hannah Ocuish, who lived with a widow woman nearby. She was examined and confessed the crime. It was a case of cruel and malicious murder growing out of a dispute that occurred in a strawberry field some days before. The fierce young savage,

nursing her wrath, and watching for an opportunity to take revenge, at length came upon her victim on her way to school alone; after coaxing and luring her into the woods, fell upon her and beat her to death. The only alleviating circumstances in the case were the extreme ignorance and youth of the criminal.

The circumstances described as alleviating were true enough. Hannah's mother was described as "an abandoned creature addicted to the vice of drunkenness." The tragic little girl, retarded and certainly underprivileged, was born at Groton and had a brother two years older than she. Some time previous to this crime, they had attacked a small girl and stripped her of her clothing and stolen from her body a gold necklace. After beating her until she was almost dead, they left her and argued about the division of the spoils. Hearing about this earlier crime, the town selectmen had taken the children from their mother and bound them out. This remedy apparently had little effect, for Hannah's conduct, as described in the evidence given at her trial, was marked with almost everything bad; theft and lying were her common vices. To these were added a maliciousness of disposition which made the neighborhood children afraid of her (from the appendix of the above mentioned sources). McDade states that Hannah could expect no mercy from the stern New England community. He adds: "When brought to the bar to receive sentence of death, her stupidity and unconcern astonished everyone. While that beloved benevolent tenderness which distinguished his honor, the chief justice, almost prevented utterance, and the spectators could not refrain from tears; the prisoner alone appeared scarcely to attend . . . at the place of execution she said very little—apparently greatly afraid and seemed to want somebody to help her." The scaffold used on this young criminal was erected in the rear of the town's old meeting house, near the corner of Granite Street. The Rev. Mr. Henry Channing, from Yale College, delivered the gallows-side sermon and entitled it "God Admonishing His People of Their Duty as Parents and Masters."[15]

It is certainly true that the history of the hangings of children is a sorry story at best. There are only a few examples. A

[15]McDade, *op. cit.,* 720.

fourteen-year-old Negro boy, named Bud Beard, on December 17, 1897 was hanged at Carrollton, Pickens County, Alabama. He had been convicted of criminal assault on the eight-year-old daughter of the farmer for whom he worked. It was stated in the press, at that time, that this was the youngest person ever hanged in Alabama. The story continued that the boy denied his guilt and died trembling. Prior to the hanging, it took prompt action by the governor to prevent the lynching of the boy. A mob had previously prevented the sheriff from taking him from the court house to the jail after the trial had begun. The "Warrior Guards" trecked across the state in an all-night forced wagon march. Their arrival at daybreak frustrated the potential lynching.[16]

Many news stories of the times and surveys clearly indicate that many minors between the ages of sixteen and eighteen have been executed through the years. One case that also springs to mind is that of a sixteen-year-old Negro boy known only as Bristol, who was hanged at Taunton, Massachusetts, December 1, 1763. He had murdered the spinster Miss Elizabeth McKinstray, for no apparent reason. The minister officiating at the gallows in his religious capacity delivered a sermon entitled *The Blood of Abel and the Blood of Jesus Considered and Improved.* How much of the awful words and thoughts associated with this death sermon was comprehended by the unlettered slave boy stimulates interesting conjecture.[17]

Pennsylvania's long history of hangings includes the hanging of two young boys, age presumably but seventeen. They were William Battin and James Burke. Battin, whose case we discuss later in another connection, was hanged at Chester on August 15, 1722 (see *infra.,* p. 84). Burke, a servant boy, killed his master, Thomas M'Auliffe, a merchant in Philadelphia, with a claw hammer as he slept. He attempted to flee the country by taking passage on a boat for Ireland under an assumed name. Officials followed him by small craft down the Delaware River and into the Delaware Bay, where his ship was told to stop and unload their killer

---

[16]For details on this case see the *Chatanooga Tennessee Daily Times,* December 18, 1897; also from the following Birmingham papers: *Age Herald,* November 5, p. 3; November 13, p. 3; *News,* December 18, all 1897.

[17]McDade, *op. cit.,* 131; later in this chapter we shall have a few words about another Massachusetts boy, sixteen-year-old Stephen N. Clarke, p. 25.

passenger. Burke was hanged on October 16, 1784 (*Pennsylvania Packet,* Philadelphia, October 18, 1784).

HANGINGS IN THE STREETS AND SQUARES

In retrospect we are likely to admit that the era of public hanging was far more dramatic, socially satisfying, even though bizarre and emotionally tense, than any other later period of the history of capital punishment in this country. The literature that reflects the practice of hanging throughout the world, most of it produced in England, is both caustic and satirical, and differs markedly from its polemic counterpart associated with the ongoing battle against capital punishment in our own country. One immediately calls to mind Charles Duff's satire, the *New Handbook on Hanging* (Chicago, Charles Regnery, 1954) and somewhat similar though far more bitter, Arthur Koestler's *Reflections on Hanging* (New York, Macmillan, 1957).[18]

It seems that electrocution and the gas chamber do little to inspire satire. Grim though any form of capital punishment undoubtedly is, it must be admitted that a certain perverted romanticism surrounded public hangings in both Great Britain and this country. Few ballads, for instance, have been composed or sung about persons who have been electrocuted or asphyxiated, as has been the case with those hanged by the neck. Contemporary newspaper accounts testify to and substantiate the judgment that a hanging, especially a public affair, is surrounded with an aura of thrills and excitement.

While the long period of county jail and state prison hangings was not and is not totally without its personalized elements, the very secretiveness of dispatching hundreds, or even thousands of lives into eternity or oblivion could scarcely compare with the earlier and livelier public hanging bees. If we dare refer to that period as glamorous, certainly the latter years may be referred to as ghoulish by way of contrast. The titillation of the riffraff elements of the general public induced by all forms of public punishments— stocks, pillories, whippingposts, and the gallows, was greatly re-

---

[18]The two mentioned do not exhaust the list. We shall later allude to other authors such as Justin Atholl, Horace Bleackley and Bernard O'Donnell. We should mention August Mencken's *By the Neck,* to which we shall refer from time to time throughout this work.

duced when hangings were taken away from the village squares
and city commons and legally spirited into the confines of jails and
prisons. By this we do not mean to advocate public hanging or a
return of the gallows or electric chair or gas chamber to areas of
public exhibition. We mean only to indicate that public execution
seemed, somehow or other, a more honest expression of what the
advocates of capital punishment seem to feel is the public sentiment.

Newspaper people of those early days (we can scarcely refer to
them as journalists) possessed little imagination when reporting
public hangings. In fact, they were treated as ordinary mundane
experiences and received but scant and sometimes even sterile
coverage, with few if any embellishments; certainly no colorful
headlines, or no headlines at all. Perhaps executions became "good
copy" only after they were removed from the public eye, but left
in the public imagination. In those early days, often only a terse
statement appeared on the inside of the local weekly newspaper
which stands today as mute proof that someone was hanged on a
certain date. For example, Philadelphia's *American Weekly Mercury* for November 5 to 12, 1741, states, "On Saturday last, John
Bullock who received the sentence of death on the 28th of last
month, for the murder of his wife, was executed." No mention of
the event itself, nor of the probable excitement surrounding it or
incidental to the death march, or procession from the jail to the
place of execution on the city's commons.

We learn nothing of the criminal himself, although the *Colonial
Record of Pennsylvania* (Vol. IV, p. 503) refers to the murderer
as "notorious and one of the blackest and most barbarous kind."
Again, in the early days, there were no roving reporters bent on
getting a story, so we find few descriptions of the holiday nature
of a public hanging until the turn of the nineteenth century. After
the era of private jail hangings came into being, and journalists
became more sophisticated, we find many a sensational headline
and story. Naturally it took the genius of the last decade of that
century to develop a workmanlike job on the story of a hanging.
There is plenty of clinical evidence to support the thesis that newspapers vie with one another to dramatize or exploit an execution.
This is particularly characteristic of our times. Even yet, none
can top the headline of the *Chicago Times* for November 27, 1875,

announcing the hanging of four persons, two in Louisiana and two in Mississippi. The startling headline, which still remains as classic of some kind, reads: *"Jerked to Jesus."*[19]

The *New York Sun* did a workmanlike job in its story of the hanging in far-off Rupley, Jackson County, West Virginia of a mass killer, John F. Morgan, ignominiously hanged on November 9, 1896. He had killed Mrs. Chloe Green, her son and daughter, with an axe. The sub-heading on the metropolitan *Sun,* in bold type read:

West Virginia Came on Horseback, in Wagon and on Foot to See the Show: Some Traveled Sixty Hours to Get There—A Celebration the Night Before—Punch and Judy Show—and Twanging Banjoes at the Jail When Morgan Sang Hymns—A Feud Crops out on the Way to the Gallows a Mile Out of Town —Farmers with Their Families and Women with Their Babies Enjoyed the Spectacle—It Was Fun for all But Morgan. (See Chap. IV, p. 202 for story.)

An episode submitted by Lewis Blake Duff may compete with this one, but in another direction. He tells us that he knew a news-boy who hawked his wares, knowing that the paper he was selling described the hanging, play by play, of his own brother.[20]

A source of more graphic description of hangings is the early diarist and local historian, who wrote something of the drama, or even the pathos, surrounding a public hanging. Their accounts, unfortunately, are usually couched in doleful or even deplorable prose. Some of the accounts tell us the victims "were taken from the gaol" and herded into a cart, usually weighted down with irons —handcuffs or leg irons—and driven slowly to the gallows, per-haps amidst the tolling of bells. How prevalent the use of bells was at a hanging is not clear. Few of our news accounts refer to the ringing of bells although such a practice in early days would have been in keeping with the mournful atmosphere. Samuel Row-land Fisher, a dissident Quaker who was sent to jail for disloyalty (in reality, a conscientious objector) during the War of Independence, kept a journal while incarcerated in the Old Stone Prison

---

[19]Herbert Asbury, *Gem of the Prairie*, New York, Knopf, 1940, p. 70.

[20]On the jacket of his book on hangings entitled *The County Kerchief,* Toronto, Ryer-son Press, 1929.

in Philadelphia. He wrote the following on November 23, 1780,
"They (David Dawson and Richard Chamberlain, the former convicted of treason, the latter for passing counterfeit money) were
taken out amidst a crowd of spectators; they walked after a cart
which bore a coffin, a ladder, etc., each had a rope around their
neck and their arms tied behind them. Dawson walked first, accompanied by a brother, two sisters, and another woman. Chamberlain was only accompanied by one of his relatives. They were
hanged on the Commons about one o'clock."

We find the notorious yet romantic story of Abraham and Levi
Doan, Torys and legally condemned outlaws of Bucks County,
Pennsylvania, in the autobiography of Charles Biddle, a prominent
Philadelphian of colonial times. As they were on their way to the
gallows in Philadelphia, on September 28th, 1788: "I met them
going in a cart . . . followed by their relatives and friends. It was
a very affecting sight, they died with great firmness." The story
of the Doan clan is a Bucks County saga. In fact, their legal-illegal
exploits have become legend throughout Pennsylvania as far west
as Washington County, and down to the northern tier of what is
now West Virginia. Abraham and Levi were but two of a remarkable family that rebelled against the patriot cause and in
reality became a fifth column. They were informers and runners
for the British, and harassed Washington's army in and around
what is now known as Washington's Crossing, prior to the battle
of Trenton. The new government could overlook the gang's horse
stealing and general highway robbery, but could not forgive their
Tory conduct, which it regarded as treachery.

> The double hanging of the Doans—they were cousins—with-
> out even the gesture of a trial, survived in the locale of their
> native heath for many years (see *The New Doan Book,* Doyles-
> town, Penna., 1952; also *Doylestown Democrat,* December 31,
> 189, which states, "It was an infamous murder (the hangings),
> since those men were protected by the treaty of peace signed in
> 1785").

Many other stories are told even today about this gang, especially about Abe Doan, supposed to have been 6'6" tall, very
heavy, with fiery red hair that was "in three fat braids down his

neck." His prowess as a broad-jumper, as well as a horseman, were equally legendary. He is supposed to have worn an "iron fist" on his right hand—a spiked gauntlet of mail from medieval times that he had obtained somewhere. It was related that he had "smashed the lives out of nine men with his 'fist.'" Other uses made of this unique weapon were "to move posts, drive spikes, and sledge beeves." Despite all of these achievements and material assets, it is also alleged that he "suffered from coughing, and twitched and shook constantly."[21]

The behavior of crowds watching public hangings is interesting in that it ran the gamut of reaction, from raucous railing against and cruelty toward the condemned, to pious sympathy. In America, however, we have found no evidence that crowds going to the place of execution were ever unruly, although at the place itself, we find many instances where they were boisterous, rude, and even unruly, but in general, those about to be hanged were not molested, nor for that matter, ridiculed. Stories originating from English history, however, indicate that in many instances the company making up or accompanying the procession to the tree were unmanageable and sometimes downright cruel to the victim. Perhaps differences in the manner of transporting the victim from the place of confinement to the scaffold prompted different crowd reaction. The British practice of being drawn on a "hurdle" or a "sled" that sometimes seemed to be the lot of the gallows victim on the way to the place of execution, was almost unheard of in most of the Colonies, although we read of such in Virginia. Being drawn was the initial part of the frightening sentence "drawn and quartered." The privilege of being drawn to the gallows was apparently restricted to slaves in this country. While some culprits convicted of crimes not capital were subject to the indignity of being attached to a horse's tail or to the tail of a cart, and flogged, such was not the fare of those who were to be hanged, at least not in the northern colonies. It may be safely stated that by and large, a condemned man or woman in Colonial America was less severely maligned or manhandled than was the case so frequently in Mother England. This, of course, does not include the handling of slaves and some persons

---

[21]Excerpts from the Washington, Pennsylvania *Observer*, January 25, 1963, from a series of articles by Glen P. Lough, Fairmont, West Virginia historian.

convicted of treason. We shall discuss some of these exceptions in our next chapter.[22]

While meeting death before hundreds, or perhaps thousands, may have had a bolstering effect on some, to others, it apparently made little or no difference. There are cases in which the victim collapsed or became demoralized or emotionally uncontrollable at the moment of his doom. One tragic figure, Samuel Brandt, hanged at Lancaster, Pennsylvania, December 18, 1773, "filled the air with unearthly screams and yells as he approached the gallows" (*The Manheim Tragedy,* Lancaster, 1858, Appendix 57).

The case of Charles R. S. Boyington is of some interest in this connection. He was hanged in Mobile, Alabama, on February 20, 1835, for the murder of Nathanial Frost. The murder was committed on May 11, 1834. He had the misfortune of walking with Frost shortly before the latter was found stabbed to death and robbed; the evidence given at the trial was slight and sketchy, and certainly circumstantial, but it served to damn him nonetheless. He was convicted and executed. As he approached the gallows, he exhibited great firmness and an unwavering step, as one writer, in describing the event, put it, "His whole soul had been steeled and nerved up to the time the ministers of the law commenced robing him for death, and fixing the fatal noose." It is well worth describing the dramatic scene occurring at Boyington's hanging.

> The blood forsook his cheeks, despair was written in awful marks upon his many features, and a scene of horror ensued that beggars description. He dashed from the foot of the scaffold among the military. But he was easily secured. Then followed a scene of horror—the hopeless agony of the criminal was displayed in obstinate resistance to the performance of the necessary duties of the agents of the law; and even when at last suspended from the fatal cord, a desperate clinging to the life he had forfeited was shown by struggles to free his arms from the pinions, and clutching at the rope. He succeeded in thrusting his hands between the rope and his throat, and thus resisting and struggling to the last, died despairingly, and, for all the human eye could see, impenitent. The last five minutes were

---

[22]For the story of hanging in England, see Justin Athall, *Shadow of the Gallows,* London, John Long, Ltd., 1954, especially Chapter 3, "The Journey to the Gallows."

marked by a horror of dying. A prostration of energy as remarkable as the sternness of nerve and wreckless levity of carriage which had signalized him during the whole of the trial.[23]

Another case mentioned by the Rev. Charles Spear, mid-nineteenth century crusader against capital punishment, is that of sixteen-year-old Stephen M. Clarke, hanged at Salem, Massachusetts,
on May 10, 1821, for the crime of arson. He had burned down a
stable owned by Miss Phoebe Cross, with the conflagration racing
to the adjoining home of Andrew Buffington. This despairing
young boy pitifully attempted to pay the sum of $100, which he
probably did not have, but hoped to produce, to the turnkey if he
would help him to escape.[24,25]

It can be said that most of those who were publicly hanged
demonstrated great fortitude and courage. Observation of cases we
have examined indicates that more heroism came from those publicly hanged than from those privately hanged. If this is true, perhaps heroism is more often elicited by stimulation from our fellow
man than from a more restricted public exposure.

Aside from those who cringed and cried to or under the gallows,
or showed heroism, many showed neither. Rather they were calm,
casual and even contemptuous or callous as they made their way
to the "tree." (In a later section we shall deal with gallows-side
demeanor of several cases that have come to our attention that fall
into these categories of behaviour, see pages 47-51.) There also
exist many cases of dull, stolid, sluggish or even stupid persons,
doubtless some of them mentally retarded, who were led to the
tree more like flabby pieces of protoplasm than vital human beings.
The Rev. Charles Spear bluntly described all public hangings:
"They generally produce a sort of stupid brutality." This was in
connection with the description of the Jacob Leadings case, Al-

---

[23]Charles Spear, *Essays on the Punishment of Death,* Boston, 1844, pp. 43-4, quoted
from *Mobile Commercial Advertiser.* The Boyington case is locally a legend poignantly and tenderly recalled. The man Boyington was a poet of sorts and was a
lover of considerable reputation. We shall deal with his case in a later connection, see
Chapter VIII.

[24]Spear states it was found necessary to force the tragic young man from his cell and
drag him to the scaffold, amidst a parade of soldiers with accompanying martial
music (p. 102).

[25]See also Louis Blake Duff, *op. cit.,* p. 129.

bany, New York, on December 29, 1840, for the murder of his wife. He was a drunkard and the father of twelve:

> He went to the scaffold perfectly indifferent and reckless and sunk in such a condition of stupid brutality as to create on the part of many disbelief of his soundness of mind. At the solicitation of some of the clergymen who were laboring in vain to arouse him to some fitter state of preparation for the awful journey to which he was soon to be dispatched, the governor respited him twice, from week to week; but to no effect.

Spear adds an aftermath to the hanging of Leadings: "Two or three days after, a fine boy about sixteen years of age, the delight of highly respectable and estimable parents hung himself from the banisters of the stairs in his father's home at Albany."[26]

In many county seats it was the custom for a squad of the military to accompany the death party. This was a precaution, not only to hold back an unruly crowd, but to frustrate any overt attempt to free the culprit, since many of them had a sympathetic following. In some instances, the drums were beaten, or martial music played to prevent the crowd from hearing what the gallows victims might say as they faced their doom. This was evident when the Quakers, Stevenson and Robinson, mentioned earlier, were hanged at Boston (see *supra,* page 11). It should be added that a military contingent lent color and even glamour to the spectacle which the crowd, in most cases, would see only once in every generation or in a lifetime, if at all. Many counties in this country have never experienced the excitement or the macabre atmosphere of a public hanging. In Bellefonte, Pennsylvania (Center County), a fifer, veteran of the War of 1812, played the *Death March* at the hanging of James Munks, on January 23, 1819. Munks had killed Reuben Guild for no apparent reason, but unwittingly dropped a tell-tale hymn book at the scene of the crime. This innocent little oversight led to his execution.

There are many examples of the holiday atmosphere connected with public hanging in the cases peculiar to America. At the place of the hanging of Stephen Arnold, at Cooperstown, New York, in 1805, on July 19th, a battalion of light infantry and an artillery

---

[26]*op. cit.,* 63n, preceding quote, 51.

company paraded through the village streets. Arnold was a schoolmaster. He had killed his six-year-old niece, Betsy Van Ambergh, because she could not, or stubbornly, would not correctly pronounce the word "gig." Fortunately, teaching methods have changed somewhat since the nineteenth century. In a cold frenzy, Arnold whipped the girl unmercifully with several sticks, one at a time, until she died. Convicted at his June trial, Arnold was paraded to the tree with the rope around his neck and with thousands of persons looking on and anticipating the hanging-bee, then the sheriff took from his pocket a note from the governor that granted a reprieve to the victim. The sentence was later commuted. The sheriff had carried the reprieve papers in his pocket all morning—such an act was often motivated by the unsympathetic feeling of the town folk against the criminal or somehow to teach the culprit a lesson. Another reason equally potent was to prevent the large assemblage from stampeding with disappointment or more likely, rage. When a crowd assembled to witness a public event, it was not considered cricket to frustrate them. The crowd certainly was out in a holiday mood, hundreds having come long distances, and concessionaires had money invested in trinkets and food to be sold at the jamboree. In short, it was suspected that they would stand a loss—in the best twentieth century tradition, the show must go on. Sheriffs themselves were local citizens who were loath to engender ill will from their friends and neighbors. The crowds of this era disliked last minute pardons or reprieves. They left such events with feelings of being cheated.

Frustration may well precipitate a riot—such was the case at Orwigsburg, Pennsylvania, the county seat of Schuylkill County, which is now Pottsville. A pathetic old man named John Zimmerman, convicted of killing his twenty-year-old daughter for making eyes at some young Irish coal miner in the vicinity, of whom the father disapproved, was reprieved at the gallows, in 1824, for reasons of insanity. The *New York Evening Post* contended that Zimmerman must have been insane "for no father in his right mind could deliberately take the life of an innocent child." Edward Livingston, the great Louisiana law-giver, and earlier distinguished New York statesman, wrote that when the crowd learned of Zimmerman's reprieve, almost literally at the gallows, "their fury knew no bounds and raised a ferocious cry, and the poor maniac was with difficulty snatched by the officers of justice from the fate which the most violent among them seemed determined to inflict." Livingston complained that public executions "were scenes of riot and every species of wickedness," added that "20,000 or even 40,000 persons are in attendance at such occasions." Furthermore, he maintained that "in the country, two or three days are employed in the merry-making, much after the manner of fairs."[28]

As we have stated above, hangings were most unusual or infrequent affairs in the bulk of the counties of the country and called for much anticipation and preparation. Certainly the most sensational case, if that is the word appropriate here, involving a frustrated crowd assembled to witness a hanging is that of David Redding of Bennington, Vermont. This incident involved more than mere public frustration—there are many amazing angles to it, and we feel compelled to tell the story of the events leading up to June 11, 1778.

Redding was arrested, indicted and convicted of nebulous charges sometimes described by the words "inimical conduct," sometimes with the charge of supplying the British with supplies on Lake Champlain, and sometimes with downright treason. Treason or whatever, he was convicted and scheduled to hang on June 4th, and a large crowd had assembled to witness the event, one that was unheard of in those parts—in an area about to become the state of Vermont. There happened to be at that time, in this small backwoods community, a lawyer of sorts by the name of John Burnham who had but recently migrated to the region. He pointed out that Redding had been convicted by a jury consisting of only six men. The conviction was therefore illegal. It was immediately thought not only just but expedient to give the victim a reprieve in order to rectify the error, that is, the error of jury, if error it was. The crowd was naturally piqued to the point of frustration and exasperation. It was fortunately appeased by the sudden appearance of their town hero, Ethan Allen, who had just returned home after a period of captivity by the British. The story goes that Allen, sensing the bad humor of the crowd on being circumvented in their attempt,

---

[28]*Remarks on the Expediency of Abolishing the Punishment of Death*, Philadelphia, 1831.

jumped upon a stump and shouted some of his immortal words, *viz.* "Attention the whole!" He then proceeded to tell them the reason for the reprieve, and advising them to return on the day a week hence, and, with a characteristic oath (so the story goes) he added: "You shall see somebody hung at all events, for if Redding is not then hung, I will be hung myself." The crowd melted away obediently, and on the appointed day, June 11th, the unfortunate Redding, after being legally convicted and sentenced by a twelve man jury, was promptly executed.

No record of the trial has ever been found; the names of the jury cannot be identified; apparently there has been, until 1945, a great deal of mystery surrounding this bizarre case. No one seemed motivated to inquire into the facts. Local historians carried on the tale without question, even on occasion embellishing it with details of their own manufacture. A local resident, long a writer concerned with social justice, John Spargo, decided to set the Redding record straight. He did so and found that Redding was actually a Tory of the neighborhood, joined Col. John Peters's Queen Royal Rangers, and engaged in legitimate activities of marauding and foraging in the countryside. Instead of being given a military trial, to which he was entitled, he was civilly tried. The trial was conducted in a rather slapstick fashion with primitive backwoods tactics and procedures, and he was ignominiously hanged. Spargo ends his factual study of the case: "The Vermonters of today cannot regard the trial of David Redding as anything other than a discreditable travesty of justice or refrain from regretting the ugly blot it has left upon the pioneer founders of the Green Mountain State, and its famous champion and leader, Ethan Allen."[29]

Redding had escaped from his captors some time before the trial, so he was carefully guarded as he went to the scaffold. We find no accurate description of the affair, but we feel that it is not out of place to transcribe Spargo's words relative to the scene:

> There came an outburst of noise, the terrible cacophony with the cries of hysterical sobbing women and the exultant shouting of blood-lusting men mingled in a dissonance of blas-

---

[29]The facts, as presented sketchily above, are from John Spargo, *The Story of David Redding, Who Was Hanged,* Bennington Museum, 1945; the above quotes are from page 53.

phemy, while the distorted body of a man dangled at the end of a rope swaying in the afternoon breeze. If Ethan Allen was among those present could he have looked at that dangling grimacing thing? Probably not. He must have looked down, I think, for surely he could not have looked towards the sky![30]

Public hangings often presented interesting choices to members of a particular community. Whether to attend a balloon ascension or a double hanging represented the dubious dilemma of Philadelphians on July 17, 1784. On that day John Downie and John Martin, highwaymen, were hanged on the city's Commons, while at the same time a Professor Cairnes, balloonist, resident of Baltimore, proposed to ascend over the city from the Walnut Street Jailyard. The event had been postponed from July 9th. Box seats within the jail enclosure sold for two dollars which was a pretty penny in those days. The crowd, however, stood across the street at Potter's Field, what is now Washington Square, but at this date we have no idea of the attendance at either of the two attractions.[31]

FURTHER DESCRIPTIONS OF PUBLIC HANGINGS

That public executions were grim and ribald spectacles is well supported by clinical evidence from across this country, as well as from that gathered from abroad, particularly from England. It goes without saying that they were debasing, as far as public decen-

---

[30]p. 51. In contrast to the admittedly large crowds which attended hangings in the first half of the nineteenth century, it must be mentioned that in the second hanging to take place in the Colony of Pennsylvaia, July 9, 1693, Bucks County, at "Tyburn," it was recorded that "There were too few there to make the affair enjoyable." The victim, Derek Jonson, was employed as a ferryman and for some reason disposed of an unknown person by dumping his body into the Neshaminy Creek, which empties into the Delaware River. Jonson was taken from the crude cabin which served as both a public-house, a court-house and jail, to a spot and hanged. The site of the "hanging tree" became known as Tyburn, presumably after the famous hanging place on the outskirts of London, now near the Marble Arch in Hyde Park. The little hamlet on the Pennsylvania Railroad between Philadelphia and Trenton, N.J., near Morrisville, is still known by that name. There is a steel company now occupying the spot that was once "court and public-house." The area, at that early time, was known as Crewcorn. The jail was so rickety, Jonson was hurriedly hanged for fear he might escape. The sheriff, one Israel Taylor, was a Quaker. He was so upset by the onerous duty he was obliged to perform for the Colony that he resigned. The Colonial Council ordered one of the victim's neighbors to harvest his crops so his widow and children might have enough money with which to buy food to subsist (*Colonial Records of Pennsylvania.* Vol. I, pp. 378-9; 382; 442).

[31]Scharf and Westcott, *History of Philadelphia,* 1884, I, 43n.; see also, Teeters, *The Cradle of the Penitentiary,* Philadelphia, Pennsylvania Prison Society, 1955, pp. 63-4.

cy, respect and morality were concerned. Most descriptive of these public debaucheries in England is Thackeray's classic example, "Going to See a Man Hanged" found in *Fraser's Magazine,* London, in 1850. Because of its import to hangings as established institutions, it seems worthy of transcription in part:

> I fully confess that I came away down from Snow Hill that morning with a disgust for murder, but it *was* for the murder I saw done . . . this is the 20th of July, and I may be permitted for my part to declare that, for the last fourteen days, so salutary has been the impression of the butchery upon me, I have had the man's face continually before my eyes. That I can see Mr. Ketch [the hangman] at this moment with an easy air, taking the rope from his pocket; that I feel myself ashamed and degraded by the brutal curiosity which took me to that brutal sight; and I pray to Almighty God to cause this disgraceful sin to pass from among us, and to cleanse our land of blood.
>
> It is curious that a murder is a great inspirer of jokes. We all like to laugh and have our feelings about it; there is a certain grim pleasure in the circumstances—a perpetual jingling antithesis between life and death, and that he is sure of his success.

He describes his approach to Newgate Prison, and then sees the scaffold:

> There it stands, black and handy, jutting out from a little door in the prison. As you see it, you feel a kind of dumb electric shock which causes one to start a little and feel a sort of gasp for breath. The shock is over in a second and presently you examine the object before you with a certain feeling of complete curiosity.
>
> Between the writing of this line and the last, the pen has been put down, as the reader may suppose, and the person who is addressing him has gone through a pause of no very pleasant thoughts and recollections. The whole of the sickening, ghastly, wicked scene passes before the eyes again; and indeed, it is an awful one to see, and very hard and painful to describe.
>
> As the clock begins to strike, an immense sway and movement swept over the whole of that vast dense crowd. They were all uncovered directly and then a great murmur arose, more awful, bizarre, and indescribable than any sound I have ever before

heard. Women and children began to shriek horridly. I don't know whether it was the bell I heard, but a dreadful feverish kind of jangling noise which mingled with the noise of the people and lasted about two minutes. The scaffold stood before us, tenantless and black. A black chain was hanging down ready from the beam. Nobody came. "He has been respited," somebody said and another said "He has killed himself in prison." Just then out of the black prison door a pale quiet head peered out. It was shockingly bright and distinct as it rose up directly and a man in black appeared on the scaffold, silently followed by about four more dark figures. The first was a tall, grave man; we all knew who the second man was "That's he, that's he" you heard the people say as the devoted man came up (Calcraft, the Hangman).

I have seen a cast of the head since, but indeed, should never have known it. Courvoisier bore his punishment like a man and walked very firmly.[32]

He was dressed in a new black suit and his shirt was open, his arms were tied in front of him, he opened his hands in a helpless kind of way and clasped them once or twice together. He turned his head here and there and looked about him for an instant with a wild, imploring look. His mouth was contorted into a kind of pitiful smile. He wasn't quite himself, and walked under the beam with his face toward St. Sepulchre's. The tall gray man in black twisted him round quickly in another direction, drawing from his pocket a nightcap, he pulled it tight around the patient's head and face. I am not ashamed to say that I could look no more, "but shut my eyes at the last dreadful act was going on, which sent the wretched, guilty soul into the presence of God. . . .

If a public execution is beneficial—and beneficial it is, no doubt, or else the wise laws would not encourage forty thousand people to witness it—the next useful thing must be a full description of such a ceremony, and all its entourages, and to this end the above pages are offered to the reader.[33]

---

[32]Francois Courvoisier, a French butler, hanged at the Old Bailey on July 6, 1840, for the murder of his master, Lord William Russell, at his residence in London. The executioner was William Calcraft, who held that position from 1829 to 1874, and was indeed devoted to his profession.

[33]This abridged account is taken with appropriate acknowledgment from Justin Atholl, *op. cit.,* pp. 82-83.

Charles Dickens also attended a public hanging—that of Frederick George Manning and his wife, Marie, for the murder of the woman's paramour. This double hanging aroused great interest, as it took place in the early morning of November 13, 1849, at Horsemonger Lane Jail. Writing a scornful letter to the *London Times* (December 13) the great novelist unleashed some of his most vitriolic prose on the rabble and their antics at the affair. He wrote, in part:

> "When I came upon the scene at midnight, the shrillness of the cries and howls . . . made my blood run cold. As the night went on, screeching and laughing and yelling in strong chorus of parodies of negro melodies, with a substitution of 'Mrs. Manning' for 'Susanna'; ruffians and vagabonds of every kind flocked to the ground with every variety of offensive and foul behavior. Fightings, faintings, whistling, imitations of Punch, brutal jokes, tumultuous demonstrations of indecent delight when swooning women were dragged out of the crowd by the police with their dresses disordered, gave a new zest to the entertainment." And finally: "When the two miserable creatures who attracted all this ghastly sight around them were turned quivering into the air, there was no more emotion, no more pity, no more thought that two immortal souls had gone to judgment, no more restraint in any of the previous obscenities, than if the name of Christ had never been heard in this world and there were no belief among men but that they perished like beasts."[34]

However, Dickens was able to benefit, to some degree, for that evening's vigil at the gallows. He immortalized one of the victims, Mrs. Manning, in his novel, *Bleak House*, in the character of Hortense, the French maid.

> Many British literary luminaries went to see a hanging for whatever reason they might later reveal to their public. Boswell, for instance, and Samuel Pepys, the latter several times. It is stated that on one occasion Pepys rented space on a "cartwheel for a shilling" but found the wobbly and uncertain perch "much to the discomfort of his legs" (Louis Blake Duff, *op. cit.*, pp. 34, 145).

---

[34]*Letters of Charles Dickens,* Macmillan, 1903, p. 200.

Justin McCarthy, in his *History of Our Times,* uses the following graphic prose to describe a public hanging in London:
"Through all the long night before the execution the precincts of
the prison became the bivouac ground for the ruffianism of the
metropolis. The roughs, harlots, the professional robbers and pros-
pective murderers held high carnival there. The air reeked with the
smell of strong drink, with filthy jokes and oaths and blasphemy.
The soul took its flight as if it were a trapeze performer in a
circus. The moral effect of the scene as an example to evil-doers
was about as great as the moral effects of a cockfight. The de-
moralizing effect, however, was broad and deep. It may be doubted
that one in a thousand of those who from mere curiousity came
to see an execution did not go away a worse creature than he had
come. As the old-fashioned intramural burial-ground made by its
vapors more corpses to fill it, so the atmosphere of the public
execution generates fresh criminals to exhibit on the scaffold.[35]

We need not go to England to be convinced of the carnival-like
and hilarious atmosphere of a public execution. At the last public
hanging in Philadelphia, which occurred on May 19, 1837 (it
was a federal offense the victim committed—piracy—and thus
not subject to the state law of April 10, 1834, which abolished
public hangings), when James Moran, a nineteen-year-old youth
was executed, the crowd was estimated at 20,000. At the John
Lechler hanging at Lancaster, Pennsylvania, on October 25, 1822,
the crowd was estimated at between 20,000 and 30,000 with upward of 2,000 coming from surrounding counties.

From the Lebanon, Pennsylvania, *Historical Society Journal,* we
find the following description of old-time executions, a sort of
composite, in their issue for April 18, 1902, as the writer places
them in retrospect:

> The scenes attending the hangings were degrading and dis-
> graceful. They were made occasions for large gatherings from
> far and near, mostly bent on idle curiosity or for a grand jollifi-
> cation and some even bent on attempting to rescue the pris-
> oner. They came in wagons, on horseback and on foot, and the
> procession continued in constantly increasing proportions down

---

[35]Quoted by Charles Kassel, "Recent Death Orgies," *South Atlantic Quarterly,* XXIII
(October 1924), pp. 305-309, at p. 305.

to the moment of the execution. Many came long distances, arriving the night before, crowding the taverns the preceding evening, or sleeping in the wagons in which they had come to town, and in which they proceeded the following day in gay procession to the place of execution. On the road to that place booths were erected for the sale of confections, eatables and intoxicants . . . The presence of the military was always required to prevent turbulance, or possible rescue of the condemned.

Jack Kenney Williams, in his *Vogues in Villainy,* which deals with crime in ante-bellum South Carolina, presents an excerpt dealing with the crowd that witnessed the hanging of the celebrated Lavinia Fisher on February 18, 1820. Mrs. Fisher and her husband robbed and killed a number of men at a tavern near the city of Charleston:

> Staid merchants were there, inwardly surprised at themselves for coming, and with them were dandies with . . . extravagantly-cut pantaloons; coon-skin capped wagoners, soldiers from the garrison of Fort Johnson; Dutch, French, and Spanish seamen; country cousins who had come to town for Race Week and neglected to go home again; free Negroes with their plump mulatto wives; slaves and white apprentice boys, all gathered around the gibbet. Little masters and misses broke from their nurses and . . . trudged to the hanging. Here and there were even fashionably clad women . . . The keepers of grog shops and sailors' boarding-houses in Bedon's Alley were there. The girls from the houses near the jail were there, on their best behavior.[36]

In Nevada, on April 24, 1868, a Frenchman, John Millian (properly Jean Marie A. Villain) was hanged for the murder of a "woman of the town and darling of Engine Company No. 1." The report of the hanging spectacle reads:

> Before 8 o'clock this morning little clumps of men might have been seen about the courthouse, and by 10, B Street was packed from side to side. A delegation from the Sisters of

---

[36]Quoted by Kenney, *op. cit.,* Columbia, S.C.; University of South Carolina Press, 1959, pp. 101-2, from Beatrice St. Julien Ravenal, *Charleston Murders,* New York, Duell, Sloan and Pearce, 1947, pp. 61-2.

Charity visited the doomed man and remained with him most
of the morning . . . about 9-1/2 o'clock a perfect torrent of
humanity poured into the city from all directions—Carson,
Washoe, Dayton, Gold Hill, Silver City, and even the cow
counties were largely represented. Men came by wagon loads,
in carriages, buggies, on horseback and afoot . . . Some time
before the prisoner was brought from the jail every available
housetop, balcony, door and window along B Street, from
Taylor to Sutton Avenue, was crowded with the curious. When
the National Guard marched down from the armory to the jail,
there was considerable stir in the crowd . . . Finally [the pris-
oner] was brought forth, and amid some half-suppressed jibes
and jeers from the heartless and degraded [he] stepped into
the carriage which was to carry him to the place of execution
. . . The streets leading out to the Geiger Grade were thronged
with people as far as the eye could reach, and along the road
beyond the Sierra Nevada works the side of Cedar Hill was
black with people. The gallows was erected just beyond the
point of the hill below the road . . . Women, with children in
their arms, hair disheveled and flying in the breeze, could be
seen hurrying across the bleak, burnt hills to catch a distant
glimpse of the horrid sight.[37]

In passing it should be noted that these garish spectacles were
not restricted to members of the male sex. The records indicate
that in the hanging-places, around the "trees," especially in the
large cities, females abounded. One comment, coming from a
source in Doylestown, Bucks County, Pennsylvania, is of interest
in this connection, only contrary to the above. The editor of the
paper, on the second day after the hanging of a celebrated Spanish
(?) adventurer, Lino Amelio Epos y Mina, which took place on
June 21, 1832, "in a natural ampitheatre on the banks of the Neshaminy [creek] on the almshouse grounds" before an estimated
assemblage of 10,000 persons, smugly wrote: "We are pleased that
there were not more than one hundred females in the vast concourse" (see Chap. V, 352 for account of this case).

Apocryphal tales have cropped up on occasion that testify to
the practice of females dressing as males in order that they be in-

---

[37](Reprinted in the Carson *Appeal*, April 26, 1868, from the *"Tresspass of Last Evening."* For further treatment of this case, see Chapter VII.

cluded in the crowd gathering around the "tree." This occurred
when they were denied the privilege of witnessing an execution,
either by convention or by official mandate. Hard facts, however,
that substantiate this are difficult to obtain. At the first hanging
within a county jail in Lancaster County, Pennsylvania, a news
report states that "females shed tears because of their hopeless
visit." A large crowd attempted to witness the affair, however, the
law prohibiting public hangings had already been passed and so
they were denied a viewing. Consequently, the disappointed females wept. This occurred at the hanging of Henry Smith, on May
11, 1838. He was executed for killing a man named Benjamin
Peart in a brawl over the theft of "two shoats."

It seems appropriate here to offer the reader a singularly punc-
tilious reporting of a private hanging. We have mentioned previously that in the days of public hangings, the daily or weekly papers,
for some strange reason, shunned reporting details of an event as
sordid as a hanging, but by the mid-nineteenth century, news
stories of such events were prevalent and quite commonplace. The
Geneva, New York *Courier,* of July 10, 1889, tells something of
the hanging of John Kelly on that date at Canandaigua, Ontario
County, New York. He had murdered Elizabeth O'Shea, house-
keeper for the man for whom Kelly worked. It seems that the victim had attempted to interfere in an "intimacy" between Kelly and
his employer's daughter. The scribe for the paper writes:

> The end is approaching fast. Kelly seems to fully realize the
> fact, and says that he is prepared to go. Last night was the
> hardest that he had experienced; at times he was very restless.
> He would sleep at intervals. Considering the circumstances—
> death staring him in the face—he stands it well and seems to
> be very cheerful this morning at times . . . Sheriff Hodgson of
> Rochester arrived this morning. He called on Kelly who was
> glad to see him and who shook hands with him . . .
>
> People are already beginning to come to the jail. Kelly's
> daughters arrived early to see their father for the last time. His
> wife and son will arrive soon.
>
> 10:00 A.M.   Quite a number of Genevans were present. Sher-
>   iff Corwin is beseeched every minute for passes.
>   The law allows but twelve persons, besides the
>   officials (eighteen) and relatives of the con-

demned. Sheriff Corwin has firmly resisted extra applications, eight in number.

Sheriff Hodgson and Sheriff Corwin have just come to the courthouse and are examining the gallows. A bag of sand is attached to the rope. The trap is sprung and the drop rests at four feet and eight inches. The mechanism works perfectly. Sheriff Corwin tried it with his weight; every part of the gallows was examined including the springs.

10:15 A.M.   The arrangements are fully completed. The sheriff is waiting for the hearse and coffin which left Geneva at 7 o'clock this morning.

10:30 A.M.   Parting between Kelly and his family—wife and son and two daughters has just been had—it was very affecting.

10:45 A.M.   Prisoner being dressed for execution, death watch present.

11:00 A.M.   Yard has been made clear and those having tickets only are admitted.

11:20 A.M.   Sheriff and jury enter jail yard.

11:35 A.M.   Borgman's hearse from Geneva came into yard with coffin.

11:40 A.M.   Kelly in his cell perfectly composed with no liquor to stimulate and is anxious to have affair over. Three priests with him.

11:45 A.M.   Jury took seats on the stand, the sun beat down upon the jurymen as though it would melt them. The procession has just started. Sheriffs, priests and Kelly walked to the scaffold. Kelly ascended the platform aided by the two sheriffs—the two priests kneeled on the ground under the scaffold. Kelly took the cross suspended around his neck and crossed himself. Sheriff strapped his legs.

11:50 A.M.   Kelly received a blessing with composure, standing fingering a little cross. The sheriff asked him if he had anything to say. Kelly made a long, rambling address. He said he would like the blessing of God on his friends in Geneva, and all over the country, that he owed no man a cent. He thanked the sheriff for his prompt attention and treatment, sympathized with the farmers and bade all good-bye.

After the cap was drawn over his face, Kelly said, "Now I am going" and in a moment he said "You are going too slow." The trap was sprung, almost while the words were in his mouth, and the body dropped at once. As the rope tightened it was shown the jugular vein was severed, and death must have been instantaneous. The trap was sprung at exactly 12:15 o'clock. The doctors stepped forward to take the pulse. We do not repeat the details. At 16-1/2 minutes pulsations ceased entirely. The head was two-thirds severed from the body.

12:29 P.M.   The body was taken down, put in the coffin, placed in Borgman's hearse and started immediately for Geneva.

Descriptions of hangings, such as we have reproduced in the preceding pages, could be duplicated or augmented by the hundreds throughout the country during that era of public executions. As McDade puts it: "Perhaps no single event brought more spectators in those years, than a public hanging. People drove for miles to be present; some camped in the vicinity for several days. The large concourse of people brought camp followers to every large gathering. Entertainers, vendors, pick-pockets, promoters, evangelists, sight-seers, peddlers and medicine men would descend on the town before the fatal day." He then says of the hanging of Joel Clough (July 26, 1833 for the murder of a widow, Mrs. Mary W. Hamilton who resisted his advances) "the gallows was erected by the road-side, about two miles from Mt. Holly, New Jersey. Around the place in every direction were the assembled multitudes—some in tents, and by-wagons, engaged in gambling and other vices of the sort, in open day."[38]

Many have pondered the questionable, if not reprehensible practice of persons setting up booths and tents to sell food and drink or hawk whatever souvenirs there were available on occasions of public hangings. But this is still done wherever crowds are likely

[38]*Op. cit.* p. xxx.

to gather to watch or anticipate some unusual event or spectacle regardless of its solemnity or tragedy. Such might be to watch the rescue of some entombed miners as was done near Hazelton, Pennsylvania in August 1963, or when, years earlier, Floyd Collins was caught in a Kentucky cave; further, it might be to watch an unusual fire or to wait for a potential riot which may never come off. It is characteristic of some members of the human race to take advantage of other people's miseries or troubles. This has been referred to by some anonymous coiner of phrases as "capitalistic opportunism." We find it today just as we read of it in the era of public hangings.

As we stated above, females attended, and in many instances, children. In New Hampshire, in 1820, Israel Wilkins[39] was hanged at Amherst for patricide. It was reported that "youngsters were called in from the playing-field to prepare to go to the hanging."

On occasion some untoward accident or tragedy would occur at a hanging, largely due to too many people descending on a small town unaccustomed to handling them. At the last public hanging at Cooperstown, New York (December 28, 1827), at the execution of Levi Kelley, a stand erected to accommodate the spectators collapsed, killing two and injuring several.[40]

The ribaldry that often developed became cause for anxiety among town officials. Mayors issued proclamations of warning, saloons and taverns were closed for a short time before and during the hanging. Yet despite such precautions, brawls and arguments took place. Even murders were committed, as a kind of catharsis to compensate for the vicarious mass sadism and pent-up tension of the attending crowd. In the John Lechler hanging, mentioned earlier (I, page 34) the mayor of Lancaster, Pennsylvania, urged tavern-keepers "for their own honour . . . to prevent gambling, drunkenness, dancing and all immoral transactions within their houses."

The local paper, the *Journal,* maintained that "the crowd retired following the hanging without any of that confusion which too often occurs and without a single incident of the most trivial

---

[39]Related to one of the writer's informants by Mr. George Woodbury, River Road, Bedford, New Hampshire.

[40]McDade, *op. cit.,* 550; also Chapter VII.

kind. Fears were entertained of the consequences [Lancaster had not witnessed a hanging since December 15, 1781, when "Negro York" had been executed for rape, a matter of some forty years] of so great a concourse of people . . . but such was the peaceful and praiseworthy conduct of all, that those who were clothed with authority saw no occasion for its exercise."

However, the cruel reality of the aftermath of this public orgy belies the benign optimistism and smugness of the editor. Wrote one correspondent: "Fifteen persons were committed to prison, one for murder, one for larceny, the rest for vagrancy." The person committed for murder was a John Wilson who stabbed Thomas Burns in a drunken brawl at a tavern. Both were on their way home from the hanging. Edward Livingston, mentioned earlier, commented on this homicide: "Wilson was apprehended and had the same irons put on him which had scarcely been laid off long enough by Lechler to get cold." As an aftermath he commented on the large number of pickpockets that abounded in the crowd watching the hanging of Lechler. The presence of pickpockets at a public hanging was always prevalent—especially in England where such an offense was for so long considered capital. It has become a cliché among many as an argument that capital punishment is not a deterrent.

The traditional revelry incidental to a public hanging is alleged to have occurred at Augusta, Maine, following the "turning off" of Joseph Sager, on January 2, 1835, for the arsenic poisoning of his wife Phoebe at Gardiner. According to a report presented to the legislature, the day was "one of drunkenness and profanity . . . with vices, quarreling and fighting carried to such an extent that it became necessary for the police to interfere, and the jail, which had just been emptied of a murderer [Sager] threw open its doors to receive those who came to profit by the solemn scene of a public execution."[41]

It has always been the contention of those opposed to capital punishment that murders are more likely to occur as the result of a hanging, whether it be before the public, or hidden behind walls. There was supposed to be a causal relationship between the

---

[41](*Report of the Committee to the Legislature of Maine, 1835,* quoted by Charles Spear, *op. cit.,* p. 61).

Lechler execution and the Wilson murder, mentioned above. There are other such conjectural chains of events. For example, Levi Kelley, at whose hanging, at Cooperstown, New York, the stands collapsed, is presumed to have murdered his victim, Abraham Spafard, because of his high suggestibility superinduced by witnessing the hanging of Jesse Strang at Albany, New York, on August 27.[42] Kelley drove to the state capital to see the spectacle and, on his return, remarked that no one who had witnessed such a dismal scene could ever commit a murder. Yet, but ten days later, he shot Spafard, who was his tenant. Spafard had defended a lame boy who had incurred Kelley's anger.[43] An aftermath of Kelley's execution was the suicide *by hanging* of one Cooke, who lived in the neighborhood and who had witnessed the event. We included earlier another similar linkage between a hanging and a tragic aftermath—the Jacob Leadings case, again in Albany, New York.[44]

Another such case was cited by Robert Rantoul, stern opponent of capital punishment of an earlier time. Writing in 1836, he stated: "In the state of Ohio, on the day on which a man was executed for murder of his wife, under circumstances of particular cruelty, another man, near the place of execution, murdered his wife in the same manner; and this is by no means the only instance where the crime seems to have been directly suggested by the punishment intended to prevent it."[45]

This conviction, held by many abolitionists, led the Rev. William Roberts, of Bristol, England, to remark that of 167 convicts under sentence of death that he had visited before their execution, 164 had witnessed at least one hanging.[46] Another Englishman, Dr. Stephen Lushington, speaking to the British Parliament, contended that "every execution brings an additional candidate for the hangman."[47]

It is difficult to prove empirically that hangings precipitate or

---

[42]See Chapter VII for story of the Strang case.

[43]This case is cited by Spear, *op. cit.,* p. 63.

[44]See *supra,* p. 25.

[45]Quoted by Spear, *op. cit.,* pp. 61-62.

[46]Cited by Andrew J. Palm, *The Death Penalty,* New York, G. P. Putnam's Sons, 1891, p. 127.

[47]Palm, *op. cit.,* p. 127.

breed murders, but there have been several homicides that have seemed to flow from the high suggestibility of persons who have witnessed hangings. The news reports dealing with this perverted phenomenon sound plausible. Palm has collected several instances of this sordid state of affairs but, unfortunately, he has not given us the dates of the newspapers. Nonetheless, we present them here, and eventually someone may have the time and the motivation to check them:

> *The Chicago Times:* "Within forty-eight hours after the hanging of the three assassins in the county jail, two men died in this city, the victims of murderous assault . . . If Chicago does not fail in the usual average, the deaths from homicide at the end of the week will considerably exceed the number of murderers killed off in the same time."

> *New York Star:* "Four men, three white and one colored, were hanged in the Tombs yesterday morning. It might be supposed that this terrible vengeance of outraged law would have at least a solemn effect upon the class whose ways and associations are leading them toward the gallows or the prison, but the night before the executions and just across the street from the Tombs, a gang of toughs passed the time in singing ribald songs and making vulgar remarks about the executions so soon to take place. The leader of the gang was hanged about a year ago."

> *Wilkes-Barre Record:* "The impressive lesson of yesterday's gallows tragedy in the jail-yard of this city did not prevent a murderous assault upon a citizen of Plymouth, who attended the execution of Volkavitch [*alias* Adam Volinski, hanged April 3, 1888, for the murder of John Bioski]. At an early hour he was found in an unconscious condition under the trestle of the Delaware & Hudson railway."

> *Pittsburgh Telegraph:* 'The lesson which may be wrought from capital punishment, so closely following the execution of McSteen (William, hanged October 4, 1883, for murder of his wife; at gallows 'was indifferent to his surroundings held bitter contempt for others, and unconcern for spiritual advice') was poorly learned in Allegheny yesterday. While McSteen hanged for the murder of his partner in marital life, John Brown, a business partner with Henry Weaver, killed him because of a dispute which involved a woman and a horse. The tragedy was one of the most bloody and determined that was ever enacted

in this vicinity" (disposition of this case not known, but the killer was *not* executed).

Pittsburgh Times: "The hanging of four men in New York Friday has been followed by as many murders in the vicinity since. The force of the admonition seems to have been lost on those for whose benefit hanging, it has been held, is the proper medicine. That branch of the argument, it is clear, will have to be abandoned. . . ."

Philadelphia Press: "On Friday last two men were hanged in New York for murder. On the following Sunday an Italian in that city stabbed another Italian to the heart, and a patrolman at Long Island City killed a police sergeant. There is no doubt about the efficacy of capital punishment, so far as the particular culprit is concerned. He can't murder anyone else, but the argument of the death penalty as a warning to other criminals is weakened by such occurrences as these two Sunday murders immediately following a double execution."[48]

Let us return to the hanging jamborees in the county seats. When William Welch, a young Revolutionary War soldier veteran was hanged at Reading, Pennsylvania, on July 17, 1784, some 15,000 to 20,000 persons attended the affair. Charles Biddle, burgess of the town at the time, accompanied Welch to the scaffold. He did so because he felt the death penalty was altogether too severe for the crime the young man had committed. It consisted of "highway robbery," which actually involved the paltry peculation of nine silver dollars from the market basket of a woman which he carried into town for her. Biddle, an influential person, bitterly denounced the court's draconic verdict. He also tells of "an old women [who] walked near seventy miles to see the hanging and being fatigued, a little before the execution, fell asleep and did not awake until it was over, when she cried bitterly."[49]

This anecdote can be exceeded by a grim tale related by Louis Blake Duff, which must have occurred in his native Canada. He tells of a woman who drove eight and one-half miles "from the Shorthills" to the jail with horse and buggy, early in the morning, to witness the hanging of her own son and on learning that he

---

[48]The above material is from Palm, *op. cit.,* 125-8.

[49]*Autobiography of Charles Biddle, Philadelphia,* 1883, pp. 192-3.

had been reprieved felt that "she had been cheated by an authority inconsiderate, unfeeling and harsh" for putting her to the trouble of getting up unduly early and trudging off in the early dawn on a futile errand![50]

It would be nice to believe that only the riffraff and the "great unwashed" attended public hangings. However, the excerpts from diaries, essays, letters and from books, written by literary men and women, or public leaders of the past, negate such a complacent assurance. Doubtless, the bulk of the "concourse"—a word very frequently used in describing a hanging crowd—were from the lower classes—the *hoi polloi,* yet there must have been a generous sprinkling of the *intelligentia* and favored classes in the crowds.

In the smaller counties, hangings were usually few and far apart in time. Sometimes a county would have but one, if at all, in its entire history. In others, they were separated by ten or twenty years, or a generation. In such localities they were regarded as an experience of a lifetime by many. It is little wonder that they were so well attended by persons coming from miles around. For example, at Woodstock, Vermont, over 10,000 persons attended the hanging of Samuel E. Godfrey on February 13, 1818. He had murdered Thomas Hewlett, keeper of the State Prison at Windsor. This hamlet, county seat of Windsor County, had but 1,300 souls in 1960; what could have been its population at the time of the hanging![51]

The lovely rural state of Vermont experienced more than one public hanging. The first of these (not counting the strange case of David Redding which we dealt with earlier, /see *supra,* 28) was that of Cyrus B. Dean, hanged at Burlington, on November 11, 1808, for the murder of Jonathan Ormsbee and Asa Marsh, two revenue officers. They were attempting to intercept potash smugglers on Lake Champlain who were aboard the craft, *Black Snake.* Dean shot the officers with a "gun nine feet, four inches long."[52] One colored man named Virginia was publicly hanged at St. Albans some time in 1820, for murder. The last one to be

---

[50]On the dust cover of his work, *The County Kerchief,* Toronto, Ryerson Press, 1929.
[51]McDade, *op. cit.,* 355.
[52]*Ibid.,* 246.

exposed to public view was Archibald Bates, hanged at Bennington on February 6, 1839, for the murder of the wife of his brother, Philorman, at Shaftesbury, some time in October, 1838. From a respectable farm family, Bates "came stealthily to the house at dusk and discharged his gun through the window," as his victim was nursing her baby. His motive was due to bad blood between them all that developed out of the distribution of their father's property.[53]

One could while away considerable time speculating as to just why people attended public hangings. Aside from the catharsis that many might be in need of, which an event of this kind might conceivably furnish, there was a maudlin or morbid curiosity in most of those who stood in the crowds. Professor Jack Kenney Williams has suggested, "Many said they were fast friends of the culprit, and had come from a sense of duty to pay him final homage. Others claimed to be relatives. Some declared they came in the hope of obtaining a souvenir. A bit of rope used in the hanging would, it was claimed, cure the worst sort of toothache; and others said it would, if used properly, ward off bad luck and evil spirits generally. If an inch or so of the rope were not obtainable, a chip of the gallows might be used in its stead. Even the bark off nearby trees was thought to possess special curative powers.[54]

TYPES OF EARLY GALLOWS

In the days of public hangings, gallowses or scaffolds were rather crude contraptions. Early periods in our history have seen limbs of trees used for this grim purpose. It is from this point of reference that the gallows gets its name "the tree." Another design consisted of two posts in the ground, with a cross-piece between them from which the victim swung—a modification of this design used a single stout post with a timber nailed at right angles at the top, with supporting boards attached.

The later refinement was a platform erected some nine or more

---

[53]Details found in *Bennington Banner,* Feb. 23, 1900.

[54]*Op. cit.,* p. 102; material compiled from several newspapers. In another connection we shall present controversial arguments as to their social value (see *infra,* page 63 superstitions).

feet from the ground, in the middle of which was a trap door swung upon hinges. This kind of folding-door would be supported at each end by a broad wedge. When the signal was given, the wedges were drawn out immediately by a cord passing through a pulley. The body fell through the space and was jerked by the shortness of the rope and thus the victim was "jerked into eternity." Louis (Louie) Miller, peripatetic homespun artist from York, Pennsylvania, in the early eighteen-hundreds, attended the Lechler hanging at Lancaster in the adjoining county (mentioned earlier) and thus described the scaffold: "It had a tremendous trap-door on the platform. And when the sheriff give (*sic*) the word the trap-door fell. Lechler was setting (*sic*) on a chair upon the door. Oh! what a crowd of people to see a poor sinner of a creature hung (*sic*) at the gallows."[55]

It may safely be stated that fully nine tenths of those hanged met their fate by being jerked in their short flight *downward*. But some were actually jerked *upward* by being catapulted in that direction. But not until hangings were transferred from open air sites into closed buildings with roofs do we find instances of such sophisticated, bizarre, and imaginative mechanisms. We shall describe them in a later chapter.[56]

ATTITUDES OF VICTIMS AT THE "TREE"

It would be a great mistake to assume that most of those hanged in this country exhibited or expressed repentance or even guilt as they stood on the gallows. Many did, but a large percentage denied their guilt up to the last second when the hood (usually black) was adjusted and the noose placed around their necks. The retributive nature of our penal philosophy urges, if not demands, wrong-doers to manifest a degree of penitence and when such an attitude is not forthcoming, little pity or grace can be expected. Society prefers to witness something like this which we find in the self-debasement of two Philadelphia burglars (John Whatnell and Michael McDeirmatt) who were hanged May 5, 1736: "During their imprisonment they appeared Penitent be-

---

[55]Courtesy, Historical Society of York County, Penna. Miller's quaint illustrations were quite familiar in the Pennsylvania Dutch countryside.

[56]See Chapter IV, p. 159-64.

wailing their Sins, and desirous of Instruction. At the place of Execution they seemed very earnest in their Supplications to Heaven for Mercy and cautioning the Spectators to take warning of their miserable and shameful end."[57]

A surprisingly large number exhibited great fortitude and courage at the "tree." A perspicacious remark on the exhibition of courage at the gallows was made by that American DeQuincey, Edmund Pearson, whose murder stories have delighted millions. Commenting on the hanging of Frederick Small at the State Prison at Concord, New Hampshire, on January 15, 1918, for the murder of his wife at their summer home on Lake Ossippee, he writes: "As with many another of his kind, better and worse, his death was apparently simple and courageous. It is one of the tormenting ironies of life that many good men do not make as good an end as those whose death is obscure and shameful."[58] On the other hand, many implored forgiveness of the survivors of persons whom they had wronged, accepted the services of the ministers of the gospel routinely, prayed for salvation in a dignified manner, and died resigned to their fate.

Overall, we find some who were quite garrulous and who showed quite some tolerance toward the sheriff or executioner. We have run across a few highly emotional persons who actually kissed the sheriff as he went ahead with his unpleasant duty. Still others enjoyed and basked in the attention they were receiving—perhaps for the first time in their lives to be the center of the stage—and made the most of it. After all, they had been the talk of the town, the focus of many news stories and perhaps some of these were embroidered with their photographs. They and their crimes were debated by hundreds during the trial period and the courtrooms were packed, with many turned away—all focusing their attention on the victims of society's jurisprudence. As Professor Williams states: "In South Carolina a few gloried in the attention they were receiving and died smiling and joking . . . . A Pendleton murderer, in 1828, entertained the multitude with a long speech in which he urged his listeners to go to church every Sunday and to take the temper-

---

[57]*American Weekly Mercury,* Philadelphia, April 30-May 5, 1736.

[58]*Five Murders,* New York, Doubleday, Doran, 1928, "The Man Who Was Too Clever," p. 50.

ance pledge at once . . . A Newberry felon, David G. Sims, sat on the edge of his gallows platform, listened attentively and added an occasional 'Amen' while the Rev. Samuel P. Pressley preached his funeral discourse. At Abbeville, a malefactor devoted the bulk of his final oration to an appeal that some one of the bystanders marry and care for his widow-to-be. 'She is a good woman and handy and no mistake' he declared."[59]

A good example of a casual, or contemptuous case comes from Washington, Pennsylvania, in the person of a seventy-year-old man named William Crawford. He was hanged on February 21, 1823. He had murdered his grown son for taunting him. The son whistled a patriotic ditty the old man disliked as it cast aspersions on the British with whom the father had fought during the War of 1812. The song was called *The Blackbird* and the son frequently baited the old man by singing or whistling it until one day "something snapped" and he killed his tormentor. The hard-bitten, unregenerate admirer of the British stood up in the death cart as it was being driven to the gallows, peeled and ate an apple as he surveyed the tag-along rabble that lined the route. To top off his disdain for the event he told the accompanying minister "to mind his own business" when asked if he wished prayers said for him.

McDade contributes a good case of casual nonchalance at the "tree" in the case of Jereboam O. Beauchamp, hanged at Frankford, Kentucky on July 7, 1826 for the murder of Col. Solomon P. Sharp, member of the legislature and one-time attorney-general of the state in an "honor affair." Beauchamp had brooded over the victim's ungentlemanly conduct in casting aside a young lady only to marry another. Beauchamp then proceeded to marry her, and challenged Sharp to a duel. Failing to gain his cooperation in this illegal deed, he stabbed him and took the consequences of the gallows. His wife shared his cell and while awaiting execution the two decided to commit suicide. The tragic wife succeeded but Beauchamp failed in his attempt. At the scaffold, he called on the military band to play *Bonaparte's Retreat from Moscow* and declared the "music delightful."[60]

---

[59]Williams, *op. cit.*, p. 103.

[60]McDade, *Annals of Murder*, xxxi; 80-89.

An example of a careless, even contemptuous, attitude at the gallows is that of John McDonald, hanged in Bucks County, Pennsylvania (place not certain), on November 9, 1785, for the murder of a farm woman and her child as they slept in their rural home. From all reports, this killer was a tough character. Charles Biddle, one-time member of the Provincial Council, has the following to say about him: "He died game, as it is called by such wretches, that is, like a hardened villain. A gentleman present when he was led pinioned and put into the cart for the execution, observed he had seen him before, wheeling oysters about the streets. 'Yes,' said he, 'you may have seen me before, and if you will wait until Jack Ketch has done with me, I'll turn around that you may see me behind.' "[61]

Then, of course, we have those calloused individuals who capitalized on their impending doom to make a play to the assembled crowd. There are many such cases in the history of hangings in Great Britain. Such cases exist in America and the following is a good example: Peter Robinson, hanged at New Brunswick, New Jersey, on April 16, 1841, for the murder of Abraham Suydam on December 3, 1840. Suydam was a bank president with whom Robinson's mortgage was held. He confronted Suydam in his own home, forced him to the cellar and dug his victim's grave— then battered him to death with the shovel. He threw the body into the hole and went on his way. Suspicion soon rested on him as he flashed the mortgage around maintaining he had paid it off, although it was generally known he had no assets. His execution, it was reported, was a "gala event" in the small New Jersey town. Robinson loved the fleeting and macabre publicity he received prior to the hanging as well as at the scaffold itself. Even at the sentencing, the rush of humanity about him was tremendous, "the ladies in particular." He slyly said to the harassed sheriff as he strove to do his duty: "Remember, you must share the fees with me that you get for hanging me." How he intended to take advantage of such monies he did not state. All through the ordeal he jested: "As I am a carpenter, I think I ought to be employed to help build my own gallows, and I should make my own coffin

---

[61] Biddle, *Autobiography*, 1883, p. 206.

. . . All I ask is a snug platform and a snug rope. And I won't have a damned priest near me." There was much more of this kind of calloused chatter. Said he: "If I could just have the big field to be hung in, and a band of music, I'd ask no more." Whether this bravado was genuine or simulated no one can say at this late date. At least, however, he put on a "good front."[62]

Another almost as contemptous was Guy Clark, hanged at Ithaca, Tompkins County, New York State, on February 3, 1832, for killing his wife, Fanny. On the way to the gallows, he amused himself by splashing the crowd's "fine feathers" with slush that was awash the board sidewalks. When admonished by the sheriff to hasten his gait, he assured him and the mob that "nothing will happen until I get there."[63]

Some of the victims of the tree had their lives snuffed out abruptly or prematurely. Perhaps these incidents were due to the nervousness of the hangman, who likely had little, if any, experience in hanging a human being. The incidents may have occurred because of a misunderstanding of signals between the sheriff and the person who released the platform. Some poignant examples of this untoward and premature last moment crudeness exist, but they seem more the result of ineptitude or nervousness rather than to any actual callousness or hostility on the part of the public servants officiating.

STATUS OF THE HANGMAN

Regardless of the victim's crime, if there was hostility against him, on the part of the officials during the time preceding or during his trial, it seems to have disappeared completely by the time the execution was to take place. There are, of course, exceptions to this. In fact, in many instances there seems to have evolved a strange affinity between officials and the gallows' victim. There are instances in which the doomed persons praised their keepers and shook hands all around before the trap was sprung. Of course, this last minute courtesy by the sheriff, hangman, and others in

---

[62]Spear, *op. cit.,* pp. 44-45; McDade, *op. cit.,* 808-812; there are several published pamphlets on this notorious case.

[63]Courtesy Mr. William Heidt, Jr., DeWitt Historical Society and Library, Ithaca, in letter dated January 7, 1964.

an official capacity cost nothing, especially when extended to those about to die.

There were mixed emotions by the crowds regarding not only the criminals, but the executioners, especially if the latter were hirelings. It was traditional in this country for hangmen to be anonymous, which explains, to a degree, why they were hated by many. Wrote the Rev. Charles Spear, in 1844: "The office of hangman is a hateful one, *detestabile carnificis ministerium.* Men scorn to give him the right hand of fellowship; they flee from him as from a pestilence."[64] Whether or not the above expressed attitude is strictly correct, we can at least state that never has a hangman in this country managed to get his name immortalized in the *National Dictionary of Biography,* or even in *Who's Who in America* (see *infra,* page 55).

Nothing like the following panegyric concerning the hangman has ever been spawned in this country, despite the fact that that craftsman has been obligated to do our "dirty work" for us. Ramon Sender has this to say about the hero in this novel, *The Affable Hangman*:

> I sometimes think there is only one man who lives the truth and who, furthermore, deserves the gratitude of all the rest and does not ask for it: the hangman. Upon his head rests all the social order known until today and still the hangman, aware of it, offers himself on a propitious object for the scorn, fear, and moral repugnance of all. Here is the martyr and hero.[65]

The only person to be involved in an execution and yet achieve distinction who has come to our attention, was President Grover Cleveland. When he was sheriff of Erie County, New York (Buffalo), he naturally inherited the onerous duty of officiating at the executions occurring in that county while he was in office. The record shows that he was obliged to hang two persons: Patrick Morrissey, on September 6, 1872, and Jack Gaffney, on February 14, 1873. Sheriff Cleveland took his duties seriously and would have "no damned foolishness from the public" at his hangings. On

---

[64]*Op. cit.,* p. 209.

[65]New York, Las Americas Co. 1963 (quoted in *New York Times Book Review,* September 8, 1963, by Thos. Curley; for other literary allusions to hangmen, see Chapter X.

the day of Gaffney's execution, the weather was cold and snow and ice were on the ground. This prompted the officials to sprinkle salt and sand in the jail yard, as a precaution against the sheriff slipping on his way to the gallows.[66]

Anonymity, then, was one of the main characteristics of hang-men in the early days of the country prior to the era in which sheriffs dispatched the distasteful function of their office (see Chapter IV, p. 175-6 for further discussion of the matter). In order to maintain this unenviable state, they were usually disguised in some manner. Sometimes their faces were blackened or they were covered with masks, some of which were reported as being hideous. At times, the local newspaper would editorialize against the practice of employing outsiders for the distasteful task, or in cloaking them with a kind of facelessness. The Crawford County, Pennsylvania, (Meadville) *Sentinel* for November 5, 1822, commented on the hanging of David Lamphier for the killing of a constable: "The practice of *hiring* a person to officiate in disguise on such occasions is highly improper. A duty so solemn, so important as that of taking life, ought to be performed by the person whom the law has designated; and we highly commend the sheriff for having performed the unpleasant task himself."

The above represents one point of view. The other is that this country has only infrequently employed trained hangmen and so has a bad record for bungling the job. There are instances where convicts were pressed into service with the reward of a pardon for negotiating the onerous chore (see *infra,* page 71). We discuss this problem in more detail in Chapter VIII. Let it suffice here to say that one of the serious criticisms directed against hanging in this country by Charles Duff, British authority on hanging, is that we have permitted most anyone to perform such an awful task (cf. Charles Duff, *The New Handbook of Hanging,* Chicago, Henry Regnery, 1955 107 ff.)

During the period of public executions, there are instances where public sentiment rose against the executioner to the extent that he was waylaid and roughly handled. The hangman who officiated

---

[66]Courtesy Dr. Louis Jones, Director, New York Historical Association, in a letter; see also, August Mencken, *By The Neck,* New York, Hastings House, 1942, p. 109.

at the hanging of Susannah Cox, of Reading, Pennsylvania, was actually "beset and soundly thrashed."

The Susannah Cox case was typical of the plight of young women in colonial and later days who loved more impetuously than wisely. The twenty-four-year-old girl was a domestic in the home of one Jacob Geehr in Oley Township, not far from the county seat. Geehr discovered the body of a baby in his woodshed. It was not until this discovery that it was suspected that Susannah was pregnant. After being sentenced, she freely admitted her crime. She went to the gallows "in City Park," clad in a white dress, decorated with wide black ribbons. Public opinion was so distressed at the execution of this young girl that the jurist who pronounced sentence was censured and badgered into resigning his post.[67]

The hangman had it within his power to make the lot of the victim somewhat easy—albeit not appreciated by that unfortunate person. It must be assumed, however, that this officiating personality was thoroughly objective in fashioning the noose and adjusting the sundry paraphernalia at the scaffold. But we detect more than a mere hint that one hangman, at least, arranged for a painless and prompt death for a beautiful female murderer, Lavinia Fisher, and for a sustained and painful torture for the woman's husband, John. The double hanging took place at Charleston, South Carolina, in the spring of 1820. Both were notorious malefactors and were finally sentenced to death for killing some patrons of a saloon-brothel. Writes a popular historian of this ghoulish episode:

> This despised creature [the hangman] had it in his hands, for once, to show both mercy and envious malice. Lavinia's beauty had stood her in good stead at last. But her affection for her husband, shown throughout the trial and at the end, had filled the hangman with hatred for him. At least this conjecture may furnish a clue as to the reason why Lavinia died so quickly and John so hard.[68]

As a parallel of the witnessing crowds manhandling of the executioner, we have found instances where the hangman was attacked

---

[67]Revival of news of the case in Reading *Eagle,* January 24, 1886.

[68]*Charleston Murders,* edited by Beatrice St. Julien Ravenel, Duell, Sloan & Pearce, 1947, p. 66.

by the person about to be hanged. At the execution of James Magowan at Harrisburg, Pennsylvania,[69] on December 29, 1806, Magowan attacked the executioner, tearing off his mask and knocking him out of the cart in which both rode to the gallows. Similar treatment was meted out to the hangman at Meadville, Pennsylvania, when George Speth Van Holland, alias Vanhollen, was executed on July 26, 1817. Van Holland, a stranger in the village, was permitted to stay overnight at the Fitzpatrick's. During the night he killed his host with an axe, obtaining forty dollars for his trouble. The title page of a pamphlet published on the case shows Van Holland jostling the hangman on the scaffold.[70]

Better treatment of hangmen in England has been the tradition although some, in the remote past, have apparently been badly treated by the mobs. More modern hangmen in that country—certainly our "Mother Country" so far as the practice of hanging is concerned—have operated public houses that have been *the* places to patronize, something akin to the popularity of restaurants and night clubs operated by baseball players or prize fighters in this country. Until his retirement, not too long ago, Albert Pierrepoint, hangman, was a public personality and seemingly well respected. He operated a pub which enjoyed the unusual but wholly realistic name of *Help The Poor Struggler*. One of his former assistants, Allenby, also operated a pub called *The Rope and Anchor*. While certainly not overpaid for their disagreeable task, four of these British hangmen have their names enshrined in the *Dictionary of National Biography,* according to Arthur Koestler.[71]

As stated above, some British hangmen have had their troubles. An early sixteenth century London hangman named Cratwell was hanged himself, in 1538, for robbing a young boy at a fair; later, the notorious John Price, who served in that capacity for one year (1714-15), was also hanged, but for murder; another, William Marvell (1715-17), was arrested for larceny as he was on his way to Tyburn, where he had a commission to hang three thugs.[72]

---

[69]McDade, *op. cit.,* 509-511.

[70]McDade, *op. cit.,* 1018.

[71]*Reflections on Hanging,* New York, Macmillan, 1957, p. 3.

[72]For a history of British hangmen, see Horace Bleackley, *The Hangmen of England,* London, Chapman & Hall, 1929.

William Brunskill (1786-1814) was obliged to petition the authorities, in 1794, for more money per hanging, lamenting that he was unable to obtain other employment due to social ostracism.[73] Louis Blake Duff tells us that one hangman of the seventeenth century—Exeter being his bailwick—Roger Gray, actually was obliged to hang his own brother. He hints that the trials and tribulations of executioners, in this country as well as abroad, sometimes drove them to suicide.[74]

Overzealous crusaders against capital punishment in this country have held the office of hangman in contempt. Earlier we mentioned the statement made by the Rev. Charles Spear that the office of hangman is a hateful one, which is typical of their attitude (see *supra.,* page 51). Andrew J. Palm, another early zealot who has been quoted earlier, writes: "A sure indication that the death penalty is repulsive to the better feelings of men is the detestation with which an executioner is regarded. Men refuse him the hand of fellowship and would sooner associate with a beast than with him whose trade is to take human life." He further quotes from the Britisher, William Ladd: "No man, however low or dispicable, would consent to perform the office of hangman; that whoever would dare to suggest such a thing to a decent man would be in danger of bodily injury."[75]

Of William Marwood, the first hangman of England to bring a certain element of respectability to the office (he served from 1874 to 1883), Palm writes: "Marwood arrived in London the evening before he was to hang Dr. Lamson in 1882 (April 28, for poisoning his young brother-in-law, a student at Wimbledon, with aconite) and he paid a visit to Lusby's music hall. He was recognized immediately and a scene of confusion ensued. He was obliged to drive away in a cab, in order to escape being mobbed.[76] Perhaps the cynic might put a different interpretation on the hangman's abrupt departure. He might suggest that it was precipitated by his *popularity* rather than through revulsion.

On the reverse side of this controversial coin, we suggest only

---

[73]Charles Duff, *op. cit.,* p. 24.
[74]*The County Kerchief, op. cit.,* pp. 151, 153.
[75]Palm, *op. cit.,* p. 94.
[76]*Idem.*

that most of the hangings within the walls of a prison or county jail have been personally carried out by the sheriff as a part of his duty, distasteful though it is. We have not heard of any county sheriff being socially ostracized for performing this onerous task. Hangings in this country have been, for the most part, local affairs, and aside from the period of public executions when professional hangmen were usually employed, it was a local man with community connections whose job it was to dispose of persons condemned to death. Today, in this country, we have work for hangmen in the states where that method is still used, so "career" personnel are in some demand and should not be discouraged through fear of social stigma. Aside from professional executioners, members of the prison custodial staff (guards) handle the infrequent assignments imposed upon the prisons by the courts.[77]

It should be stated that hangmen have been known in both Great Britain and this country (we imported the term) as "Jack Ketch." There was such a person—a hangman—whose real name was Richard Brandon. He held office from 1663 to 1686. The story is that he badly bungled the hangings of Lord Russell, in 1683, and the Duke of Monmouth, in 1685. He was thoroughly hated by everyone and was finally turned out of office for insulting the sheriff, Pasha Rose, who was also a butcher. Rose was installed but later he "had to be hanged," so Ketch was reinstated and served for some time.[78]

As stated above, Marwood gave some dignity to the job. He had followed the notorious hangman-institution, William Calcraft, who served in that capacity from 1829 to 1874, a period of forty-five years! Marwood not only lent dignity to the profession, but it was he who introduced several innovations—such as the "long drop"—which revolutionized hanging by making it more efficient and less painful. He and his equally well-known successor, James Berry, who served between 1886 and 1891, left a unique heritage for later hangmen to emulate.[79]

---

[77]A humorous or, perhaps, satirical article dealing with some infrequently discussed elements of this profession may be found in *Esquire*, "Young Man, Be An Executioner," by Gerald Walker, August, 1963, pp. 62-3.

[78]Bleackley, *op. cit.*, p. 5.

[79]See Justin Atholl, *The Reluctant Hangman*, London, John Long, Ltd., 1956.

Public hangings were not cheap affairs. What they cost the tax-payers in various decades could probably be ascertained by a careful check of those records that have survived the ravages of time. Professor Williams states that in "ante-bellum days in South Carolina the cost was one hundred dollars.[80] However, there are few published accounts, and, of course, the price varied from place to place and with the times. It is quite possible that hangmen were better paid then than now (see *Esquire* article, *loc. cit., supra.*).

Aside from the *cost of hanging* a person, the hangman, whether he was anonymous or the constable or keeper of the local jail, was usually given a swig of toddy or punch, sometimes before and sometimes after the hanging. We append here two itemized accounts presented to the sheriff of Philadelphia County for specified hangings:

1. For executing "Negroe Peter," October 12, 1782, for murder: William Will, Esq., (Sheriff) to John Reynolds (jailer) Dr.

October 11, 1782

To makeing the Gallows & Putting it up L1.10.0
To a Rope for Negroe Peter. 0.10.0
To a Coffin for Ditto. 1.10.0
To Cash Henry Byrnes for Hanging Negroe Peter. 3.10.0
To Liquor for the Constables 0.12.0

2. For executing Dawson & Chamberlain, both on November 25, 1780, and James Sutton, on November 29

	Dr. 1780	*Dollars*
October 24th	To 3 Bowls of punch as putting up the gallows	
	To Hang Dawson & Chamberlain	90
October 25th	To 3 Bowls and a half of Toddy after the Execution	70
October 28th	To 3 Bowls of Toddy at putting up gallows on the Island	
October 30th	To Toddy for the Constables for Hanging Sutton	85

(Negroe Peter was hanged for murder, Dawson for treason, Chamberlain for passing counterfeit money and Sutton for piracy.)

---

[80]*Op. cit.,* p. 101, from accounts of Sheriff A. C. Bomar, November 20, 1838 (penal papers).

We do not know what a dollar was worth at that time, but comparatively, it cost about as much to supply three and a half bowls of toddy as to execute two criminals. On the other hand, it seems to have cost about three times as much to hang a man in the Negroe Peter case as to purchase his coffin.[81]

PLACES OF EXECUTION

Public hangings were generally held in the public squares or commons. A few victims were taken "to the edge of town," or to "the depot" or "behind the jail or courthouse." Many county seats had their "Gallows Hill" which was usually public property or, perhaps, leased for the occasion of a hanging. One man, Charles Getter, was hanged on an island in the Delaware River off the town of Easton, Pennsylvania—on October 11, 1833, for killing his wife—and to this day it is called Getter's Island. Raphael Semmes reports that some early hangings took place on islands in Maryland; Jacob, a Negro slave, on October 4, 1664, on Spesutie Island at the head of Chesapeake Bay, for the murder of his mistress, wife of Col. Nathaniel Utie, by stabbing. In sentencing this poor wretch, Governor Charles Calvert said: "You, Jacob, shall be drawn to the gallows at St. Mary and there hanged by the neck until you are dead." Another Maryland felon, John Dandy, was hanged on an island in the Patuxant River—date not known—for beating his servant boy, Henry Gough, to death. Dandy lived at Newton.[82] August Mencken tells of the hanging on Smith's Island, on July 26, 1906, of William Lee, a Negro, convicted of raping two white women in Somerset County, Maryland. He was tried in Baltimore.[83]

Pirates, especially, were hanged on islands in New York City (Bedloe's) and in the Delaware River off Philadelphia, during colonial days and some years later. Three such renegades, Joseph Baker, or Boulinger, Joseph Berouse, or Brous, and Peter Le Croix, part of the crew of the ship *Eliza,* seized the boat and murdered

---

[81]The above data are from State Record Office, Harrisburg, Pennsylvania. A news story from Delaware in October 1965 states the cost there as $450 with $300 of the amount going to the hangman.

[82]These cases are cited by Semmes, in *Crime & Punishment in Early Maryland,* Baltimore, Johns Hopkins Press, 1938; from bibliography (Jacob, XLIX, 486, 489-91; Dandy, X, 522, 534-45).

[83](*By the Neck,* pp. 27-32; story in Baltimore *Sun,* July 27).

three of the crew and wounded the captain. However, the master,
Captain Wheland, was able to regain possession of the vessel and
bring it into port at St. Kitt. The men were then brought to Philadelphia on the United States sloop of war, the *Ganges*, convicted
and hanged. The news account emphasized the supplication and
prayerful mien of the men as they knelt for an hour or more before
the gallows. A large crowd on the island and on boats plying in
the river made the triple hanging a gala event in the life of the
staid Quaker city.[84]

In the hinterland counties, in the early days, sheriffs were sometimes hard put to rent private land for their hangings, due to repugnance of the owner to have his field tramped down by the
crowds or due to some superstition he might possess regarding an
affiliation with such an event. Under such conditions, the sheriff, in
desperation, might set up the hanging-tree at a street intersection
of the county seat. In such instances, to add to his woe, persons
opposed to capital punishment might denounce him for using such
conspicuous public intersections for so grim a spectacle. It was a
wise sheriff, indeed, who managed to preempt an open site large
enough to permit a crowd of several thousands to attend a hanging.
In the case of the only public hanging at Norristown, Montgomery
County, Pennsylvania (the writer's home county), on April 12,
1788, when John Brown paid the penalty for burglary, the sheriff
was desperate in his effort to find a suitable place for his scaffold.
He finally managed to locate a spot behind the jail, but even here,
many citizens objected to it. The sheriff's answer was that he
could not get permission of "any holders of land in or near the
place to permit him, as an officer, to fulfill the performance of
that which was required of him by law".[85]

The following two cases deal with persons convicted and hanged
for piracy, but both are somewhat dubious so far as actual piracy
was concerned. The first, Albert W. Hicks, has often been referred to as the "last pirate" hanged in this country. Hicks did
commandeer a sloop, but he committed the dastardly crime of
murdering the entire crew of four. It was the oyster sloop *E. A.*

---

[84]McDade, *op. cit.*, 62-64; Poulson's *American Daily Advertiser*, Philadelphia, May 9.
[85]William J. Buck, *History of Montgomery County in the Schuylkill Valley*, Norristown, Pa. 1859, pp. 90-91.

Johnson, out of New York City for Deep Creek, Virginia, and the date of the tragedy was March 21, 1860. In his own words, Hicks maintained "the Devil took possession of me," so he determined to murder the crew, which he did. His victims were the captain, named Burr, a sailor named Johnson, and two boys named Oliver and Smith Watts. The craft was later picked up deserted, its decks covered with blood, by the schooner, *Telegraph* and was towed into New York Harbor. Hicks was soon apprehended and convicted of piracy and murder. He was taken on board the *Red Jacket,* along with 1,500 others who had been invited to witness the execution, and transported to Bedloe's Island, where he was hanged. However, as the hour of the hanging had been slightly changed, the captain of the boat had a little time to kill so he "gave the passengers a little excursion trip to enable them to view the *Great Eastern* (the vessel later laid the second Atlantic Cable), the monster ship which had just made her first voyage to America and was lying near the foot of Hammond Street."[86]

McDade refers to the execution of Hicks as follows: "In New York Harbor, in the sight of a hundred vessels, in the best maritime tradition."[87]

The following case is bizarre indeed. It is included at this point in our narrative only because the victim of the hangman's noose was convicted of piracy although he neither shanghaied a vessel nor a crew. The case deals with Nathanial Gordon, from Down East (born in Portland, Maine in 1832), at twenty-eight, the master of the small 500-ton vessel, the *Erie* out of Havana on April 17, 1860. On that date, he was headed for Africa with a crew of four who were apparently ignorant of the boat's destination.

The little vessel's cargo out of Cuba consisted of 150 hogsheads of liquor and a consignment of various kinds of meat and rice. It arrived at the mouth of the Congo River on the west coast of Africa in the latter part of July and there, to the consternation of the crew, 897 Africans, consisting of men, women, and children were driven aboard and herded between decks. With the greatest

---

[86]Thomas S. Duke, *Celebrated Criminal Cases of America,* San Francisco, The James H. Barry Co., 1910, p. 614. Hicks was hanged July 13, 1860.

[87]*Op. cit.,* 473; for a graphic description of the hanging scene, see Louis Blake Duff, *op. cit.,* p. 108.

possible haste, Captain Gordon started back to his home base, Cuba. However, an American war vessel, the *Mohican,* was lying in the river at the time and its captain had been informed of the wholesale kidnaping which was obviously illegal. Overtaking the *Erie,* the *Mohican* towed it to Monrovia where the helpless cargo was released but not before eighteen of them had died of suffocation in the fetid hold. Gordon was returned to the United States where he was tried on a strange charge defined as piracy. It was dated May 15, 1820, and referred to as the Fifth Section United State Statutes. It reads as follows:

> If any citizen of the United States, being of a ship's crew of any foreign vessel, owned wholly or in part or navigated for any citizen or citizens of the United States, shall forcibly confine or detail or aid and abet in forcibly confining or detaining on board such vessel, any negro or mulatto not held in service by the laws of either the States or Territories of the United States, with intent to make him a slave, such person shall be adjudged a pirate and on conviction shall suffer death.

Gordon's conviction under this statute was allegedly the only one which terminated in the death penalty.

In sentencing the unhappy man, the jurist, Judge Simpson, had these words to say:

> Think of the cruelty and wickedness of seizing nearly a thousand human beings, who never did you any harm, and thrusting them between the decks of a small ship, beneath a burning tropical sun, to die of disease or suffocation, or be transported to distant lands, and consigned, they and their posterity, to a fate far more cruel than death.
>
> Think of the sufferings of the unhappy beings whom you crowded on the *Erie;* of their helpless agony and terror as you took them from their native land, and especially think of those who perished under the weight of their miseries on the passage from the place of your capture to Monrovia. Remember that you showed mercy to none—carrying off, as you did, not only those of your own sex, but women and helpless children.

Gordon's wife and mother tried desperately to see President Lincoln, hoping he might stay the execution. In this they were bitterly disappointed through a cruel turn of fate; on the day they were in Washington the great president's son, Willie, died—February 20, 1862.

Gordon attempted suicide in his cell the day preceding his execution. Some of his relatives, when visiting him, had given him some cigars. At 3 A.M. on the day of his execution February 21 he was seized with convulsions. The prison physician diagnosed his illness as strychnine poisoning and, after working over him for several hours, brought him around to a condition in which he could be hanged. It was believed he obtained the poison in the gift cigars.[88]

SUPERSTITIONS SURROUNDING THE HANGING TREE

Much superstition is woven in and around the practice of hanging with the hanging itself, with the gallows, the rope, the shroud, the hangman, and, no doubt, even the weather and the nature of the crowd.

Perhaps the first recorded superstition was that connected with the cart that carried several of the doomed "witches" to the gallows at Salem, Massachusetts, on September 22, 1692. It is stated that "the Cart going to the Hill with these Eight to Execution, was for some time at a sett; the afflicted and others said, that the Devil himself ordered it."[89]

As late as the 1870's, we learn of ghosts hovering around the gallows at Fort Smith, in the Indian country, where "Hanging Judge" Isaac Parker kept it and the hangman, George Maledon, busy disposing of the outlaws of that territory. Glenn Shirley tells us of the ghosts standing on the scaffold, of strange spirits leaping the walls with ropes around their necks, and, in one tale, of a group of such creatures actually holding a meeting to discuss the idea of making an attack on the jail.[90]

Pennsylvania, like most of the states, is replete with superstitions regarding hanging victims. A slave, "Negro Bob" (Robert Waldron), whose case is embalmed in legal decisions (involving the

[88]The above data comes from Thomas S. Duke, *op. cit.*, pp. 604-5, from Thomas Sutton, *History of New York Tombs.*

[89]George Lincoln Burr, *Narratives of the Witchcraft Cases,* New York, Barnes & Noble, Inc., 1914, p. 367, *by permission.*

[90]*Law West of Fort Smith,* New York, Holt, Rinehart and Winston, Inc., 1957, p. 81; see pages 398-404 for discussion of that era in our social history, Chapter IX.

legality of a slave's testimony in a court trial) (see Chapter VII, Boyington case p. 313 for similar situation, also V, p. 65 Carawan case), was hanged at Easton, Northampption County, on October 25, 1795, for killing another slave named David. He is supposed to have haunted the hanging site—"the scene of many fearful tales of ghosts, sprites, and hobgoblins; the school boy hastens to pass it on his return from the out lots before the shadows of the night present to his terrified vision the body of Bob swinging stiff, and black, and stark in the wind, or standing with his bloody axe over his victim as he did years ago."[91] The otherwise docile Bob, ferocious at the scene of his crime, had declared he "would split the skull of any fellow who would be saucy;" apparently David took the dare and lost.

Spooks have been identified and accepted without question in other Pennsylvania communities where hangings took place. James Munks, mentioned earlier (Bellefonte, Centre County), haunted the community for years (p. 26). A tale from Carlisle, Cumberland County, same state, is of interest. Edward Donnelly, hanged February 8, 1808, for killing his wife (he burned her body in the fireplace), is supposed to still converse with people who take the time to go down to the "eastern end of Main Street at the Fork of the Trindle Spring and York Roads and halloo at the spot, 'Donnelly, what were you hanged for?' and the answer comes back loud and strong 'For nothing.' "[92]

Still another Pennsylvania saga carries with it a degree of superstition: the case of Cap'n James Fitzpatrick—"Sandy Flash" immortalized by Bayard Taylor in his historical novel, *The Story of Kennett* (1869). This swashbuckling Chester County Tory was the romantic stereo-type of the gentleman highwayman who, in the tradition of Robin Hood, Dick Turpin or Jack Sheppard, was beloved by the simple folk and who often robbed the rich to give to the poor. An outside member of the famous Doan gang, members of which he met from time to time in Philadelphia or in their hideaways in Bucks County, Sandy Fitzpatrick could "do everything well" and was "brave and heroic," albeit unlawful. He was

---

[91]Quoted in the *Easton* (Pa.) *Free Press* (from a reprinting from an issue in 1835), July 20, 1871.

[92]From *Old Home Week Letters,* No. 5, 1909, Carlisle.

hanged September 26, 1778, at Chester, the victim of betrayal by a woman. Cap'n "Fitz's" horse can be heard nowadays—or so some people think—galloping at night among the hills and caves of Chester and Delaware Counties (the caves are named for him),[93] along with the horse that belonged to the brother of Elizabeth Wilson, a tragic young woman who was also hanged at Chester on January 3, 1786, and whose story will be related later (see Chapter II, p. 123). Amos Wilson "went into a depression" in his attempt to rescue his sister from the gallows, and having failed, spent the remainder of his life as a hermit in the hills of Pennsylvania. Their poignant story is a classic.

Far from Pennsylvania, in the Tarheel State of North Carolina, it is said that for many years, the unquiet spirit of the Rev. George Washington Carawan, convicted for the murder of his schoolteacher neighbor, in 1853, walks the shore of Juniper Bay. He did not hang, however, but committed suicide in the court room. We shall defer this story until later (see Chap. V).

One superstition or, apparently, a practice from England, and one that finds no counterpart in this country, was that in which a parent who took his children to witness a hanging would, of necessity, be obliged to spank them afterward, in order to impress on their minds the awful lesson of the gallows.[94]

Perhaps the most ghoulish superstition we have encountered in our study was the belief on the part of any criminal who might witness a hanging that bones from the hands of the victim of the "tree" would serve as charms "to open the door of any home without detection."[95]

The Rev. Charles Spear, whose stories on capital punishment of a bygone era have been incorporated earlier, supplies us with a strange case that is pertinent. He tells of the notorious Charles Gibbs, hanged in New York City on April 22, 1831, for piracy. He writes: "A witness was present (at the execution) who declared positively that he had seen Gibbs hung (sic) on a former occasion for the same crime, at some port in South America. He

---

[93]For more on Fitzpatrick, see *infra*, page 71.

[94]William Andrews, *Bygone Punishments*, London, 1899, p. 224.

[95]Clifford Kirkpatrick, *Capital Punishment*, Philadelphia, Yearly Meeting of Friends, 1925, p. 26; quotes from S. Baring-Gould, *Strange Survivals*, p. 244.

insisted that he recognized him beyond the possibility of a mistake, by certain peculiar marks of identity" (*op. cit.,* pp. 55-56).

BUNGLING AT THE TREE

Bungling of executions has, through the years, been regarded as well-nigh scandalous. All through hanging history, in England, such emergencies were anticipated and dealt with on a pragmatic basis. In most instances, a second rope was always handy in case the first one broke. However, in the old "strangling" days, the hangman might be obliged to beat upon the breast of his victim in order to hasten death, or pull on his legs if the rope was too short or if the poor wretch did not seem to be strangled sufficiently. It was not unusual for the friends of the condemned to offer such help so as to end any suffering that might result from bungling. Such were regarded as friendly gestures. Despite the fact that professional executioners have always graced the English scaffolds— men schooled in the art of hanging—many victims were bungled or botched out of the world.

In our own country, from colonial times, we find many cases of sheer bungling. Earlier we cited the case of Mary Martin, hanged some time in 1646, at Boston, for infanticide, and whose execution was undoubtedly bungled (see page 9). She hung by the neck for quite a spell after she was pushed from the ladder.

Perhaps the best-known example of a frustrated hanging is that of Will Purvis who was actually freed after the hangman had made three abortive attempts to snuff out the alleged killer's life. This was in Mississippi, on February 7, 1894.[96]

Perhaps the most colorful case from Pennsylvania is that of the Delaware Indian, Mamachtaga, hanged on December 20, 1785, at Hannas Town (Greensburg) Westmoreland County, at the time a backwoods outpost. This child of the forest holds the dubious distinction of being the first to be hanged for murder west of the Alleghenies, and thus deserves a few lines here. The story as related by state historians is as follows: He was convicted of killing two men, John Smith and Benjamin Jones, in a drunken orgy, on Killbuck Island, not far from Pittsburgh. His trial took place in

---

[96](See page 228 Chapter V) for this story and also the classic John Lee episode from England.

the log cabin home of Robert Hannas, the sheriff, and was presided over by the Chief Justice of the Commonwealth, Thomas McKean. The unlettered Indian was defended by the outstanding frontiersman advocate, Hugh Brackenridge. When brought into court, the pathetic and confused defendant refused to plead not guilty because, as he said, he had actually killed the two men. He admitted he did not know what he was doing since he was drunk. But he simply could not fathom the casuistry of the Anglo-Saxon jurisprudence with its legal fictions that almost insisted that he declare himself "not guilty." Chief Justice McKean explained in sonorous pontifical terms that drunkenness was no excuse for murder; yet this was not a premeditated crime.

One may well visualize the awe and reverential fear of Mamachtaga as he viewed the Chief Justice and his associate jurists attired in scarlet robes, enunciating the hocus-pocus of the legal jargon that was the white man's burden inherited from the English common law. The grave demeanor, and glittering robes of the justices reflected in the crude candlelight of the cabin undoubtedly made a deep impression on the Indian. As one historian put it: "He could not believe they were mortals, but regarded them as divine personages." As one views this case today, it is obvious that the cards were heavily stacked against this trusting primitive.

Jurists, witnesses, jurors, and lawyers were herded together in a small crowded room. The jurists themselves occupied common hickory chairs raised on a clapboard platform. After his conviction and sentence to death, the little daughter of the jailer fell dangerously ill. Mamachtaga said if they would let him go into the woods he could find some roots that would cure her. He went, obtained the roots, and the little girl's illness was cured. The day before the hanging he asked for permission to go to the woods again, this time to get some roots to paint his face. The jailer went with him, he found the desired roots and returned to the jail. The next night he was hanged, in all the painted glory of a Delaware warrior.

The gallows, it was reported, was merely a cross-piece structure, with a ladder leading up to the noose which was thrown across the crossbeam. A rope was placed around the Indian's neck and he was shoved off the ladder by the sheriff. The first time *the rope broke.* The poor Indian, struggling and bewildered as he felt himself partially strangling supposed that was all, laboring under the delusion that this was it! But he had not reckoned with the caprice of the white man. The sheriff procured another rope and he was again compelled to ascend the ladder. This time the majesty of the law was vindicated by the death of the frightened red man for a crime, as one historian put it "committed in a frenzy fit, occasioned by whiskey the white man had given him."

We stated above that this was the first hanging for murder west of the mountains. This is correct but, sheer minutes before, "a simple-minded white man," one Joseph Ross, was hanged at the same place on the same gallows, convicted by the same court, for the crime of buggery.[97] The gallows in this backwoods region "was erected on a hill west of Hannas Town known until recently as Gallows Hill . . . the executions took place at night and were witnessed by a great number of people."[98]

We have no way of knowing just how many hangings took place in other states in which the rope broke. Judged by the several instances we have found in our own intensive study of Pennsylvania hangings, it would seem that, overall, these abortive hangings happened frequently. When it did happen, it caused confusion and even consternation at the worst, and embarrassment at best. It is of some interest to learn that the notorious pirate, Captain William Kidd, suffered this same fate when he was hanged at Execution Dock, in London, in 1701.[99] During the interval in which another rope was being sought he took the minister's advice to use the time for further supplication. This he did and expressed his charity for the world and hopes of salvation.

There has been little editorial censure directed against the sheriff in charge of an execution in which the rope broke. Yet it has always been his responsibility to see that everything operates

---

[97]*Colonial Records of Pennsylvania,* XIV, p. 588, December 1, 1785.

[98]Sources: J.W.F. White: The Judiciary of Allegheny County, *Pa. Mag. of Hist. & Biog., VII:* 147-9, 1883; also, A.A. Lambing: *Allegheny County: Its Early History & Subsequent Development,* 1888; also Hugh Henry Brackenridge: The Trial of Mamchtaga, a Delaware Indian, the First Person Convicted of Murder West of the Allegheny Mountains and Hanged for His Crime, *West, Pa. Hist. Mag.,* I:27-36, 1918; John N. Boucher: *Old and New Westmoreland,* 1918 Ed., I, 208; and Archibald Loudon: *Indian Narratives,* 1829, I, 38-50; and CR XIV, 585, November 25, 1785.

[99]Justin Atholl, *Shadow of the Gallows,* p. 62.

smoothly and that no such ghastly crisis such as this occurs. In England, when Captain Kidd was subjected to this crisis, the *Newgate Calendar Improved* made the following critical comment:

> In cases of this distressing nature . . . the sheriff ought to be punished. It is his duty to carry out the sentence of the law into execution, and there can be no plea for not providing a rope of sufficient strength.[100]

Unfortunately, we have little clinical evidence of the reaction of the victim to such an occurrence. Doubtless he was so bewildered that he possessed no coherent thought he could express. His semi-conscious state must have been akin to a nightmarish trance. In all the instances with which we are familar, another rope was quickly obtained and the poor frightened wretch dispatched before he could speak. A few of our Pennsylvania cases will suffice to indicate the trauma of these fiascos.

A slave named Christian Sharp, or "Kit," was being returned to the South by a "Negro drover," one Robert Carlile of Woodford City, Kentucky. As they passed through Washington, Pennsylvania, Sharp suddenly turned on his captor and killed him. The Negro was hanged on November 21, 1828, but not without the rope breaking. The same thing happened when Charles Getter was hanged at Easton, on October 11, 1833. The news report states: "He had been raised scarcely three feet when the *rope broke* and he fell. His face was uncovered but he lay without life for half a minute . . . Even this terrible interlude in the solemn scene which chilled the look of almost every spectator, had no effect upon his iron nerve."[101]

Then there was the case of Cornelius Jones, hanged at Honesdale (Bethany) Wayne County, November 13, 1817, for the murder of his step-father. At the hanging, near the courthouse, the *rope broke*. The report read: "Before it could be readjusted, he recovered his power of articulation and begged most piteously not to be hauled up again. . . He was dropped a few inches off the ground where he ended his life in horrible agony, while the crowd

---

[100]*Ibid.*, p. 55.

[101]As reported from news story in the Pennsylvania House of Representatives, "On the Expediency of Abolishing Public Executions," read in the House December 12, 1833.

turned away appalled at the sickening scene."[102] We quote the dirge phantasy of Jimmie Quinn later. His execution at Lebanon, same state, was also marred when the *rope broke*.

The story to end all rope breakings comes from Bellefonte, Centre County, Pennsylvania. When Dan Byers, a Negro, was hanged there, on December 13, 1802, the *rope broke*. The crowd immediately began to shout: "Dan's free!" The people surged forward but were thwarted by the military squads present. A spectator, standing nearby, took Dan by the arm and said, "Dan, you've always been a good boy; go up now and be hung (sic) like a man." It was reported "Dan obliged!"[103]

This paternalistic attitude, nurtured by the "spectator" who, undoubtedly, was a representative citizen of the community, reminds us of the bit of repartee that took place during the hearings of the British Royal Commission on Capital Punishment, during 1950. The hangman, Pierrepoint, had testified that he had experienced but one "rough or awkward moment" during his professional career, and that was when a "foreigner"—a spy—"had kicked up rough" at the gallows. The payoff to this was when the hangman's testimony was substantiated by the Under-Sheriff of London County who said unblushingly:

> He was a foreigner, and I have personally noticed that English people take their punishment better than foreigners . . . He just dived at the Executioner with his head, and then he just fought with everything he had.[104]

Incidentally, the philosophy expressed above is in the same tradition as that advanced by many editors and news commentators who condemned our own Caryl Chessman for fighting so tenaciously through the courts to save himself from the gas chamber at San Quentin prison for alleged kidnaping. They contended that he was "playing with the courts" and "making a mockery of justice" by writing and presenting writs to the California and federal courts to stave off the sentence of death imposed upon him. The "for-

---

[102]From the *History of Wayne, Pike and Monroe Counties, Pa.*, by Alfred Mathews, 1886, pp. 181-2.

[103]John Blair Linn, *History of Centre & Clinton Counties*, Pa. 1883, pp. 44-5.

[104]RCM 302, quoted by Arthur Koestler, *op. cit.*, p. 4.

eigner" in England who resisted hanging was participating in "unseemly conduct" and it was not quite "cricket" for Chessman to fight for his life with the only weapon he had at his command—the legal right to present writs to the courts. Chessman was gassed on May 2, 1960, after remaining in the death house for some twelve years!

To return to the subject of ropes breaking at hangings. Just the opposite might conceivably happen—that of the rope being too long or too short. The highwayman, Fitzpatrick—"Sandy Flash" mentioned earlier in another connection (Chap. I, p. 64) was the victim of such a situation. Ashmead, the Chester County (Pennsylvania) historian, reports the story of his hanging:

> Tradition has it that after the rope was adjusted about his neck and the cart drawn from beneath the gallows, he (Fitzpatrick) fell to the earth on his feet, and that by standing on his toes the strain on his neck was removed. This the hangman saw and, springing upon the shoulders of the doomed man, the increased weight forced the body until Fitzpatrick was actually strangled to death.[105]

PARDONS, REPRIEVES AND COMMUTATIONS OF SENTENCE OF DEATH

In both periods of our study of hangings—the open and public era and the so-called private period—we find many persons either pardoned completely or who have had their sentence commuted to a prison term. In the colonial period, some were pardoned "at the gallows," or pardoned "providing they leave the country forthwith" or, at least during the War of Independence, to go on board a frigate or join the continental army. A few such cases that have come to our attention are herewith included.

First is the strange case of Isaac Bradford, doomed to die in Philadelphia for burglary. The date of his execution was set for July 2, 1737, along with two others, one of whom was a woman. The Provincial Council offered Bradford a pardon, conditional on whether he "did the office of Executioner" on his companions in misery. This "very hard choice," so stated by the local newspaper,

---

[105]Quoted by Henry Ashmead in *The New Doane Book*, Doylestown, Pennsylvania, 1952, in section (356-69) entitled "Fitzpatrick, Chester County Outlaw."

did not seem to bother Bradford since he did escape the noose.[106]
The female alluded to was Catherine Conner who had been pardoned the previous year because of her pregnant condition. Apparently, she was a confirmed burglar and eventually was obliged
to suffer on the gallows.

Another case was that of John Benson, another case from
Philadelphia, pardoned "under the gallows" on May 12, 1764. His
two doomed companions were not so lucky. The local paper stated
it as follows:

> Benson seemed particularly affected not knowing any thing
> about his reprieve till the others were turned off, having gone
> through all the solemnity of that dismal scene, being blind-fold-
> ed, tied up, as he imagined and about to step into Eternity . . .
> His concern, it was thought, was the greater, as all alone, we
> hear, he flattered himself with being saved, always declaring his
> Innocence of the Crime for which he was ordered to die; but
> his Behavior in going to, and at the Tree, showed that he had
> lost all Hopes of that Kind.[107]

Benson, alias Brinkloe, was a transported felon from England, of
which there were many in the seaboard colonies. In fact, much of
the conventional crime during the colonial period was due to these
thousands of cashiered or departed riffraff from the Mother Country. The practice was stopped in 1776, when we became embroiled
with England. Benjamin Franklin, years before, had remonstrated
with the London government against sending felons to America.
When he was told it was absolutely necessary to remove them
from England, and therefore the colonies must take them, he
replied by asking the British ministers "if the same reasoning would
not justify the Americans in sending their rattlesnakes to England."[108]

Relative to the cases of pardon providing the persons left the
colony, two Pennsylvania cases are of interest. Both parties involved were given this alternative to save their necks; both, for
some reason, returned. One, a person named Jacob Dryer, was

---

[106]*The American Weekly Mercury,* June 30-July 7, 1737; the two executed at the time
were Catherine Conner and Henry Wildeman, both for burglary.

[107]*Pennsylvania Gazette,* May 17, page 2.

[108]*Journal of Prison Discipline and Philanthropy,* Philadelphia, Oct. 1859, p. 15.

given a second pardon; the other, one Robert Elliott of Chester, was hanged May 12, 1787. His pardon had read: "on condition he transport himself beyond the seas, not to return to the United States." His offense was burglary.

Earlier, we had something to say about Stephen Arnold of Cooperstown, New York, who was granted a reprieve "at the tree." The sheriff had carried the paper around with him all day before he told him of his good fortune (see *supra,* p. 26). We speculated on the reasons for such behavior on the part of this particular sheriff. Here we might ponder just why, in other cases, some of which we cited above, such refined sadism was generated by withholding the good news of a pardon until the culprit was "at the tree" or until *after* his wretched but not so fortunate companions had been executed.

It is not known how many persons have been lost to the gallows only because the official word of pardon or reprieve did not arrive in time to stay the springing of the trap. Opponents of capital punishment have often cited this calamity as a valid argument against the permanency of the death penalty. Few cases, however, can be mobilized for proof. Former Warden Clinton T. Duffy, of California's notorious San Quentin prison, mentions such a case in his work *Eighty-Eight Men and Two Women.*[109] A reprieve —not a commutation—is involved but at such a time, any *stay,* however brief, is desperately hoped for by the victim and his friends. The man was Joseph Regan who had been sentenced to death for his part in killing a police officer. His co-defendant, Carl Fellows, had also been sentenced to death but he escaped that dismal fate. Regan, unfortunately, was hanged two minutes prior to the receipt of the "magic words" that came cracking through the telephone wire from the governor's office to the prison. The date was August 18, 1933.

A quaint but intriguing custom found in colonial times, but inherited from England, was that if a female sentenced to death or, in fact, was being tried for some serious illegal sex act, a special panel of females was empowered to examine her for possible pregnancy, referred to sometimes as "in a peculiar situation." If

---

[109]New York, Doubleday, 1962, p. 87. Copyright 1962 by Clinton T. Duffy and Al Hirshberg. Reprinted by permission of Doubleday & Co. Inc.

she were so found, she might be spared the rigors of a trial or pardoned even though she had been condemned to death. Such a case is recorded in Chester County, Pennsylvania, in 1689. A young woman was on trial for "carnal intercourse" and a jury of women reported "that they cannot find she is pregnant neither be they sure that she is not." Nevertheless, punishment was delayed (so reported by George Smith, *History of Delaware County,* one time part of Chester County, 1862, p. 174). We referred to the case of Catherine Connor above. She was spared the gallows once, in Philadelphia, in 1735, because of pregnancy but on her second offense of burglary, she was hanged—in 1736.

A similar case was reported from New York City, in 1736. A female sentenced to death for burglary "pleaded her belly, upon which a Jury of Women found her Quick with Child and she was reprieved."[110]

A gruesome case involving this custom comes to us from England. It is the case of Mary Bateman, sentenced to death at Leeds for murder and fraud, in 1809. Upon being sentenced, she turned to the jailer and told him she was pregnant. Immediately, the judge ordered the doors of the courtroom closed and proceeded to garner twelve matrons to ascertain the truth of her contention. It seems that this task was considered somewhat distasteful for the ladies, since they all made a dash for the doors. However, they were apprehended by the bailiffs and pressed into service. Their verdict was that Mary Bateman was not in that state. Hence she was hanged. However, upon dissection, after the hanging, it was established that the matrons of Leeds had been in error (see the Bathsheba Spooner case, Chapter VII p. 305). This, in itself, was a sad commentary on the case, but to add shocking insult and ignominy to the penalty of taking the poor woman's life, her body was despoiled, due to the ghastly custom that still lingered on in Yorkshire at that late date, to wit, "her skin was tanned and distributed in small pieces to different applicants."[111]

Jack Kenney Williams tells of some pardoning incidents in early South Carolina history, when, as he states, an inordinate

---

[110]Story appearing in the *Philadelphia Mercury,* April 29-May 6, 1736.

[111]Justin Atholl, *op. cit.,* p. 180; for details of this practice see Louis Blake Duff, *op. cit.,* Chapter XVI, "Human Hide."

number of pardons was written by various governors. Sometimes, these acts of gubernatorial grace met with approval back home, although in many cases they did not. He gives an example of a Newberry felon whose pardon was delivered as he stood on the gallows with the rope about his neck. On being freed he was severely beaten by some of the disgruntled crowd. Williams also cites an instance of a prosecutor who, after winning a conviction, worked for the criminal's pardon. He stated: "I think the conviction was righteous but I should regret the execution of the poor old convict . . . He is seventy-three years old, has an aged wife, and a most pitiable family of idiot children."[112] Williams further states that it was not unusual for citizens' petitions to be hastily formulated and presented to the governor for the pardon of some convicted felon. This practice, too, was not unusual in the early days of most of the states. In fact, the personnel of juries who rendered the decision of guilt and doomed the felon to the "tree" might conceivably be the source of circulating petitions for pardon of the culprit.

Today, as we read of abuses in the pardoning power of state boards or governors, we tend to recall that these same abuses came down through our history of crime and its quaint folklore and legend.

Yet caution should be suggested before we condemn our forbears for being too lenient in disbursing pardons to convicted murderers. There were many instances when petitions and influence had little effect on a governor or board. We have the record of one such case that is of some interest. It is that of one Joseph Blundin who was hanged in the small county-seat of Bucks County, Pennsylvania—Doylestown—on August 14, 1835, for the provoked murder of Aaron Cuttlehow—somtimes referred to as the "horrible cradle murder." This is a reference to a harvesting device, not to be confused with a child's bed. In the heat of a July afternoon, the victim began badgering Blundin, for some reason, and in a fit of rage, Blundin struck him down with the scythe he was using. Certainly, it was not a premeditated killing but the jury thought otherwise. Blundin was a brother of the deputy-warden (known usually as the "principal keeper") of the state

---

[112]*Op. cit.*, p. 105.

penitentiary at Philadelphia and a highly respected public servant. The Quaker warden, Samuel R. Wood, who had more than a modicum of influence in state political circles, tried desperately to prevail upon his friend, the governor, to pardon the doomed man. Petitions of influential citizens were carried to the capitol but the governor was adamant; he refused to issue a pardon. The unhappy Blundin attempted suicide by jumping from his cell and was badly crippled. It was necessary to hang him as he sat in a chair.

SERMONS DELIVERED AT THE TREE

It was the practice in early times to publish sermons delivered at the gallows as well as confessions of the victims who were about to die for their crimes. There is a vast literature in these areas and hundreds of such works can be located in the various state and local libraries throughout the country. Many collectors and bibliophiles own their own private collections of such items.

Let us attend first to the sermons that were delivered by local ministers either at the jail before the procession to the "tree" began, or at the gallows itself. Delivering and publishing sermons in connection with these exciting, but macabre, public events was a widespread practice. Two reasons may be adduced for this universal practice in early times. One was to remind the sinner of his enormous crime and urge his repentance with an accompanying warning to others not to become enmeshed in such sordid trouble; the other was to pick up in legitimate fashion a little money to augment the minister's usual paltry income. Local persons were more likely to invest a few pennies in these published broadside sermons than to spend time listening to the minister at his weekly Sunday sermon. As to the facts of the crime, few may be gleaned from the sermons themselves. As Thomas McDade states, "Most of such printed sermons contain few if any facts of the crime or of the person involved. Full of hell-fire and Old Testament theology, they contributed nothing to the subject of murder in America."[113]

Miller and Johnson, in their scholarly work, *The Puritans,* have this to say of these sermons: ". . . they represent a class of literature which publishers willingly undertook in anticipation of profitable sales. Such accounts supplied the public with what we might

---

[113]*Op. cit.,* p. v.

call the murder novels of their day. They presented the horrors of sin with enough lurid details to arouse interest, and concluded with edifying advice. The custom of publicly addressing the condemned man in the presence of the gallows was brought from England; the twentieth century mind revolts from the barbaric practice, yet the rite was universal in English-speaking communities till well into the eighteenth century."[114]

In the vernacular of the times the wording on the face of the pamphlet might read: "printed by the name of the distributor and sold from their fists through every quarter of the city."[115]

Allegedly the first "book" printed in Boston was a sermon preached by the eminent divine, the Rev. Increase Mather, at the hanging of two wretches on March 18, 1675, and entitled *The Wicked Man's Portion.*[116] Their names were Nicholas Feavor and Robert Driver. Samuel Sewell, the noted diarist and jurist, wrote in February 13 of that year: "A Scotchman and Frenchman—two servants—killed their Master, knocking him in the head as he was taking Tobaco. They are taken by Hew and Cry and condemned; Hanged, Feavor born in the Isle of Jersey; Driver born in the Isle of Orknye in Scotland. Executed March 18."

An earlier publication, however, presumably told of the hanging of the Quakers, the plight of whom we dealt with earlier (see *supra,* p. 10). The published pamphlet comes from England and, apparently, there seems to be no Massachusetts printed copy extant. The title of the London pamphlet is: *"A Declaration of the General Court of the Mass, Holden at Boston in New England October* 18, 1659, *Concerning the Execution of Two Quakers by their Order in New England.*[117]

Some years later, again in Massachusetts, one James Morgan was subjected to three sermons delivered at the gallows or nearby, as he was being fixed to be "turned off." This occurred at Boston, on March 11, 1685. Morgan had been convicted of killing a man

---

[114]Perry Miller and Thomas H. Johnson, *The Puritans,* American Book Co., 1938, p. 413.

[115]From death pamphlet of one John Jubheart, hanged in New York City on September 6, 1769, for coining and passing counterfeit dollars.

[116]McDade, *op. cit.,* p. xvii.

[117]Charles Evans, *The American Bibliography* (14 vols. with index), Peter Smith, N.Y. ed., 1959, item 51.

in a drunken brawl "by running a spitt into his belly a little above the navell."

Since an eye-witness, James Dunton, an "eccentric book-seller," witnessed this man's hanging and wrote in considerable detail concerning it, we feel inclined to give the case considerable space. It may well be considered typical of the times. The unhappy Morgan was subjected to the three sermons in his behalf, two on Sunday prior to the hanging and the third on Thursday, the hanging day, March 11. The Sunday morning sermon, delivered by the Rev. Cotton Mather (son of Increase, mentioned above) was entitled: "Look unto Me and be ye saved, all the Ends of the Earth" (Isaiah 45:22); the evening sermon of the "Lord's Day" was delivered by the Rev. Joshua Moody and entitled: "Tho' thou wast angry with me, thine anger is turned away" (Isaiah 12:1); and on the fatal Thursday, a sermon without a formal title, by the Rev. Increase Mather.

Part of the terrible words of the first sermon by Cotton Mather were: "My request unto you is, That you wou'd at this hour think of an Interest in Christ. Surely when the Executioner is laying the Cold Cloth of Death over your Eyes, the look, with the Shriek of your Soul, will then say 'O now a Thousand Worlds for an Interest in Jesus Christ,' Surely a few minutes after that, when your naked Soul shall appear before the Judgment-Seat of the Most High, you will again say, 'an Interest in Jesus Christ, is worth whole mountains of gold' . . . The sharp Ax of Civil Justice will speedily cut you down; O for a little good Fruit before the Blow! Manifest your penitence for your Iniquities by a due care to excel in Tempers quite contrary to those ill habits and Customs whereby you have heretofore blasphemed the Worthy Name of Christ and Christianity: Especially employ the last minutes of your life in giving a Zealous Warning unto others to take heed of those things which have been destructive unto you. . .!"

The Rev. Joshua Moody continued in the same awful vein. In part, he soberly stated: "You seem to bewail your Sin of Sabbath-breaking; Well, know that you shall never have another Sabbath to break. The Lord help you to keep this as you ought. It is a very awful thing to us to look on you, a Person in your Youth, Health, and Strength, Breasts full of Milk (sic) and Bones moistened with Marrow, and then to think that within so many Days, this Man, tho' in his full strength, must Dye; And methinks it should be much more awful to you . . ."

On the gallows, the Rev. Increase Mather said in part to the tortured victim: "Consider what a Sinner you have been; the Sin which you are to dye for, is as bad as Scarlet; and many other Sins has your wicked life been filled with. You have been a stranger to me; I never saw you, until you had committed the Murder for which you must Dye this Day; but I hear by others that have known you, how wicked you have been; and you yourself have confessed to the World, That you have been guilty of Drunkenness, guilty of Cursing and Swearing, guilty of Sabbath-breaking, guilty of Lying, guilty of Secret Uncleanness . . . and that which aggravates your Guiltiness not a little, is, That since you have been in Prison you have done Wickedly; You have made yourself drunk several times since your Imprisonment; yea, and you have been guilty of Lying since your condemnation . . . And what misery you have brought upon your poor Children? You have brought an everlasting Reproach upon them. How great will their shame be, when it shall be said to them that their Father was hang'd? not for his Goodness, as many in the World have been; but for his wickedness: Not as a Martyr, but as a Malefactor. . ."

The observer, Dunton, continued by stating that the sermons were preached in an "auditory" of the New Church, but, as he remarked, "the Gallery crack'd with as much Awfulness, and so pathetically apply'd to the Poor Condemned Man, that all the Auditory were very much affected." He continued:

> After he had been about an Hour at the Gallows and had pray'd again, his Cap was pulled over his Eyes, and then having said, "Oh Lord, Receive my Spirit; I come unto Thee O Lord; I come, I come, I come," he was turned off and the multitude by degrees dispersed. I think during this Mournful Scene, I never was more serious nor had greater Compassion.

The faithful scribe then finished his communication to his London friend, a Mr. Larkin, by these words in an altogether different vein: "But from the House of Mourning, I rambled to

the House of Feasting; for Mr. York, Mr. King, with Madam
Brick, Mrs. Green, Mrs. Toy, the Damsell and myself, took a
Ramble to a place call'd Governor's Island, about a mile from
Boston, to see a whole Hog roasted, as did several other Bos-
tonians. We went all in a Boat; and having treated the Fair Sex,
returned in the Evening."[118]

Toward the end of that century, some time in 1698, we find
two divines delivering sermons at the executions of two "Un-
knowns." One by the Rev. Samuel Willard is entitled, *Impenitent
Sinners Warn'd of their Misery and Summoned to Judgment . .
Two Sermons in Boston November 6 and 10, 1698; Occasioned
by the Amazing Instance of a Miserly Creature, Condemn'd for
Murdering Her Infants*; the other by the Rev. Increase Mather on
November 17, entitled, *The Folly of Sinning Opened and Apply'd;
In two Sermons Occasioned by the Condemnation of One that was
Executed at Boston in New England on November 17.*[119] It is pos-
sible that both sermons were preached in connection with the
same victim of the gallows. We have failed to locate the identity
of this female.

The case of Esther Rodgers of Ipswich, Massachusetts, at and
over whom three sermons were delivered by the Rev. John Rogers
(similarity of names purely coincidental) at her ignominious execution, on July 15, 1701, might well belong to our next chapter;
this, because she was gibbeted—the only female subjected to this
cruel and humiliating fate in the colonies—and there we deal with
this and other sanguinary, strange and esoteric penalties. Her
crime was infanticide, committed at Newberry, on November 12,
1700. The titles of the sermons are: *Death the Certain Wages of
Sin to the Impenitent; Life the Sure Reward of Grace to the Penitent; and The Only Way of Youth to Avoid the Former, and At-
tain the Latter.* These sermons, it was stated at the time, "were
occasioned by the imprisonment, condemnation, and execution
of a young woman who was guilty of murdering her infant be-
gotten in whoredom." Samuel Sewell noted in his *Diary,"* July
15, To Ipswich: to Try Esther Rogers (sic); July next Morn

---

[118]Letter to Mr. George Larkin, London, Printer, at the Two Swans, without Bishop-
gate; in Miller and Johnson, *op. cit.,* p. 414-26.

[119]Evans, *op. cit.,* p. 879.

ask'd Advice . . . brought in Guilty of Murdering her Bastard Daughter, July 17: Mr. Cooke pronounced sentence. She hardly said a word."[120] The place of execution and humiliation was known as Pingrey's Plain, often referred to as Gallows Lot.

On July 10, 1726, William Fly, Samuel Cole, and Henry Grenvil were hanged for piracy at Boston. They had seized a vessel, the *Elizabeth* as she sailed from Jamaica in May. They threw the mate and captain overboard and changed the name of the ship to *Fame's Revenge* and started out on a further career of piracy and plunder. They preempted a man named Atkinson, a passenger, as one of their prizes—actually a hostage—but this proved their undoing. He, with some other crew members, watched their chance and captured the vessel—a kind of counter-piracy! They brought the ship to Boston and turned the pirates over to the authorities. They were soon convicted and executed. The Rev. Benjamin Colman preached their death sermon which is entitled *It is a Fearful Thing to Fall into the Hands of the Living God.*[121]

Then we have the sermon preached at Falmouth, Maine (at the time a part of Massachusetts) by the Rev. Ephraim Clark at gallows-side where Solomon Goodwin was hanged on November 12, 1772. He had killed David Wilson, quite possibly accidentally —when he and his victim, were drunk and out in a canoe, the preceding May. In the published sermon there are "seventeen pages of mournful admonition to the waiting prisoner, exemplified by this quotation: 'There you stand a condemned malefactor, full of all the horrors of a shameful and painful death. Oh! sad state indeed! But your present distress, however great, is nothing compared with the horror that your poor soul will be filled with instantly it leaves your body, if you are found in an unconverted state.'[122]

There are many doleful sermons recorded in the literary heritage that survives; that is, if we may dignify this material by that designation. There is the sermon preached over Thomas Starr at Haddam, Connecticut, on the date of his hanging, June 14, 1797. He had been condemned for the penknife slaying of his kinsman,

---

[120]*Massachusetts Historical Society,* 5th Series, Boston, 1879, Vol. VI, p. 39.
[121]McDade, *op. cit.,* 308.
[122]*Ibid.,* item 361.

Samuel Cornwell, on July 26, 1796. The minister was the Rev. Enoch Huntington.[123]

Confessions and Gallows-side Speeches

The tone of many of the gallows-side speeches of our victims, when they indulged in such last-minute, often time-consuming acts or maneuvers, was often likely to be similar to the sermons. Penitence was most likely to be the conspicuous feature of such speeches, or perhaps the word harangues might be better to express what took place at the "tree."

Six pirates were hanged on June 30, 1704, on the "Charles River, Boston side" and a "broadside" was published on the event. It purported to be the "last dying speeches" of these miserable men who were Capt. John Quelch, John Lambert, Christopher Scudamore, John Miller, Erasmus Petersen, and Peter Roach. The title of the publication is: *An Account and Behavior and Last Dying Speeches of the Six Pirates that Were Executed on Charles River, Boston side, on Fryday, June 30, 1704.*[124]

The following is a combination of a sermon and a dying speech. They are associated with David Wallis, a sailor who killed the young cook of a vessel because he didn't like the food served up on the mess. The title tells something of the story: *The sad effects of sin, A true relation of the murder committed by David Wallis, on his companion Benjamin Stolwood; on Saturday night, the first of August, 1713, With his carriage after condemnation; his confession and dying speech at the place of execution, &c. To which are added, the sermons preached at the lecture in Boston, in his hearing, after his condemnation: and the day of his execution, being Sept. 24, 1713.*[125]

It may be noted that titles of sermons, gallows speeches and pamphlets are, in general, quite verbose. One may probably learn all worth knowing about a case merely by reading the title.

The Edward Hunt case, at Philadelphia, November 19, 1720, represents one of the most poignant speeches made at gallows-side. His offense was counterfeiting, but, in actuality, treason, since the

---

[123]*Ibid.,* item 906.
[124]*Massachusetts Broadsides,* No. 265.
[125]McDade, *op. cit.,* 1034.

heinous offense of making spurious money was treasonable against
the mother country. So far as the records show, his was the first
execution to take place in Philadelphia (but not in the colony
of Pennsylvania). It has often been conjectured that others must
have been hanged in that city or country prior to Hunt's execution
but we have found nothing to substantiate such speculation.

John Fanning Watson, early Philadelphia historian of the nineteenth century, states in his *Annals*: "Edward and Martha Hunt,
Man and Wife, sentenced to death for making and passing counterfeit money."[126] In the *American Weekly Mercury* for November
25, 1720, we find this headline: "The Dying Speech of Edward
Hunt, forger taken in the Rebellion at Preston and Transported
a bound Servant to the Island of Antigua, before his Execution
upon the 19th inst. at Philadelphia where he had been legally
convicted of High Treason and most justly condemned for Counterfeiting Spanish Silver Coin, made current by Act of Parliament
within all His Majesty's Colonies of America."

The paper prefaces Hunt's remarks with this statement: "Tho'
it is evident that the following speech was intended to misrepresent
the Administration and Justice of this Government, as well as to
infuse both ill Principles and Practices into the minds of the
People, yet the Falsehoods, Contradictions and silly Evasions
therein contained, will as plainly appear to every impartial and
honest Reader, that it has been thought proper to publish this
extraordinary Piece here, from the Copy which was this Morning
delivered to the Governor by the Reverend John Vicary, Minister,
who acknowledged That the same had been communicated to
him by the Criminal in Gaol, who afterwards read it publickly
at the place of Execution, and then delivered the paper to the said
Mr. Vicary, desiring it might be printed."

Hunt, in a very specious argument, maintained that he did not
know he was doing wrong or violating the King's laws in counterfeiting coins, which, of course could not excuse him from the
gallows since counterfeiting was a capital offense. He stated, however, "I am the first unhappy Instance of this kind (but not the
last) that ever suffered in the King's Dominions, pray God it may
be a warning to all, not to offend wilfully in the same that I did

---

[126]Vol. I, p. 308.

through ignorance. For if I had known it, I would not have taken all the World to have done it. God give me a patient Resignation to submit to his blessed will, in whatsoever he pleases."

Another Pennsylvania case is worthy of relating at this point. On August 15, 1722, at Chester, William Battin, an indentured servant, was hanged for "divers horrid, complicated crimes" which, in reality, were arson and murder. He was a seventeen-year-old who had arrived from England, after his father had despaired of him as a thief and runaway. He landed in Philadelphia and was "bought" on the dock by a Chester County farmer who took him into his home. He absconded from him and in due time, was passed on to a neighbor. One evening, when his new master and his wife were off on a social call, Battin carelessly lighted a torch and went into the attic in search of apples to eat. The place caught fire and in his dull mind a mixture of fright and irresponsibility congealed, so that he ignored three small boys who were asleep under the rafters, sons of his master, and ran for help. Help finally arrived but too late; the children were dead. Battin's grievous mistake was that he had assured his master and mistress that the children were safe yet he knew he had neglected to save them. He was convicted of arson, which at the time was a capital offense, and murder, and thus was hanged. He was an ignorant, socially irresponsible young boy. Today the disposition of such a case might well be totally different.[127] Battin was convinced that he had been "enslaved by the Devil."

On September 27, 1733, Rebecca Chamblitt of Boston was hanged "for concealing the birth of her spurious male infant." A pamphlet was issued entitled: *The Declaration, Dying Warning and Advice of Rebecca Chamblitt a Young Woman Aged near Twenty-Seven Years, Executed at Boston . . . being then found Guilty of Felony, in Concealing the Birth of her spurious Male Infant . . ."* Another was entitled: *Lessons of Caution to Young Sinners,* a sermon delivered by Thomas Foxcroft.[128]

The case involving two men, Matthew Cushing and John Ormsby, is of some interest. Both were executed at Boston at the

---

[127]See *The American Weekly Mercury,* Philadelphia, August 16-23, 1722, for his last words and confession.

[128]McDade, *op. cit.,* 167; also *Massachusetts Broadsides,* No. 623.

same time, October 17, 1734, the former for burglary, the latter
for murder. Pamphlets were struck off for both and we here append the titles: Cushing: *The Declaration and Confession of . . .
A Young Man about Twenty-Two Years who was Try'd for burglary . . . which he Delivered to Us . . . and Confirmed the same
before Credible Witnesses the Day of his Execution.*[129] Ormsby:
*The Last Speech and Dying Words of John Ormsby who was ap-
pointed to be Executed at Boston Neck the 17th of October 1734;
Written by his own hand the Day before he was to Suffer.*[130]

The pamphlets published on the Whiting Sweeting case of
Albany, New York, merit special mention at this point. Fully
fourteen publications emerged from the presses from 1791, the
year of the trial and execution of Sweeting, to 1797. Sweeting,
hanged at Albany on August 26, 1791, was, according to Mc-
Dade, "the victim of the strict code of the eighteenth century that
one who encompassed the death of another is guilty of murder."
The story of the case is briefly this: A constable of Stephentown,
New York, led a small posse armed with a warrant to arrest Sweeting for trespassing. He was cornered in the woods at night and in
attempting to escape, lashed out against his pursuers. In so doing,
he struck one of them, one Darius Quimby, with a knife from
which his victim died. Sweeting was tried, convicted and hanged
for "murder." There were those, even at that time, who felt the
penalty too severe. The case is well remembered in local circles
and is frequently quoted in American criminal history. One of the
pamphlets "written by himself" was published "for the benefit of
precious souls."[131]

A bit of doleful doggerel, purported to have been written by an
Irish roustabout named Jimmie Quinn, of Lebanon, Pennsylvania,
about to be hanged for the murder of his wife, Biddy on February
9, 1827, might well end this chapter. Quinn was a laborer brought
into the peaceful Dutch country to help dredge a canal. Given
much to drink he had overindulged at the town's annual cherry
festival and had gone home and picked a quarrel with his spouse.
It ended in a senseless murder and he suffered for his deed on

---

[129]*Massachusetts Broadsides,* No. 642.
[130]*Massachusetts Broadsides,* No. 652.
[131]McDade, *op. cit.,* 960.

"Gallows Hill" of the little community county-seat. On the front of the pamphlet relating details of the sad event, one notices embellished the following dirge which shares the page with a likeness of a coffin. The words reflect the victim's phantasy or soliloquy, probably written by someone other than Quinn himself; it reads:

O, thou gruesome gallows-tree; Built, O horror, built for me;
Lord of Heaven, on bended knee, Do I cry in fear of Thee.
Gallows-tree! Thy timbers strong Feed my anguish all day long,
Telling me that soon my light Must go out in blackest night!
When I leave my prison cell Shall I go to Heaven or Hell?
Lord, in Thee I place my trust, Thou are kind as well as just,
Terror makes my spirit sore, — How I wish that all were o'er!

Time for me is but a span, Yet I'd warn my fellow-man,
Here upon perdition's brink, Warn him' gainst the curse of drink.
Rum, alas! has been my bane, Cause of crime, disgrace and
    shame!
Lord, Thine ear in mercy lend, Help, O, help me face the end!
Glad, I'll die on scaffold tree, And atonement make to Thee,
Fain to reach that heavenly plain, Washed and cleansed from sin
    and pain.
Soon will come my fearful end! Thou, O Christ, wilt stand my
    friend;
Thee, I feel — Thy power and might! Now, O World, good
    night! good night![132]

There are hundreds of these pamphlets and broadsides extant, most of them carrying the same messages of tragedy, penance or remorse, and grovelling degradation. Few express the heroic, although there are signs of dignity and courage in some. As a last example, we quote this title of a pamphlet associated with the hanging of John Harrington at Cambridge, Massachusetts on March 17, 1757, for the murder of Paul Learned: "The Agonies of the Soul Departing out of Time unto Eternity."

---

[132]Originally printed in German and published by *Der Pennsylvanischer Beobachter* and appearing in English translation in a paper read by S. P. Heilman, M.D., before the Lebanon (Pa.) County Historical Society on April 18, 1902 and appearing in *Proceedings* II, No. 5; courtesy, Mr. Ray S. Bowman, secretary.

Chapter II

EXCESSIVE RETRIBUTION AND PURITANICAL ZEAL IN EARLY DAYS

GIBBETING

G IBBETING, or suspending an already-hanged body in a frame, was not uncommon in some of the American colonies. It was quite venerable as a practice even at that time, both in England and on the Continent. It was widely resorted to in England, during the 1700's, and we may note that some towns had their permanent gibbets which are used as landmarks for the aid of travelers: "You pass Panmeris Hill, and at . . . Hilldraught Hill, on the left, ascend a small hill with a gibbet on the right."[1]

Gibbeting is sometimes referred to as "hanging in chains." It is usually thought of as actually placing the hanged body—on rare occasions still alive—in an iron frame that crudely encased the contour of the human form. It was a penalty that was associated with ignominy. Shame and deterrence were its salient features. It was a penalty more debasing than hanging.

Many Negroes, in colonial times (in this country) were gibbeted, or, as stated in the southern colonies, "hanged in chains." Surviving evidence indicates, however, that it was by no means rare for a white man to be subjected to the penalty, especially for the crimes of piracy and treason (some of these will be identified later). Records also indicate that at least one woman was sentenced to gibbeting.

Professor Thorsten Sellin has made a fascinating study of gibbeting in this country, as he relates the story of an iron frame that is in the Atwater Kent Museum at Philadelphia. He tells us

---

[1]William Andrews, *Bygone Punishments*, London, 1899, p. 38.

that so far as he can learn, this gibbet—fashioned for the punishment of an eighteenth-century pirate named Thomas Wilkinson was never used.[2]

Another gibbet is on display in the Essex Institute at Salem, Massachusetts. These two are the only such contraptions surviving in the country. The Massachusetts gibbet was used to encase a woman, one Madam Dodier, in 1763 (this did not occur in this country, however, but in St. Valier, Quebec).

As stated above, hanging in chains and gibbeting were terms used interchangeably. There seems to be no evidence, however, that any person was actually hanged in chains in this country, although the term was frequently designated in the court's sentence. In England, however, where chains were used, the device consisted of a heavy chain, about twelve feet in length, divided in the middle by a curved iron bar or narrow saddle which fitted the crotch of the body. A hinged iron neckband, which could be passed through the links at the height of the neck, locked the head in place, holding the body upright and the two ends of the chains were attached to a ring which was attached to a hook which was attached to the arm of the gibbet.[3]

Hanging in chains and gibbeting were closely associated. This may be plainly seen from the following couplet as quoted by Andrews:

> That the wretch in his chains, each night took the pains,
> To come down from the gibbet—and walk

At least, this was the belief of the good people of Pendleton Moor, where stood the gibbet.[4] It should be pointed out that hanging in

---

[2]Wilkinson, of Philadelphia, was convicted of piracy and sentenced to be hanged and gibbeted. The execution was set for May 23, 1781, on "Windmill Island in the Delaware River" and afterwards "the body . . . to be taken down to Mud Island . . . and hanged in chains." However, due to the intercession of several influential citizens, including the great patriot, Stephen Decatur and another privateer captain, Thomas Truxton, he was reprieved and then pardoned. The Provincial Council was obliged to pay one David Henderson the sum of £17.16 sterling for fashioning this curiously wrought instrument of infamy. It will be noted that this culprit was sentenced to "hang in chains" but, in reality, it was a gibbet that was prepared. As mentioned above, the two penalties were used interchangeably.

[3]So described by Sellin, "The Philadelphia Gibbet-Iron," *Journal of Criminal Law, Criminology and Police Science,* Vol. 46, No. 1 (May-June, 1955), pp. 11-25.

[4]Andrews, *op. cit.,* p. 51.

chains occasionally refers to the "bilboes" which refers to an iron bar with ankle rings attached—a device usually used to shackle offenders at sea. Still another variation is known as "breaking on the wheel" in which the body was impaled upon a wheel on top of a pole. We have few instances where this punishment has been imposed on culprits in this country.[5]

Just plain gibbeting, however, took place in many of the American colonies. Pennsylvania was one of the exceptions and even in that colony we have seen that there were no qualms among the dispensers of justice to resort to it on at least one occasion. Massachusetts furnishes a bizarre instance in the gibbeting of Mark, a slave. Mark and two females, Phillis and Phoebe, were tried for poisoning their master Captain John Codman, of Charlestown. Phoebe was acquitted, but Mark and Phillis were convicted. "The fellow was hanged and the Woman burned at the Stake about Ten Yards distant from the Gallows . . . They died very Penitent."[6] Mark is a figure whose ghoulish form of death ties him uniquely to famous people in American history. McDade, in the *Annals of Murder* tells us, "That Mark was made of no common clay is attested to by the fact that in June, 1758, an army surgeon, Dr. Cabel Ray, passed Mark still hanging there—on the Charlestown Commons—and noted in his *Diary* 'His skin was but very little broken, altho' he had hung there over three or four years.' "[7] That noted, although somewhat alarming American patriot, Paul Revere, in describing his famous ride on April 15, 1775, referred to passing the place "where Mark was hung in chains."[8]

Customs peculiar to the time seem to foster such grisly conjecture. In order to preserve the bodies in the gibbet, it was the

---

[5]The last person to suffer this painful penalty in France was Jean Calas, a citizen of Toulouse, in 1761. He had been unjustly accused and convicted of murdering his son who actually committed suicide. Voltaire spent three years attempting to right the wrong inflicted upon the family by the court of that day, and while he could not bring Calas back to life, did manage to stir up France to rectify the wrong to the family and to abolish that awful penalty.

[6]*The Boston Evening Post,* for September 22, 1755.

[7]McDade, *op. cit.,* xxxiii.

[8]Quoted by Abner C. Goodell, "The Murder of Captain Codman," in *Proceedings of Mass. Hist. Soc. 20:* 147, March, 1883, and cited by Sellin, *op. cit.,* p. 16. It should be noted that Revere may have merely passed the site of the gibbeting, and not actually seen the body.

practice to dip them in tar. As Sellin describes the gibbet: "The post was often studded with nails and bound with iron bands to prevent its being cut down, and the body either literally hung 'in chains' or was enclosed in a framework of iron bands, which formed a kind of lattice-work cage for head, torso, and limbs. The part enclosing the head would usually have a ring bolt by which the entire contraption could be suspended from the arm of the gibbet."[9]

If the body of Mark had been dipped in tar, it is quite possible that he might still have been hanging at the time of Revere's ride. A ballad comes down to us concerning these benighted slaves:

> What sad and awful scenes are these
> 　　Presented to your view;
> Let everyone Example take
> 　　And Virtue's ways pursue.
>
> For here you see what Vice has done
> 　　In all its sinful Ways;
> By Mark and Phillis, who are left,
> 　　To finish now their Days.
>
> Their Crimes appear as black as Hell
> 　　And justly so indeed;
> And for a greater, I am sure,
> 　　There's none can this exceed.
>
> Three were together in their Crime,
> 　　And one by Law is clear'd;
> The other two must suffer Death,
> 　　And 'twas but just indeed.
>
> Their Master's Life they took away,
> 　　And that they thought with Ease,
> By poys'ning him from Time to Time
> 　　Which killed him by degrees.[10]

Another ballad comes down to us from Francois Villon, the

---

[9]Sellin, *op. cit.,* p. 14; see also Andrews, *op. cit.,* p. 39.

[10]Olive Wooley Burt, *American Murder Ballads,* "Copyright © 1958 by Oxford University Press, Inc., pp. 154-155. Throughout this work we have drawn heavily from Mrs. Burt's collection of ballads. We have both her permission and that of the publisher's and at this point we wish to make proper acknowledgment.

swashbuckling French vagabond, who allegedly left the following epitaph, in the form of a ballad of sorts, when it was certain that he and his companions were to be executed. The poet, Swinburne, translates it as follows:

> The rain has washed and laundered us all five
> And the sun dried and blackened; yes, pardie,
> Ravens and pies with beaks that rend and rive
> Have dug our eyes out, and plucked off for fee
> Our beards and eyebrows, never are we so free,
> Not once, to rest, but here and there still sped,
> Drive at the wild will by the winds change led,
> More pecked of birds than fruits on garden-wall,
> Men, for God's love, let no gibe here be said,
> But pray to God that he forgive us all.[11]

The business of setting an example, of offering deterrent, was not left to gibbeting alone. Such a plight sometimes went along with burning at the stake, this especially when a male and a female were convicted of the same crime and were Negroes. The male was usually gibbeted, and the female burned at the stake. A companion piece to the gibbeting of Mark and Phillis comes from Schoharie, New York, where two unnamed Negroes, a male and a female, were convicted of the murder of one Trucax, probably on January 2, 1716. Their sentence read as follows: "The negroe man was burned half an hour until dead, and then hanged in gibbets where he is to remain, and the wench was burned one hour and afterwards to ashed." Another sentence, quite emphatic, but probably customary at the time, reads: "a negroe . . . first hanged on the gallows till Dead, Dead Dead, and afterwards Hanged in Gibbets where he was to remain for forcing a little girl of thirteen years to lay with him."[12]

In Virginia Colony, Anthony Arnold, one of the leaders in Bacon's Rebellion, was sentenced to be hanged "in chains in his own County, and bee a more remarkable Example to the rest." This was in 1676. Two years later, Thomas Hellier, an escaped convict from England and who had murdered his master, Cut-

---

[11]Louis Blake Duff, *The County Kerchief,* Toronto, The Ryerson Press, 1949, p. 193.
[12]Both of the above quotations are from Sellin, *op. cit.* p. 18.

beard Williamson, his wife and her maid, was "hanged up in chains at Windmill Point on James River" on August 5, 1678. This was only one of several cases in the Old Dominion that were gibbeted—hanged in chains.[13]

One Mecum, or more properly, Jeremiah Meacham, of Newport, Rhode Island, was gibbeted "in chains" and set atop Miantonomy Hill for the murder of his wife. A Scot, he was described as "a madman who sat on top of his house and, on being induced to come down, murdered his family." The Rev. Nathaniel Clap, a local divine, preached a sermon for the benefit of the poor wretch whose crime was committed on March 22, 1715; its title, *The Lord's Voice, crying to His People.*[14]

In 1712, in New York City, as the result of a Negro conspiracy, several of the participants were burned at the stake, one was broken at the wheel, and Adrian Hoagland's slave, Robin, was sentenced "to be hung in chains alive and so continue from lack of substenance until he is dead."[15]

In our preceding chapter we dicsussed the case of the only female ever gibbeted in this country. She was Esther Rodgers and had murdered her illegitimate daughter (*supra,* (ms.76) Chap. I).

The cost of gibbeting a culprit came high for the taxpayer. We have already perused the bill submitted for fashioning the gibbet iron for Wilkinson of Philadelphia. Curiously, this device was a total loss since the pirate was pardoned.

On May 13, 1724, a John Rose Archer, age twenty-seven, William White, age twenty-two, and William Taylor, age unknown, were tried for piracy by a court of admiralty in Boston. On June 2nd, Archer and White were executed; what became of Taylor is not recorded. The Rev. Cotton Mather, that ubiquitous Puritan divine, ministered to them in their last agonizing days and it would seem did not make their last moments too easy as he preached to them, the sermon bearing the title: "The Converted Sinner . . . A Sermon Preached . . . in the Hearing and at the Desire of certain

---

[13]See Sellin, *op. cit.,* p. 19, for original sources.

[14]McDade, *op. cit.,* 675.

[15]Julius Goebel, Jr., and Frank Naughton, *Law Enforcement in Colonial New York,* Commonwealth Fund, 1944, p. 118; cited by Sellin; see pages *infra* ms. for account of the Negro conspiracy of 1741, in the same city.

Pirates a little before their Execution, To which is Added, A More Private Conference of a Minister to them."

A newspaper report of the double hanging indicated that after their death, they were conveyed to an island where White was buried, and "Quartermaster Archer" was *hanged in irons, in order to serve as a lesson to others.*[16]

On that same day Robert Dobney presented a bill for twelve pounds and ten shillings "To Making of the Chains for John Rose Archer one of the Pyrats and the hire of a man to help fix him on the Gibbett att Bird Island." The Marshall of the court also presented the following bill for "Sundrys by him Expended:"[17]

```
To the Executioner for his Services I paid him...... 12.00.0
To Mr. Joseph Parsons for Cordage I paid his Bill.... 2.17.6
To Boat hire and Labourers to help Sett the Gibbet
    and attendance at the Execution and Diging the
    Grave for White............................... 3.10.8
To Expenses on the Sheriefs officers and Constables
    after the Execution at Mrs. Gilbert's her Bill....... 3.15.8
                                                       _____
                                                       £22 .03.10
To George. Mayo, Blockmaker, his Bill                   1. 5. 0
                                                       _____
                                                       £ 23. 8.10
```

Many other cases could be recorded here, but compared to plain hanging, cases of gibbeting were in the minority. There were, however, punishments that were imposed in colonial times that were even more hideous, if it is possible to think of anything more socially corrupting and revolting than an ill-smelling corpse dipped in tar "hung on high to poison half Mankind."

OTHER FRIGHTFUL PUNISHMENTS

Beheading and dismemberment of the body, even quartering the corpse and scattering the remains around was not unusual. Drawing

---

[16]One Bumstead wrote in his diary that he took his wife and children and six more persons to the castle on Governor's Island to see the pirates "in Gibbets on Bird Island" (*The Boston Gazette*, June 7 and 8, 1724).

[17]The above material is from Sellin, *op. cit.*, pp. 13-14, original sources being primarily from John Franklin Jameson, *Privateering and Piracy in the Colonial Period*, Illustrative Document, New York, Macmillan, 1923, pp. 338-45.

and quartering was a punishment that found many precedents in England. It was often referred to in early times as "godly butchery," allegedly because of divine authority supporting the penalty. Andrews contends that Lord Coke found Biblical justification for the hideous punishment.[18] Drawing and quartering is described as applied to traitors as follows: "He is to be taken from the prison and laid upon a sledge or hurdle (or to the tail of a horse) and *drawn* to the gallows . . . and then hanged by the neck until he be half dead, and then cut down; and his entrails to be cut out of his body and burnt by the executioner; then his head is to be cut off, his body to be divided into quarters, and afterwards his head and quarters to be set up in some open places directed . . . The headsman, or hangman, commonly sliced open the chest and cut thence the heart, plucking it forth and holding it up to the populace saying, 'Behold the heart of a traitor' "[19]

Andrews tells us further that this penalty was first inflicted in England, in 1241, on one William Larise, a pirate and son of a nobleman. The last victims of the draconic punishment were three persons convicted of treason at Derby. They were subjected to the gory penalty of quartering, after being drawn on a hurdle by a horse to the place of execution. The penalty was inflicted on November 8, 1817.[20]

The spectacle was surveyed by a huge crowd, but as the head of the first victim was exhibited "there was a terrifying shriek set up, and the multitude ran violently in all directions as if under the influence of a sudden frenzy." The poet Shelley is said to have witnessed the bloody ordeal. He wrote: "When Edward Turner saw his brother dragged along upon the hurdle he shrieked horribly, and fell into a fit, and was carried away like a corpse. How fearful must have been their agony sitting in solitude that day when the tempestuous voice of horror from the crowd told them the head so dear to them had been severed from the body! Yes, they listened to the maddening shriek which burst from the multitude; they heard the rush of ten thousand terror-striken feet, the groans and hootings

---

[18] Andrews, *op. cit.*, p. 79.

[19] *Ibid.*, p. 80.

[20] (The victims' names were Jeremiah Brandreth, William Turner and Isaac Ludlam [Ibid., p. 81].)

which told them the mangled and distorted head was then lifted in the air."[21]

Beheading and dismemberment of the corpse, as well as quartering and "scattering" the portions were not unusual even in the American colonies. Close scrutiny of the records offers mute testimony of the degradation of the human body far beyond mere hanging. At Lewes, Delaware, while under control of the Dutch, a "Turc," a servant of the English, was hanged on Sunday, October 19, 1662 for resisting and wounding his captors, "the head afterwards to be cut off and placed upon a post or stake in the Horekill."[22]

In June, 1733, in Goochland County, Virginia, two Negro slaves, Champion and Valentine, who had murdered Robert Allen, probably their overseer, were sentenced to "have their heads and quarters set up in severall parts of the County," which was done. The undersheriffs who handled this piece of human butchery charged 2,000 pounds of tobacco for, as they stated, "providing Tarr, burying the Trunk, cutting out the quarters a Pott, carts and horses carrying and setting up the heads and quarters of the two negroes at the places mentioned by the court." Another Negro, one Peter, from Orange County, Virginia, killed his master and escaped on a horse. He was captured and his head was cut off and "put on a Pole near the Courthouse to deter others from doing the Like." In 1767, four Negroes from Alexandria who conspired to poison their overseers—but apparently not successful, "had their heads cut off their bodies and fixed on the chimneys of the court house." It appears it was not unusual for decapitated Negroes to have their heads exposed on posts at crossroads in the Virginia colony.[23]

Two more grim and terrifying cases are to be found in the history of the Virginia colony. In Surrey County, in 1710, two slaves had plotted a rebellion: one was an Indian named Salvador, the

[21]*Ibid.,* p. 84; Shelley's pamphlet is entitled: "We pity the Plumage, but forget the Dying. An address to the People on the Death of the Princess Charlotte. By the Hermit of Marlow." The death of the Princess and the executions of the traitors occurred on the same day.

[22]*Pennsylvania Archives,* 2nd Series, Vol. VII, p. 691.

[23]Arthur F. Scott, *Criminal Law in Colonial Virginia,* Chicago University of Chicago Press, pp. 195-196.

other a Negro named Scipio, both were charged accordingly. As punishment, the following was ordered: "Salvador to be hanged and his body disposed of *viz,* his head to be delivered to the sheriff of James City County and by him sett up at the city of Williamsburg. Two of his quarters likewise delivered to the sd. Sheriff of James City and the other two delivered to the Sheriff of New Kent County to be sett up in the most publick place of the said County and the other two quarters to be disposed of and sett up as the Justices of the County of Surrey shall think fit to direct."[24] The body of the other slave, Scipio, was to be disposed of in Gloucester, Lancaster, Kent and Queen Counties.

To keep the record clear, the following case comes from the archives of Rhode Island. However, the case is one of suicide, not execution—dismemberment of the body is still present however, and hence gives us reason to report it here. In 1706, a slave murdered his mistress and committed suicide by drowning. His body was washed up at Kingston and the General Assembly "ordered his head, legs and arms to be cut off and hung up in some public place near Newport, and that his body be burned to ashes."[25]

The punishments of decapitation and dismemberment were not reserved, however, for slaves or Negroes—white men were also subjected to such indecencies, at least in the sentence of the court. Sellin gives the following gruesome example that comes from Frederick, Maryland, during the War of Independence. On August 15, 1781, the *Pennsylvania Gazette* (Philadelphia) carried the following notice:

> At a special court, lately held at Frederick Town, Maryland, Peter Sutman, Nicholas Andrews, John George Graves, Yost Plecker, Adam Graves, Henry Shell and Caspar Fritchie [shades of the fictional Barbara of the same place during the War Between the States] were found guilty of high treason . . . for having recruited and sworn in troops to fight for England; Judge Hanson imposed the following sentence on them: "You will be carried to the gaol of Frederick County, and there be

---

[24]*Ibid.,* p. 195.

[25]Edward Field: *State of Rhode Island and Providence Plantation at the End of the Century; A History.* Boston and Syracuse, Mason Publishing Co., 1902, Vol. 3, p. 148; cited by Sellin, *loc. cit.,* p. 17.

drawn to the gallows of Frederick-Town and be hanged thereon; you shall be cut down to the earth alive, and your entrails shall be taken out, and burnt while you are yet alive; your head shall be cut off; your body shall be divided into four parts, and your head and quarters shall be placed where His Excellency the Governor shall appoint—So Lord have mercy upon your poor souls."[25a]

Records indicate that although sentence was pronounced, it was never brought to conclusion. It seems the parts of the sentence beyond the hanging were not carried out, nor were all of the culprits hanged. One report states two; another, three.[26]

We should note that in sentences of drawing and quartering, the "drawing" refers to the trip made to the site of the quartering. There is confusion as to just what drawing means—the penalty could be construed to mean literal drawing of the entrails of a human being at the scene of the medieval butchering. As far as our researches carry us, this does not appear to be the case. The word is more associated with being drawn on a sled or hurdle, or perhaps a cart. The purpose of the ride was to humiliate, and although records indicate that while the ride may have been fraught with considerable physical pain, this was not the actual purpose of the drawing. As described by Scott, in the *History of Torture Throughout the Ages,* "The ancient methods of execution in which the limbs and body were literally pulled apart by main force, or cut up into sections by an executioner lived long in European civilizations. Quartering would appear to be a development of disemboweling, as the practice of cutting open the abdomen and removing the bowels, before the body was divided into sections, persisted for a long time. An analagous method of execution, prescribed for traitors, was to remove the heart in addition to or instead of the bowels, before quartering." Scott further describes a pronounced sentence: "That the traitor is to be taken from the prison and laid upon a sled or hurdle and drawn to the gallows,

---

[25a]Sellin, *op. cit.,* p. 20.

[26]Sources: J. Thomas Scharf, *The History of Western Maryland,* Vol. I, pp. 141-3; T. J. C. Williams, *History of Frederick County, Maryland,* 1910; and Esther Mohr Dole, *Maryland in the American Revolution,* 1941, who states "we have no information as to whether it [the sentence] was carried out in all its horrible details."

or place of execution, and thence to be hanged by the neck until he be half dead, then cut down; his entrails to be cut out of his body and burnt by the executioner . . ."[27] The implication is clear, then, that "drawing" refers to the trip to the place of "punishment" and not any performance at the place of punishment.

PRESSED TO DEATH
(The Case of Giles Corey)

The case of Giles Corey represents the single instance of a culprit being condemned by a court to be "pressed to death." Technically, this form of torture was known as *peine forte et dure*. This peculiar but extremely painful penalty was early associated with persons refusing to plead either guilty or not guilty at the bar. It was a modification of the earlier and more widely-used punishment of starving such dissidents to death or until such time as they were ready to plead. This peculiar form of persuasion is alleged to have come into existence because of the folk belief that truth could actually be pressed out of the accused if enough weight was put upon the body. According to English common law, the penalty did not constitute torture.[28]

The methods were justified by jurists of the day, since if a person brought before the bar of justice remained mute his refusal to plead balked every effort of justice. Legally it was impossible to convict a person who refused to plead and the court could not enter a plea for the accused.[29]

Andrews, our authority on bygone punishments, describes the penalty as it was originally applied in England:

> The prisoner shall be remanded to the place from whence he came, and put in some low, dark room, and there laid on his back, without any manner of clothing except a cloth around his middle; and that as many weights shall be laid upon him as he can bear, *and more;* and that he shall have no more substenance but of the worst bread and water, and that he shall not eat

---

[27]George Ryley Scott, *The History of Torture Throughout the Ages*, London, Luxor Press, 1959, p. 212.

[28]Scott, *op. cit.*, pp. 87, 156.

[29]*Ibid.*, p. 87.

the same day on which he drinks nor drink the same day on which he eats; and he shall so continue until he die.[30]

Later modification of the punishment included the tying of the individual's arms and legs to four corners of the "low dark room."

> "The criminal is sent back to the prison whence he came and there laid in some low dark room upon the bare ground on his back, all naked except his privy parts, his arms and legs drawn with cords fastened to several parts of the room; and there is laid on his body iron, stone, or lead, as much as he can bear; the next day he shall have three morsels of barley bread, without drink; and the third day shall have to drink some of the kernel water with bread. And this method is in strictness to be observed until he is dead."[31]

The logic, of course, behind this protracted torture was that given enough time and enough pain, the person would plead guilty or not guilty, thus recognizing the jurisdiction of the court, rather than protract the current agonies he was in. Other refined gestures of torment were invented, or were already established by the earlier inquisition to attempt to compel the victim to plead or confess; notable among them were twisting the thumb with whipcord, or thumbscrews.[32]

As stated above, the only case that has come to our attention in which a person was subjected to the penalty of being pressed to death is the case of Giles Corey. His ordeal took place in Salem, Massachusetts, on September 19, 1692. Corey refused to plead, consequently the crime for which he was pressed was that of "standing mute." Burr, in his *Narratives,* describes this case:

> He pleaded not guilty [of witchcraft] but would not put himself upon Tryal by the Jury and knowing there would be the same witnesses against him, rather chose to undergo what Death they would put him to. In pressing, his Tongue being prest out of his Mouth, the Sheriff with his Cane forced it in again,

---

[30]Andrews, *op. cit.,* p. 88.

[31]Scott, *op. cit.,* p. 185.

[32]*Ibid.,* p. 87.

when he was dying. He was the first in New England that was pressed to Death.[33]

The Salem hysteria struck the Corey family twice. Mrs. Corey was hanged for witchcraft on August 19, 1692. A portion of the damning testimony had been given by her husband and her four son-in-laws. Giles later recanted, but his testimony apparently bore more weight than his recantation.

Giles Corey himself was regarded as a stubborn person among his contemporaries. At the time of his wife Martha's, trial he was a confused old man of eighty, possessed of admirable qualities, to be sure, but he was not an altogether upright citizen and had few friends. An entry in the *Diary* of Samuel Sewell, dated September 19, 1692, narrates that about noon Corey was pressed to death. The entry for September 20th reads: "Now I hear from Salem that about eighteen years ago he (Corey) was suspected to have stamped and pressed a man to death, but was cleared. It was not remembered until Anne Putnam was told of it by said Corey's spectre, the Sabbath day night before the execution."[34] The tale bore some credence. Local gossip had it that in 1676, Corey had beaten a man named Goodell and he died either as a result of the beating or because of his impaired health. Goodell worked for Corey, and it is believed that Corey became angry at some misconduct on the part of Goodell.[35]

Samuel Sewell received the story he recorded in his *Diary* from Thomas Proctor, whose wife was hanged as a "witch." He wrote it in a letter. He maintained that his daughter, Anne, who had been "grievously tormented by witches," had been confronted by the spirit of a man in a "winding-sheet" who had claimed he had been murdered by Giles Corey. He went even further and contended he had been pressed to death. Sewell, of course, believed the tale. The Corey case was dramatized by playright Arthur Miller in *The Crucible*. With all faults considered, as we regard Corey

---

[33]George Lincoln Burr, *Narratives to the Witchcraft Cases,* Barnes & Noble, 1914, p. 367, see also, Charles W. Upham: *Salem Witchcraft,* New York, Frederick Ungar, Vol. I, 181-91; Vol. II, 334-43.

[34]Stated by Peleg W. Chandler: *American Criminal Trials,* Boston, 1841, Vol. I, p. 123n; his source, Washburne, *Judicial History of Massachusetts,* p. 148.

[35]Upham *op. cit.,* Vol. I, p. 185; Vol. II, pp. 341-3.

today, he must be remembered as a person of heroic stature; a "man of granite."

A somewhat hoary broadside related the tragic stories of Giles Corey and Goodwife Corey. Here is a portion of the ballad as it involves Giles:

"Giles Corey and Good Wyfe Corey—a Ballad of 1692"[36]

Giles Corey was a Wizzard strong,
    A stubborn Wretch was he,
And fitt was he to hang on high
    Upon ye Locust Tree.

So when before ye Magistrates
    For Tryall he did come,
He would no true Confession make
    But was compleatlie dumb.

"Giles Corey" said ye Magistrate,
    What hast ye here to pleade,
To those who now accuse thy Soule
    Of Crimes and horrid Deed?

Giles Corey—he sayde not a Word,
    No single Word spake he;
"Giles Corey," sayeth ye Magistrate,
    "We'll press it out of thee."

They got them a heavy Beam,
    They layde it on his Breast,
They loaded it with heavy Stones,
    And hard upon him preasst.

"More weight!" now sayde this wretched Man,
    "More weight!" again he cryde,
And he did no Confession make
    But wickedly he dyed.

———————

Dame Corey lived but six days more,
    But six Days more lived she,
For she was hung at Gallows Hill
    Upon ye Locust Tree.

[36]Olive Woolley, Burt: *American Murder Ballads*, New York, Oxford University Press, 1958, p. 107. See Chapter III, pages 144-6 for other verses dealing with Martha Corey.

BURNING AT THE STAKE

Burning a person to death was an almost universal form of punishment in medieval times and actually carried over into more modern sophisticated eras. In the Middle Ages, it was most frequently invoked to stifle heresy against the *status quo* whether religious or secular. Savonarola was burned in 1498, John Huss in 1419 and Servitus in 1553. Then, too, we have the case of Joan of Arc, who was burned to death at Rouen, France, in 1431. Some three hundred persons—Protestant—suffered this fate under Mary I (Bloody Mary) between 1555 and 1558.

In simple form, the victim was burned to death promptly, but it was not uncommon for the unfortunate wretch to be snatched from the flames after being thoroughly seared, left for an interval to suffer from his burns, and then to be returned to the stake at a later date. History records single burnings, multiple burnings, and many tortures utilizing heat and flame. During the years of the Spanish Inquisition, it was necessary that the full court of Spain be present at the burnings of heretics.

> "At the place of execution there are so many stakes set as there are prisoners to be burned, a large quantity of dried furze being set about them. The stakes of the Protestants, or, as the Inquisitors called them, the professed are about four yards high and have each a board whereupon the prisoner is seated within half a yard of the top. The professed then go up a ladder between two priests, who attend them the whole day of execution. When they come even with the aforementioned board, they turn about to the people and the priests spend near a quarter of an hour exhorting with them to be reconciled to the See of Rome . . . a general shout is then raised when the priests get off the ladder, the universal cry is: 'Let the dogs beard be made' (which implies singe their beards)". . . . "The intrepidity of the twenty-one men and women in suffering the horrid death was truly astonishing; . . . the near situation of the King to the criminals rendered their dying groans very audible to him; he could not, however, be absent from this dreadful scene as it is esteemed a religious one and his coronation oath obliges him to give sanction by his presence to all the acts of the Tribunal."[37]

---

[37]Scott, *op. cit.*, p. 73.

Fire appears to have been considered as versatile an instrument as it was plentiful. Parts were burned off, whole bodies were burned, persons were fried, with or without shortening, in great large frying pans, others were boiled, others were simply suspended from poles over flames while other such niceties as were thought necessary were performed on the writhing victim.

There is an element of calculated cruelty in making use of this penalty, not present in hanging. Without condoning hanging, it is obvious that it is far more humane than burning. It is quicker; it is supervised by an "expert" (although all too frequently this safeguard was overlooked especially in our own country), and officially there is no element of vindictiveness as was so often the case in early burnings. It also appeals less to the primordial ferocity inherent in many person.

Burning at the stake, as practiced in this country, was generally reserved for Negroes, the depressed, if not despised, people. It was considered not only as a prime deterrent, but as a horrible example and lesson to the survivors of subservient groups. It was a symbol of the caste system, especially as we have known it and seen it reflected in the racial struggle in this country. The punishment was legally invoked primarily as a deterrent penalty against assaulting a white person or of conspiring to escape bondage. The fear of rebellion on the part of the Negro in colonial America was almost pathological therefore burning at the stake seemed justifiable to prevent such untoward contingencies. It seems appropriate to cite a few cases to more fully document our position. We have already mentioned the New York Negro conspiracy of 1712 (p. 114) and we shall more fully describe the more serious one of 1741.

New Jersey records several cases of Negroes being burned at the stake. Some time in 1716, month and day not mentioned, an un-named Negro was burned alive for the murder of his master.[38] A Negro was burned in 1729 at Perth Amboy for the murder of Thomas Cook, a tailor.[39] Negro Jack, of Bergen County, was

---

[38]Charles J. Boyer, "Jersey Justice in Olden Days," *Proceedings, New Jersey Historical Society, 16:* 257-83, July 1931.

[39]Harry B. and Grace M. Weiss, *An Introduction to Crime and Punishment in Colonial New Jersey.* Trenton, The Past Times Press, 1960, p. 49, from *Archives* Vol. XI, p. 201.

burned to death on August 16, 1735, for assaulting his master, Peter Kipp.[40] and "two Negroes," at Amboy, on June 21, 1750, for the murder of Mrs. Obadiah Ayers.[41] Others were: a Negro belonging to Robert L. Hooper at Rocky Hill, Somerset County, in January 1739, for the murder of a small son of the overseer and for setting fire to a barn.[42] Two more Negroes were burned "on the east side of the Hackensack River" near the home of Dierach Van Horn, for arson (they burned seven barns). The date of these burnings was May 14, 1741.

It should be noted that the burnings listed above for New Jersey took place actually in the colony of East Jersey, rather than in the Quaker colony of West Jersey. The latter colony, together with that of William Penn's colony (prior to his death in 1718), did not allow brutal punishments of any sort.[43]

The only person legally burned at the stake in the Pennsylvania colony was a white woman. We will describe this episode below. There were several Negroes hanged in the colony, but none burned, so far as records indicate. One reason for this may have been because Negroes were chattels and slave owners were loath to tolerate economic loss without protest. In fact, laws that now appear quaint serve as mute testimony to the grim economic realism of the times. Laws were passed in some states which provided for compensation to slave owners whose human property suffered hanging. Pennsylvania's law dates from March 5, 1725. We have a few examples from the Commonwealth that indicate the invocation of that legislation. A Joseph Richardson, of Chester County, was allowed $55 when his female slave, Phebe, was hanged in March, 1764, for burglary "of Divers Goods and Chattels;" Andrew Long, of Franklin County, and the master of the slave Jack Durham, was compensated in the sum of $80 for his loss—Durham was hanged at Chambersburg on July 8, 1788; and as late as 1802, a slave owner of Bellefonte, Centre County, was allowed $214 for the loss of his slave, Dan Byers, by execution on December 13. These funds, of course, were paid out of the local treasuries. A

---

[40]*Ibid.*, pp. 88-89.

[41]*Ibid.*, p. 31.

[42]Written up in Boston *News Letter January*, 18-33, 1739.

[43]For a contrast of penalties in the two Jerseys, see Weiss & Weiss, *op. cit.*, Chapter 1.

case from Georgetown, Kentucky has come to our attention which follows this pattern. The female slave, Nancy, property of Walter Rhodes, was hanged on September 30, 1803, from a tree "in a little thicket on the Georgetown and Lexington Road" for arson—she had burned down a barn belonging to her master. This gentleman was awarded $300 for his loss "for the value of the said slave."[44]

Now let us narrate the case that may well be the only instance of a white person legally burned in this country. The case is that of Catherine Bevan, of New Castle (now in Delaware, but at the time, 1731, one of the "lower counties" of Penn's colony). It does seem paradoxical that this single burning case should have happened in the colony of Pennsylvania, characterized by its humanity. William Penn had died in 1718 and a rigorous penal code had been adopted by the Provincial Council—a council dominated by Anglicans, rather than by Quakers. It was under the auspices of the new penal code that Mrs. Bevan met her sorry end.

The New Castle matron had grown tired of her husband, Harry, and so had entered into a pact with her servant, Peter Murphy, to rid herself of him. She sent Murphy to the village to purchase some "rat bone" or "Roman vitriol" to "get rid of rats" (a reason still invoked for the purchase of lethal commodities). Mrs. Bevan began feeding her aging spouse the poison. The old man, apparently of hardy stock, did not die according to his wife's timetable; she became impatient with the sluggishness of the deadly potion, and called upon her servant to help her choke the old man to death. In reality they beat their victim to death.

Murphy was sentenced to hang; Catherine was sentenced to "burn." In early English history, the punishment for a woman who poisoned her husband to death was to burn, accompanied by hanging. The theory behind this extreme penalty was that before the flames from the lighted faggots could reach the female culprit, she would be strangled by the rope placed around her neck by the executioner. On occasions, however, theory was not put to practice—something might go wrong. Something did go wrong in the case of Catherine Bevan. At the place of execution

---

[44]B. G. Gaines, *History of Scott Co. Kentucky,* Georgetown Printery 1905, p. 385.

each of the two schemers blamed the other for the murder. As the contemporary news story records the event: ". . . Neither said much; the Man seemed penitent, but the Woman appeared hardened. It was design'd to strangle her before the Fire should touch her; but its first breaking out was in a stream which pointed directly upon the rope . . . and burnt it off instantly so that she fell alive in the Flames, and was seen to struggle."[45]

Justin Atholl, narrator of tales of the gallows in Britain, relates a case somewhat similar. Elizabeth Wright, a coiner [counterfeiter], was taken in a cart to the gallows along with others doomed to die. When prayers were finished she begged hard to be hanged as was to be their lot. Yet she was fastened to the stake and "burned to ashes." But, fortunately for her, the executioner, seeing the flames reaching up to her before she could be strangled, beat her to death with blows on her breast.[46] Catherine Bevan, of New Castle, had no such good luck![47]

We mentioned above that Pennsylvania was one of two colonies originally established along humane lines, so far as penalties for crimes were concerned. A fact that is little known, however, is that William Penn, overcome with the lawlessness so prevalent even in his humane and docile colony, felt compelled to invoke a drastic code in 1700, ratified in 1701 as the Newcastle Code. It called for mutilations, brandings, floggings and even castration for certain offenses.[48] The great Penn wrote to the Provincial Council from London that persistent rumors reaching him complained not only of crimes in low places but even among those who were charged with serious responsibilities in his colony. He ruefully concluded: "There is no place more overrun with wickedness, Sins so very

---

[45]*Pennsylvania Gazette,* Philadelphia, September 9-23, 1731.

[46]*Shadow of the Gallows,* London, John Long, Ltd., 1954, 169.

[47]The only other person burned at the stake in Pennsylvania (an illegal lynching) was a Negro named Zachariah Walker. He was dragged from a hospital bed, in Coarseville, Chester County, on August 13, 1911, to a field on the outskirts of town and burned to death. He had killed a night watchman. For further details of this case, see M. A. De Wolfe Howe: *John Jay Chapman and His Letters,* Boston, Houghton, Mifflin, 1937, pp. 215-219; 329; 473-475.

[48]For rape, second offense, sodomy and beastiality by a married man; *Statutes at Large,* II, 8, 183; III, 202; repealed and reenacted in 1705 with castration omitted; see Lawrence H. Gipson, *"The Criminal Code of Pennsylvania" J. of Amer. Inst. of Crim. Law and Criminol.,* VI, 3 (1915) 323-44, citation at 330.

Scandalous, openly Committed in defiance of Law and Virtue; facts so foul I *am* forbid by common modesty to relate ym."[49] In 1698, according to Professor Lawrence P. Gipson, "Pennsylvania was called 'Ye Greatest refuge and shelter for pirates and rogues in America.' "[50] What a contrast to Penn's fervent hopes when he conceived his "Holy Experiment" and to the glorious reputation so frequently tendered it by early historians!

Presumably following some of the southern colonies in dealing with Negroes, the Provincial Council of Pennsylvania, in 1701, passed an act which placed the trials of Negroes in the hands of two specially designated justices of the peace before a jury of freeholders. These officers had the power to "hear, try and determine" the offenses of "murder, manslaughter, buggery, rapes, attempts of rapes, and other high and heinous enormities and capital offenses."[51] All of these offenses, when committed by Negroes, were made capital. None of the records of these special courts remain, so we can only surmise what penalties were imposed and carried out. The first Negroes to be hanged in the colony—so far as the records show—were "Negro Caspar" and "Negro Joe," at Philadelphia, for burglary. The date was some time in November, 1762.

As for the penalty of castration, which we alluded to above, and invoked by the Newcastle Code of 1701, we have no knowledge that it was ever imposed on anyone. Pennsylvania may be the only colony wherein this drastic penalty was ever placed on the statute books.

The metamorphosis that transpired with the passage of this severe code can only be explained by the fact that Pennsylvania Colony was transformed from a mild haven for law-abiding, tolerant and kindly people into a receptacle for transported felons and other riff-raff from the mother country. As Gipson puts it:

> From prosecuting cases of larceny, slander, swearing, Sabbath breaking, assault and battery, drunkenness, the selling of

---

[49] (*Colonial Records of Pennsylvania,* Vol. I, p. 525, February 9, 1697).

[50] *Loc. cit.,* p. 341. Some of the above material has previously appeared in the *Journal* of the Lancaster County (Penna.) Historical Society and is referred to by permission of that society; see Teeters, "Public Executions in Pennsylvania," V64, No. 3 (Spring) 1960, pp. 85-164.

[51] *Statutes at Large,* Vol. II, pp. 77-9.

rum to the Indians, and immorality . . . the authorities at the
close of the century and from then on were called upon to deal
with burglaries, counterfeiting, highway robbery, petit treason,
horse stealing, rapes, homicides, infanticides, and murders.[52]

The extreme sanctions passed in 1701 proved to be so repugnant
to the mother country that their repeal was ordered by the Crown
within a few years. As Herbert W. K. Fitzroy says:

> The more extreme punishments were permitted to be con-
> tinued for but a few years, since in 1705 we had the rather
> unusual spectacle of the English Privy Council disallowing laws
> of the Quaker province because of their *unusual cruelty*—the
> laws involving castration because it was "a punishment never
> inflicted by any law of Her Majesty's dominions", and the laws
> providing enslavement because "selling" a man "is not a pun-
> ishment allowed by the laws of England."[53]

In 1718, the colony went all out, now that Penn was dead and
the Quakers were losing their influence, in setting up a sanguinary
code. On May 31st, an act designating thirteen capital crimes was
passed. The Anglicans, who dominated the colony by this time,
gained the reluctant support of the Quakers by permitting them
their beloved "right of affirmation" in legal matters. From this
date on, to 1786, when a reforming zeal began to permeate the
colony—now a state—Pennsylvania executed its fair number of
criminals convicted of such offenses as arson, rape, burglary, robbery and murder. But, aside from that one lone case of Catherine
Bevan, recorded earlier, there were no burnings in the colony.

Another paradox one finds in examining early criminal law in
Pennsylvania is the reluctance to pass laws making horse-stealing
capital. So far as we know, not one single person was ever hanged
in the colony or state for this offense. How many were hanged in
other jurisdictions we have no way of knowing, aside from negotiating a careful check, state by state.

Generally speaking, horse-stealing has been considered one of
the most serious offenses, especially in a new country, when a horse
was almost indispensable for rapid travel. The horse thief was both

---

[52]Gipson, *loc. cit.,* p. 341.

[53]Punishments of crime in Pennsylvania, *Pa. Mag. of Hist. & Biog., 60*:250, 1936.

a menace and a swashbuckling, almost romantic, outlaw. While the offense was never declared capital, by statute, in Pennsylvania, it was so considered at common law; thus there were some who were convicted of the crime and sentenced to death and a few that were pardoned, or their sentences commuted.[54] The Act of 1767 was the first to legislate against the offense, calling for penalties such as fines, the pillory, the whipping post and imprisonment. Later acts increased the severity of the punishments to embrace branding, the cropping of ears, and hard labor in a house of correction. It is true, however, that a few persons were hanged who were definitely horse thieves but they were indicted and convicted of such crimes as robbery (usually highway) or burglary.

The Last Legal Burning in the United States

In August, 1825, a slave, "Negro Jack" was tried by an inferior court of "the magistrates and five freeholders," for the offenses of rape and murder, in the county of Abbeville, South Carolina. He was sentenced to be chained to a stake and set afire. In this case, the court decided to "make of him a dreadful example to his race." In general, rape and murder and other capital crimes were punishable in South Carolina by hanging, but there were early statutes that permitted burning.

As a result of this one legalized burning, the state repealed all sections of the code that permitted courts to pronounce the sentence of burning of slaves in capital cases in 1833. The added provision reads: "On the conviction of a slave or free person of color for a capital offense, the punishment shall be by hanging and not otherwise." Below is the constable's expense account[55] itemized for the state treasurer:

State of South Carolina
August 1825, to Thos. Goodman, Const. Dr.
    To Summons five freeholders at 54¢. $2.70
    To Summons one Magistrate. 54
    Guarding of Negro Jack four days. 6.00
(Continued)

---

[54]See Teeters, *Scaffold & Chair,* Philadelphia, Pennsylvania Prison Society, 1963, Part I, pp. 23-4.

[55]Courtesy Jack Kenney Williams; material sent to writers.

feeding Negro Jack four days................ .50
To waggons & teams one day a getting of
      lightwood for to burn Jack............ 6.00
4 hands one day extra of the driving for
      the Waggons 2.00
paid black Smyth for Ironing of Jack.......... 2.50
two bottles of Spirits Turpentine at 56-1/4..... 1.12-1/2
Chains for to confine Jack when burnt........ 3.00
Execution of Negro Jack.................... 3.00

                         —————
                        $27.36-1/2

South Carolina
Abbeville District   I, John G. McGhee one of the Justices of the peace for Abbeville district hereby certify that Thomas Goodman is a constable for this District, Regularly appointed, that I believe the charges in the above account are just and reasonable.

                         John G. Mc Ghee

22nd. November, 1825

Early Hangings for Sex Crimes

In the early Anglo-Saxon penal codes, certain sex crimes were traditionally considered capital. Among these were rape, bestiality, sodomy and buggery. These terms, with the exception of rape, were used interchangeably throughout the colonies. For the purposes of this work, the distinctions between the terms are less important than the fact that all of the offenses were identified as sexual aberrations or perversions.

Historically, such offenses have always been codified in the law as being offensive to the general public, although it is now recognized that there is a profound difference between what a man prescribes for others and what he practices himself. Despite codification, we find none of these offenses, with the exception of rape, listed today as capital crimes. Historically, however, scarcely a colony imposed a penalty short of death, at one time or other in its history, and many were the times that the penalty was invoked. We do not pretend to have collected all of the cases that ended in the gallows for sex offenders. There were probably hundreds of them during colonial times. We do, however, have a fair sprinkling of them which we shall review here.

We know little about our first case, other than that one Hackett (or Hatchet) was hanged in Massachusetts Bay Colony for "bestiality," some time in 1641.[56] The following year, 1642, Thomas Graunger, a lad of sixteen or seventeen years, and a servant of Roxbury, in Plymouth Colony, was hanged for buggery. Governor Bradford describes the case as follows: "a very sad spectacle . . . horrible it is to mention . . . first the mare, then the cow, and the rest of the lesser cattle, were kilt before his face, according to the law, Leviticus 20:15 and he himself was executed."[57]

We find no other cases even remotely related to sexual perversion until 1674, when one Benjamin Gourd, age seventeen, of Roxbury, was hanged on April 2nd for bestiality (sodomy). The sentence called for his death and "the mare you abused before your execution in your sight shall be knockt in the head."[58]

In the Jerseys (both East and West), we find few cases of trials for "unnatural" crime, and only one person whose name is identified actually hanged for the offense. In 1688, a John Laurie of East Jersey was indicted for having relations with "a Certaine Mare att the stable of Miles Foster of Amboy." He was acquitted but had to remain in prison for a year for his good behavior.[59] In 1692, the Negro servant of Isaac Marriatt, place not mentioned, was indicted and tried for a similar offense with a cow. He was sentenced to be "hanged by the neck till the body be dead, dead, dead and God have mercy on thy Soule; and that the Cowe with which thou committed the Buggery shall the same day be slaine." However, the human victim escaped jail and that was the end of the case. It may be surmised that the cow was reprieved under the circumstances.

There are occasional cases referred to in some of the Jersey counties but the only ones that seem to have been actually hanged were Charles Conoway of Salem County, executed sometime in 1757, and John Taylor of Burlington County. The latter was con-

---

[56] Winthrop's *History*, Vol. II, pp. 58-60.
[57] Bradford's *History*, pp. 474-5; P.C.R. Vol. II, p. 44, 1742.
[58] Source: Sewell's *Diary* for April 2, 1684.
[59] Weiss and Weiss, *op. cit.*, p. 87.

victed of "that detestible crime bestiality" and sentenced to hang on December 4, 1774.

The only case we could find in Pennsylvania was that of Joseph Ross, hanged at Hannas Town (now Greensburg), Westmoreland County, on December 20th, 1785. We mentioned this case in our previous chapter as the first person hanged west of the Allegheny Mountains (see Chapter I, page 112). There are doubtless many other cases of persons hanged in the colonies for the so-called "unnatural" sex crime, but the above are all that have been brought to our attention.

We have about a dozen cases of persons hanged for rape during the latter part of the seventeenth century. Doubtless there were many more but their records have not been examined, if they exist. As in our times, we would probably find some confusion in the definition of intent of rape except in the cases in which Negroes or Indians were concerned. Rapes, assaults, or "muggings"—and perhaps even simulated rapes with fraud, blackmail, coercion or extortion accompanying them, would probably all be thrown into the hopper if we had all the facts with the records.

Our first case lists Tom, an Indian, 1674, in Massachusetts Bay Colony; victim, "a squaw."[60] The following year, in the same colony, we find Samuel Guile being hanged for the rape of Mary, wife of Samuel Ash.[61] In 1676, one Basto, a Negro slave, committed rape on his master's child and was hanged.[62] In 1681 we find William Cheny hanged for the rape of a servant with the intriguing name of Experience Holdbrooke, but one may wonder what kind of experience she had had before she ran afoul of Cheny.[63] We skip down the coast to New Jersey, first to East Jersey and, more specifically to Monmouth County. Here we find the case of Tom, a Negro, hanged in 1690 for rape, victim not identified; the place, Freehold.[64] We find a hanging at Salem, West Jersey, in

---

[60]*Court of Assistants,* Mass., Vol. I, pp. 21-22, 1674.

[61]*Ibid.,* p. 50, 1675.

[62]*Ibid.,* p. 74 (also Sewell's *Diary,* June 22, 1676).

[63]*Ibid.,* p. 199, 1681. See Edwin Powers, *Crime and Punishment in Early Massachusetts,* Beacon Press, 1966, Chapter 9.

[64]Source: Freehold, *Transcript,* compilation, April 15, 1892; courtesy Mr. Robert Van Benthuysen, secretary, Monmouth Co. Historical Association, Freehold.

1763, possibly on March 29. It was of a Negro, not identified, for the rape of "an idiot girl."[65]

Some ten years later, on December 5, 1774, again in what was earlier called West Jersey, this time at Burlington, Peter Galwin "a school teacher," was hanged for "rape of a girl of ten." Other charges were "assaults with intent to ravish infants." One more case from Jersey, disposition of which is problematical is that of a sixteen-year-old Dutch boy, servant of a Mr. Lippincott of Haddonfield, who enticed his master's nine-year-old daughter from home on the pretense of picking grapes. After ravishing the child, he murdered her and buried her body in the woods. His bestial crime occurred in August, 1770. He was arrested and held in the Gloucester jail. We have no record of what happened.[66]

A few other cases that have come to our attention are a drummer boy named Pierre Berge, attached to Cadillac's troops somewhere in Michigan who was hanged in 1705 (no date given), for criminally assaulting a girl named Susanne Capelle; he was also known as La Tulipe.[67] James, a Negro slave, is the first rape case in Philadelphia of which we have record—on August 7, 1736 (fully fifty years after colonization).[68] Arthur, a Negro, was hanged at Worcester, Massachusetts, October 20, 1768, for the rape of Deborah Metcalfe[69] and Bryan Sheehan at Salem, same colony, on January 16, 1772, for the rape of Abial, wife of Venhamin Hallowell of Marblehead.[70] In that same year we find another case in Pennsylvania, that of Patrick Kennedy, hanged in Chester County, on May 2nd. He, together with three others raped Jane Walker, of "Thornberry Township" but he, alone, was hanged.[71]

It is quite likely that there were many more persons hanged for rape in the other colonies the records of which have not come to our attention. In general, however, there seem not to have been

[65]Weiss and Weiss, *op. cit.,* p. 60, from *N. J. Archives,* Vol. XXVI, p. 400.

[66]*Ibid.,* p. 60; *Archives,* Vol. XXVII, p. 236.

[67]Louis H. Burbey, in *Michigan Historical Magazine,* Vol. V, No. 4, 1938, pp. 443-457.

[68]*American Weekly Mercury,* Philadelphia, July 29-August 5.

[69]*Massachusetts Broadsides,* No. 1426.

[70]*Massachusetts Broadsides,* No. 1633; also Evans, 12559.

[71]*Pennsylvania Colonial Records,* Vol. X, pp. 43-4; also Henry Ashmead, *History of Delaware County,* 1884, p. 165.

too many cases. An exhaustive, tedious and time-consuming search of the existing records and court dockets might unearth many such cases but such is not our task so far as this work is concerned.

EARLY MASS HANGINGS—NEGRO CONSPIRACIES

Perhaps the largest group of persons to be hanged *en masse,* in the history of this country, consisted of thirty-eight Sioux Indians at Mankato, Minnesota, on December 26, 1862. This group did penance for the whole tribe which had risen up against the whites and slaughtered almost five hundred men, women, and children.[72] We shall discuss this grim episode in detail in a later chapter (see Chapter IX).

The earliest mass executions (by shooting rather than by hanging) is recorded in Samuel Sewell's *Diary* in the following manner:

> *September 13, 1676:* The Afterpart of the day very rainy. Note: there were eight Indians shot to death on the Common, upon Wind-mill hill.

There appears no other information. Again, in Massachusetts, in the same year, 1676, there is recorded that "Four Concord Englishmen were hanged for killing three Indian women and three Indian children."[73]

One of the most spectacular mass executions took place in the summer of 1741, in New York City. It occurred as the result of an alleged Negro conspiracy which also involved some white victims. There was considerable difference of opinion at the time as to whether or not there actually was a conspiracy. This controversy still reverberates today. Certainly the recorder of the city, Daniel Horsemanden, who wrote about the incidents of that era, believed there was a plot. His book, entitled *Journal of the Proceedings in the Detection of the Conspiracy, formed by some White People, in Conjunction with Negro and Other Slaves, for Burning the City of New York and Murdering the Inhabitants* was published in 1744. Later writers have paid little heed to the events and George Bancroft, the historian, disposes of it in these few words: "Once," he writes regarding slaves, "an excitement against

---

[72]Paul L. Wellman, *A Dynasty of Western Outlaws,* Pyramid Book, Doubleday and Company, 1964, p. 216; Wellman gives the number hanged as thirty-nine.

[73]*Court of Assistants,* Vol. I, p. 71, 1676.

them raged in New York, through fear of pretended plot, but the frenzy grew out of a delusion."

Plot or no plot, four white persons, two men and two women, were hanged; eighteen Negroes were also hanged, and eleven other Negroes were burned at the stake for their alleged participation in the "plot." All were legally tried and convicted, albeit during a period of panic. Many others escaped the death penalty through the route of pardon or for turning informer on those who were executed.[74] Thomas Sutton, in his *The New York Tombs.* says regarding these executions (1874, p. 150):

> The Negroes . . . were chained to a stake and burned to death in a valley between Windmill Hill (site of the old Chatham Theatre) and Pot Bakers' Hill, midway between Pearl and Barclay streets, where public executions were performed for some years after. John Huston [Hughson] white, who was one of the principals in the last outrage (1740-41) was bound in chains on a gibbet at the southeast point of Rutger's Farm—not ten yards from the present southeast corner of Cherry and Catherine streets. Carson, a negro, was also hanged in chains on a gibbet at the southeast corner of the old powder house on Magazine street. At this time a general alarm prevailed and the scenes of the arrest, trial and execution at the Collect Pond, where the Tombs now stands [1874] kept up a continual feverish excitement.

Riots and incipient plots among Negroes at that time were not unusual. These people were slaves not far removed in time from Africa, with no education or sense of responsibility coupled with a just cause. It was not difficult for some to be emotionally fanned into a frenzy against the injustices heaped upon them by their masters or the white man in general. Punishments for insubordination and for assaulting slave owners were extremely severe, as we have indicated earlier. All of the colonies suffered plots, riots and uprisings of slaves from time to time. We have already mentioned the conspiracy in New York City in 1712; there was another in 1734, and in 1738, there was a serious riot in South Carolina.

The story of the great conspiracy of 1741, in New York, starts with the robbing of the home of a merchant named Hogg, in

---

[74]The material here is from Peleg W. Chandler, *op. cit.*, Vol. I, 213-54.

February. Suspicion immediately rested upon the operator of a "low tavern" named John Hughson "where Negroes were in the habit of resorting." Hughson had a sixteen-year-old indentured servant named Mary Burton, who informed against him, so he confessed the crime. A certain Peggy Carey, in one place referred to as "a woman of infamous character" and in another, as a "prostitute," was also apparently involved in the robbery. Not long thereafter, the government house, the king's chapel, the secretary's office, the barracks, and the stable were all burned at midday. This conflagration was soon followed by other fires, and it gradually became evident that they were all caused by incendiaries.

At this particular time, a Spanish ship had brought into the port a large number of Negro slaves who were immediately sold. They were dissatisfied with their lot and grumbled so loudly that they were immediately suspect as incipient trouble-makers. Fires continued throughout the city which prompted rewards to be offered for information as to the culprits. Mary Burton, the indentured girl, immediately came forward and informed that three Negro slaves, Caesar, Prince and Cuffee, had met at her master's (Hughson) house and had concocted an ambitious plan to burn the whole city and massacre the inhabitants. She further implicated her master, his wife, Sarah, and Peggy Carey. She further maintained that Hughson was planning to set himself up as king and the Negro, Caesar, as governor.

At this juncture of the fantastic but potentially alarming state of affairs, legal action against the alleged conspirators began. Peggy Carey was promised immunity if she would confess and implicate Hughson. She refused by saying that "if she should accuse any body of such things she must accuse innocent persons, and wrong her own soul." But later she reconsidered—due to a charge against her for receiving stolen goods—and contended that Hughson was behind the plot. With this "deposition" on the books, it seemed easy to enmesh others into the net of guilt. During May, June and July, a great many Negroes were indicted and tried for conspiracy. One prosecutor spoke to the jury as follows:

> The monstrous ingratitude of this black tribe is what exceedingly aggravates their guilt. Their slavery among us is generally soft-

ened with great indulgence. They live without care; and are commonly better clothed and fed, and put to less labor than the poor of Christian countries. But notwithstanding all the kindness and tenderness with which they have been treated . . . yet this is the second attempt of the same kind, that this brutish and bloody species of mankind have made within one age.

These helpless and ignorant Negroes were sentenced in the following brutal charge:

> You that were for destroying us without mercy, you abject wretches, outcasts of the nations of the earth, are treated here with tenderness and humanity . . . you have grown wanton with excess of liberty and your idleness has proved your ruin, having given you the opportunity of forming this villainous and detestable conspiracy. What hopes can you have of mercy in the other world.[75]

Most of the Negroes stoutly maintained their innocence; some confessed—it seemed to be saved from a hideous death—but the sentencing went blithely on. On June 8, six Negroes were condemned to be chained to the stake and burned; on June 10, four more received the same fate. On June 13, an additional five were convicted and later sentenced to death. The trials continued and more victims of the justice of the "master race" were condemned and sentenced.

John Hughson denied any guilt in the conspiracy, but to no avail. He died on the gallows "expecting a rescue." His wife "was senseless, and Peggy Carey met her fate with less composure than either of the others."

The fourth white person to become involved in this hysterical frenzy was the Rev. John Urie, former secretary of the South Sea Company and a "non-juring" clergyman, a man of considerable education. He came to New York for the purpose of teaching school. He became involved through Mary Burton and a soldier who had been accused but had escaped indictment, one William Kane. These two villains cooked up a transparent story in which they placed him at Hughson's in the role of encouraging the Negroes assembled to burn and pillage, set fire to the king's house

---

[75]Chandler, *op. cit.,* pp. 218-219.

and, to add fuel to the iniquities allegedly perpetrated by the ignorant blacks, they also associated him with a Romish plot which,
at that time, was an apparent "red herring" in various parts of the
New World. The testimony was strong against the accused man,
despite his pleas of innocence and impeccable reputation as an
educator. He was executed on August 29. At the gallows he said
among other things:

> In the presence of God, the possessor of heaven and earth;
> I lift up my hands and solemnly protest I am innocent of what
> is laid to my charge. I appeal to the great God for my non-
> knowledge of Hughson, his wife, or the creature that was hanged
> with them [Peggy Carey]. I never saw them, living, dying, or
> dead; nor ever had I any knowledge or confederacy with white
> or black, as to any plot; . . . and I protest that the witnesses
> were perjured; I never knew them but at my trial.[76]

After the last execution had been consummated (that of Urie),
a day of thanksgiving to Almighty God was observed by public
command, "for the deliverance of his majesty's subjects here from
the destruction wherewith they were so generally threatened by
the late execrable conspiracy."

A very few months later it was learned that some Negroes in
Queens, Long Island, celebrating Christmas holidays were suspected of engineering another plot. Immediately, several were arrested
and one was actually executed. Mary Burton, the informer, was
given the reward of one hundred pounds for "disclosing" the
earlier plot. Over one hundred fifty were taken into custody during the great community frenzy. We have already mentioned the
number executed. In addition, fifty were transported to the West
Indies and sold. Thus ended the great and amazing New York
Negro conspiracy of 1741. This hanging orgy, together with that
occurring a hundred or more years later—of the thirty-eight Sioux
Indians in Minnesota—represents the largest number of persons
executed for the same offense.

A Mass Hanging—The Wheelbarrow Men of Philadelphia—1789

October 12, 1789: Philadelphia: five hangings at once: all

---

[76]Chandler, *op. cit.*, p. 249.

"wheel-barrow men"—felons from the county jail who were condemned earlier by a strange law to sweep the streets "publickly
and disgracefully weighted down with irons." It was the Act of
September 15, 1786, fathered by the Chief Justice of Pennsylvania,
Thomas McKean. While this act was a step in diminishing the
number of capital crimes, its passage was ill-advised. The convicts, with heads shaved and wearing a garish garb of many hues,
slouched out of the jail gate, each pushing a wheelbarrow in which
rested a huge heavy iron ball attached to a chain, the other end
of which was riveted to the ankle. Guards carrying "blunderbuses"
marched alongside. To make the picture more degrading, each
contingent was followed by crowds of the city's riffraff and idle
curious.

The wheelbarrow men were employed at digging ditches, cess-
pools, foundations and at "sweeping and scraping." The more
malicious of these derelicts would curse the idlers who looked on
their misery, and, on occasions, hurl their iron balls at them and
perhaps hit them. This law had many critics, especially among
the members of the prison reform society *The Philadelphia Society
for Alleviating the Miseries of Public Prisons* which had been established on May 7, 1787, with the specific objective to work for
the repeal of this unpopular law.

Before it was finally repealed in 1790, many frightful tragedies
occurred. There were escapes from the jail, incipient riots took
place so that it was necessary for armed guards to come out in
force. The crime that led up to the mass execution of October 12,
1789, consisted of the murder of John McFarland, a drover, in
his home within a half block of the Commons, where these five
criminals were to be hanged not long afterwards. The five men—
John Burnett, Francis Burns, George Cronen, John Ferguson, and
John Logan—escaped jail one night and bludgeoned McFarland
to death and stole a large sum of money from the house. The
story of the crime reads almost like a modern thriller. The wife of
one of these criminals went along. It should be stated that all of
these men were transported criminals from England—the dregs
from the jails of the mother country. The news account reads:

> After reaching the drovers they forced an entrance after
> vainly demanding admission. The light of a lantern, carried by

Logan's wife, revealed one of the brothers, who was instantly knocked down with an iron pump-handle. Meanwhile the (other) brother fled to the loft where he was pursued by the murderers. In desperation he squeezed himself into a place in which it was after considered almost incredible that a human body could have been so forced.

The robbers, having lost their light could not find him, and descended the stairs. On relighting the lantern, Logan's wife perceived that the drover whom they had previously slugged, was not dead. "Damn him," cried the woman, "he's not dead yet, I'll finish him." And she raised his head with her hands and battered it against the wall till she thought life was gone. Having then secured the money, $2,000, they fancied they heard an alarm and hastened away. Most of the booty they hid in Potter's Field (now Washington Square) and then went straight to the grog-shop in the lower part of town . . . In a riot with some sailors the 'barrow men were badly beaten and one of them was found in the street. He confessed the crime and his accomplices were caught.[77]

These five transported criminals and "wheelbarrow men" were hanged and a broadside was struck off in commemoration of the spectacle. This is the largest group ever hanged at one time in Philadelphia. Characteristic of the journalism of the day, little of the event appears in the paper. The article merely gives the names of those hanged and adds: "the behavior of these unhappy men appeared penitent and suited to their deplorable situation."

MORE FEMALES HANGED IN THE EARLY DAYS

In our first chapter, we mentioned a few cases of females hanged for various offenses. Other hangings occurred during the early colonial days although we have scant information on them.

The first and only female to be hanged in Plymouth Colony was Alice Bishope, for the murder of Martha Clarke, "her owne child, the fruit of her own body," in 1648. During the 1640's some females were hanged for witchcraft, but we shall discuss these in the following chapter. We also find a case in Maryland

---

[77]This account is from the Philadelphia *Dispatch,* June 19, 1866; contemporary sources are: *Penna. Packet & Daily Advertiser,* September 22, 1789, for the account of the crime and the issue of October 13, for account of the executions.

of a woman hanged some time in the 1660's for infanticide. Her name was Elizabeth Greene. Other cases include Maria, servant of Joshua Lamb, of Roxbury, Massachusetts, for the then capital crime of arson. She was obliged to share the spotlight at the "tree" with Jack, servant of Samuel Wolcott, of Wethersfield, same state, also for arson. We also find the case of Elizabeth Emerson, probably of Haverhill, who was hanged some time in 1691 for the death of her two "bastard children." We have no record indicating other hangings during this early period of colonization.

Later periods provide us with cases on which we have more information. Patience Samson, *alias* Boston, was a twenty-three-year-old half-breed Indian, living at Falmouth, Maine (a part of Massachusetts at the time) in 1735. For some reason, not now known, she waylaid eight-year-old Benjamin Trot and drowned him in a well. For this, she was hanged at York on July 24. According to a pamphlet published in Boston in 1738, she led a "life of swearing, lying, and drunkenness." She brought it to an end in a senseless murder.[78]

A sermon preached at Portsmouth, New Hampshire by the Rev. William Shurtleff, calls our attention to the hanging in that city on December 22, 1739, of two "criminal" females, for the murder of their "bastard children." The victims were Sarah Simpson and Penelope Kenney and were the first *women* (and perhaps *the* very first) hanged in New Hampshire. The title of the sermon preached in their presence was "The Faith and Prayer of a Dying Malefactor."[79]

Some thirty years later, in 1768, New Hampshire was shocked to learn that Ruth Blay, a school mistress and member of a well-known family of South Hampton, Rockingham County, had disposed of her illegitimate child. She was indicted, convicted and hanged at Portsmouth. It could not be ascertained whether or not the child had been stillborn or killed upon birth by the unhappy young woman. The Blay family petitioned the governor to intercede but he did not until it was too late.

On the day of the execution, December 30, hundreds of people

---

[78]Listed by McDade *op. cit.,* 123.

[79]*Ibid.,* 874.

gathered at the "Training Field," a plot of ground set aside by the town of Portsmouth for a cemetery. However, at the time of the hanging it had not yet been placed in use. The sheriff drove the death cart to the place of execution with the girl, dressed in her wedding gown, sitting beside her coffin in the traditional manner. The sheriff, getting impatient as he waited for the noon bells to ring, gave the order for the rope to be loosed. At that same moment, it is reported, a messenger arrived from the governor with the long-looked for reprieve but it was too late.

The mob, angered at the turn of the event, stoned the sheriff's house and then burned it down. In addition, they hanged the official in effigy. The tragic victim was buried in the "Training Field" and thus became the first occupant of the newly-created Auburn Cemetery. Ironically it was later learned that the victim's child had actually been borne prematurely and had actually never lived at all.[80]

A case of hanging for infanticide is also recorded at Saybrook, Connecticut, the principal being Catherine Garret, an Indian servant girl. She was "turned off," probably at New London on May 3, 1738. The sermon preached on the occasion by the Rev. Eliphalet Andrews runs to thirty-seven printed pages in a pamphlet published after the girl's death. It also includes a short account of her behavior after being condemned and also her dying words.[81]

Still other cases of females who were hanged for their "vicious and criminal" acts were: Margaret Sexton, New Castle, now a part of Delaware but, at the time, in Pennsylvania Colony, who was hanged in June 1757, for killing her four-year-old step-son. Her crime was described by the Provincial Council as a "most barbarous and wilful act."[82] And the mulatto, Elizabeth Moore, of York, Pennsylvania, who poisoned her nine-year-old son whom she had placed out in a foundling home. She took him for a walk in the woods and killed him so he "could join his baby sister in Heaven"—a daughter she had killed some time earlier and for which crime she had not been detected.

---

[80]*The New Hampshire Sunday News,* May 7, 1961, article by George Woodbury, "The Tragic Fate of Ruth Blay," courtesy Misses Marjorie Calkins, Manchester, and Catherine McGettings, of Lebanon, New Hampshire.

[81]McDade, *op. cit.,* 332.

[82]*Colonial Records,* Vol. VII, June 4, 1757.

A different kind of crime was committed by "Negress Chloe," a slave belonging to a Mr. Carothers of Cumberland County, same state (Carlisle, county seat). She was hanged on July 18, 1801, for murdering the two daughters of her master's (they were four and six), in order to "bring sorrow to her hated mistress."[83]

The Mournful Story of Elizabeth Wilson's Betrayal

Perhaps the most pathetic of the really poignant cases in which a female was hanged in this country—not excepting the tragic Esther Rodgers at Ipswich, Massachusetts, who was hanged and gibbeted (see Chapter I, page 80)—is that of Elizabeth Wilson, a simple farm girl of Chester County, Pennsylvania, who was hanged at Chester on January 3, 1786. She was condemned for the murder of her ten-day-old twin boys whose bodies were found by hunters not far from her home.

The story is much involved and, apparently, is a true and classic case of the old-fashioned and maudlin motif—betrayal of a trusting girl by a heartless fiend. Most of the facts can be substantiated from various reliable sources, but it must be admitted that legend is interwoven in the story to some degree. The girl left her farm home to visit relatives in Philadelphia and, quite probably, to get away from her humdrum life for a more exciting one in the big city. While employed at a tavern—some stories say the Indian Queen, others, the Cross Keys—she met a man who seduced her on the promise of marriage. His name (or so he maintained) was Joseph Deshong, allegedly a former sheriff of Sussex, New Jersey County. We have not been able to substantiate this, however.

The happy girl returned home to prepare for marriage and motherhood. But before long she realized that Deshong's promises were false. After the birth of his children, the bogus ex-sheriff promised to meet her at Newtown Square, near her home. As Charles Biddle, distinguished member of the Pennsylvania Executive Council at the time, a man of impeccable reputation, tells us in his *Autobiography*:

> He persuaded her to take a walk saying he intended to put the children out to nurse; then when they got into the woods he took them from her and laying them down the inhuman monster

[83]*The American Volunteer*, Carlisle, Pennsylvania, December 23, 1869.

put his foot on their breasts, and crushed them to death. He then threatened to murder her if she ever mentioned a word about what he had done.

Far off in New Hampshire, at Portsmouth, the plight of this young woman was reported in the local paper, *The Mercury and General Advertiser,* dated January 25, 1785:

> About a week ago a woman was committed to the Chester gaol on suspicion of murdering her two suckling infants, whose bodies were found under some brush. A traveler passing by, observed his dog scratching among the brush, and presently brought out the head of a child in its mouth. This induced the master to light and examine further, where he found the bodies of two innocent babes, who had been put to death not long before. The woman was charged with the murder which she denied, but acknowledged placing the children by the road-side in order that any person passing that way, and who had humanity enough, might take them up. The head that the dog brought out had been cut off; and the woman was seen suckling the children near the spot but a little time before the bodies were discovered.

The distraught young woman refused to say a word and apparently was in shock. Her brother, hearing of her plight as he worked on a farm near Lancaster, hastened to the Chester jail where, on sustained and sympathetic questioning, she told him her story. He resolved to bring the betrayer to book. The story of his frantic but futile attempt to rescue his sister was told later by Charles Biddle whose veracity can scarcely be doubted.

The brother, William (sometimes referred to as Amos), hastened to Philadelphia to secure witnesses against the seducer Deshong and had been successful. He appeared at the home of Benjamin Franklin, at the time President of the Council, in hopes he might obtain a reprieve for his doomed sister whom he knew to be innocent. But for some reason, now obscure, Franklin was not available and after considerable maddening delay, Wilson went to the State House where he told his story to Biddle. Biddle, vice-president of the Council, scribbled off a reprieve ordering the Chester sheriff to delay the execution. Wilson dashed off on his horse to deliver his priceless news. What happened thereafter is told in a news story many years later:

> . . . The brother had succeeded in obtaining a pardon . . . his horse foamed and bled as he spurred him homeward. But an unpropitious rain had swollen the stream (the Schuylkill River at Philadelphia) so that he was compelled to pace the bank with brain bursting and gaze upon the gushing waters that threatened to blast his only hope. At the earliest moment that a ford was practicable he dashed through and arrived at the place just in time to see the last struggle of his sister.[84]

Actually, he arrived twenty-two minutes too late. The sheriff had sent his deputies out a distance from the gallows charging them to signal him immediately they might see the brother racing to the spot with the pardon. Another version of the drama is that Wilson, impeded by the river ford and storm, plunged into the ice-filled river with his horse and swam the turbulent stream.

There is quite a literature regarding this case. To add to the drama, Wilson, completely stunned by the death of his sister on the gallows, retired to the hills near Harrisburg and lived the life of a hermit. He made and sold grindstones for a living and died some forty year later in isolation, "estranged from life."[85]

---

[84]Harrisburg *Intelligencer,* October 13, 1821.

[85]Harrisburg *Intelligencer,* October 13, 1821; see pamphlets, "A Faithful Narrative of Elizabeth Wilson," etc., Philadelphia, 1807 and "The Pennsylvania Hermit, a Narrative of the Extraordinary Life of Amos Wilson," Philadelphia, 1839. An even earlier pamphlet, dated 1822, was published at Boston and entitled, "The Sweetness of Solitude or Directions to Mankind how they may be Happy in a Miserable World and Insure a Glorious Inheritance in That Which is to Come," by Amos Wilson. This pamphlet was published for a John Wilkey who claimed to have been a friend of Wilson's and who discovered his body in the cave where he expired.

Chapter III

THE TREATMENT OF WITCHES
(Hanged Not Burned)

T HERE IS A COMMON NOTION in our country—perpetuated even by writers on American history—that persons were burned "at the stake" in colonial times for witchcraft. We often hear some mention made of the "witchburning era," although it is possible that this expression is used symbolically rather than literally. While many persons were burned to death as witches in England and elsewhere in Europe, we have been unable to find a single case of anyone suffering this penalty for that offense on the North American continent.

An interesting bit of folklore, somewhat to the contrary, comes from South Carolina. It seems that around 1712, several individuals suspected of "wizardry" were seized by a Vigilance Committee and condemned to be burned. They were "actually roasted by the fire" but apparently not fatally.[1] Persons were hanged for the crime of witchcraft.

Aside from the case of Rebecca Fowler, of Calvert County, Maryland, persons were hanged for witchcraft only in the colonies of Connecticut and Massachusetts. Many were tried elsewhere but were either declared not guilty or were not sentenced to death. Many in these two colonies were also declared not guilty or escaped hanging. The colony of Pennsylvania, for instance, had but three cases of persons charged with witchcraft. All were found not guilty in regular court procedure. These trials were held when witchcraft was not a capital offense and when it was declared capital (in 1718) no cases appeared in the courts.[2]

---

[1]Cited by the author of "Witchcraft in Connecticut, 1647-1697," *New Englander: Yale Review, VIII*:788-817, citation, page 789 (November, 1885); but even if they were burned, it was not a *legal* penalty.

[2]*Colonial Records of Pennsylvania,* I, December 27, 1683, pp. 94-96 (Margaret Matson and Getro Hendrickson) and II, March 21, 1701, 20 (Robert Guard and wife).

One would think the colony of Virginia might be listed in the practice of hanging witches, but such is not the case. Two females were put to death at sea *en route* to Virginia on separate occasions on a charge related to witchcraft. Each was charged with precipitating violent storms that jeopardized the voyages.[3]

There were persons charged with witchcraft but the few who were convicted were only fined. The so-called "Virginia Witch," Mrs. Grace Sherwood, Princess Anne County (*circa* 1705) was tried in a desultory fashion for the offense—she was ducked in water, but the results were dubious and inconclusive as to her guilt. She was imprisoned to await the judgment of the general court but later released and never really tried. She lived on for some years following this 1705 difficulty.

It is not our purpose to indict our ancestors for what they did at Salem or elsewhere where persons were hanged for witchcraft. This has been done elsewhere. There have been many authoritative treatises written on the events that led up to this frightening episode. The authors come to different conclusions; some are understanding if not apologetic; others are caustic and almost uncompromising in their indictment of those who harassed elderly men and women literally to death in the name of religious fervor. The practice of witchcraft was prevalent throughout the Middle Ages in Europe and the belief in demons, witches, wizards and sorcerers and the afflictions for which they were presumed to be responsible, as well as hexing and black magic, were brought to these shores by the colonists.[4] Poole, an authority on witchcraft, estimates that as many as 30,000 persons were executed in England for the offense of witchcraft, with some 75,000 in France and in excess of 100,000 in Germany. Hanging and burning were the rule in those countries.[5]

While there were a few persons living at the time of the orgy of witch hanging in our own colonial times who questioned the

---

[3]These poor females were named Mary Lee, (in 1654) and Elizabeth Richardson (in 1658). The method of exacting the death penalty is not recorded. Arthur P. Scott, *Criminal Law in Colonial Virginia*, Chicago, University of Chicago Press, 1930, p. 241.

[4]See Perry Miller and Thomas R. Johnson, *The Puritans*, American Book Co., 1938.

[5]Wiliam F. Poole, "Witchcraft in Boston," a chapter in Justin Winsor, *Memorial History of Boston*, Boston, 1881, 4 vols., citation Vol. II, p. 131.

action of the officials and in varying degrees deplored the debacle, it should be pointed out that "at that time anyone in his right mind believed in witchcraft."

We might make mention of one distinguished contemporary who did not subscribe to the guilt of the condemned. Thomas Brattle, a learned astronomer, graduate and later treasurer of Harvard University, penned a letter to a friend (name unknown) on October 4, 1692, less than a month after the last of the hangings in which he said, albeit cautiously: "As to the late executions, that in the opinion of many unprejudiced and considerable spectators, some of the condemned went out of the world not only with as great protestations, but also with as good shows of innocence, as men could do . . . they wished, and declared their wish, that their blood might be the last innocent blood shed on that account."[6]

To those living today there may be an element of shame as well as remorse hovering around us when a discussion of the events of that dismal era takes place, but we must suggest that there are many historical occurrences that should cause us equal shame.[7]

The total number of persons hanged in colonial times for witchcraft was 35, as estimated by these authors. Poole's figure is thirty-two. However, he does not list them.[8] Many more were indicted and tried, some of whom were condemned but not hanged. Judging from experience in England, it is surprising that more were not hanged in the colonies. It was a period of great strain, of religious orthodoxy, bigotry, of superstition and fanatical zeal bordering on hysteria. Radical and repressive measures seemed expedient and even necessary.

About one half of those hanged were executed at Salem, Massachusetts. We shall, therefore, tell the story of Salem Village and then list all known cases that were actually hanged so far as we can ascertain.

The chain of events that led to the Salem frenzy came almost a half century after the first person was hanged for witchcraft in this country (see our list, page 136).

---

[6]George Lincoln Burr, *Narratives of the Witchcraft Cases,* New York: Barnes & Noble, Inc., 1914, p. 177, *By permission.*

[7]One authority who makes no apologies for those who persecuted the victims is Charles W. Upham in *Salem Witchcraft* New York, Frederick Ungar, 1959 reprint, 2 vols.

[8]Poole, *op. cit.,* p. 133.

Early cases were sporadic and did not represent the mass hysteria that characterized the Salem episode. There was a kind of contagion of demonism, voodoo, hexing, jerking and sorcery that took hold of a number of adolescent girls of the village in early 1692. It began in the devout home of the Rev. Samuel Parris, onetime student in theology at Harvard and later in business in the Barbadoes. He had arrived in Salem Village in 1689 and began to minister to his small flock of Puritan stock. He brought with him from the West Indies a couple of servants, or slaves; one was a Negro crone named Tituba who looms large in our story; the other known as Indian John. They were man and wife; and as Upham maintains, "they may have originated the 'Salem witchcraft.' "[9]

There assembled around the female Negro servant the small daughter of the minister, Elizabeth, aged nine (usually called Betty) and her twelve-year-old cousin, Abigail Williams who lived with the Parrises. These children found it pleasant to tarry in the kitchen and listen to the dronings, mumblings and incantations of Tituba. It is possible, as suggested by Arthur Miller in *The Crucible,* that the slave sought to entertain the girls with tales of witchcraft and spells. The girls spread word abroad among their friends that this scintillating creature was a sure source of entertainment, however scarey it might have been, as well as instruction and discipline in the esoteric arts of the occult. From time to time, the following came to sit at the feet of Tituba: Mary Wolcott, age sixteen; Elizabeth Booth, age sixteen; Susannah Sheldon, age eighteen; Sarah Churchill, age twenty, servant of John and Elizabeth Proctor, the former to be hanged in time; Mercy Lewis, age nineteen, who worked for the Putnams, and perhaps the most susceptible of all, sickly, high-strung, twelve-year-old Ann Putnam, a child already pre-psychotic, if we could diagnose her in modern nomenclature. These children formed Tituba's inner circle, the coterie from which sprang the evil that ended in nineteen tragic, mostly ancient men and women, being hanged on Gallows Hill during the late summer and fall of that frightening year of 1692.

The first sign of trouble was the strange behavior of Betty Parris in early January. Her mother and father noted that she

---

[9]Upham, *op. cit.,* Vol. II, p. 2.

began to turn sickly. She developed a sense or irresponsibility and showed signs of immobility of features, especially of face and hands. Her cousin Abigail began to show symptoms of a kind of affliction but with rather curious gestures. She began to run about on all fours, barking and braying like various animals. Upon inquiry it was found that some of the others from Tituba's voodoo sessions began to act as if possessed. Mary Wolcott and Susannah Sheldon fell into convulsions at their place of abode; Mercy Lewis, maid of the Putnam's and the ailing child, Ann, began to suffer horribly. The record shows that these maladies became contagious, especially among the adolescent maidens of the village.

Rev. Samuel Parris began to quizz Tituba and to call in some of his religious colleagues and soon it became known what had happened. The girls were apparently hexed, or bewitched. When questioned they confessed that Tituba and a couple of elderly women in the village were at the bottom of it all. From that point on, the villagers were in a shocking turmoil, possessed with a kind of debasement and defilement the like of which no modern in this country can contemplate.

The documentation of this awful period in our history is abundant. We have taken our facts from George Lincoln Burr's *Narratives of the Witchcraft Cases,* Charles W. Upham, *Salem Witchcraft,* with occasional reference to Marion Starkey's *The Devil in Massachusetts,* the last source being a more popular, but well-documented account of the phenomenon.

The initial hearings in the long agenda of cases began on March 1, in the Meeting House—Ingersoll's *ordinary* was not considered large enough—with Judge or Magistrate John Hathorne hearing the evidence. The first two to appear for interrogation were two elderly women of the village, Sarah Good and Sarah Osborne. The former was hanged (see below), the latter grew ill (she was a sickly woman) and died in jail. Marion Starkey writes of these two victims:

> The querulous voice of poor sick Sarah Osborne grew daily fainter until at last on May 10 she died. Sarah Good gave birth; just when, no one bothered to record. In fact, for all the records show she may have brought a suckling babe to prison with her. All that interested the authorities was that she left the child die.

Anyway, it did die, the prison with its fetid air, its cold floors and its meager fare serving ill as a creche. But Sarah was left her pipe, and when good people of Boston came to the prison to look at the witches much as they might look at caged animals, she begged tobacco of them.[10]

Among the many records surviving the witch episode is that of the Boston jailer's bill for "caring for" these old women: It is dated May 29, 1692 and charged "against the country": "To chains for Sarah Good and Sarah Osburn, 14 shillings; To the keeping of Sarah Osburn from the 7th of March to the 10th of May, when she died, being nine weeks and two days, 1 1. 3s. 6d."[11] We shall discuss the charges against the victims of this long ordeal later, on an individual basis, and more specifically against those who were finally hanged. Their monotony is exceeded only by their delusionary absurdity.

The court was convinced that prosecuting these old men and women on the charges of sick adolescent girls and effecting their executions by hanging would accomplish a great service to the community. The crime and sin of sorcery or witchcraft was a disgrace in the sight of God and must be atoned. The frightful diary of that year has few counterparts for anxiety, apprehension and sorrow in the history of the American scene. Wrote Cotton Mather at its conclusion:

> And now Nineteen Persons having been hang'd, and one prest to death, and Eight more condemn'd, in all Twenty and Eight, of which above a third part were Members of some of the Churches in N. England, and more than half of them of a good Conversation in general, and not one clear'd; about fifty having confest themselves to be Witches, of which not one was Executed; above an Hundred and Fifty in Prison, and above Two Hundred more accused; The Special Commission of Oyer and Terminer comes to a period which has no other foundation than the Governour's Commission . . .[12]

The Rev. Cotton Mather obviously believed a disagreeable, yet

[10]Starkey, *op. cit.,* p. 47. New York, Knopf, 1949; by permission of author; 1961 ed. Doubleday & Co., Inc.

[11]Upham, *op. cit.,* Frederick Ungar, 1959 ed., Vol. II, p. 32.

[12]Burr, *op. cit.,* Scribner's Sons, 1914, p. 373.

necessary job had been completed and had been exceedingly well done!

It seems important, at this point, that we append a portion of the indictment charging witchcraft, for the sake of its language. It reads:

> The accused "wickedly and feloniously hath used certain detestable arts, called witchcraft and sorceries, by which said wicked arts" the said bewitched "was and is tortured, afflicted, pined, consumed, wasted and tormented against the peace of our sovereign lord and lady, the King and Queen, and against the form of the statute in that case made and provided."[13]

THE ROSTER OF THOSE HANGED FOR WITCHCRAFT

It seems appropriate to identify all cases hanged in the colonies for witchcraft and add a few remarks about each, if possible.

1. *Achsah Young* was first person credited to be hanged. The date varies by one day and by the colony; his first name also varies, *viz.,* John M. Taylor gives the name as Alse and his home as Windsor, Connecticut.[14] Joseph Nathan Kane, in *Famous First Facts,* (p. 482), states that Young was from Massachusetts and was hanged on May 27, 1647. George Lincoln Burr gives Connecticut as the colony and May 26, 1647, as the date.[15] This person is undoubtedly the same as "One ... of Windsor," mentioned by Governor John Winthrop of Massachusetts Colony, although he states this witch was from Hartford.[16]

2. *Margaret Jones* was hanged at Charlestown, Massachusetts on June 15, 1648. She was suspected because after having angry words with some of her neighbors "some mischief befell" them; also because of certain things that were supposed to be bewitched or possessing a charm, on being burned, she was concerned."[17]

---

[13]Burr. *op. cit.,* p. 380.

[14]*The Witchcraft Delusion in Colonial Connecticut, 1647-97,* New York, The Grafton Press, 1908, pp. 145-6 where he states his sources.

[15]*Narratives,* p. 408 n.

[16]*Journal, II*:374 (ed. of 1853); see also, William F. Poole, in his chapter entitled "Witchcraft in Boston," p. 1 in Justin Winsor, *Memorial History of Boston,* Boston, 1881, II, 133n; Poole lists the date as 1646 and refers to the person as a "woman of Windsor."

[17]Burr, *op. cit.,* p. 408.

Also, on being examined, she had a "malignant touch," the mark of a witch, "a teat . . . as fresh as it had been newly sucked," and an impertinence during her trial.[18]
Her knowledge of "physic and medicine" also militated against her.

3. *Mary Johnson* was tried and condemned as a witch on December 7, 1648, and hanged some time the following year; "a not too bright servant girl" from either Wethersfield or Hartford, Connecticut. She was charged with "familiarity with the Devil" and said "a Devil was wont to do her many services" and that "her Master once blamed her for not carrying out the Ashes and a Devil did clear the Hearth for her afterward."[19]

4 and 5. *John and Roanna Carrington,* actual hanging uncertain; residents of Wethersfield, Connecticut; trial February 20, 1650; accused of familiarity with the Devil. Certain diaries contend that these persons were hanged but official records do not so indicate.[20]

6. *Mary Parsons* (and possibly her husband, Hugh), of Springfield, Massachusetts, was hanged at Boston or Springfield on May 29, 1651.[21] "Her Familiarity with Satan was this: She had lost a child and was exceedingly discontented at it and longed 'that she might see her Child again' and at last the Devil in likeness of her Child came to her Bed side and talked with her, and asked to come into bed with her, and she received it . . ."[22] She also used "divers devilish practices by Witchcraft to the hurt of the persons of Martha and Rebecca Moxen, daughters of the minister of Springfield," and "for murdering her own child."[23] She swore her innocence to the first charge but did acknowledge herself guilty to the murder of her child.

7. *Goodwife (Goody) Bassett,* of Stratford, Connecticut, undoubtedly hanged some time in 1651.[24] When condemned, she said another witch lived at Fairfield and she named Goodwife

---

[18]Poole, *op. cit.,* pp.135-6.

[19]Burr, *op. cit.,* p. 135; p. 410; Poole gives the date of her hanging thus: "1650?"; for more data on this case see Donald Lines Jacobus, "Connecticut Witches," *New Haven Geneological Mag., IV*:951-8, May, 1927.

[20]"Witchcraft in Connecticut, 1647-97," *Yale Review, VIII*:788-815, November 1885; the diaries mentioned are George Brinley of Hartford and Matthew Grant.

[21]Poole, *op. cit.,* p. 137.

[22]Burr, *op. cit.,* p. 410.

[23]Poole, *op. cit.,* p. 137.

[24]Burr, *op. cit.,* 410.

Knapp; later she meant Goodwife Staples. The court trial for Goodwife Bassett was held in May, 1651. In *Historical Sketches,* the authors, B. W. Hinks and B. L. Swan (1871) state that the place of execution is pointed out to visitors; that the name of the stream that passes it is Fellows Brook and nearby is Gallows Swamp.[25]

8. A *Mrs. Kendall,* of Cambridge, Massachusetts, was hanged sometime in 1651. The principal witness against her was a Watertown nurse who testified that she "did bewitch to death a child of Goodman Genings of Watertown." Genings, however, did not so accuse her but she was nevertheless hanged.[26]

9. *Goody Knapp,* of Fairfield, Connecticut, was hanged sometime in 1653.[27] Peleg W. Chandler identified this person as Elizabeth Knap who possessed ventriloquist powers, alarmed the people of Groton as the demon railed at public officials of the town."[28]

10. *Mrs. Ann Hibben* was hanged at Boston, ANNO 1656; "widow of one of the foremost men in Boston, William Hibben, a merchant.[29] "She was also the sister of Richard Bellingham who was deputy-governor at the time of her execution on June 19, 1656."[30]

As there are no records of her case extant, we know very little about her aside from what was written concerning her disposition a century later. It was stated that due to financial losses to her husband before he died, she increased in "natural crannedness which made her turbulent and quarrelsome, brought her under church censure, and at length rendered her so odious to her neighbors, as to cause some of them to accuse her of witchcraft."[31]

11 and 12. *Nathaniel and Rebecca Greensmith,* of Hartford, Connecticut, were hanged in January 1662. "Well to do but not reputable people; she was referred to as a 'lewd and ignorant woman'; they lived next door to people named Coles and Ann

[25]Jacobus, *op. cit.,* p. 954; see also, Orcutt, **History of Stratford,** Vol. I, p. 147.

[26]Burr, *op. cit.,* 409.

[27]Witchcraft in Connecticut, 1647-97, p. 794.

[28]*American Criminal Trials,* 2 vols., Boston, 1841, 1842, Vol. I, p. 74; there may have been two Knaps; see Poole, *op. cit.,* p. 159.

[29]Burr, *op. cit.,* p. 410n.

[30]Poole, *op. cit.,* p. 138.

[31]*Ibid.,* p. 139.

Coles implicates several persons as witches. Rebecca had been married twice before she married Greensmith . . . others implicated for bewitching the Coles were Judith Varlet and Goodwife Ayres."[32]

She confessed that she and others had familiarity with the Devil. She and her husband were indicted December 30, 1661. The Hartford records show that one Daniel Garrett was allowed six shillings per week for keeping the two victims as well as handling their fees to be paid out of the Greensmith estate.[33] It was also recorded that the two of them were hanged on Gallows Hill on the bluff a "little north of Trinity College." This location "afforded a good view of the execution to a large crowd on the meadow to the west."[34]

13. *Mary Barnes,* of Farmington, Connecticut, was hanged probably sometime in March, 1662. She and Elizabeth Seager were ordered to appear in court on charges of practicing witchcraft on January 6. The Seager woman was found not guilty but Mary Barnes was and sent to the prison at Hartford.[35] Daniel Garret was allowed two shillings per week for three weeks to be paid by the woman's husband.[36]

14. *Mrs. Henry Lake,* of Dorchester, Massachusetts, was hanged sometime in 1684, "whom the Devil drew in by appearing to her in her likeness, and acting the part of a Child of hers then lately dead, on whom her heart was much set."[37]

15. *Rebecca Fowler,* of Calvert County, Maryland, October 9, 1685, was the only person hanged in this colony as a witch.[38] At the same time, one John Cowman was accused of the crime and taken to the gallows, but, with the rope about his neck, he was freed. This was done, so it was said, to impress upon him that "he was obligated to the lower house of the Assembly for interceding in his behalf."[39]

---

[32]Burr, *op. cit.,* pp. 19-22.

[33]*Witchcraft in Connecticut,* pp. 808-809.

[34]Taylor, *op. cit.,* p. 100.

[35]*Witchcraft in Connecticut,* p. 809.

[36]*Idem.;* see also Taylor, *op. cit.,* p. 152.

[37]Quoted in a letter from Nathaniel Mather to his brother, Increase, from Burr, *op. cit.,* 408n; also Poole *op. cit.,* 133n.

[38]Raphael Semmes, *Crime and Punishment in Early Maryland,* 1938, p. 168.

[39]So stated in the *Report of the Commission on Capital Punishment* to the Legislative Committee, Maryland, October 3, 1962, p. 2.

16. *Goody Glover* was hanged at Boston, on November 16, 1688. She was charged with bewitching the children of John Goodwin, a Mason; the Boston merchant, Robert Calef, wrote: "she was a despised, crazy, ill-conditioned old woman, an Irish Roman Catholic who was tried for afflicting Goodwin's children;" Cotton Mather wrote knowingly of this case since he maintained he had seen the results of this woman's influence on the Goodwin children."[40]

"While on trial her house was searched and several small images or puppets, made of rags and stuffed with goat's hair were found . . . and the woman acknowledged that her way of tormenting the objects of her malice was by wetting her finger and stroking these images."[41]

THE SALEM VICTIMS OF THE TREE

The following pathetic and tragic victims to superstition and colonial hysteria and bigotry were all hanged at Salem, Massachusetts. A few facts about each follows:

17. *Rebecca Nurse* (or Nourse) was a respected matron of seventy-one years of age, wife of an energetic and prosperous farmer, and mother of several fine children loyal to her throughout her tragic ordeal. She was initially acquitted by a jury, but later condemned like the others, with approximately the same charges against her by witnesses. There were testimonials that she was a good woman, a worthy Christian, and an excellent mother, doing, it was said, an extraordinary job rearing her children. One deposition regarding her good character was signed by thirty-nine of her neighbors.[42] Yet she was hanged on July 19. Writes Charles W. Upham regarding the Nurse case: "There is no more disgraceful record in the judicial annals of the country, than that which relates the trial of this excellent woman."[43]

After her body was thrown into a crevice on Gallows Hill, with the others hanged that day, her faithful children, at night, stealthily removed it and carried it to some unknown place. Year later, a granite shaft was raised over what traditionally

---

[40]Burr, *op. cit.,* p. 123-6; also Chandler, *op. cit.,* Vol. I, pp. 75-7; Poole, *op. cit.,* p. 142.

[41]Poole, *op cit.,* p. 143; the date of her execution is from Samuel Sewell's *Diary,* Vol. I, p. 236; see also Poole, *op. cit.,* p. 142 n 1.

[42]Burr, *op. cit.,* p. 360.

[43]Upham, *op. cit.,* Vol. II, p. 286.

was believed to be her grave and beside it a slab testifying to the neighbors who spoke in her defense when such an action took great courage.[44]

18. *Susannah Martin,* of Amesbury, had developed a reputation of a witch many years before and as she survived that charge unscathed she almost relished the reputation that had been fashioned about her. She was recognized as a neat, trim dresser with not a pin out of place. At first, she took the charges with a sardonic mien and a look of contemptuous scorn as her adolescent accusers confronted her at the hearing; one of these stated that he had threatened to throw her into the brook for hexing him, whereupon she flew low over the bridge and escaped; another claimed she flew in through the window one night, took hold of his feet, drew his body into a heap, and lay on it for two hours during which time he could neither speak nor stir; still another that a cat came into his window one night, took hold of his throat and almost killed him. He then remembered that Susannah Martin had threatened him thusly. He yelled out: "Avoid, thou she-devil. . . . Avoid." At that, the cat left him.

Still another witness claimed his "pious and prudent wife" was constantly in fear of this woman who often confronted her and then suddenly disappeared. Another swore she had bitten him on the finger, some eight years previously—one night— and he still had the scar from it. At the conclusion of her trial it was recorded: "This woman was one of the most impudent, scurrilous, wicked creatures in the world; and she did now throughout the whole trial discover herself to be such an one. Yet when she was asked what she had to say for her self her Cheef Plea was, That she had Led a most Virtuous and Holy Life."[45] Her character comes down to us as one displaying great energy of spirit and of language.[46]

19. *Elizabeth How* of Ipswich; had a blind husband; local gossip maintained she was a witch and had been denied membership in the church. Several witnesses swore she had afflicted and tortured them and went into a swoon when she touched them; that they were visited by ghosts who had been murdered

[44]For more details regarding this case, see Upham, *op. cit.,* p. 286.

[45]Burr, *op. cit.,* pp. 229-236.

[46]Upham, *op. cit.,* Vol. II, p. 270.

by her; even her brother-in-law, John How, on refusing to speak
in her behalf, contended that some of his cattle "were Bewitched
to Death, Leaping three and four foot high, turning about,
Squealing, Falling, and Dying." Another witness testified that
she choked one of his oxen with a turnip. Her blind husband and
her daughters stood by her in her ordeal but to no avail. Some
witnesses contended that she had been baptised by the Devil
at New-Berry Falls.[47] Upham described Elizabeth How thus
"Her gentle, patient, humble, benignant, devout and tender heart
bore her . . . with a spirit of saint-like love and faith, through
the dreadful scenes."[48]

20. *Sarah Wild* (or Wildes) was a farmer's wife with a strong
sense of property rights. Her accusers claimed she sent demons
after people who borrowed anything belonging to her without
her approval, sometimes overturning their hay wagons; she is
remembered as patient and humble but a firm and faithful suf-
ferer.[49]

21. *George Jacobs,* of Salem, was condemned as the others
and had his property confiscated. He was toothless, lame, grey,
and got about only with the aid of two canes, but at the trial,
he stood "like a giant" in stature and vigor. The hardest blow
of all for Jacobs was that his granddaughter, Margaret Jacobs,
testified against him; after his execution she recanted; her "letter of Shame" was written in the "Dungeon of Salem prison,"
dated August 20, 1692.

A shameful indignity was visited on this decrepit old man.
He was ruthlessly examined for a traditional "witch's teat" and
"one was found under his right shoulder." As one witness who
had examined him described it: "About a quarter of an inch
long or better, with a sharp point dropping downward, so that
I took a pin and run it through the said teat; but there was
neither water, blood, or corruption nor any other matter."[50]

A point of interest regarding Jacobs is that the precise spot
where lies his remains is known—the only reliable grave (the
Nourse grave is traditional) extant of all those hanged as
witches. The legend is that a grandson located the old man's

[47]Burr, *op. cit.,* pp. 237-240.

[48]Upham, *op. cit.,* Vol. II, p. 270.

[49]*Idem.*

[50]Upham, *op. cit.,* Vol. II, p. 274; see also, pp. 312-321.

body at the place of execution, strapped it onto a horse, brought it home to the farm and buried it. Two weathered stones marked the spot for years. In 1864, the remains were exhumed and reverently lifted for examination, after which they were again interred. The skull was in excellent condition and the skeleton indicated that Jacobs had been a very tall man. A metallic pin was found in the grave with his remains.[51]

22. *John Willard,* of Salem Village, had been employed to "fetch in several who had been accused; this he could not do and soon he was accused himself. Having made his escape, he was apprehended about forty miles from Salem, as Nashwag, ancient name for Lancaster. Judge Samuel Sewell wrote in his *Diary* on the day Willard and the others were executed: "This day, George Burroughs, John Willard, Jno. Proctor, Martha Carrier, and George Jacobs were executed at Salem, a very great number of Spectators being present. Mr. Cotton Mather was there, Mr. Sims, Hale, Noyes, Chiever, etc. All of them (the condemned) said they were innocent . . . Mr. Mather said they all died by a Righteous Sentence. Mr. Burroughs, by his Speech, Prayer, protestations of his Innocence, did much move unthinking persons . . . which occasions their speaking hardly concerning his being executed." In the margin of the page, Sewell later wrote: "Doleful Witchcraft."[52]

The accusing girls who damned Willard, enmeshed in this hysterical morass, testified that he was seen to "suckle the apparitions of two black pigs in his breast and along with other wizards to kneel in prayer to the black man with a long-crowned hat" after which they vanished from sight.[53] Willard appears to have been an honest and amiable person, an industrious farmer, with a comfortable estate, a wife and three young children.[54]

23. *John Proctor* of Salem Village was described as "a person of decided character; impulsive and imprudent, of a manly spirit, honest, earnest, and bold in word and deed; he saw through the whole thing and was convinced that it was the result of a conspiracy, deliberate and criminal, on the part of

---

[51]*Ibid.,* Vol. II, p. 320

[52]Burr, *op. cit.,* p. 361.

[53]Upham, *op. cit.,* Vol. II, p. 323.

[54]*Ibid.,* p. 321.

the accusers. He gave free utterances to his indignation at their conduct, and it cost him his life.[55]

While Proctor was in prison with his wife—she was later reprieved due to pregnancy—the sheriff went to their home and seized all their goods, "Provisions and Cattle." He sold the cattle at half price and killed others, and "put them up for the West Indies." Furthermore, "he threw out the Beer from the Barrel and carried away the Barrel, emptied a Pot of Broath, and took away the Pot, and left nothing in the house for the support of the Children." None of these goods was returned. Proctor asked the Rev. Nicholas Noyes to pray for him but he was denied by that man of God because he "would not own himself to be a witch." He wrote a complaint from his prison cell in which he protested his innocence and bitterly complained of the tortures inflicted on his son, William (as was done also to the two sons of Martha Carrier), which consisted of "tying them Neck and Heels till the Blood was ready to come out of their Noses" in order to extract a confession of witchcraft from them.[56]

24. *Martha Carrier* of Andover; there were several witnesses against her, including her own sons and several of her neighbors who actually said they were in confederacy with her in the Black Art of Witchcraft. Her sons (see above) frankly and fully confessed "not only that they were Witches themselves (one, Richard, was but sixteen), but that this, their Mother, had made them so. "This Confession they made with great show of Repentance, and with much Demonstration of Truth. They related Place, Time, Occasion; they gave account of Journeys, Meetings, and Mischiefs by them performed; and were very credible in what they said." However, it was stated that this evidence of the sons was not produced against their mother at the trial as there was apparently plenty of other testimony to condemn her.

Cotton Mather, in his writings, stated regarding Martha Carrier: "This Rampant Hag . . . was the Person, of whom the Confessions of the Witches, and of her own Children among the rest, agreed, that the Devil had promised her, she should be Queen of Hell.[57]

[55]Upham, *op. cit.*, Vol. II, p. 304.

[56]Burr, *op. cit.*, pp. 360-363.

[57]*Ibid.*, pp. 341-344.

25. *George Burroughs* was reputed to have been the most notable of all those hanged for witchcraft in the colony. He was a graduate of Harvard, of the class of 1670, and became pastor in Salem Village in 1680. Within three years, he became involved in a parish quarrel not of his making and found it expedient to leave. He went to Maine, to the town of Wells, where he remained until he was arrested for "afflicting" some persons in his old habitat of Salem Village. In the language of Mather, he was accused by five or six of the "Bewitched, as the Author of their Miseries; Accused by Eight of the Confessing Witches, as being an Head Actor at some of their Hellish Rendezvoucez, and one who had the promise of being a King in Satan's Kingdom, now going to be Erected; he was further accused by nine persons for extraordinary Lifting, and such Feats of Strength, as could not be done without a Diabolical Assistance . . ." He was also accused of tormenting his "two successive wives." It was also recorded that the night before some of the executions there was a great witch meeting at which the sacrament was administered; that Burroughs was present and took leave of his companions, bidding them hold fast to the faith and make no confessions.[58]

This man was no mean personage. His exploits, whether for good or ill, were deemed suspect in such a hysterical climate. His conviction was a foregone conclusion. Two items of further interest concerning this defendant are his execution and burial and the apologia of Cotton Mather concerning his status. First the details of the hanging:

> Burroughs was carried in a Cart with the others through the streets of Salem to Execution; when he was upon the Ladder, he made a Speech for the clearing of his Innocency, with such Solemn and Serious Expression, as were to the Admiration of all present; his Prayer (which he concluded by repeating the Lord's Prayer) was so well worded, and uttered with such composedness, and such (at least seeming) fervency of Spirit as was very affecting, and drew Tears from many (so that it seemed to some, that the Spectators would hinder the Execution). The accusers said the black Man stood and dictated to him.

---

[58]Peleg W. Chandler, *American Criminal Trials,* Boston, 1841-2; Vol. I, p. 121; as to his trial, *ibid.,* 114-21.

The Rev. Cotton Mather's remarks to the assembled awed crowd, at the moment of the "turning off" of Burroughs, are revealing of the sore dilemma of the God-fearing, sincere, but stiff-necked and deluded spiritual leader of that day. It reads: "Being mounted on a horse, Mr. C. Mather addressed himself to the People, partly to declare, that he (Burroughs) was no ordained minister and partly to possess the People of his guilt; saying, That the Devil has often been transformed into an Angel of Light; and this did somewhat appease the People, and the Execution went on . . ."

To climax this regrettable episode in our history we find Burroughs humiliated even further by the method of disposing of his body. We read: "When he was cut down he was dragged by the Halter to a Hole, or Grace, between the Rocks, about two feet deep, his Shirt and Breeches being pulled off, and an old pair of Trousers of one Executed, put on his lower parts (one might wonder whose), he was so put in, together with Willard and Carryer, and one of his Hands and his Chin and a Foot, of one (of) them being uncovered."[59]

Upham, quoting from a contemporary source states of this victim: "Being a little man he had performed feats beyond the strength of a giant; had held out a gun of seven feet barrel with one hand, and had carried a barrel of cider from a canoe to the shore." An accuser claimed that it took Burroughs less time to go from one place to another; thus he was in league with the Devil. This intelligent victim of the hysteria was astounded "at the monstrous folly and falsehood with which he was surrounded. He was a man without guile and incapable of appreciating such wickedness. He tried, in simplicity and ingeniousness, to explain what was brought against him; and this, probably, was all the 'twisting and turning' he exhibited."[60]

After the victims of August 19 of that fateful year were finally "turned off," the court proceeded to condemn others. From the records we find:

> *September 9:* Six were tried, and received Sentence of Death, *viz., Martha Corey,* of Salem Village, Mary Easty of Topsfield, Alice Parker and Ann Pudeater of Salem,

---

[59]Burr, *op. cit.,* pp. 215-222.

[60]Upham, *op. cit.,* p. 297.

Dorcas Hoar of Beverly, and Mary Bradberry of Salisbury; September 16 Giles Corey was put to death.

September 17: Nine more received Sentence of Death, *viz.,* Margaret Scott of Rowly, Goodwife Redd of Marblehead, Samuel Wardwell, and Mary Parker of Andover, also Abigail Falkner of Andover, who pleaded Pregnancy, Rebecka Eames of Bosford, Mary Lacy, and Ann Foster of Andover, and Abigail Hobbes of Topsfield.[61]

The following were hanged on September 22—the others were spared:

26. *Mary Parker:* little information regarding this victim has been unearthed; she was the widow of Joseph Parker, lived at Andover; she had a reputation of being somewhat of a "distempered mind, incapable of the care of her estate"; she had been accused by Mercy Wardwell and William Barker—both self-confessed witches—and of joining with them to afflict Timothy Swan; several persons in the court who had been restored by her touch.[62]

27. *Alice Parker,* of Salem: no data available; apparently no kin of Mary Parker (above).

28. *Mary Esty* (or Easty), wife of Isaac, of Topsfield. She was the sister of Rebecca Nurse. When she took farewell of her husband, children and friends, she was, as reported by those present, "Serious, Religious, Distinct and Affectionate as could well be expressed, drawing Tears from the Eyes of almost all present. It seems besides the Testimony of the Accusers and Confessors, another proof, as it was counted, appears against her, it having been usual to search the accused for Tets (sic) on some parts of her Body, not here to be named, was found as Excrescence, which they called a Tet."[63]

This doomed woman presented a petition to the judges protesting her innocence begging them not to spill more innocent blood. Upham says of Mary Esty's appeal: "It would be hard to find, in all the records of human suffering and of Christian deportment under them, a more affecting production. It is a most beautiful specimen of strong good-sense, and the true elo-

---

[61] Burr, *op. cit.,* p. 366.

[62] Courtesy Miss Irene McCarthy of Andover, Mass. in letter dated July 5, 1963, taken from archives of the Andover Historical Society.

[63] Burr, *op. cit.,* p. 368.

quence of a pure heart; and was evidently composed by her own hand. It may be said of her—and there can be no higher eulohium—that she felt for others more than for herself."[64]

29. *Martha Corey,* wife of Giles Corey who was pressed to death "for standing mute" (see Chapter II, pages 98-100). The case against this poor woman was a strong one, if we may count what was considered as evidence at the time as valid. There were at least ten or more "afflicted Persons" involved in her case, *viz.,* "Four Married Women . . . an Ancient Woman named Goodal, three Maids . . . three girls from nine to twelve Years of Age," these last being Elizabeth Parris, Abigail Williams and Ann Putnam.

At her examination, "they did vehemently accuse her . . . of Afflicting them by Biting, Pinching, Strangling, etc. and they did in their Fit see her Likeness coming to them, and bringing a book to them . . . they Affirmed, she had a Yellow-Bird that used to suck betwixt her Fingers." This, and much more similar hysterical testimony doomed the accused; so she went to her death on the appointed day "concluding her Life with an Eminent Prayer upon the Ladder."[65]

Perhaps the most tragic aspect of this victim's plight was that her husband, Giles, who was pressed to death, initially became involved in the witch hunt that permeated the community and even testified against his wife. However, later he "saw the light" and recanted, but too late to save her or himself. The poor woman's four sons-in-law also testified against her.

A ballad, relating the story of Giles and Martha Corey, is appended here. The portion dealing with "Goodwyfe Corey" follows:

> Come all New England men,
>   And hearken unto me,
> And I will tell what did begalle
>   Upon ye Gallows Tree.
>
> In Salem Village was the place
>   And I did heare them saye,
> And Goodwyfe Corey was the Name,
>   Upon that paynfull Daye:

[64]Upham, *op. cit.,* Vol. II, p. 127.

[65]Burr, *op. cit.,* pp. 155, 367. Upham refers to Goodwife Bibber as a "falsedefamer"; both she and Goodwife Goodall were "hangers-on" to the adolescent circle sponsored by Tituba.

This Goody Corey was a Witch
    The people did believe,
Afflicting of the Godly Ones
    Did make them sadly Greave.

There were two pyous Matron Dames
    And goodly Maidens Three,
That cryed upon this heynous Witch
    As you shall quickly see.

Goodwyfe Bibber,[65] she was one,
    And Goodwyfe Goodall two,
These were the more afflicted ones
    With Pyts and Pynchings too.

And those three Damsels faire,
    She worried them full sore,
As all could see upon their arms
    The divers Markes they bore.

And when before the Magistrates
    For Tryall she did stand,
This Wicked Witch did lye to them
    While holding up her Hand.

'I pray you all Good Gentlemen
    Come listen unto me,
I never harmed those two Goodwyfes
    Nor yet these Children Three.

'I call upon my Savior Lord'
    (Blasphemeously she sayed)
'As witness of my Innocence,
    In this my Hour of Need'.

The goodly Ministers were shockt
    This Witch-prayer for to hear,
And some did see ye Black Man there
    A-whispering in her Eare.

The Magistrates did say to her.
    'Most surely thou dost lye!
Confess thou here thy hellish Deeds
    Or ill Death thou must dye.'

> She rent her Cloathes, she tore her Haire,
>   And lowdly she did crye,
> 'May Christe forgive mine Enimies
>   When I am called to dye.'

> This Goodwyfe had a Goodman too,
>   Giles Corey was his Name,
> In Salem Gaol they shut him in
>   With his blasphemous Dame.[66]

30. *Ann Pudeater* of Salem is distinctive because she was selected to be *post-humously* pardoned for her "crime" of witchcraft and the record expunged. This was done with some fanfare in Massachusetts, in 1959. The proceedings were televized with Senator Leverett Saltonstall and other dignitaries participating with eulogies in behalf of the woman so bitterly wronged over 250 years ago.

This Salem resident had previously been married to one Greenslitt who had abandoned her and their five children. She later married John Pudeater who died in 1682. However, he had left each child a small legacy and at the time of the trials they were living at Casco Bay. The records seem to indicate that Ann was a kind neighbor. In her pitiful petition to the judges who were about to condemn her, she begged that they pay no attention to the untrue statements rendered against her by her accusers.[67]

31. *Wilmot Read* of Marblehead (also spelled Willmot Redd). Upham refers to this person as a female, *viz.,* in her approach to death "probably adhered to the unresisting demeanor which marked her examination. It was all a mystery to her; and to every question she answered, 'I know nothing about it.' "[68]

32. *Margaret Scott,* of Rowly, was condemned on September 17; widow of Benjamin who died some time in 1671 (will dated June 6); had two sons, Benjamin and John and daughter Mary; was found guilty of "certain detestable arts called witchcraft sorceries" and was hanged; she was an adopted daughter of Mary Smith and Samuel Scott.[69]

---

[66]Olive Woolley Burt, *American Murder Ballads,* New York, Oxford University Press, 1958, pp. 105-106; the portion of the ballad relating the Giles Corey episode is in our Chapter II, page 101.

[67]Upham, *op. cit.,* Vol. II, pp. 329-330.

[68]*Ibid.,* p. 325.

[69]Data supplied courtesy Mrs. J. Dudley Perley, president Rowly Historical Society in letter dated June 16, 1963; also letter dated June 21.

The Rev. Nicholas Noyes, present at the mass hanging on this day, "turning him to the bodies, said, what a sad thing it is to see eight Firebrands of Hell hanging there."[70]

33. *Samuel Wardwell,* of Andover, had originally confessed to witchcraft but later repudiated it and, of course, went to his death; his indictment read: "wickedly and feloniously a covenant with the Evil Spirit and Devil did make." At the execution, while he was speaking to the assembled crowd, protesting his innocence, "the Executioner, being at the same time smoking Tobaco, the Smoak coming in his Face, interrupted his Discourse; those accusers said that the Devil did hinder him with Smoak."[71]

34. *Bridget Bishop,* alias Oliver: she lived at Salem Village (Danvers) and ran a couple of *ordinaries* (taverns), one in Salem Village, the other on the outskirts of Salem Town. There was gossip about her handling of these taverns—she permitted young people to frequent them at unseemly hours to play "shovelboard" and keep the town in nightly turmoil. She was a strange dresser and wore a "red paragon bodice."[75] She had long been under suspicion and twelve years earlier had been similarly charged. There were many witnesses at the trial who maintained that she had either pinched, choked or bitten them. One "afflicted" stated that she had "taken her from her wheel," carried her to the river, and threatened to drown her. It seems that she attempted to force those who testified against her to sign a book (the Devil's book) which she referred to as "ours." Another testified that she had seen Bishop in a field at a "General Meeting of Witches . . . and there partook of a Diabolical Sacrament in Bread and Wine." Several others complained that she had bewitched them, their testimony being obviously similar. One other witness, John Bly, stated that when he was employed by her to take down the cellar wall he found several "poppets"—images that witches were supposed to make of their victims—made of "rags and Hogs Brussels (sic) with Headless Pins in them, the Point being outward." Many years earlier, when she had been under suspicion, she had been falsely accused of bewitching a child to death by the child's father; he

---

[70]Burr, *op. cit.,* p. 369.

[71]Burr, *op. cit.,* p. 367; Upham, *op. cit.,* Vol. II, p. 332.

[72]Starkey, *op. cit.,* pp. 99-101.

had later recanted on his death-bed.[73] Bridget Bishop, first of
the Salem victims, was hanged on June 10. On that day High
Sheriff George Corwin trundled her up Gallows Hill with a
large crowd looking on, and hanged her "from the branches
of a great oak tree."[74] Upham tells us that the only death warrant that survives of all those hanged is that of Bridget Bishop.
An envelope that once contained all of them was found in the
records but only Bishop's was inside.[75]

35. *Sarah Good:* she, with Sarah Osborne, were, as we have
seen, the first to be arraigned. The accusers were the hysterical
children comprising Tituba's "inner circle." Sarah Good and
her husband were without any status to speak of in the village,
living as they did in a state of poverty and hiring themselves out
to anyone who would employ and tolerate them. Sarah was
described as a powerful "hag," pipe-smoking and shrewish.
While there may have been pity expressed by the free and the
stable element of the town for some of the victims of this con-
vulsion, there was little for Sarah Good. She had a four-year-
old child, Dorcas, who is alleged to have been bewitched. Upon
her examination, it was stated "that when she cast her eye upon
afflicted persons they were tormented . . . they had often been
bitten by her and produced marks of a small set of teeth." This
young child was remanded to gaol and "lay there seven or eight
months and being chained in the dungeon was terrified." Her
father, some eighteen years later, maintained "that she hath ever
since . . . had little or no reason to govern herself."

Sarah Good had a sharp, if not vile, tongue, or so it was
claimed. When she was at the gallows and was urged to repent,
as she was accused of being a witch by the Rev. Nicholas Noyes,
she exploded: 'You are a lyer; I am no more a Witch than you
are a Wizard, and if you take away my life, God will give you
blood to drink." Awaiting trial, she had been kept in the Salem
gaol in chains because the afflicted contended that they experienced no relief unless she kept "in fetters.[76]

One further word about the indominable Sarah Good: "In

---

[73]Burr, *op. cit.*, pp. 223-229; abstracted from Cotton Mathers *Wonders of the Lnvisable World.*

[74]Starkey, *op. cit.*, p. 154.

[75]For further details of Bishop's trial and execution, see Upham, *op. cit.*, Vol. I, pp. 191-197; Vol. II, pp. 156-167.

[76]Burr, *op. cit.*, p. 349.

the summer of 1692 when several persons were committed to prison in Boston for 'Having an Hand in that most Horrid and Hellish Witchcraft which has brought in the Devile upon several persons of the Country at such a rate as is the just Astonishment of the World," then it was that Mercy Short—who had been captured by the Indians but who had been rescued—being sent by her Mistress upon an Errand to the Prison, was asked by one of the Suspected Witches (Sarah Good) for a little Tobaco; and she affronted the Hag by throwing a Handful of Shavings at her and saying, 'That's tobaco good enough for you' —whereupon the wretched Woman bestowed some ill words upon her, and poor Mercy was taken with. . . . Fits as those which held the Bewitched people then Tormented by Invisable Furies in the County of Essex."[77]

In Chapter I, in our discussion of superstition surrounding the gallows, we mentioned at the outset the remark that has come down to us from the witch hangings, *viz.,* "The Cart going up the Hill with these Eight to Execution (September 22) was for some time at a Sett; the afflicted and others said, that the Devil himself ordered it."

Upham ventures the speculation that it was no wonder the cart was brought to a halt, primarily because of the roughness of the journey up to the hill. He states "the route must have been a cruelly painful and fatiguing one, particularly to infirm and delicate persons as many of them were."[78] All eight of them, on this day, were herded into the one cart and laboriously rolled to their doom.

There was a crowd present to see the mass hanging. As Upham puts it: "People left their business and families, and came from distant points, to gratify their curiousity, and enable them to form a judgment of the phenomena here exhibited. Strangers from all parts swelled the concourse, gathered to behold the sufferings of 'the afflicted' . . . and flocked to the surrounding eminences and the grounds immediately in front of Witch Hill."[79] We find this description no different from many we recorded in Chapter I when public hangings were the mode.

---

[77]*Ibid.,* p. 260, quoted from "A Brand Pluck'd Out of the Burning."
[78]Upham, *op. cit.,* Vol. II, p. 332.
[79]*Ibid.,* pp. 381-382.

Whatever the reasons for or explanations of this hysterical "jag," the community of Salem soon developed deep feelings of remorse and shame. Despite the fact that there were many still under suspicion when the court adjourned to meet later, no others were ever hanged, although a few were convicted and then reprieved. A metamorphosis had taken place, and, as Peleg Chandler states: "The change in the public mind was complete and universal. Bitter was the lamentation of the whole community for the sad consequences of their rashness and delusion; contrite for all of the actors who had been in the tragedy. The indignation of the people, not loud but deep and strong, was directed with restless force against those who had been particularly active in these insane enormities."[80]

And thus ended the witch hunt, perhaps the most disgraceful episode in our nations history!

---

[80]Chandler, *op. cit..* Vol. I, pp. 31-32.

Chapter IV

HANGINGS INSIDE—
FAR FROM THE MADDING THRONGS
PUBLIC HANGINGS GRADUALLY OUTLAWED

T HERE IS SOMETHING akin to immortality about murder and hanging. There are the ballads about them—sad, maudlin, flippant, or gory; there are the publications about many of them—confessions, sermons, trial accounts, and mere single-sheet broadsides; and the wide variety of bibliographies in various collections, public and private. Each town has its particular "never to be forgotten" crime. This heritage justifies the startling statement made in the opening sentence.

It is sometimes said that capital punishment would be abolished overnight if executions were more personalized and open to the public. There are those who believe that the clandestine almost "star chamber" executions, now consummated in this country in gas chambers and "little green rooms," go far in perpetuating the death penalty. It is their contention that open-air hangings on the squares of the county seats, or, perhaps, in great amphitheatres or stadiums would bring an abrupt halt to capital punishment.

There is little evidence available to support such a hope. Our several states went through a long period when public executions were the mode, when crowds of 10,000 to 20,000 or more witnessed the events, but capital punishment still persists. It took a long time even to move these public orgies from the open air to more private and cloistered sanctuaries—the county jails or state prisons.

This is not an exposition on the persistence of capital punishment. Suffice to state that it persists today in thirty-seven of our states, although we must admit, or contend, haltingly and without much enthusiasm. A few abolished it and then reinstated it. Most recent of these is Delaware which abolished the penalty in 1958 and reinstated it in 1961; their present method is hanging. Parenthetically, Delaware is the only state that clings to flogging as a penalty that can be imposed by a court. The American people are capricious and unpredictable about the death penalty and it would seem that it will remain with us for many years to come, if even in a desultory fashion.

The first person to protest against all kinds of public punishments was the famous Philadelphia colonial physician and signer of the Declaration of Independence, Dr. Benjamin Rush (1745-1813). In 1787, he read a paper at the home of Benjamin Franklin before a group of professional citizens of the city in which he denounced all forms of public punishments such as hangings, the use of the stocks and pillory, and whipping-posts. He called these degrading and ineffectual in reforming the culprit. He heaped scorn on those who advocated such instruments of torture such as the post and the hanging tree. He further contended that public punishments tended to result in the opposite attitudes toward crime and criminals by society than those intended by the defenders of such penalties. In many instances, he said, sympathy rather than vengeance for the criminal resulted, and, as he further stated: "Murder is propagated by hangings for murder."[1]

Rush wrote another pamphlet in 1792, which dealt more specifically with the abolition of the death penalty. The following year, the brilliant William Bradford, attorney general of the Quaker state, penned his views on the same subject which concurred substantially with those of Dr. Rush. Both men were pioneers in urging the abolition of the penalty of death.

Within the movement to abolish capital punishment, the movement to abolish public hangings operated. It became a movement within a movement. One became a dynamic of the other.

While sensitive persons recoiled from public hangings and lent their weight and influence to the movement to bring an end to the long-lived, entrenched but disgusting spectacles, it was not until April 10, 1834 that Pennsylvania became the first state to legislate against public hangings. New Jersey was not far behind, on March 3, 1835, followed by New York on May 9 of the same

---

[1] So stated in his pamphlet entitled *An Inquiry into the Affects of Public Punishments upon Criminals and upon Society*, Philadelphia, 1787.

year and Massachusetts on November 4. New Hampshire followed on January 13, 1837.

The laws of the various states that were passed in the 1830's and 1840's were quite similar. They called for executions (hangings) inside the county jails or in the state prisons. They stipulated that a physician should be present, a minister of the victim's own choosing, and a certain number of local witnesses to be selected by the sheriff. In addition, the victim was generally permitted to name a few whom he might wish to be present. The sheriff usually was given the right to exclude any person whom he might consider objectionable or embarrassing.

Few inside hangings conformed precisely to the letter of the law. Sometimes hundreds and even as many as a thousand persons jammed or crammed into the close confines of the jails to see a victim "turned off." It is hardly a debatable question whether or not hangings began to be "private" or not; hangings merely became less public.

Inside hangings might be within the walls of the jail building or merely within the outer walls, that is, in the jail yard. When they were in the yard, more of the determined curious could witness the event by climbing nearby poles or trees, or by gaining a vantage point in some neighborhood building. There was nothing to prevent the owner of such strategically-situated structures from selling window or even roof-top space to anyone who wished to spend the money for a kind of "ringside" seat. In some instances, canvas was stretched around the courthouse grounds and the hanging negotiated there. Such was the case at Emporium, county-seat of Cameron County, Pennsylvania, when two victims were hanged in 1909. The canvas was stretched from the jail to the lawn which obstructed the view from the front, but a fairly clear view from the other sides was obtained by the crowds. *Private* appears to be a matter of definition.

IS HANGING PAINFUL?

On February 27, 1662, Samuel Pepys, diarist, recorded: "All the doctors at the table concluded that there is no pain at all in hanging, for that do stop the circulation of the blood and so stops all sense and motion in an instant."[2]

---

[2]Quoted by Justin Atholl, *The Shadow of the Gallows*, London, John Long, Ltd., 1954, p. 98.

The comparable amount of pain imposed upon or experienced by one who undergoes the death penalty by hanging, decapitation, lethal gas, electrocution, or shooting, has long been a conversation piece in all countries. Generally, the talk gravitates around the amount of *physical* pain with little discussion regarding psychological pain or uneasiness or despair of the victim or his family. The physical pain will always remain a matter of conjecture since none return to describe it. It is quite commendable that societies have, in general, been assiduous in constantly perfecting the techniques of imposing the death penalty so as to reduce, if not completely guarantee, the elimination of pain to the victim as he pays the "ignoble" penalty for his crime. This concern is a wondrous example of social ambivalence.

Practically all of the evidence adduced indicates that hanging, if properly done, is painless. This does not necessarily mean that death is instantaneous but does mean that unconsciousness results as soon as the drop is sprung and the body is abruptly halted in midair. Some persons who have survived hanging—that is, an abortive hanging—contend that they felt no pain. Such evidence, however, comes almost exclusively from England. We find no testimonials of this sort in the United States. In earlier times, in the mother country, there were actually many who survived. Atholl quotes from the *Quarterly Review* an issue as late as 1849:

> An immense number of persons recovered have recorded their sensations and agree . . . that an easier end could not be desired. An acquaintance of Lord Bacon who meant to hang himself partially lost his footing and was cut down at the last extremity . . . and declared he felt no pain and his only sensation was fire before his eyes which changed first to black and then to sky blue.[3]

Atholl records several such testimonials, all from Britian.

In fact, the thought of hanging being painless and actually generating a pleasurable sensation for the condemned raised not a little protest as its being a deterrent. In 1701, for instance, a tract was published entitled "Hanging Not Punishment Enough for Murthererers, High-Way Men and House-Breakers!"[4]

[3]*Ibid.*, p. 106.
[4]*Ibid.*, p. 107.

Our own Henry L. Mencken wrote some years ago that in his judgment, "hanging, if competently carried out, is a humane method of putting criminals to death, though it is not quite as quick as electrocution . . . The blow delivered to the criminal's head when he reaches suddenly the end of the rope . . . in most cases causes immediate unconsciousness, or, at all events, such a shattering of the faculties that he is hardly able to suffer."[5]

We are, of course, discussing the question of pain to the person *being hanged,* not the psychological pain experienced by the witnesses. A priest, some years ago, commenting on the painfulness of asphyxiation in the gas chamber, admitted that the victim probably suffered little but the sensitive witnesses probably suffered much from the ordeal. Hanging has always been a brutal spectacle to behold, painful or not. Ben Hecht in his inimitable style describes the process in this manner:

> A hanged man dies in a few seconds if his neck is broken by the drop. If his neck isn't broken, due to the incorrect adjustment of the noose, he chokes to death. This takes from eight to fourteen minutes.
>
> While he hangs choking, the white-covered body starts to spin slowly. The white-hooded head tilts to one side and a stretch of purpled neck becomes visible. Then the rope begins to vibrate and hum like a hive of bees. After this the white robe begins to expand and deflate as if it were being blown up by a leaky bicycle pump. Following the turning, vibrating, spinning, and pumping up of the white robe comes the climax of the hanging. This is the throat of the hanging man letting out a last strangled cry or moan of life.[6]

We must continuously stress the fact that competence in the art of hanging is an extremely important factor in assaying the degree of suffering involved. As we have pointed out and as we shall adduce in this chapter, there has been much bungling in the practice of hanging throughout the centuries and this hazard must be assessed in discussing the efficacy of hanging as opposed to other methods of invoking the death penalty such as electrocution

---

[5]In the *Foreword* of August Mencken's *By the Neck,* New York, Hastings House, 1942, p. vi.

[6]*Gaily, Gaily,* p. 48. Copyright 1963 by Ben Hecht. Reproduced by permission of Doubleday & Company, Inc.

and the use of lethal gas. We do not mean to imply that we approve of any form of capital punishment only that each method has a degree of pain.

Charles Duff, in his book *New Handbook on Hanging,* states positively: "Dislocation of the neck is the ideal to be aimed at" in hanging a person. Regardless of how the operation is verbally described, the objective is to break the neck of the victim. However, in earlier times and to considerable degree today, the victim's neck was not and is not broken. Up until the introduction of the so-called "long drop," most persons were in reality, strangulated. Lack of skill in designing the "fatal" knot, or carelessness in placing it at the proper angle of the neck, precluded the possibility of sudden death or dislocation of the neck. It was during this period, prior to the eighteenth century and, in many areas long afterward, that the victims of the "tree" were left dangling or "dancing in the air," in their death contortions.

The knot, properly prepared, should be placed on the lower left jaw. At the drop, it tends to throw the head back which is proper since it snaps the neck. If the knot is on the right hand side of the neck, the head will be thrown forward and cause strangulation. This is confirmed by the former hangman, Pierrepoint, as he was queried before the Royal Commission on Capital Punishment in 1950:

> Q. The knot, as you showed us, must always be under the angle of the left jaw?
> A. Yes.
> Q. That is very important, is it?
> A. Very important.
> Q. Why is it very important?
> A. If you had the same knot on the right hand side it comes back behind the neck, and throws the neck forward, which would make a strangulation. If you put it on the left hand side it finishes up in front and throws the chin back and breaks the spinal cord.
> Q. It depends on where he is standing on the trap?
> A. No, I do not think so. *The knot is the secret of it, really* (italics added). We have to put it on the left lower jaw and if we have it on that side, when he falls it finishes

under the chin and throws the chin back; but if the knot is
on the right-hand side, it would finish up behind the neck
and throw the neck forward, which would be strangulation.
He might live on the rope a quarter of an hour then.[7]

According to Justin Atholl, in England the knot is no longer
used for hangings. The popular executioner—if a hangman can
ever be labeled "popular"—William Marwood, who reigned at the
gallows from 1874 to 1883, developed a technique of inserting a
metal eye in the end of the rope and of using a leather washer to
prevent the rope from slipping as it passed through.[8]

The Royal Commission was an extremely thorough probe into
the many ramifications of capital punishment, exclusively hanging
in England, and much testimony was supplied by the experts, both
for and against the death penalty. To objective students and
scholarly observers identified directly or indirectly with this commission or of its report, nothing connected with the process of
hanging was expressed with certainty. For example, skepticism
was expressed by the *Encyclopedia Britannica* (1955 edition) after
the commission had published its report, relative to the certainty
of immediate death:

It is said (italics added) that the dislocation of the vertebrae
causes immediate unconsciousness . . . the heart may continue to
beat for up to twenty minutes but this is thought to be a purely
automatic function.[9]

Nevertheless, the introduction of the "long drop" which changed
hanging from sheer, crude strangulation or suffocation to sever-
ance of the spinal cord, brought about a new dispensation in the
art. The height of the drop in ratio with the weight of the victim's
body plus the skill in adjusting the knot, theoretically revolutionized hanging. The British hangmen, professionals as they are, are
in office long enough (they also serve as apprentices) to become

[7]Arthur Koestler, *Reflections on Hanging,* New York, Macmillan, 1957, p. 141 (from
testimony of Royal Commission on Capital Punishment, 1950, 8428-31).

[8]*The Shadow of the Gallows,* 1956. In a letter to the writer he maintains "they still
call it the noose even though there is no knot."

[9]Quoted by Koestler, *op. cit.,* p. 140.

"experts." We have pointed out earlier that the sheriff in this country can hardly hope to qualify as a professional hangman since even in the days of public and more frequent hangings, seldom was he called upon to "execute his art of execution."

It is not surprising that in due time a table was compiled which indicated just how long the drop and the amount of weight should be in terms of the size and the weight of the victim. If this ratio between length of drop and weight of victim was not correctly correlated to a nicety, there would be danger of the person being decapitated and thus creating a horror as well as a gory tableau. We have mentioned such catastrophes elsewhere (see pp. 173-8) The British formula, computed in stones is here changed to pounds and thus gives a rough idea of the length of the drop for each victim (or client as he is referred to some times in British jargon):[10]

Weight	*Drop*
196 lbs.	8 ft.
189 lbs.	8 ft. 2 in.
182 lbs.	8 ft. 4 in.
175 lbs.	8 ft. 6 in.

The long drop was used after a fashion by various British hangmen but it was the "Jack Ketch" of his day, William Marwood (incumbent from 1874 to 1883) who first put the principles into operation. His successor, James Berry (1884-1892) and referred to by Atholl as "The Reluctant Hangman," experimented on and improved the procedure. But despite his efficiency he had the misfortune, in misjudging his calculations, to decapitate a victim, one Robert Goodale.[11]

We cannot state that hanging is not painful. Perhaps, if properly done and, when so, nothing interferes for the operation to proceed "according to plan," the victim suffers little if at all. We cannot agree that any person should be hanged. We may close this section with a beautifully satirical thought on hanging as expressed by Charles Duff, mentioned earlier. "But enough has surely been said

---

[10]Adapted from Louis Blake Duff, *The County Kerchief,* Toronto, The Ryerson Press, p. 152, 1949.

[11]Atholl, in *The Reluctant Hangman,* John Long, Ltd., 1956, p. 114.

to show that, in Old England at least, hanging is well done from the beginning to end. Let us forget the heads occasionally pulled off by bad hangmen, and the strangulation that may happen, through no *fault* of the hangman. All we need to remember are those impressive words uttered by the august judges: 'To be hanged by the neck *until dead.' Until Dead*—those are the operative words. In Executing the Judgment of Death, the hangman never fails; and nothing else matters to the State."[12]

IMPROVED GALLOWS IN THE PRIVATE ERA

In due time improvements were made in the scaffolds on which our victims were hanged. In the latter part of the era, the "long drop" was introduced, probably from England, or possibly through Yankee ingenuity, which, to a degree, made the grisly business more scientific.

Professional hangmen sometimes invented their own scaffold-machines and carried, or shipped them about from one county-seat to another. Such apparatuses were sometimes referred to as "galloping-gallows." A few professional hangmen developed a reputation but such was more or less local in character. We have never evolved a national "Jack Ketch" as we have a "John Henry" or a "Paul Bunyan." A few persons, however, come to mind who are remembered for their profession as hangmen; one, James Van Hise, from Newark, New Jersey, who, it is reported, "sprung the trap on at least eighty-five persons, using his own patented gallows." Another, known as the "celebrated Atkinson," was not averse in "explaining the workings of his simple but deadly apparatus" to all inquirers. These two were, of course, from only the eastern seaboard states of Pennsylvania and New Jersey.[13]

In his work, *Law West of Fort Smith,* Glenn Shirley tells us of George Maledon who was hangman of the bad men of the Indian country. They had been sentenced to death by the "Hanging Judge," Isaac C. Parker, during the late 1800's. Of Maledon, known as the "Prince of Hangmen," it was said "he never smiled, took a natural pride in his ability to always break the neck

---

[12]Duff, *op. cit.,* p. 178.

[13]See Teeters, *Scaffold & Chair,* Pennsylvania Prison Society, Philadelphia, 1963, p. 22.

of his victim"and who "after retirement toured the West with rope and other gruesome instruments of his office."[14]

In a kind of reverse, we learn of one E. P. Davis, State Electrician for the State of New York, visiting Philadelphia on March 10, 1908, to witness the hangings of two Chinese, Jung Jow and Mock Kung (Tong murderers), admitted he had never seen a hanging prior to that day; yet he had officiated at 110 electrocutions in his own state.

In our study of types of hangings, we learned that many victims of the "tree" were jerked *upward* rather than dropped *downward*. August Mencken, in his book *By the Neck,* described one such gallows or scaffold which was used in the Wethersfield, Connecticut, penitentiary for the hanging of the debonair, swashbuckling, but ruthless Gerald Chapman, robber and killer, on April 6, 1926, before that state turned to electrocution:

> To one end of the fifty-foot rope, which goes up through a hole in the ceiling, is a weight carefully balanced, in this case, against the 135 pounds of Chapman's frail body. On the other end, inside the death chamber, was the noose, which was held by a hook in the wall, and, as it was behind Chapman as he entered the room, it probably was not seen by him. The weight is held three feet above floor level and is connected by a steel rod to the plunger at the point where the warden stands . . . Fifteen seconds after Chapman entered the room there was a sudden click as the trigger released the weight and his body *shot upward.* Save for the click there was not a sound. The body hung suspended at a height of twelve feet. The neck vertebrae had snapped and death had been practically instantaneous . . . Those at the drum on which the rope was wound began slowly to turn the windlass and the body was lowered almost imperceptibly until the feet were a foot from the floor.[15]

---

[14]New York, Holt, Rinehart & Winston, 1957, p. 115. For details see Chapter IX, For other anecdotes regarding this legendary hangman, see Homer Croy, *He Hanged Them High,* New York, Duell, Sloane & Pearce, 1952 (this is actually the story of Judge Isaac Parker). Another valuable source not only on Judge Parker and his court but on much criminal history of the Indian Territory is . . . *Hell on the Border* by S. W. Harman, a newspaper editor who was for many years a close observer of the court and knew the judge and many of the chief figures as well. Paul I. Wellman, *A Dynasty of Western Outlaws,* Doubleday 1961.

[15]New York, Hastings House, 1942, pp. 24-25.

The method of hanging Chapman represents the ingenuity of a hanging in a state prison. An earlier case of this kind, that is, one in which the victim was catapulted *upward* is associated with a celebrated crime of murder known as the Udderzook case—locale, Chester County, Pennsylvania. William Eachus Udderzook was hanged in the West Chester county jail on November 12, 1874, for the murder of his brother-in-law, Winfield Scott Goss, the motive being insurance money.[16]

On the outside cover of a pamphlet published on this notorious case may be seen a likeness of an executioner raising a hatchet to cut a rope on the side of the gallows. This released a 300-pound weight that fell and jerked the victim's body *upward*. While this method of hanging a person is bizarre and unusual, several instances have been recorded. One, presumably hanged in this manner, was Benjamin F. Hunter, at Camden, New Jersey, on January 10, 1879, for the murder of John M. Armstrong in an insurance scheme.[17] He was hanged as he sat in a chair. He had attempted suicide by slashing the veins in his feet with a concealed knife and almost died.

However, we find a much earlier gallows that shot the victim up rather than down. On November 30, 1842, at Lockport, New York, in Niagara County, David Douglass, the lone person ever hanged in that county, met his death by being jerked upward. He had been convicted of the murder of a "nameless roommate" in a drunken brawl. As stated, "the body was jerked *up* instead of dropping *down*." It is reported that the old scaffold was stored for many years in a barn and may still be seen in the Lockport Museum.

Another interesting feature of the case is that John Greenleaf Whittier, learning of this hanging, wrote a stinging poem concerning it, entitled *A Human Sacrifice*. Always a zealous opponent of capital punishment, the Quaker poet was incensed by, and contemptuous of, a Lockport clergyman who believed in the death penalty. This cleric felt it was justifiable "by the awful dread and horror it inspired." This local divine, the Rev. William Wisner,

---

[16]McDade, *op. cit.*, 1012-3, also "immortalized" by Edmund Pearson, in *Murder at Smutty Nose and Other Murders,* New York, 1926. "A Demnition Body," pp. 70-93.

[17]McDade, *op. cit.*, 494.

sent his account of the hanging to the *New York Tribune,* in which he related the story of his "attendance upon a criminal at the time of his execution in western New York;" he described "the agony of the wretched being, his abortive attempts at prayer, his appeal for life, his fear of violent death; and, after declaring his belief that the poor victim died without hope of salvation, concluded with a warm eulogy upon the gallows being more than ever convinced of its utility."[18]

Whittier's long poem opens with the prisoner's dream carrying him back to his happy childhood and from there on carries through six more stanzas describing the horror of his sensations on the scaffold. He ends the poem with this warning:

> Oh, never yet upon the scroll
> Of the sin stained, but priceless soul,
>   Hath Heaven inscribed *Despair!*
> Cast not the clouded gem away,
> Quench not the dim but living ray,
>   My brother-man, *Beware!*
> With the deep voice which from the skies
> Forbade the Patriarch's sacrifice,
>   God's angel cries, *Forbear!*

Few descriptions of gallows, scaffolds and/or traps exist in printed form. It seems incumbent that we append here a technical description of one that comes from the Otsego, New York *Republican,* Cooperstown, New York, dated November 20, 1879. It appeared shortly after Myron A. Buel was hanged (on November 14) for the rape and murder of fifteen-year-old Mary Catherine Richards, daughter of his employer, at Plainfield. He had made advances to her previously but on the fatal day, June 25, 1878, he attacked her in the cow barn with a milking stool. He then strangled and raped her. He was twenty-one years of age and a hard-working boy with a good reputation. We insert an account. It may be seen that the gallows had been previously constructed and used for another victim, Felix McCann, at Norwich, Chenango County, on June 6.[19]

---

[18]In material sent the writer by Mr. Clarence O. Lewis, Historian Niagara County, Lockport, New York.

[19]The writers are indebted to Dr. Louis Jones, Director of the New York State Historical Association, Cooperstown, for the material abstracted below.

The gallows arrived by express from Norwich and was erected on the east side of the jail, which had been enclosed by Sheriff Clark with a high, board fence.

"The gallows, when placed in position, was tested by the Sheriff with a bag of sand weighing 155 pounds, and was found to operate satisfactorily.

"The gallows consisted of two bottom or bed-pieces, each nine feet long. Framed into these, were sleepers upon which was laid a flooring for the condemned man to stand upon. Rising from the center of each bed-piece was an upright post, eleven feet and three inches high, strengthened on either side by braces framed into the bed-pieces. Across, from post to post, stretched the cap-piece, measuring eight feet and three inches between the posts. One end of the cap post extended over the upright twenty-two inches. In the center of the cap-piece was a pulley-wheel, and in the extended-end just mentioned was another pulley-wheel. The rope passed up over the center pulley then ran along the upper-side of the cap-piece to the second pulley, then extended down and was attached to the weight.

"The trap that held the weight consisted of a brace of iron, in the end of the horizontal arm of which was fastened another arm by means of a pivot. This second arm lay upon the first arm and extended about an inch beyond it in the shape of a half hook. Upon this hook was hung the weight by a staple. This second arm thus became a lever—the long arm of the lever lying along the horizontal arm of the brace, and the short arm extending beyond the brace and holding up the weight. About three inches from the upright post was a small arm rising perpendicularly, about four inches long. This was fastened to the brace by a pivot, and had a notch in it which slipped over the long arm of the lever. A small rope was hitched to the upper end of this perpendicular arm, then passed over a pulley and through the upright post, and then down to the hand of Sheriff Clark when it was pulled; that brought the perpendicular arm of the small lever over towards the upright post, and released the long arm of the horizontal lever, which flying up, allowed the weight to drop off. There was provided about three feet of slack, so that the weight fell three feet before the rope became taut—then it fell three feet more, jerking Buel up that distance. It was a very ingenious contrivance.

"The weight was a block of iron about one foot square and fifteen inches high, and weighed three hundred and ten pounds. It had been used in the executions of several others in the surrounding counties.

"The rope was about thirty-three feet in length, and three eighths of an inch in thickness, and was made for the execution of McCann, and consisted of four hundred and fourteen strands of shoe threads twisted together. Two of these strands, on a test trial, sustained a weight of twenty-two pounds. The knot was the usual hangman's knot. The whole apparatus of death was painted black."[20]

New York State, during the 1870's and 1880's, used this same scaffold or one similar to it, aided by one or, perhaps, two, weights of over 300 pounds as many as thirteen times. The *upward* technique was apparently quite popular in that state during the period.

Buckshot and Water-trap Scaffolds

We mentioned the Gerald Chapman hanging above. He was apparently doomed to hang on a strange and ingenious device that had been used in the state prison of Connecticut for many years. The operation depended on buckshot for timing purposes. Mencken, in describing the apparatus on which Chapman died, stated: "When it [the device] was first installed, the condemned man, upon entering the chamber, stood upon a small trap in the floor. His weight released a quantity of buckshot which slowly rolled down a slight incline until their weight released a trigger which held the weight. It was decided, however, that this method was illegal, as it virtually *compelled the prisoner to commit suicide,* and it was abandoned for the present apparatus" (italics added).[21]

This buckshot device had been conceived and invented by a prisoner named John Rabbitt, a machinist, whose hometown was Stamford. He was later pardoned for his unique services to the state. The first person to be hanged on this mechanism was John Cronin from Hartford on December 18, 1894. In the story of his execution from the *New York Times* of that date, we find this

---

[20]From *The Otsego Republican,* Cooperstown, Otsego County, New York, Thursday, November 20, 1879.

[21]Mencken, *op. cit.,* p. 25.

summary description of the Rabbitt apparatus: The condemned man steps on a two-foot square iron plate and his weight opens a sliding valve in the bottom of a container of fifty pounds of buckshot. As the shot runs out, a lever connection holding the weight in place is released, and the weight drops. The weight is six feet off the floor and weighs 312 pounds. When the weight tautens the rope, and the knot behind the left jaw breaks the neck, the body is jerked six feet in the air and is dropped to within two feet of the ground. By foot pressure on a lever, the movement of the buckshot can be accelerated or retarded. The time to hang a man is thirty seconds or less.

Like buckshot, water has been used as a timing device in effecting a hanging. A few examples have come to our attention. First, let us look at the state of Idaho, which incidentally still clings to hanging. We know that at least two men were shot into eternity by means of this ingenious timing device. These were Noah Arnold, hanged in the Boise prison on December 19, 1924, and John Jerko, hanged July 9, 1926. An eye-witness to these executions states that there was a water-trap used to control an automatic trip. When the weight of the victim's body was placed upon the trapdoor it would lower approximately two inches. At this point, a valve in a water line would open, thereby filling a container. When the weight of the water in the container reached a certain level, this automatically released the trip on the trapdoor. After these two hangings took place, the water method was apparently abolished, since it was found that in cold weather the water would freeze.[22]

Another water contraption was at least devised in the state prison of Colorado, at Canon City, back in 1892. A summary in the *New York Times* (January 24, 1892) describes this as an ordinary scaffold to which was attached a 370-pound weight. The weight was connected to a beam which was perfectly balanced by a two-gallon keg of water. The beam was attached to an upright from the floor and pivoted freely, while the weight was so balanced that it would slide off when the beam was vertical. The barrel had its bunghole plugged and a cord went through to the

---

[22]Courtesy L. E. Clapp, warden, in letter dated February 21, 1965.

platform in the adjoining room. When the prisoner, "noosed, black-capped and strapped" stood on the platform, his weight pressed down on it, the cord was drawn taut which released the plug of the keg. Water started to run out, the time and amount being recorded on a meter clock. When the keg was empty, the beam tipped and the weight came off and fell the required distance onto a mattress. The rope immediately tightened and the victim was jerked upwards the necessary distance.

Water was used in somewhat similar fashion in the hanging of Tom Horn, the controversial "Jekyl and Hyde" nemesis of Wyoming cattle rustlers, at Cheyenne, on November 20, 1903. Horn had been employed and brought into the district during a period of cattle warfare. He was accused of being a kind of "hired killer" and in his operations allegedly killed a fourteen-year-old boy, Willie Nickell, in a case of probable mistaken identity. The crime was committed on July 18, 1902, and Horn was convicted on October 24. Horn was real but the circumstances surrounding his function and his crime are somewhat nebulous and legendary.

The gallows, a strange mechanism, had been fabricated by James P. Julian, a noted "architect" and was referred to as a "weird classic in Rube Goldbergism." It was designed for a hanging in 1892 and made use of a water can from which trickled the water to spring the trap. While the contraption was supposed to work efficiently, human error in adjusting the weight of Horn to the drop caused his strangulation, so that it actually took seventeen minutes for death to occur.

One local historian described the uncanny execution, in part, by these words: "Instantly the sibilant sound of running water permeated the breathless stillness; the instrument of death had begun to operate. To the straining ears of the listeners that little sound had the magnitude of a rushing torrent."[23]

Neither buckshot nor water was used at the gruesome hanging of Charles W. Nordstrom in the King County, Washington, jail at Seattle, on August 23, 1901, for the murder of his employer William Mason. This case is legendary in the state for several

---

[23]Dean F. Krakel, *The Saga of Tom Horn,* Laramie (Wyoming) Printing Co., 1954, p. 263. By special permission of author.

reasons. He was reprieved several times while his case was reviewed by many courts. His attorney was the colorful later senator
from Illinois, James Hamilton (Ham) Lewis. The condemned man
languished in jail for nine years, an almost unheard of phenomenon
at that time. Local gossips circulated the story that several brand
new scaffolds had to be built before the unhappy man went to
his doom. Because of the man's tragic emotional state and to
control his desperate struggles, the sheriff lashed him to a plank
in which condition he was dropped. When the sheriff sounded a
bell, three deputies, each clutching a rope behind an alcove,
pulled simultaneously. None, of course, knew which held the fatal
cord. (courtesy Charles Zibulka, Spokane, Washington).

Many years earlier, at the hanging of Albert L. Starkweather,
at Hartford, Connecticut, on August 17, 1866, for the murder of
his mother and sister, the sheriff had conjured up an ingenious
contrivance for dispatching the unhappy youth. It merely consisted of a spring that was placed under the bottom step of the
stairs leading to the platform. After fixing the noose and cap the
sheriff slowly walked down the stairs and when his weight rested
on the bottom, the deadly little metallic gadget released the trap.

HANGMEN'S ROPES

The names of the artificers of the ropes used in colonial times
are lost in oblivion. Nowhere have we come across a scintilla of
information regarding just who may have supplied that most important of all appurtenances to a hanging, the rope. Nor have we
unearthed any written or printed material dealing with the mysteries incidental to its manufacture. We believe they were always
handmade and we also believe it must have taken a reasonable
amount of dexterity and skill to make one that could be guaranteed
to work effectively and efficiently. Locally it is quite possible that
some of these artisans left their imprint on their townsmen and their
names may be preserved in the archives; we have just not discovered any of them.

We have some knowledge of a person who turned out such
products of his craft for well over a hundred hangings—in and
around western Pennsylvania. He lived in a more modern era, that
is, during the latter part of the nineteenth century. He was W. P.

Bobb, of Allegheny (Pittsburgh) County, who, when he was in his prime around 1890, was sixty years of age. This craftsman liked to believe that he supplied the rope with which Charles Julius Guiteau was hanged at Washington, D. C., on June 30, 1882, for the assassination of President James A. Garfield (see Chapter IX, page 393). He was one of a score who were asked to send a rope for that purpose. While he was never officially informed whether or not his product was used, he was satisfied by the public accounts that it was his handiwork since it was announced that there were 110 strands in the death rope rather than the forty-six that was the accustomed number.

According to information that originally came from this veteran artisan, hemp is always used in the hangman's rope. Flax, he said, would do, but hemp is longer and stronger. It is first beaten and hackled until it is soft and tender and then it is twisted into strands. It is made in four parts, one of which is used as the heart with the other three twisted around it. When finished, it is perfectly round and smooth, about 9/16 of an inch in thickness. It is usually twenty-five to thirty feet long. It requires twenty-one feet to perform an execution properly, the surplus being used in cases of accidental breakages. The knot is usually tied by the manufacturer so that the executioner has nothing to do but slip the noose over the victim's head.[24] A rope used in Huntingdon County, Pennsylvania, for the hanging of Frank Calhoun, on May 8, 1913, for the murder of Benjamin Galloup—a "triangle" murder of sorts, is in the archives of that county's historical library. It is thus described:

> It is a half-inch rope of four strands and twenty-seven feet long. At one end is a twelve-inch loop and above the loop the end of the rope is wrapped around the other part of the rope *seven times,* and fastened to form the knot, which is placed directly under the left ear of the man to be hanged. In addition to the rope there were three 1-1/4 inch straps; one to go around the waist and two shorter ones to strap arms to the waist strap.[25]

Information coming from the state of Washington where hang-

---

[24]The source for this material was a short piece written by C. Lee Berry of Williamsport, Pennsylvania and supplied the writer by Mrs. Margaret Lindemuth of that city.

[25]Excerpt from the *Huntingdon Daily News,* date not available. See *supra,* page (p. 162), for description of rope used in hanging of Buel at Cooperstown, New York.

ing is still the mode of executing, states that the ropes used there "have no heart" (sic) and are of but three strands and are "approximately twenty-one feet long;" further the length of drop is "dependent upon the man's height and weight."

A weird tale connecting a curiosity about rope fashioning or noose-making and an actual hanging case comes from the files of J. Francis McComas, as related in his work *The Graveside Companion.*[26] He tells of the hanging of William G. Smith, at the San Quentin prison, the second last person to be hanged in the State of California on September 8, 1939. Smith was sent up to prison for burglary and as he sat around in his cell he became more than intrigued with ropes. He worked in the furniture factory which, at the time, housed the gallows. He could scarcely keep his attention from the death machine and all that it implied. He wanted to know how the ropes were assembled, hardened and stretched; how the victims of the San Quentin "tree" were measured and weighed before they went to their doom; and what the relationship was between their weight and the "drop." In the process of garnering this macabre data, Smith proved to be too garrulous for his own good; in fact, it proved his own undoing. In the process of his research, he confided to a cell mate that he had actually killed a man, one Elmer Cox. His fellow convict became a "squealer" and Smith was returned to Sacramento to stand trial for the murder. He was soon convicted and was sent on his way for the last and fatal ride to the big gray house on San Francisco Bay where he paid the penalty for his crime and for "talking too much." Perhaps he picked the wrong hobby.

The former warden of this "Big House," Clinton T. Duffy, tells of another inmate in for second-degree murder who was also obsessed with the engine of doom. He worked in the sash and blind shop leading off from which the old "gallows room." This inmate confided to the warden that he loathed the gallows—as did also Warden Duffy—and swore that some day he would destroy it. He was warned not to do so, as it would not rid the state of the death penalty and would engulf him in trouble. But he brooded over this ghastly penalty, all too close to his day-by-day existence. This unhappy and obsessed inmate, one John Lee How-

---

[26]New York, Ivan Obolensky, Inc., 1962, p. 287.

ard, had killed his roommate in Pasadena and had been in the San Quentin establishment since 1929. He had been conscious of some hangings during the period and when the last victim of the rope met his doom—Lisemba-James on May 1, 1942, (see Chapter IV, p. 203), this seemed to release some of his compulsive inhibitions. He stole into the gallows room and literally destroyed the San Quentin "tree." As Duffy describes the destruction: "The overhead cross-timber, which had a groove cut into it from the friction of hundreds of ropes had been smashed to pieces. So had the platform and the two painted traps and the thirteen steps and the booth and long table for the string-cutting guards. Even the restraining board had been ripped from the wall beside the scaffold and torn to pieces. Only the metal mechanism had been left intact. A crowbar stood against the wall."[27]

Clinton T. Duffy was associated with many hangings in the prison where he was employed for so many years, latterly as its warden. This was, of course, prior to the introduction of the gas chamber. In his book, he describes the preparation necessary to hang a victim and tells something of the equipment needed and mentions the grim surroundings of the gallows and scaffold. He first mentions the procedure by which a man is hanged: three officers at a table, each controlling a string which, when cut, on signal from the hangman, releases the deadly trap. But only one string can do the deed and only the hangman knows which of the officers controls the right string. One might well wonder to what extent we go to absolve ourselves of guilt. Duffy describes something that we have thus far not seen mentioned—a "restraining board" which may never, or certainly seldom, needs to be used. It is "five feet long and ten inches wide, with straps spaced several inches apart." It is ever near by, in case a man slowly moving to his doom may become panicky or violent so necessitating his being strapped to it and carried to the gallows. The former warden's description of the rope and the drop is of importance at this point:

The length of the rope was also very important. There was

---

[27]*Eighty-Eight Men and Two Women,* New York, Doubleday, 1962, p. 15. Reprinted by permission of the publisher.

a measuring rod at the side of the gallows indicating the length best suited for a man's height and weight, but the executioner had to take other factors into consideration, too. The condemned man's age and strength, and even his occupation, might have some bearing on the length of the drop. The older the man, the weaker he might be and the shorter the rope. However, an older man used to physical work might require more rope than a younger man who had led a sedentary life, for his muscles would be harder and more resistant to pressure.

As to the preparation of the rope the warden states:

> Off the gallows room was the storage area for stretching the ropes to eliminate any bounce or spring. This was necessary in order to make sure the neck would be broken. Even the slightest slack might cause only partial strangulation, prolonging the death throes. Each rope was suspended from the ceiling and attached to 150 pound weights for about two years. On the day before the execution, the hangman selected the proper rope and had it put on the scaffold.

And as a final word relative to the anxieties of the hangman in his preparations he states:

> . . . To make sure nothing could go wrong, the executioner spent long—and agonizing minutes carefully weighing and measuring and inspecting the condemned man.[28]

While hemp has been used in the vast majority of hangings, both in Britain and in this country, on rare occasions, the rope is made of silk. The advantages of such aristocratic material, according to the doughty and garrulous Samuel Pepys, as far back as the 1600's, was "it being soft and sleek it do slip and kills, that is strangles presently, whereas a stiff one do not come so close together and so the party may live longer before killed."[29] Pepys, of course, was writing during the period of strangulation—not "neck-breaking" or vertebrae dislocation.

The classic example of the person hanged with a silken rope was that of Earl Ferrers (Laurence Shirley) hanged at Tyburn, London, on May 5, 1760, for the murder of his steward in a frantic

[28]Duffy, *op. cit.,* pp. 47-48. Reprinted by permission of the publisher.
[29]Atholl, *op. cit.,* p. 109.

rage. His execution was, perhaps, the most "magnificent" in the annals of British hanging,[30] and we in this country have nothing to compare with it.

In early English days, when there was a stiff competition for hemp between the fleet and the gallows—and presumably that did happen—a bit of doggerel appeared which read:

> Scarce can our fields,
> Such crowds at Tyburn die,
> With hemp the gallows
> And the fleet supply.

It is apparently true that even in our own country, during the all-out mobilization for production during World War II, hemp became so scarce the War Production Board was obliged to issue a directive (April 1944) that Manila for ropes be used even "to carry out the death sentence of the court."[31]

There is a legend that the number of loops making up the hangman's noose is some specific number. This number is variously mentioned as thirteen, nine, seven, or five. There may well be such a legend but the writers' limited check shows the number "seven" most prevalent in the nooses that have come to their attention. However, one occasionally finds one with more loops which leads to the tentative conclusion that perhaps the number depended on the person fashioning the deadly rope. A sample check made of the numerous ropes that have survived in Philadelphia's old Moyamensing Prison, in which some sixty-seven persons were hanged from 1834 to 1916, indicated that all of the nooses were shaped by seven loops.[32]

A legend similar to that regarding the loops is that there are (or were) thirteen steps leading up to the platform of the scaffold. However, in the accounts of the hangings in which the number of steps appears we find no specific number prescribed. The number ranges from eight to sixteen. Former warden, Clinton Duffy, men-

---

[30] *Ibid.*, p. 49.

[31] This information as well as the above verse, from Louis Blake Duff, *op. cit.*, p. 46.

[32] The official directions for conducting military executions indicate in an illustration of a noose that six loops are employed: *Procedure for Military Executions*, Headquarters, Dept. of the Army, Washington, D.C., AR 633-15, April 1959, Figure 7, page 21.

tions thirteen,[33] but in the U.S. Army manual, mentioned above, one can count sixteen in the model found on page 16. Information coming from the state of Washington on this point states: "there is no specific number of steps leading up to the scaffold as the cell where the man spends his last hours is on the same level." However, this may apply only to the set-up in the Walla Walla prison, where the hangings for the state still take place.

There are undoubtedly hundreds of remnants of ropes, pinions, hoods and shrouds, and other hanging paraphernalia "stashed away" in historical museums, county jails, state prisons, and in private collections in this country. The same holds true of scaffolds. Other scaffolds were preserved—and still may be—because one or more of their intended victims have absconded and, according to law, must be hanged in the event they are apprehended, even though the method of execution in the jurisdiction has changed from hanging to another.

THE SAD HISTORY OF BUNGLING AT THE GALLOWS

The new technique in hanging that we described earlier—the shooting of the victim *upward* instead of *downward* was no guarantee against fiascoes occurring at the scaffold. Andrew J. Palm, arch-foe of capital punishment, whom we have mentioned earlier, tells of a repugnant case that occurred on August 1, 1884, in the Raymond Street jail, in Brooklyn. It involved the Negro killer, Alexander Jefferson, who had been convicted of the berserk murders of two persons, one an innocent bystander, when he fancied himself betrayed by his irresponsible mistress-sweetheart. With only a small group present at the hanging, the unhappy man came "quivering and praying from his cell, strong in courage but frightened at the thought of a slow lingering death." He commented to the sheriff that he was not afraid to die, but that he dreaded a possible blunder. He must have entertained a premonition because a blunder did occur. As Palm tells the hideous story of the hanging:

> He never flinched while he stood under the gallows. He even smiled at some acquaintances . . . the sheriff wiped his brow

---

[33]Duffy, *op. cit.*, p. 47.

and the hangman, Joe Levy, with the blow of an axe, cut the rope in his pen. The two weights, of 206 and 120 pounds, fell . . . and Jefferson's body was raised about five feet in the air. It fell back limp when suddenly it began to writhe in agony. The movements at first were not violent, but presently the legs, which had not been pinioned, were drawn up toward the body, the knees reaching almost to the chin, while the arms were extended pleadingly towards the occupants of the balconies right and left. The man kicked furiously and moaned so piteously that a thrill of horror went through the audience. The sheriff was bewildered. His face turned pale and his eyes filled with tears. The hangman was called from his pen to witness his clumsy work. He looked at his struggling victim, but said he could do nothing for him. Jefferson freed his hands sufficiently and clutched the noose, but, being unable to loosen the rope, he tore the black cap from his face and stretched out his hand imploringly toward the audience. The appearance of his face was terrible. After eight minutes of agony, which must have been horrible, the contortions began to lessen, and finally ceased.[34]

The above ghastly spectacle was the responsibility of a professional hangman. Yet it was, in the last analysis, the sheriff of the county within which jurisdiction a hanging took place, who was held accountable for the official execution. The sheriffs of this country, through the years, have stood up to their austere duty superbly and with admirable fortitude. We mentioned earlier that Grover Cleveland, when he was sheriff of Erie County, New York, dispatched his distasteful task on two occasions(Chapter I, p. 52).

On the other hand, there are instances when sheriffs blanched at the prospect of swinging a doomed person into eternity. One, a Philadelphia sheriff, collapsed; it is a wonder that more of them did not! In the late 1890's (November 30, 1897), at the hanging of George Douglas at Pittsburgh, the news report stated that the victim "at his own accord walked the thirteen steps alone; the sheriff gave the lever a mighty jerk and then almost ran to the corridor."

There is little to wonder at the fright of the sheriff as he approached the "point of no return" at the gallows. Most of them

---

[34]*The Death Penalty*, New York, G. P. Putnam's Sons, 1891, p. 105. (Andrew J. Palm)

were completely inexperienced, especially in the smaller counties where hangings were not too frequent. There was simply no way for them to become inured to the ordeal. A story comes from New Hampshire where the sheriff from the county in which a man is sentenced to death must journey to the state prison with his victim and officiate at the hanging. On November 3, 1961, the following conversation took place at the home of the sheriff of Hillsboro County and a member of the staff of an Episcopal bi-monthly magazine. The sheriff had before him the task of hanging two persons who had been condemned to death:

Q. Sheriff, have you ever executed anyone before?
A. No.
Q. Have you ever assisted in an execution?
A. No.
Q. Have you ever seen a hanging?
A. No.
Q. Have you ever seen *any* kind of an execution?
A. No.
Q. Sheriff, have you ever studied any of the material available on this subject . . . the British or American Army manuals on hanging . . . the mathematical equations such as the formula whereby the weight of the body should be proportionate to the circumstances and length of the rope?
A. No. I really don't know much about it—maybe we can get a Canadian.
Q. Supposing you can't locate one?
A. I guess I'll have to learn.

The reporter then added the following:

I guess so—at least I hope so—desperately. I remember the large sheet which was recently installed in the execution chamber of the Washington State penitentiary at Walla Walla. The sheet, which hangs from the gallows platform to the floor, is designed to protect witnesses. At a recent hanging, the front row of witnesses was sprayed with blood from the severed jugular vein of a man whose head was nearly torn off. There are numerous records of complete decapitation in those [states] that still persist in this most gruesome of all four types of United States executions.[35]

---

[35]Quoted from *Concern,* Bi-monthly Journal of Opinion, New London, N.H., courtesy of the Rev. Lester Kinsolving; issue, November 17, 1961.

This small county sheriff, described by the reporter as "an elderly, soft-spoken, affable individual" was facing this double hanging but a few days off at the time of the interview (they were Russell Nelson and Fred Martineau, for kidnap-murder).

In our account of the era of public hangings, we described several instances in which the rope was either too long or too short and often snapped in two. These embarrassments continued during the later period and probably still do. Bungling, amateurism, defective ropes or other untoward incidents continued. A shocking case occurred in Washington, D.C., on April 2, 1880, at the hanging of James Madison Wyatt Stone for the murder of his estranged wife, Alberta. He was completely beheaded in the fall. The body fell to the ground while the head clung to the noose after which it dropped, spattering the beam with gore.[36]

A strange contrast was the equally shocking case, this time in Oregon, prior to that state's adoption of lethal gas in which a cripple had to be hanged. A special "sled" designed for the purpose carried him into the death chamber and the rope inadvertently caught on it in such a manner "that it gave sufficient support to enable an elongated strangulation which took twenty-three minutes—during which time the officials pondered the legality of either a shooting to end the victim's agonies—or running the legal risk of cutting him down."[37] This same source contends that not only decapitation sometimes happens but instances have been known in which the victim's "face has been torn off." And the source adds "at best there is always the chance of popped eyes, purple countenance, swollen tongue and exploded veins—but these are covered up by the black hood."

The hanging of Thomas H. (Black Jack) Ketchum at Clayton, Union County, New Mexico, on April 26, 1901, is just such a case. Ketchum, a notorious train-robber, was finally apprehended and condemned to death for that crime. He was shackled—he had lost a hand in an earlier robbery—and taken from the Santa Fe territorial prison in an armoured car to the place of execution. He was a heavy man, about two hundred pounds, and it can be as-

---

[36]See August Mencken, *By the Neck,* pp. 93-97.

[37]*Concern,* see *supra,* p. 175. Oregon, by referendum, abolished the death penalty in November, 1964.

sumed that the drop was not long enough for his weight. His head was literally torn from his body. Just before the gruesome drop, it is alleged the calloused outlaw waved to the crowd and shouted: "I'll be in hell before you can eat your dinner, boys" (courtesy Mr. Charles Zibulka, Spokane, Washington in material sent to the writers).

A shocking case of downright bungling was that of Robert Fogler, hanged at Washington, Pennsylvania, on May 15, 1867, a case in which the rope was too short. His victim was named Robert Dinsmore. The story of the bungling comes from the *New York World*, for May 17, with the headline reading: *Horrid Blundering of the Executioner:*

> In an instant the trap fell and the prisoner was suspended with his toes touching the ground. A cry of horror ran through the crowd. The sheriff regained his composure and called for assistance, when several men mounted the scaffold, but a strong nerved individual in the assemblage took the rope in his hands and actually held the quivering lump of flesh suspended some one foot from the ground while the sheriff and his deputies prepared the tackle to run it up again. For several minutes the body underwent severe contortions and death was far from being an easy one. His neck, it was afterwards discovered was not broken, and he died from strangulation.

One of the grimmest cases recorded was that of John Coffey who was put to death on October 16, 1886, at Crawfordsville, Indiana. Quoting again from Palm, who in turn uses a "newspaper" as his source, we read:

> The execution . . . yesterday was one of the most horrible affairs of its kind ever witnessed. When the drop fell, the *rope broke* and the body dropped to the ground. The neck was not broken, but the shock caused the blood to spurt from the wretched man's ears. He was carried back up the scaffold stairs, and, while the rope was being adjusted he regained consciousness and begged to have the cap removed and make another speech. This was refused and the drop fell again. The rope broke a second time, but the body was caught before it reached the ground. It was lifted up and held in place by deputy sheriffs while the noose was again adjusted, when the drop fell again.

The rope held and Coffee was slowly strangled to death, dying in twelve minutes. The spectators were overcome with horror.[38]

Palm supplies us with another bungling case—this time from Pennsylvania. It is the case of Andrew Tracy, a young lawyer of Smethport, McKean County. He was hanged December 4, 1879, for the murder of his cousin, Mary Riley, who refused to marry him. The execution was reported in the local paper, or, as Palm put it, by "the ever-present reporter [who] described the beautiful example—set by our law":

> Precisely at 1:45 the sheriff severed the rope that held the drop and Tracy fell with an awful thud. The knot had not been tied perfectly and the weight of the body caused it to slip out, and the prisoner fell through the drop, striking the stone floor, a distance of seven feet.
> Something like a groan went up from the spectators at this unexpected, horrible accident. Tracy struck on his feet, but in a second, his arms and legs being tied, toppled over on his head and struck the hard wall, relapsing into insensibility. The sheriff and attendants reached up and caught him, and raised him to his feet. Recovering his senses, Tracy exclaimed "I forgive my enemies" and continued to repeat the litany of his religion. While adjusting the rope a second time he fainted again, and was launched into eternity, unconscious of the means used.[39]

Charles Duff, in his *New Handbook of Hanging* tells the story of a bungled hanging at Amite, Louisiana, of six Italians on May 9, 1924, as revealed by an eye-witness, Clem Hearsey in his book entitled *The Six Who Were Hanged*. These men had been condemned to "die by the neck" for murder of one Dallas Calmes at Independence, Tangipahoa Parish. The story of this gory episode is herewith presented by Duff:

Captain Rennyson, accompanied by the hangman, known only as 'Joe the Hangman,' arrived from New Orleans with 100 feet of rope which had apparently been tested in the prison there. Joe is described as "a bowed man, with stiff sandy hair, short grey moustache, tobacco-stained, and fiercely bushy eyebrows, a sort

---

[38]Palm, *op. cit.,* pp. 103-104.
[39]Palm, *op. cit.,* p. 104.

of 'jack' carpenter and iron-worker. He is sixty-one years old, lives in Carrolton, and before hanging these six Italians had hanged ten or a dozen men in the Parish Prison at New Orleans." In a more gratuitous vein the writer states: "he is a butcherly worker, and has such little skill that his victims are lucky indeed if their necks break on the drop. He is calloused and hardened as is natural for a man of his trade and when on a 'job' must have a drink of whiskey (not unknown among hangmen, especially in earlier times) every now and then." The hangman began his grisly work. Whether or not he dispatched his unenviable task efficiently and in a humane manner, the reader must be the judge. The quote from the report is from Hearsey:

> The double rope was coiled in two lengths of fifty feet and fitted to the staples over the traps. Joe, his face hidden by his black mask, deftly made his nooses and retired to the kitchen where he clamoured for a drink of whiskey. All the whiskey that could be obtained had been given to the condemned men as occasional stimulants during the night just passed, and the hangman had to be content with strawberry wine. It was not to his palate . . .
>
> Three steps at a time the masked hangman ran up the gallows and first rushed to Deamore (one of the victims) to groom him for the hard passing. Deamore stood impassive as the hangman wrapped the strands of rope about his legs, and attached cords to his manacled wrists. Leona (another of the six) turned and watched the deathsman at his task . . . The two bodies fell, came up with a sudden jerk which visably stretched the neck several inches . . . It was clean, quick work from the hangman's standpoint.
>
> Giglio and Rini (the fifth and last victims) felt the summons before they heard it . . . The hangman crouched like an ugly poison spider between the two, raised his lever, and crash went the double trap . . . Rini hung motionless, but Giglio spun twice on the rope, and vented a deep and long-sustained groan as his chest heaved and his shoulders and arms were drawn up in an ugly movement. Giglio groaned again, and there was a wheezing gurgle in his throat as he gasped for breath. His chest rose and fell rapidly, and his wrists twisted and turned as though trying to free themselves of the manacles, but soon the body seemed

to stretch downwards and then it hung as motionless as Rini's
. . . the men were pronounced dead in less than fifteen minutes.

A description of the bodies, as they appeared later, on the train,
as they were taken from the death house to a point where they
could be claimed by their relatives:

> In the baggage car . . . going to New Orleans were six cof-
> fins and each contained the corpse of a hanged man. Deamore's
> neck was so swollen and distorted that the undertaker used
> more than a hundred pounds of ice to reduce the ugly folds of
> discolored flesh. The rope had mangled Deamore's neck, and
> had the drop been greater, the man's head might have been
> torn from his shoulders.

Duff, of course, considered the job done by "Joe the Hangman,"
as a very incompetent piece of work. As he states: "[He] was not
an artist but a very roughneck type of executioner. How he got
the job one cannot understand, unless it was by political influence. Nobody can say that this sort of thing and the mess made
of Deamore are good for hanging."[40]

Grim and disgusting though this bungling episode undoubtedly
was, it did not descend to the lowest depths of human depravity
that characterized an earlier episode involving Italians, in that
same city of New Orleans, some thirty-five years earlier—in 1890.
Eleven men of Italian stock were shot to death—lynched—in the
cells of the county jail by a mob deliberately called by a few
well-known citizens. These victims had stood trial earlier (on
December 11, 1890), for the murder of Chief of Police David C.
Hennessey, but none had been found guilty. They were awaiting
a new trial, amidst the disgust and anger of the community that
had been outraged because of what they deemed to be a lapse in
the administration of justice.

In broad daylight, the mob collected at Clay Square on that
fatal day and were addressed by "three of the leading lawyers of
the city who stated that the time had arrived when the people must

---

[40]Charles Duff, *op. cit.*, pp. 109-11; Louis Blake Duff (not to be confused with Charles
Duff), in *The Country Kerchief*, pp. 130-133, tells of another double hanging in
Louisiana that was badly botched; of Adam and Delisle, New Orleans the locale.
In Chapter I, we mentioned a satirical article on hanging as a profession. We refer
to it again: see Gerald Walker, "Young Man, Be An Executioner," *Esquire Magazine*,
August 1963, pp. 62-63.

administer justice themselves." They marched on the arsenal where shotguns and rifles were furnished and thence to the jail where doors were battered down in order to reach their victims. The following almost unbelievable statement was made by the mayor of the city, named S————. Upon being asked if he regretted the killing of the Italians "is said to have replied":

> No, Sir, I am an American citizen and I am not afraid of the devil. These men deserved killing and they were punished by peaceable and law-abiding citizens. They took the law into their own hands and we were forced to do the same.

President Harrison, acting for the responsible citizens of the United States, willingly paid a stiff indemnity to the Italian government for this shocking illegal mass lynching.[41]

Before passing on to our next section dealing with gallows tidbits, we wish to include the story of an unusual aftermath of a bungling episode as recorded by Paul Wellman, in his story of the murder of the distinguished citizen of Rock Island, Illinois, Col. George Davenport, in 1845.[42] When the three men who engineered the crime were hanged, one of them, Aaron Long, had to withstand the ordeal of witnessing the dangling and lifeless bodies of his two confederates—his own brother, John, and Granville Young. The rope which had been chosen by which to hang him had snapped at the scaffold. While a new one was being prepared, the hood was taken from his face and he heard the sonorous voice of the clergyman intone: "You see before you the dead bodies of your brother and Young. They have gone and you must soon follow. You have no hope of escape. If you are guilty, confess your guilt to God." It is further recorded that he confessed his guilt.[43]

GALLOWS TIDBITS

Even the devil is entitled to his "due," so hangmen and county sheriffs must be given the benefit of the doubt; they must have

---

[41]The above material is from Thomas S. Duke, *Celebrated Criminal Cases in America,* San Francisco, James H. Barry, Co., 1910, pp. 444-446.

[42]See Chapter VI, (p. 272) for story of the murder as found in Wellman's *Spawn of Evil,* New York, Doubleday, 1964, pp. 285-289.

[43]*Ibid,* pp. 331-332.

been (and still are) anxious to negotiate a successful hanging—one that is expeditiously dispatched with as little embarrassment as possible; one that causes the hangman no serious concern, no discomfort to witnesses, nor unfavorable news stories or editorials in the local press. We have a few asides on some successful executions: one at Reading, Pennsylvania (July 9, 1914), "was so successful that not a sound was heard" and, as an afterthought, "the rope was cut to pieces and distributed to the spectators." At the Gottlieb Williams hanging, at Philadelphia on June 4, 1897, it was reported: "There was no hangman dressed in prison garb with his head hid [sic] behind a mask . . . everything was conducted with the utmost propriety; but for the gallows which was in full view the purpose of the procession would scarcely have been divined."

Anxious as the sheriffs were to carry out a successful hanging, it is doubtful that any of them went so far as to ask for a testimonial from the attending physician. We find something of that sort in England, when the official executioner at the time, James Berry, received the following:

> I have never seen an execution more satisfactorily performed . . . This was gratifying to me.
> Your rope was of excellent quality; fine, soft, pliable and strong. You adjusted the ring [the noose] directed forward in the manner in which I have recommended in my pamphlet, *Judicial Hanging.* You gave a sufficient length of drop, considering the weight of the culprit, [Peter Cassidy, hanged on September 2, 1884] and completely dislocated the cervical vertebrae between the atlas and the axis—the first and second vertebrae. . . . The pinioning and other details were carried out with due decorum. (Signed James Barr, M.D.)[44]

For an economical hanging, we have the following "exhibit." The first and only hanging to take place in Pike County, Pennsylvania (county seat, Milford) occurred on December 7, 1897, when Herman Paul Schultz was executed for the murder of his wife, Lizzie. The occurrence was conspicuous, at least, if not notorious for its economy and probably has few, if any, equals in

---

[44]Justin Atholl, *op. cit.,* p. 153.

that category: "District Attorney Van Auker received $14, defense attorney J. H. Vanetten, nothing; the sheriff's fee was $15 but as he paid $10 for the noose, he will net only $5; the county received $15 from the Anatomy Board for the body which will pay the sheriff's fee."[45]

Most of our tidbits of hanging lore come from the Commonwealth of Pennsylvania. It is our studied opinion, however, that much of what we have learned from that state can be duplicated in most, if not all, of the other states through the years.

Earlier, we stated that fragments of ropes used in hanging were highly prized. Sometimes they were given away by the sheriffs, sometimes sold, and sometimes merely preempted by zealous spectators. Sometimes, of course, officials would deny this ghoulish hawking on the part of the rabble. In one case in Schuylkill County (Pottsville), on March 12, 1908, "some of the several hundreds in the prison yards made a rush for the death rope, pieces of which were distributed to the lucky; the carnation he [the victim] wore was sent to a member of the deathwatch; pennies, pins, and other trifles were taken as souvenirs."[46]

The frenzy for souvenirs of the occasion of a hanging sometimes took a strange twist. We found in the early archives of New York City, the execution of a so-called traitor, Jacob Leisler, on May 16, 1691. He was actually a Popist, a follower of William and Mary, and was charged and convicted of "treason." After the hanging, his followers cut his clothing to pieces and "his hair was divided as the precious relics of a martyr."[47]

Often, small sums were charged the public to view the body after the victim was "turned off." The proceeds went either to the members of the family or were used to defray the cost of the funeral. For example, in the William Hummel case (Lycoming County, Pennsylvania, June 5, 1900), "the sheriff charged a dime to look at the culprit after he had been sentenced [and hanged]; feeling ran so high against him that he was hanged in effigy."[48] In

[45]See Teeters, *Scaffold & Chair,* 1963, p. 135.

[46]Pottsville *Republican,* March 12; the victim of the gallows was Charles Werzel.

[47]So stated by Peleg W. Chandler, *American Criminal Trials,* Vol. I, "Leisler's Rebellion," pp. 265-6, Boston, Timothy Carter, 1842.

[48]Williamsport *Gazette & Bulletin,* June 6.

a case at Carlisle, Cumberland County, same state, "thousands of persons crowded the entrance of the jail; bystanders paid a nickel each to view the body and the money was used to bury him" (Charles Salyard, hanged March 1, 1894).[49] A bizarre incident occurred in the Frank Calhoun hanging at Huntingdon, Pennsylvania, on May 8, 1915. After the hanging, in order to satisfy the curiosity of the public his body was placed "in the window of a furniture store next door to the undertaker's establishment."[50]

In the mass hangings of six Mollie Maguires at Pottsville, Pennsylvania, on June 21, 1877, when the first contingent of that terroristic society met their doom, "fully 3,000 men and women and even little girls with school books under their arms wandered into the jail yard to see the scaffold."[51]

LAST REQUESTS OF THE CONDEMNED

It is only recently that anyone has attempted to collect (if not to analyze) the last thoughts, actions, and requests of the condemned. The noted German criminologist, Hans von Hentig, has made a study of these, at least in earlier eras, in his book *Von Ursprung der Hankersmahlzen* (concerning the victim's last meal, favor, request, etc.). He covers such items as last meals, drinks, boutonniere, kind words and other whimsies. He also refers to the condemned asking for forgiveness or for abjectly asking for punishment, uttering praise of, or imprecations upon, the hangman or the witnesses. One of the cases murmured (probably apocryphal), as he was being led to the gallows: "This is going to be a lesson to me."[52]

We occasionally find just the reverse of such requests. At Salt Lake City, Utah, one Joe Hill, or Hillstrom, was about to be led to his doom (shot, not hanged) for the murder of a small-time grocer and his son, in the act of robbing the establishment. Hill had become something of a martyr among the more radical labor

---

[49]*The American Volunteer*, Carlisle, March 7.

[50]Stated in a letter from a local resident to the writer.

[51]See Chapter IX, for the story.

[52]Tuebingen, Germany: J.C.B. Mohr, 1958; as the American reviewer, Hans A. Illing (*Federal Probation*, June 1959, p. 75) states: "A wide range of human emotions and situations is covered, both from ancient and modern times."

elements of the area, so that almost every movement of his in the jail and every detail of the case was followed in the press. On the day of the execution, November 19, 1915, the prison physician said to Hill: "You have a pretty stiff ordeal ahead of you . . . How about a slug of whiskey?" Hill answered: "I don't want no whiskey. I ain't never drunk the stuff and I don't intend to start now." Remarked the doctor wryly: "Perhaps you're right, Joe. It might be habit forming."[53]

The preceding case, focused around a notorious labor leader, made the creation of a ballad almost inevitable. Part of it is hereby appended:

> I dreamed I saw Joe Hill last night,
> Alive as you and me.
> Says I, "But Joe, you're ten years dead!"
> "I never died," says he,
> "I never died," says he.[54]

Another story about a last-minute request, again probably apocryphal, is the English victim of the noose who asked not to be "turned off" on the coming Monday, as it would "be such a terrible way to start a week."

Some last-minute requests indicate a braggadocio not compatible with the solemnity and "permanence" of the occasion. Alan J. Adams stood on the scaffold at Northampton, Massachusetts, on April 16, 1881, as the sheriff was about to read his death warrant for the murder of Moses Dickinson at Amherst "about Thanksgiving Day, 1875." His reaction to this sober but necessary ritual was "Damned if I care what you read; you had better go get yourself a drink to steady your nerves."[55] Jack Allen, hanged at Monticello, New York, July 20, 1888, asked for a drink of whiskey on the scaffold. On being refused, he placed the noose about his neck and gave the signal, "Let 'er go, Gallagher!"[56]

Then there is the bizarre case of Pat Harnett, hanged in the

---

[53]Olive Woolley Burt, *American Murder Ballads,* New York, Oxford University Press, 1958, p. 96.

[54]*Ibid.,* p. 95.

[55]Quoted by Palm, *op. cit.,* p. 105.

[56]*Ibid.,* p. 105.

Ohio State Prison, at Columbus, on September 13, 1885. The night before the event, he was asked if he would like to go up on the wall and look at his last sunset. He accepted the offer and "gazed at it intently for some time, and a halo lit the sky; the attendants expected to hear some expression of regret or sentiment; but they were shocked to hear him say: 'When that sun goes down again I shall be flying about among the little angels.' "[57] But Harnett, at that moment, could not have anticipated the botch that would be made of his hanging. As Andrew Palm tells the story:

> The rope allowed a fall of more than seven feet, and one of the most sickening and revolting scenes in the history of Ohio executions followed. As the body dropped to a standstill, a heavy gurgling sound was heard, and soon the blood in torrents commenced pouring on the stone floor below. The black cap was raised slightly and it was found that decapitation was almost complete, the head hanging to the body by a small piece of skin at the back of the neck. During the half minute or more that the heart beat, the blood was thrown against the platform above from the gash caused by the head being pulled back on the shoulder. The strong men who had charge of the execution turned to avoid the scene, and stood fixed for a time, looking each other in the eye. Finally Coroner Carrick, more thoughtful than the rest, though unable to speak above a whisper, called for help to take the body down before it should disconnect from the head and fall. The heavy clothing of the murderer had by this time become soaked and running with blood from every wrinkle and seam. Those who lifted it up until the rope could be untied were smeared with blood, and as the body was lowered to the pools of gore below, the gasping trunk was exposed in all its horror.[58]

There can be little doubt that many last-minute requests have been made, but most have been lost to posterity. Wardens and sheriffs have kept their own counsel regarding many of these, since so often they were pathetically intimate and personal. On occasions, however, we learn of a request that bears preservation. Clinton Duffy tells of one he received from an obscure Chinese

---

[57]*Ibid.*, p. 102.
[58]*Ibid.*, p. 103.

named Leong Fook, scheduled for the gallows on April 5, 1929, in the San Quentin Sash and Blind shop, where it reposed at the time. A resident of Tulare County, he had murdered his landlady, Jean Leong Gat. For months prior to his execution, this impassive Oriental had maintained a stony indifferent silence, speaking to no one, asking no favors, nor apparently giving any concern to his impending doom. But after being transferred to the "holding cell" the day before, he suddenly began screaming and calling for the warden. After much persuasion to communicate what was troubling him, he suddenly blurted out that he wanted his dentures and eye glasses to be placed in the coffin with his body as he could make use of them in the hereafter. This unusual, but understandable request was, of course granted him.[59]

DRESS AT THE GALLOWS

In our earlier section dealing with public hangings, we made no references to the garb or clothing worn by those sent to the hanging "trcc." This was because we found no special mention of this matter in news items or records. However, McDade states that in the early years, the victim "often wore a white shroud." He continues: "When William F. Hooe was hanged at Fairfax Court House, Virginia, on July 3, 1826, he was dressed in a long white shroud and white gloves; his face was entirely concealed by a long loose white cap, over which he wore a black fur hat." The shroud had a functional use, as it covered the victim's arms and hands so that they could not be raised to obtain relief from the rope when the drop was made. Later, leather pinions or, in some instances, mere cloth restraints, were used to prevent freedom of such movements. McDade adds: "The trimming in black on the cap had some significance for James Reynolds, hanged in New York City (November 19, 1825), was clad in white trousers, white frock, and a cap of the same material trimmed in black." (Reynolds murdered Capt. W. M. West, owner of a freighter on which he was employed. He killed his victim and threw the body into the river tied to a large stone. He attributed his ruin to "the company who lured him to houses of ill-fame.") McDade states

---

[59]Duffy, *Op. cit.*, p. 58.

that the shroud seems to have disappeared before the middle of the nineteenth century and that donations of hanging suits came sometimes from unexpected sources. He cites the case of John W. Cowan, hanged at Cincinnati, Ohio, for the murder of his wife and two children, on October 10, 1835. He was presented with a black suit for the occasion by "some gentlemen of the Ohio Medical College." Of course he had compensated for this by signing over his body for scientific purposes and dissection.[60]

Many of our Pennsylvania gallows victims insisted on going to their doom dressed in sartorial splendor. Many idiosyncracies were noted during the period of private, county jail hangings. We may start with the case of Matthias Stupinsky, hanged in Philadelphia August 6, 1852 (with his brother Blaise), for the murder of a young jewelry peddler. He was "dressed in a blue frock coat, black pants, and black silk vest."[61] A few years later, again in Philadelphia, in the same Moyamensing Prison, Peter Mattocks (hanged May 23, 1856) was "clad in a white flannel shroud open in front, with a white muslin turban, ornamented by himself with bows of white ribbon."[62] William Seeley Hopkins, hanged at Bellefonte, Centre County, Pennsylvania on February 20, 1890, wore "a black cutaway coat, dark striped trousers, patent leather shoes, standup collar and a white tie." This case is of interest for several reasons. He killed his mother-in-law and his wife, Maggie, on September 21, 1889. He lived with his in-laws and constantly quarreled with them. He accused his wife of infidelity so on the night of the murder he slept in the cellar. As his wife prepared breakfast, he sneaked upstairs and shot her. Next he went to the bedroom of his mother-in-law and shot her. At the execution the rope broke twice; the jail was crowded. After the murder, he tried suicide twice but he went to the gallows in a paralyzed state; he was stoical at the hanging and encouraged the sheriff's deputies "who faltered at their grim task."

Perhaps the most splendid person to be hanged in Pennsylvania, at least, was John "Jack" Kehoe, a powerful member of the Mollie

---

[60]McDade, *op. cit.,* p. xxxi. (Hooe, a gambler, was badly in need of funds, enticed his victim, William Simpson, to a lonely road near Centreville, Virginia and shot him.)

[61]Philadelphia *Public Ledger,* August 7.

[62]*Ibid.,* May 24, 1856.

Maguires, a terroristic group whose story we shall relate later (See Chapter IX, pages 390-393). Kehoe was hanged at Pottsville, Schuylkill County, on December 18, 1878. He wore "a garrick—an overcoat and cape combined—over his shoulders, glistening new patent leather slippers and a flower in his lapel." After the execution, "the body was cut down and placed in a handsome coffin and sent to his home at Girardsville on a special train placed at the disposal of his relatives."[63] It was not unusual for victims of the gallows to wear flowers in their buttonholes—usually carnations.

Impeccable dressers at the gallows could be found in all states. The Knapp brothers—John Francis hanged at Salem, Massachusetts on September 29, 1830 and his brother, Joseph, Jr. on December 31, 1830, wore expensive outfits. The former was dressed "genteely in a dark frock coat and pantaloons, black silk vest and boots." The latter was "very neatly dressed in a dark cloth frock coat, blue pantaloons, light vest, boots, etc." He also "had a white handkerchief in the breast pocket of his coat which he took in his hand and held there till his death," despite the fact that his arms were pinioned in the conventional and required fashion. The Salem newspaper expressed hope that few, if any, females would attend the executions of these brothers, but it was forced to admit that of the 4,000 or so spectators there were many females present; but it added "a very small proportion of these were inhabitants of the town." Later, it expressed satisfaction that at the hanging of the second brother—three months after the first—the number of the fair sex was "greatly reduced."[64]

The gay Lothario dresser in Minnesota was Harry Hayward who was hanged at Minneapolis, on December 11, 1895, for the ruthless murder of Kitty Ging.[65] He was attired in a fashionable cutaway coat and pinstriped trousers as he walked to the gallows.[66]

---

[63]*Miner's Journal*, Pottsville, Pennsylvania, December 19, 1878.

[64]Edmund Pearson, *Murder at Smutty Nose*, New York, The Sun Dial Press, 1926, "The Salem Conspiracy," 173-189, at 186 and 187; see our discussion of this famous case, Chapter VI, p. 269.

[65]See Chapter VI, p. 273 for our discussion of this case.

[66]See Walter N. Trenerry, *Murder in Minnesota*, Saint Paul, Minnesota Historical Society, 1962, p. 153.

However, no Beau Brummel's hanging wear could begin to compare with that of the Earl Ferrers (Laurence Shirley) hanged at Tyburn, May 5, 1760. He wore a white satin suit—his wedding suit—and was pinioned with a black silk sash. We mentioned earlier that he was hanged with a silken cord.[67]

MASS KILLERS

There have been innumerable examples of mass murder in this country and some of such gruesome episodes have passed without the perpetrators being brought to book. Generally, this is due to the culprits having fled and never been captured or because evidence has not been sufficient to initiate court proceedings. Two notorious mass killers who cannot come within the purview of this work are Belle Gunness, of LaPorte, Indiana, and the Bender family, of near Parsons, Labette County, Kansas. In neither case were the guilty parties apprehended. Briefly, however, the former represented a kind of early "lonely heart" scheme by which Belle Gunness enticed her victims to her farm through newspaper advertisements, and then murdered them for what money they possessed.[68]

The Bender family murdered travelers who stopped at their farm-house-inn during the 1870's. These were lonely, frontier times and the area was also lonely. The perverted leader of this totally-perverted family was the daughter, Kate, who claimed to be a healer of sorts and so advertised her gifts in the newspapers. When the law attempted to close in on the nefarious deeds of this family of murderers, they fled to parts unknown. Some think they were apprehended and disposed of by irate neighbors.[69]

The two female Bluebeards, Belle Gunness and Kate Bender, escaped the noose, but their male counterpart Johann Hoch whose exploits we now review, met that fate in Chicago, on February 23, 1906.

---

[67]Horace Bleackley, *The Hangmen of England,* London, Chapman & Hall, 1929, p. 102.

[68]For details of this macabre story, see Stewart Holbrook, *Murder Out Yonder,* New York, Macmillan, 1941, Chapter VII, "Belle of Indiana," pp. 126-144; also Thomas S. Duke, *Celebrated Criminal Cases In America,* San Francisco, James H. Barry Co., 1910, pp. 437-443, section entitled "Mrs. Belle Gunness, The Arch-Fiend who Required a Private Graveyard for her Numerous Victims but who was Subsequently Murdered and Cremated with her Three Children." Belle's ghastly deeds took place in the early 1900's.

[69]For the story of this murdering clan, see Thomas S. Duke, *Celebrated Criminal Cases of America,* 1910, pp. 348-353. "The Hideous Murders Committed by the Bender Family in Kansas"; McDade, *op. cit.,* 97-98.

Hoch was born in Strasburg, Germany, in 1860. His father and two brothers were ministers and he, too, was educated for some laudable career. He abandoned the idea and emigrated to the United States. In due time, he settled in Philadelphia where, on October 20, 1904, he married Caroline Streicher. Tiring of this woman in the short period of eleven days, he took leave of Philadelphia and wandered to Chicago where he registered at the hotel-home of a Mrs. Kate Bowers. Borrowing some money from a bank, on nothing but his word that he represented Armour & Co., he purchased a cottage "for him and his wife." Next he inserted an advertisement in a local German-language paper, to wit:

> Matrimonial: German; owns home; wishes acquaintance of widow without children; object, matrimony; Address M. 422 Abend Post, December 3, 1904.

Marie Walcker, a hard-working forty-six-year-old divorcee answered the ad as follows:

> Dear Sir: In answer to your honorable advertisement I hereby inform you that I am a lady standing alone. I am forty-six and have a small business, also a few hundred dollars. If you are in earnest I tell you I shall be. I may be seen at 12 Willow St.
> Marie Walcker

Marie operated a small candy shop to which Johann Hoch made haste. In a short time, they procured a license and were duly married. Thus, Hoch became a bigamist. He also became possessor of the trusting female's savings. Mrs. Walcker had a sister, Mrs. Fischer, who had a saving account of close to $900. Soon Mrs. Hoch became violently ill and died. The physician diagnosed her ailment as "nephritis and cystitis." But it soon developed that the trusting wife had been given arsenic by Hoch. She died January 12, 1905. When the sister became suspicious, sometime later, she notified the Chicago police and Hoch was arrested. However, this action did not materialize until the "Bluebeard" Hoch had disposed of a dozen females. He was tried and convicted of the murder of Mrs. Walcker and subsequently hanged.[70]

---

[70]For details, see Duke, *op. cit.*, pp. 431-437; see also, Edward H. Smith, *Famous American Poison Mysteries*, London, Hurst & Blackett, Ltd., 1927, "The Stockyards Bluebeard," pp. 92-106.

The Infamous Mudgett — Alias H. H. Holmes

On May 7, 1896, in Philadelphia's Moyamensing Prison, the most amazing mass killer of them all—that is, Herman Webster Mudgett, alias H. H. Holmes—was hanged for the murder of an obscure man named Benjamin F. Pitezel, his erstwhile partner in a confidence game. It was merely by chance that this fantastic person was tried for murder in Philadelphia and that the crime on the indictment was for the murder of his partner, rather than for any one of his many other victims.

One hardly knows just where to begin telling the story of the man Mudgett-Holmes. The literature, none of it definitive nor carefully compiled, is prodigious, but it is widely scattered and confusing so far as fact and fiction are concerned. For instance, the number of his victims ranges from a few to over a hundred, if we may judge from the pamphlets published concerning his almost unbelievable exploits. One of the most widely-circulated, published by that indefatigable purveyor of murder stories, E. E. Barclay, of Philadelphia and Cincinnati, is entitled *Holmes the Arch-Fiend, or a Carnival of Crime . . . Twenty-Seven Lives Sacrificed to the Monstrous Ogre's Insatiable Appetite* (1896).

Who was this arch-fiend, monstrous ogre, and mass killer? Born Herman Webster Mudgett, in 1861, he was a native of the small town of Gilmanton, New Hampshire, the alleged locale of "Peyton Place." He studied medicine at the Universities of Vermont and Michigan but obtained no degrees at either institution. Later he gravitated to the Chicago area around the time of the Columbian World's Fair. Not being too faithful to the institution of marriage, he early became a bigamist, so that as we review his exploits, we find his love life obscure, labyrinthian, and confused in most of its details.

He found employment in the Englewood section of the city as a drug clerk and with his winning and "taking" ways, he soon took over the business which was owned by a trusting female named Holden. She merely disappeared; disappearance of persons affiliated with Mudgett, or H. H. Holmes, the name he invariably went by (no one knows what the initials denoted), became the paramount element in his truly zany career. How many persons who disappeared were murdered, there is no way of knowing. It is because of the disappearance of so many persons that the figure of one hundred or more is sometimes used to signify his high murder rate.

The strange metamorphosis that turned a soft-spoken drug clerk into an "ogre" or "Bluebeard" who built a murder "castle" in Englewood is one of the many mysteries of this case. We know that sometime after he disposed of his druggist employer, he made contact with girls and young women who, in turn, also disappeared. Probably to facilitate these disappearances, Holmes proceeded to build himself a structure at 63rd and Wallace Sts. in Chicago, ostensibly to "let out" rooms to persons visiting the World's Fair. The building, or hotel, was cunningly designed; probably no other building was ever erected that was so bizarre and uncanny in its appointments. We learn through published pamphlets, which came later, that "it was a nightmarish conglomeration of trapdoors, sliding panels, secret stairways, soundproof rooms, torture chambers, an operating room with a butcher's table, a crematory with vats of acid and quicklime to dispose of his victims." When the castle was raided, the place was found to be filled with "scores of bodies, parts of bodies in various degrees of decomposition." Most, if not all, were of females. It was his practice to hire "sweet young things" to serve as receptionists and secretaries, and, in short order, to dispose of them.

They may have been murdered and their bodies "sent down the chute" to the cellar abattoir—or that is what it appeared to be—where dissection and an acid bath awaited them. This part of the Mudgett-Holmes tale is almost unbelievable but, in general, is true. His objective has never been precisely defined. One rumor is that he prepared cadavers for anatomists. But fact and legend are so closely intertwined that thus far, no definitive work on this man's incredible career has emerged.

One description of Holmes's castle refers to the "forty rooms on the second floor" where he had his personal quarters, "with hinged walls with no doors or windows, dead-end passages, black closets, dummy elevators and a couple of 'slick' chutes into the basement." His neighbors, once friendly, gradually became suspicious of the sly but mysterious "goings-on" and this easily turned to anger, as Holmes continued his blatant activities. At the height of their anger and frustration, he was in Philadelphia where he overstepped himself by commiting an obvious, open and above-board murder. Back in Chicago, his "friends," marched on his castle—actually, they charged rather than marched—and burned it "to the ground." This was on the night of August 19, 1895.

The downfall of this strange creature came by way of the "murder for insurance" route. It is believed he illicitly obtained the legacies of some of his young female victims, as well as others. Pitezel, the partner he murdered, was certainly involved in some of his financial machinations. Yet the "ogre" not only killed him, but had earlier disposed of three of the man's children. A Philadelphia detective later found their bodies buried in cellars of houses as far apart as Irvington, Indiana, and Toronto, Canada.

The trial and hanging of Holmes-Mudgett were Philadelphia sensations. He was defended by distinguished trial lawyers and, of course, denied his guilt to the end. He claimed he had never killed anyone—except two young women in illegal operations—that he knew nothing about the Pitezel children's deaths. At the gallows, he showed remarkable courage. The news stories stated that "he died as he had lived, a man of incomparable coolness and assurance." One paper put it in the following words: "This frail, pale man with the quiet manner and the soft cultured accent of speech, walked to his death as if to a business or social engagement." Apparently due to an inordinate fear of the dissecting table —with which he was so familiar—he asked to be buried in cement, a request which was granted.

Cement was poured into the rough-box coffin and his body placed therein just as it was rolled from the gallows in Moyamensing Prison. He was buried in a Catholic cemetery in one of the city's suburbs. The contemporary press was full of news and features about this amazing but socially perverted man who, without doubt, was the "criminal of the century." He held many interviews with citizens and reporters and to the last conferred on a professional and friendly basis with his lawyers. One gets the impression that Holmes possessed great personal magnetism that appealed both to males and females.

Two of the more reliable works dealing with the case are Frank P. Geyer's *The Holmes-Pitezel Case*: *History of the Greatest*

Crime of the Century and of the Search of the Missing Pitezel Children (Philadelphia, 1896) and George T. Bizel's *The Trial of H. H. Holmes for the Murder of Benjamin Pitezel"* (1897).[71]

Thomas McDade, in his *The Annals of Murder,* has this to say about the Holmes case, in part: "To those Americans who take special pride in native talent and industry, it may be comforting to know that Herman W. Mudgett, our greatest mass murderer, was of good Yankee lineage . . . No period of his life seems to have been free of deceit, fraud, misrepresentation, or chicanery of some sort . . . The full toll of his victims will never be known but it was surely over a score." He then adds: "There is no adequate full-length study of this extraordinary criminal."[72]

Edward H. Rulloff — Professor Edward Leurio

After one reads of the amazing criminal career of Edward H. Rulloff, murderer, burglar, philologist, "scientist," confidence man, kidnaper, etc., he must come to the conclusion that here was no ordinary man and, further, to venture the appraisal that he, like Mudgett-Holmes with whom he must compete for dubious criminal honors, was a "sociopath" or psychopath.

Barclay, the publisher who had a penchant for turning out stories of murders, real and imaginary, refers to Rulloff as "the perpetrator of eight murders, numerous burglaries and other crimes . . . a man shrouded in mystery! A learned ruffian! Was he man or fiend?" This man's amazing career which ended on the gallows at Binghamton, New York, on May 18, 1871, is well related by Stewart H. Holbrook in his fascinating work, *Murder Out Yonder.*[73]

The criminal episodes in his life as Rulloff vie with his pseudo-scientific activities as Professor Edward Leurio, philologist and word-designer, linguist and "Master of the Universal Language." Born Edward Howard Ruloffson, in 1819, near St. John, New Brunswick, of Dutch ancestry, we find him first in the small town

---

[71]See also, John Bartlow Martin, *Chicago Murders,* edited by Sewell Peasley Wright, Duell, Sloane & Pearce, 1945; Charles Bowell, *The Girls in Nightmare House,* New York, Gold Medal Books, 1955; Herbert Asbury, *Gem of the Prairie,* New York, Knopf, in Chapter VI, "The Mansion on Sixty-Third Street," Asbury has a picture of the "castle" and of a likeness of Holmes, p. 179.

[72]McDade, *op. cit.,* (item) 703.

[73]New York, Macmillan, 1941.

of Dryden, Tompkins County, New York, in 1842, working as a laborer on a canal. He was affable, intelligent, and friendly. In September of that year, he was offered the position of teacher in a small private school in the town. Testimony indicates that he was an excellent teacher, possessing the capacity of stimulating his young scholars. Especially did a charming sixteen-year-old girl find Rulloff not only erudite but scintillating. She was Harriet Schutt, member of a large and respectable family of the small community. It seemed to be love at first sight, and, despite opposition from her family, she married him a year or so later.

With marriage, Rulloff dropped his teaching and became "Dr." Rulloff, botanical-physician and herbist. His young wife soon found that the charming young school master had his dark side. He was arrogant, moody and high strung on occasions. Within a year, the young "doctor" took his wife to Lansing, not far from Lake Cayuga, where Rulloff's' phony medical practice began to thrive. A child was born to the couple in 1845, but it seems that the "physician" had little time for his newborn infant or his wife. In some mysterious manner, Rulloff "disposed" of his dependents, actually, as it was learned later, by killing them and sending their weighted bodies to the bottom of the lake.

Thus began a cat-and-mouse game between the wily Rulloff and the wife's relatives, neighbors and friends. "Where were his wife and child," they asked. "Gone visiting—out to Ohio," answered Rulloff. But the law caught up with him, albeit with few clues to go on. The victims had vanished, it was true, but as there was no *corpus delicti,* he could not be tried for murder. Lake Cayuga had been dragged but no bodies were found. Rulloff, however, was tried for abduction and was convicted. He received a ten-year sentence in the Auburn State Prison.

This resourceful and amazing man permitted not a day nor an hour to pass without absorbing new knowlege or demonstrating before admiring staff and convicts his erudition. In the carpet factory where he worked, he designed new patterns, both intricate and artistic. He studied in his cell whenever he had free time. In short, he took advantage of every available hour, served his time and was released a free man.

The authorities were again attempting to prosecute Rulloff for murder, but with no *corpus delicti,* the conviction obtained could not stand up before a higher court. While awaiting the decision of that higher court, Rulloff escaped from jail, assisted by the deputy-sheriff's son. The clever Rulloff fled to Meadville, Pennsylvania, where he applied to Allegheny College for a teaching position. Such was not available but he was given *entree* to certain academic circles and for a time he showed off his learning not in philology but in certain scientific areas—the result of his incarceration at Auburn prison!

Getting into some embarrassment at Meadville, which was inevitable, Rulloff took off and wandered to New York City and Brooklyn, where he "tied in" with a couple of ex-convicts named Dexter and Jarvis, the latter was the deputy sheriff's son who had assisted him in absconding from jail. This New York period (1865-70) is supposed to have been the heyday of this fantastic man's career. He became three different persons, maintaining three different establishments. He endeavored, in his own strange way, to be respectable, although at the same time he was living off the ill-gotten loot from his convict friends whom he controlled. As his other self, "he lectured and taught languages, word structure, philology and word building, in his various haunts and was known at 170 Third Avenue, Manhattan, as Professor Edward Leurio, master of twenty-eight languages."

Arch criminal though Rulloff undoubtedly was, his delusions of grandeur were sincere. He was determined to be a great scholar, despite the fact that his background could never establish such a status. He had to fail, but death alone would have to intervene before such a fate would be realized.

At this period in his life, Rulloff (Leurio) habitually dressed in frock coat and silk hat. He was the great philologist and tried desperately to gain recognition before the American Philolological Association. At its annual meeting, at Poughkeepsie, in 1869, Rulloff-Leurio was permitted to present his project before the members. Later, when he asked the Society to publish his work, he was told that it did not come within the scope of the Association. True to his psychopathic disposition, Rulloff was enraged. Back in New York City, he confided to his burglar friends that they needed funds badly and, for some strange reason, they de-

cided to rob a silk shop in Binghamton. On the night of August
21, 1870, his two henchmen entered Halbert Bros. store on Court
Street. Rulloff, in his ubiquitous frock coat, was the lookout. Two
clerks, Gilbert Burroughs and Frederick Merrick, were asleep in
the store but were awakened by the stealthy noise of the intruders.
They saw the burglars piling silk bolts upon the counters and
rushed them. A shot rang out and Merrick fell dead; Burroughs
was wounded. Afterward the wounded clerk testified that the man
with the revolver was Rulloff, dressed in a silk hat and frock coat,
wearing a black beard.

The three fled; Rulloff's two associates drowned as they attempted to swim the Chenango River. The "master," Rulloff, who
made his getaway, was finally apprehended and identified by the
fact that his left foot had no big toe; he had once been obliged to
cut it off himself! He went on trial, January 5, 1871, was found
guilty of the murder of Merrick and sentenced to death. Even as
he awaited hanging, he became something of a sensation. He
busied himself with his "universal method" of language which had
always been close to his heart. New York celebrities paid him
notice. Horace Greeley had some contact with him and the city
newspapers referred to him as the "Learned Murderer." At least
one volunteer offered to be hanged in his stead.

It is alleged that Rulloff spent his last night alternately boasting
of his achievements and in blasphemy and obscenity. He refused
any religious comfort and "was hanged in front of the jail" at Binghamton, on the appointed day, May 18, 1871.

He had told his counsel earlier that he did kill his wife and baby
in 1845; beat them to death with an iron pipe and wrapped their
bodies with steel wire, attached a heavy piece of mortar to his
wife's body and a flatiron to that of the child, put them in a chest
and dumped their bodies into Lake Cayuga from a rowboat.

Thomas McDade, in abstracting the remarkable career of this
strange creature makes this statement relative to his end: "As no
one claimed his remains, a Dr. George Burr was permitted to remove his head for study, and there were many comparisons of
Rulloff's brain with those of Daniel Webster and Thackeray, to
the disadvantage of the latter. His brain, which found a final rest-
ing place in Cornell University, fared better that the rest of his

remains, which disappeared after they were dug up by body snatchers."[74]

In comparing Rulloff with Herman Webster Mudgett, we find them similar in most respects. They must have been totally amoral; neither would tolerate interference with his selfish plans. Those who do not recognize such a clinical entity as sociopathy may manufacture their own to fit these two strange human beings.[75]

The Robert McConaghy Case — Huntingdon, Pennsylvania

In the little mountain town of Huntingdon, Pennsylvania, on November 6, 1840, Robert McConaghy, sometimes referred to as a "butcher" of human beings, paid the penalty of death by hanging. He had been convicted for the mass killing of the William Brown family, all of whom were his kinsfolk. In an outburst of pent-up hatred and fury, he choked, shot, or beat to death his mother-in-law, Rosanna, referred to as "the old woman," and her five children (his wife's brothers and sisters) ranging in age from ten to twenty-one, and then shot his father-in-law who fortunately survived his wounds. The human slaughter took place in broad daylight on May 30. Several pamphlets were published concerning this crime, one by the officiating ministers. At the gallows, the rope broke, and not until that moment did McConaghy confess his crime. He was, of course, promptly hanged with a second rope which is always in reserve.[76]

Excerpts from the sentence pronounced by the presiding judge state: "Your case is without parallel in criminal jurisprudence [words so often stated in American courts] . . . John, a young man in the vigor of manhood—twenty-one—you by falsehood and cunning brought to his father's dwelling, and the moment he reached it, from your covert, you sent a rifle ball through his breast; Elizabeth and Jacob—seventeen and fourteen—you early on the fatal day seduced from their mother's side and through the brain of the latter you sent a rifle ball and the skull of the former you beat in with stones. George and David—sixteen and ten—you

---

[74]McDade, *op. cit.*, p. 249, item 835.
[75]Sources: much of the above material is from Holbrook, *op. cit.*, pp. 145-168.
[76]*Ibid.* 645-7.

entrapped in a different direction; the former you treacherously disabled by a strike from your gun, and then you probably shot him and cut his throat. The child David fled; you sent a rifle ball after him . . . you then followed the child, seized and choked him until his life was extinct. You returned to the house and there your aged mother-in-law was engaged in baking and you struck her senseless; then cut her throat. You covered her up in bed. And then, with your rifle you went into the barn to await the arrival of John; and, in reaching his father's dwelling you killed him. You dragged him under his mother's bed—washed up the floor—then returned to your hiding place in the barn . . .to await the return of your father-in-law. You took the handle off his door and when he came to it, he could not find entrance; he turned partly around looking for his wife and you fired and missed him. You took up your other weapon of death and fired and slightly wounded him. His eagle eye saw you; and you fled in his presence from your hiding place. For barbarity, treachery and depravity, your cruelty and wickedness have not been surpassed by the pirates of the West Indies or the savages of the wilderness."

Samuel Mohawk — Cornplanter Indian — Butler, Pennsylvania

Had the judge who invoked those fearful words that appear above, in connection with the McConaghy case, been around four years later he would have seen another similar case—one that matched the brutality of his charge. It was the case of a Cornplanter Indian named Samuel Mohawk who, in a drunken frenzy, murdered Mrs. James Wigton and her five children at Slippery Rock, Butler County, Pennsylvania, on June 30, 1843. Mohawk had been born on the Cattaraugus reservation in New York State and had attended a Quaker school. He killed his victims, one by one, with a stone. At his execution, which took place at Butler on March 22, 1844, the husband and father of the victims was present —but not inside. He wrote that "he and a great crowd filled the town and crowded the walls of the jail but did not notice Mohawk drop but did see the body on the gallows."[77] If there was the

---

[77]From the Butler *Eagle,* sesquicentennial edition, July 1, 1950.

slightest extenuating circumstance connected with this mass murder, it was that the Indian was drunk!

The Anton Probst Case — Philadelphia

On April 7, 1866, the hired man of Christopher Deering, one Anton Probst, a German, brutally and senselessly murdered an entire family, plus two—seven in all—and within two months was hanged in the Philadelphia prison. Roger Butterfield, in an article on the case refers to the crime as "the bloodiest, most brutal and senseless that Philadelphia has ever known."[78] This is no doubt true—but no more so than the McConaghy wholesale killing, discussed above.

The locale of this butchery was in the "Neck" area of South Philadelphia near the Delaware River which, at the time, was farmland. Deering, on the fatal day, had driven into the city to meet a niece, Elizabeth Dolan, aged seventeen, who lived at Burlington, New Jersey, and was coming to visit her relatives. While he was absent, Probst must have gone berserk or have become overpowered with cupidity and greed—for his crime was motivated, at least to some degree, by robbery. He procured an axe and started out to eliminate all around him. He first killed a fellow farm-hand, Cornelius Corey, an apprentice of Deering's; then Mrs. Julia Deering, wife and mother, in her thirties; then one by one, the children: John, eight; Tom six; Annie, four; and the baby, Emily.

He then lay in wait for the return of the owner of the farm, Deering. As he drove into the yard with his house guest, Probst murdered him, and also the girl, before they could discover the results of his gory deed. He then left the premises with about $200 in cash and some trinkets.

The crime went undetected for some days and it was not until neighbors noticed something amiss—no smoke from the chimneys —that the bodies were discovered and the full import of the crime became obvious. Probst was immediately suspected. He had been "living it up" at the various taverns in the city with his ill-gotten loot. He was arrested, convicted and hanged without delay and in record time. If "short shrift" of a killer was the purpose of the

---

[78]*Town Crier,* Philadelphia, July 14, 1930 in an article entitled "Murder at the Neck."

court as reflected by the public, this was one such action. The crime was discovered on April 11, four days after it had occurred; Probst was convicted on April 28, the death warrant issued on May 8, and he was hanged on June 8. In another connection, we discuss some of the unusual tests made of Probst's cadaver by the medical men of the day.[79]

There have been mass killers through every decade in this country—many more than can be recorded here. Details of some of these are lost in oblivion or are familiar to only those living in the vicinity. A couple of such cases are the John F. Morgan and Abel Clemmons cases from West Virginia and the Stephen Lee Richards butchery in Nebraska. The first dealt with a greedy, financially-strapped man who stayed overnight with the Pfost-Greene families, with intent to rob them as they slept. This occurred in Jackson County, in 1897. They were all friends and neighbors; yet this did not deter Morgan from "first crushing the head of Jimmie Greene with a stone and then killing Mrs. Chloe Greene and Matilda Pfost with an axe." He was caught almost immediately and hanged at Ripley, the county seat.[80] The second case from West Virginia which is legendary is the Abel Clemmons case. Hanged at Morgantown (at the time Virginia), on June 30, 1806, he had brutally murdered his wife and eight children the preceding November at Clarkesburg. There are several pamphlets surviving relative to this mass killer.[81]

The killer from Nebraska was referred to as the "Nebraska fiend." He murdered nine persons, including the members of the Harlson family. Richards was twenty-five years of age, but his murderous exploits were notorious. He was hanged at Minden, Kearney County, April 28, 1879.[82]

His crimes bring to mind the mass murders of Charles Starkweather in the same state who was executed (by electrocution) on June 25, 1959 for killing a dozen persons. He was aided and accompanied through the midwest by an adolescent girl who was

---

[79]See Chater V, p. 217; McDade, *op. cit.*, pp. 772-775.

[80]McDade, *op. cit.*, 742; see also, *New York Times Sun*, Sunday, December 19, 1897 (see our Chapter I, headlines, p. 21).

[81]*Ibid.*, 181-182.

[82]*Ibid.*

sent to prison for life. Their murderous fling was completely ruthless and meaningless.

Wife-killer James-Lisemba — California

The last person to be legally hanged in California might be called a mass killer; at least, he managed to dispose of some wives by diabolical murder processes. Born on a cotton patch in Alabama and bearing the strange name of Major Raymond Lisemba, he learned the barber trade in Birmingham, and, in due time, wandered into Colorado and later to California. He seems to have had unfortunate experiences with his wives, not only in disposing of them but in collecting their insurance. However, he was persevering. One wife went out with him for a boatride and returned alone, terror-stricken and soaking wet; what finally became of her we are none too sure. Another wife was critically injured when her car plunged down a mountain, but surgeons saved her life. Still another was found drowned in her own bathtub in a Colorado mountain cabin.

Lisemba assumed the name of Robert S. James and continued his grim work with women. He married Mary Emma Busch in Los Angeles and immediately insured her life for a large amount of money. Next he prevailed on a "wino" to procure some rattlesnakes for him. With these he attempted to get rid of his bride by strapping her to a kitchen table and inducing the snakes to bite her. However, he became impatient with this technique and finally drowned her in the bathtub. He was arrested and investigated. It was found that he had a record of incest and seduction. During his stay in San Quentin prison's Death Row, this lecherous cottonpicking barber got religion and occupied his time by teaching a Bible class. He was hanged May 1, 1942 at the age of forty-eight.[88]

REVENGE OR SPITE MURDERS

There are probably many instances in which persons have gone to the "hanging tree" as the result of killing someone who

---

[88]Data from J. Francis McComas, *The Graveside Companion*, New York, Ivan Obolensky, Inc., 1962, pp. 303-305. The first legal hanging after California became a state is alleged to have been José Rodriguez, who was executed on Russian Hill, San Francisco on December 10, 1852. He and José Forner got into a fight over a gambling debt and the latter was killed; perhaps manslaughter rather than murder.

had testified against them for earlier crimes of theft, robbery, poaching, trespassing, or other noncapital offenses. Our only way of knowing just what cases follow this pattern is by checking whatever news stories indicate this actually happened. That it is a very definite pattern in criminality is generally accepted by criminologists and we have examples of it in this study.

We start with the case of John Stephens, a mulatto who lived in the Indian country. He was sentenced to be hanged on January 14, 1887, by Judge Isaac C. Parker, the "hanging judge" of Fort Smith, now Arkansas. Stephen's crime was the murder of Mrs. Annie Kerr who had testified against him in a larceny case. He hacked her and her sixteen-year-old son to death with an axe. He then rode to the home of a Dr. Pyle, who had also been a witness against him at the earlier trial, and beat him so badly that he died five days later.[89]

The following case, usually referred to as the "Meeks Massacre," presents a slightly different angle. Gus Meeks, his wife and children, were murdered by George and William Taylor "somewhere between Browning and Hamphrey, at the foot of Jenkin's Hill, Linn County, Missouri." The date was May 11, 1894, the motive, to prevent Meeks from testifying against them at an upcoming trial for stealing cattle. A banker in Browning became suspicious of the Taylor's taking ways and started to investigate. Meeks, who worked for the Taylors, was the only person who could testify against them. He agreed to leave town with his family for $500. After they were on their way, the Taylors followed them and killed them all, except little Nellie who was four years old. While the Taylors went after a harrow to eradicate their marks, she crawled out of the straw (badly wounded) where she was hidden and made her way to the Cotter homestead. The Taylors, learning of their imminent danger, left town. Four months later, they were apprehended in Arkansas and returned to Missouri to stand trial. The brothers were tried in Carroll County through change of venue and sentenced to death. They escaped; but one, Bill, was recaptured and hanged at Carrollton, on April 30, 1896.

This case possesses many ingredients that make for survival. It

---

[89]Glenn Shirley, *Law West of Fort Smith,* New York, Holt, 1957, pp. 220-221.

was a brutal mass killing, with a motive to silence someone from testifying; the principals were well known in the community—even surrounded with an air of distinction; there was a survivor who added a tincture of romance (see below); and there are ballads that grind out the story in perpetuity. McDade says of this case:

> "For sheer senseless and fiendish brutality, it is hard to match the killing of the Meeks family."[90]

Nellie, the lone survivor, a few years later joined a tent show and sang a ballad about her sad experience. In the bloody encounter with the killers, Nellie had received a terrible blow on the forehead with an axe which left a dent. At the appropriate place in her morbid song, probably with dramatic fanfare and flourish, she would brush back her golden curls so the sympathetic, and, no doubt, tearful audience could see her "dent." Through the kind permission of Mrs. Olive Woolley Burt, of Salt Lake City, we reproduce the ballad she sang for many years thereafter to earn her living:

> I'm Mister Meeks' little girl, and if you'll lend an ear,
> I'll tell you all the saddest tale, that ever you did hear.
> We lived upon George Taylor's farm, not very far from town,
> One night when we was sleeping the Taylor boys came down.
> They wanted to take Papa away, but Mama said no,
> We could not be left there alone, we all would have to go.
> We got into the wagon then and went to Jenkins Hills
> And when we started up the slope the team suddenly stood still.
> And then those wicked Taylor men, they jumped on us with an axe,
> And though we begged on bended knees, our heads they cruelly cracked.
> They killed Mama and Papa, too, and knocked the baby in the head;
> They murdered my brothers and sisters, and left me there for dead.
> But God did not forsake me, And I lived to tell the tale;
> The Taylors were arrested and put in Carrolton jail.
> And now my little song you've heard, it's sad for me to tell;

---

[90]McDade, *op. cit.*, 963.

I'm left an orphan here alone in this wide world to dwell.
I want you all to pray for me, That I'll meet my family dear
In heaven above, where all is peace—
And there'll be no murderers there.[91]

THE TOM DULA SAGA OF NORTH CAROLINA

On the very first page of this book we briefly made reference to the story of Tom Dula, of North Carolina, the ne'er-do-well or mountain hero about whom millions of teen-agers and others, not so young, sang a few years ago in "hootnannies" and other folk gatherings. The story belongs to Manly Wade Wellman who revived it in his exciting work, *Dead and Gone.*[92]

Tom came back from the War Between the States and settled restlessly in his native habitat in Happy Valley, Wilkes County. The glamour and excitement of a war is a sharp contrast to the humdrum boredom of a mountain fastness, and a restless young man, especially when he is endowed with good looks, is likely to search for some stimulation out of the ordinary.

This hero of the Yadkin River country is described as about six feet tall, with dark curly hair, and generally regarded as handsome. He liked the girls and the girls liked him; he played a fiddle and a banjo and with these and a war record of which any man could be proud, it is understandable that he turned to the girls for stimulation rather than to hard work or other serious pursuits.

One of the girls he sparked, Laura Foster, became his victim. In circuitous fashion, he started with Laura, leaned toward her cousin Pauline Foster who, in her turn, introduced him to Mrs. Ann Melton. As Wellman described this siren: "Here was a woman who at first sight would make a man's mouth go dry to its roof and his eyes protrude like door knobs."[93] The woman also had land and money. Her maid was Pauline Foster and it was sometime in 1866 that Tom first "dallied" with the lovely and cultured Ann. By May of that year, he was apparently well ensconced in the favors—and clutches of this scintillating young married

---

[91]*American Murder Ballads,* pp. 235-236; this is only one of several ballads about this notorious case. Mrs. Burt includes two others.

[92]Chapel Hill, University of North Carolina Press, 1954, pp. 172-187.

[93]Wellman, *op. cit.,* p. 174.

woman, her unrecorded husband, James Melton, notwithstanding.

On the 26th of that month, Laura Foster "turned up missing." It was believed that she had eloped. It was further hinted that her elopement mate was Tom Dula, but it soon appeared that neither he, nor Bob Cummings, the local school teacher who was sweet on Laura, were missing. The plot, of course, thickened. It was not until June 10 that the mountain mystery was cracked with the discovery of Laura's body in a thicket known as "Bates Place." Her horse had been found, tethered to a tree, and faint with hunger. After digging up the remains of the girl, they were taken to Elkville where it was established that Laura had been murdered by some party unknown—by stabbing. As Laura had been pretty chummy with a number of young bucks from the mountain area, several were immediately suspected of the foul play. But due to some clever sleuthing by the spurned lover, Bob Cummings, Tom Dula, a Jack Keaton, and Ann Melton became deeply involved. Keaton was able to establish an alibi but Tom and Ann were not so fortunate and thus were bound over for the fall term of court.

There was a change of venue from Wilkes County to Iredale County, of which Statesville is the county seat. Tom was defended by his old commanding officer and one-time governor of the state, Zebulon Baird Vance, but to no avail. He was found guilty at both trials and was sentenced to be hanged. Before he met his death, he absolved Ann Melton, taking all the blame himself.

The scaffold was made of "mountain pine, two stout uprights and a crossbar." The *New York Herald* described Dula in this fashion: "He fought gallantly in the Confederate service where he established a reputation for bravery, but since the war closed, he became reckless, demoralized and a desperado, of whom the people in his community had a terror. There is everything in his expression to denote the hardened assassin—a fierce glare of the eyes, a great deal of malignity, and a callousness that is revolting."[94]

Hanging day for Tom Dula was May 1, 1868. Arriving at the gallows, in the traditional manner, with cart, crowd and officials, Tom made a long rambling speech about the nice clean rope that

[94]*Ibid.*, p. 183.

had been thrown about his neck, stating that he "should have washed his neck." The dread moment arrived, the trap was sprung and Tom Dula was, like so many other victims of the "hanging tree," swung into eternity. His neck was not broken—"he dangled and strangled to death." His body was claimed by some relatives.

Laura Foster's body lies in an unmarked grave; Ann Melton survived the scandal for some years and was killed when a wagon overturned on her. It was believed by many that "on the night she died, the room filled with a crackling sound as of burning meat, and a black cat was seen to climb the wall. Happy Hollow dwellers have been persuaded to think that Satan came in person to receive Ann Melton to hell."[95]

The Tom Dula story has become a legend and the haunting ballad with its one or more versions, in itself a legend, was actually composed, according to Wellman, by a school teacher named Thomas C. Land. In Chapter I, we referred to the version that was revived not too long ago and became a favorite juke-box record among adolescents—and many others. Here is the version reproduced from Wellman's work:

> Oh, bow your head, Tom Dula,
> Oh, bow your head and cry;
> You've killed poor Laura Foster
> And you know you're bound to die.
>
> I take my banjo this evening,
> I pick it on my knee;
> This time tomorrow evening
> 'Twill be no use to me.
>
> I had my trial at Wilkesboro,
> Oh, what do you reckon they done?
> They bound me over to Statesville
> And there's where I'll be hung.
>
> Oh, pappy, oh, pappy,
> What shall I do?
> I have lost all my money
> And killed poor Laura, too.

[95]*Ibid.*, pp. 186-187.

Oh, mammy, oh, mammy,
Bow your head and cry,
I've killed poor Laura Foster
And I know I'm bound to die.

Oh, what my mammy told me
Is about to come to pass;
That drinking and the women
Would be my ruin at last.[96]

---

[96]Wellman, *op. cit.*, pp. 185-186.

Chapter V

A WIDE RANGE OF CASES

THE ROLE OF THE MEDICAL MEN AND THE HANGING PRACTICE

A CLICHE SOMETIMES HEARD in connection with an impending execution is that the doctor says the victim is too ill to be hanged!

Nothing has been found in colonial statutes specifying just how persons condemned to death were to be executed, except from the specific announcement of the judge "to be taken from the jail to the place of execution and there to be hanged by the neck until dead." We can find no mention of an autopsy nor that a physician was to be present. Who (other than the hangman or sheriff) pronounced the victim dead is a matter of conjecture.

In the statutes of the various states that brought about the abolition of public hangings, we find mention made of the presence of a physician being necessary to a well-conducted legal hanging, whether it be within the walls of a jail or of a state prison. When hangings became a private, or less public, affair, the presence of a medical man at the scaffold was expected. His affirmation of death was mandatory.

As to the disposition of the body after hanging, no doubt, in most cases, the relatives or friends were given possession of the remains, which were properly interred in some cemetery of the survivors' or victim's choice. We have found at least one case in which the disposition of the person's body was stipulated in the death sentence. In Ste. Genevieve County, Missouri, Peter Johnston was condemned to death for the murder of John Spear in Big River Township. He was sentenced to hang on August 3, 1810, and a part of the court's sentence was that his body "be turned over to Dr. Walter Fenwick for dissection." The record states that he was hanged on that date on Academy Hill.[1] Many, also, were buried in the Potter's Field of the town where the hanging took place or in the prison yard. So far as the clothing worn by the victim of the gallows is concerned we have found almost no evidence that it was taken from the cadaver by friends or looters. The only such unseemingly instance of this that we have noted is in connection with George Burroughs, one of the alleged witches who were hanged at Salem.[2]

However, many of the cadavers were turned over to physicians or anatomical groups by county or state officials or by the victims themselves in a previously arranged agreement. The role of medical science and the prerogatives of physicians—aside from the mere pronouncement of death—represents a singular area of our study of hanging in this country.

The earliest case we have discovered in which medical men preempted the body of a victim of the "tree" was that of the Negro slave, Julian, hanged at Boston in 1733. We shall deal with this case below (see pages 218-20). A second, revealing more factual information, was that of the famous Bennington, Vermont, case of David Redding, hanged under tragic but colorful circumstances on June 11, 1778. We have discussed this case earlier (Chapter I, page 28). Dr. Jonas Fay, brother of the sheriff who officiated at the Redding affair, asked for and received the cadaver for "anatomical purposes." After applying lye and quicklime to reduce it to a skelton, he found he was unable to articulate it. We now know that the small-town physician had little knowledge of anatomy and failed to make the realignment of the bones that probably resulted from the hanging procedure. At any rate, he got rid of the skeleton by presenting it to a friend, a Dr. William Towner, of Williamstown, Massachusetts, who was able to fix it for functional and exhibition purposes. Later it was turned over to interested persons in Bennington.[3]

We know a little more about our next case, a hanging that occurred during our second period of hangings in the county jails.

---

[1] Source: Goodspeed's *History of Southeast Missouri*, (1888), reprint, 1964, p. 311.

[2] See Chapter III, page 142; source, Burr, *Narratives*, pp. 215-222.

[3] See John Spargo, *The Story of David Redding Who Was Hanged*, Bennington Historical Museum, 1945, pp. 51-52.

It is that of Joshua Jones, executed at Coudersport, Potter County, Pennsylvania on May 31, 1839, for the murder of his wife as she slept.

There was nothing unusual about his crime. He killed her, went after his cows, and then announced to the neighbors that she had died from self-inflicted wounds. It was the aftermath of his conviction and sentence which set the case apart from the ordinary run-of-the mill murder episodes. Jones made a compact with two physicians, Drs. Thorp and French, whereby they could have his remains for ten dollars cash and a promise that they would educate his son. With the ten dollars, Jones "enlivened his prison fare" with choice tidbits of food. On the day of his hanging, he had one dollar bill left, so he placed it between two slices of bread and ate it. A fascinating ballad emerged from this hanging and the contract made between Jones and his medical friends. According to the ballad (reproduced below) the physicians had agreed to do what they could to restore life to the body after the "tree" had done its grim work. Realizing the number of inept hangings at that time, with strangling much more prevalent than the more permanent dislocation of the vertebrae—neck-breaking—such a pledge does not seem too fantastic. The plight of Jones's poor wife who was murdered seems to have escaped the folk composer of the ballad.

Joshua Jones's skeleton was long in the possession of the French family, but in the flood of 1911 it was washed away. However, the skull was retrieved and this may still be seen in the county historical society's headquarters at Coudersport. Here is the Jones ballad:

The Ghost of Joshua Jones Appears

Come list ye doctors all to me For Jones's ghost I truly be—
Come look at me now if you can, I am that slaughtered, mangled
    man.
When on earth my name was Jones, Composed like you of flesh
    and bones,
But for the murder of my wife The people they did take my life.

You came to me, 'twas in this wise; You told to me some dread-
    ful lies.
You said you would bring me to life Although I murdered my
    dear wife.

My body then I willed to you, And you agreed your best to do
To bring me unto life again, When on the gallows I was slain.

You did not do as you agreed Before my death, when you did
  plead.
You let me hang an hour almost Until that I gave up the ghost.
You took me down with wicked hands Conveyed my corpse to
  distant lands,
There to dissect this frame of mine—which you did mangle like
  the swine.

You brought disgrace upon Whitesville⁴ By taking me to the old
  oil mill,
You cut me up there, slice by slice, For which I blame Squire
  Avery Rice.
A Christian he is said to be, But think, oh think, Squire Rice, of
  me.
When you address the throne of grace I'll stare you then full
  in the face.

And now, you villains, Thorp and French, You burnt my gar-
  ments, root and branch,
My coffin burned to boil my bones, Because I was the murderer
  Jones.
You snapped my jaws at boys you know—Old Satan will serve
  you just so.
You threw my flesh about the floor, The like was never seen
  before.

A coat of tar awaits you all; a storm of feathers will on you fall;
It shall be done, for it is right. Oh, how you'll look in such a
  plight!
You must not come where I do dwell, You're neither fit for
  heaven or hell.
Vile vagabonds you all will be In time and in eternity.

If you by chance to heaven soar, Then Gabriel bolts on you the
  door;
And if to hell you all should fall, All hell will be in an uproar
  squall.

---

⁴Whitesville, N.Y. is where Jones's body was dissected; it lies just across the border
from Coudersport. We are indebted to Mrs. Olive Woolley Burt, *American Murder
Ballads*, Oxford University Press, 1958, pp. 19-21, for this ballad.

Repining ghosts will cry, 'Avaunt, Lord God of Hosts, hell they
  can't haunt.'
Raging devils will break their chains, And kick you back to
  earth again.

At the consummation of all things, You will not come to Priests
  or Kings,
You, Dr. Thorp and Dr. French, Will be burnt, both root and
  branch,
Unless you do your sins confess, To God and man your wickedness;
And pray to God you to forgive, And like a humble Christian
  live!

Two other humble victims of the hanging tree whose remains
were sold to physicians were: Henry Kobler Musselman, hanged at
Lancaster, Pennsylvania, on December 20, 1839, for murder of an
itinerant peddler, Lazarus Zellerbach, who sold his remains to Dr.
Samuel Kerfoot for five dollars; John McNab, "seducer and murderer" of Sarah H. Furber of Manchester, New Hampshire, who,
sometime in 1848, sold her body to Dr. Oliver Wendell Holmes,
of the Boston Medical School, for ten dollars. This latter is not a
case of outright murder but rather of an abortion which ended
fatally. A broadside was struck off about the Furber case and a
wheezy ballad poem contrived. Here it is:

Lines Composed on the Abduction
and Cruel Murder of
Miss Sarah Furber
Late of Nottingham, N.H.   Tune: The Aatchers
Dedicated to her dear parents
By Mrs. Lucy Hall

A maid of twenty summers went forth with joy and mirth
To toil for life's own blessings amidst the din of earth.
She left her place of childhood, and friends to her so dear,
And joined the scenes of mirth with hearts that were not pure.

A manly face and favor attracted her free heart,
She thought him pure and lovely, in all his acts of mirth.
But ah, she little knew him, a fallen, sinful lew [sic]
Beneath a smiling face lay thoughts of darkest hue.

Time showed her sad condition, with thoughts of sad regret,
She saw her wide digression from paths of rectitude.
But O, what silent grief, which none but like has known,
Of youthful virtues wasted, and seeds of misery sown.

In men of art and science, she thought a sure redress,
For all her grief and sorrow, in long oblivion rest.
O cruel, hellish practice, which none but fiends should know,
Yet in our land of science it's practiced not by few.

No mother's voice to sooth her, no father's gaze to cheer,
No sister's heart to feel for, no brother's hand so dear;
But near her bed is standing a fiend in human form.
He feels no sad emotion to see the maniac mourn.

Now in that lonely sick room no mourner yet has come,
She sleeps her long, long slumber, till God shall call her home.
O young and joyous maidens, remember well these lines,
Fear not to shun temptation, for they impair your mind.[5]

Viewing this tragedy in the light of present day mores it seems preposterous that a medical man (of the stature of Dr. Oliver Wendell Holmes) would purchase the remains of an aborted female from a wandering wastrel such as McNab.

In those days there were many bodies spirited away by physicians or snatched from graves by ghouls. Whether the members of the medical profession bought the cadavers outright, or whether they were legally entitled to paupers who were executed, there was a public condemnation of the practice of having persons dissected on the anatomical table.[6]

The body of John Earls of Lycoming County, Pennsylvania (Williamsport), was tampered with after the execution on May 24, 1836. He had killed his wife two days after she had given birth to a child. He sat at the foot of the bed and watched her sip a cup of hot chocolate in which he had placed a pinch of arsenic. Upon hanging for his crime, he was buried outside the jail, the first legal victim of the "tree" in the county. Physicians spirited away his remains. Legend has it that the skeleton of Earls was displayed in a local tavern for many years.

------

[5]Price: two cents. Burt, *op. cit.*, pp. 38-39.
[6]See Funston ballad—last verse; Chapter VI, page 284.

One case in Philadelphia which caused much protest was that of Arthur Spring. He was a "hardened" criminal who served time in Sing Sing, New York prison. He had murdered two women in the Quaker City on March 12, 1853, in brutal fashion, while robbing their home. He had committed a long string of crimes and had at least one other murder to his credit; he had killed a toy merchant. Roger Butterfield, a devotee of unusual murder cases, has done a piece regarding that one crime entitled "The Man Who Forgot His Umbella."[7] Feeling ran high against Spring throughout the city. But the aftermath of his hanging on June 10 was macabre in the extreme.

No sooner was the trap released than his body was wheeled out of the death corridor and carried by van to a medical laboratory for dissection. The amphitheater was filled with the town's riffraff as well as with medical students, physicians and others. One report stated that the exhibition was "blessed with the follies of phrenology contributing largely to enliven it." Further editorial comment called attention to the ribald remarks of the crowd and the levity and smugness of the dissecting physicians as the process unfolded.[8]

The press had already complained that well over a thousand persons had witnessed an earlier hanging in that same city—that of a colored man named James Morris on January 15, 1841. The editorial protests against the crudities of the examining and dissecting physicians were extremely bitter. One stated: "Yet this was the solemn consummation of justice! If private executions are to be thus perverted, humanity, decency, and common sense will cry out against them. The sheriff bears the responsibility of the execution; and in sanctioning these inhuman, impious and beastly outrages he makes himself liable to prosecution . . . If he has the right to do this, he has the right to chain a convicted criminal down to the dissecting table and give him up, as Morris was given up, a living subject, to the doctors."[9]

Another hanging victim, in the same gloomy Philadelphia prison, whose body was tampered with in an experiment, was Gerald

---

[7]*Town Crier,* Philadelphia, October 6, 1930.

[8]As reported by the *J. of Prison Discipline & Philanthropy,* VIII, No. 3 (July 1853) 147-8.

[9]Philadelphia *Public Ledger & Transcript,* January 16, 1841.

Eaton, executed April 8, 1869. His body was taken to a local medical college "where a galvanic battery and mustard were used, in addition to 'rolling' [*sic*] in an attempt to resuscitate him." This might be called a humanitarian gesture in addition to having scientific validity. The physicians worked for two hours without success. The body of the notorious mass-killer, Anton Probst, whose case we described in the previous chapter (page 201) "afforded the physicians a field day, putting it [the body] through all kinds of tests, including one to test the theory that the retina of the eye of dying persons retains the last image seen." Probst's head and right arm appeared in a New York City museum of anatomy and science for some time after his execution.[10]

Other off-beat experiments were made on the bodies of several hanged persons that rivaled even the bizarre tests made on Probst's corpse. Phrenology was a semi-respectable "science" during the early part of the nineteenth century and it is not surprising to read of masters of that cult being called in for post-mortems concerning the possible causes of crime. For instance, Joseph Christock (hanged in Schuylkill County, Pottsville, March 30, 1911) was examined by a phrenologist long after that subject had fallen into disrepute. The "specialist," after making measurements, announced that this killer, who had murdered the mother-in-law of his employer, had the "cunning of a fox and if aroused would become as cruel as a tiger." Many years before, a tramp named Harris Bell who was hanged at Honesdale, Wayne County, Pennsylvania, on September 29, 1848, was written up as a case in the *American Phrenological Journal* (Vol. XII, 1850). It was stated at the time that he had committed murder because of a "vice he had contracted when young." A phrenologist, present at the hanging of Albert Starkweather, at Hartford, Connecticut, in 1866—he had murdered his mother and sister while they slept in a vain hope of getting the family farm—reported that "his conscientiousness was weak; his hope large."[11]

When gambler Harry Hayward was hanged in Minneapolis for the murder of Kitty Ging (December 11, 1895), "criminologists"

---

[10]McDade, *op. cit.*, 772-775.

[11]*Ibid.*, 905.

were curious about the weight of his brain. Obsessed at the time with the Lombrosian thesis that there are "born criminals—atavistic or "throwbacks" to an earlier human order—they found "three of the four Lombrosian stigmata—a symmetry of skull, brain and face the protusian [sic], of front teeth and the narrow and sharply arched palate" which, apparently, "labeled the dead man as a dangerous biological phenomenon somewhat below the savage and above the lunatic."[12]

Skeletons, whole or partial, may be found scattered in medical laboratories and colleges, but generally they do not lend themselves to identification. There is one, however, reposing in a junkyard on the outskirts of Angelica, Allegany County, New York, which is all that remains of David Carpenter. He was hanged on April 16, 1869, for the murder of his brother. His cadaver was first utilized for medical purposes, in a university in New York City, after which the skeleton was shipped back to his home county. Here it was used for "educational purposes" in a local high school, after which it came into the possession of a second-hand junk and antique dealer where it may be found today.

The terrestrial remains of many of the victims of the hanging tree have been subjected to indignities of a wide variety. Society seems reluctant to afford them even a modicum of human dignity either before or after death.

The Ballad of Julian

We mentioned the Julian case earlier in this chapter. The subject of this case was the first we have in our records whose body was taken to medical persons for dissection. It was hoped, at the time, that the students who procured the body "would dissect it in a most accurate manner and that their critical inspection would prove of singular advantage."[13]

We seldom find criminal immortality ascribed to a simple Indian, but such is the case of Julian, hanged on March 22, 1733. The closest we might come to this phenomenon is the gibbeting of the Negro Mark and the burning of his co-conspirator Phillis

---

[12]Walter N. Trenerry, *Murder in Minnesota*, St. Paul, Minnesota Historical Society, 1962, p. 153; by permission; see our Chapter VI, pp. 273-5, for story of this case.
[13]Burt, *op. cit.*, p. 150.

for poisoning their master in 1758 (see Chapter II, page 89.)

In September 1732, Julian, a slave belonging to Major Quincy of Bridgewater, Massachusetts, ran away. A reward was offered for his capture and John Rogers of Pembroke set off in search of the errant absconder. Julian eluded capture until finally he was cornered by his pursuer in a cornfield. Julian pulled a knife and stabbed Rogers to death. Subsequently, he was convicted and hanged, his body being turned over to the medical students for dissection.

There are two broadsides extant that tell of Julian's plight. One, entitled "Advice from the Dead to the Living or a Solemn Warning to the World," is embellished with a woodcut showing the Indian brandishing a knife, his victim lying on the ground, and a preacher wielding sticks as he pursues the frightened killer. Another is entitled "Poor Julleyoun's Warnings to Children and Servants to Shun the Ways of Sin." Then there is an admittedly spurious broadside, decorated with an hourglass, a skull, pick and shovel, with a note at the bottom, to wit: "Published at His Desire in the Presence of Two Witnesses." Two ballads of the case of Julian come from the collection of Mrs. Olive Woolley Burt which we append here:

> The Prisoner owns his bloody Act, and saith the sentence on
>   his Fact,
> Was pass'd on him impartially, and therefore doth deserve to
>   die.
>
> By his Account he first was sold, when he was not quite three
>   years old,
> And by his Mother in his Youth, instructed in the ways of Truth.
>
> Was also taught to Write and Read, and learned his Catechise
>   and Creed,
> And what was proper (as he saith) relating to the Christian
>   Faith.
>
> His pious Master did with care, by Counsels warn him to
>   beware
> Of wicked Courses that would tend to his Destruction in the
>   End.

When twenty Years were gone and past, by his Account, he
    took at last,
To Drinking and ill Company, which proved his fatal Destiny.

From Sin to Sin advancing thus, by sad Degrees from bad to
    worse,
He did at length commit the Crime, for which he dies before his
    Time.

He prays his sad untimely Fall, maybe a Warning unto all,
That they no such like Steps do tred,
Nor lead such Life as he had led . . .

Julian's advice to children goes something like this:

Poor Julleyoun doth cry aloud
To all this numerous thronging crowd
To hear his dying doleful cries,
To learn from him how to be wise.
Beware of Lying, Stealing, too,
And joining with a Wicked Crew,
Who will the Sabbath Day Profane,
The Sacred Name of God blaspheme.[14]

Another ballad dealing with an Indian—however, not with medical dissection—but one who committed murder, is associated with the case of Moses Paul, hanged at New Haven, Connecticut on September 2, 1772. He had killed Moses Cook of Peterburg in a tavern brawl at Bethany, on December 7 the previous year— with a club "not with a flatiron as was supposed." The condemned man asked the Rev. Samson Occum, an Indian missionary of the gospel to preach a sermon at the gallows. Occum had quite a reputation as he had visited England where he had been hailed as the first Indian divine to honor that country. A great crowd was present at the hanging of Paul at New Haven, since it was the first such spectacle held there since 1749. The poor Indian victim, as well as those about him, blamed drink for his downfall. A broadside which reproduces the ballad shows the Rev. Occum preaching

---

[14]Burt, *op. cit.,* pp. 151-152

to a crowd while the miserable victim stands mournfully on the gallows:

> My Kindred Indians pray attend and hear,
> With great Attention and with Godly Fear,
> This Day I warn you of that cursed Sin,
> That poor despited (sic) Indians wallow in.
>
> 'Tis Drunkeness, this is the Sin you know,
> Has been and is poor Indians' overthrow;
> 'Twas Drunkeness that was the leading Cause,
> That made poor MOSES break God's righteous Laws.
>
> When Drunk he other evil Courses took,
> Thus hurried on, he murder'd Moses Cook
> Poor Moses Paul must now be hanged this Day,
> For wilful Murder in a drunken Fray.
>
> We've nothing valuable or to our Praise,
> And well may other Nations on us gaze;
> We have no Money, Credit or a Name,
> But what this Sun doth turn to our great Shame.
>
> Mean are our Houses, and we are kept low,
> And almost naked, thieving as we go;
> Pinch'd for Food and almost starv'd we are,
> And many times put up with stinking Fare.
>
> Our little Children hovering round us weep,
> Most starv'd to Death we've nought for them to eat;
> And all this Distress is justly on us come,
> For the accursed use we make of Rum.
>
> My kindred Indians, I entreat you all,
> In this vile Sun never again to fall;
> Fly to the blood of Christ, for that alone
> Can for this Sin and all your Sins atone.
>
> Tho' Moses Paul is here alive and well,
> This Night his Soul must be in Heaven or Hell;
> O! do take Warning by this awful Sight,
> And to a Jesus make a speedy flight.[15]

The above, of course, is more the sermon than the ballad. The

---

[15]Burt, *op. cit.*, pp. 152-153.

missionary is advising his followers that their salvation is to avoid rum and strong drink.

The above case of the doomed Indian, Moses Paul, was a digression from our discussion of the role of medical men and their body-snatching practices in early days of hanging. Our first case was that of Julian. Our second case is an interesting one— that of a doomed man who escaped the noose by means of a most unpopular pardon. He was Ebenezer Richardson, the "Informer" of Boston during pre-Revolutionary War days. We feel justified in including it because of the phenomenon of dissection—and a ballad.

We are all familiar, after a fashion, with the so-called Boston Massacre which occurred on March 5, 1770, when an altercation took place between a small group of citizens and the soldiers of the city guard. A mob gathered, and, in exasperation, the soldiers fired, killing three men. This incident has been immortalized in song and story embellished with patriotic fervor and chauvinistic zeal.

It appears that one Ebenezer Richardson, an employee of the Boston Custom House, and known by his neighbors as *The Informer,* became identified with that Boston Massacre. A few days after the tragic event of March 5, Richardson became involved in a skirmish. In the melee, he shot and killed an eleven-year-old boy named Christopher Sneider. The boy became a martyr. Richardson was tried for murder and convicted. He was sentenced to hang, but Governor Hutchinson refused to sign the death warrant. The unpopular killer remained in jail for two years until a King's Pardon set him free. The public's indignation was exemplified by the number of broadsides and pamphlets struck off against the man who had escaped what is believed to be just desserts. There is no evidence that Richardson felt at all disposed toward the ideas expressed in the rash of ballads and broadsides that emerged during this hectic period in American history.

When Richardson was pardoned a black-bordered broadside appeared urging the residents of Boston to remember the *Boston Massacre* and crying for the punishment of Richardson. Its front cover shows British soldiers bayoneting women and children. The Ebenezer Richardson ballad is herewith reproduced:

Injured Boston now awake While I a true confession make,
Of my notorious sins and guilt, As well the harmless blood I've
  spilt.
Woodburn, my native place can tell, My crimes are blacker, far
  than Hell,
What great disturbance there I made, Against their people and
  their head.

A wretch of wretches prov'd with child, By me, I know, at
  which I smil'd,
To think the Parson, he must bare The guilt of me, and I go
  clear.
And thus the worthy man of God Unjustly felt the scourging rod,
Which broke his heart, it prov'd his end, And for whose blood
  I guilty stand.

The halter now is justly due, For now I've killed no less than
  two,
Their blood for vengeance loud doth cry, It reached the ears
  of Heaven on high.
But yet still wicked, yet still vile, I've lived on honest merchant's
  spoil.
For this I justly got the name, The INFORMER, though with
  little gain.

Little indeed when I compare, The stings of conscience which I
  bear,
And now I frankly own to thee, I'm the INFORMER, I am he.
By my account poor Boston's lost, By me in only three years
  past,
Full sixty thousand pounds—yea more May still be added to
  the score.

But what's all that to this last crime, In sending Sneider out of
  time.
This cuts my heart; this frights me most; O help me Lord, I see
  his ghost.
There—there's a life you now behold, So vile I've been—alas,
  so bold;
There'd scarce a lawyer undertake To plead my case, or for
  me speak.

On Tuesday next I must appear, And there my dismal sentence
hear;
But O my conscience guilty cries, For conscience never can
tell lyes.
And now, alas, my injur'd friends, Since I can make you no
amends,
Here is my body you may take, And sell, a notimy to make.

In essence, the promise of his body after he would be "turned
off" was all he had to offer for his perfidy—perhaps the most
ignominious part of a hanging. But, of course, these words were
put into his mouth through the broadside by those who held
nothing but contempt for him.[16]

FICTIONAL HANGING CASES

One of the hazardous elements in our study of hangings, or of
one dealing with murders is the existence of publications recording
fictional crimes or hangings. Several exuberant publishers placed
before an avid public many cases that simply did not exist. McDade
in his *The Annals of Murder* has recognized this irritating penchant
of certain well-known literary entrepreneurs of the past. As he
puts the matter: "It is difficult to identify single examples of such
work; the best clues lie in the publishers." He then cites the names
of E. E. Barclay, A. R. Orton, and Nathaniel Coverly "who made
a practice of publishing cases purporting to be genuine." Barclay
who did a "land office" business in grinding out murder stories,
first from his headquarters in Philadelphia and next, from Cincinnati, apparently turned over a new leaf after the War Between
the States and "went straight, or genuine."

McDade states that most of the fictitious cases are about female
murderers or multiple murders. One fetching example he cites is:
*The Three Sisters: or the Life, Confession, and Execution of Amy,
Elizabeth and Cynthia Halzinger Who were Tried, Convicted and
Executed at Elizabethtown, Ark., Nov. 30, 1855 for the Awful
and Horrible Murder of the Edmonds Family, Consisting of Seven
Members; Together with the Speech of the Eldest Sister, Amy, on
the Gallows. Edited by the Rev. O. R. Arthur, Published by A. R.*

---

[16]Burt, *op. cit.*, pp. 179-182.

Orton, Baltimore, Philadelphia, New York and Buffalo, 1856.[17]

There is no town by that name in that state although there is a small place named Elizabeth, population little more than one hundred, in Fulton County. But the county seat, where hangings almost always took place, is Salem.

Another fictional case is that of one Ann Walters "the celebrated female murderess who was tried, condemned, and sentenced to death at Georgetown, Delaware, and in which she confesses to have been guilty of ten murders."[18] It is quite probable that this Ann Walters is confused with a nebulous but real case of a Patty (Mrs. Lucretia P.) Cannon who allegedly led a notorious and murderous life in Sussex County, Delaware, of which Georgetown is the county-seat (*circa* 1829). The sketchy story— fact mingled with fiction—tells of a woman with three accomplices named Joseph and Ebenezer Johnson and James Melson who trafficked in kidnaped Negroes (Patty seemed to have lived across the state line in Maryland) and well-heeled strangers. Several skeletons (one of them a child's) were dug up by a tenant on a farm belonging to Patty Cannon near her home, although within the state of Delaware.

This precious quartet was indicted but court records are no longer extant so there is no accurate way of knowing what happened to them. Rumor and spurious pamphlets indicate that the Johnsons were hanged, and that Patty committed suicide. How much credence we can put on the story that her father, L. P. Hannon, had been hanged at Montreal for murder and that her brother, James, suffered the same fate at Kingston (Ontario) for horsestealing is dubious. These data come from a pamphlet entitled: *Narrative and Confession of Lucretia P. Cannon, who Was Tried, Convicted and Sentenced To Be Hung At Georgetown, Delaware With Two Of Her Accomplices Containing An Account Of Some Of The Most Horrible And Shocking Murders And Daring Robberies Ever Committed By One Of The Female Sex,* published anonymously in New York in 1841. The Rev. Charles Spear, Boston crusader against the death penalty, must have known of

---

[17]McDade, *op. cit.,* p. vi.

[18]From a pamphlet published at Boston, no date, and cited by McDade, 1037. The date may have been 1850.

the Patty Cannon case because he wrote about her "destroying herself after arrest by poison."[19] However, he may have got his information from the quasi-spurious pamphlet.

The vague and questionable pamphlet telling of the crimes of Ann Walters is associated with two other persons who were undoubtedly real as were their crimes. The first has to do with one Mary Runkle of Utica who murdered her husband, John, on August 20, 1847. She was hanged in the Whitesboro, Oneida County, jail on November 9 of that same year. (In early days Rome and Whitesboro shared honors of county seat with court terms being alternated between the two towns.) McDade said of the pamphlet struck off regarding this case: "A first-person recital that sounds like fiction."[20] The other person associated with the Walters account but, of course, having nothing to do with her fictional career, was the Rev. Enos O. Dudley who was himself hanged at Haverhill, New Hampshire, on May 23, 1849. We shall briefly elaborate on this case later. (See page 264).

A dubious case, not yet substantiated, is that of one Pamela Lee, of Pittsburgh, who supposedly murdered her husband and was convicted on December 19, 1851, in the Allegheny County court. She was sentenced to be hanged. In the published pamphlet, her husband, for some strange reason, is referred to as Moses Worms. Her *modus operandi* was the old standby, arsenic. In one of the two pamphlets telling of her exploits and doom, she is supposed to have murdered her first victim's daughter also. There is a discrepancy in the dates of her execution and confession:

1. Private history of Pamela Lee, who was convicted at Pittsburgh, Pa. December 19th, 1851, for the wilful murder of her husband, and sentenced to be hanged on the 30th day of January, a.d. 1852. Written at her request and according to her dictation, and prepared by the Rev. Augustus Dimick, Pittsburgh, Pa. 1852. Copyright by Lucas & Grant.

2. Trial, Conviction and Confession of Pamela Lee, who was sentenced to be hanged at Pittsburgh, Pa. January 28, 1853

---

[19]*Essays on the Punishment of Death,* Boston, 1944, p. 55.

[20]The name of the pamphlet is: *Life and Confession of Mary Runkle . . . for the Murder of Her Husband John,* Troy, N.Y., 1847; McDade, *op. cit.,* 843.

for the murder of Moses Worms and daughter. Written at her request and prepared by Rev. Augustus Dimick, Pittsburgh, Pa. 1853.

The following case, from Pennsylvania, is unquestionably fiction. A publication outlining the crime may be found in the Harvard Law School Library. The pamphlet tells nothing of the crime itself —aside from the mere mention of murder; The title page tells all:

Narrative of the pious death of the penitent Henry Mills, who was executed at Galesboro' (Penn.) on the 16th of July last [1817] for the murder of his wife and five children! To which is annexed his serious and solemn address to youth . . . To this work will be found annexed some further particulars of the horrid murder committed by Mills, which have not before been published. Boston: printed by Henry Trumbull, 1817.

No evidence of this crime can be found. There is no such town as Galesboro although there is a Galesburg (Centre County) which, on a map of 1882 was spelled Galesburgh. However, trials and public hangings in 1817 occurred in county seats and the county seat of Centre County is Bellefonte. There is practically nothing in the pamphlet but crude exhortation and weasel penance.[21] Another similar case, from Philadelphia, is that of a so-called John Myrick. The title of the pamphlet telling of this case—unquestionably fictional—is *The Life and Confession of John Myrick who was Executed for the Murder of his Wife and Children: Philadelphia, printed by James Chattin, 1755*[22] No such case can be found in any records of the City of Philadelphia.

Still another case, probably fictional, is that of Mary Jane Gordon of Vasselboro, Maine whose pamphlet reads: *Life and Confession of . . . who was tried, condemned and hung [sic] on the 24th of February, 1847. For the Murder of Jane Anderson, a native of Vasselboro, Maine. Her trial, her counsellor's debates, judge's charge to the jury . . . Carefully collected by the author, J. S. Calhoun, attorney at law, Augusta, Maine. Published for the author, 1847.* McDade has this to say about this case: "This work

---

[21]This case is listed by McDade, *op. cit.,* 682-683, but recognized as fictional.

[22]Listed by Evans, *American Bibliography*, item 7494.

appears to be fiction, though the title page sounds authentic enough. This conviction is borne out by the existence of another printing of this work with a Covington (Ky.) imprint in which Jane Anderson [the murder victim] becomes a native of Covington . . ."[23]

The state of North Carolina is the locale of this fictional mass murder. The title of the pamphlet telling us about it is *A faithful Account of the Massacre of the Family of Gerald Warson, of Fayetteville County, N.C. by John Jackson, the father-in-law of said Watson which horrid Catastrophe took place July last [1818]; Jackson had for a time been subject to Fits of mental derangement, which, it is supposed, was the Cause of his perpetrating the dreadful Deed . . . Boston, printed for N. Coverly, 1819.* And again McDade writes of this: "This sounds like fiction, and Coverly, the publisher, produced a quantity of this kind of work. There is a general vagueness in details in the story. Reputedly, Jackson killed his daughter and four of her children while her husband was away."[24] As there is no hanging involved or even suggestion of such an ending, this case is peripheral to our main consideration.

The Gallows — Almost

Opponents of capital punishment are constantly looking for and listing cases of innocent persons who have been executed. Without entering into this controversial—even inflammatory—debate, it is of pertinence, in our story of hangings and aborted hangings, to relate the story of Will Purvis who was freed from death because of the fact that the "rope broke." The case is a classic and is well described by Edwin M. Borchard in his scholarly work of some years ago, *Convicting the Innocent.*[25]

THE CLASSIC CASE OF WILL PURVIS — MISSISSIPPI

Purvis, a youth of nineteen, living near Columbia, Mississippi, was a member of the Ku Klux Klan, as were many of his neighbors

---

[23]*Ibid.,* 367.

[24]*Ibid.,* 500.

[25]New Haven, Yale University Press, 1932, pp. 210-17, courtesy Banks-Baldwin Law Pub. Co., Cleveland, Ohio; see also, August Mencken, *By the Neck,* New York, Hastings House 1942, pp. 49-57, "The Hand of Providence," also New Orleans news item, June 6, 1920.

and acquaintances. Early in 1893, the hooded band in that county, Marion, flogged a Negro employed by one of its other members, Will Buckley. Enraged that the Klan had perpetrated this on his own hired hand, Buckley swore he would reveal the secrets of the organization to the authorities. This he did soon thereafter when the grand jury met. On his way home, accompanied by his hired hand and his brother, Jim, he was ambushed and shot down by persons concealed in the brush alongside the road.

Within a few days, Will Purvis was arrested for the crime, and in due time, was indicted for the killing. He was found guilty and sentenced on August 5, 1893, with hanging to be carried out on February 7, 1894. The scaffold scene was typical of those days in a rural community with some 5,000 persons milling about, intent upon a conventional hanging. There were many in the mob who could not believe that Purvis was guilty, but many others believed justice was about to be done.

As the rope was placed around his neck, the deputy-sheriff, seeing an "ungainly string dangling from the knot," cut the string flush with the knot, "while the minister droned his prayer 'God save this innocent boy.'" When everything was ready, the executioner, taking his hatchet, cut the rope holding the trap and Purvis's body dropped with a sharp jerk. But the knot, instead of tightening around its victim, untwisted, and Purvis fell to the ground unhurt. As Professor Borchard describes the event:

> An indescribable horror shook the spellbound onlookers. Purvis staggered to his feet, the death mask falling free from his head, and, turning to the sheriff, said simply: "Let's have it over with." With his hands and feet still bound, Purvis stepped up the first step of the scaffold before the awed silence was broken. A wave of emotion seized the crowd. Some ascribed the incident as significance far beyond the natural import—that divine intervention had saved Purvis.[26]

While the officials were preparing another rope, murmurs were heard from members of the crowd. A kind of groundswell developed, led by Dr. Ford, a local physician, and the Rev. J. Sibley, urging that Purvis be freed. There were cries of "Don't let him

---

[26]Borchard, *op. cit.,* p. 213.

hang," on the one hand, and, on the other, equally vocal cries of "Hang him—he's guilty." The officials were obviously perplexed. On the advice of an attorney who was present, the sheriff began to prepare another rope to carry out his sworn duty. The physician, Dr. Ford, asked for a vote from the crowd as to a decision, and the majority demanded that Purvis be freed. The sheriff, realizing that it would be futile to proceed, loosened the bonds of the prisoner and returned him to jail.

A subsequent decision of the state supreme court demanded that Purvis be hanged according to his sentence, and set a new date—July 31, 1894. Upon hearing of this, some of the culprit's friends spirited him away from his home. As there was to be a gubernatorial election soon, one of the candidates promised that if he were elected, he would commute Purvis's sentence to life imprisonment. He won and Purvis was sent to prison.

Two years later, the state's star witness, the brother of the murdered man, contradicted his previous testimony which completely nullified the state's case against Purvis. Consequently, he was not only freed from prison but given a full and unconditional pardon. From then on he took his place in the community, married and had a large family. He became a prosperous farmer but realized there still hovered over him a dark cloud—he had not been vindicated of the murder of Buckley.

In 1917, Joe Beard, an aged member of the town, "got religion" at a revival meeting of Holy Rollers and confessed he had done wrong. Shortly thereafter, he became fatally ill and, on his death bed, assumed full blame for the Buckley murder. He further maintained that Purvis, a member of the Klan at the time, refused to have anything to do with the proposed manhandling of Buckley and withdrew from the group. At a later meeting of some of the members, Beard and Louis Thornhill were given the task of disposing of Buckley for telling Klan secrets. Thornhill, according to Beard, fired the shot that killed Buckley. He, it seems, lost his nerve and Buckley's companions, his brother and his Negro hand, escaped death.

At last, Purvis was vindicated, and, in time, he was awarded the sum of $5,000 for his services as he labored for four years in the state penitentiary. So this case assumed the proportion of a classic because "the rope slipped."

AN ENGLISH COUNTERPART — JOHN LEE

The counterpart of the Purvis case is that of John Lee, saved from the gallows at Exeter jail in England on February 23, 1885, for the murder of Miss Emma Keyse, for whom he worked on November 15, 1884. Lee denied his guilt up to the last and many were willing to agree to his innocence, especially after the gallows failed to end his life. The executioner was the respected James Berry who held the post from 1884 to 1892 and who, in later years, was an uncompromising opponent of capital punishment. Lee, in addition to denying his guilt, insisted that he "would never hang." Berry examined the gallows in the coach-house of the jail and, while he was none too pleased with it, apparently passed it as satisfactory for its grim work.

Everything was in readiness; the straps were placed on the condemned man, his head was covered with the white hood, and the chaplain was intoning the last prayer. The signal was given, the lever pulled, but the doors to the trap struck. Berry pulled frantically but the doors would not budge. In embarrassment, all present did what anyone would do in such a situation—they tried to be helpful. Lee was unpinioned and stood aside while the hangman examined the faulty doors. Strangely, they were found to be in good working order. For a second time, Lee stood upon the trap and the ritual was repeated. Again, the signal was given and again the doors refused to yield. All save Lee were, almost in a state of shock. Once again, he stood aside and the doors were examined. They appeared in good shape. The condemned man was readied for the third time and, unbelievably, the same painful procedure was repeated. Lee just would not die! At this juncture, the under-sheriff ordered him to be taken back to his cell with the execution postponed until the Home Secretary could be apprised of the uncanny occurrence.

In short order, Lee was given a respite and then the sentence was commuted to "penal servitude for life" which, in those days, meant twenty years. In time, he was released and it is believed that he married and emigrated to America.

There were many reasons advanced as to the cause of this mishap at the "tree." There were those, of course, who maintained it was the Divine Will interceding. Lee himself offered no explanation except that he was convinced, as he had vehemently contended

earlier, he would not hang. The best explanation advanced was
that the board of the platform nearest the trap was warped and
when the condemned man stood on it, it jammed the mechanism.
When he stepped off, it fell back into place. Whatever the explanation, John Lee holds the distinction of being the only man sentenced to die in Great Britain who was saved because the hangman
could not legally kill him on the gallows. It is believed that Lee
and Purvis are in a class by themselves.[27]

STRANGE CASES NOT SO FORTUNATE

Not so fortunate as Purvis or Lee was Jack O'Neill, who was
hanged at Greenfield, Franklin County, Massachusetts on January 7, 1898—one of the last persons to be hanged in the Bay
State (the electric chair was installed in 1900)—for the murder
of Hattie Evelyn McCloud. He was convicted of strangling his
victim in a country lane at Buckland, near Shelburne Falls, on
January 8, 1897. He denied the killing to the last, maintaining
he was a "dupe of racial bigotry" when this prejudice was still
widespread. He said calmly, as he stood at the gallows: "I shall
meet death like a man and I hope those who see me hanged will
live to see the day when it is proved that I am innocent—and it
will be, some time."

And it was—at least to the satisfaction of many Massachusetts
citizens. Eddie Collins, ace Boston news correspondent in Cuba
at the time, interviewed a soldier who was fighting in the Spanish-
American War, and obtained a confession. The man, from Shelburne Falls, was a member of the Sixth Massachusetts militia. He
readily confessed that he was the killer. Collins flashed this news
to the *Boston Post* but not in time to save O'Neill.[28]

Nor did a repentant confession of two robbers in Rhode Island
save Dr. Hamilton from the gallows in the murder of a Dr. Saun-
derson in 1825—details now obscure. Hamilton's pistol was found

---

[27]For details of the Lee case, see Justin Atholl, *The Reluctant Hangman,* London, John
    Long, Ltd., 1956, pp. 124-134; see also, *The Man They Could Not Hang: The Life
    Story of John Lee* (Babbacombe Lee), Arthur Westbrook Co., Cleveland.

[28]Details regarding this case may be seen in the *Boston Post,* June 26, 1950; summar-
    ized by Sara Ehrmann in *Federal Probation,* March 1962, p. 19, an article entitled
    "For Whom the Chair Waits."

near the dead man's body. The robbers admitted that they stole it.[29]

The strange case of Burton, of some Missouri county, vintage of the 1840's, is worth recording. The facts are obscure, the locale more so, and thus far, the case cannot be identified. However, there are allusions to it and these emerge from reliable sources, despite their antiquity. The Rev. Charles Spear of Boston relates the bare facts as follows: Burton, in love with a beautiful and socially prominent girl, was disappointed by her refusal to marry him. She plighted her troth to another and this anonymous person "betrayed" her. Angered and humiliated the young woman killed this person and Burton permitted himself to be accused and tried for the crime. Apparently, he had some confidence that he could not be convicted on whatever evidence that might be presented. Unfortunately, he guessed unwisely and was hanged. The date was probably in 1842. The report continues by stating "when she learned he had sacrificed himself for her," she proceeded to write and "publish the whole history of her wrongs and her revenge . . . she was from a genteel family, very proud."[30]

A travesty of error is recorded in Dutchess County, New York, the time being in the first instance, 1806 and in the second, some ten years later. It involves the murder by and subsequent hanging of Jesse Wood. He was convicted of killing his son Joseph in a brawl, in which another son, Hezekiah, was also involved. Allegedly, the father was drunk and his shotgun went off, killing the quarreling son. He was convicted largely on the testimony of the other son, Hezekiah. The hanging took place at Poughkeepsie on December 5, 1806.

Consternation must have been rampant in the Hudson River communities when, with the appearance of the Poughkeepsie *Daily Herald* of January 15, 1817, it was reported in a righteously indignant story that the surviving son of the hanged man had, on his death-bed, confessed to the crime of a decade earlier. The language used in the article reflected shock, dismay and condemnation, as it described the perfidy of this son Hezekiah.

---

[29]So stated by Clifford Kirkpatrick, "The Death Penalty," from Senate Report, Rhode Island, 18.

[30]Sources, L. Marie Child, *Letters From New York*, 1943, Letter XXXI, November 19, 1842; and Charles Spear, *Essays on the Punishment of Death*, Boston, 1844, p. 116; Spear may have obtained his facts from Mrs. Child.

If the surprise of the natives was immense upon reading of this, it can scarcely be imagined when, one week later, the same paper —dated January 22—published a correction, or retraction by stating that upon enquiry it was found that "Mr. Hezekiah Wood was still living in Fishkill where he always maintained that the story of his sickness and confession was as incorrect as that of his death."[40]

The Stephen Boorn Case — Vermont

The locale of this strange case is Manchester, Vermont, the time, 1812. The alleged victim was one Russell Colvin, brother-in-law of Stephen and Jesse Boorn, a man with little mental strength but with a periodic impulse to wander far from the small hamlet where he earned a precarious living.

On May 10 of that year, Colvin disappeared, but for some time, no one paid too much attention since this was his wont. But after a while, one of the Boorn clan, Uncle Amos, maintained he had a dream. He saw Russell in that dream and he, Russell, told him he had been murdered. Furthermore, he told Amos where his body could be found; in a hole that had once been a cellar in Manchester. In truth, some bones were found, in addition to a couple of knives that were later identified as once belonging to Colvin. Gossip, hysteria, fright, and small-town provincialism, if not ignorance, managed to construct a case of murder. A step further and the finger of guilt was placed on Stephen and Jesse Boorn, Colvin's own kinsmen.

Before proceeding with the bizarre elements of this story, let it be stated that the case is famous in legal annals for two good reasons: first, two defendants were convicted for murder without a body having been found; second, because a grand jury indicted on almost no solid, substantial evidence. Jesse contended that Stephen had fought with Colvin and Stephen insisted he had not; yet in time, Stephen confessed to killing Colvin!

He told a vivid story of participating in a fight with the victim over some trivial matter, of how he hit him with a club and actually killed him. He also stated in his confession that he took the body and "put him [it] in the corner of the fence by the cellar hole

---

[40]Courtesy Mrs. Amy Ver Nooy of Poughkeepsie.

and put briars over him . . . and when it was dark went down . . . and dug a grave as well as [he] could." He signed this fantastic, imaginative and damning confession on August 27, 1819. He and his brother, Jesse, were tried in November and both were condemned and sentenced to death. The date set for the execution was January 28, 1820. A petition to the legislature for their reprieve resulted finally in Jesse's receiving such grace, but Stephen was denied by an overwhelming vote of ninety-seven to forty-two. Jesse was taken to the state prison at Windsor and Stephen was jailed, pending the date of the hanging.

Then something amazing happened! The Hon. Leonard Sergeant, one of the defendants' attorneys, *decided to advertise for Russell Colvin.* He did this against the advice of his legal colleagues, and despite public ridicule. The first notice appeared in the Rutland (Vt.) *Herald* for November 26, 1819, in the Albany *Daily Advertiser,* and in the New York *Evening Post.* The notices simply stated that an innocent man was about to die for the murder of Colvin who had disappeared seven years earlier, urging anyone who might have information concerning the missing man would do well by communicating with the writer.

It was by reading the *Post* article, allegedly by pure chance, that one Taber Chadwick of Shrewsbury, Monmouth County, New Jersey, recognized Russell Colvin as a man who had worked on a farm of William Polhemus of Dover, New Jersey. He responded with a leter to the New York paper and, in short time, Manchester officials had gone to the designated village and enticed the wanted man back to his native heath. He was identified and recognized "beyond all doubt" as Colvin and, after another trial, Stephen Boorn was discharged, a free man.

A still further melodramatic angle was injected by some of the zealous opponents of capital punishment during the last half of the century. William S. Balch of New York City is the authority for the following description of the Boorn case:

> The day of the execution at length arrived. Hundreds of people from the hills and vales were gathered around the gallows, to witness the dying struggles of a poor unfortunate fellow-sinner. The hour had arrived, and the elder Bourne, still avowing his innocence, wan and weak, was led forth into the ring, and

stood beneath the horrid engine of death. The sheriff was about to adjust the halter, and draw the dismal cap, when a cry was heard from behind the ring, "Stop! Stop! For God's sake stop!" All eyes were directed that way; when, to the astonishment of all, the *murdered* Colvin was led into the ring, presented to the sheriff, recognized by the assembled neighbors, and greeted by Bourne, with feelings better imagined than described; and the doomed to return home in disappointment—as some remarked, "without seeing the *fun* they anticipated."

Mr. Balch continues by stating that had Colvin's return been delayed by a "single hour, an innocent man would have been hurried out of the world as a felon, leaving a wife and children, and friends to lament his untimely death; humanity to weep over the mistakes, and weaknesses, and cruelties, of human legislation; and judges and juries to reproach themselves for taking the fearful responsibility of destroying a life which they could not restore when their errors were clearly manifested."[41] The fact is that Colvin actually returned to Manchester *six weeks* before Boorn was to have been hanged. He appeared on the scene on December 22, 1819.[42] Balch is reported to have been "born and reared in the vicinity of the place where the facts occurred" but sometimes abolitionists are tempted to employ literary license and more, to prove their resentment and disgust for capital punishment.

Colvin "the dead man" returned to New Jersey and the Boorn brothers went off to Ohio. There was much speculation about this case in local circles and, in time, it became a notorious, if not distinguished case in the law books.[43] Edmund Pearson, who presents this as one of his famous cases, has this to say about Stephen Boorn's confession: ". . . it was probably incited by fear, and made in hopes of reducing the charge to manslaughter." Rumors persisted, too, that perhaps the New Jersey Colvin was an imposter, despite the fact that he was identified and recognized by many townsmen and, actually, beyond "any count."

---

[41]Quoted by Spear, *op. cit.,* pp. 110-111.

[42]McDade, *op. cit.,* 111.

[43]See John H. Wigmore, *Principles of Judicial Proof,* pp. 559-564.

The Boorn men asked the state for compensation for false arrest but their claims were denied.[44]

A well-known case from Cooperstown, New York is the Stephen Arnold affair, which we mentioned earlier in another connection (Chapter I, page 26). Arnold, a school teacher, had beaten his six-year-old niece, Betsy Van Ambergh, to death and was doomed to die. But in the nick of time, on the day of the public hanging, July 19, 1805, he received a commutation. This case is interesting because it was so obvious that the crowd was disappointed and the sheriff had catered to them by withholding the pardon—he carried it in his pocket—until the procession arrived at the tree.[45]

The Strange Case of Farnsworth

Reverberations of a strange incident that occurred in Genesee County, New York—Batavia the county seat—occasionally resound as old-timers and raconteurs of murders, trials, hangings and the like, settle down to swap stories. One that still baffles persons learned in the law has to do with a chap named Farnsworth who wandered into the vicinity sometime during the year 1822. Facts are scarce and hazy but it is well known that he was arrested for forging United States Land Warrants. A federal district court was ordered held which was convened in July of that year. Hon. Roger Skinner presided, and Jacob Sutherland, later a jurist on the Supreme Court Bench of New York State, was appointed to prosecute.

Farnsworth was indicted, tried and sentenced to death! It was apparently believed at the time that the only proper penalty for so dastardly a deed was death and, accordingly, he was a doomed man. However, his counsel, General Ethan Allen, prepared a petition and sent it to President Monroe in Washington, begging for a reprieve for the unhappy culprit. Time sped quickly by and at last the day arrived for the execution of Farnsworth. On the

---

[44]For further details about this strange case, see Pearson, *Studies in Murder,* New York, Macmillan, 1924, "Uncle Amos Dreams a Dream," pp. 265-285; McDade's listings, 111-114. McDade states that this case "is a constant reminder that innocent persons can be convicted." See also Sherman Moulton, *The Boorn Mystery,* Montpelier, Vt., Vermont Historical Society, 1937.

[45]See also the Zimmerman case at Orwigsburg, Pennsylvania in Chapter I, p. 27.

eve of that potential, a courier arrived from the President granting a six-month stay. It is reported that "a vexed, disappointed, chagrined assembly of thousands who had flocked to the village to witness the struggles of Farnsworth being launched into that 'undiscovered country' would not leave until the turnkey admitted them into the back gate of the jail to see the 'monster' at a shilling a head."

Subsequently, the president, on examining the charge and record, concluded that Farnsworth had violated no law of the United States and granted him a pardon.[46]

William Freeman Comings — New Hampshire

Another who escaped the hangman's noose through a strange quirk of fate was William Freeman Comings, of Haverhill (and of other hamlets), New Hampshire, condemned to die on October 30, 1844 for the murder of his wife on September 9, 1842. Controversy in the state over the death penalty, at that particular time, capriciously, but literally, snatched this unhappy and unsuccessful tanner and farmer from the jaws (but perhaps one should say, *noose*) of death. It is a strange but not especially dramatic story—certainly not nearly so dramatic as the Stephen Boorn case, which we have just related.

At a reasonably early age, Comings was working as a tanner in Andover, and, there, fell in love and married one Adeline Tenny whose father, Captain Tenny, held a fairly high social position in the community. This was in 1832 and things were none too good in that area economically. Comings found it difficult at that time, and, actually, for the remainder of his life, to achieve any degree of financial security on his own; he was bedeviled by one small failure after another in fairly rapid succession. His wife, probably prodded on by her socially proper father, decided that it would be best for her "to return to the old home" because she seemed unhappy that her ill-fated spouse could not make ends meet.

At the time, Comings was living at Bath, another small town in the state and while there he met the Abbott family, one member of which was the comely Sarah Ann. This was in 1841. In June of

---

[46]Data through courtesy Miss Charlotte M. Read, Holland Land Office Building Museum, Batavia, N.Y.

that year, he wrote ". . . I discovered that Sarah Ann was frequently gazing at me, and, as she caught my eyes, turned hers off with a deep sigh." This was the beginning of an irresistable affinity that was to precipitate the young but unsuccessful small-town bumpkin into tragedy. For, in due time, his wife, Ann, probably overwhelmed with a feeling of guilt on leaving her spouse, decided to return to him. Her husband was lodging in the Nemiah Hoskins home, so she moved in with him. But by this time, the two illicit lovers were holding clandestine trysts and contemplating elopement, as well as discussing the possibility of a divorce, in order to resolve the impossible situation.

The die was cast for all the parties enmeshed in this sad triangle of love and possession. It seemed to the unhappy man that there was nothing to do but to judiciously get rid of the unreasonable wife. So, on the morning of September 9, 1842, it appeared that Adeline had hanged herself from the bedpost with a handkerchief. Despite skepticism on the part of many persons, a court of inquest ruled that Mrs. Comings did "voluntarily and feloniously, as a felon of herself, kill and murder herself against the peace and dignity of the State." In justice to the bereaved husband, he tarried a while to see if an indictment for murder might be forthcoming but, as nothing as formidable as that occurred, he injudiciously left the state. He did nothing to cover up his departure which certainly was "open and above board."

It was at this juncture that many skeptics looked upon the young man's departure as an incipient mark of potential guilt. So, action was soon taken to bring him back for further questioning. He was picked up at Rensselaerville, New York, and promptly returned to stand trial for murder. The grand jury indicted him for strangling his wife, of hanging her with an handkerchief "of the value of fifty cents, of beating, bruising, wounding and striking her with his hands, fists, feet, and knees on her head, breast, heart, abdomen, and stomach." It occurs to us that the wording of this indictment is at least unique in court annals.

After an exciting trial in which many witnesses for both sides paraded through the court-room, including several medical men, Comings was convicted and sentenced to death. But at this point of time, there was much controversy throughout the State of New

Hampshire concerning the death penalty. A bill to abolish "that barbarous penalty" was introduced in the senate in June, 1844, only four months before Comings was slated to die on the gallows. Mindful that a candidate for the hangman's noose was languishing in the Plymouth jail in Grafton County, a special plebiscite was promulgated to sense popular opinion on the penalty of death for murderers. As David Brion Davis, who has narrated and documented this unusual story, relates it: "Thus his life was placed directly in the hands of the citizens of New Hampshire. It was a dramatic moment, some two years after Adeline Comings' death, one year after the trial, when the voters . . . ruled that a man should not live."[47]

The vote stood: affirmative, 11,241; negative, 21,544. The governor, who had hoped for a resounding repudiation of the death penalty, was disappointed. It was just not considered quite cricket to hang Comings after the voter let-down at the polls. Thus a petition was introduced in the House to commute his sentence. In desultory fashion, as even such momentous issues are often handled in legislatures, with some pulling and hauling, on December 18, but eight days before the hanging was to have taken place, the members of that body voted 154 to 84 to give the governor the power to commute sentence. Two days later, the senate concurred and the governor acted. Comings was sent to state prison at Concord and remained there until June, 1853 when he was pardoned by executive clemency. It is believed he went West, perhaps to the Oregon country. Sarah Ann Abbott, his paramour, married a man named Bishop in 1845 and died in Quebec in 1882.

Here, then, is a case of a person saved from the "tree" because of a heated controversy over capital punishment. New Hampshire still retains the death penalty, and is one of the seven states that persist in the use of the hangman's rope and noose, but finds it difficult actually to snuff out the life of a murderer. Public hangings were abolished in 1837 but for years after that date executions could hardly be labeled private (see Chapter VI, p. 296, for discussion of this).

---

[47]This and other material comes from Mr. Davis's "Murder in New Hampshire," *The New England Quarterly*, V. 28, No. 2 (June 1955) 147-63; cit. at 161.

The following case deals with one whose life was placed in "double jeopardy" and still hanged. The full story is, perhaps, not known; only the bare facts have come to our attention. It is the fate of one James Mobley of Washington, Wilkes County, Georgia, in colonial times. He is supposed to have been acquitted by a jury of the charges of "Horse Stealing and Hogg Stealing and other misdemeanors." But for some strange reason new evidence was trumped up and displayed to another jury a few days later—he languished in jail in the meantime—which declared him guilty and he was sentenced to hang. The hanging took place on August 25, 1779.[48]

THOSE WHO CHEATED THE GALLOWS

By Escaping

To hear the solemn voice of a judge, as he sentences a person convicted of an offense deemed at the time as capital, in the awful tones so characteristic of the courtroom—*to be hanged by the neck until you are dead,* must have struck terror in the hearts of many. Few could be so composed as to take such a sentence casually, despite apparent outward composure. It is quite possible that a fair percentage believed that under no circumstances would that awful penalty be carried out; there were many ways of circumventing the law. There was hope of a new trial, of a pardon, a commutation, or at least a reprieve or stay of execution which would delay the sentence being carried out. Then, as a last resort, there was a bare chance of escape; and if such failed, perhaps suicide as the lesser of two evils! There were many escapes and many suicides through the years. There are cases of persons condemned who were taken from the officials or jails and lynched· Still others died of natural causes—and even of fright. We shall briefly discuss a few such cases.

Escapes

One of the most notorious cases that stirred the country at the turn of the century was that of the "Biddle Boys"—Edward and

---

[48]Source, Ulrich B. Phillips, *Life and Labor in the Old South,* Little, Brown, 1963 edition, p. 351; see also, Washington (Ga.) *News Reporter,* August 25, 1922.

John (alias Wright) condemned to death in Allegheny County (Pittsburgh, Pennsylvania) for the murder of police officer James Fitzpatrick on April 11, 1901. Both had long criminal records, were natives of Amherstburg, Ontario—their father had gone there to escape the Civil War draft—and had served prison sentences in the Joliet, Illinois and Columbus, Ohio prisons. The killing of Officer Fitzpatrick occurred in connection with the robbery of a grocery store in which two female decoys had been used; their names were Jessie Bodine and Jennie Zebers. Another person involved was Walter Dorman who turned state's evidence and thus saved himself from the death penalty.

It is alleged that Jessie Bodine killed the grocer, but she was never tried for the offense. The Biddles were arrested and stood trial for murder. John was slated to hang January 14, 1902, and Edward on January 16. Up to this point, the story is little different from hundreds of others that have taken place in the annals of murder. But from here on, things began to take an unusual turn.

After receiving a short respite until February 25 and 27, respectively, the men escaped. It was on a cold and blizzardy night, January 30. The escape was made possible by the aid of Sheriff Peter Soffel's wife, Kate, who actually went along with the absconders in a bobsled. Edward and the female had apparently fallen in love as she ministered to the needs of those incarcerated in her husband's jail. By an ingenious set of signals, in which mirrors were used to communicate, Mrs. Soffel agreed to chloroform her husband and to supply the Biddles with the necessary guns and the conveyance for the getaway. They escaped, but their freedom was short. They were apprehended near Butler, Pennsylvania, not too far away, several shots were fired, and the desperadoes captured and returned to the Allegheny County jail. In a subsequent trial, Kate was convicted and sentenced to two years in prison. After her release, she tried a theatrical venture but the authorities stopped her performance. She next became a dressmaker and finally ended her days in a mental hospital.

Both Biddles died of the wounds they received during their capture. There were ugly rumors that they had been brutally handled by the officers. A drama was woven around this colorful case entitled *A Desperate Chance* which, many years later, was adapted into a motion picture with the same title.[49]

We found several cases of escapees in our intensive study of Pennsylvania, all, strangely enough, after the period of public hangings, which ended in 1834. We have no explanation as to the reason condemned criminals did not abscond prior to hanging during the early period, in this state or others, unless it is because the spread of time between the sentence and its execution was so brief.

The earliest case that caught our attention in Pennsylvania was that of the Flannagan brothers of Cambria County (Ebensburg, county seat). They had been condemned for killing a Betty Holder on July 3, 1841 at Loretta, as they passed through the town. It was reported that they were "in search of plunder." Condemned to death on October 5, they made their escape from the Ebensburg jail the following day and were never again heard from. The news story tells us that their escape was effected "by the heroic devotion of a sister."[50]

The Patrick Moran (Boran) case emanating from Schuylkill County (county seat at the time, Orwigsburg), is of more than passing interest. Moran pleaded guilty to the murder of one Larrabee Brennan, which he committed on September 7, 1847. In the *Miners' Journal* (Pottsville) we find: "while he [Moran] pined away in jail he seemed to have acquired an escape complex." Later, a John Ennis was found guilty of a misdemeanor in secreting a file in a bundle of "segars" and handing it into Moran's cell. A later story tells of Moran's escape with five companions through "an incision in the wall." This despite the fact that Moran was heavily manacled.

A story from Tennessee tells of the escape of James Foreman who ambushed a wealthy Cherokee half-breed and was condemned to death. While he was waiting for a decision from the supreme court relative to his case, he escaped into Indian terri-

---

[49]For a popular account of this case, see Arthur Forrest, *The Biddle Boys and Mrs. Soffel: The Great Pittsburgh Tragedy and Romance,* Baltimore, L. & M. Oppenheimer, 1908; see also, Thomas S. Duke, *Celebrated Criminal Cases in America,* pp. 565-568.

[50]Henry Wilson, *History of Cambria County,* 1907, Vol. I, p. 177.

tory. This was in 1835 and the scene probably Nashville.[51] The only significance of this obscure case is the legal jurisdiction of that territory at that time—Tennessee or the federal government.

Suicide

The suicide route seems to have held out much more promise for the condemned in by-passing the hangman's noose than did escape. Many cases scattered over the entire country have come to our attention. A few of these merit our attention, primarily because of their renown among devotees of murder, mayhem, and the area of crime in general.

We may begin with the case of John C. Colt, brother of the inventor of the revolver that was to become a household word, especially in the West. Colt, the killer, had murdered one Samuel Adams, a printer, on September 17, 1841, in New York City, not with a revolver but with a hatchet. In order to conceal his crime, he was about to ship the body of his victim to New Orleans but it was discovered before the ship could leave port. He was eventually convicted and sentenced to death. However, the day before the fatal day he surprised everyone by marrying Caroline Henshaw in his death cell. One of the witnesses to this most unusual matrimonial incident was no less a person than John Howard Payne, the composer of *Home, Sweet Home*. One hour before the scheduled hanging Colt stabbed himself through the heart and succumbed to the wound. The date of this impromptu event was November 18, 1842, a full year after he had committed his crime.[52]

A contemporary militant crusader against the death penalty, Mrs. L. Marie Child, wrote of this suicide in the following satirical vein:

> We were to have had an execution yesterday; but the wretched prisoner [Colt] avoided it by suicide. The gallows had been erected for several hours, and, with a cool refinement of cruelty, was hoisted before the window of the condemned; the hangman was all ready to cut the cord; marshals paced back and forth, smoking and whistling; spectators were waiting im-

---

[51]McDade, *op. cit.*, 311.

[52]*Ibid.*, 205-207.

patiently to see whether he would "die game." Printed circulars had been handed abroad to summon the number of witnesses required by law; "You are respectfully invited to witness the execution of John C. Colt." I trust some of them are preserved for museums. Specimens should be kept, as relics of a barbarous age, for succeeding generations to wonder at.[53]

Mrs. Childs commented that females were incensed that they did not receive tickets of admission to witness the hanging. She continues with her bitter denunciation:

> And there the multitude stood, with open watches, and strained ears, to catch the sound, and the marshals smoked and whistled, and the hangman walked up and down, waiting for his prey, when, lo!—word was brought that the criminal was found dead in his bed! He had asked one half hour alone to prepare for his departure; and at the end of that brief interval, he was found with a dagger thrust in his heart! The tidings were received with fierce mutterings of disappointed rage!

Coincidentally, at that hour, a fire broke out at the very top of the cupola of the New York City Prison. As Mrs. Child described the conflagration: "The wind was high, and the flames rushed upwards as if the angry spirits below had escaped on fiery wings."[54]

Another strange quirk associated with this case is that Colt's brother, Samuel, inventor of the famous firearm, was called upon to demonstrate his array of pistols before the court, despite the fact that the murder weapon had been a hatchet. As McDade states: "the relevance of this display is obscure."[55]

DR. VALOROUS P. COOLIDGE: The Valorous P. Coolidge case is one that frequently comes up in discussion of suicide as a way to avoid hanging. It is the story of a physician who found himself in financial straits and unwittingly killed someone from whom he hoped to extract money. His victim was Edward Mathews, of Waterville, Maine, known to have possessed some money, whom he enticed into his office. First, however, he had cleverly urged

---

[53]*Letters from New York,* New York, Chas. S. Francis Co., 1843, p. 207.

[54]The above quotes from Mrs. Child's work are from Charles Spear, *Essays on the Punishment of Death* (privately printed) Boston, 1844, pp. 208-209.

[55]McDade, *op. cit.,* item 205.

his assistant, Flint, to stay away for a while. He gave his victim a wee bit of brandy in which was another "wee bit" of hydrocyanic acid. To finish up the job he struck his victim several times with a hatchet. He then sought out his assistant whom he told a "cock and bull story" of how Mathews had inconsiderately died in his office of natural causes. He urged Flint to assist him in carrying the body to Kennebec River, but as an afterthought, decided to bury the body in the cellar. It was discovered the next morning. A coroner's jury, which actually included Dr. Coolidge, performed an autopsy which certainly bestows on the doctor-murderer some kind of macabre-distinction—that of probably being the only person in this country, at least, to legally and professionally examine his own victim.[56]

But the hands of a cruel fate clutched out and caught the shrewd Waterville physician. He was convicted and sentenced to death. But, clever to the last, he cheated the hangman's noose and committed suicide almost immediately after being sentenced. As Olive Woolley Burt, collector of ballads has demonstrated: the case called for a ballad and it was duly composed. It consists of twenty-six verses but only the following seem pertinent:

The Ballad of Edward Mathews

Poor Edward Mathews, where is he? Sent headlong to eternity,
The mortal debt by him is paid, And in his narrow bed he's laid.

No more will anguish seize his soul; No more will poison fill his bowl;
No more will fiendship clutch his throat, Or o'er his mangled body gloat.

O V. P. Coolidge how could you So black a deed of murder do?
You on your honor did pretend To be his nearest earthly friend.

You knew to Brighton he had gone, And watched each hour for his return,
The hay for cattle which he drove You swore within your heart to have.

---

[56]Dr. Palmer of Rugeley of England also shares this distinction. Bleakley, in his *Hangmen of England,* says of this man: "the greatest name in the criminal calender of nineteeth century England . . . wholesale poisoner, who murdered his wife, his brother, several of his friends and probably all of his five children." London, Chapman & Hill, 1929, p. 215.

You failed in that but did succeed, By promising a mortgage
deed,
Of all on earth that you possessed So that he could in safety rest.

The money from the bank he drew And brought with faithful-
ness to you,
Not dreaming of your vile intent, Alone into your office went.

You said, "Dear Mathews, worthy friend, Our friendship here
shall never end.
A glass of brandy you must drink; 'Twill do you good, I surely
think."

He drank the liquor you had fixed, With Prussic acid amply
mixed.
Then cried, "O Lord! What can it be? What Poison have you
given me?"

You seized his throat and stopp'd his breath,, Until your friend
lay still in death;
Then with your hatchet bruised his head, After he was entirely
dead.

His money then you took away, And hid his watch out in your
sleigh;
Then called to your confederate And all your doings did relate.

I have a secret, Flint, you said, And if by you I am betrayed
The state will me for murder try And on the gallows I must die.
That cursed Mathews, don't you think? Came here and did some
brandy drink,
Then instantly he fell down dead, And I have thumped him on
the head.

Where can we now his body thrust, So that no one can us mis-
trust,
In younder room his corpse is laid, I wish the river were its
bed.

The murder we have done this night, Tomorrow will be brought
to light,
But my good character and name Will shield me from all harm
and blame.

We dragged his lifeless form away, Into a cellar there to lay,
Until someone by chance did see His mangled, bruised and dead
body.

O, Edward Mathews, could you know The scathing pangs I un-
dergo,
You surely would look down from Heaven, And say let Coolidge
be forgiven.[56a]

Several persons condemned for murder and sentenced to death
in Pennsylvania have committed suicide. This is doubtless true in
most, if not all, of the states. Most of these suicides, as well as the
cases in which they have been involved, are obscure and are not
known to many persons beyond the immediate vicinity or county
in which they occurred. A couple of those that happened in
Pennsylvania deserve some attention.

The first case is that of Emanuel Ettinger, one of four persons
who participated in an inept robbery and murder in Snyder County
back in 1877. The quartet, aside from Ettinger, consisted of Jonathan and Uriah Moyer, brothers, and Israel Erb, all natives of
the county. Living in a shack on Jack's Mountain, near Truxelville,
were a seventy-seven-year-old recluse and his wife, John and
Gretchen Kintzler. They were known to be surly, unapproachable
people and Kintzler, a rugged, Pennsylvania Dutch grubber, was
known to own both guns and pistols; he was referred to as *"Der
alt Donner Wetter."* It was believed by many that the Kintzlers
kept a large sum of money in a strong-box hidden in the rafters
of their cabin.

On the night of December 2, 1877, the four men set out for
what they referred to as a "coon hunting" expedition to the mountains. They arrived at the Kintzler cabin, broke in, murdered the
couple in cold blood, ransacked and burned the cabin, and fled
with but $150. The crime itself was nothing unusual. The four
were apprehended and condemned. The Moyers were sentenced
to death and eventually were hanged in the Middleburg jail. Erb
and Ettinger were also sentenced to die but both escaped the
noose. Erb's sentence was commuted and Ettinger ended his own
life in the jail.

Ettinger swore he "would never hang." It is believed he had
secreted strychnine on his person some time before and used it to
end his life. News accounts are confused as to whether he died

[56a]Burt, *op. cit.*, pp. 83-87.

of typhoid fever, or of eating ground glass. However, after burial his body was exhumed and an autopsy made when the strychnine version was substantiated. The date of his death is October 21, 1881. The Moyer brothers were the only persons ever hanged in Snyder County.[57]

Abram I. Eckerd of Luzerne County, Pennsylvania, a school janitor, killed his employer, Frederick T. Rittembender, on May 14, 1896, because the latter had chided him for carelessness in his work. After his conviction for murder, the family appealed to the governor for clemency, stating that "as a child he had been blown up in a well in which he was working so that it was doubtful that he had been rational when he perpetrated the crime." Such a reason for clemency might be more favorably received today than it was in 1896. Eckerd was doomed to die. But on the night before the scheduled hanging, he was visited by his wife, five children and his four sisters. The next morning, he took "enough morphine to kill ten men." It was reported that "seven or eight doctors worked over him," his fate being in doubt for many hours. The sheriff was loath "to carry him to the gallows at the appointed time" so he set "a dead-line of three o'clock." But Eckerd cheated the hangman; he died at 11:40 a.m., December 8, 1896. Prisoners and members of the family were questioned as to the possible source of the poison but to no avail. The sheriff was caustically criticized by the local press but the unpleasant incident was soon dissipated by more interesting and worthwhile events in town and country.[58]

Another Pennsylvania suicide case whose renown has spread beyond its locale, Philadelphia, is that of one George Twitchell, who ended his life in old Moyamensing Prison on the eve of his scheduled hanging, April 8, 1869. Twichell beat his mother-in-law, Mary H. Hill, to death with a poker and threw her body out the window to make it look like suicide. His wife, Camilla, was acquitted of participation in the crime. Another prisoner informed a guard that Twitchell was about to take his own life but he arrived at the cell too late. Physicians found a bottle of potassium

---

[57] For details of this notorious case, see George F. Dunkelberger, "The Kintzler Murder," in Snyder County *Historical Bulletin*, Vol. II, p. 3: January 1942, pp. 22-5.

[58] From news stories in Wilkes-Barre *Record*, December 9 and other contemporary dates.

cyanide in the victim's boot, the contents half gone. A druggist friend of Twitchell's was accused of smuggling in the poison but he was never prosecuted. This case is well publicized with pamphlets and is well known to bibliophiles of murder.[59]

Still another well-known case of suicide of a person condemned to death by hanging is that of Dr. Thomas Thatcher Graves. The doctor had been convicted of poisoning Mrs. Josephine A. Barnaby, a wealthy widow of Providence, Rhode Island, after acting as the lady's medical advisor and confidante. The widow died of arsenic poisoning while visiting friends in Denver. Her death occurred under mysterious circumstances. Upon her arrival in that western city, she found a parcel which contained a bottle of "very fine whiskey" from her friends "in the woods back home." Without too much skepticism, she and a friend took a swig of the elixir but to their sorrow. The friend survived, but Mrs. Barnaby succumbed.

It was Dr. Graves, the kindly consulting physician, and not Mrs. Barnaby's "friends in the woods" who had sent the lethal gift from Providence. Of course the gentleman in question denied the charge vehemently. He was "merely her friendly advisor" although he knew she had riches. Condemned to death by a Denver jury, Dr. Graves, on September 3, 1893, committed suicide, ironically, by poisoning himself. Throughout his ordeal, he maintained he was being persecuted. He left two notes that are of some interest. In one, he said: "Upon my solemn Masonic oath, I, T. Thatcher Graves, did not have anything to do, in any way, shape, manner, or deed, with the death of Mrs. Barnaby. I wrote this knowing what the future will soon have in store for me;" the second: "To the Coroner of Denver: Please do not hold any autopsy on my remains. The cause of death may be rendered as follows: Died of persecution; worn out; exhausted."[60]

A strange case, some details of which are preserved, locale Northampton, Hampshire County, Massachusetts, is worth telling because of a "twist" in the tale. Jonathan Jewett, in the "common

---

[59]Listed by Wm. Barker, Great Falls, Va., in his *Bibliotheca Criminalis Et Juridica*, privately compiled.

[60]For further material on this fascinating case, see Edmund Pearson, *Five Murders*, New York; Doubleday, Doran, 1928, "The Doctor's Whiskey," pp. 175-199.

gaol," for murdering his father, and under sentence of death, was advised by his fellow prisoner, George Bowen, to cheat the gallows by committing suicide. Jewett took the advice seriously and ended his life on November 9, 1815—method not stated. Bowen was tried for the *murder* of this gallows cheater but was acquitted. There is a published pamphlet on Bowen's trial which took place on January 12-14, 1825.[61]

The William Beadle case—one of mass murder of his wife and four children, ending in his own suicide—is a classic case that has had wide circulation—enough to merit a ballad which we append below. A resident of Wethersfield, Connecticut, back in 1783, Beadle began to brood because his business was falling off. He suddenly became engrossed in reading and soon his business went completely to "pot" so that his family actually began to want. Losing his head completely—figuratively—that is, he became convinced that all prophecies were false and that no future state for those who suffered here on earth existed. Obsessed by his strange delusion, he drugged his wife and children, before they retired, on December 11, 1782, and, while they slept, stabbed them all. After performing this shocking deed, he shot himself. He sent word to the neighbors that "the populace should remain as collected in their minds and persons as he was."

If this were merely a mass murder and a suicide of the perpetrator, it would hardly be included here. But it is the aftermath that justifies its inclusion. At the inquest, it was concluded that Beadle was of *a sound mind and,* therefore, must suffer infamy for his crime. According to the tradition of the times, his body was exposed on two barrels with the bloody knife with which he stabbed his loved ones, tied to his breast. He was buried at night. At both buryings, at his, and that of his victims, a balladeer sold a broadside struck off for the occasions. It was entitled: *A Poem Occasioned by the Most Shocking and Cruel Murder That Ever Was Perpetrated in Human Life. He Violated Nature's Great Original Law, Defy'd Eternal Justice, and Seal'd His Own Perdition.* On the front, it depicts Beadle wielding a knife, attacking his little son and daughter as they sit playing with a toy sword and a doll. It

---

[61]McDade, *op. cit.,* 124.

also depicts six coffins with skull and crossbones. Here is the ballad:

> A bloody scene I'll now relate, Which lately happened in a neighb'ring state,
> A murder of the deepest dye, I say, O be amaz'd! for surely well you may.
> A man (unworthy of the name) who slew Himself, his consort, and his offspring too;
> An amiable wife with four children dear, Into one grave was put—Oh drop a tear!
> Soon in the morning of that fatal day, Beadle, the murd'rer sent his maid away,
> To tell the awful deed he had to view; To their assistance the kind neighbors flew.
> It truly gives me pain for to pen down, A deed so black, and yet his mind was sound.
> Says he "I mean to close six persons eyes, Through perfect fondness and the tend'rest ties."
> Detest the errors, to this deed him drew, And mourn the hapless victims whom he slew;
> And pray to God that Satan may be bound, Since to deceive so many he is found . . .
> Fly swiftly round, ye circling years, Hail the auspicious day!
> When love shall dwell in every heart—Nor men their offspring slay![62]

Our inclusion of the Beadle case, in which there was no conviction and thus no hanging, establishes a kind of precedent for us to include two more similar cases, but briefly. The first one is that of Captain James Purinton of Augusta, Maine. On July 8, 1806, he ran amuck and slaughtered his wife and six of his seven children. He then took his own life. The seventh child died of its wounds later. A curious incident in the case is that Purinton's Bible was found open at Ezekiel, Chapter 9: "Slay utterly old and young, both maids and children . ." Several publications were struck off regarding this gruesome case.[63]

---

[62]Burt, *op. cit.*, pp. 6-7.

[63]McDade, *op. cit.*, 776-779.

One more such case—but this time on the distaff side—was that of a Mrs. Sims of Medina, Michigan. The tale is told in the title of a pamphlet: *Fearful Tragedy in Medina, Michigan: Four Murders and A Suicide. Mrs. Sims Slaughters Entire Family of Four Children and Then Ends Her Own Existence.*[64] It is possible, too, that there were those whose attempted suicides at least delayed the scheduled hanging. One dramatic case that has been recorded by Clinton T. Duffy, excerpts from whose book we have drawn earlier, is that of one George Costello who had been condemned in the slaying of a bank teller in Oakland, California. He was scheduled to die on October 17, 1929, but he attempted suicide by slashing his throat. The warden received an urgent letter from the prison physician, Dr. W. F. Goddard, which stated that the unfortunate man would be able "to mount the scaffold on schedule (but) the wound would open when he dropped (and) that considerable hemorrhaging would result, and the doctor could not guarantee that the head wouldn't be completely severed." A hurry-up appeal was dispatched to the governor who "graciously" gave the man a reprieve until December 13, so that his self-inflicted wound would adequately heal so as to avoid possible decapitation.[65]

Natural Causes and Fright

There are doubtless many cases of persons who became ill in jail or prison, not of their own doing, while under sentence of death and who succumbed, thus cheating the gallows. Perhaps the first persons to be recorded who died of illness while awaiting their potential hanging were two females who had been accused of witchcraft. These were Sarah Osborne and Sarah Daston. Both died in the Ipswich jail, the former on May 10, 1692. Her home

---

[64]Published in Adrian, Mich., 1866; McDade, *op. cit.*, 875. Other suicides listed by McDade are: Adonijah Bailey, for murder of Jeremiah W. Pollock, Brooklyn, Windham Co., Conn., ca. Nov. 1825; item 58; Robert Bush, for wife murder at Springfield, Mass. Nov. 12, 1828, item 151; George W. Green, Chicago banker, who killed his wife sometime in 1855; item 383; Samuel Leonard, another wife killer, West Springfield, Mass. December 25, item 601; Samuel Perry, who also killed his wife on June 1, 1826, probaby at Utica, N.Y., item 739; and Abner Rogers, Jr., killer of Charles Lincoln, warden of State Prison at Charlestown, Mass., in January 1844, despite the fact that he was acquitted by reason of insanity; item 826.

[65]Duffy, *op. cit.*, pp. 51-53.

is still standing in Salem.[66] The latter was described as an "unsavory old woman, far gone in age (she was eighty) and malice." However, she was cleared of all charges but as she could not pay her jail fees she remained in jail until she died.[67]

Aside from a few cases that we have unearthed in Pennsylvania, none has come to our attention in which hanging has been permanently interrupted due to fatal illness. However, we are confident that there have been many such cases. We know, also, that today, in the era of legal electrocution and asphyxiation, many have deferred their exit from life because of illness and even death of natural causes. One of the ironies of capital punishment is the care given a condemned person who becomes ill. Some have contended that society is more concerned in keeping such a person alive medically (so he can physically pay his debt to society by means of the death penalty) than to maintain and improve the health of underprivileged people on the outside of prison. An interesting bit of clinical evidence of this comes from the press, under the enlightened regime of Warden Lewis E. Lawes, of Sing Sing prison:

> Ossining, New York, September 15 (1929): Three expert surgeons, sent here by the state of New York, fought tonight to save the life of Frank Plaia. Frank Plaia's life is most valuable to the state of New York. The state of New York will electrocute Frank Plaia in Sing Sing prison after he recovers. The sentence passed upon Plaia said he must die by the passage of a current of electricity through his body. So the state, through the Sing Sing warden and three surgeons, fought to keep Plaia from dying from appendicitis Saturday night and today. He was taken from the death house, under guard, to the new hospital a quarter of a mile away. The three doctors performed the operation. A guard watched and a guard is at Plaia's bedside. He must die for a murder in Nassau County. The operation was pronounced a success. Plaia, it is said, will be healthy and strong again when it is time for him to die.[68]

Whether or not a person can die of sheer fright is a moot

[66]Marion Starkey, *The Devil In Massachusetts,* pp. 35-47; see also, *supra.,* Chapter III, p. (ms. 6).

[67]*Ibid.,* pp. 237-238.

[68]Springfield (Mass.) *Republican,* September 16, 1929.

point. We cannot enter into such a discussion here. We can only report the cases in which local news stories indicate death "by fright" of those who awaited an engagement with the hangman.

The first is that of Charles Keck, of Lehigh County, Pennsylvania, awaiting death by hanging in the jail at Allentown. Convicted of the death of Mrs. Jeanette Nipsches of Ironton (Smoketown), which occurred on November 18, 1891, his case was complicated by the fact that the victim's husband also died in the shooting spree. Public opinion was definitely mobilized against Keck—he had been a friend of the Nipsches couple. An effigy of him had been strung up on a homemade scaffold erected in the street of Smoketown. There were many respites allotted the condemned man, but the final date of the hanging arrived. He died on November 9, 1892, at 9:30 in the morning; the day he was to hang. The gallows had been ready to receive him for some days. He had admittedly been a victim of asthma and, despite the clamor of the mob that he had cheated the gallows by taking poison, the physicians maintained that he died of "nervous prostration superinduced by fear and terror of imminent execution." They had made an autopsy and found no trace of poison.[69]

The second case, again from the Keystone State of Pennsylvania, comes from Beaver County (Beaver the county seat), and deals with Charles Hickman, scheduled to die on June 22, 1911, by hanging. He had been convicted of murdering his wife on February 2, 1910. He swore he would never hang, a boast perhaps overdone through the years by imminent victims of capital punishment. He escaped jail twice and then died, only two hours prior to his scheduled rendezvous with the "tree." The attending physician "speculated" that he died of "fright" or from natural causes or from "eating cucumbers which gave him cholera morbis."[70]

Lynching to Cheat the Gallows

We have studiously refrained from the temptation of recording lynching and vigilantism in this study of hanging. The lynching

---

[69]Allentown (Pa.) *Daily Chronicle & News,* November 10, 1892.

[70]For details see *Pittsburgh Post,* July 19, 1911. For account of other cases in Pennsylvania, see Teeters, *Scaffold & Chair,* Philadelphia, Pennsylvania Prison Society, 1963, pp. 237-238.

record in this country has slowly and painfully improved through the years, but there are some cases in which persons accused of crime, while awaiting trial or, for that matter, being escorted to jail by officials, have been snatched by a mob and lynched. But we are interested in cases in which persons have been lynched while under sentence of death.

We submit a few cases in this section in which persons were lynched by angry mobs, before the regular legal processes could be consummated. There is no doubt that there have been many such incidents throughout our early history. The first has to do with Adolphus F. Monroe, who was taken from the jail at Charleston, Coles County, Illinois on February 15, 1856, by a mob and lynched. Their anger had been aroused because the governor had respited the condemned man for three months on the date set for his execution. Monroe had murdered his father-in-law, Nathan Ellington, Esq. The victim had a jaundiced opinion of his son-in-law and after an altercation of words, hit him with his cane. Monroe promptly pulled a gun and shot him dead.[71]

Another case is that of David F. Mayberry who was convicted at Janesville, Rock County, Wisconsin, on July 11, 1855, for the murder of Andrew Alger with a hatchet. Before he could be sent to prison to serve his sentence—-not death, because that state had abolished capital punishment two years previously—a mob seized and hanged him in the streets. Mayberry knew Alger was returning home with a large sum of money. He met him on the road at Harmony and killed him while riding with him. Whether the lynching would have occurred had there been a death penalty is purely conjectural. It is the sort of question on which proponents and opponents of capital punishment have spent many hours expressing themselves.[72]

Two additional cases come from Missouri. The first has to do with the lynching of A. W. Smith who killed John Vincent in February 1844, in Madison County. A group of the victim's friends, assembling at Fredericktown and imbibing rather freely of whiskey, decided to take the lethargic law in their own hands.

---

[71]McDade, *op. cit.*, 696.

[72]The Mayberry case is listed by McDade, *op. cit.*, 674.

They dragged the victim from the jail, drafted a Methodist minister to offer a prayer and proceeded to lynch the unhappy murderer. Subsequently, several of the crowd were indicted; but for some strange reason, all who were awaiting trial died within a year. Thus no one was convicted of the clandestine lynching bee.

The second case is even more unusual. Mary Layton was cruelly murdered by her husband James, in Perry County, a crime that was described as "the most atrocious ever committed in the county." Through a change of venue, Layton was tried and convicted in St. Francois County and sentenced to death. On the date of his scheduled execution, June 17, 1843, he received a reprieve. Incensed by this unexpected event, the crowd divided into two groups to vote on whether or not to lynch the unpopular murderer. The affirmative group "carried the day and Layton was taken from the jail" and hanged "to a beam placed across the 'stray pen' on the public square in Farmington."[73]

A much more recent case of this type is that of the Leo Frank lynching that occurred in Atlanta, Georgia, in August 1915. Frank, a northern Jew, had been convicted of the rape-slaying of 14-year-old Mary Phagan on April 26, 1913 "Confederate Memorial Day." Frank, an intelligent and sensitive college graduate, had come South to marry the daughter of a pencil manufacturer and assumed the position of manager of the factory. The young victim had been employed in the plant and on the fatal day had come to Frank's office for her pay. Some time later her body was found in the cellar of the factory and Frank was accused of the crime. Feeling ran high prior to and during the trial. Prejudice and inordinate fear manufacturing supplanting the agrarian way of life of the region stirred up mass hysteria which made justice in the courtroom impossible. The unlucky Frank was convicted, largely on testimony of an illiterate Negro who worked at the plant was sentenced to be hanged. An appeal to the Supreme Court was denied. But friends and defense attorneys prevailed on the governor to commute the death sentence which was done despite the unpopularity of the action. In August, 1915, a mob kidnaped Frank from the state

---

[73]These two cases are reviewed in Goodspeed's *History of Southeast Missouri*, first published in 1888, and reprinted 1964 by Ramfre Press, Cape Girardeau, Mo., pp. 341, 346.

prison, hurried him to the outskirts of Atlanta, and lynched him. Many articles and books on the case (see Harry Golden, *A Little Girl Is Dead,* Doubleday, 1965).

Hanging of Persons "Tired of Life"

One strange breed of *homo sapiens* is, perhaps, more prevalent than the apparent data indicate. We refer to the person who is tired of life, wants to leave its trials and tribulations, but is pathologically afraid to do so. He is afraid of suicide but not murder and subsequent execution. His road to death, then, is to stalk an unknown prey and kill him. Bizarre though this may sound to average normal people, we have found some cases in our research that bear out this strange compulsion.

Our first case is from Philadelphia, the man's name, John Bruelman, jeweler and a lieutenant in the Provincial militia. He was executed October 22, 1760, for the murder of Robert Scull, a man he did not know, had never seen until he fired the fatal shot and, of course, held him no grudge. The incident as reviewed in the *Philadelphia Dispatch,* June 17, 1866 is as follows:

> John Bruelman committed a murder in August of this year [1760], which made a profound impression at the time. A gentleman named Robert Scull was playing billiards one afternoon at the Centre Square Tavern, in Market Street, West of Schuylkill Eighth Street when Bruelman presented a loaded gun at Scull, as he was about to strike a ball, and saying, I will show you a fine stroke. He then discharged the piece. Scull dropped the cue, and fell severely wounded, and died in three days.
>
> Upon such petty trifles life may depend. Had Dr. Cadwalader been in a bad humour he might have fallen the victim; and had Scull happened to arrive at the billiard-room a little later another unoffending man would have perished in his stead, Bruelman declared that Scull had done him no injury, but that he was weary of life, and had committed the crime to escape from the toils and troubles of the world. In later years such evidence of insanity would have ensured his acquittal; but in 1760 people were not eager to sympathize with crime.[74]

---

[74]Bruelman was hanged October 22; see Henry Simpson, *The Lives of Eminent Philadelphians* (for sketch of Dr. Cadwalader) 1859, p. 159; also Thorsten Sellin, "The Death Penalty," a report prepared for the American Law Institute, Philadelphia, 1959, p. 66.

A second case from Philadelphia is that of Henry Halbert a thirty-year-old German immigrant from Luneberg who killed the son of Jacob Woolman in the outskirts of the city, on August 30, 1765. In the words of the Rev. Henry Melchior Muhlenberg, noted Lutheran minister who attended Halbert prior to his execution: "he purposely cut the throat of this twelve-year-old boy *in order that he might lose his own life* (italics added). Halbert had led a dissolute life "drinking, whoring, cursing, swearing, breaking the Sabbath, and keeping all manner of debauched company." He was hanged October 19, at Centre Square in Philadelphia, after which his "last speech and confession was published."[75]

In the *Dispatch* article, quoted above, a hint was suggested that such cases would be recognized as insane and "acquitted" even in 1866. At least, today, psychiatrists would be called in—that is, in many jurisdictions—to examine persons laboring under a suicide complex or some sort of delusion and, perhaps, be spared the death penalty, or even a court trial for murder. However, such disposition to a mental hospital, as is often suggested or urged, is by no means a certainty in any state even today.

Halbert not only asked the "Lutheran School boys in the city should sing Hymns at the Gallows in the German language" but insisted on speaking at the scaffold. His dying words were:

> Attend good people, see my final end; Take warning by your
>   sinful dying Friend,
> I am condemned to die, and die I must, I die for Murder, and
>   my Fate is just;
> I beg that God my sins may now Forgive, And die in Peace
>   with all good Men that live.

He wrote a letter which he headed: "A Letter from the criminal to the father of his murdered son."

Ministers of the Gospel and Murder

None of the professions—medicine, dentistry, law, engineering, or the ministry— has been completely free of crime and some members of these crafts have been executed for murder and other felonies. Some day, we hope that someone will catalogue the cases

[75]McDade, *op. cit.*, 425; see also *Journal of Henry Melchior Muhlenberg,* Philadelphia, 1958, Vol. II pp. 264-265. Courtesy Fortress Press, Philadelphia.

of professional persons that have been involved in murder and other capital crimes. In this section, we wish to survey the profession of the ministry—but in only a few instances. One may read of many cases which might belong here, but only in a few instances was the death penalty invoked and carried out.

For example, the man in the case we are now about to discuss was actually sentenced to be hanged—but he shot himself; thus we might have included him in our section on suicide. Yet we thought his case would be more appropriate in this section.

The Rev. George Washington Carawan was a colorful North Carolina character. Actually, he was an athiest turned cleric after he had "seen the light." His habitat was in the Lake Mattamuskeet region of Hyde County. He might be thought of as a kind of circuit rider, serving several flocks of the Baptist persuasion.

He had quarreled with his school-master neighbor, Clement H. Lassiter, so that "bad blood" persisted between them for all time. Lassiter was well liked and Carawan was at least suspected of being shrewd and conniving; he was also feared by many.

On November 15, 1852, Lassiter, who had decided to go elsewhere for a teaching post, bade his many friends goodbye and started off on foot. He was never seen by them alive again. Carawan ambushed him, killed him and buried his body, witnessed and aided by a slave boy named Seth. In short order, the minister was arrested and taken to the dungeon-jail at Swanquarter, county seat of Hyde County. The defendant's able lawyers rightfully insisted that feeling was too prejudiced against their client and begged for a change of venue. The request was granted so Carawan went on trial at Washington, Beaufort County, in the Fall term of 1853. Circumstantial though the evidence was, the self-assured "sky pilot" was convicted, despite the fact that southern law and tradition forbade Seth, the Negro eye-witness slave, to testify against his master.[76]

After the jury had been polled and Carawan realized that he was doomed to die on the gallows, he suddenly pulled a gun from his waistcoat and aimed it at the prosecutor, Edward J. Warren. He pulled the trigger and shot Warren, who fell to the floor but

---

[76]See other such cases, Chapter I, p. 63, Negro Bob; and VII, p. 313 f., Boyington.

was almost unscathed. The beleaguered parson then turned the gun on himself and fired a bullet into his brain. He died almost instantly. This story, told so graphically by Manly Wade Wellman, ends with the burial of Carawan whose remains were first deposited in a spot of earth on the county almshouse grounds where, ironically, once stood a gallows. Later, his body was removed by relatives (he had a wife and several children) and friends, and laid to final rest at Juniper Bay.[77]

The Case of the Rev. Abner Vance — Virginia — 1810

The person of the cloth whose story may be almost literally dredged up from the dim annals of history—1810, to be exact— is that of the Rev. Abner Vance, who lived on the Big Sandy River, Russell County, Virginia. Vance owes his death on the gallows, in the county seat at Abingdon, to a "double-cross," according to Mrs. Olive Woolley Burt, who has supplied us with a ballad concerning the case. Briefly, the story is this: A wealthy neighbor by the name of Lewis Horton seduced the Baptist preacher's young daughter. Vance tried to prevail on the farmer to marry her, but he refused. Angered and disappointed, Vance shot and killed Horton. He then left the country and remained free for several years. For some unaccountable reason, he persuaded his son to turn him in and thus receive the hundred-dollar reward that had been placed upon him. He was subsequently tried, convicted, and hanged.

On the jury was a man named Johnson. Vance, for a good reason, had expected this jury to stand for acquittal. Johnson's son-in-law had earlier killed a man and Vance had been on his jury. He had voted for an acquittal which resulted in a hung jury. Because of this obligation Vance felt that the juror, Johnson, would reciprocate. But he was bitterly disappointed as the jury rendered a verdict in the first degree, so the poor preacher went to his death on the gallows.

A ballad survives with legend suggesting that Vance himself was the composer, writing it as he saw his scaffold being constructed. It is, like so many others, a mournful dirge, without much

---

[77]See Wellman, *Dead and Gone; Classic Crimes of North Carolina*, Chapel Hill, University of North Carolina Press, 1954, Chapter 3, "The Preacher and the Gun."

rhyme and rather humdrum and uninteresting as to the facts of the case. Here are a few of the verses reproduced, as are most of the ballads in this book, from Mrs. Burt's collection:

> Green are the woods where Sandy flows, And sweet peace dwell-
> eth there.
> The red buck roves o'er the wooded knobs, In the valley safe
> lies the fear.
> But Vance shall no more the Sandy behold, Nor drink its crystal
> wave;
> The partial judge has spoke his doom, The hunter has found his
> grave.
> The judge called me an incarnate fiend, Though Elliott I tried to
> save;
> I wished as a juryman to let him free, Humanity belonged to
> the grave.
> The friendship I have showed to others Has never to me been
> shown;
> Humanity belongs to the brave of heart And I hope it is my own.
> 'Twas on the advice of McFarlan That Judge Johnson did me
> call;
> I was taken from my native home And confined in a stone wall.
> My persecutors gained their request, Their promise they made
> good;
> For they have oftimes swore they would never rest Till they
> gained my heart's blood.
> Daniel Horton, Ike and Bill A lie against me swore,
> In order to take away my life That I might be no more.
> But I and them together must meet, Where the truth of all
> things is known;
> And if I have shed innocent blood, I hope there's mercy shown.
> I will stand before the Judgment Seat, Where everyone must
> stand some day;
> And I pray that mercy may be shown to me, And my foes, too,
> had better pray.
> Bright shines the sun on Clinch's hill, And soft the west wind
> blows;
> The valleys with bloom are covered, Perfumed with the sweet
> red rose.

But Vance shall Sandy no more behold, Now smell its sweet
  perfume;
This day his eyes must close in death, His body be confined to
  the tomb.

Farewell, my friends and children dear, To you I bid farewell;
The love I have for your precious souls No mortal tongue can
  tell.

Farewell to you, my loving wife, To you I bid adieu;
And if I reach fair Canaan's shore, I hope to meet with you.

An older and shorter version is the following:

I've killed a man, I don't deny; He threatened to kill me.
The jury said I must die, Judge Johnson did agree.

The friends that should be true to me, A lie against me swore,
In order for to take my life That I should live no more.[78]

A slightly different version of the Vance ballad is reproduced
in the Lomax collection of ballads entitled *Our Singing Country*.[79]
We learn that the seducer, Horton, attempted to escape Vance's
wrath by swimming a stream near the parson's home; also, that
Vance's brother-in-law, Frank Browning, was present at the hanging and that the condemned man asked him "to turn his back
when the trap fell." It seems that a reprieve had been granted but
it failed to arrive.

Rev. Cyriacus Spangenburg — Pennsylvania — 1795

A case that pre-dates the Vance tragedy is that of an obscure
cleric of the German Reformed Church of Bedford, Pennsylvania,
by the name of Cyriacus Spangenburg. The details of his crime
are sketchy at best, but we do know that he killed one of his
parishoners, by the name of Jacob Glessner, with a dagger which
he suddenly pulled from his ministerial robe. He was hanged for
his crime on October 10, 1795. His case is recorded in the state's
legal annals primarily because it was the first to come before the

---

[78]Burt, *op. cit.*, pp. 221-224.

[79]John A. and Alan Lomax, *Our Singing Country*, New York Macmillan, 1941, pp.
  322-323.

courts after the law of April 22, 1794, was passed limiting the death penalty to first degree murder only.[80]

Not so obscure, nor so far back in time, is the case of the Methodist minister of Belvidere, Warren County, New Jersey, the Rev. Jacob S. Harden, who was hanged on July 6, 1860, for the arsenic poisoning and subsequent death of his wife. Harden, pastor of the Methodist Episcopal Church of Hunterdon County at Mount Lebanon, had been told by a fortune teller that his wife had not long to live. It is recorded that the wife's mother was "the real cause of the crime for she hounded him until he reluctantly married the girl," although this would hardly exonerate him from the crime of murder. A pamphlet was struck off at that time that dealt with this sordid crime. Part of its title refers to it as "The Life, Confession and letters of Courtship of Jacob S. Harden."[81]

Another Methodist minister, the Rev. Enos Dudley, was hanged at Haverhill, New Hampshire, on May 23, 1849, for murdering his wife the previous March. They lived at Grafton.[82]

Rev. Ephraim K. Avery: Rhode Island — 1832

The following case does not merit a place in this work about hangings, simply because the preacher involved was acquitted of a bare-faced murder and left the scene of his evil deed and churchly duties. It is included because it is notorious case and is recalled in murder circles from time to time. It has to do with the Rev. Ephraim K. Avery, of a Methodist church of Bristol, Rhode Island. His alleged victim was Sarah Mariah Cornell, factory girl of Fall River, Massachusetts, whom he apparently murdered on December 22, 1832. Proof of the notoriety or fame of this case is that McDade, in his *Annals of Murder,* has listed twenty-one items dealing with it.[83]

The facts in the case are these: the body of the victim was found hanging from a frame of a haystack in Tiverton, Rhode Island, not too far from Fall River where the girl lived. It might well have

[80]Solon J., and Elizabeth Buck, *The Planting of Civilization in Western Pennsylvania,* Pittsburgh, University of Pittsburgh Press, 1939, pp. 450-2.

[81]McDade, *op. cit.,* 438.

[82]Source, J. O. Bettinger, *History of Haverhill, N. H.* 1888, 397.

[83]McDade, *op. cit.,* 33-53.

passed for a suicide, except for a note that the girl had left in her handbag. It read: "If I should be missing enquire of the Rev. Mr. Avery of Bristol—he will know where I am." Despite the aura of respectability that usually surrounds a man of the cloth, it was common gossip that Avery had been more than passingly familiar with Miss Cornell and when it was discovered that she was five months pregnant, it took little deduction to associate the cleric with her untimely death. And besides, the gentleman had been seen wandering in the vicinity of the place where the body had been found hanging in such a manner as to suggest self-destruction.

He was brought in for questioning but was dismissed by the magistrate. Had he not disappeared from the community, Mr. Avery might have got away with his crime; but unwisely, he took off and was found by officers sent out by irate citizens to look for him. He was found at Rindge, New Hampshire, and was returned to face the music of an outraged community.

The trial at Newport lasted twenty-seven days, which was long for that era. It is reported that 196 witnesses were questioned, which, in itself, is worthy to report. The minister was acquitted and, perhaps, on the basis of the evidence, it was a fair verdict. To this day, however, a cloud surrounds the name of the Rev. Ephraim Avery just as a fairly large one hangs over the name of that more notorious New England spinster, Lizzie Borden who, on August 4, 1892, allegedly "took an axe and gave her mother forty whacks, and when she saw what she had done, she gave her father forty-one" and was subsequently acquitted by a Fall River jury.[84]

After extricating himself from the law and the social stigma surrounding the Cornell murder, Mr. Avery wandered out to the Western Reserve of Ohio where he lived to a ripe old age—perhaps free of the pangs of conscience.

---

[84]McDade lists but four items (115-8) for the Borden case, as opposed to twenty-one for the Avery case; yet the Borden case is much more notorious and famous.

Chapter VI

MURDER FOR GREED,
ANGER AND LUST

T HE ANNALS OF MURDER are full of cases showing elements
of greed, anger and lust. Many of those we have related in earlier
chapters show one or more of those motives that we deal with
in this chapter, but we have found it more convenient to place
them elsewhere rather than in this connection. We shall first
deal with some cases that involve cupidity or greed, some in high
places and some in low places. Later we shall include some cases
from New Hampshire which involve anger and lust as their special
ingredients. Our first case involving greed is related below.

The Smutty Nose Murder Case

One of Edmund Pearson's best known stories is the murder at
Smutty Nose. The title is intriguing but, in reality, it is merely the
name of a small island, one of a cluster lying off the coast of
Maine, known as the Isles of Shoals. The trial that grew out of
the murder which took place on the lonely island was held in the
small town of Alfred, county seat of York County, in 1873. Pearson gives credit for the story to Celia Thaxter, a contemporary
writer who knew of some of the principals in the case. Her true
story is entitled *A Memorable Murder* and, as Pearson stated "her
essay represents one of the rare instances in which an American
author of first-rate ability has told the story of an actual murder,
related it as fact and not as fiction, used the real names of persons
and places, and published the work in anything less ephemeral
than a daily newspaper."[1]

---

[1]*Murder at Smutty Nose and Other Murders,* New York, Sun Dial Press, 1926, p. 321;
Mrs. Thaxter's story was published in the *Atlantic Monthly,* May, 1875, Vol. 35, pp.
602-615; reprinted in *Stories by American Authors,* Charles Scribner's Sons, 1884, pp.
267-291.

The murders at Smutty Nose were committed on the night of March 5, 1873, by Louis Wagner, a stoic German who was familiar with the life that went on in bleak fashion on the island. The inhabitants were few and the victims were two womenfolk of fishermen who had come a few years earlier from Norway. The men took their daily catch into Portsmouth, New Hampshire, less than ten miles away by boat. These fishermen and their wives were John Hontvet and his wife, Maren; his brother, Matthew; Maren's brother, Ivan Christensen and his wife, Anethe; and Karen, a spinster and sister of Maren. In the 1870's, there had lived with the Hontvets the man Wagner, who was engaged in various jobs—sailor, fisherman, and the like. He was also familiar with the seafaring ways and activities of the island folk. He developed a notion that there was money on the island, possessed by these simple, hard-working Norwegian-Americans. He laid his plans to purloin whatever cache there might be, come what may.

He carefully checked the comings and goings of the fishermen. He knew they would be obliged to tarry at Portsmouth after disposing of their fish, in order to meet the train from Boston that brought them their bait. He got into a dory and started rowing the ten miles to Smutty Nose. Upon arrival, he cautiously reconnoitered. The women were in bed, so he carefully slipped into the home of Hontvets. Maren, sleeping on a couch in the kitchen, heard a noise and called out, "John, is that you?" No sooner had she spoken than Wagner picked up a chair and attacked the bewildered woman in the dark. The other women screamed as they heard the commotion and ran downstairs. In the deadly struggle that ensued, Wagner murdered Karen with an axe and turned on Anethe. Maren in wild disarray and indescribable terror ran from the house with the dog who followed her. She heard Anethe's screams as she sought some place where she could escape the terrible fate that might befall her. The woman finally realized it was Wagner. His gutteral German accent betrayed his presence. Methodically, the killer searched the humble home but found little of value. As he left Smutty Nose, he had less than twenty dollars in his pocket, a poor haul for the murders he had committed in his inordinate greed.

The killer was apprehended and taken to Alfred and lodged in

jail, pending indictment and subsequent conviction of murder.
After he was sentenced to death he escaped jail by placing a dummy in his cot. His freedom was short-lived, for within a few days
he was arrested in Farmington, New Hampshire. Maren Hontvet
recovered from her ordeal in the bitter cold and snowy night in
the cove with scant clothing to protect her. She was the star witness against Wagner, who from the start simulated a contrite and
abject sinner. He played this role to the last. He was hanged at the
state prison at Thomaston on June 24, 1875, along with John
Gordon who had killed his brother, his wife and infant in Waldo
County.

Pearson intimated that these were Maine's last hangings. This is
incorrect. It is true that the state abolished capital punishment in
1876, but it was reinstated in 1883 only to be reabolished permanently in 1887. During that interim, three others were hanged in
the Thomaston prison yard. Raffaele Capone and Carmen Santore,
Italian laborers on the Shore Line Railroad were convicted at
Bangor, for murdering a fellow worker, Pasquele Coscie, and
hanged on April 17, 1885. A few months later, on November 20,
Daniel Wilkinson was hanged for the killing of a Bath police officer, William Lawrence. Wilkinson was definitely the last person
to be executed in Maine.

The Nelson E. Wade Case of Pennsylvania

One of the pamphlets published on the Nelson E. Wade case is
entitled *The Wonderful Murderer of the McBride Family.*[2] Often
referred to as The Linden Tragedy, it represents an excellent case
of greed, robbery, murder, and mystery.

John McBride and his wife, Isabella, were an elderly, miserly
couple living in the small town of Linden, Lycoming County,
Pennsylvania. They were indeed rich but they guarded their
money, which they kept in their own home, with a kind of pathological tenacity. As they had been bothered by thieves on numerous occasions, they are supposed to have kept some vicious dogs
on the premises to guard their gold.

Sometime during 1873, Nelson Wade passed by the house, stopped, and asked for a drink of milk. True to form, the couple tried

[2]By G.P.I. Orthodox (no date).

to make him pay for the milk. At this lack of traditional hospitality, he set upon them, beat them to death, and ransacked the place looking for gold. Here, legend and fact become confused. Legend insists that Wade obtained some $60,000 and that he didn't get it all. Regardless of the amount, his undoing resulted almost immediately when he visited a bawdy house where he gave the girls some gold pieces from his ill-gotten stock. He was caught, convicted and hanged at Williamsport, the county seat, on November 6, 1873.

In 1960, the house which, in that remote era, had been the "bawdy" house was torn down, but contrary to expectations, no gold was found. However, it has been believed through the years that Wade successfully hid large sums of the McBride loot.

Fact, however, and not legend, tells of the strength of the man Wade. During his incarceration, he broke no less than seven pairs of handcuffs; consequently, a large iron collar was forged to go around his neck with a seven-foot chain attached to it and to a ring-bolt riveted to the floor of his cell. At the execution, the rope broke and he had to be carried to the second noose.[3]

The Knapp-Crowninshield Case: Greed on a High Level

On the night of April 6, 1830, eighty-two-year-old Capt. Joseph White, retired wealthy ship-owner was murdered as he slept in his palatial home, on Essex Street, in Salem, Massachusetts. Aside from his wealth, it was hard to believe that anyone would deliberately enter his peaceful home (which still stands in lovely Salem) and kill him in cold blood. He was alone in the big house at the time, as his housekeeper-niece, Mrs. Beckford, had gone to Wrenham, not too far away, to visit her daughter, Mrs. Joseph J. Knapp, Jr.

It was known that Capt. White had numerous relatives who were more than passively interested in him, his health and his fortune. None came under suspicion for some considerable time. Due to a quirk of fate—which so often shatters the potentially perfect crime—the brothers, John Francis Knapp and Joseph J. Knapp,

---

[3]Williamsport *Gazette & Bulletin,* November 7, 1873; also information from an informant.

Jr., the latter being the husband of the victim's grand-niece, were suspected, indicted, convicted, and hanged for the crime. John Francis was hanged on September 28, 1830; Joseph J. on December 31, the same year. The details of this New England crime are extraordinary.

The fascinating element in this classic case is that the Knapps did not actually commit the cowardly murder themselves, but hired someone to perpetrate it. That someone was a seamy character named Richard Crowninshield (his name sounds aristocratic, at least) who, apparently, agreed to commit the foul deed for one thousand dollars. Joseph Knapp arranged to leave a window in the White mansion unlocked for the murderer's convenience. Crowninshield entered the old man's bedroom, knocked him unconscious, and then stabbed him with a stiletto thirteen times. The killer's brother, George, was also involved as an accessory.

A local committee of vigilance enlisted and received the eager but patently bogus support of the Knapp brothers. Due to a damaging letter of extortion sent to Joseph Knapp by a convict who had vague knowledge of the plot, the brothers were eventually trapped and arrested for masterminding the crime. Crowninshield committed suicide in his cell at Salem, but in due time, the wheels of justice began to turn and enmeshed in the mechanism were the brothers Knapp who paid the ultimate penalty for their greedy and murderous scheme.

Daniel Webster participated in this famous case as the prosecutor. He said of the case: "It is a most extraordinary case. In some respects, it has hardly a precedent anywhere; certainly none in our New England." He is alleged to have made another interesting observation at this trial. It seems that a convict was brought in to the courtroom to testify, although there were objections to the impropriety of such an action. Webster apparently said that "truth was truth, if it came from the bottomless pit."[4] Edmund Pearson has immortalized this case in his title: *The Salem Conspiracy: or, the Lamentable Death of Captain White.*[5]

---

[4]Thus quoted by the Rev. Charles Spear, *The Irremediability of Capital Punishment,* Boston, 1844, p. 112.

[5]In his *Murder at Smutty Nose and Other Murders,* 1926, pp. 173-189; see *supra,* Chapter IV, page 187, for allusions to the clothing the killers wore to the gallows. This case is also discussed by Thomas S. Duke, *Celebrated Criminal Cases of America,* San Francisco, James H. Barry Co., 1905.

There were many publications regarding this sensational New England case.[6] There even developed a ballad, sung to the tune *Auld Lang Syne,* which ran as follows:

> O what a horrid tale to sound,
> In this our land to tell,
> That Joseph White of Salem Town,
> By ruffian hands he fell!

> Perhaps for money or for gain,
> This wicked deed was done;
> But if for either, great the pain
> This murderer must be in.

> O the infernal of the damn'd,
> To murder in the night;
> With cruel arm and bloodstain'd hand
> Which pierced the side of White.
> Thou harden'd hearted monster devil,
> To thrust the dirk of death,
> You will be plac'd upon the level,
> For time will stop your breath!

> (three stanzas omitted)

> Calmly he laid in sweet repose,
> The ruffian forced the room,
> And with his dirk he did dispose
> Of him who'd done no harm.
> Great God, how can these things be so,
> When man is left alone?
> Poor feeble wretch, he does not know
> How wicked he has done

> (last four stanzas omitted)

The suicide of Crowninshield prompted another ballad associated with this case:

> Silence does dwell in the murderer's cell;
> No sound of clanking chain,
> Of fearful moan or stifled groan,
> Shall echo there again.
> Poor wretch, thy name shall be spar'd the shame
> Of vile, disgraceful death,

---

[6]See McDade, *op. cit.,* items, 562-573.

Expos'd forlorn to the public scorn,
While fleets thy passing breath.
      (five verses omitted)
See where he stands with clenchéd hands,
In restless agony.
Say, doth not hell in that bosom dwell?
Ah, whither can he flee?

At still midnight see the ghost of White
Streaming with blood appear,
Ill can murd'rer brook that dreadful look
His pulses stop through fear.
      (one stanza omitted)
Had Crowninshield in the bloody field
Died, like a warrior brave,
Glory had been his portion then,
He had slept in a soldier's grave.

Be thy name forgot; who can tell the lot
Where departed spirits roam.
Haply at last all they penace past
Thy God shall receive thee home.[7]

The Col. George Davenport Murder — Illinois

Lonely but wealthy old men have always been the prey to avaricious people, sometimes men, sometimes women. The Knapp case is a most intimate case because it involved kinsfolk, even if only by marriage. The case which follows deals with the murder of an elderly man who happened to be alone when he was set upon and beaten to death. The time was fifteen years after the Salem tragedy and the locale, on Rock Island in the Mississippi, under jurisdiction of the State of Illinois.

The victim was Col. George Davenport, wealthy and respected retired soldier—veteran of the War of 1812 and the Indian wars —who gave his name to the town across from Rock Island, that of Davenport, Iowa.

On July 4, 1845, the townsmen of Rock Island decided to lay an ambitious patriotic celebration, in honor of the Declaration of

---

[7]From Olive Woolley Burt, *American Murder Ballads,* New York, Oxford University press, 1958, pp. 87-89. Verses omitted by that author.

Independence, to which all were enthusiastically invited. The Davenport household, family and servants, all attended, except the colonel who was indisposed. He felt it best to remain in his comfortable home. This, of course, proved to be a tragic mistake. It was believed by certain greedy robbers in the vicinity that Davenport kept large sums of money in his mansion house and they proposed to relieve him of it. The story is as old as thievery and robbery. The men rowed to the island, entered the house and bludgeoned the old man to death. They got very little cash for their trouble, but they became objects of one of the most ingenious detective thrillers up to that time. One Edward Bonney, after considerable sleuthing, brought the murderers to book. Eight persons were tried for the heinous crime and three were hanged on October 19, 1845.[8]

INSURANCE POLICIES AND GREED
The Hayward-Ging Case — Minnesota

One of Minnesota's most notorious cases is the Harry Hayward-Kittie Ging affair which involved a diabolically-contrived murder of the girl by the man in 1895. The locale was Minneapolis and the murder spot, a road skirting Lake Calhoun. The victim, Katherine Ging, fancy milliner and dress designer, was in love with Hayward, the wayward son of a respectable family. At the time, both were twenty-nine years of age. Hayward, referred to in some of the contemporary news articles as a "tin-horn gambler," was proud of his adeptness at faro. It was also stated that he never did a single day's work in his life, living either off his family or by his wits.

He met Kitty Ging at a boarding house and prevailed on her to move into his father's apartment hotel, the Osark Flats. He began to show his victim some attention after he deduced that she had considerable money. As she was in love with him, she was blind to the fact that her feelings were not reciprocated; he was using her for her money. She lent him funds to play faro and after

---

[8]These were John and Aaron Long, and Granville Young. Bonney wrote his memoirs in 1850, entitled *The Banditti of the Prairies;* for contemporary account of the crime see Paul I. Wellman, *Spawn of Evil,* New York, Doubleday, 1964, 285 ff. See also, McDade, *op. cit.,* 243; also, *Journal of Illinois Historical Society,* (Winter, 1959).

certain intimacies, he had her insured, declaring himself the beneficiary.

Hayward's next move was to find some way to dispose of Kitty
and thus cash in on her insurance. He threw discretion to the
winds. First, he tried to enlist the services of his rather dull-witted
brother, Adry. This not-so-simple objective failed. Next, he turned
to the janitor of the apartment house, Claus A. Blixt, a frightened
Swedish laborer. By intimidating him with threats of killing his
wife, he succeeded in obtaining the consent of this man to engineer
a buggy ride with Miss Ging as guest. The scheme was to take
her to the outskirts of the city to meet Hayward. She was then to
be killed. This is exactly what happened.

While Hayward set up a perfect alibi by escorting a society
belle to the theatre, Blixt picked Kitty up in a rented buggy, with
Hayward promising he would soon meet her near the shore of the
lake. Blixt drove out into the outskirts of the city, shot the woman
and pushed her body out on the snowy ground. The murder was
committed December 3, 1894. The body was soon discovered and
within four days the mystery was solved. Shrewd as Hayward was
purported to be, he actually talked himself into being a prime suspect. He was arrested, tried, convicted and finally hanged on
December 11, 1895.

He went to the gallows—painted red at his request—wearing a
frock coat and pin-striped trousers. It is alleged his last words
were: "Pull her tight; I'll stand pat." The literature that has grown
up around this case shows Hayward to have been an utterly selfish
creature, greedy for money and without any of those sensitivities
normally associated with human beings. The amazing thing about
the case is that Katherine Ging could not divine his motives. He
actually despised her, if we may believe that he made the following
statement about his victim: "Every time I go into her room she
puts her arms around me, and I would like to put a knife into
the God damned bitch . . . If there was a dog and her, I would
rather shoot her and let the dog go."

Prior to his execution, some person smuggled cylindrical re-
corders into his cell and allegedly recorded some of his statements
as well as his last words before he walked to the scaffold. Occurring at an early date, this event is of some interest to criminolo-

gist. A legend went the rounds that Hayward actually did not
die but was resuscitated by members of a secret order (later
identified as the Masons). As we have noted throughout our study
of executions, there is nothing unique about such a legend. Blixt,
the unwitting but real murderer, was given a life sentence and died
in prison in 1925. Even Kitty Ging is remembered by a ballad
which goes like this:

Minneapolis was excited, and for many miles around,
For a terrible crime committed, just a mile or so from town,
It was a cold and winter's eve, and a villain did reply
Tonight she takes that fatal ride, and she will have to die.

Chorus

The stars were shining brightly and the moon had passed away,
The roads were dark and lonely when found dead where she lay.
Then telling the tale of a criminal, she was his promised bride
Just another sin to answer for; another fatal ride.

When for pleasure she went riding little did she know her fate,
That took place on the lonely night, on the road near Calhoun
Lake.
She was shot while in the buggy, and beaten ('Tis true to
speak!)
Until all life had vanished—then was cast into the street.

He was at heart a criminal but a coward of a man!
And so he sought another to execute his plan.
It was a cold and bloody plot it was a terrible sin
To take a life so kind and true as she was then to him.[9]

A Triple Hanging — The Thayer Brothers of Buffalo, New York

Seldom do we hear of three brothers being hanged at the same
time, for the same crime. The only case that has come to our attention is that of the Thayer brothers—Israel, Isaac, and Nelson—
who were executed at Buffalo, New York, on June 17, 1825,

---

[9]The material above is taken from: (1) Walter N. Trenerry, *Murder in Minnesota*, St.
Paul, Minnesota Historical Society, 1962, pp. 135-155 (including the ballad); and (2)
Stewart H. Holbrook, *Murder Out Yonder*, New York, Macmillan, 1941, "Kitty
Ging's Buggy Ride," pp. 69-93; the ballad is also reproduced in Olive Woolley Burt's
American Murder Ballads, pp. 97-99.

for the murder of an itinerant boarder named John Love. Love lent the Thayers a sum of money which they refused to return. In order to relieve themselves of embarrassment over their debt, they decided to kill their creditor. They waited till "hog-killing" time, so that any suspicious blood around the premises could more easily be explained.

Their story regarding Love's disappearance—that he had left the country because the sheriff was after him for forging checks—belied the brothers' efforts to collect outstanding sums of money owed to Love. Thus, local suspicion was aroused and subsequently the trio was arrested, convicted and hanged for the murder. The victim's body was found in a nearby woods. The trial took place on April 21-23.

Several ballads evolved from this case and these were hawked at the hanging tree which stood in a field outside Buffalo, Erie County. All were very long, according to the murder-ballad expert, Olive Woolley Burt, one consisting of twenty-three verses. Here are some verses of one of those that went the rounds at the time:

> Again the murderer's ruthless hand has stained with blood our
>   happy land!
> Again the hapless victim dies, to lust of gain a sacrifice.
>
> Three brothers bent on crime and blood, in bold defiance of
>   their God,
> More monstrous than the savage fiend, have murdered Love,
>   their nearest friend.
>
> And now condemned in jail they lay, waiting, in bitter grief, the
>   day
> When they must yield their forfeit breath, and share the mur-
>   derer's shameful death.
>
> "We long had planned the fatal deed, and on the horrid crime
>   agreed;
> And none except the eyes above, to view our deeds, we mur-
>   dered Love!"
>
> "With hearts as hard as devils have, we hollowed out the shal-
>   low grave;
> And calmly hoped no human eye would e'er the mangled corpse
>   espy."

"The gallows now must end our days, and we must walk the
    unknown ways
Of that dark world beyond the tomb, where all must meet their
    fatal doom."

The remaining verses of the ballad beg for forgiveness. Mrs. Burt
has in her collection other Thayer ballads. One, an extremely
illiterate affair, and which was actually published, goes like this:

> with Nelson Thair Love made his station
> thrue the summer there to staye
> Nelson had two brothers, Isaac and Israel
> Love lent them money there debts to pay.
>
> First Isaac with his gun he shot him
> He left his gun and went away
> then Nelson with his axe he chopt him
> till he had no life that he could perceeve.[10]

The Murder of Thomas Walsh — Willow City, North Dakota — 1902

Another murder for greed that ended in a hanging which has a
ballad attached to it, occurred far from Buffalo, New York—in
North Dakota. Thomas Walsh, an elderly farmer living in Bottin-
eau County, was shot dead as he lay in bed, on July 5, 1902. The
killer, William Ross, stole his victim's horse and what money he
could find. He was soon apprehended, convicted, and hanged on
March 6, 1903. The more significant feature of this humdrum
pedestrian crime is that it was North Dakota's last legal hanging.
North Dakota abolished capital punishment in 1915. Here is the
ballad associated with this crime:

It's a sad and cruel tragedy I am going to relate,
Happened near Willow City in the North Dakota state;
There lived a good and kind old man alone upon his farm,
Not even a little child can say he ever did them harm.

But a cowardly assassin butchered him and left him in his gore,
And there John Cudnie found him lying dead upon the floor.
But our officers were wide awake, they all did use their wits,
And the villain soon was captured by Sheriff Billie Pitts.

---

[10]*Ibid.*, pp. 76-78.

The jury came into the court, twelve men were in the gang,
It was then and there decided little Willie he must hang,
So on next Friday morning these words Judge Cowan said,
That Willie Ross must hang by the neck until he was dead.

People called him Little Willie and his other name is Ross,
Was convicted of this awful crime tho defended by Ben Goss.
So now your trial is over, you're a poor unlucky chap,
With a rope around your neck, and you'll wear a nice black cap.

So, Sheriff Thomas Gardner, you do your work right well,
And William Ross will play in luck if he don't land in hell.
So on next Friday morning will be the end of murderer Ross,
He had friends, though 'twas not Jesus; but Charlie Brown and
  Bennie Goss.

Oh, for killing Thomas Walsh it was my great mistake,
And I'll get hemp rope for breakfast, dead sure that is no fake.
So now I'll say good-bye, bid you all by me take warning,
If you do, you won't hang by your neck on a cold and frosty
  morning.[11]

William Udderzook — Pennsylvania

We referred to the William Udderzook case earlier in connection with an ingenious method of hanging—upward rather than downward.

The case, which had its locale in the sleepy village of West Chester, Pennsylvania, during the 1870's, is not notorious or famous because of the type of scaffold used, but because it was a fantastic example of murder-for-insurance. It was a case worthy of the great Edmund Pearson and he handled it in his own inimitable style.[12]

William Eachus Udderzook was convicted of murdering his brother-in-law, Winfield Scott Goss, alias Alex C. Wilson, for insurance, in which Udderzook's wife, Eliza, was the beneficiary. The story of this almost unbelievable crime began on February 2, 1872, with the discovery of a body thought to be that of Goss, in his own house, in Baltimore County, Maryland. The house had been set afire and the body was burned beyond recognition. Almost a year and a half later, on July 9, 1873, a John Harford

[11]*Ibid.*, pp. 82-83.

[12]See *Murder at Smutty Nose and Other Murders,* New York, Sun Dial Press, 1926, in
  story entitled "A Demonition Body," pp. 70.93.

was traveling on a lonely road in Chester County, Pennsylvania, and noted some "buzzards presumably interested in a dead snake." On July 11, a partly decomposed body was found on the site which later the state contended was the actual body of the missing Goss, whose alleged remains had been found earlier in the charred remains of his home. However, in the interim, the widow of Goss, sister of the criminal finally hanged, demanded that the insurance companies pay her the $25,000 which had been placed on the life of her husband. The companies demurred to such a degree that Udderzook, actually hiding Goss under various aliases, finally thought it expedient and wise to dispose of the bothersome relative actually and completely. This he did by bludgeoning him to death and hiding the body in the woods where the cadaver had attracted the ubiquitous buzzards. Udderzook and his sister, the saddened Mrs. Goss, were in a dubious position to collect the insurance money even though Goss was really departed. The killer was found guilty on November 9, 1873. Due to writs of error and other legal maneuvering, he was not taken to the gallows until a year later on November 12, 1874. Three weeks before he was "to be jerked upward rather than to be swung downward," Udderzook wrote somewhat feelingly, concerning the disposition of his remains: "It is my desire that my remains will rest in Baltimore if not in the same lot, at least in the same cemetery with those of Mr. Winfield Scott Goss, a friend ever dear to me, that our bodies may return to the mother dust, and our spirits may mingle together on the bright sunny banks of deliverance, where pleasures never end, . . ."[13] It is now obvious, if it wasn't at the time, that he really meant the Goss whom he killed and whose body he left in the woods, and not the "other" Goss, found in the charred ruins of his home which remains, it would seem, may most likely have been a cadaver from some medical school.

THE HAZARDOUS PLIGHT OF EARLY PEDDLERS
Jost Folhaber, the German Peddler of Mahoney Mountain — Pennsylvania

After this country was initially settled along the Eastern Seaboard, a slow migration to the western lands began to take place.

---

[13]McDade, *op. cit.*, 1012.

People pushed out to the hinterland, taking their chances with Indians, inconveniences and loneliness. It was a way of life that attracted many. It was not unusual to find itinerant peddlers roaming through the mountains of the long Appalachian chain serving the needs of those sequestered folks.

The life of a peddler was at best precarious, especially if he penetrated into the mountain fastnesses which were served by narrow dirt or muddy roads or ruts, with no canals or railroads. It is little wonder that we read on occasions of a holdup or even of the murder of a peddler as these harmless and inoffensive small-time merchants went about their business serving mankind.

The first such crime to come to our attention was the murder of the German Peddler, Jost Folhaber, in what was then Berks County, Pennsylvania (now Schulylkill County). The murder occurred on August 11, 1797. Today, one may see the grave of this humble merchant. It was on this spot where he was cruelly shot down by an assassin. This peddler's grave consists of a pile of stones on a lonely road—even today—between the village of Brandonville and the borough of Mahoney City, not far from a small creek anciently known as Waste House Run.

On August 1, 1797, there appeared at Reich's tavern a well-dressed game hunter named Benjamin Bailey who claimed his native habitat as Morristown, New Jersey. As was the custom of the times, the stranger offered to supply the tavern with game meat, while he was a guest, in return for his lodgings. Some days later, the peddler, Folhaber, arrived at the mountain inn, on horseback. After engaging him in conversation, Bailey soon learned the immediate plans and itinerary of the merchant.

The next day, shortly after the peddler left for his daily trek through the mountain trails, he had a follower. While Bailey was afoot, he had no trouble in overtaking the unsuspecting Folhaber as he stopped now and again to pick berries along the trail. At what Bailey thought was a propitious moment to commit his crime, he took aim with his gun and fired, hitting the peddler in the back. He then rushed to the spot where his victim fell and dispatched him into eternity with blows from a tomahawk. Upon searching for loot he was shocked and bitterly disappointed. All he found were a few coins worth only a few paltry dollars and some clothing of no special value.

The details of Bailey's capture, trial and execution follow in the usual pattern. His crime was not particularly ingenious; rather it was one of sheer greed mingled with cruelty. The trial, held at Reading, the county seat, created a great deal of excitement in that small village. The trial judge was Jacob Rush, brother of the eminent physician, Dr. Benjamin Rush. The victim's widow was present as well as Reich, the tavern owner, and his family, all of whom testified against the defendant Bailey. It did not take long for the jury to pronounce him guilty. He was sentenced to death.

Bailey was hanged in the square at Reading, Pennsylvania, on January 6, 1798 before a crowd estimated at 6,000. A curious sequel to this tragedy was the discovery, in August of 1880, of some copper coins which it is believed were hidden by Bailey after he had committed his murder. Some boys, playing in the vicinity at a place known as Lawton's Patch, stumbled onto the coins.

One commentator dwelling at some length on this mountain tragedy, has this to say: "It is a notable commentary upon the fate of the principals that whilst the bones of the assassin were left to moulder among the undistinguishable tenants of the Potters Field—those of his humble victim still repose after the lapse of more than a century [he was writing in 1905] on the lofty mountain top—his place of sepulture known to all men, cared for by the public, and visited by hundreds who have heard the pathetic legend that attaches to "The German Peddler's Grave." On the face of the granite slab appears these words:

The Peddler's Grave
JOST FOLHABER
DIED AUGUST 11, 1797

Near this spot was committed the first known murder in this section. Folhaber, a travelling peddler, was ambushed, cruelly murdered and robbed. He and his horse were left to die by the wayside.

His assassin was tried, found guilty and hanged.

Erected by E. T. Everett & Sons[14]

---

[14]"The German Pedlar's Grave," in publications of the Historical Society of Schuylkill County, Penna. Vol. I, No. 3 (1906) pp. 183-192, paper read before the Society by D. C. Henning March 29, 1905. Thanks to Dorothy Scheer of Philadelphia for her research on and interest in this case.

THE PLIGHT OF SOME OTHER PEDDLERS

Earlier we mentioned that one Henry Kobler Musselman of Lancaster County, Pennsylvania, sold his body to a local physician just prior to his execution.[15] This Musselman, with an accomplice, murdered an itinerant peddler, Lazarus Zellerbach, but only after a terrific struggle had taken place in a field near the town. At the hanging, which took place on December 20, 1839, Musselman swore vehemently, as God was his judge, that he was not guilty. The news report stated that only "a few physicians and their students amounting to only thirty attendants" witnessed the spectacle. Both principals in the crime were from Bavaria, but were unknown to one another.

A similar peddler-murder occurring on August 19, 1853, is that of Hiram Williams, a German-Jew from New York City, who was hawking his wares in the Troy-Albany New York area. An ex-convict named Warren Wood accosted this inoffensive man near Greenville and walked with him for a while. Believing him to have a large sum of money on him (a common misconception about peddlers) he dropped back a few steps, drew a pistol and shot Williams. He threw his victim's body into a stream, and pelted it with stones after picking the victims' pockets.

The peddler, however, was not dead. He succeeded in hailing a passing stage and was taken to Greenville where he told the authorities of the encounter with Wood and the ensuing robbery-assault. He lived just long enough to identify his assailant by means of a "daguerrotype" local rogues gallery. Wood was apprehended in New York City, returned to stand trial and was convicted. He was sentenced to death and, after some delays, was hanged on June 20, 1854. The episode inspired a ballad which follows:

The Murdered Pedlar

Vouchsafe thine aid, ye wondrous nine,
To pen each sad and mournful line,
A tragic scene transpired of late,
The truth of which I shall narrate.

On the Plank-Road in Greenville Town,
A Jewish Pedlar was shot down.

---

[15](Chap. V, p. 214); McDade, 708.

Ah, by a wretch called Warren Wood,
Who shot the Pedlar in cold blood.

Hiram Williams was the Pedlar's name,
Who had obtained an honest fame.
He met with Wood in Greenville town,
Where, sad to tell he shot him down.

When first he shot, the Pedlar cried,
What'er you want shall be supplied.
His pocket book to Wood he gave,
In hopes of this his life to save.

Again he shot! O cruel man!
What mortal can your feelings scan.
Infernal spirits astonish'd stood,
Awhile to gaze on Warren Wood.

Who did the Pedlar's head then pound
As he laid bleeding on the ground.
Until he thought him truly dead,
And then the monster quickly fled.

Back to New York he sped his way,
To promenade with Ladies gay,
In Cherry Street they did him take,
He now his pleasure must forsake.

Though filled with dread and guilty fear,
Before the Pedlar must appear.
Thou art the man the Pedlar said,
As he then raised his dying head.

I know that coat, the boots likewise,
A dying man will tell no lies.
To jail the murderer then was sent,
His awful crimes there to lament.

On January next, the twentieth day,
The Sheriff must the law obey,
Upon the gallows him suspend,
And thus poor Wood his life will end.

Let all a solemn warning take,
And every wicked way forsake.
For soon we all will usher'd be,
Into a vast eternity.[16]

---

[16]Burt, *op. cit.*, pp. 78-80.

The Postboy Murder — Ohio — 1825

A murder, involving not a peddler, but a "postboy," and which ended in a hanging, occurred in Ohio, on September 9, 1825. It seems that William Cartmell, the postboy, was shot from ambush as he was carrying the mail from Coshocton to Freeport, in Tuscarawas County, eastern Ohio. William Johnson, who lived in Steubenville, not far away, was accompanying the victim. He had stopped behind briefly to get a drink of water from a roadside spring. When he heard a shot, he rushed to the scene and found another, John Funston, with the dead man.

Johnson was accused of murder but he swore he was innocent. He maintained he could recognize the murderer and begged the authorities to gather the young men of the vicinity and bring before him for identification. This was done and he pointed out Funston to the officials. Aside from the identification, there was other evidence against the suspect. Funston was convicted and hanged on December 30, 1825, at New Philadelphia, the county seat. He confessed his crime and laid it to his "greed for gold." Six of the nine verses of a ballad concerning this affair follow:

John Funston, a youth of but twenty years old,
With light hair and blue eyes, he ventured so bold;
He was young, fair and handsome with light hair and blue eyes,
He wrought his own ruin by seeking a prize.

He murdered William Cartmell, a youth of renown,
On the road leading from Freeport to Cohocton Town.
He murdered him and robbed him of money and goods,
And made his way home through a thicket of woods.

Soon after young Johnson to prison was bound,
He denied all the charges against him were found;
He said he was nigh when young Cartmell was shot,
Just hearing the gun, he came up to the spot.

Soon after, John Funston was sporting with joy,
On the money he took from the poor murdered boy;
Squire Major then took him and brought him straightway,
To New Philadelphia, his actions to try.

The jury found him guilty and unto him they said
'You must hang by the neck until you are dead!'
On the twentieth of December in the morning quite soon,
He called to the sheriff to confess what he'd done.

The doctors stood 'round him, his pulse for to feel,
Thinking at night his dead body to steal;
'Tis forbidden by law and considered not right,
To steal the dead body of Funston at night.[17]

(incomplete)

The Rosensweig-Blank Case — Pennsylvania — 1893

Our victim was one Jacob Marks; the killers were Harris Blank and Isaac Rosensweig; the scene of the crime, "Dutch Mountain" in Wyoming County, Pennsylvania; the time and place of the double hanging, May 18, 1893 at the county seat, Tunkhannock. Marks, like all peddlers, carried some money and trinkets. The killers lay in wait for their victim and bludgeoned him to death. They made off to New York City, thence to the middlewest and later to Montreal where they were captured and returned to expiate their wanton crime.

The local paper, *The New Era,* on the date of the hanging, made the following statement (which is open to some doubt): "It is said to be the first instance in which capital punishment was ever visited upon members of the Jewish race upon the Continent of America." This is not correct, even for the state of Pennsylvania. One Martin Weinberger was hanged at Pittsburgh (Allegheny County), on September 2, 1884, almost ten years earlier, for the murder of one Gottfreud in a business dispute. The *Pittsburgh Post* for that date stated that "the Jewish rites were performed in his cell." We have no further evidence that there were earlier cases of persons of the Jewish faith being hanged for murder.

One interesting sidelight about the Rosensweig case is this: "He wrote a rather pathetic letter in reply to one sent to him by a Towanda [Pennsylvania] woman in which she exhorted him to seek Christ as his Savior; he wrote that Christ might be the true Savior but as he had been taught by his mother to regard him as an imposter she could hardly expect him to break the faith he had clung to all his life."[18]

OTHER CASES OF GREED

The thread of avarice runs through many murder cases, espe-

---

[17]Burt, *op. cit.,* pp. 81-2.
[18]*The New Era,* Tunkhannock, Pennsylvania, May 18, 1893.

cially where money or financial assets are involved. At this point, we wish to insert some details of a Philadelphia case which may be labeled low-level greed. It has to do with the murder of Mrs. Sarah Cross by two men "of colour," John Joyce, alias Davis, and Peter Matthias, for which they were hanged publicly on March 11, 1808. The case is actually an ordinary run-of-the-mill affair and gained notoriety only because the two killers were defended by Nicholas Biddle, financier and Richard Rush, later United States Attorney General and statesman. The confessions of the two men were published, thus bequeathing to posterity a pamphlet that may be found in some law libraries.[19]

The story is briefly this: Mrs. Cross, the victim, kept a small shop in Black Horse Alley in downtown Philadelphia. On December 18, 1807, thirteen-year-old Anne Messenger was sent to the shop to get some licorice for her guardian and noted that the shutters were drawn, which was a bit unusual. In peeking through the keyhole she saw Joyce shaking Mrs. Cross by the neck. The girl pushed open the door and rushed in only to be seized by the assailant. He immediately locked the door of the shop with one hand and held a rope which was about the shop-keeper's throat. She was dead. Matthias appeared from upstairs and the two men forced the girl to hold a lighted candle while they rifled the shop. Being satisfied they had everything of value they left after shoving the girl into the street. This star witness was able to identify the two killers the following day when they were apprehended. They were indicted, convicted and hanged for this atrocious crime.

Matthias was a neighborhood fiddler, living within a block of the widow Cross's little shop; Joyce was a mere roustabout. Both were contrite throughout. The trial created considerable local attention due to the reputation of the attorneys and the Chief Justice who presided at the trial.

GREED AND BANK THEFTS

Greed is often associated with bank thefts, whether it be outright robbery, embezzlement or shrewd manipulation of the records. Generally, in more recent years, bank thefts have not called for the death penalty so that professional bank thieves have been

---

[19]Listed by McDade, *op. cit.,* 543-545.

fairly careful to abstain from murder unless cornered. We insert here what may be considered the first bank robbery in the country; but, unfortunately for the perpetrator he botched his job and killed an employee and thus was condemned to death. This bungling job may have resulted from the fact that Edward W. Green, of Malden, Massachusetts was really not a desperado or professional but the postmaster of the town!

Green, twenty-seven years of age and a partial cripple, found himself short in his postal accounts—perhaps due to his "secret drinking habits" of which some of the towns people had been privy. On December 16, 1863, finding the town bank manned solely by a seventeen-year-old youth, Frank Eugene Converse, son of the bank's president, he decided to rob it. Obtaining a gun he entered the bank and shot the teller—if that was the title in those days—through the head and skipped with $5,000. He was quickly apprehended and soon confessed, telling where the money could be found. Appeals were made for commutation of the death sentence but the governor refused to act, so Green was hanged on April 13, 1866. McDade, in his *Annals of Murder* (item 381) states, in presenting data on the Green case, that Homer Croy, in his work *Jesse James Was My Neighbor*,[20] "On February 13, 1866, ten men rode up to the bank in Liberty, Missouri, and the first bank robbery took place in America." McDade then makes the assertion that "staid New England Malden, Massachusetts is entitled to that dubious honor." But the two crimes, so widely separated by geography, had very little in common!

The Malden Public Library was presented to the town by the victim's parents as a memorial to him, in 1883. A painting of young Converse hangs in the library painted in 1886 by Albion H. Bicknell.

Liberty, Missouri and Malden, Massachusetts may have been the locales for *bona fide* bank robberies, but public funds were mulcted from official hands by greedy thieves long before the turn of the nineteenth century. We have no data on these early peculations, but we know of two persons who were hanged in Pennsylvania for crimes associated with such public monies. One

[20]New York, Duell, Sloane & Pearce, 1949.

John Tomlinson, alleged member of the Bucks County Doan gang, notorious and scintillating Tory highwaymen,[21] was hanged at Newton, same county, on October 17, 1782, for "robbing the county treasury" in that town. He "was buried on his own farm." In that same state, on September 26, 1778, "Capt. Sandy Flash" Fitzpatrick was hanged at Chester for "larceny and burglary"— actually he was the prototype of the "highwayman" and was guilty of many and sundry crimes. He robbed "tax collectors" of the day and when he was captured in the home of a Capt. McAffie by his female servant, Rachel Walker, they shared a reward of $1,000, which was considered large for those days.[22]

It would be an interesting exercise to see just who the first real bank robbers were and what penalties were exacted.

NEW HAMPSHIRE MURDERS AND THEIR BALLADS

All states have had their murders of greed, lust, white cold anger and other such motives and all states have some identifying ballads which have survived. But perhaps no other state has had so many associated with it as New Hampshire. We have made no scientific survey to substantiate this statement, but in recording the cases incorporated in this book, we find the Granite State bobbing up more than would seem average. We can find no explanation as to the reason this small New England state should stimulate its homespun balladeers and bards to create mournful dirges associated with murder and hanging; suffice to say that many survive and we shall attempt to relate the crimes and executions associated with them regardless of the underlying motives of the crimes.

The first we ran across was the murder of Capt. Peter Downe, by Elisha Thomas, locale and date—New Durham in February 1788. The weapon was a knife and the motive was anger at the victim for separating Thomas from someone with whom he was quarreling. Thomas expressed deep remorse for his impetuous act —the victim was his friend—but it did him no good in escaping the death penalty. While languishing in the jail at Dover, he attempted to escape by climbing into the chimney flue but in this

---

[21]See Chapter I, p. 21.

[22]For further details of the Fitzpatrick case, see Chapter I, p. 64.

he failed. He was hanged at Dover at the foot of Swazey's Hill on June 3 (or 5th) 1788. He left a wife and six children. A ballad of twenty-four rather repetitious verses survives this early case. Here is a sample:

Unhappy man, I understand You are condemned to die;
In a few days you must away To vast eternity.

Your fate is sad, but not too bad, But mercy you may have;
If speedily to Him you fly, Who sinners came to save.

Behold the lamb, the great I AM, The hapless sinners' friend,
Was made a curse, and died for us, That we might not be damned.

But to conclude, O may that God Who gave his only Son,
Give you his Grace, in Heaven a place, For Jesus' sake— Amen.[23]

Josie Langmaid — Pembroke Schoolgirl — 1875

Earlier we mentioned the lonely mountain grave of the peddler Folhaber, murdered in 1797 in Pennsylvania. This mute reminder of a cruel murder parallels the erection of a loving monument to an innocent schoolgirl of Pembroke, New Hampshire, who was struck down on October 4, 1875. She was Josie Langmaid, a student at Pembroke Academy, less than two miles from her home. As a rule Josie was accompanied to school by her step-brother; but on this fateful morning she was obliged to go alone; she never reached the academy. She was waylaid by a killer, knocked down with a club, her head severed from her body with a razor, and then despoiled sexually. The murderer, one Joseph LaPage, alias Joseph Paquette, a French-Canadian wood-cutter, threw her mangled body into a nearby swamp, not more than a half mile from the school.

That evening, searching parties scoured the terrain looking for the missing girl. One of the seachers was LaPage. Her headless body was found and the following day the head was found behind a stump in Giles Swamp, wrapped in her blue cape. A Boston detective was placed on the case. Suspicion rested on LaPage first, because his hob-nailed boots coincided with marks found on the

---

[23]Burt, *op. cit.*, p. 237; data from John Scans, *History of Strafford County, N.H.*, Chicago, 1914, pp. 64-68; *Massachusetts Broadsides*, 2523, a pamphlet.

girl's body and second, he furnished an ironclad alibi except for one hour on the morning of the crime. He was brought to trial on January 4, 1876, and hanged at the state prison at Concord on March 4, 1878. It was later discovered that LaPage had murdered Miss Marietta Hall, a school teacher of St. Alban's, Vermont, the previous year.

The townspeople of Pembroke were overwhelmed at the brutal crime perpetrated on so young and lovely a person and were moved to erect a monument to her memory. In addition there is a ballad extant, crude though it is. Thanks again to Mrs. Burt's collection, we reproduce it:

> Kind people all, both far and near, Attend a while and you
>   shall hear;
> How that a lady of renown Was murdered in fair Sunlock Town.
>
> 'Twas in the morning very cool, As Josie started for her school;
> Then on her body marks did show, Some skilful hand had dealt
>   the blow.
>
> The wretch who did the wicked deed, Was one LePage, a chop-
>   per by trade;
> He often had outraged other young maids, And took the life
>   of Josie Langmaid.[24]

A more complete, and probably more accurate version of the Josie Langmaid ballad has been preserved in one of the collections of Helen Hartness Flanders which follows:

> Come all young people, now draw near;
> Attend a while and you shall hear,
> How a young person of renown
> Was murdered in fair Suncook Town.
>
> It was in the morning very cool
> When Josie started for her school,
> And many the time that road she passed
> But little thought she it would be her last.
>
> It was at the foot of Pembrook Street
> La Page lay ambushed with a stick;
> Long time ago his plans were laid
> To take the life of the fair maid.

---

[24]Burt, *op. cit.,* p. 57; case cited by McDade, *op. cit.,* 580-582; also Concord *Daily Monitor,* March 15, 1878.

The mother watched with eager air,
Hoping her daughter would appear,
But when the shades of night drew near
Her darling child did not appear.

The weeping father and the son
All thro' the woods their search begun,
And found at last to their surprise
The murdered child before their eyes.

Her head was from her body tore,
Her clothes were all a crimson gore,
And on her body marks did show
Some skilful hand had dealt the blow.

This monster now so deep in crime,
He thought the peoples' eyes to blind,
But found at last to his mistake,
They had him fast behind the grate.

It was at Concord he was tried.
Unto the last his crime denied,
But he was found to guilty be
And the judge said, "Death is your plea.

"And now, La Page, your work is done
And you like Eveuse must be hung,
For we must all examples make
Till crime shall cease in the Granite State."[25]

The Daniel Farmer Case — Amherst, New Hampshire — 1822

Daniel Davis Farmer was executed for the murder of the widow, Ann Ayer, at Amherst, New Hampshire, on January 3, 1822. The crime occurred at Goffstown, on April 4, 1821, although Farmer was a resident of Manchester. The victim had the reputation of being a "worthless woman" so that few were much concerned at the crime. Allegedly, Farmer had struck his victim several blows in a deep-seated fit of anger. She had accused him of "fathering her child" which, of course, he could not accept. He was hanged "on a cold day" with 10,000 "witnesses" to the event. He prepared a pamphlet to be published after his death, "a valedictory

[25]Used by permission of Helen Hartness Flanders as published in *Vermont Folk-Songs & Ballads,* Stephen Daye Press, Brattleboro, Vt.; 1931, pp. 72-73. (Copyright held by Helen Hartness Flanders).

address, with some of his correspondence during his imprisonment."[26]

This case has something worthy of note. It is represented by religious murder ballad samplings, as preserved by Burt. She points out that sectarianism was introduced in this case to explain the probable fate of Farmer. The creator of the ballad contributes not one word of the crime or of the criminal's life. As Mrs. Burt states: "It is entirely an adjuration to Farmer, and to all youths, to shun crime, or suffer the consequences, not only in this world, but also in the next." Calvinism and predestination are the *motif* of a second ballad, signed by "J.G." with Farmer's murder as vehicle for stating his views regarding the religion of the day:

Thoughts

Occasioned by the Seeing of the Execution of Daniel Davis Farmer At Amherst, January 3, 1822—Keeping an Eye on Calvinism

O! Did the God, the God of love decree
That this poor Farmer should a murderer be,
And after years of sin and murd'rous strife,
That on the gallows he should end his life?

Not only so, did he predestinate
That endless torments in a future state
Should be his lot and final destiny
For sinful deeds which God did fore decree?

If this be true, O! what a wretch forlorn!
Good had it been if he had not been born.
O! must he sin through life by God's decree,
And for it suffer endless misery?

O, Mr. Calvin, if thy creed be right,
Doth not THY GOD in tormenting delight?
No wonder then, for thy religion's sake,
Thou caused Servetus to burn at the stake.[27]

Some forty years earlier than the Josie Langmaid murder, the townsfolk of Hopkinton, Merrimac County, in the same state, erected a monument to mark the spot of the murder of Mrs.

---

[26]McDade, *op. cit.*, 299-300.

[27]Burt, *op. cit.*, p. 108.

Sally Cochrane, which occurred on June 23, 1833, at the hands of a dull-witted youth of eighteen, Abraham Prescott. The boy lived with the Cochranes and one day he went "strawberry picking" with his victim and for no apparent reason bludgeoned her to death with a stake. He returned home and immediately apprized the husband of what he had done. His defense, for some reason now obscure, contended that Prescott was a somnambulist with some incipient insanity. He was tried in Concord but hanged at Hopkinton, on January 8, 1836.[28]

Again we rely on Mrs. Burt's collection for the ballad created for the Prescott case which allegedly was written by a "private individual at the Bar." There are twenty stanzas but only seven seem to be necessary to tell the story of the crime:

Ye people all assemble here, To see me suffer death,
Draw nigh the guilty wretch and hear Words of my dying breath.

Insanity I do not plead—'Tis useless now, and vain;
Therefore I pray you all take heed, I shall not long remain.

The trees and flowers and all were bright, 'Twas strawberry time, and she
Thinking no harm in broad day-light Went to the fields with me.

She had a mother been to me, In health and sickness kind;
O what a wretch was I, to be
To all her goodness blind!

We picked some berries red and rare, Red as her blushing face—
Then with a stake I killed her there, All in that lonely place!

I feared her husband's wrath, for he I once had tried to kill;
I fear'd his rage would murder me, I fear his person still.

The grave awaits me, I must go, My parents farewell, ye;
May you more sorrow never know, May you all happy be.[29]

The Almy-Abbott-Christie Warden Case

Perhaps the most famous, or notorious case coming out of New Hampshire is that of the Frank C. Almy - George Abbott affair. It has to do with the murder of a young girl, of near Hanover,

---

[28]McDade, *op. cit.*, 769-771; also, *History of Pembroke, N.H.*, Vol. I, 1895.
[29]Burt, *op. cit.*, pp. 66-67.

by Almy, who had worked as a farm-hand for the victim's father. Almy was madly in love with the girl. The sad case of Christina Warden including the dual life of Almy, alias Abbott, has been preserved for posterity by Stewart H. Holbrook in his *Murder Out Yonder*.[30] He labeled it "The Crime of the Vale of Tempe" because such a place exists near the Dartmouth College campus and has long been famous as a beauty spot. Christie Warden was actually murdered in this lovely spot by the love-maddened Almy.[31]

Born George Abbott, he was a member of a well-known family of Puritan descent, in Salem, Massachusetts. Early in life he showed signs of dissipation. His mother died when he was born and, in due time, his father shipped him off to an uncle who lived in the village of North Thetford, Vermont. George soon showed signs of delinquency when he stole from school acquaintances and village shops. He was seventeen years of age when he was sent to prison for a term of four years. After his release, he continued to be a menace to the community and subsequently was again sent to prison for a fifteen-year stretch. This was in 1881 and he was then twenty-four. It was in this state prison at Windsor that George Abbott demonstrated the kind of man he actually was. He did what had been considered impossible; he escaped by fashioning a ladder through inexhaustible patience and cunning skill. Opened in 1809, this prison had never experienced an escape, but George Abbott made it.

After some wandering about, Abbott—who now took the name Frank Almy, spotted a farm near Hanover owned by Andrew Warden and there sought work. The farm was on the Lyme Road "a bit more than a mile from Dartmouth Hall." The Wardens had two daughters, Christie, aged twenty, and Fanny, aged sixteen. From the start Fanny disliked the new hired man and did not hesitate to show him her distrust. Christie, on the other hand, was interested in the young floater. Being a very active person in community affairs, she enlisted Almy's interest in Grange programs as well as other rural activities. They picked flowers, popped corn, took hikes and attended various meetings together. It could not be denied—it was a budding courtship with affection mutually

---

[30]New York, Macmillan, 1941.

[31]Francis Lane Childs, Hanover, N.H. Bi-Centennial Book, 1961, in a sketch by Robert P. Richmond, pp. 161-172.

exchanged. Fanny's attitude toward Almy turned from distrust to implaccable hatred. Before matters could come to a head, Warden notified Almy that he had no more work for him. The man left, or so it appeared. He traveled to his home town, Salem, but soon returned to his old haunts to be near Christie Warden. He hid in their barn, secreting himself in the hay and venturing out at night to obtain food and hoping to obtain a fleeting glimpse of the girl he allegedly loved. For thirty-two days he remained there, foraging for food and checking on the family activities through a knot-hole in the loft. His objective was to await the chance of seeing his lady-love alone, something that was difficult since Christie was hardly ever alone. At last he sensed his chance. He saw the two girls and their mother wending their way through the "Vale of Tempe" returning home from a meeting of the Grange. He approached them with a revolver in his hand. In the frightening confusion the women screamed and Almy fired—at Christie. He had killed her, the girl he claimed he loved. Her body was found later, almost stripped of clothing. The murder was committed on July 17, 1891. A posse was formed to hunt down the killer, although he eluded them for some time. One day, quite by accident, it was discovered that he was hidden in that same Warden barn, in the hayloft, deep in the hay. After a brisk fight in which some shots were fired, Almy was captured. During this stay in the barn he had actually spent many nocturnal hours at the grave of his victim, Christie Warden whom he loved.

After he was apprehended and a checkup was made, it was discovered that he and George Abbott were the same; a startling, almost horrifying surprise. Here the arch-thief and escape artist Abbott had been accepted by a God-fearing family and was actually on the verge of marrying the lovely Warden daughter. Fanny, of course, was vindicated in her appraisal of Almy. He was a villain in disguise. On the witness stand she said, "His cruel eyes glistened like a serpent's." Abbott-Almy was hanged at Concord state prison on May 16, 1892. A lewd ballad survives the case— a ballad that Stewart H. Holbrook maintains is "absolutely worthless because it is consciously humorous, something that should not occur in a song about a tragedy."[31a]

[31a]In a footnote to page 190, *op. cit.*

Almy's execution, like so many others, was bungled. As his body hurtled through the trap, the knot in the rope became loosened, adding several inches to its length. His feet struck the stone pavement in the death house. The sheriff and his assistants immediately pounced upon the bewildered victim and drew him into the air. He was unconscious when he was dropped the second time and died after some nine minutes.[32]

Almy was presumably buried in the prison yard at Concord but his grave has never been located. This quandary led to the legend, or belief, held by many at the time, that his body was exhumed and spirited away to the Dartmouth Medical School for dissection and experimentation, a not uncommon practice in years gone by.[33] A verse of the alleged Almy ballad—sung to the tune "Ta-ra-ra-Boom-de-ay," is:

> So they hanged him by the neck,
>> On the gallows, yes, by heck!
> So he rests beneath the sod,
>> For Almy's gone to meet his God.[33a]

The End of Public Hangings in New Hampshire

Before leaving the subject of hangings in New Hampshire—most of which were colorful, quaint, or notorious—a few words should be incorporated here regarding what is supposed to be the state's last public execution, that of Samuel Mills, at Haverhill, on May 6, 1868. While public hangings were allegedly abolished in the state by the act of January 13, 1837, more than one public or semi-public execution took place after that date, culminating in the Mills hanging. For instance, Andrew Howard was hanged in Strafford County (presumably at the county seat of Dover) some time following July 8, 1846—the original date when a large crowd assembled to witness the affair but which had to be postponed due to a last minute reprieve from the governor.[34] Three

---

[32]As reported by Richmond, *loc. cit.,* p. 172.

[33]*Granite Monthly,* Vol. 97, No. 4 (October 1897) pp. 223-8.

[33a]*Note:* The Vale of Tempe in Hanover, adjacent to the Dartmouth campus, is now part of an eighteen-hole golf course and college ski jump.

[34]Howard had killed Phebe Hanson on September 19, 1843; source, John Scabe, *History of Strafford County,* 1914.

years later, on May 23, 1849, the Methodist minister, the Rev. Enos G. Dudley of Grafton, was hanged at Haverhill for the murder of his wife the preceding year. We have no information, however, regarding the attendance at this execution.[35]

The Mills execution holds the distinction of being the last public affair. It was witnessed by one Elmore Whipple of Franconia and this gentleman had a sense of the historical importance and so related the details to Ella Shannon Bowles many years later. It is from her article, entitled "The Last Public Hanging in New Hampshire" and that we tell the story of Mills and his murdered victim.[36]

There are many legends and old-wives' tales built about the Mills case. Among them are that Mills treacherously slew his best friend, a bachelor named George Maxwell; that he was both dexterous and powerful, possessing almost superhuman strength, agility and skill and defied capture with great and even an admired tenacity; and that his execution was surrounded with a heavy aura of doubt as to whether or not it was a public spectacle. Certainly the crime and the hanging created a great stir in the mountain villages around Haverhill—Franconia and Lisbon, for example—so that every detail of fact and fancy concerning the saga became woven into the local fabric of White Mountain history and folklore.

Samuel Mills was an immigrant miner from England. He was employed by a mining company at Lisbon that was engaged in digging for minerals on the "Dodge Farm." There were iron and copper deposits in the vicinity so it was not unusual to see many "rough customers" about. Mills was described as having a "bull neck, twenty-one inches 'round." On Saturday night, December 8, 1866, he called on his friend Maxwell, who lived alone. The two were well acquainted and met frequently to play cards. Mills had heard that Maxwell had a sum of money cached away in his home —a sum of $1,200, obtained by selling a piece of farmland. The avaricious Mills, after arriving at his friend's home, took a steelyard, or balance, that hung over the kitchen door, and slugged the startled Maxwell so that he died from the force of the blow.

---

[35]Sources: J. O. Bettinger, *History of Haverhill, N.H.*, 1888, p. 397; McDade, *op. cit.*, 1036.

[36]*Yankee: A Yankee Magazine for Yankees Everywhere*, Vol. IV, No. 4 (April, 1938).

Mills then went into the victim's barn, hitched up the team, and made off.

The sleepy village of Franconia had never witnessed such a crime. Excitement was indescribable as posses were formed and searching parties scoured the woods. There was no trace of Mills and after some six weeks, the townsfolk returned to normalcy. The authorities, however, could not give up. A private detective from Boston was brought into the case and, while his efforts seemed to local people somewhat desultory, it was privately known that he was gradually unearthing important leads. He found that the man for whom he was looking wore an abnormal-type shoe with a turned-over heel. He got a drawing from a dentist of the mouth of the culprit and built up a composite likeness of Mills, no actual photographs, of course, being available. These laborious bits of detective work soon paid off. Mills was finally found in Galena, Illinois, far from the scene of his crime.

He was eventually returned and tried for the murder and convicted. He managed to escape from the Haverhill jail on two occasions. A revolver, and some poison, smuggled into him, tempted him to commit suicide but he shunned that way out of his fateful dilemma.

The eye-witness of the hanging, Whipple, contended that it was a public hanging despite the fact that local history contends that it was not. There were not many present since the sheriff refused to wait for the train to arrive from Littleton with its capacity crowd of interested folk. Whipple describes the gallows as a "rough hemlock joist, projected five or six feet from the window of the cell, on the second floor of the jail, fronting the east and in full view of the street and surrounding fields." He describes the floor or platform of the scaffold as "made of rough boards thrown across the jail yard walls, about three feet lower than the jail window. Near the center of this floor the trap was arranged; beneath it the earth was removed to give a fall of nine feet." There was a fence about as high as "my piazza" built around it so "when the body dropped it couldn't be seen."

Whipple did admit that the Mills hanging was not as "brutal" nor as "public" as an earlier one which he probably did not witness —that of Josiah Burnham, hanged on August 12, 1806 for the murder of two cell-mates (Russell Freeman and Joseph Stark-weather), in the Haverhill jail where they were all incarcerated for debt. Burnham was defended by the court-assigned young Daniel Webster at Plymouth. According to Whipple, Burnham was hanged "on a gallows built right out in plain sight on Powder House Hill and [he] had to ride to it sitting on his coffin" before 10,000 people with "the Rev. David Sutherland of Bath preaching a sermon two hours long, preceded by singing and prayer."[37]

The Mills hanging was quicker and more expeditious. He was "laced in a white canvas bag and he descended to the scaffold without any trouble. He conversed at some length with the sheriff and with a couple of English friends who were in the crowd. These men waved to him and said 'Good Bye, Samuelly,' for that is what they called him." This was the end of a "desperate" murderer of the White Mountains a century ago and, with almost "unanimous" agreement, the last "public" hanging in the state. After this date, all condemned to death have been hanged in the state prison at Concord. State law requires the county sheriff to officiate at any hanging from his county.[38]

---

[37]See also McDade, *op. cit.*, 145.

[38]Much of the information regarding New Hampshire hangings has been obtained through the courteous help of Marjorie Calkins of Manchester and Catherine McGettigan of Lebanon, both of New Hampshire and formerly students at the University of New Hampshire.

Chapter VII

A FURTHER POTPOURRI OF CASES

M ANY MURDER CASES are known only to small local communities or regions. This is especially true of early cases when knowledge of their details could be disseminated by word of mouth. As journalism developed, more people became knowledgeable of such important incidents as killings. Some murders, committed in isolated culture pockets and prosecuted in backwoods county seats, in time developed into legends. Some of the following cases fit into such categories. Geographically, they range across the country and in point of time, they cover a spread of many years. All deserve a place in this book, even though some are not what a good raconteur of murder stories would consider first-rate. We start with the Frankie Silver case:

Frankie Silver — North Carolina — 1833

A crime—and a hanging—make up the Frankie Silver story, and a gruesome one it is. She was the only female hanged in the state of North Carolina. Her end came ignominiously on July 12, 1833, at Morganton, Burke County, her crime being the wilful murder of her husband, Charlie, on December 22, 1831.

The couple, together with their young child, lived at Deyton Bend, on the "Toe" River (Estadoe) on the line between Yancey and Mitchell Counties. Theirs had been considered a perfect match by an attractive backwoods girl of her strong backwoods man, but it ended in murder. The night of the killing he had taken his axe, chopped down a tree, and split it into firewood against the few days he was to be gone hunting game in the mountains. He never went. She knocked him cold with that same axe, as he slept on the cabin floor with their baby girl in his arms. She coolly cut up the body and stuffed it piece by piece into the fireplace and watched it burn until is was completely consumed—or almost completely.

The next morning, she nonchalantly appeared at the cabin home of her in-laws, telling them how she had tidied up her kitchen and had finished her chores which, in itself, seemed to them a bit strange. Frankie was usually not that energetic. As Charlie failed to show up around the mountain area, people began to be curious. A posse set off to find him, while suspicious neighbors began investigating about the Silver cabin. Before long, vague remnants of Charlie were found in the fireplace ashes. Bones and teeth, a buckle and other artifacts were discovered. It did not take too long for Sheriff John Boone, a nephew of the more famous Daniel, to place Frankie under arrest.

She was soon convicted and sentenced to be hanged, but this clever mountain female was not to be disposed of so easily or so quickly. With the aid of a wooden key, whittled into shape by one of her cooperating kinsfolk, Frankie escaped from jail. Dressed in men's clothing and with her hair shorn, she got away in a wagon hidden under some hay. But her time out of jail was limited, due to the efficiency of Sheriff Boone who captured her. She was hanged "near the Old Buckhorn Tavern, nine miles west of Morganton."

Post-mortem stories of just how she had murdered her Charlie indicated that she had taken the baby from his arms as he slumbered, struck him a horrible blow with the axe and then calculatingly hacked the body to pieces. She saw to it that each piece of human flesh and bones was burned in the fire which she kindled and rekindled with the wood that her victim had chopped for her convenience. The burning was an all-night ordeal for this amazing woman. She showed no signs of concern, hysteria or remorse so far as her foul deed was concerned.

Legends soon built up around this mountain tragedy. It was alleged that she composed her own gallows speech and read it before the crowd and that she insisted on finishing a piece of cake at the place of execution before she would permit the sheriff to "turn her off." Manly Wade Wellman has gathered the facts on this case and Olive Woolley Burt has published a ballad that may still be sung in the hills of the Tarheel State. In fact, Mrs. Burt

tells us that Muriel Early Sheppard, in her *Cabin on the Laurel,*
mentions it.[1]

There are some who feel that the famous Frankie and Johnny
ballad, known to most school boys and girls, and regarded by
Mrs. Burt as "one of the finest examples of American folk song,
actually unknown as to origin and age," refers to this North Carolina saga. However, there appears to be little really factual association since, as Mrs. Burt states, Frankie and Johnny is a "city song,
with pawnshop, hotel, saloons, and so on, whereas Frankie Silver
lived in an isolated mountain cabin, and, so far as it is known,
Charlie never 'done her wrong.' "[2] So far as we know, the motive
for the frenzied murder was jealousy, since it was apparent that
Charlie did pay some attention to other girls at mountain parties.
Here is the Silver ballad:

I Try That Awful Road

The jealous thought that first gave strife
To make me take my husband's life;
For days and months I spent my time
Thinking how to commit this crime.

And on a dark and doleful night
I put his body out of sight;
With flames I tried him to consume
But time would not admit it done.

Judge Donnell has my sentence passed;
These prison walls I leave at last;
Nothing to cheer my drooping head
Until I'm numbered with the dead.

But O that dreadful judge I fear;
Shall I that awful sentence hear?
'Depart, ye cursed, down to Hell,
And forever there to dwell.'

Then shall I meet that mournful face
Whose blood I spilled upon the place,

---

[1] Chapel Hill, University of North Carolina Press, 1935. For the story of this case, see
Manly Wade Wellman, *Dead and Gone,* Chapel Hill, University of Carolina Press,
1954, pp. 155-171.

[2] Burt, *op. cit.,* p. 17.

With flaming eye to me he'll say,
Why did you take my life away?

His feeble hands dropped gently down,
His chattering tongue soon lost its sound,

My mind on solemn subjects rolls,
My little child—God bless its soul.
All you that are of Adam's race,
Let not my faults this child disgrace.

Farewell, good people, now you see
What my bad conduct brought in me;
To die of shame and of disgrace
Before this world of human race.

Awful, indeed, to think of death,
In perfect health to lose my breath;
Farewell, my friends, I bid adieu,
Vengeance on me must now pursue.

Great God, how shall I be forgiven?
Not fit for earth, not fit for Heaven.
But little time to pray to God,
For now I try that awful road.[3]

Wellman says of this crude ballad: "The language . . . is somewhat labored, but there is circumstantiality in it." And so there is!

The Roxalana Druse Case — Herkimer, New York

Some fifty years later—specifically, February 28, 1887—another female was hanged for literally butchering her husband near Herkimer, New York. She was the forty-year-old farm-drudge wife of Will Druse, a close-fisted aging and bearded patriarch. She killed him on December 18, 1883, with an axe after the shots she fired from a pearl-handled revolver failed to dispatch her victim. On the fatal morning, before breakfast, a quarrel developed over Roxie's alleged extravagances at the general store. Apparently this was an old story, and, through the years, the maligned wife had reached the "breaking point." As he sat at the kitchen table, she cowered in the pantry fearing for her own life—he had threatened to kill her with an axe—and suddenly she remembered the pearl-

---

[3]Reproduced from Burt, *op. cit.,* pp. 17-18. and substantiated with Wellman, *op. cit.,* pp. 169-170.

handled revolver that lay out of sight in the cupboard. She slowly
and dispassionately withdrew the lethal weapon from its resting-
place and slipped quietly to the kitchen. She stole up behind her
spouse and pulled the trigger of the gun. She fired three shots,
all of which entered the neck and shoulders of her husband. He
slumped to the floor but was certainly not dead—yet. She called
her two children, Mary, aged eighteen, and George, eleven, who,
with a visiting nephew, Fred Gates, aged fourteen, had gone out-
doors during the quarrel. They returned to the house and Roxie
ordered the young nephew to continue shooting the helpless victim.
Still the old man did not yield to death. The crazed woman
picked up the kitchen axe and with two furious blows managed
to sever her spouse's head from his body. She then ordered the
children to help her cut up the inert body into pieces small enough
to stuff into the pot-bellied stove that reposed in the parlor. Still not
satisfied with her insane work of the morning, she waited until
the next day when the ashes had cooled, and, assisted by the terrorized children, she took them to Wall's swamp, a half-mile from
the house and buried them. Roxie was cool and collected throughout. She ordered the boys to hitch up the horse to the cutter while
she prepared the ashes for their resting-place. She, aided by her
daughter, not only scoured the flours in the effort to remove the
blood, but actually repapered where stains appeared on the walls.
But despite all of her efforts, it was not long before the evil deed
became known. Neighbors had seen and smelled the black acrid
smoke that emerged from the chimney of the house and thought
it strange. When a day or two later no sign was seen of Will Druse
suspicions were compounded. County officials were notified and
subsequent protracted questioning of Fred Gates broke the case
wide open. Despite some sympathy on the part of neighbors who
petitioned for reprieves—she was given two by the governor—
Roxie was ultimately hanged in the Herkimer County jail. Over
one thousand spectators milled around the old jail and a sixty-man
military contingent known as the Remington Rifle Corps from
Mohawk kept order. During Roxie's long stay in the jail she
occupied a cell which many years later—in 1908—Chester Gil-
lette would also occupy pending his removal to the Auburn prison
to be electrocuted for the murder of Grace Brown. This was the

saga made famous by Theodore Dreiser's adaptation, *An American Tragedy*.[4]

Bathsheba Spooner, Beautiful, Disgruntled Colonial Wife — Worcester, Massachusetts

A more sophisticated, but equally brutal murder of a man by his spouse was that of Joshua Spooner by his dissatisfied wife who answered to the Biblical name of Bathsheba, at Brookfield, Massachusetts, in 1778. Not courageous enough to do it herself, she hired two British soldiers to carry through her evil intent. Her young lover was also involved in the clandestine deed. The case, like so many described herein, is a classic.[5]

Before relating details of this fascinating case it should be stated that, contrary to general belief, Massachusetts Colony probably executed more females than did any other. For instance, prior to Bathsheba's execution, which occurred on July 2, 1778, our records indicate that twenty-eight other females were hanged (counting, of course, those convicted of witchcraft) and that at least two others were hanged afterward. These were Abigail Converse at Northampton, on July 6, 1788, for infanticide (Evans item, 20955), and Rachel Wall at Boston on October 8, 1789, for highway robbery (Evans item, 22235, also *Massachusetts Broadsides,* 2129).

Bathsheba was the daughter of Judge Timothy Ruggles, a wealthy squire and Tory General who had served under Lord Amherst. The local patriots had confiscated his estate and he had fled to Nova Scotia, leaving his thirty-two-year-old daughter behind. She was married to a man some thirty-seven years her senior and, though they had been married a dozen years, they were at the time of the tragedy, extremely incompatible. Spooner was a frequenter of the local tavern and had a considerable reputation for being a heavy drinker. It was said of Bathsheba that she was "attractive, intelligent and imperious" and that she "dominated her husband."

---

[4]For details of the Roxie Druse story, see Marilyn M. Jackson, *Oh Roxy, Don't* (purported to have been the victim's last words), Herkimer County, N. Y., Division of Archives & History, June, 1954.

[5]Listed by McDade, *op. cit.,* 897-903; also described by Peleg W. Chandler, *American Criminal Trials,* Boston, 1841, 2 vols.

At the time of the story, a dashing young man named Ezra Ross—a patriot soldier—had been picked up by Spooner in a wounded condition and carried to his home for a kind of Samaritan recuperation. Both husband and wife tended the young soldier but almost immediately the woman and the soldier fell madly in love. In almost no time at all, she suggested to Ross that he dispose of her no-longer-wanted spouse, but he seemed to be somewhat dilatory in going through with the frightening deed. It was at this point that the wily but desperate female hired two itinerant British soldiers to negotiate the scheme. Aided, at least passively, and perhaps even actively, by Ross, the three beat Spooner to death on his own doorstep, stripping him of his silver shoe buckles and stylish clothes. They then threw his body into a well, the crime taking place on the night of March 1, 1778.

The three men—young Ross, James Buchanan and William Brooks—and the conniving Bathsheba were all tried, convicted and hanged at Worcester.[6] This was, in reality, the first capital case in the state under American jurisdiction. Prior to the hanging, a movement was launched to postpone Bathsheba's execution on the grounds that she might be pregnant. A group of physicians contended she was, but the court appointed twelve midwives who, upon examination of the distraught young matron, found otherwise. After the hanging a post-mortem corroborated the diagnosis of the physicians.[7]

The scene of the quadruple hanging was one of tremendous excitement and confusion. Shouts, ribaldry and evidence of true sympathy, especially for the young woman and her lover, were to be heard and seen. A contemporary account later reported:

> The terror which her punishment was intended to produce was neutralized by the pity of her sufferings. Her appearance was so calm and her end so peaceful, that it was forgotten how deeply her hands were stained with blood. The tragedy was long recited around the hearths of those who saw her die, and the obdurate wickedness of the heroine was almost disregarded in the admiration excited for her beauty, her energy and her fortitude.

---

[6]For a recent account of the crime with its many fascinating details, see George Minot, "The Day They Hanged a Woman in Massachusetts," *Boston Herald,* January 5, 1964.

[7]See a similar unfortunate case of Mary Bateman of Leeds, England, cited in Chapter I.

There has been created a considerable literature regarding this sensational case although so far as is known, it did not merit a ballad. In this respect it has not developed the same folk reputation as so many of that era managed to achieve. As we read of the beautiful but cunning Bathsheba today, we cannot avoid making the statement that she did at least deserve a ballad in order to bring her into that charmed circle whose specific murders are remembered through the years by this classic art form.

Bridget Dergan, New Jersey Slavey and Her Evil Deed — Hanged 1867

A case, equally repugnant as the Bathsheba Spooner affair, but this time involving a most unattractive female of the servant class rather than of the aristocracy is that of Bridget Dergan (or Durgan). She was hanged at New Brunswick, New Jersey on August 30, 1867, for the murder of her mistress, Mrs. Ellen Coriell. We gather from contemporaries of the day that they recoiled at the thought of this slavey's crime since they referred to it as "fiendish."

According to the few details we have on the case, this twenty-four-old "Irish servant possessed an ugly and forbidding countenance" and literally "butchered" her victim, "hoping to take her place in the affections of the husband of her lovely and innocent victim." Mrs. Coriell was the wife of a prominent physician of New Market, New Jersey. She tolerated this unsavory and troublesome wench as long as she could, but as matters became unbearable she ordered her to leave the premises. Flying into a rage Bridget obtained a knife and stabbed her victim to death.

While this case, crude and sordid as it was, did not seem to elicit a ballad, it did prompt pamphlet scribblers of the day to write it up and display their wares for sale. There are at least two publications available.[8]

Ann Carson, Quaker City Coquette

Few cases possess the important ingredients of romance, frustration, daring and actual glamor of the Ann Carson-Richard Smyth case—locale, Philadelphia, during the second decade of the 1800s. The story begins with the flowering of the beautiful Ann Baker,

---

[8]McDade, *op. cit.,* 274-275.

daughter of a proud ship-captain who gave her a glorious "coming-out" party. Captain Baker dreamed big things for his darling daughter who was from her early 'teens one of the toasts of the city's men-about-town. In due time, the salty captain married her off to what he considered a great "catch," to his old friend, a sea-faring man, John Carson, many years the girl's senior. In shipping circles, at least. Carson was considered quite a catch for Ann, but it was obvious to all that she was not happy with the trumped-up match. However, as she was a dutiful daughter, she made the best of it and settled down to keep house for Carson and to bear him children.

Some nine years after they were married, in 1810, Carson left on one of his long voyages. After he had been gone for a long period of time, and having heard that he had died in England, the lovely Ann opened a crockery and china shop to support herself and children. She was wont to flirt with the good-looking swains of the city and despite her coy discreetness, developed a reputa-tion of being a coquette. Before long, she "just happened to meet" the dashing young Irish lieutenant, Richard Smyth (or Smith), who had distinguished himself in the War of 1812. He was, from all reports, a "fast worker." Following a few short friendly calls to the crockery shop, Smyth invited the lovely Ann to take a ride with him in his gig the following Sunday. She consented. They drove to a tavern in outlying Frankford where they had a sumptu-ous dinner. On his way out to the tavern Smyth had summarily stated that he was going to marry the young "widow"—that day. True to his threat, while at dinner, a minister appeared on an order previously issued by Smyth. They repaired to another room at the inn and Ann Carson, over "oh, so feeble" protests, became Mrs. Richard Smyth. And here her troubles began. Shortly thereafter, like Enoch Arden, Captain John Carson returned home from the sea. He had hardly landed on the dock when he heard the bad news and realized he had his work cut out for him if he were to repossess his legal and rightful spouse. There immediately began a series of meetings between the captain and the younger newly-married pair, as well as between Carson and the young women's parents. It would seem that no one wanted trouble from the affair. Yet it was obvious from the start that Ann would never return to the captain and that the dashing Irishman, Smyth, would never tolerate such an action. Something had to give. One day, January 20, 1816—when Carson came to the home of the Smyths, an argument began, developed into a scuffle, and ended in a shooting. Carson dropped from a bullet shot from a gun held by Smyth and died some time later, on February 4. It was a homicide but whether in "self defense" or not was the perplexing question.

The case became a sensation in the Quaker City. While the public was definitely sympathetic to Smyth, sober legal minds realized that he was a doomed man. The trial was exciting but the defendant was convicted of murder in the first degree by a supine jury that took its orders from Judge Rush. The fiery lieutenant and dashing lover of Ann Carson was hanged on August 10. A large crowd awaited his exit from the jail and accompanied the procession to the place of execution which is now the city's Logan Circle. The news account of the event states that Smyth "was arrayed in a blue surtout [a close-fitting garment] reaching to his knees." It further stated that "the concourse of people at the place of execution was immense and all seemed to lament the necessity of enforcing so awful a punishment."

The doughty, but distraught wife did not accept such a cruel fate passively. She fought and it is this fight that adds both pathos and admiration to Ann's brave but sordid future. First she attempted to bribe the jailers of the Walnut Street jail in Philadelphia to release her lover-husband. They refused. Next she attempted to corral some desperadoes to storm the Bastille-like establishment. This desperate plot also failed. But Ann Carson Smyth was not to be daunted. She had other cards to play in her obsession to free her husband or at least, perhaps, to obtain his pardon. But instead of attempting this move through respectable channels, the determined woman settled on a wild move—to kidnap the governor and force him to sign a pardon for her man.

She gathered some confederates together and they moved to Selins Grove, a small town not far from the capitol, Harrisburg, and lay in wait for Governor Simon Snyder. It was believed he would pass the tavern where they were concealed on his way to the executive mansion. But law officers somehow learned of the plot, swooped down on the conspirators and arrested them. They were taken to the Dauphin County jail at Harrisburg and eventually placed on trial. Lieutenant Richard Smyth was hanged while his sorrowing wife languished in jail awaiting her future. She was acquitted of all the crimes with which she was charged and eventually returned to Philadelphia.

But something had happened to this beautiful wife, erstwhile coquette. Instead of accepting her fate up to that point, she plunged into a life of wrong-doing. She became affiliated with a counterfeiter ring composed of thugs and other persons unworthy of this carefully-reared young woman. After a short period of lawlessness, she and the band were arrested and sentenced to the same prison from which Smyth had emerged to be driven to his doom.

And again, instead of accomodating herself to her lot, Ann began to quarrel with the female harpies of the jail, including the blowsy matron, one Sarah Maland. Eventually she was beaten up in a prison brawl and lodged in the prison hospital where she soon succumbed to her wounds. It is more than a rumor, perhaps, that Ann Carson Smyth actually died from typhus which she contracted from the infected bedding that she unfortunately inherited when she was dispatched to the prison sick bay. She died some time in 1824, in her thirty-eighth year. This amazing story was carefully written up, first in a curtailed autobiography and then later embellished and brought up to the date of her death by a female friend who was a writer, a Mrs. Clark.[9]

Even in a city as large as Philadelphia, one occasionally hears, to this day, an allusion to the Ann Carson affair. There is a kind of heroic halo built around the woman, or at least around her memory. She has descendants still living in the city and so far as it is known they are proud of some of her exploits and of some of her sterling qualities. One never hears of Smyth, but of course, he left no known descendants.

Professor Webster — Dr. Parkman: Harvard University — 1849-1850

Notorious cases are frequent and intriguing. The social history

---

[9]There is a substantial bibliography regarding this case; Mrs. E. Clark, *The Memoirs of the Celebrated and Beautiful Mrs. Ann Carson, Daughter of an Officer of the U.S. Navy . . . whose Life Terminated in a Philadelphia Prison*, 1838.

of our country fairly exudes cases—and we mean cases that end in hanging—that people write and talk about for years after; even generations after they occurred. Such is the Professor John W. Webster and Dr. George Parkman case, the locale of which was Harvard University's Medical School in 1849. The details are macabre, sordid and repugnant, yet fascinating.

Dr. George Parkman, prominent Bostonian—donor of the Parkman Chair of Anatomy[10] (brother of the Rev. Fr. Parkman, and uncle of the later famous historian, Francis Parkman) and Professor John W. Webster, occupant of the Chair of Chemistry and Mineralogy—were the principals. Parkman, a little on the order of Ichabod Crane, so far as physique is concerned, with elongated body and prognathous jaw, had lent Professor Webster a sum of money [some said about $450] some years previously. Later, he lent him an additional sizeable amount, taking a cabinet of minerals as collateral. Then Webster did the unpardonable; he offered Parkman's brother-in-law the opportunity of purchasing the minerals which, of course, he no longer really owned. Parkman was not only impatient to get some of his money back from the harassed professor, but was also outraged at what he thought was Webster's perfidy. He was determined to bring the matter to a head by demanding his money at once.

He made an appointment with Professor Webster at the laboratory of the Medical School for Friday, November 23, 1849. This was the last time Parkman was seen by anyone. He simply disappeared. As Parkman owned several tenement houses it was at first believed that someone had done him in while he was collecting rentals.[11] His family immediately became alarmed, and by Monday, a sum of $3,000 had been posted for information leading to "his return to his home and to his important duties."

The solution of the baffling disappearance and subsequent murder of the Boston Brahmin is generally credited to the janitor of the building in which Webster had his office and laboratory. The janitor, Ephraim Littlefield, on being questioned, stated that he had remembered that Parkman had been to the office previously on a "dunning and threatening expedition" as much as a week

10Occupied by Dr. Oliver Wendell Homes.
11Duke, *op. cit.,* pp. 551-557.

prior to the day of his disappearance. In addition, on being pressed, he ventured that he had seen the victim come to Webster's bailiwick on the fatal day and had not seen him emerge. On still further musing, he recalled that Webster had barred him from the laboratory and he had also suspected that a very bad fire had been set by the professor, a most unusual incident. Although the premises had been searched twice with no success, Littlefield decided to make a personal, thorough investigation of the cellar and privy in Webster's office. He dug for two days, uncovering five layers of bricks in the cellar in order to reach the privy vault. His efforts were extremely fruitful; he found some of the remains of the distinguished Dr. Parkman.

Littlefield's find was indeed gruesome. There was first the victim's pelvis, then next a leg. On further examination, after Webster's arrest, there were uncovered the victim's teeth in the furnace, bits of bone in the grate and, of all things, the "thorax and a thigh in a tea chest."

Famous Harvard savants attended the trial and some were even witnesses. Dr. Holmes, who had his office near that of Professor Webster's, Drs. W. T. G. Morton, and C. T. Jackson, discoverers of ether, and Jared Sparks, biographer of George Washington were among them. There was practically no defense worthy of the name. Webster confessed but maintained the murder was not premeditated. He stated that he had been greviously taunted and badgered by his impatient creditor. He said that on the day Parkman came to his office demanding a settlement he theatened him with exposure and that in the heated argument, he picked up a heavy root that was nearby and killed him.

Webster was hanged on August 30, 1850. Efforts were made to have his sentence commuted but they proved bitterly futile. Webster, like Parkman, had excellent, if not impeccable, connections. As to education, he was a graduate of Harvard, the class of 1811; he held the degrees of Master of Arts and Medical Doctor. He was a member of the Academy of Arts and Sciences and of the London Geological Society. He studied in London with John Keats. His wife, Harriet Fredericka Hickling, was an aunt of William Hickling Prescott, famous historian and author of *The Conquest of Peru.*

Many legends, stories and anecdotes remain to this day regarding this gruesome and, actually, pathetic case. Here was a scholar and, presumably, a gentleman, literally hounding a more or less improvident and harassed financial failure, taunting and threatening him to the point of fanning him into a state of "white anger" with the result murder and awful retribution on the hanging tree. How happier everyone in and around Harvard University, Cambridge and Boston would have been at that time—and perhaps since—had it never happened.[12]

The Boyington Tragedy — Mobile, Alabama — 1835

In their zeal to cite cases of persons executed unjustly or who later turn out to be innocent—perhaps through the guilty person's death-bed confession, crusaders against capital punishment sometimes give us a few vague elements of a case which, on reasonable investigation, lead into a blind alley.

In such a case, we attempted to run down some details allegedly from Louisiana, and discovered an amazing case from Alabama. In an authoritative source, it was stated that someone named Boynton was hanged in Louisiana for murdering a man. A tavern-owner, a few months later, believing himself to be on the point of death, confessed to the crime for which he had purposely contrived to fasten on the victim.[13] This case has not yet been identified. But there is the legendary Boyington case of Mobile, Alabama. The only similarity is the name but that is enough to make it possible for the Mobile case to come to light.

We mentioned this case earlier in connection with the last-minute attempts made by the victim of the gallows to escape his fate.[14]

Charles R. S. Boyington and Nathaniel Frost were friends and roommates in a rooming house in Mobile, Alabama. Frost, a young printer in delicate health had gone for a walk with Boyington early in the afternoon of May 10, 1834. The following morning, Frost's body was found "barbarously assassinated near the

---

[12]See Pearson, *op. cit.,* pp. 94-114; also McDade, *op. cit.,* 1053-70, eighteen items published in this case!

[13]Clifford Kirkpatrick, *Capital Punishment,* Philadelphia, Yearly Meeting of Friends, 1925, p. 47.

[14]See Chapter I, p. 24.

Old Church Street Cemetery in a wooded space under a large chinquapin tree on the west side of Bayou Street south of Government Street." The body was "shockingly cut and mangled."

Boyington, also a journeyman printer but out of work at the time, was immediately suspected since he was the last person seen with the victim and it was learned that he had "precipitately left town on the night of the murder." He, like Frost, had come to Mobile only a short while before—from New England; Boyington, apparently a native of Litchfield, Connecticut and a seafaring man. It was immediately conjectured that the motive for the crime was "plunder, as the pockets of the deceased were rifled of about fifty or sixty dollars and also of a Lepine watch with gold chased edge."

Frost, the victim, had a reputation for being a kindly young man and it was believed that he had been supporting Boyington during his period of enforced unemployment. Another feature of this amazing case is that the murderer was engaged to be married to "Madamoiselle Rose de Fleur . . . the beautiful daughter of Baron de Fleur, a French political duellist-refugee." He composed poems to her and the two exchanged letters during their brief courtship interspersed with meetings at various trysting-places in old Mobile. There is feeling even today that Boyington may have been innocent—yet the facts are that he presented practically no defense in his behalf. Perhaps, in these modern days, this unfortunate man could not have been convicted of first degree murder.

A few days after the murder of Frost, Boyington was apprehended. He had taken passage on an Alabama river boat, hoping, it was believed, to escape to the North. He was arrested at Claiborne, Alabama and returned to Mobile. He was seen throwing the stolen Lepine watch into the river and when he was searched a fair sum of money was found on his person. Since he had received no money throughout the winter from his work, the presence of the bills in his pocket suggested the amount stolen from his victim.

Trial was commenced on May 29 and sentence of death pronounced November 29. Higher courts refused to intercede, thus dooming the young man who presented no alibi, excuse or rebuttal for the crime of which he had been accused. During the interval awaiting execution, the Rev. William T. Hamilton had several meetings with Boyington. The condemned murderer was tolerant of the minister but made no confession, insisting always that he was innocent and, furthermore, repudiated all religion, including a belief in God. The young man was deeply moved by the efforts of the kindly man of God but he remained adamant to the last.

On the day of execution Boyington, dressed in a conventional black suit and silk hat, was permitted to walk behind the cart and coffin. He was accompanied by the Rev. Mr. Hamilton and another spiritual advisor. Earlier in this work, we described that ghastly hanging and need not repeat the details here. Suffice, however, to state that Boyington entertained the hope—almost to the point of being pathological—of escaping. He used every pretext to kill time—appealing to his counsel, the sheriff, the minister, and other officials to ward off the impending doom of the event. Writes one who attended the sordid affair:

> He was clinging to the hope that escape he would by some means. To this prospect he bent all his thoughts, on it he kept his mind fixed, and he never suffered himself to look steadfastly and fully on the certainty that he would die. "He laid all his plans—took all his measures—and regulated all his intercourse with others in anticipation of that hope being realized—determined, so far as he was concerned, to bring his rescue or escape."

The account of the hanging states that when everything was in readiness and no more time could possibly be "killed" by Boyington, he yelled and jumped, bound though he was, into the horrified crowd. The military contingent present fixed bayonets, picked up the pitiable Boyington and restored him to his place on the gallows. Thus he was hanged.

The tragic young man was buried in Potter's Field of the Old Church Street Cemetery on the Bayou Street side, not more than sixty yards from the scene of the crime. A huge live-oak eventually grew out of the grave and became known in Mobile as the Boyington Oak. Legend has it that friends of the murdered Nathaniel Frost erected a headstone for the grave but today this is gone, leaving only the old oak tree. Children made the grave a kind of sanctuary where they brought flowers through the years. Legend has it also that for years prior to the War Between the

States, on All Saints Day, a woman would come to the grave, burn a candle and place a bouquet of white flowers in the small urn that stood by. It was conjectured by many that the woman must be the one-time beauty and sweetheart of Boyington, Rose de Fleur.

The mystery of the Boyington case persists. Killer of a good friend, or not, he is kindly remembered by posterity. A Mobilian, Dr. Erwin Craighead, one-time editor of the Mobile Register, in a literary sketch of writers of his city, states: "It is . . . true that few persons have left so profound a mark upon their time as he [Boyington]; for there never has been for long a cessation of the discussion of what is known here as the Boyington case." Speaking of the poems Boyington composed, he further states: "Some were printed in the local newspapers and have considerable merit." Here are a few samples of his poems that have survived. They were written to and for his Rose de Fleur:

To Rose

I saw a lovely butterfly Light on the bosom of a winter rose;
He kissed the stamens one by one, Then flew away as in a love-sick pose.

Each eve I came into the garden To look upon this lovely flower;
And came to me the sudden thought, "I'll place it in my lady's bower."

Then when I started forth To pluck this lovely flower,
The butterfly returned in haste, And with him came a shower.

The raindrops beat down the rose Until it hung low its lovely head,
And when I returned next eve I found, too, the butterfly was dead.

So if I had been the butterfly And you the lovely winter rose,
I would do the same, methinks, And call down the blinding snows!

True love is the greatest thing In life a man can own;
Oh, 'tis you, my lovely Rose, I love and you alone!
Mobile, December 5, 1833

To a Butterfly at Christmas

Oh, care-free creature, Flitting here and flitting there;
You should be tucked in From this chilly air.

You press each flower With a kiss and a smile;
I wish I were a butterfly For just a little while.

Oh, to be a care-free creature, You never fret or cry,
Whose happiness is only Flowers and rainless sky!
Then take me with you To Titania's flow'ry home,
There to rest in peace, Never more to roam.

Boyington left several poems, some of which he wrote while he awaited his fate in a jail cell. He sent them to the various Mobile newspapers and fortunately, for that portion of posterity that might be labeled Boyington devotees, they have been collected, together with some of his love letters to his Rose de Fleur, by Francois Ludgére Diard, in his compilation on the facts of and speculation on the bizarre saga of Mobile. Much of the material herein incorporated is from that source.[15]

Periodically, repercussions of this famous Mobile case are experienced—usually in letters to the papers. It is the kind of case that will never die. A hundred or two hundred years later, some vague, almost forgotten element will come to light to be debated over modern cracker barrels. Some years after the murder, it was revealed that a young slave girl, one Patsy, the property of the father of a friend of the man who wrote a letter to the local paper —note the circuitous route of the piece of information—saw two men quarrelling at the time and place when Frost was being killed. Later she identified the assailant as Boyington. But, true to the traditions of the time, Patsy could not testify in a court of law. Here, at least, seemed to be an eye-witness of the crime. Boyington legends will persist as long as time![16]

A Strange Civil War Murder and Hanging — Dr. David M. Wright — Norfolk, Virginia

A murder and a hanging which should never have happened

---

[15]Privately printed and copyrighted by M. Diard, Mobile, Alabama, 1949.

[16]*Ibid.*, p. 58; see Chapter I, p. 63, for similar situation in a Pennsylvania case, that of "Negro Bob."

occurred at Norfolk, Virginia, during the War Between the States. Perhaps because there are so few professional men and women who are eventually executed for murder, the compiler of such events checks more carefully his list of victims, so that none shall be overlooked needlessly.

Poignant is the case of Dr. David M. Wright, originally from Edenton, North Carolina. He later moved to Norfolk where he practiced medicine and was highly respected. The case has to do with war nerves during those hectic days when many, not in the services of North or South, kept their trigger fingers alert and their guns in convenient but dangerous places.

Wright was of strong southern sympathies, and on July 11, 1863, as he was watching a company of Negro soldiers pass by, he hissed at an officer. He was immediately ordered arrested. As this humiliating gesture was about to be consummated, he drew a pistol and fired point-blank at an officer, Lieut. A. L. Sanborn who immediately fell dead. It was a tragic impetuous act, but it was certainly not premeditated. Nevertheless, he was convicted of first degree murder and sentenced to death.

While awaiting execution Dr. Wright attempted to escape, dressed in the clothes of his daughter who had visited him, with other members of the family, in his cell. Had he not tripped as "she" was leaving, he might well have eluded detection. He took the affair coolly and in a gentlemanly manner and eventually approached the hanging tree with great courage. Efforts were made to obtain a reprieve from President Lincoln but they failed. Dr. Wright was hanged on "the old fairgrounds" of Norfolk on October 23, 1863. A final word in the news report concerning the execution states that "the family which he leaves is large but in affluent circumstances."[17]

The Wright tragedy, being of the vintage of the War Between the States, prompts the inclusion of a well-known case of that same era, despite the fact that it did not end in a hanging. Those familiar with the famous murder cases of this country would certainly include that of Miss Mary Harris who, in 1865, murdered Adoniram J. Burroughs in the national capitol of Washington.

---

[17]This case is included in August Mencken's *By the Neck,* New York, Hastings House, 1942, pp. 146-150, "The Frustrated Escape."

Apparently, by all traditional standards, the man Burroughs—brother of the president of the old University of Chicago (obviously the pre-Harper era)—was a cad. The story is that he tried to entice his fiancee, Miss Harris, into a house of assignation to frame her, so he could break off his engagement with her. He then married another woman. The abandoned woman, probably white with rage, followed him to Washington and shot him to death in the corridor of the Treasury Building. The case was an open and shut one in the area of male gallantry for wounded and wronged womanhood; thus Mary Harris was acquitted with the jury out for less than five minutes!

An interesting sidelight on the case is that Mary Todd Lincoln, the president's wife, sent Mary flowers when she was in jail awaiting trial.[18]

The Jesse Strang Case — Albany, New York — 1827

In our first chapter, we dealt with the strange phenomenon of high suggestibility of some persons to commit murder after witnessing an execution. This happens more times, it seems, than to be mere coincidence. Levi Kelley (Cooperstown, New York), was hanged December 27, 1827, for the murder of Abraham Spafard, and the case seems to be a crystal-clear aftermath of the execution at Albany, of Jesse Strang, which occurred on August 24 of that same year.[19]

No compiler of murder cases that occurred in central New York State could possibly overlook the Strang saga. It is certainly Albany's most famous, or notorious, case largely due to the prominence of Strang's victim, John Whipple. Thomas McDade, in his account of the crime, states that the murder was unusual on two counts: "One, the actual killing followed months of the most careful planning and preparation; and two, the guiding genius of the crime was his wife,"—that is, the victim's. The killer, Strang, using the alias of Joseph Orton—he had abandoned his wife and children—hired himself out to Whipple on the Van Rensselear estate. Orton, or Strang, and Elsie Whipple—fully ten years younger than

---

[18]McDade, *op cit.*, 445.
[19]See Chapter I, page 40.

her husband, pretty, calculating and cunning, became enamoured and the plot to kill the husband was hatched. The lovely Elsie Whipple was definitely the instigator.

The hired man, Orton-Strang, made three attempts to finish off the unsuspecting victim with arsenic poisoning, but to no avail. In their state of frustration, the pair decided to shoot him. Mrs. Whipple supplied the money for Orton to buy a rifle and to practice with it. In order to insure success of a rifle ball shot through the window pane of Whipple's room, the would-be killer practiced in the woods. Their "scientific experiments" proved that shots fired through glass would not be deflected from their course.

Strang killed his victim as planned on May 7, 1827. But the killer, like so many, showed too much interest in the case. For instance, he served on the coroner's jury which found Whipple the victim of murder by "persons unknown." Both Strang and Mrs. Whipple were soon arrested and tried separately. He was convicted and she was acquitted, since Strang could not testify against her. The execution, as well as the procession to the scaffold, were all-time "highs" for the sophisticated city of Albany. There were many pamphlets published regarding this notorious case.[20]

The Talberts of Maryville, Missouri

Another case in which a man was shot and killed through an open window is that of the Talbert (or Talbott) affair near Arco, Nodaway County, Missouri, on September 18, 1880. On that night, Dr. Perry H. Talbert, a prominent and wealthy physician who had served as a surgeon in the Northern Army in the War Between the States, was shot and killed. One version of this case is that Talbert was a martinet, thoroughly hated and feared by his wife and children. The story is that the wife, the former Belle McFarland of Page County, Iowa, a hired man named Wright, and two of the sons, Albert, aged twenty-one, and Charles, aged sixteen, entered into a conspiracy to dispose of him. There are two versions of the heinous crime; one is that the wife held back the curtain of a window so that the hired man could shoot the victim. The other version states that Charles, the younger son, shot his

---

[20]McDade, *op. cit.*, 932-43.

father—through a window—with a rifle. Both the wife and Wright were cleared of the crime, but both sons were hanged at Maryville on July 22, 1881. Local lore contends that the Charles was actually innocent.[21] An interesting ingredient of this story is that a detective, posing as a "bank robber," gained the confidence of the sons, and they told him the whole story.[22]

WOMEN OF THE STREET AND MURDER

The Ellen Jewett Case

One notes in the archives of murder the number of women of easy virtue whose lives have been snuffed out by jealous boy friends or avaricious hangers-on who, in many cases, are tempted by greed to gain possession of money or baubles usually worn by such pathetic creatures. The perpetrators of such murders are seldom unknown to their victims.

Perhaps the most sensational of such murders was that of Ellen Jewett, a very beautiful prostitute of New York City who was brutally murdered on Saturday night, April 9, 1836, allegedly by a nineteen-year-old youth named Richard P. Robinson. There was no hanging in this case, but its notoriety has secured for it a place in any mythical murder hall of fame.

Ellen Jewett had been killed with a hatchet and the killer had tried to burn the premises. Robinson was immediately suspected since he had been with the woman on the evening of the murder and was generally known to be her "boy friend." He was indicted and tried. Great legal talent was mobilized for the case and the young defendant was acquitted. Several pamphlets were published on the case.[23] One has the interesting title; "Robinson Downstream: Containing Conversations with the 'Great Unhung' Since his Acquittal."

The illustrious journalist of the day, James Gordon Bennett, did the case justice in his papers; he actually took "a peep at the famous bordello on Thomas Street where the murder was committed."

---

[21]Sources: *History of Nodaway County*, 1882, courtesy Mrs. Catherine Johnson of Stansberry, Missouri.

[22]As stated in listing by McDade, *op. cit.*, 962.

[23]*Ibid.*, 812-822.

Kesiah Stowe — Philadelphia Victim — 1823

One of the earliest of this type of case that has come to our attention is that of William Gross, ne'er-do-well son of a prominent Philadelphia family and himself a trusted employee of the Bank of Pennsylvania. He murdered his mistress, Kesiah Stowe, who maintained "a house in Currant Alley, between 10th and 11th, Walnut and Locust Streets" in the City of Brotherly Love. He was extremely jealous of her attentions to others, so one night as she returned home from a frolic "glowing with excitement, fresh from a ballroom, with all her imperfections on her head," he plunged a butcher knife into her pretty body.[24]

He was publicly hanged on February 7, 1823. The picture or cut on the front cover of a pamphlet published on this case shows the older type of cross-beam gallows with cart being drawn underneath and with a disguised hangman poised on a ladder. A squad of the ubiquitous military may also be noted.

The John Millian-Julia Bulette Case — Virginia City, Nevada — 1868

A legal hanging that occurred in the virgin mining country of Nevada is authentic, notorious, glamorous—if that word dare be used—and well worthy of being preserved here.

The victim of the hanging tree set up in Virginia City, Nevada, on April 24, 1868, was John Millian, more properly known as Jean Marie A. Villain, erstwhile native of St. Malo, France. Quite obviously an adventurer, he first arrived in California in 1849, wandered around for some time, returned to France, and again entered the country in 1853.

He eventually gravitated to the mining town of Virginia City and became employed as a laundryman. On the night of January 20, 1867, he and two acquaintances decided to rob a woman of the town named Julia Bulette, darling of the rough-and-ready males who worked hard in the mines and who frequented the bawdy-houses. It is reliably recorded that Julia was the mascot—or something of the sort—of "Engine Company No. 1" of the town. There is no record that Millian knew the woman but certain-

---

[24]McDade, *op. cit.*, 397-398.

ly he knew of her material wealth consisting of clothing and jewelry. While in the process of robbing her house as she allegedly slept, he heard muffled cries and saw the other thieves running out of the dive with loot in their arms. When officers entered the establishment they found the woman's body badly bruised, which indicated she had been beaten to death. Robbery was undoubtedly the motive, since a great deal of clothing and jewelry were taken.

Millian was not arrested until about four months later, when some of the loot was found and traced to him. He had followed in the elaborate funeral procession of the dead but strangely respected woman; one who was regarded as "very kind-hearted and benevolent." The suave Frenchman was convicted and sentenced to death. He was hanged on April 24, 1868, in the presence of a large and rather unsympathetic crowd.[25]

The doomed man read his last remarks in his native tongue which, of course, was understood only by few. The news story continues: "Not the least tremor, not the quivering of a muscle, nor the rush of blood or the slightest paleness was noticeable about him." He apparently died bravely.[26]

Other Such Cases

A similar case occurred in sleepy Vermont in the late 1870s. A prostitute of Rutland, one Ann E. Freeze, was robbed and had her throat cut by John P. Phair. In order to cover up the tracks of his crime, he set fire to her place. He left the vicinity and was not brought to book for five years. Items belonging to his victim and pawned by him in Boston led to his undoing. He was hanged in the state prison at Windsor on April 10, 1879.[27]

A kind of switch in the old familiar story is the case of William W. Lee of Henderson County, Illinois, who operated a bawdyhouse at East Burlington. In his brothel, he had as one of his best "money-makers" one Whiskey-Jess" McCarty. Known far and wide in such circles, this prostitute was known as an "old-timer" who caused Lee some trouble. One day, in a frenzy, Lee beat the

---

[25]See *supra.* for description of the crowd; Chapter I, p. 35.

[26]For details, see Carson City *Appeal,* April 26, 1868, a reprint of the Virginia *Trespass.*

[27]McDade, *op. cit.,* 743.

woman to death and threw her body into the Mississippi River. He was hanged at the county seat, Aquawka, by Sheriff George Bell on June 16, 1876. His brothers published a pamphlet including an authentic account of the trial and a copy of the dying confession. They were so motivated because they believed it would "prove a warning to others" not to live in sin.[28]

MURDER IN CHURCH BELFRIES

We all know that murder is committed in all kinds of outlandish places; in boats, on docks, in graveyards, in pool halls, and in brothels. We also know of some committed in church belfries. There have doubtless been some committed in and around the outside of churches, cathedrals, cloisters, and other such sanctuaries; perhaps enough to warrant some original research by devotees of murder.

One of the most sensational murder cases of the late nineteenth century was that of William Henry Theodore Durrant of San Francisco who was convicted and hanged for the brutal slaying of Blanche Lamont in the belfrey of Emmanuel Church of the Bay City in 1895. This was unquestionably a murder made to order for yellow journalism which was emerging during that era. But the case gained some significance as it reminded many of the earlier murder of five-year-old Mabel Young in the Warren Avenue Baptist Church belfrey of Boston by the sexton, Thomas W. Piper, in 1876.

An earlier crime had shocked the nation and had been well covered by the press as well as by a rash of post-execution pamphlets.[29] The titles of two of these indicate the nature of the crime: "The church belfrey murder in Boston, or the cruel fate of the beautiful, innocent little Mabel H. Young, who was so cruelly butchered by the sexton . . ." and "The Boston fiend! Many long hidden mysteries at last disclosed. Full account of the atrocious crimes of Thomas W. Piper." The killer used a cricket bat to bludgeon the child to death. It was established that he had previously murdered another girl and had attacked several others. He was hanged at Boston on May 27, 1876, on the gallows used for

---

[28]*Ibid.*, 600.
[29]*Ibid.*, 750-4.

the execution of Professor John White Webster on August 30, 1850.[30]

The Durrant case became even more notorious and sensational —even international in scope. The young killer was a medical student at Cooper Medical College in San Francisco and, at the time of the crime, was acting superintendent of the Sunday School at the Emmanuel Church. He was twenty-four years old and came from a respectable family.

On April 13, 1895, the mutilated body of Minnie Williams was found in the library of the church. She had been choked to death and her body perforated by a table knife, pieces of which protruded from her wounds. On the following day the naked and badly decomposed body of Blanche Lamont was found in the belfrey of the same church. Her clothing was found hidden in the rafters.

It did not take long for suspicion to rest on young Durrant. It was believed he was engaged to Miss Lamont and he knew both girls intimately. The space of nine days intervened between the two deaths. Seduction seems to have been the motive. Despite the reputation Durrant had for being a "good boy," he was soon arrested and in due time brought to trial for the murder of the Lamont girl. But it took approximately three years and three stays before he was delivered to the hangman at the San Quentin prison on January 7, 1898. Known as the "crime of the century"—how many of these we have each decade or each generation—William Henry Theodore Durrant held the spotlight for a long period of time for that day. The murders were indeed gruesome; the execution and the preparation thereof were both unique and gripping. An account of the event is well documented by the news story from the *San Francisco Chronicle* for January 8, 1895, the day following the event.

Quite a large crowd of witnesses were permitted within the whitewashed walls of the death-house where stood the grey-drab gallows. Sheriffs from many hinterland counties had saved their prisoners from the trek to San Quentin against the day of Durrant's execution—thus to witness the affair at state expense. Many

---

of these gentlemen appeared at the bayside dock of the prison with their "shooting-irons" in their belts; these, of course, had to be checked before entering the death room. A strange feature of the hanging was the presence of the victim's distraught father who wanted to be with his son until the very last. He was accompanied by a friend who supported him as he sobbed throughout. After the execution both parents ate a "hearty" meal at the prison! The *San Francisco Chronicle* described the event in these words:

> To the unlearned observer it would have seemed a gala day in San Quentin. Everything from a dog cart to a carry-all had been pressed into service to bring the eager and expectant spectators from the trains. There were all sorts of men. Some were prominent and others were of the ordinary prize-fight push. There were a few lawyers, many doctors, a smattering of deputies, a number of saloon keepers and several gentlemen from political and other walks of life. It looked like a sporting crowd, for the men of position had worn their oldest clothes by way of disguise and in all that assemblage there was but one man in decent black . . . The crowd looked more like an assemblage of Wyatt Earps than ever when the warden, standing on a flight of steps warned it to leave its shooting irons outside the gate and live without cigars for a few moments.

The victim was given ample opportunity to speak, and speak he did. It was believed by the representatives of the press that Durrant had composed and memorized his death remarks. He swore he was innocent of the brutal crimes but, as is usual in most cases, he forgave all of his "persecutors."

The drop fell and Warden Hale remarked: "It was the most successful execution that has ever taken place in this institution. There was not a hitch . . . I have never before seen a condemned man meet his fate so calmly and with less apparent fear."[31]

Thomas S. Duke of the San Francisco police force, at the time of the Durrant affair, wrote that in his judgment the young killer

---

[31]The San Francisco *Chronicle,* January 8, 1898, reproduced in August Mencken, *By the Neck,* pp. 36-48: "Far From the Sunday School;" see McDade items, 276-8; a thorough account of this case is *The Girl in the Belfry,* by Joseph Henry Jackson and Lenore Glen Offord, New York, Gold Medal Books, 1957; see also account in Kenneth Lamott, *Chronicles of San Quentin,* New York, David McKay Co., 1961, pp. 157-60.

was and had always been a "degenerate." He grudgingly admitted that the young man—for he was only twenty-seven at the time of his execution, having been born in 1871—was attractive to women. He states that many women showered him with attention and one, especially, daily presented him with small bunches of sweet peas so that she became known as the "Sweet Pea Girl." Capt. Duke also stated that Durrant's sister, who was in Europe as a concert singer, even before the crimes were commited, was known as "Maude Allen." He said "she was creating a sensation with the "Vision of Salome Dance.""[32]

TRUNK OR BARREL MURDERS THAT ENDED IN HANGING

Earlier we briefly mentioned the case of the Irishman of Greensburg, Pennsylvania, Hugh Corrigon, who killed his wife, known locally as "Big Mary," stuffed her body in a barrel and burned it. He committed suicide before the hangman could dispatch his legal duty. This was in 1856.

About the same time, in 1858, Henry Jumpertz, of Chicago, murdered his mistress, Sophia Elten Werner, on March 6, and stuffed her cut-up body into a whiskey barrel and shipped it off to New York. The killer, a journeyman barber, was convicted in January 1859, but what his fate was, we are not certain.[33]

In 1880, in San Francisco, George Wheeler, enraged at his paramour sister-in-law, strangled her to death and stuffed her body into a trunk in their flat. He immediately gave himself up to the police but in court he fought hard. It took four trials to convict him and lead him to the gallows where he was hanged on January 23, 1884. The case is a strange one although the trunk plays only an incidental part in its unfolding. Wheeler, wife and sister-in-law, Della Tillson, migrated to California from Massachusetts where, even at the early date, he and the younger girl had had an affair serious enough to bring forth a baby belonging to Wheeler. Apparently, it was believed a new life should be attempted in the Golden State. They settled in the small town of Cisco, Placer County. In time, the lovely Della met a young man

---

[32]*Celebrated Criminal Cases of America,* 1910, 114-122, quote on p. 122.
[33]McDade, *op. cit.,* 546.

named George Peckham. Immediately Wheeler insisted that his sister-in-law should have nothing to do with this interloper that dared enter his miniature harem. Disgusted, he took his wife and sister-in-law to the big city of San Francisco to be rid of the man Peckham. This however, did not work. Wheeler learned that there were clandestine meetings between Della and the unwanted swain. It was this that enraged the jealous Wheeler to the point of murder. It is indeed strange that he took the trouble to stuff the victim's body into a trunk when he was so eager to give himself up to the police.[34]

Some years later, in 1886, a young man of twenty-five, Walter Lennox Maxwell, applied some chloroform to C. Thomas Preller, a sleeping roommate, in the Southern Hotel, St. Louis. The result was death which later proved to be murder. The motive, with a tinge of homosexuality, was robbery. Both men were British and had met on the vessel, *Cephalonio,* bound from Liverpool for Boston. This was in January, 1885. Each had gone different ways but agreed to meet in St. Louis later. Maxwell, whose real name was Hugh Brooks, was described in court testimony as a "sponger and impersonator." After killing his victim, he stuffed the body into a trunk and made off for Auckland, New Zealand, via San Francisco. After clever detective work by St. Louis and San Francisco operatives, his whereabouts was ascertained and President Grover Cleveland signed extradition papers which brought him home to face the charge of premeditated murder. He claimed Preller died from an overdose of chloroform which he, with his knowledge of medicine, gave him in his attempt to relieve the pain of a stricture by inserting a catheter in the urethra. This defense was unique, but it failed to save him. He was sentenced to death and was hanged at St. Louis, on August 10, 1888.[35]

In this Maxwell case, as well as in the John Colt case (discussed in our previous chapter), it will be noted that the bodies were placed in trunks but were discovered exclusively because of the stench emitted therefrom. Colt, at least, disposed of his gruesome trunk by having it hauled to a ship in the harbor of

---

[34]Duke, *op. cit.,* pp. 68-70.
[35]McDade, *op. cit.,* 673; for more details see Thomas S. Duke, pp. 486-95.

New York to be sent off to New Orleans. Maxwell merely left town without bothering to dispose of his trunk and shortly thereafter the horrible odor reached the noses of some of the help in the Southern Hotel.

A NUN MURDER IN A HOSPITAL

In the last analysis a church belfry is an isolated place for a murder to be committed and trunks and barrels are unusual receptacles to receive bodies or parts thereof. But seldom do we hear of a murder of a nun in a hospital. Persons have gone berserk in mental institutions and killed innocent bystanders but not many have been killed in a city hospital. We have found one such case in St. Joseph's Hospital at Reading, Pennsylvania, which occurred on the afternoon of June 23, 1892. Few details are available but we know the victim was a young nun, Sister Mary Hildaberta, born Tillie Shannter at Huntingdon in the same state. She was affiliated with the hospital as a nurse and one of her patients was an Italian immigrant named Pietro Buccieri, aged thirty-eight. He was a shoemaker by trade and in an unfortunate accident in which a lamp exploded in his shop he had become crippled and required hospitalization. Whether crazed by pain, or perhaps by pain and the heat of a June day, or for some other obscure reason, he jumped from his bed and ran into the hospital kitchen. There he attacked the young nun with a knife—she had just served him his lunch—and stabbed her to death. He was sentenced to death and died on the gallows on June 29, 1893.[36]

THE KIDNAPING SCOURGE

No more contemptible crime exists than that of kidnaping, especially if it involves a child. It is doubly reprehensible if the parents of the victim are kept in agonizing suspense while attempting to negotiate, in order to effect the safe return of the helpless hostage. During the uneasy and frustrating period between the snatching of the victim and the conclusion of the case, the public is naturally incensed and extremely angry. It becomes even more so because of the periodic news releases by press, radio and television. An indescribable fury, almost savage in nature, follows

---

[36]*Berks & Schuylkill Journal,* Reading, Pa., July 1, 1893.

in the wake of the cases that end in the murder of the victim. Millions of people vicariously live the agony of the parents in such pathetic cases. Many persons, opposed to the death penalty, break at this point and join the proponents of the noose, chair or gas chamber, justifying their change of attitude by the ghastliness of the criminal's callousness.

The American public has always followed kidnapings with a personalized identification. Starting with the Charlie Ross case of the 1890's to the much more recent 1963 strange case of the abduction of Frank Sinatra, Jr., persons in all walks of life read, listened to and looked at every shred of information available to them at the time. The most notorious cases, prior to the most famous of all time, the Lindbergh case, were the Ross tragedy, followed by the Billy Whitla and Eddie Cudahy abductions. In the Ross case, the four-year-old son of a Germantown (Philadelphia) grocer, Charles Ross, Sr., was taken by two men in a buggy as he and his seven-year-old brother played in front of their palatial home, on July 1, 1874. He was held for $25,000 ransom which was never paid; nor was the child ever returned. But, so far as kidnapings go, it still remains the classic case since, for a quarter of a century or more, various persons have attempted to pass themselves off as the lost victim.

The case was partially cracked when two burglars, Joseph Douglas and William Mosher, were shot to death attempting to rob a Brooklyn home and one of them, Douglas, in a dying statement, maintained that they had abducted Charlie Ross. Sometime later, a confederate, an embittered New York City ex-policeman named William Westervelt, was tried and convicted in a Philadelphia court for being an accessory to the crime. He was convicted on October 9, 1875, and served seven years in the Eastern State Penitentiary of Pennsylvania.

The Eddie Cudahy case with its locale in Omaha, Nebraska, involved the abduction and safe return of the fifteen-year-old scion of the multi-millionaire packer, Edward Cudahy, Sr. The boy was forced into a buggy near his home, on the night of December 18, 1900, and held for $25,000 ransom "in gold pieces." He was released unharmed the following night, after the father had quickly responded to the ransom note and turned over several bags of gold on a lonely road. Two men were eventually tried for the crime and amazingly, they were acquitted. One, James Callahan, was apprehended almost immediately but could not be convicted. Some six years later, the notorious burglar and bank robber, Pat Crowe, gave himself up, made favorable terms with the police and was acquitted by an Omaha jury. The father and the city had placed a $55,000 reward on the kidnaper's arrest and conviction but one of Crowe's stipulations for giving himself up was that the reward be rescinded. This was done and, after his raw acquittal, Crowe toured the country, lecturing on crime and religion. He died at a ripe old age and has become something of a legend.

The Billy Whitla case also ended happily—that is, the abducted eight-year-old boy was returned to his home in Sharon, Pennsylvania, after a ransom of $10,000 had been paid by his lawyer father. The ruse, so often used, of enticing the victim from the school-room was successfully used by the kidnaper, James H. Boyle. He and his wife, Helen McDermott Boyle, on the day of the kidnaping, March 18, 1909, took the boy to Cleveland. Here he was hidden in an apartment until the ransom was forthcoming. He was then delivered by street-car to the Hotel Hollenden in that city. Boyle was later convicted and sent to prison for life and his wife to a term of twenty years. Boyle died in prison on June 23, 1920, and his wife served ten years. The Whitla boy was the nephew of the Sharon philanthropist and steel magnate Frank Buhl.[37]

But the most sensational and poignant case of all time was the Charles A. Lindbergh case of 1932—the kidnaping of the baby from his nursery, his subsequent death at the hands of the kidnaper, and the electrocution of Bruno Richard Hauptmann, convicted of the heinous offense. The sensational violation of public decency set off one of the most thorough and dramatic manhunts in the history of American crime. It also precipitated a series of laws that had for their purpose the punishment of those who would dare to participate in this basest of all crimes. In 1934, the federal

---

[37]These three cases are summarized from Edward H. Smith, *Mysteries of the Missing,* New York, Dial Press, 1927; Ross, pp. 1-22; Cudahy, pp. 133-52; Whitla, pp. 153-170. See also, Duke, *op. cit., pp.* 536-50.

government passed the so-called Lindbergh Law which permits the F.B.I. to enter a case after twenty-four hours on the assumption that the victim had been transported over state lines. There was a provision in the legislation that imposes the death penalty if the kidnaped person is injured in any manner. Since that date, relatively few persons have been executed for kidnaping even when murder is or was involved. During the past twenty-five years, over 500 cases have been investigated by the Federal Bureau of Investigation and almost 1,000 persons have been convicted. Less than fifty have been sentenced to death and only a few have been executed.

We shall deal with two more kidnaping cases in this section: one, the notorious Hickman kidnaping in California in late 1927; the other, the Arthur Gooch case, of Oklahoma, the first person to be hanged under the federal kidnap law. We shall dispose of the Gooch affair first, because it is colorless and caused little public concern. It is important only because the person hanged may be remembered as the *first* that ran afoul of a new federal sanction.

Gooch was what is called in modern parlance, a confirmed criminal. At the time he planned his final escapade he was incarcerated in a local Oklahoma jail where he had, as a cellmate, one Ambrose Nix. These two worthies escaped and fled to Paris, Texas. Here they seized two police officers and carried them into Oklahoma. In a melee, Nix was killed and one of the officers was pushed through a glass show-case and severely injured—all making for a capital offense under the new federal law. Gooch was eventually hanged for his crime in the Oklahoma State Prison at McAlester on June 19, 1936. Until near the last he had expected a commutation from President Franklin Roosevelt, but it did not come. Bitterly he insisted that "the President did not read [his] letter to Mrs. Roosevelt and did not personally investigate the case, or he would have given me a break." The Oklahoma gunman left behind him "an appeal to youth" which warned them "of the pitfalls which are in wait for all boys and girls of this world in the shape of whiskey and a good time."[38,39]

---

[38]*Daily Oklahoman,* Oklahoma City, June 19-20, 1936.

[39]August Mencken includes the Gooch case in his potpourri of hangings, *By the Neck.* New York, Hastings House, 1942, "The Lindbergh Law's Debut," pp. 1-5.

The William Edward Hickman-Marion Parker case of Los Angeles in 1927, in all of its brutality, was the second of three ghastly kidnap episodes involving children of a decade that has since been referred to, rightly or wrongly, as "flaming" and "lawless." First there was the Loeb-Leopold case of 1924, which shocked the nation; then the Hickman affair, and finally the tragic and completely senseless kidnaping of the Lindbergh baby in 1932, which practically numbed the rational sensitivity of the nation. All were different in most particulars but, in essence, they were quite similar in that all of the victims were children and none of them was safely restored to their families but were murdered.

Hickman, a good-looking, relatively bright mid-west boy of twenty, decided to kidnap the daughter of a man whom he knew. On December 15, 1927, he went to the school where the twin daughters of Perry M. Parker—Marion and Marjorie—aged twelve attended and told the teacher that he, a "fellow employee," had been asked to take the "younger girl" to her father. He did not know there were two daughters nor that they were twins and the teacher unwittingly asked, "Which one? Marion?" to which the quick-witted Hickman answered in the affirmative. This initial piece of thoughtlessness on the part of the teacher together with a short history of stupid errors and professional ineptness on the part of the police, made it possible for a rank amateur to culminate a kidnaping, a cunning extortion, and, finally a murder involving almost unspeakable dismemberment.

The girl was given over to the "nice-looking young man" and immediately he sent the father a ransom note demanding a surprisingly small amount of money—$1,500. The distraught parent did exactly what Hickman warned him not to do, but what almost every parent would do; he notified the police. From then on, Hickman played a cat-and-mouse game with the police with the heartbroken father in the middle. The kidnaper wrote several letters, all signed "The Fox" and at times included letters written in the handwriting of the girl Marion. After about a week of toying with the father Hickman finally made contact, obtained the ransom money (of marked bills) and disposed of the lifeless mangled body almost before the eyes of the father. After the full enormity of the baseless crime became known, the public unleashed a strident call to all-out action by the police in bringing the "fiend" to book. Tips of all kinds were turned over to the police, rewards in excess of $50,000 were offered for the capture of the perpetrator of the foul deed, and the newspapers and radio stepped up their hour-by-hour coverage beyond anything that had up to that point ever been dispensed.

The kidnaper was traced to Oregon through a car he had stolen and by means of marked currency. He was apprehended by two Pendleton, Oregon police officers and gave himself up without a struggle. This was on December 22, one week after the crime. He still had $1,400 on his person. He was returned to Los Angeles where a large crowd waited for him at the railroad station. He was soon brought to trial, convicted and sentenced to death. It turned out that this "fine-looking" young man had been engaged in burglaries and murders prior to this last of his crimes. He had actually killed two other persons while on a jag through the middle west. Contrary to most stories about criminals, Hickman had come from a middle-class home, was graduated from high school, never drank nor smoked and had actually worked in a Los Angeles bank; it was there that he was acquainted with his victim's father. However, he owed Parker no malice. He merely selected the man's small daughter as victim because he knew of her existence. This young terrorist was hanged at San Quentin prison on October 19, 1928. It was reported that his last request was for a bunch of flowers which was granted. As to the last moments we have this conjecture:

> About the actual hanging of the Fox, reporter-witnesses—of which there were many!—are in some conflict. There is no doubt that Hickman made good his boast to fellow inmates of the Row that he would walk to the gallows unaided. Most say he fainted under the rope and was unconscious when the trap fell. One report has it that the executioner—yielding to personal contempt for Hickman—so adjusted the noose that the kidnap-murderer would strangle to death rather than receive the more merciful fate of a broken neck.[40]

---

[40]This material, together with the quotation, is from J. Francis McComas, *The Graveside Companion,* New York, Ivan Obolinsky, Inc., 1962, "Our Younger Brothers," pp. 61-90; quote at p. 89.

Human feelings are difficult to gauge and we cannot read the minds of hangmen or others whose official duty is to execute for society. Does such a person permit himself to identify with the victim he executes? Perhaps not, but how do we know? In the above statement regarding the hangman of William Hickman we note that a report states that he did—and negatively. This is quite possible. But in all of the news stories of hangings that have come to our attention the above is the first mention of such an attitude on the part of a hangman. How many others might have felt this way and thus caused bungling or unnecessary suffering or a prolongation of the death throes we can never know; merely speculate.

Hickman was the last person to be hanged in the State of California prior to the introduction of asphyxiation in a gas chamber. The first person to be hanged apparently was one Jose Rodriguez shortly after California became a state. He was executed on Russian Hill in San Francisco for the murder—in a fight—of one Jose Forner. The first person hanged in San Quentin, following the passage of the law making "inside" executions mandatory was one Jose Gabriel, alias Indian Joe, "a friendless and simple-minded murderer of an aged farm couple." This was in 1893.[41]

Approximately two years and eighteen victims after the hanging of Hickman in San Quentin—on October 2, 1930—a sex-kidnap-murder case shocked the state of California, although not necessarily the nation, as did the Hickman affair. This case, with a twenty-two-year-old man named Gordon Stewart Northcott as its principal, has been described by Clinton T. Duffy. At that time he was an assistant or clerk to the incumbent Warden James B. Holohan, and was pressed into playing an important role in the drama that occurred during the last forty-eight hours prior to the hanging.

Northcott had been convicted of the murder of an unidentified Mexican boy along with two American youngsters named Nelson and Lewis Winslow in Riverside County. This person has been described by Duffy as loathsome, a pervert, a pathological liar, a sadistic degenerate and a cold-blooded, heartless, physical misfit who, convicted of only three murders, had, "by his own admission,

---

[41]So stated by Kenneth Lamott, in *Chronicles of San Quentin*, New York, David McKay Co., 1961, p. 156.

been responsible for several times as many." He told Duffy that he did not know the "exact number of people he had killed" but maybe "eighteen, nineteen, or even twenty." In 1928, he lived with his mother and a nephew on a ranch in Riverside County. His father had died in an insane asylum and an uncle had "beaten several murder raps by providing alibis" but had finally been convicted and was serving a prison term in San Quentin.

This patholgoical young man had a penchant for kidnaping young boys, sometimes in pairs or even in groups of threes, and keeping them captives for weeks while coercing them to submit to various kinds of sexual perversion and then finally killing them. It was established that in some cases, prior to burying them, he dismembered them. In his sadistic abuses he was assisted by his mother, especially in the case of two young brothers, ages eight and ten, who participated in her son's perverted orgies. The boys were killed at the ranch and their bodies buried. It was later learned that mother and son had kidnaped a ten-year-old Mexican boy, had taken him to the ranch where he was sexually abused and murdered. This young degenerate was apprehended for his crimes, convicted and sentenced to death. His mother, equally as guilty of these unnatural crimes, was spared the death penalty—perhaps because she was a woman—and sentenced to life imprisonment.

Aside from the impending execution, this might have been the ending of the Northcott monstrosity. But there was more to come, as we may learn from Warden Duffy's account. Approximately forty-eight hours prior to the scheduled execution, two ladies dressed in black appeared at the prison where they asked to speak to Warden Holohan. They were mothers of three of Northcott's victims, one the mother of the two young brothers. They were making a desperate effort to learn where this young sex fiend had buried their children. Duffy volunteered to try to obtain this information from Northcott. The story progresses, step by step, in the attempts to pin the man about to die to a plausible story concerning the killings and disposition of the bodies. It is during this poignant account that we learn how a psychopathic liar operates. Once he will agree to speak truthfully. Then he will repudiate what he has said; perhaps even contending that he is innocent of all wrong-doing. At one point, Northcott agreed to tell the truth if confronted by the mothers. After some discussion among the prison officials, this unusual procedure was consummated. Yet Northcott did not communicate the truth. He lied. This was learned when the warden dispatched some men to the Riverside ranch and dug where it was stated the bodies were to be found.

In short, Northcott went to his death without confessing where the boys' bodies were buried. The night before the hanging, the young sex murderer enjoyed his last inning. He feigned suicide by screaming to the officer guarding his every moment that he had taken poison. The prison physician rushed to the holding cell but it was medically established that he was faking or, perhaps more likely, was "scared to death." After begging not to be obliged to see anything—his head was hooded—and not to be obliged to walk too fast, he was led limply to the gallows and hanged. He died whimpering. Many, of course, did and still do. But a large percentage of those who have lived by crime do approach the hanging tree gamely. The evidence indicates that Northcott did not.[42]

Two others were hanged at San Quentin technically for kidnaping, but actually for "breaking prison." These were Joseph Kristy and Alexander McKay, on May 22, 1936. These men, with two others, Rudolph Straight and Fred Landers, had surprised Warden James B. Holohan as he was entertaining the members of the Prison Board in his home, in January, 1935. The inmates ordered the men to strip and when the warden resisted he was shot. The thugs changed into civilian garb, seized a prison car and swiftly made for the gate, holding the board members as hostages. They were captured soon afterwards but not without a gun battle in which Straight was killed. The warden recovered and Landers was spared execution because he had insisted that the warden's life be spared. The charges against the men were "kidnaping for the purpose of breaking prison."[43]

THE PEARL BRYAN TRAGEDY — OHIO AND KENTUCKY — 1897

The annals of crime catalogue several murders of pregnant fe-

---

[42]For an account of this case, see Duffy, *Eighty-Eight Men and Two Women,* Doubleday, 1962, pp. 60-72.

[43]Duffy, *op. cit.,* Chapter 8.

males by those who find it embarrassing to have them close to
their private lives—such as a threat to their reputation, or to their
domestic tranquility or to their pocketbooks. One of the most intriguing—and notorious—is that of the murder of a nineteen-year-
old girl named Pearl Bryan, a native of Greencastle, Indiana.
Hanged for this crime at Newport, Kentucky, on March 27, 1897,
were Scott Jackson and Alonzo Walling, dental students of Cincinnati, Ohio. The story is as follows:

Pearl Bryan left her home in January 1896, ostensibly to look
for a job in the big city—of Cincinnati. Her parents never saw
her alive again. It seems that at the Indiana House in that city,
she met two dental students who were friends of William Wood,
son of a Greencastle minister who, apparently, was responsible for
Pearl's pregnant condition. The two friends accepted the onerous
role of amateur abortionists and loyally undertook to save their
friend's reputation back home. Unfortunately for all concerned—
that is, for all but young Mr. Wood—the boys gave Pearl too
much cocaine so that she died. Frantically, the unwilling killers
took her body across the river to Ft. Thomas, Kentucky, and
buried it, after severing the head from the torso. This was presumably done to make identification more difficult.

On February 1, the body was found near the Alexandria Pike
out of Ft. Thomas and was taken to a Cincinnati morgue to await
identification. This was accomplished by means of the webbed toes
of the victim. A bloody satchel was found which raised conjecture
that this may have been used to carry off the victim's head. However, the head was never found.

Pearl's body was removed to her home town of Greencastle and
a monument was erected over her grave. This proved too much
of a temptation for souvenir hunters and it was chipped away gradually, save for the base. It is said that this may still be seen in the
town cemetery. The two abortionist-murderers were tried and
hanged in Kentucky. There was a rash of ballads on the Bryan
case. The following are typical:

> Young ladies, if you'll listen, a story I'll relate,
> Which happened near Fort Thomas in the old Kentucky state;
> It was January the 31st, that awful deed was done,
> By Jackson and Walling, how cold Pearl's blood did run.

But little did Pearl Bryan think when she left her happy home,
That the grip she carried in her hand would hide her head away;
She thought it was a lover's hand she could trust both night and
    day,
But alas! it was a lover's hand that took her life away.

But little did Pearl's parents think when she left her happy home,
That their darling child in youth would nevermore return;
Her aged parents, you know well, a fortune they would give,
If Pearl could but return to them, a natural life to live.

Now all young girls take warning, for all men are unjust,
It may be your truest lover; you know not whom to trust;
Pearl Bryan died away from home on a dark and lonely spot,
My God, believe me girls, don't let this be your lot.

Some random verses, some indicating confusion with the facts, are
also of interest:

Next morning the people were excited, they looked around and
    said;
'Here lays a murdered woman, but where, oh where is her head?'

In came Pearlie's sister, fell down on her knees;
Pleading to Jackson, 'Give sister's head, oh please.'

Jackson was so stubborn, this is what he said,
'When you see your sister in Heaven, there will be no missing
    head.'[44]

One of the numerous pamphlets published on this case is entitled
"Headless, yet Identified"![45] No data have come to light that indicate that Pearl's seducer, allegedly William Wood from her old
home town, was ever brought to book for his participation in the
evil deed.

THE TRAGEDY OF MOUNTAIN MEADOWS AND THE EXECUTION OF JOHN D. LEE

**Mountain Meadows
A Favorite Recruiting Place
on the Old Spanish Trail
In this vicinity — September 7-11, 1857 occurred one of
the most lamentable tragedies in the history annals of the**

---

[44]Burt, *op. cit.,* pp. 31-2.
[45]McDade, *op. cit.,* 502-4.

**West. A company of about 140 migrants from Arkansas
and Missouri led by Captain Charles Fancher, en route to
California, was attacked by white men and Indians. All
but 17 small children were killed. John D. Lee, who confessed to participation as leader, was legally executed here
March 23rd, 1877. Most of the emigrants were buried in
their own defense pit. This monument was reverently-
dedicated September 10th, 1932, by the Utah Pioneer
Trails and Landmarks Association and the people of
southern Utah.**

A tragedy occurs, someone is held responsible, and is penalized. Years later, when sober consideration is given the event and
all involved, as well as all who remember, are dead, new apprais-
als are made. Often these new judgments are mere rationaliza-
tions or complete "white-washings." Witness the tragedy of the
hanging of the New England men and women for alleged witchcraft. This was admittedly a hideous episode in our history, but
there are those who rationalize these hangings because "every-
body" believed in witchcraft at the time.

In the story of the massacre at Mountain Meadows, so briefly
but so poignantly etched above, a Mormon bishop "participated
as leader" of the massacre party and was shot for his crime on
March 23, 1877. It took almost twenty years to bring him to his
moment of expiation. He was the only person punished for this
perfidious slaughter, but as one person puts it today: "Calmer
judgment now absolved him of some of the bitter responsibility
. . . All evidence indicates that these southern Utah men were
acting on their own initiative, and that Brigham Young . . . had
no knowledge of the affair until it was an accomplished fact."[45]

Brigham Young did act honorably in this most unfortunate tragedy, despite the fact that Lee had reported to him that the slaughter
had been committed by the "Pahute Indians . . . because the emigrants fed the Indians poisoned cattle." Later, when the true facts
came to light by slow piece-meal shreds of evidence, Brigham
Young cooperated with the federal authorities. Lee was actually
convicted by a jury entirely composed of Mormons.[46]

---

[45]Olive Woolley Burt, *op. cit.,* p. 114.
[46]See Thomas S. Duke, *op. cit.,* pp. 323-326.

Bishop Lee was not hanged, but shot. Thus we insert another case in this compilation of hangings that does not belong. The only justification for the inclusion is that to most Americans this tragedy is unknown and does bear telling and retelling. It is the kind of episode that seldom gets into the school boy's history book, probably due to its unsavory elements. The admittedly regrettable incident has been immortalized by a ballad which is also worthy of insertion here:

Come all you sons of liberty, unto my rhyme give ear, —
'Tis of a bloody massacre, you presently shall hear. —
In splendor on the mountains some thirty wagons came,
They were awaited by a wicked band, oh, Utah! Where's thy
    shame?
On a crisp October morning at the Mountain Meadows green,
By the light of bright campfires, Lee's Mormon bullets screamed.
In Indian garb and colors those bloody hounds were seen
To attack the little train all on the meadows green.
They were attacked in the morning, as they were on their way,
They forthwith corralled their wagons, and fought in blood
    array.
When Lee, the leader of the band, his word to them did give,
That if their arms they would give up he'd surely let them live.
When once their arms they did give up thinking their lives to
    save,
The words were broken among the rest, which sent them to their
    grave.
When once they had give up their arms and started to Cedar
    City,
They rushed on them in Indian style, oh, what a human pity!
They melted down with one accord like wax before the flame;
Both men and women, young and old, oh Utah, where's they
    shame?
Both men and women, young and old, a 'rolling in their gore,
And such an awful sight and scene was ne'er beheld before!
Their property was divided among this bloody crew;
And Uncle Sam is bound to see this bloody matter through.
The soldiers will be stationed throughout this Utah land,
All to find those murderers out and bring them to his hand.
By order of their president this awful deed was done,
He was leader of the Mormon Church, his name was Brigham
    Young.

Of Lee's execution, a one-verse ballad survives:

> See Lee kneel upon his coffin, sure his death can do no good;
> Oh, see, they've shot him see his bosom stream with blood![47]

SOME CLASSIC CASES

We have one last series of crimes to set down in this chapter before we continue. We might refer to these as the Nashville murders. While the execution of three persons at a time has not been unusual and perhaps this number can scarcely be referred to as a mass hanging, there was a "mass hanging" at Nashville, Tennessee, on February 10, 1843, that must have caused somewhat of a ripple of excitement. The victims of the gallows and *their* victims were: Zebadiah Payne, murderer and robber of William Coltart—Payne waylaid him, cut his throat robbed him and fled to Texas from whence he was eventually returned and hanged; Willis Green Carroll, for the murder and robbery of the Rev. Isaac Lindsey—both men set off from Nashville carrying a large sum of money; they crossed the Cumberland River at Watson's Ferry where, apparently, Carroll shot his companion and fled to Arkansas; and Archibald Kirby, Pine Mountain assassin of Mrs. Polly Hunter—he had four years previously been acquitted of the murder of Peter Elrod. This day must have been a busy one for officials, including the hangman and his assistants.[48]

Three brothers hanged at one time is unusual and we have discussed such an affair earlier, that of the Thayer Brothers of Buffalo, New York, in 1825.[49] There are many cases of two brothers being hanged at one time and for the same crime, either for burglary or murder and perhaps, for other heinous crimes. We have no authentic information concerning a double or triple hanging of sisters. Although we mentioned such a case in an earlier connection. We refer to the obviously fictional case—supposed to be a valid one—of the three Halzinger sisters who were allegedly hanged at a place referred to as Elizabethtown, Arkansas, on November 30, 1855, for the murder of the Edmonds family.[50] Nor

---

[47]The above verses from Burt, *op. cit.,* pp. 119-120.

[48]All cases listed in McDade, *op. cit.,* 734-5.

[49]See pp. 275-7.

[50]Chapter V, p. 224, "Fictional Cases."

have we heard of authentic cases wherein any other family combination of two or more members have been hanged, except one instance in New York State, and one in Iowa. In the former there was a lapse in time. We refer to the hanging of an Indian female named Mary Antoine which occurred at Peterboro, Madison County, in that state in 1814, and of her father, Abram, hanged September 12, 1823, at Morrisville, same county. The two cases are closely related. The father killed one John Jacobs, a half-breed, because he had been the chief witness against his daughter. The daughter allegedly killed a "female" who had "alienated her husband's affection." Despite public sympathy being associated with the Indian Abram, the law was obliged to take its course.[51]

The Iowa case was of a father and son, hanged at the same time in the state prison at Fort Madison. They were Philip Heiney, aged seventy-two, and his son, William, aged forty-five, executed for the murder of Robert Raebel of Lake Okeboji. The hangings took place on March 29, 1946. Iowa abolished the death penalty in 1965.

There are doubtless others but they have not come to our attention.

---

[51]J. H. Smith, *History of Chenango and Madison Counties,* 1880, pp. 546, 635.

Chapter VIII

THE POISONERS

HOW MURDEROUS ARE FEMALES?

O F FIFTY-FOUR MURDER CASES involving the use of poison, listed by Thomas McDade in his *The Annals of Murder,* he notes that in only seventeen was a female charged with the crime.[1] This admittedly superficial analysis may come as a shock to many, since it is traditional in this country to believe that it is the female that resorts to poison to commit a murder. There are those sentimental persons who hold a strong conviction that the female is less dangerous than the male, that she is more to be trusted, that she tends to be more moral and, perhaps, should not be executed, even though the death penalty is thought proper for male killers. Quite a literature could be adduced to support this opinion but an equally large bibliography could be produced to refute it. One rather quaint warning comes from an early nineteenth century Pennsylvania legislator, Thomas B. McElwee, who was deeply engrossed in an investigation of the state penitentiary at Philadelphia in 1835. One of the charges against the management at the time was that the wife of the deputy-warden, a Mrs. Blundin[2] was "carrying-on, carrousing, drinking, etc." within the portals of the prison. He bitterly penned these words and added them to his minority report:

> I have no faith in the ethereal qualities of the feminine gender and believe much evil could be accrued to society by stuffing their heads with the idea that they are angels, goddesses, etc.,— "Heaven bless the mark!"—when their faults, their follies, and their vices drive men mad and produce fatal disruptions in families. We call them angels when the violence of their passions

---

[1]McDade, *op. cit.,* p. xix.

[2]See Chapter I, page 75. Joseph Blundin, this woman's brother-in-law was hanged for murder at Doyestown, Bucks County, Pennsylvania on August 14, 1835.

render the domestic sanctuary a pandemonium—when it ought
to be a paradise. We call them goddesses when, in fact, lamentable experience admonishes us, that they possess all the ungodly
properties annexed to the poor dwellers on this terrene globe;
and if there is in their composition, an admixture of heavenly
qualities, it is sprinkled so sparsely that much research is necessary to enable us to detect its existence.

The dagger is not less penetrating and effectual because it
is wielded by a woman—the poisoned chalice less bitter, or less
fatal because administered by her we love, in whose keeping
we have placed our honour and our life. When Charlotte Corday
plunged her murderous knife into the bosom of Marat, did he
omit to die because the blow was given by a woman? The annals of mankind are filled with Parysites, Xantippes and Cleo-
patras. While I recognize in its fullest extent the validity of the
claim of every female to courtesy and protection from man, I
reject with indignation the requisition of homage to a sex which
should only be preferred to piety and virtue. Virtue, piety and
amiability are the sole ornaments of woman. Sex cannot ob-
literate a crime or adorn a vice. I never will worship at the
shrine of vice and immorality, though their altars may be decorated with the image of a woman.[3]

To keep the record balanced, we feel obliged to quote from a
more gallant gentleman, Hon. Roscoe Conkling, New York political leader of the past century. He writes in no uncertain terms:
"At no time should a woman's life be put in danger. Our civilization surely is too far advanced to permit the killing of a woman
by process of law. It is bad enough, God knows, to hang a man.
A woman's life should never be taken, even though she has been
found guilty of the awful crime of murder. The hastening to eternal
judgment of a woman's soul, by order of a civilized judge, in a
civilized court, of a civilized country, is a blot upon the manhood
of this nation."[4]

The position regarding this debatable question that one might
take is that the responsibility of females for their crimes is likely

---

[3] *A Concise History of the Eastern Penitentiary of Pennsylvania, Philadelphia,* Neall &
Massey, 1835, pp. 26-27.

[4] Quoted by Andrew J. Palm, *The Death Penalty,* New York, G. P. Putnam's Sons,
1891, p. 153.

to be based largely upon prejudice against or in their favor by
jurists, juries, and the general public.[5]

Crime statistics in our own country, in recent years, indicate
that females are more prone to commit murder, compared to males,
if we appraise all of the offenses committed by both sexes. The
difference is not great but the modest disparity does dispel the
notion that actually the gentler sex is not so gentle. Whether or not
they are arrested, convicted, or punished for their crimes leads us
to the endless controversy involving differential treatment by authorities and courts. A concluding statement might well be that if
capital punishment is to persist, females should not be immune to
the penalty.

In earlier times, slaves often resorted to poison to rid themselves
of their masters. We mentioned the Mark-Phillis case in Massachusetts in 1755.[6] Another poison case, similar to this, occurred at
Burlington, New Jersey, on June 1738. The *American Weekly
Mercury* (Philadelphia, but date-line Burlington) for June 8,
states: "two Negroes were found guilty . . . of poisoning sundry
persons [and] were executed here last week." This is an interesting,
but obscure, case. It is mentioned by the noted Philadelphia historian, John Fanning Watson in his *Annals,* as follows: "1738:
Three Negro men were hung for poisoning sundry persons in Jersey.
They said they had poisoned Judge Trent the founder of Trenton."[7]

Arsenic was the most common poison used, especially when a
more medically conscious period emerged sometime after the early
1800's. In the Catherine Bevan case at New Castle, Pennsylvania
Colony, in 1731, when this maritally unhappy matron poisoned
her spouse, she used "rat bone, or Roman Vitrol."[8] Other forms
of poison that have been catalogued by McDade in his *The Annals
of Murder,* are: strychnine, laudanum, and prussic acid. At least
in one case, John Hendrickson, who murdered his wife in 1853
at Bethlehem, Albany County, New York, a poison known as
aconite was used. Hendrickson, a twenty-year-old ne'er-do-well,

---

[5] For an interesting account of this question, see Bernard O'Donnell, *Should Women
Hang?* London, W. H. Allen, 1956.

[6] See Chapter II, pages 89-90. Mark was gibbeted, Phillis burned.

[7] *Annals of Philadelphia,* Vol. II, p. 309, 1858 edition.

[8] See Chapter II, 107.

killed his young wife of nineteen, and seven other persons in the house at the time all made an attempt to conceal his wife's murder. He was subsequently hanged.[9] This case has notoriety because it is believed it was the first time that the poison *aconite* was used in this country.

Another notorious case in which the poison antimony was used is that of Mrs. Elizabeth Wharton, who is alleged to have poisoned General W. S. Ketchum in late 1871, in Baltimore. She was a widow, and a good friend of the general but apparently owed him a large sum. He left Washington for Baltimore to collect the debt. His body was returned to Washington two days later without a stomach; it was being analyzed. The medical men found the general had been poisoned by imbibing "harmless" lemonade spiked with antimony (tarter emetic). A sensational trial followed but the comely widow was acquitted of any wrongdoing.[10]

SOME CLASSICAL CASES

In mentioning the Wharton case we feel under some compulsion to say a few words about some of the cases that developed a far-flung notoriety but which did not end in hanging. There is the famous Lydia Sherman case. This woman (referred to at the time as the modern Lucretia Borgia) poisoned three husbands and six of her children and doubtless several others, in and around New York City (her children were buried in Trinity Churchyard) and Derby, Connecticut. She merely found a family "discouraging" and disposed of it with arsenic. She was tried at New Haven, given a second degree prison term, and died in the Wethersfield, Connecticut prison, on May 16, 1878. Thanks to Mrs. Olive Woolley Burt we have a ballad about the case:

> Lydia Sherman is plagued with rats;
> Lydia has no faith in cats.
> So Lydia buys some arsenic,
> And then her husband he gets sick;
> And then her husband, he does die,
> And Lydia's neighbors wonder why.

---

[9]McDade, *op. cit.,* 468-470.
[10]*Ibid.,* 1076-1080.

Lydia moves, but still has rats;
And still she puts no faith in cats;
So again she buys some arsenic,
This time her children, they get sick,
This time her children, they do die,
And Lydia's neighbors wonder why.

Lydia lies in Wethersfield jail,
And loudly she does moan and wail,
She blames her fate on a plague of rats;
She blames the laziness of cats.
But her neighbors questions she can't deny —
So Lydia now in prison must lie.[11]

The Sarah Jane Robinson case is worthy of bare mention here despite the digression from strict adherence to subject matter. An Irish immigrant to Massachusetts as a child, Sarah Jane Tennent settled, grew up, and married. During the 1880's, several of her kinsfolk mysteriously died. It turned out Sarah Jane was responsible for their deaths. The rollcall of her victims, according to McDade, included her husband, her own two children, her sister, her brother-in-law, a nephew, and a landlord. The poisonous agent was, again, arsenic. She was first tried for the murder of her son, but the jury disagreed. Next she was tried for the murder of her brother-in-law, Prince Arthur Freeman, was convicted and sentenced to death. The penalty was subsequently commuted to life imprisonment. She died twenty years later in prison.[12]

Still another notorious dispenser of poison was the Cambridge, Massachusetts, nurse whose murders are reported so delightfully by Ellery Sedgwick, in his *The Happy Profession.*[13] Her name was Jane Toppan and Sedgwick had been one of her patients when he was a Harvard student. Fortunately for him, her chore in ministering to him happened to be between her insane attacks when she was obsessed to dispose of her patients. Apparently, she would work heroically and lovingly to pull her patient around to good health and then decide on death as their next status. She "played"

---

[11]Burt, *op. cit.,* p. 5.

[12]For details concerning the above notorious cases, see McDade: for the Sherman case, items 866-8; for the Robinson case, item 823.

[13]Boston, Little, Brown, 1946, pp. 81-84.

with them with morphia and atropin in a thoroughly objective manner until they succumbed. The number of her victims is estimated as somewhere between thirty and one hundred. She was put away in the mental hospital at Bridgewater. Sedgwick quotes from one of his professors regarding Jane and her evil work: ". . . she seemed to find the criminal enjoyment of doing aesthetic work to which danger appears to add zest."

There were some persons who manipulated poison simply to dispose of unwanted spouses and often, so far as we know, for reasons other than the existence of a third party of whom they were enamoured. We have some such "triangle love" cases that we shall describe later (See *infra*, page 352). We found many "non-triangle" cases in our earlier study of Pennsylvania murders. A few humdrum examples suffice. There was John Earls of Lycoming County (Williamsport) who gave his wife—two days after she had borne him a child—some hot chocolate in which he had slipped some arsenic. He sat at the foot of her bed and watched her die. He was hanged on October 16, 1835. For many years thereafter, his skeleton was on display at a local tavern. At the other end of the state, at Erie, two years later, Cornelius Henry Francisco "not having the fear of God before his eyes and being moved and seduced by the Devil did advise and cause his wife [of but three weeks] to take, drink, and swallow down her body four ounces of laudanum . . ." He was hanged for murder on March 9, 1838.

Our next case is a reversal to those above. This was the female, Lena Miller, of Clearfield, same state, some twenty-five years later. Lena was tired of her spouse, reason not expounded. She gave him just plain rat poison after spending some time experimenting with other less well-known lethal concoctions. She tried "tea made of laurel leaves, the filings of a brass buckle, laudanum, indigo, a small green snake boiled in coffee." She was hanged on November 13, 1867, a badly-disillusioned female.[14]

The most like the *Arsenic and Old Lace* classic that we have come across in our investigation into poison-murder cases is the

---

[14]M. L. McQuown, *History of Capital Crimes, etc. in Clearfield County* (Pa.), published by The Raftsman's Journal, 1914.

"motherly old lady" from Pittsburgh, one Martha Grinder, who was hanged for her maniacal poison jamboree on January 19, 1866. If one ponders on the fact that so few females are executed for their crimes, it is almost a coincidence that less than two years and 200 miles separate this case from the Lena Miller affair related immediately above.

There is no doubt of it, Martha Grinder was a confirmed arsenic poisoner but no one suspected her for a long, long time. She loved to do little homey favors for people, especially for those less fortunate than she. But she also dearly loved to kill! There is no way of knowing exactly how many victims she could chalk up to her deadly pastime. She is alleged to have said: "I love to see death in all of its forms and phases, and left no opportunity unimproved to gratify my taste for such sights. Could I have had my own way, probably I should have done more." Many of the recipients of her favors suddenly or eventually died, from her potions and at her pleasure. Finally, a young bride named Mary Caroline Carothers moved close to Mrs. Grinder's residence but in short time she became ill, presumably shortly after she had eaten some food prepared by the motherly Martha—she wanted to be friendly to her new neighbors. The young bride immediately left for her mother's home where she was attended by a physician but it proved too late. She died and the subsequent autopsy implicated Martha Grinder. She was immediately jailed and later indicted and convicted for murder and soon sentenced to death. She went to the scaffolds in the Allegheny County (Pittsburgh) jail and died "like a man." She was amazingly calm during her stay in the jail and made it a point to make friends with both inmates and jailers. She was interested in everything about her and had but one worry, it seems, to "look nice when she walked to the gallows."[15] The agents used by Mrs. Grinder were arsenic and antimony.

But to get back to a few more cases of poisoners who were bored with their mates. One, of some interest, is that of Mrs. Elizabeth Ragan, a piquant twenty-two, of Piqua, Ohio (ca.1855) who wished to dispose of her mate. She appealed to James P. Mowrey, suggesting that he lure her husband, Arthur, off on a

---

[15]Pittsburgh *Post*, January 20, 1866.

trip and dispatch him by inserting some arsenic into his favorite food, oysters. Mowrey was a little dilatory in acting so she sent her child to the druggist with a note to "buy three cents worth of arsenic." It seems that the apothecary was not disposed to sell less than ten cents worth at a time so the two conspirators each contributed a nickel toward the lethal concoction. The husband was accordingly eliminated and the widow confessed.[16]

A Philadelphia case involving murder by poison (in 1831) was disposed of legally in such a manner that the details surrounding it demand its inclusion here even though it ended in an acquittal. The facts are these: Mrs. Joanna Clew was indicted for the murder of her husband in April of that year. She had used a lethal dose of arsenic mixed with molasses. The jury was kept in seclusion from Saturday evening at half past ten o'clock until Monday morning at ten o'clock, "without meat or drink, fire or candle." After the first twenty-four hours had expired, the court ordered food to be supplied, with the consent of the counsel for the Commonwealth as well as for the defendant, "provided the jury would receive it." The majority, acting within the framework of the common law, refused to accept it. Later on that day, two of the jurymen, Ebenezer Ferguson and Andrew Hooten, declared that if they were longer confined their lives would be placed in jeopardy. Ferguson, seventy-six years of age, declared "poor health and unable to walk without assistance;" Hooten maintained he was ill from "billious fever." In consequence of this, the jury was discharged without arriving at a verdict.

In December 1831, Joanna Clew was again put on trial. Her counsel pleaded a "former acquittal" insisting that his client's life had been in jeopardy and "could not again be endangered." The Pennsylvania Supreme Court concurred with these views and decided there must be an overruling to justify the discharge of a jury in a criminal case. But as all that was necessary was meat and drink for the jurors, juries in subsequent cases would be supplied nourishment. The female poisoner, however, went free. An earlier case similar to the Clew case was that of Samuel Alwine who had been murdered in 1822 by three persons. One of the jurors held

---

[16]McDade, *op. cit.,* 702.

out against an agreed verdict, stating he would "perish before he would agree." At that time the law was to deprive the juries of food until they did reach a verdict.[17]

TRIANGLE MURDER CASES

The illicit love or triangle case is a well-known and prevalent phenomenon in this country. Disgruntled spouses, all too often "misunderstood" by their mates, meet the "understanding" type, handsome, affluent, and masculine on the one hand, beautiful, haunting perhaps, and affectionate, on the other. Not often are these ideal qualities actually present, but to an unhappy spouse it is not difficult to see them in one who is willing to enter into an illicit, perhaps passionate, partnership.

One of the best known and well-documented of the early period is the Chapman-Mina affair which had its setting in a rural section of Bucks County, Pennsylvania, near the present day environs of Philadelphia, in Bensalem Township. The time was 1831. While this case should take its place in the era of public hangings, it would almost have to stand there alone, so we have taken the liberty of anchoring it in our poison era which, as we stated earlier, began to shape up around the beginning of the nineteenth century. While there were doubtless triangle affairs in colonial and later times in this country, few actually made a reputation firm enough to be preserved in that select but intangible "Murder Blue Book" or equally intangible "Murder Hall of Fame." The Chapman-Mina case definitely rates such a reputation.

The principals in this triangle affair were Mrs. Lucretia Chapman (past forty and buxom), her husband, "Dr." William Chapman, operator of a school for stammerers in the hamlet of Andalusia, and Sr. Lino Amelio Epos y Mina, *alias* Carolina Estradas de Mina, *alias* Celestine Armantarius, *alias* Amalia Gregorio Zarrier, a bogus Spanish (actually born in Trinidad, Cuba) adventurer or "soldier of fortune." The story goes that this dark, handsome Latin, twenty-two years old and but five feet two inches tall, stopped by the door of the Chapman home and told an imaginative tale of being the son of the Spanish governor of California. Lu-

---

[17]For details of these cases see *Philadelphia Dispatch,* July 8 and 15, 1866.

cretia Chapman seemed greatly impressed by this gallant confidence man and invited him to partake of their hospitality. (There is another version of the story that states they had actually met on the Boston-Philadelphia steamboat some days earlier,[18] within an astonishingly short time, Mina had taken over the household, aided by Lucretia and resisted by Dr. Chapman who really didn't count for much in his own home. The two connivers made a veritable love nest of the rural retreat of the naive and helpless voice professor and, in due time, he was found dead. Mina, to prove himself helpful in the mournful crisis, shaved the corpse.

With their victim in his grave the couple went off to New York and were married. But then the authorities began a sober investigation of Chapman's sudden death. They found, for instance, that some ducks in the Chapman home had died suddenly and this barnyard tragedy had been caused by some soup thrown out by Lucretia a day or so before the doctor's death. Arsenic seemed to be the cause of it all and this was traced to a purchase made by Mina at the apothecary shop of a Philadelphia merchant. He said he wanted it to "stuff birds" with. It was also noticed that the Chapman family silver had disappeared from the home. Evidence piled up. It was discovered that the couple was in the process of swindling activities in the vicinity of the city. This led to their arrest. They were both charged with murder; the woman was acquitted, the man condemned to death.

The little "Spaniard" was hanged at Doylestown, on June 21, 1832, "in a natural amphitheatre on the banks of the Neshaminy [Creek] on the almshouse grounds." He was permitted to ride to his doom in an open "dearborn" instead of the traditional cart. He was accompanied by a priest and all reports indicate that he was courageous to the last. Mrs. Chapman, after her acquittal, left the county and became a "strolling player" and died in Florida around 1840. She was the daughter of Thomas Winslow, a notorious counterfeiter of that day.[19]

Mina was, without question, a man of charm and mystery. The story, as related above, states that he arrived at the Chapman

---

[18]See below for further details.

[19]Adapted from notes by George MacReynolds, archives, Bucks County Historical Society, Doylestown, Pennsylvania.

home, unknown by the mistress of the establishment. One other
account, widely current at the time, states that the two had met
on a steamboat trip from Boston to Philadelphia. Mina, however,
had known her as a Miss Wilson. At the time he had a large
amount of valuable jewelry on his person so it was but natural
that, being a stranger, he should avail himself of her kind suggestion that he stay with a friend in the downtown section of
Philadelphia—on Pine Street. He soon learned that various pieces
of his jewel collection were being extracted from his room and,
upon complaining to the authorities, instead of obtaining redress,
was thrown into prison. This came to pass, it seemed, by the
arts of the female Wilson [or Mrs. Chapman] and her confederates.
He spent some little time in prison but was eventually pardoned
by the governor. He went immediately to his late rooming house
where he finally learned that the Miss Wilson was, in reality, Mrs.
Lucretia Chapman of Andalusia. He set off for the Chapman
abode which he reached about twilight. The matronly Lucretia
was naturally agitated but in her embarrassing situation she hastily
decided to befriend him. She begged him not to expose her to her
husband and children and in this he acquiesced. The husband, however, refused him entry but the cunning wife prevailed upon the
suspicious spouse to permit the charming Mina to tarry tempo-
rarily. During the following days the two were frequently together,
either at Andalusia, or on jaunts to Bordentown, New Jersey or
to visit the Mexican consul in Philadelphia. They frequently took
one of the woman's children with them for appearance's sake.

The above version of the Mina saga is not reported in the conventional news reports of the case. However, it is recorded in
some detail in the Lancaster, Pennsylvania *Journal,* June 29,
1932.[20]

Another strange poison murder that cannot be overlooked is that
of John Van Valkenburg of Johnstown, Fulton County, New York
killed by his wife Elizabeth. She hanged for her crime on January

---

[20]Source, *Saturday Courier* (date and place of publication not stated); probably the
Saturday preceding, June 23, two days after Mina's execution. This case is listed in
McDade, *op. cit.,* 169-173; and a pamphlet not listed: *Sketch of the Life & Con-
fession, etc. . . . .* by George N. Thompson in *Confessions, Trials & Biographical
Sketches of the Most Cold-Blooded Murderers who have been executed in this Coun-
try,* Hartford, Conn., S. Andrus & Son, 1844.

24, 1846. One-time resident of Bennington, Vermont, Elizabeth explained her motive as well as her *modus operandi* frankly and with candor. It seems her husband had the "disgusting habit" of drinking and she was determined to cure him of the vice. The poison agent was arsenic which she placed in his tea and even in his brandy in small doses. There was little sympathy for Eliza‑ beth Van Valkenburg in the neighborhood or at the state capitol so she was dispatched on the gallows. It was known that she had disposed of an earlier husband by means of the murder route.[21]

The Ann Simpson (North Carolina) and Ann Bilansky (Minnesota) Poison Cases

Two intriguing stories of callous poisoning by females of their spouses are wrapped up in somewhat of a mysterious set of flimsy circumstances that prompts at least a hint that they are connected, a "two-in-one" possibility. We refer to the Ann Simpson story of "Old Fayetteville," North Carolina and the Ann Bilansky case of St. Paul, Minnesota.

The Simpson story involves a young, beautiful and calculating female who "got her man," an unsuspecting spouse several years her senior and who "got away with it" with an acquittal. We refer to Ann Carver Simpson, delightfully "immortalized" by Manly Wade Wellman in his fascinating work dealing with murderous intrigue—but not altogether hanging—*Dead and Gone*.[22]

And yet we are not sure of Ann Simpson's ultimate fate be‑ cause of the nebulous romantic myth or legend that seems to have enveloped her name. This legend ties her in with one Ann Bilansky, hanged at St. Paul, Minnesota, some years after the Fayetteville affair. We shall explore this amazing story of the two women, if only briefly.

Alexander Simpson, a hard-working carriage-maker in his thirties finally came to the conclusion that he should turn from business for a time and enter the fields of romance and matrimony. Who, in old Fayetteville, North Carolina, could be more alluring than the sixteen-year-old Ann Carver? So, in 1846, he took her

---

[21]McDade, *op. cit.*, 1022.

[22]Chapel Hill, University of North Carolina Press, 1954; see chapter entitled "Arsenic and Old Fayetteville."

for his wife and set her up in a lovely home where they dwelt in connubial bliss for quite a time. For some reason—certainly not because Simpson needed extra cash—two young, but respectable boarders who worked at the carriage-shop were also domiciled in the spacious love-nest. As might be expected, the comely Ann Simpson gave considerable attention to these young men. After bearing her husband two children, both of whom died in infancy, marital apathy began to set in which was obvious to alert observers throughout town. The troubled young matron began to associate with fortune-tellers and sooth-sayers which resulted in her beginning to make frivolous — yet deadly serious — predictions about death and other alarming matters.

On one evening in November 1849 Ann served her husband and their boarders an interesting drink—probably indigenous to the region—called "syllabub," consisting of wine, whipped cream and spices. This was the favorite drink of the frail but trusting husband and he quaffed of it freely. The two boarders turned it down because, as they stated, they belonged to the *Sons of Temperance!* The following day, November 8, Alexander Simpson died of arsenic poisoning.

There is no further need in elaborating this case except to relate that Ann Simpson was indicted for murder—but before an all-male jury—and was acquitted. After her freedom, she left town and settled in Charleston, South Carolina. Friends back home noted in a paper some time later—for April 4, 1852, the *Weekly North Carolinian,* that the lovely Ann had become Mrs. Charles Young. That, in itself, would be nothing unusual except that not too long thereafter it was rumored in Fayetteville that there had been a separation and that Mr. Young had died suddenly and "untimely."

Our story leaves Ann Simpson and continues with Ann Bilansky. We start with the reproduction of a strange news clipping—undated—from the Milwaukee *Sentinel* which, according to Mr. Wellman, our source, was reproduced in a Charleston newspaper and may be seen today in the North Carolina Room of the library of the State University. It seems important to this compiler that the clipping be inserted here:

Singular Development — The Murderess of Two Husbands
The *Sentinel* says it is believed from recent developments

that Ann R. Bilansky, who was executed at St. Paul, Minnesota, for the murder of her husband by administering arsenic, was the same person who on the 8th of November, 1849, poisoned Alex. D. Simpson, her husband, in the town of Fayetteville, N. C. In that case arsenic was the agent employed, and after the death of Simpson his wife was arrested, but succeeded in escaping to Charleston and hence to Havana, where she remained until about May, 1850. She returned to Fayetteville on the 7th of November following, surrendering herself for trial, and was acquitted.

On the trial of Mrs. Bilansky at St. Paul, she stated that she had resided at Fayetteville, N. C. where her husband died. The Christian names of the two women are identical, and many circumstances in St. Paul subsequent to her execution have been called to mind which tend to the belief that she and Mrs. Simpson were the same person.[23]

Perhaps before we explore the legend it would be expedient to tell the story of the arsenic murder of Stanislaus Bilansky, elderly Polish saloon-keeper of St. Paul on March 11, 1859, for which his wife, Mary Ann Evards Bilansky, was tried, convicted and hanged. Her execution took place on March 23, 1860; she is the only female ever to be executed in the state of Minnesota.

This saga starts when a young man named John Walker became ill in St. Paul and wrote to his "aunt," Mary Ann Evards, a widow living in Fayetteville, North Carolina, to come up to care for him. This she did. Walker took her into his own quarters and soon he recovered completely. It so happened that he was a friend of a disgruntled widowed, saloon-keeper named Bilansky. For some reason, even then obscure, he brought the two together and subsequently Ann Evards married the Polish immigrant. Walker moved into the nuptial home with little more than a token objection from the testy, but hard-working husband. At the trial there was testimony that Ann entered Walker's bedroom many nights and stayed for hours. It was further revealed that Bilansky knew of these nocturnal illicit amours but did little more than grumble to saloon patrons.

It was also brought out in court that Ann bought arsenic at a drugstore and subsequently the old gentleman grew quite ill with

[23]*Ibid.*, p. 41.

many of the symptoms of arsenic poisoning and soon succumbed. But for some time his wife escaped detection—if not suspicion—but was eventually arrested for the crime. There was a sensational trial but inexorably the wheels of justice stopped with a conviction in the first degree of murder for the scheming Ann. She was sentenced to death but fought hard for a retrial, a commutation. She lost consistently. Yet, this amazing woman had a trump card up her sleeve. She escaped from the jail while awaiting the gallows—in the split second when the guards were looking the other way. Her freedom was shortlived. She was hanged in the county jail of Ramsey County—St. Paul—on March 23, 1860 with some 1,500 persons milling about outside the walls.[24]

Now to the myth—if it is a myth. Certainly the two writers quoted above—Messrs. Wellman or Trenerry—take no stock in the story. And for good reasons. Here are at least some—perhaps the most obvious.

The two women did not resemble each other. Ann Simpson is described (perhaps unilaterally but accurately by the police of Fayetteville) as "a woman of small stature, very black hair, dark complexion, large black eyes, small nose and large mouth, with her upper lip slightly protruding."[25] Ann Bilansky is described as follows: "a tall, blond, grey-eyed, vivacious and talkative widow of thirty-four [in 1858]."[26] The sheriff was more specific as he gave out her description after she escaped jail. He wrote: "Tall in stature, long-featured, sharp visage, teeth a little projected—the two front teeth in the upper jaw lapped—is very talkative, uses good language, voice rather masculine, grey eyes, light hair, Roman nose."[27]

As to the ages of the two women: Ann Simpson was sixteen at her marriage in 1846, which would make her but thirty in 1860, when Ann Bilansky was hanged. Ann Evards Wright Bilansky was thirty-four when she answered her "nephew's call to go from Fay-

[24]For more information concerning this fascinating case, see Walter N. Trenerry, *Murder In Minnesota,* St. Paul, Minnesota Historical Society, 1962, pp. 25-41; the case was mentioned many years ago in *History of St. Paul,* by J. Fletcher Williams, 1876.

[25]Wellman, *op. cit.,* p. 24.

[26]Trenerry, *op. cit.,* p. 28.

[27]*Ibid.,* p. 36; his source, St. Paul *Pioneer & Democrat,* July 27, 1859.

etteville to St. Paul to nurse him back to health." This was in May 1859. Thus she was thirty-six at the time of her execution.

A third difference. While it is merely rumored that Ann Simpson is buried in Fayetteville—"she was brought back one dark night and secretly buried at the edge of Person Street."[28] It is more often accepted that the remains of Ann Bilansky, who accepted Catholicism a day or two before her execution, lie in the St. Paul Catholic cemetery.

While there is much material for romanticism in the stories of these two husband poisoners, as perhaps also in several other cases described in these pages, both were mere amateurs compared to Lydia Sherman, Martha Grinder and a few others who knew poisons and their effects as well as many druggists and physicians, how to use them, and who had no compunctions in using them whenever the spirit moved them. Perhaps these professional poisoners were insane whereas the husband poisoners were merely bored with their spouses; some were not even enamoured of others.

The Harris-Hellum Case — Monroe, Louisiana

Another triangle murder that ended in a double hanging—bereft of finesse, romanticism, and sophistication—unfolded and climaxed at Monroe, Louisiana (Ouachita Parish), on November 26, 1875. It has to do with one Harris, whose wife, Alcee, twenty-four, enamoured of a "charcoal darky,"—that is what the papers called him—was brutally disposed of by the pair. It was a sordid, clandestine affair throughout. The habitually neglected husband stood as much as he thought he could and then begged his wife for a better understanding. She acquiesced to him, but in reality, merely agreed to sit down over a glass of beer and try to make amends. Surreptitiously she had connived to have her lover, named Tony Hellum—referred to by the papers also as "an ebony Don Juan"— to "check him off" after she had put him into a deep sleep with a potion slipped into his beer. The plan worked beautifully. After Harris had succumbed to the knock-out drops, Hellum entered the home and bashed in the victim's head. The two dragged his body into a shallow grave and went about their unholy amours. The body was soon discovered by alert dogs, hired for the occa-

---

[28]Wellman, *op. cit.,* p. 41.

sion, and the two conspirators were eventually brought to book for their deed. They were convicted and hanged on the courthouse lawn at Monroe.

This grimy episode might have escaped our attention had it not been identified with a singular piece of journalism which caught our attention. This triangle murder has been set apart by a "heady" journalist of the day—the headline writer for the *Chicago Times.* Whoever he was, he can make some bid to fame—however dubious—for creating perhaps the most flamboyant set of headlines in the history of the press. We referred to this in an earlier connection.[29] In writing up this story as it came over the wire from the Ouachita (La.) *Telegraph* (November 27, 1875) at the masthead we find: *Jerked to Jesus: Four Senegambian Butchers Were Wafted to Heaven—Two of Them, from Louisiana, Died with the Sweet Confidence of Pious People.*[30]

A couple of these crimes come from Pennsylvania. The first one, which ended in the hanging of both principals on September 28, 1858, at Danville, Montour County, was the Twigg-Clark affair. The male lover was William John Clark, the female accomplice in killing the unwanted wife, Catherine Ann, was Mary Twigg. Clark gave the unsuspecting wife a poisonous potion concocted "by mingling white arsenic with magnesia water."

The second case was more involved. Catherine Miller, "in her twenties," of Lycoming Country (Williamsport, county seat) connived with her paramour, George W. Smith, "twice her age," to dispose of "for all time" her husband, Andrew, whom she could no longer tolerate around the house. They lived at a place called Jersey Shore on the Susquehanna River (not, as one might think, on the seacoast), actually in the hinterland of the state. The mode of killing the victim is obscure but we know that after life became extinct the scheming pair hung his body to a rafter in his barn to make it appear a suicide. Going further in their diabolical plot they placed the blame for the murder—when the authorities finally established this fact—on a friendless colored man of the town

---

[29]See page 21.

[30]Two others were hanged the same day at Sardis, Mississippi, for murder. The word "senegambian" refers to natives of a part of Africa. See Herbert Asbury, *Gem of the Prairie,* Knopf, 1940, p. 72.

named John Brown. This poor unknown was tried but soon freed. In due time, the secret was exposed and the couple were convicted and hanged on February 3, 1881, at Williamsport.

The Cannon-Nettles Case — Goosecreek, South Carolina

One that might be referred to as the Goosecreek case is probably worth recording. It involves Joshua Nettles and his illicit sweetheart, Elizabeth Cannon, a much-married woman. On the night of October 24, 1804, at Goosecreek, South Carolina, Nettles murdered John Cannon and put the victim's body in bed with the wife, Elizabeth. Her job was to conceal the crime. Not much was accomplished by the conspirators, since Nettles was convicted and hanged while Elizabeth was, true to southern chivalry, acquitted.[31]

A poem—it can scarcely be called a ballad—was composed in 1805 regarding this foul deed. The author, Amos Taylor, contended (in the title) that it "should be pasted on the walls of every house in America." It consists of forty, four-line verses and crudely tells the facts of the crime. The poem implies that Mrs. Cannon's children, especially her twelve-year-old daughter, were implicated in the crime, being privy to their mother's clandestine amours with Nettles. At the trial, the wicked woman derived the benefit of her children's testimony which helped bring about her aquittal.[32]

The Amasa Fuller Case — Indiana — 1820

In the annals of murder, as we know it in this country, there are two rather quaint social concepts that call for at least passing mention. The first is the functioning of "southern chivalry" as it is occasionally reflected in jury acquittals of female murderers. An excellent example of this gallantry is the case of Ann Simpson of "Old Fayetteville," which we described earlier.

The second element in the murder "mores" is the "unwritten law," which alleges to shield a man from legal action—or from

---

[31]McDade, *op. cit.,* 715.

[32]The only source of this poem, entitled, "The Charleston Tragedy: A New Song," is the Huntington Library, San Marino, California. Referred to in *Proceedings,* American Antiquarian Society, April 15, 1959, pp. 45-6; 54.

paying the penalty—if he shoots or kills his wife's illicit lover. Such a philosophy often rears its head in the acquittal of a man whose wife makes of him a cuckold. Perhaps the most notorious case of this is that of Daniel E. Sickles, one-time congressman from New York, who, after an extremely unpleasant murder trial in which he was acquitted, went on to become a general in the War Between the States, losing a leg at Gettysburg, and still later becoming ambassador to Spain.

The facts are that Sickles found his wife unfaithful to him and proceeded to shoot and kill her lover, Philip Barton Key, who was none other than the son of Francis Scott Key, the author of our National Anthem. This startling affair took place on the streets of Washington, D.C., on February 27, 1859. The victim was well known and capable, being at the time United States District Attorney. Sickles was tried and acquitted.[33]

But not so fortunate was the obscure Amasa Fuller of Lawrenceburg, Dearborn County, Indiana, in 1820. While he lost his life on the scaffold for his murder he, at least, has become immortalized by a ballad. The facts of the case are simple. He left town on a business trip and while gone, a good friend, Palmer Warren, wooed and won away from him his betrothed. Flying into a rage at such short-term loyalty, Fuller disposed of the lover but spared the woman. The ballad goes as follows:

The Ballad of Amasa Fuller

Ye sons of Columbia, Attention I crave, While a sorrowful story I'll tell;

It happened of late in Indiana State, Where Fuller, a hero, did dwell.

Like Samson he courted his lady fair, Intending to make her his bride;

But like Delilah fair she did his heart ensnare, And robbed him of his honor and his life.

He gave her a gold ring to prove he was true, He gave her a token of his love;

They then both agreed to be married with speed, And they swore faith by the powers above.

---

[33]McDade, *op. cit.*, 869-872.

But this fickle maid she vowed again to wed With young
    Warren who lived in that place;

And this was the fatal blow that caused his overthrow, And
    proved to be her shame and disgrace.

When Fuller came to hear he was deprived of his dear Who
    had vowed by the powers him to wed,

Unto Warren he did go with his heart full of woe, And thus
    unto Warren he said:

'Now Warren you have wronged me to gratify your case You
    reported I had left a prudent wife;

You must admit it all before I break the law, Or Warren, I'll
    deprive you of your life!'

Then Warren he replied, 'Your wish must be denied, Since my
    heart to your darling is bound.

And further I must say this is my wedding day, In spite of all
    the heroes in this town!'

Then Fuller in a passion of honor and love, Which after all
    caused many for to cry,

With one fatal shot he killed Warren on the spot, Saying, 'Lord,
    I am ready now to die.'

The girl she was shunned for the evil she had done, For she
    caused two men to die at last;

And all the people knew it was her who caused the woe, And
    her heart it was troubled by the past.

For Fuller was condemned by the courts of Lawrenceburg,
    And sentenced to die a shameful death;

To swing beneath the sky on a gallows tree so high, And have
    a hempen rope choke off his breath.

The time at length arrived when Fuller was to die, He smiled
    and bade the audience adieu;

Like an angel he did stand, for he was a handsome man,
    On his breast he wore a ribbon of blue.

And one other verse found in some versions of the lugubrious
tale:

All ancient histories, so we understand, And the Bible we have
    to believe,

Say the woman is sensual, and the downfall of man, Just as
    Adam was beguiled by old Eve.[34]

---

[34]Burt, *op. cit.*, pp. 51-2.

A few pertinent verses appearing in the Flanders version:

> Then Fuller he was taken by the honorable board By the laurel
> of Auburn to die
> Such an ignominious death for to swing above the earth Like
> Homer on the gallows so high.
> Ten thousand spectators they smote upon their breast And the
> guards they dropped tears from their eyes
> Saying 'Curs-ed was she—she has caused his misery And she
> ought to in his stead have to die.'
> Come all you young married men who has got a prudent wife,
> Be loving, be true and be kind.
> You may look in the book of Moses, of Genises, and Job And
> the truth of my story you'll find.
> For love it is a lottery and he who wins the prize, She may be
> pleasing to his mind and his eyes
> But the man who never marries is the man that's counted wise
> So ladies and gentlemen 'Good-bye.'

THE JEREBOAM O. BEAUCHAMP CASE —
KENTUCKY, 1826

Another spectacular case possessing many of the conventional elements of southern chivalry and masculine gallantry, albeit some of it frayed, is the Jereboam O. Beauchamp trial and hanging at Frankfort, Kentucky, in 1826. Equally as strange as anything created by a master fiction writer are the facts of this case as gleaned from the many publications that survive those exciting days in the heart of the Bluegrass State. The story is briefly as follows: a member of the legislature and one-time attorney general of the state, Col. Solomon P. Sharp, had seduced a beautiful and accomplished young lady named Ann Cooke. He then allegedly discarded her in order to marry another. The gallant Beauchamp, an attorney, on learning of Scott's perfidy, courted the sullied Miss Cooke and offered to marry her. But this embittered young female set a price for her hand; Beauchamp must avenge her dishonor at the hands of Scott by slaying him. First, her champion tried to engage Scott in a duel. Failing in this, he called at the colonel's residence one night, well disguised, and as he appeared at the door, stabbed him to death. Of course the killer was immediately suspected, was soon tried and quickly convicted of first degree murder. The comely female, now Mrs. Jereboam Beauchamp, shared his cell as he awaited execution. In that interim they agreed to a suicide pact by stabbing themselves. On the day of the scheduled hanging, July 7, 1826, they went through with their plan. The wife succumbed but the gallows claimed its victim. Beauchamp was carried to his doom in a wounded condition. The two tragic figures were buried at the same time in a common grave. An ironical twist was that Beauchamp asked the military band that was present to play *Bonaparte's Retreat from Moscow* and it is reported that he declared it well played.[35]

The Fisk-Stokes Affair — New York City — 1872

The following triangle affair which did not end in a hanging—merely a short prison term for the killer—but with a ballad eulogizing a millionaire roué, who was laid low by a bullet, belongs here, if at any point in this work. Few such triangle affairs have "caught the imagination"—to help perpetuate a corny phrase—of the American people in any era. The principals were notorious, rich and powerful and the pawn female equally notorious and unscrupulous. They were Col. James Fisk, Jr., Edward S. Stokes and Helen Josephine (Josie) Mansfield, an actress darling of that period.

Fisk, stock broker, promoter and manipulator of railroads who, with Jay Gould had "stolen" the Erie railroad from Cornelius Vanderbilt, was the victim of the murder. The wielder of the gun and perpetrator of the deed was Edward S. Stokes, a wealthy associate of Fisk in the oil business. Becoming embroiled in business deals the two tycoons became insanely jealous when the latter, Stokes, "stole" Fisk's mistress Josie Mansfield. Infuriated at this, Fisk retaliated by impugning Stoke's business dealings and Josie's "good name." In retaliation for this public exposure Stokes, on the afternoon of January 6, 1872, followed Fisk to the Broadway Central Hotel and shot him on the stairs. Fisk died the following day. After considerable legal maneuvering and sensational newspaper coverage, Stokes was convicted of "third degree manslaughter" and sentenced to four years in Sing Sing prison. It is

[35]McDade, *op. cit.*, p. xxxi; also 80-9.

reported that the sentence was not too severe for the gentleman manipulator, since in a nearby stable he was permitted to "keep a coach and four and take rides about the country-side!" For some reason, the sympathy was all with Fisk although he was generally believed to be a ruthless unprincipled "Casanova, vicious in business as he was in love." The story is that his body lay in state in his colonel's uniform in his opera house "while angry crowds stormed the Tombs and threatened to lynch his assassin." The Fisk story is an American saga. Born in Pownell, Vermont, he was first a country peddler and later a roustabout in Van Amberg's circus. His financial manipulations have become a legend.[35] Olive Woolley Burt, collector of ballads, says of the Jim Fisk ballad, "it shows mass hysteria in a striking manner." It is herewith reproduced:

The Ballad of Jim Fisk

If you listen to me, I will sing you a song,
Of this glorious land of the free
And I'll show you the difference between rich and poor,
In a trial by jury, you'll see.

If you've plenty of money you can hold up your head
And can go from your own prison door,
But they'll hang you up high if you have no friends,
They'll let the rich go, but hang up the poor.

I'll tell you of a man who is now in his grave,
And a better man never was born.
Jim Fisk was his name, and his money he gave
To the outcast, the poor and forlorn.

Everyone knows he loved women and wine,
But his heart, it was right, I am sure;
He lived like a prince in his palace so fine,—
But he never went back on the poor!

Jim Fisk was a man with his heart in his hand,
No matter what people may say; He done all his deeds, both
the good and the bad,
In the broad open light of the day.

---

[35]For details see Thomas S. Duke, *Celebrated Criminal Cases in America*, San Francisco: 1910, pp. 629-35.

With his fine six-in-hand on the beach of Long Branch
He cut a big dash to be sure;
But Chicago's big fire showed the world that Jim Fisk
Would never go back on the poor.

When the news it was spread that the humble that night
Were starving to death, slow but sure,
Jim Fisk loaded up the Lightning Express
To feed all the hungry and poor.

Now what do you think of the trial of that Stokes
Who murdered this friend of the poor?
If such men go free, is anyone safe
To step outside his own door?

Is there one law for the rich and one for the poor?
It seems so from all that folks say.
If they'd hang up the poor, why shouldn't the rich
Swing high in the very same way?

They shouldn't show favor to friends or to foe,
To a beggar or prince at your door;
The millionaire should pay for his crimes also—
We should never go back on the poor.[36]

---

[36]Burt, *op. cit.*, pp. 48-50.

Chapter IX

HANGINGS IN THE INTEREST OF NATIONAL SECURITY

NECESSITY FOR NATIONAL SECURITY

T HE DEFENSE OF THE STATE has always been uppermost in the minds of the people. Public representatives are responsible for that security and, in general, handle their difficult task satisfactorily. However, there are times when their zeal does not square with tolerance and compassion. This is particularly true during and immediately following war or during periods of national unheaval or hysteria when certain basic rights may be summarily abrogated or carelessly considered.

As we look back at some of the acts of security consummated to protect the national interest, we feel from our vantage point, that they were unjust. Such may be the hangings of Mrs. Mary Suratt, one of the alleged Lincoln conspirators and, perhaps, that of Capt. Henry Wirz, unhappy commandant of the notorious Andersonville prison during the War Between the States.[1]

During the War of Independence, it seemed necessary for both the British and the American patriots to court martial and punish alleged spies, deserting soldiers, traitors, and others deemed dangerous to the security of the armies. The hangings of Capt. Nathan Hale and Major John André that occurred in that long conflict are sagas of the period. Capt. Hale, twenty-one-year-old Connecticut school-master was captured by the British and condemned to hang at a trial held on a spot not far from the present United Nations building. He was hanged on September 22, 1776, a little further north on Manhattan Island near Third Avenue and 66th Street where stood at the time the Dove Tavern. Major André, associated

---

[1]See below for discussion of both of these cases.

in a plot with Gen. Benedict Arnold, was hanged on October 2, 1780, at Tappan, New York, not far from the New Jersey line. There were many more who were hanged or shot by the patriot army during the long conflict. It is not our purpose here to deal with these executions despite the fact that they come within the purview of national defense.[2]

We may, however, describe briefly a few cases in order to demonstrate the hysteria and injustice rampant at the time. On November 4, 1778, two tragic figures went to the gallows in Philadelphia. They were John Roberts, miller, and Abraham Carlisle, house carpenter. The charge against them was that they had enlisted with the enemy and attempted to persuade others to do so. Both were members of the Society of Friends. Many leading citizens begged that they be not executed and "387 Philadelphians . . . came forward" in their behalf. No mercy was shown and they were hanged. The historians, Scharf and Westcott, writing in 1884, made this statement: "Their execution and the seizure of their property appears to this day to have been dictated by the desire to satisfy popular clamor rather than a spirit of justice."[3]

Another case, even more tragic, was that of David Dawson, executed in the Public Square of Philadelphia on November 25, 1780, convicted of treason. Actually, Dawson had refused to surrender to the proclamation under the Act of Attainder and was guilty of joining the British army and passing between New York and Philadephia. A prominent Quaker of that day, Samuel Rowland Fisher, languishing in jail himself and keeping a day-by-day Journal, writes on the day of Dawson's execution:

> The taking of the life of D. Dawson seems to me to be a greater act of Cruelty in the present Rulers [the patriots] than anything they have heretofore done for they never gave him even a Shadow of a Tryal in their own fashion and they have executed him merely as what they call a proscribed person because he came into the City while the British army lay here,

---

[2]A compilation of those persons shot or hanged in Pennsylvania at the hands of American military or civilian authorities may be found in Teeters, *Scaffold & Chair*, Philadelphia, Pennsylvania Prison Society, 1963, Part I, p. 18. The total is, perhaps, less than twenty-five in both the War of Independence and the War of 1812.

[3]*History of Philadelphia*, 1884, Vol. I, p. 394.

the circumstances of which was [sic] that he was coming from his abode with his Waggon, that being in danger of his life from some of Washington's men, he fled into the city and left and lost his Waggon, Horses, provisions, etc. He never acted in any manner under Brittish, nor had he taken the Test to the present Usurpers, he did not go with the Brittish army to New York, but had secreted himself in various places till he was betrayed by James Reed last Spring and taken prisoner.[4]

One of the better known to historians of this period is Thomas Hickey, hanged in New York City, near the Old Bowery, on June 28, 1776, for plotting to turn General Washington over to the British. Fully 20,000 persons witnessed the hanging. He had been arrested for attempting to pass counterfeit money and became talkative while in jail. He told of a conspiracy involving some 700 enlisted men from the Continental Army who would defect to the British, taking their commander with them. He was turned over to Washington, court-martialed, and hanged.[4a]

New York had trouble with Tories, deserters, and traitors, as did all of the colonies. For instance, on May 15, 1778, two men were hanged at Albany in the presence of a "prodigious number of spectators," and again, on May 19, at a mass trial, ten persons were found guilty of various charges and most of them hanged.[5]

Perhaps the most notorious of these Tories was Claudius Smith who has come down to us by the sobriquet "Cowboy of the Ramapo Mountains" and hanged for his misdeeds, including the murder of Major Nathaniel Strong, on January 22, 1779. He shared the gallows that day at Goshen, Orange County, New York, with two others of lesser reputation, Thomas Delamar and James Gordon. Delamar and Gordon were hanged for burglary. Smith and three of his sons terrorized the neighborhood by their pillaging depredations, stealing horses and delivering them to the British in New York City. After Smith had murdered Mayor Strong, a bounty was placed on his head by Governor Clinton and the

---

[4]*Journal of Samuel Rowland Fisher* (privately printed), p. 107.

[4a]Louis Blake Duff, *The County Kerchief,* Toronto, Ryerson Press, 1949, p. 28. For story see Douglas Southall Freeman, *George Washington: A Biography,* IV, Chap. 5, 115-26.

[5]John Spargo, *The Story of David Redding Who Was Hanged,* Bennington, Vermont, 1945, p. 41; Spargo cites James Thacher, M.D., *A Military Journal During the American Revolutionary War,* ed. 1823, p. 157.

man-hunt was on. He was apprehended on Long Island and eventually brought back to Goshen where he met his end from the bough of a cottonwood tree."[5a]

An interesting case comes from Peekskill, New York, in which a tree is honored for assisting in the hanging of a Tory during the War of Independence. It seems one Daniel Strang, an American, was "strung up" by patriots on June 27, 1776. In 1912, the Sons and Daughters of the Revolution thought it no more than right that a plaque be set up "in honor of this tree" (known as the Spy Oak) so that posterity might give pause to the fate of spies. The tree was blown down by a hurricane some years ago.[6]

We mentioned earlier the activities and fate of members of the Doan gang of Bucks County, Pennsylvania, who turned Tory during the War of Independence. They harassed Washington and his men around the country-side now known as Washington's Crossing, New Jersey and Pennsylvania. Levi and Abraham Doan were hanged as outlaws in Philadelphia.[7]

A quaint and obscure case comes from New Jersey folklore. It is that of the Robin Hood of Mordecai Swamp, Joe Mulliner. He was accused of "chasing cattle into the woods, scattering pigs into the pineland forests, stopping occasionally to pillage and murder." He aroused the ire of the patriots because he refused to bow to their arguments to repudiate the British or to join them. In short, he preferred to be neutral at a time when such a position was extremely unpopular. Whether or not he ever murdered anyone is debatable. He was legally hanged in one of three places—Pleasant Mills, Woodbury, or Burlington, all in New Jersey. It was sometime in 1781—so say the local amateur historians. Regardless of the year, there is enough evidence that he was disposed of on the gallows "in the interest of national security."[8]

In other wars—the War of 1812 and the War Between the States—we would probably find several others. In our next chapter

---

[5a]Samuel Eager's *History of Orange County*, Newburgh, N.Y., 1846-7, p. 557; courtesy Harry Hawkins Smith, curator, Historical Library, Goshen, N.Y. and Genevieve Van Duzer, secretary, Hist. Soc. of Town of Warwick, N.Y.

[6]Source, Miss Greta Cornell, Ossining Historical Society in letter dated June 30, 1964.

[7]See *supra*, (Chap. 1).

[8]For account of this nebulous case, see Henry Charlton Beck, Hanged in Three Places, Buried in Two," *New York Folklore Quarterly*, Vol. III, No. 3 (1947) pp, 242-246.

we tell of the hanging and shooting of three members of the crew of the *Niagara* on Lake Erie for desertion in 1813. The case of marine James Bird is especially of interest.

One fascinating but almost completely forgotten case, not associated with a war, is identified with alleged piracy but contains the overtones of national security. This threatened piracy occurred on the brig *Somers,* of the American Navy, in 1842. Three enlisted men were involved—or at least were hanged "at the yardarm," at sea, without a trial, for conspiracy to murder the officers and preempt the ship. The vessel was returning home from a voyage to Africa and the affair took place in the Caribbean not far from St. Thomas. The alleged ringleader was an eighteen-year-old midshipman named Phillip Spencer, son of the incumbent Secretary of War in President John Tyler's Cabinet, John Canfield Spencer, and grand-son of the distinguished New York State Supreme Court jurist, Ambrose Spencer. It was alleged that he was aided by two others of the crew—actually more but the two in question were hanged with Spencer; they were the ship's acting boatswain, Samuel Cromwell, and an ordinary seaman, Elisha Small. They were discovered in their plot on November 26 and reported to the commander of the vessel, Commodore Alexander Slidell MacKensie, who ordered them placed in irons and on December 1, 1842, summarily hanged them.

Upon return to this country, MacKensie reported immediately to his superiors and eventually was court martialed amidst considerable bitter criticism in many circles. However he was acquitted of any wrong-doing, the circumstances being carefully weighed and balanced off against the need for "national security." One distinguished American was shocked at the turn of events—a young midshipman hanged at sea without the semblance of a trial, and an acquital of the commanding officer by court martial—and this was the novelist, James Fenimore Cooper. He caused the story and the court proceedings to be published so we may now make our own decision relative to the young man's actions and, perhaps, his guilt.[9] A note of interest is that the young midshipman wrote all of his notes in Greek and he was but eighteen!

---

[9]*Proceedings of the Navy Court Martial of Alex. Slidell MacKenzie, with an introduc-*tion by James Fenimore Cooper, pub. by Joel F. Langley, 1844.

JOHN BROWN'S BODY — AT HARPER'S FERRY

Sometimes a villain becomes a martyr and sometimes a fanatic evolves, after his death if not before, into a patron saint of not only his followers, but of millions of others who have little knowledge of his acts. Certainly John Brown, the fanatic abolitionist, belongs to this category. Long before he met his downfall at Harper's Ferry, scene of his miniature rebellion, he was known in and around Kansas as a murderous fanatic. He was obsessed with freeing the slaves at all costs and, aided academically by a few intellectuals from the North, he went about his business in a bungling manner.

In July 1859, the bearded crusader established himself on a small farm in Maryland, about five miles from Harper's Ferry where a federal arsenal was located. He and his group of insurrectionists remained there, conditioning the arms sent to them from the North. On October 16, the group marched on Harper's Ferry. There they seized the arsenal, but in their zeal they immediately brought in troops. These consisted of the Jefferson Guards from the Charlestown, Virginia barracks and subsequently a brigade of federal troops from Washington, the latter under the command of Col. Robert E. Lee. The incipient plot was crushed. Brown and his men had barricaded themselves in the engine house in the town but they were soon flushed out and captured.

Louis Blake Duff, who calls Brown's subsequent execution "the most notable hanging case in America," states that accompanying Colonel Lee were such luminaries as Tom (later to be called "Stonewall") Jackson, young Lieutenant Jeb Stuart and, of all unlikely persons, John Wilkes Booth.[10]

After his capture, Brown was moved to the Charlestown jail and was placed on trial October 25. He was convicted of "treason, conspiring with slaves to rebel and first degree murder" for which he was sentenced to death.[11]

Brown's execution was resplendent with military pomp. No civilians were permitted to view the hanging which irritated the old abolitionist. Prior to his execution, Brown was busily engaged

---

[10]*The County Kerchief*, p. 13.

[11]The material in this section from August Mencken, *By the Neck*, pp. 179-186.

in writing letters. Some days he sent out as many as eighteen. Many northern sympathizers came to Charlestown to see him or to bear him gifts but, aside from his wife, he saw none of them. Mrs. Brown's fate was especially poignant since she had also lost two sons, Oliver and Watson, in the abortive plot. She was obliged to make arrangements for the transport and eventual burial of her three loved ones.

The Baltimore *Sun* for December 2-3, 1859, describes the scene in Charlestown: "As the fatal hour draws nigh in which that bold, bad man, John Brown, is to pay the penalty . . . everything gives token of the serious impressiveness and importance of the occasion. The town presents now, more than ever, the unusual scene of a military encampment in time of national peace. It is filled with troops who are constantly marching and countermarching, and enlivened with the strains of martial music from the regimental bands. The drills and dress parades of the soldiery are accompanied and animated by the presence of fair ladies and brave men. The streets and balconies have been thronged by the ladies as well as by the citizens and the military, watching the movements of the troops, and the air of apprehension which at one time existed has disappeared."

The domination of the spectacle by the military may best be visualized by the fact that after John Brown was standing on the trap with his arms pinioned and his face hooded, it seemed necessary for the troops to "march and countermarch" as if "an enemy was in sight." This lasted for nearly ten minutes and prompted Brown to exclaim: "Don't keep me longer than necessary."

At this distance, it would seem that many elements in the making of a martyr were present. The tense era in which the episode occurred when the country was a tinder-box of inflammable anticipation of conflict, the heroics (to many) of Brown and his little band of dedicated but ill-guided followers, the military pomp incidental to the execution—all preceding the actual outbreak of war, made martyrdom a situational imperative.

Brown met his doom on December 2, 1859. His wife took charge of her husband's and sons' bodies and transported them to Albany, New York. From there she had them interred at the family burial ground at North Elba, in upper New York State.

Emerson, in far-off Concord, where the fiery abolitionist had many warm friends, on learning of Brown's end, stated prophetically: "It is easy to see what a favorite he will be with history."[12]

THE HANGING OF THIRTY-EIGHT SIOUX INDIANS — MANKATO, MINNESOTA — DECEMBER 26, 1862

The hanging of thirty-eight human beings at one time must be a record for mass executions. It is difficult today to visualize thirty-eight gallows set up on a mass scaffold for the expressed purpose of snuffing out the lives of so many human beings, even though it was deemed they deserved such a fate for their crimes.

These thirty-eight hangings that took place on December 26, 1862, are in excess by twelve of all those persons hanged in Minnesota from 1860 to 1906.[13]

This mass killing was different! These men were eliminated as an object lesson to hundreds of Indians who, in their hatred for the white man, were subject on occasions to swoop down on lone settlers or settlements and massacre innocent men, women and children. Violence begets violence. This was the philosophy of the West as it was being settled. The Mankato mass hanging episode cannot be fairly or accurately judged today, one hundred years later. All we are concerned with here is the story of the hangings, which is almost unbelievable. It is doubtful that more than a mere handful of Americans (certainly outside Minnesota) have ever heard of this episode in our history.

The events leading up to the mass hanging are these: during the War Between the States when most of our national attention was focused on that event, the Sioux Indians in the Minnesota frontier murdered five white settlers. Those involved in this initial attack were joined by others under the leadership of Little Crow and, thus augmented, they swooped down on the inhabitants along the Minnesota river and slaughtered some 400 men, women and children. General John Pope of the federal army was sent in pursuit with his cavalry and in a series of battles defeated Little Crow and his warriors. Out of the Indians left alive, 303 were

---

[12]Duff, *op. cit.,* p. 14.

[13]Walter N. Trenerry, *Murder in Minnesota,* Minnesota Historical Society, 1962, see pages 219-225. Minnesota abolished the death penalty in 1911.

rounded up and sentenced to death. Public feeling in the area ran high with demands for all of the captives to be executed. But President Lincoln interceded, selected thirty-eight of the overall group who seemed to be the ring leaders and who appeared to be the "most ferocious," and agreed to their execution.[14]

Because of the unique features of this unusual historical event, we take the liberty of paraphrasing the facts concerning it from the St. Paul *Pioneer,* December 28, 1862.[15] The reporter commented, as follows, on what he saw when he first arrived at the scene in Mankato: "We saw none of the indications of mere idle curiosity which commonly stimulates the gathering of crowds to witness an execution, but in place of that, there was a desire to be present from a sense of duty, to witness the death of a horde of savage fiends who had desolated a whole frontier, and to give countenance by their presence of the justice of the sentence of the military court . . ."

As early as December 22, a series of military orders had been issued to guarantee peace and decorum among troops and citizens alike for a radius of ten miles from the scene of the wholesale hangings. The Indians about to die were isolated from their fellow prisoners and the death warrant signed by President Lincoln was read to them. It was interpreted to them in the Dakota language by a chaplain. This death warrant is of interest a hundred years later. It read:

> The commanding officer . . . has called to speak to you upon a very serious subject . . . Your Great Father at Washington, after careful reading what the witnesses have testified in your several trials, has come to the conclusion that you have each been guilty of wantonly and wickedly murdering his white children; and for this reason he has directed that you each be hanged by the neck until you are dead . . . Good ministers, both Catholic and Protestant, are here, from amongst whom each of you can select your spiritual adviser, who you will be permitted to commune with constantly during the four days you are yet to live.

At the end of each sentence, in the reading of the warrant, the

---

[14]The foregoing material is taken from Mencken, *By the Neck,* p. 151.
[15]As found in Mencken, pp. 151-159.

condemned indulged their usual grunt or signal that they understood the meaning of the somber words. Many smoked their pipes in complete composure throughout the reading ceremony and some, nonchalantly, filled theirs with the native tobacco called *kinne-kinnick*. They were all chained in pairs during the days preceding the mass execution.

On Tuesday evening, the condemned proceeded to fall into a death dance accompanied with wild Indian chants. Because of some official apprehension, it was decided that their chains should be riveted to the floor, so as to prevent some unforeseen pandemonium. On Thursday, the day preceding the executions, the doomed men began to distribute their belongings, consisting of somewhat pathetic trifles—locks of their hair, coats, blankets and advice.

On Friday morning, the reporter found them all sitting about, smoking and chatting in a desultory fashion until "old Tazoo" broke out "in a death wail in which one after the other joined until the prison room was filled with a wild, unearthly plaint which was neither of despair nor grief but rather a paroxysm of savage passion, more impressive to witness and startling to hear." After this demonstration, they settled down into a quiet and composed attitude punctuated occasionally by quiet mutterings.

Prior to the time for the final mass killing, the warriors began to prepare themselves for death. "Most of them had little pocket mirrors . . . and they employed themselves in putting on the finishing touches of paint and arranging their hair according to the Indian mode. Many were painted in war style, with bands and beads and feathers, and were decked as gaily as for a festival."

At the "call for death" they arose and almost casually walked toward the gallows. The *Pioneer* reporter describes this final scene: "As those at the head of the procession came out of the basement we heard a sort of death-wail sounded which was immediately caught up by all and chanted in unison until the foot of the scaffold was reached . . . At the steps there was no delay . . . The Indians crowded after Capt. Redfield [the officer in charge of the hangings] as if it were a race to see who would get up there first. They actually crowded at each other's heels and as they got to the top each took his position without any assistance from those detailed for the purpose. They still kept up a mournful wail and occasionally there would be a piercing scream." After the ropes were adjusted around the neck of each of thirty-eight victims of the white man's strange kind of justice, the scene called forth the following from the reporter of the event:

> Then ensued a scene that can hardly be described and which can never be forgotten. All joined in shouting and singing . . . the tones seemed somewhat discordant and yet there was harmony in it. Their bodies swayed to and fro and their every limb seemed to be keeping time. The drop trembled and shook as if all were dancing. The most touching scene was their attempts to grasp each other's hands, fettered as they were . . . . Three or four in a row were hand in hand swaying up and down with the rise and fall of their voices. One old man reached out on each side but could not grasp a hand. His struggles were piteous and affected many beholders.

It seems that the purpose of their singing and dancing was only to sustain each other in their last ordeal; that there was nothing defiant in their actions. As the last moment rapidly approached, they each called out their name and shouted in their native language: "I'm here! I'm here!"

A muffled tap of the drum sounded but it was quickly drowned out by the voices of the victims and then—the drop fell and the bodies came crashing down. Aside from the struggling that almost always takes place at a hanging, the dreadful event was all but over. One by one the struggles ceased. The physicians moved in and pronounced that life was extinct in each case. Following this necessary routine, the United States mule teams appeared and the bodies were taken down and dumped into the wagons without ceremony. And, as the *Pioneer* reporter closed his account: "The bodies were carried down to the sandbar in front of the city and all buried in the same hole. The half-breeds were buried in one corner so they would be disinterred by their friends. Everything was conducted in the most orderly and quiet manner."

As Louis Blake Duff states, in telling the story: "Captain John Duly brought down the axe with a resounding blow. The great platform dropped with a crash. One Indian, a heavy man, broke his rope and fell down the river bank. Soldiers grabbed him and ran his body up one of the spare ropes. In twenty minutes the thirty-eight were pronounced dead."[16]

Thus ended, perhaps, the largest wholesale mass hanging in the annals of this country. How necessary it was cannot be honestly assayed today. It was part and parcel of that bloody and almost senseless era in which the march of empire seemed to be of extreme importance to national pride. Were not Indians the "white man's burden"?

THE FORT SAM HOUSTON HANGINGS — 1917

Perhaps the second greatest mass hanging that occurred in this country was of thirteen Negro soldiers of the United States Army at Fort Sam Houston, San Antonio, Texas, on December 11, 1917, as one of the results of race riots that occurred in Houston on August 23. Known as "The Texas Mutiny," it had its incipient beginning when a Negro soldier, belonging to the 24th Infantry, 3rd Battalion, stationed at Camp Logan, engaged in an altercation with a city police officer. There had been previous clashes between the Negro soldiers and the city's white policemen and between soldiers and white workmen. On being arrested, the police officer hit the Negro on the head with a pistol and when he attempted to run away, the officer fired three shots after him. Rumor spread to the camp that the soldier had been killed which, in fact, was not true. As a result 118 soldiers broke camp, armed themselves and began a reign of terror which ultimately ended on that day with the death of fifteen civilians and white military personnel. Growing out of this unfortunate incident were three separate trials which eventually resulted in a large number of convictions of mutiny. Three groups of soldiers were sentenced to be hanged. In all, twenty-two Negro rioters were executed at three different times. The largest number was the thirteen who met their death on the above date. Five others were sentenced to be hanged on September 7, 1918, and four additional at a later date, not verified.

Duff, quoted earlier, states that the police officer had attempted to arrest a colored woman and the soldier interfered by demanding her release. Regardless of the incident, it was permitted to flare

---

[16]*The County Kerchief*, pp. 88-89.

into a full-fledged race riot. Duff further stated that the thirteen
who were hanged went to the gallows singing "Lord, I'm Going
Home."[17] The contemporary press reflects the bitterness of that
dark day in San Antonio. The *New York Times* writes of the
hangings:

> In the dark of night army motor trucks conveyed the lumber
> for the scaffold to a little clearing in the lonely mesquite thicket
> on the Government reservation where the Negroes . . . were
> to die. There, by the light of the fires, army engineers erected
> the death traps to which, at five o'clock in the morning other
> motor trucks hurried the condemned Negroes and the officers
> and men of the military guard. It was the army motor truck
> that enabled the officers in charge to keep secret the time and
> the place of the hanging. It was the army truck that so quickly
> obliterated all traces of the execution and carried the bodies to
> a place nearby which is as indistinguishable as the execution
> site, before official announcement had been made of how the
> order of the court martial had been carried out.[18]

Langston Hughes, in his work dealing with the crusade of the
National Association for the Advancement of Colored People,
writes of this incident:

> The Negro soldiers, desperate over the brutalities of the
> Houston police and the taunts and insults of white civilians,
> had used their weapons in retaliation during the riots . . . after
> a number of Negro soldiers had been beaten and disarmed.
> The military court-marshal of these soldiers was the largest
> mass murder trial in the history of the United States. Negroes
> did not feel that these men had been given a fair chance.
> The *New York Age* cried: "So sure as there is a God in
> Heaven, at some time and in some way full justice will be done."
> The NAACP sent Martha Gruening, a white writer, to the
> scene of the Houston riots; her findings were reported in *The
> Crisis.* Just before Christmas the thirteen Negro soldiers were
> hanged.[19]

---

[17]*Ibid.,* pp. 85-86.

[18]December 12, 1917, page 7, col. 1.

[19]*Fight For Freedom: The Story of the NAACP,* p. 40; published by permission of the
Berkley Pub. Co., Inc., see also *The Crisis,* November 1917, 14-19 . . . article by
Martha Gruening ....

During the year 1945, fourteen Nazi prisoners of war were hanged at the United States Disciplinary Barracks at Fort Leavenworth, Kansas—but not all at one time. They had all been convicted of the same crime—that of murdering a fellow prisoner of war in a camp at Papago Park, Texas, allegedly for traitorous action against their homeland. Of the number hanged, five met their fate on July 10, two on July 14, and the remaining seven on August 25. Some Nazi spies were electrocuted in the District of Columbia jail during wartime but these executions are outside the purview of this study.

THE HANGING OF THE LINCOLN CONSPIRATORS IN WASHINGTON, D.C.

The details of the greatest conspiracy ever hatched in this country, that which culminated in the assassination of Abraham Lincoln, are too well-known to more than mention here. Our special interest is the execution of four persons, one a woman, who were convicted of participation in the senseless crime.

While there are areas that still baffle students of this episode in our history, most of the larger elements have long been established. The leader of the conspiracy, for instance, was John Wilkes Booth, whose role of assassin was unfortunately successful. His colleagues either did not respond to the perverted "call of duty," or botched their specific job. Several who were originally involved in the plot were not hanged. Some were sent to exiled imprisonment on Dry Tortugas, one of the Florida keys.

Those hanged, after what passed for a trial before a military commission, were George A. Atzerodt, who had been charged to kill the vice-president, Andrew Johnson, but who lost his nerve; David E. Herold and Lewis T. Payne, who attacked and wounded Secretary Seward, and Mrs. Mary E. Surratt, at whose boardinghouse the conspirators, with Booth, had met while planning their action. It was initially decided to kidnap President Lincoln, take him to Richmond, and force the federal government to exchange prisoners. But before this nefarious scheme could be consummated, the war was over. Booth and his henchmen then resolved on more serious objectives, the assassination of the president and other key members of the hated federal government.

It was on the evening of April 14, 1865, when the dreadful plot was put into effect. Booth shot the president and escaped to Virginia where he was apparently shot in a barn by a cavalry trooper, Boston Corbett. There has lingered through the years a vague belief that Booth actually got away and lived to a ripe old age. His fate, of course, is not a part of our story. The others were quickly rounded up, tried and sentenced.

The first stage in the dramatic event that was to take place on July 7, 1865, when the four condemned were to die, involves the manner in which the defendants received the news of their impending doom at the hands of Major-General W. S. Hancock. The prisoners were incarcerated in the Washington Arsenal at the time. Payne was the first to receive the decision of the tribunal. As the press reported the reception: "It did not seem to take him by surprise, as doubtless he had anticipated no other sentence and had nerved himself accordingly."[20] "Herold received the sentence at first with apparent unconcern, but afterward shed tears, while Atzerodt was completely unnerved, and groveled on the floor of his cell in abject horror." The most pathetic one of the group, Mrs. Surratt, "particularly sank under the dread announcement and pleaded for four days additional time to prepare herself for death" which was, of course, denied. The news report continues:

> The excitement in Washington and throughout the country on the announcement of the result of the trial, and the immediate execution ordered by the President, was very great. The most strenuous efforts were made to obtain a reprieve for Mrs. Surratt. By permission of the authorities, the daughter of Mrs. Surratt passed the night previous to the execution with her mother in her cell. The entire interview was of a very affecting

---

[20]The bulk of this material is taken from the news account of the New York *Weekly Tribune,* July 15, 1865, entitled "The End of the Assassins;" the authors are indebted to Mrs. Sara Ehrmann of Brookline, Massachusetts, Executive Secretary of the *American Society for the Abolition of Capital Punishment,* for this material. Another source is August Mencken's *By the Neck* (pp. 133-9) newspaper account of the hangings from the *Daily National Intelligencer,* Washington, D.C., July 8, 1865. See also, *Life Magazine,* April 16, 1965 for story of the plot entitled "A Hundred Years Ago." The magazine photographs for the first time the coarse canvas hoods designed by Secretary Stanton which the male conspirators were required to wear so as to render them incommunicado. The hoods are kept in the Smithsonian Institute.

character. During the morning the daughter proceeded to the Metropolitan Hotel and sought an interview with General Hancock. Finding him, she implored him in pitiable accents to get a reprieve for her mother. The General, of course had no power or grant to obtain such a favor and so informed the distressed girl in as gentle a manner as possible.

All Thursday afternoon, the day before the executions, the distraught daughter made frequent and desperate attempts to get to President Johnson for a possible reprieve for her mother. But the chief executive was well guarded by his aides and it is extremely doubtful that he would have acted in this matter. The daughter returned to the prison and requested the priests to prepare her mother for death as there was no hope. In the meantime, a delegation of priests managed to obtain an interview with President Johnson. They urged a short reprieve, at least, "on the grounds that the rites peculiar to their church required three days in which to prepare the doomed woman for death." However, the President insisted that the sentence be carried out as designated. Mrs. Douglas, widow of "the late senator [Stephen A. Douglas] made two personal attempts to gain a reprieve for Mrs. Surratt but the president was adamant."

Five of Herold's seven sisters "dressed in full mourning, and heavily veiled" attempted to see the chief executive but were also denied an audience. They then addressed a note to Mrs. Johnson which was not delivered on account of her illness. Next they tried to get a note through to the president's daughter, Mrs. Patterson, but she, too, "was indisposed." A frantic, last-minute legal maneuver to obtain a writ of habeas corpus for Mrs. Surratt also failed. Here is the official denial as signed by President Johnson:

Executive Office, July 7, 1865

To Major-General W. S. Hancock, Commanding, & c.

I, Andrew Johnson, President of the United States, do hereby declare that the writ of habeas corpus has been heretofore suspended in such cases as this; and I do hereby especially suspend this writ, and direct that you proceed to execute the order heretofore given upon the judgment of the Military Commission; and you will give this order in return to this writ.

Scene at the Hangings

From the *Daily National Intelligencer,* Washington, D.C.:

"The day of the execution was light and clear and at an early hour in the morning double guards were stationed all along Four-and-a-half Street from Pennsylvania Avenue to the Arsenal grounds. At the main entrance a strong guard was posted and no one was allowed admittance except such persons as carried passes signed by General Hancock. Early in the day a crowd began to assemble in the neighborhood but their pleadings for admission were unavailing . . . Those who held tickets, after reaching the Penitentiary building, passed around to the west gate of the wall and entered the yard where the scaffold was erected. . . .

"During the entire morning, the spiritual advisers of the condemned were with them. At 11 o'clock Herold was lying upon a cot and was pale and nervous. His sisters were with him and he listened attentively to all that the Rev. Dr. Olds had to say to him. Payne sat upright in his cell, listening to what was said relative to his salvation. Fathers Wiget and Walter were exceedingly earnest with regard to Mrs. Surratt and prayed with her the entire morning. Her daughter was with her up to 12 o'clock and Mrs. Surratt gave her directions as to the disposition of her property after her death. Atzerodt was counseled by the Rev. Dr. Butler. He was visited during the morning by his mother and his wife,[21] and before being taken to execution he made a statement to Dr. Butler relative to his part in the crime.

"At half past twelve o'clock Herold's sisters, seven in number, passed from the cell of their brother after having bid him a farewell until eternity. They were weeping bitterly and their tears and moans told sensibly upon the stoutest hearts present. A few minutes afterward all who were in the building were ordered to go around and enter the west gate. . .

"The scaffold was erected during Thursday night. It was erected in the south yard of the building and was twenty feet long, fifteen feet wide, and ten feet high to the floor and twenty

---

[21]The New York *Weekly Tribune* says of Atzerodt: "In conversation with his former mistress he could be distinctly seen. He frequently used his handkerchief to remove the perspiration from his face, and occasionally sobbed quietly, as she addressed him, apparently in a feeling manner."

to the beam. A beam ran through the center of the platform, east and west, and upon each side of this beam and on the west side of the platform was a drop. Each drop was six feet long, by four feet wide and over each drop and suspended from the top beam hung two ropes made of strong hemp, the slip noose of each rope being formed by nine twists and a knot. The drops were suspended by uprights which, being knocked away, would allow the drops to fall. The steps leading to the platform were on the east side and it was intended that the prisoners would face the west. A few feet southeast of the scaffold four graves, each one four feet deep, seven feet long and three feet wide, had been dug and were intended for the reception of the remains of the condemned prisoners. Beside these graves the coffins, made of plain pine boards, had been placed."

The following is from the New York *Weekly Tribune,* July 15, 1865:

"At ten minutes to 1 o'clock Gen. Hancock personally posted the sentries around the scaffold, and the outer guards were ordered to come to attention, preparatory to the appearance of the prisoners. At precisely 1 o'clock Gen. Hartranft and Staff emerged from the Prison, and a moment after were followed by the condemned.

Mrs. Surratt came first, dressed in black, supported on either side by an officer and followed by her spiritual advisers . . . She wore a black bonnet and veil as on the trial, and had to be almost entirely supported by the officers attending her.

Next came Atzerodt, also supported by a soldier on either side, and dressed about as he was on the trial, and bareheaded. He was attended by his spiritual advisers. Then came Herold, dressed in his ordinary prison clothes, with a slouch cloth hat on, the brim being turned down. He, too, was much prostrated and had to be supported. He was followed by his spiritual advisers . . . . Payne alone came bold and erect, without any support, a guard walking on either side of him. He was dressed in a blue shirt and pants, with a rather jaunty straw hat on, and was followed by his spiritual advisers. . .

"Payne alone of the prisoners, ascended the scaffold without the support of his attendants. Four wooden armchairs had been placed there for the reception of the prisoners and they were seated as follows: facing West, Mrs. Surratt, on the North next to the prison; Payne sat next; Herold next, and Atzerodt next; Mrs. Surratt and Payne opposite one drop, and Herold and Atzerodt opposite the other, the five-eighths manilla rope, with its ominous noose, dangling before each respectively, the nooses reaching to within an average of eighteen inches from the floor.

"On the prisoners being seated, or rather sinking into their chairs, the findings and sentences of the Military Commission, as approved by the President and already published, was read in a clear calm voice by Major-General Hartranft, standing in the middle of the platform.

"The appearance of the prisoners as they sat there in a row facing the West, and the crowd and Gardiner's photographic instruments peering from the upper windows of an opposite building, and the ropes swaying in the breeze immediately before them, was that of agony ineffable. The thought came rushing upon the mind of the spectator: 'Oh! What they would not give if they could undo the fatal acts that have consigned them to this agony and infamy!'

"Mrs. Surratt was very much prostrated, and seemed to be kept alive almost entirely by the spiritual consolations of her advisers who were unremitting in their attention to the end . . . When about to rise from her chair for the purpose of being pinioned, she inquired what she should say on the scaffold and, upon being answered "O, nothing—what do you desire to say?" replied, "That I am innocent."

Prior to the drop, the condemned Payne (which was an alias for his real name, Lewis Thornton Powell) thanked General Hartranft and all the attending officers for their courtesies throughout his ordeal in prison. This was followed by the spiritual advisers of Atzerodt and Herold who also expressed thanks for their treatment on the part of the officers. Prayers were then uttered by the various ministers and all was in readiness for the fatal denouement, which final climax the entire country awaited.

"On the conclusion of the prayers . . . the prisoners were led forward . . . and the ropes adjusted around the neck by different persons. About the same time, Mrs. Surratt seemed, by a desperate mental effort, to nerve herself up specially for this occasion, looking forward and around her, for the only time, with an air of mingled determination and resignation. Her bonnet and veil were removed previous to the putting of the noose upon her neck.

"Payne held back and was particular about having the noose adjusted and secured by tightening above his 'Adam's apple,' as if it had been the adjustment of a cravat for a festive occasion.

"Herold and Adzerodt, during the process of adjusting the ropes, looked as if experiencing ineffable agony, as well as Mrs. Surratt, who was now bordering on a fainting condition and was kept conscious only by the assiduous fanning and other attentions of her attendants. Payne stood erect and unsupported, and he alone, it was said by one of the spiritual advisers, had come upon the scaffold without indulgence in stimulants, which he had steadily refused, saying that he wished to die with an unclouded mind. . . .

"At the conclusion of the address of Atzerodt's spiritual attendant and his deeply solemn and feeling petition to Heaven for Divine clemency, he was conducted to the drop by his attendants, and while the white cotton bands were being tied about his legs and arms, exhibited great weakness and emotion, being scarcely able to remain in an erect position. The noose was then placed about his neck, and previous to its final adjustment he addressed a few inaudible words to his executioner, and the rope was removed. Gen. Hartranft then approached, when Atzerodt evidently repeated his request, and the noose was then drawn over his head, when he exclaimed in a terrified voice, "Gentlemen, take warn . . ." probably intending to say, what his agonized feelings prevented him from expressing: "Gentlemen, take warning by my example." A moment after and he tremblingly ejaculated, "Good bye, gentlemen, who are before me now." And, after a short interval added, "May we all meet in the other world."

As the rope was being adjusted to his neck, and just before the drop fell, he cried out in a rather loud voice, "Don't choke me." These were the last words he uttered, which were succeeded by several audible groans.

"At this juncture the noose and white caps having all been adjusted, Capt. Rath, Assistant Provost-Marshall, having immediate charge of the execution, stepped in front of the scaffold, on the ground, and motioned to all attendants on the scaffold to step back off the drops, which they did, the proper ones still reaching forward and supporting their charges respectively on the drop. Immediately on this movement, Capt. Rath also gave the signal for the props to be knocked from under, which was done by a swinging scantlin for each shoved longitudinally; and the four conspirators, having fallen about five feet each, were left dangling spasmodically in the air.

"The contortions of Payne were the greatest, attributable to his highest physical condition. Herold died next hardest. The deaths of Mrs. Surratt and Atzerodt were comparatively easy. Mrs. Surratt, on falling, made a convulsive effort to bring her hands around her right side in front of her and they remained in such contorted position until she was cut down. After the convulsions of all were over, Mrs. Surratt, Payne and Atzerodt hung with their heads bent forward, while that of Herold inclined back, which later was said by experts to be the only execution on correct principles.

"After the bodies had hung about twenty minutes they were pronounced lifeless by the surgeons officiating, and were cut down, laid on the rough pine boxes, respectively, which had ranged in front of them, and were there examined again. The neck of Mrs. Surratt was pronounced positively broken and that of Herold probably.[22] The knot had caught under the base of the skull, in the case of Payne and Atzerodt, in such a manner as to make it uncertain about their necks having been broken. The bodies were put in the boxes in the same order in which they had been hung. A small bottle containing the name of each person was put in with the corpse, and [they] were buried in four graves, about five feet deep, that had been dug in the east side of the yard . . .

"A late dispatch says that the military authorities at Washington, after due consideration, have concluded to deliver the bodies of the four executed convicts to their friends for burial. The disinterment will take place immediately. Much sympathy is expressed for Miss Annie Surratt, who took her mother's fate so hardly and made such strenuous personal efforts to procure her pardon, and also for the friends of Herold and Atzerodt . . . A very bitter feeling exists in relation to Mrs. Surratt's summary execution among quondam Rebels, and, particularly, among the Catholics

---

[22]The Washington *Daily National Intelligencer* account states "not a neck was broken so far as the surgeons could ascertain."

of the city, who, it is rumoured, intend to call meetings for the purpose of denouncing the action of the Military Commission and the President."

THE COMMANDANT OF ANDERSONVILLE PRISON — CAPT. HENRY WIRZ

This generation of devotees of history and the historic novelist have become aware, to a degree at least, of Andersonville Prison, thanks in large part to MacKinlay Kantor. Yet few persons know much about that cesspool prison and the human misery that flowed from it. The following few words are all that may be found in one of our popular, contemporary encyclopedias that cater to our growing generation of school children:

> *Andersonville,* Georgia: village 52 miles s.w. Macon; pop. 281; site of Civil War Confederate prison in which over 12,000 died; burial ground now a national shrine.

The commandant of that unhappy prison was Capt. Henry Wirz. He was hanged at Washington, D.C., on November 10, 1865, a victim, many people have since said, "of Civil War fever." He had the misfortune of being the commandant of the worst of all prison camps, Andersonville, in southern Georgia. Over 12,000 Union soldiers died during its existence and the hundreds of stories that came out of this fetid miasma of human degradation can scarcely be duplicated in this country at any time or at any place.

The blame for this tragic episode can scarcely be placed on any one person. As Sherman is supposed to have said, "War is hell;" and Andersonville prison was indeed a part of this hell. There is little doubt that a complex of conditions existing at that specific time of the War Between the States largely set the stage for the situation at this camp and Capt. Wirz, a rather ineffectual person, was caught in a vice from which he was unable to extricate himself.

The period immediately after war's end was charged with vindictiveness and malice, despite the kindly words of President Lincoln who became a martyr to compassion and justice. Wirz, a native of Switzerland who had emigrated to this country in 1849, became a kind of physician on a Louisiana plantation. At the outbreak of the war, he enlisted as a private in the Confederate Army and was assigned as a clerk in the Richmond prisons. Sometime in 1863, he was placed in charge of the Andersonville prison, a position which no one could have filled satisfactorily, given the existing conditions. At his trial, he was charged with everything from murder on down the list of offenses. There seems to be a feeling that he was convicted on very dubious evidence. But he was sentenced to hang. That took place only a few months after the Lincoln "conspirators" were led to their doom.

The *New York Tribune,* for November 14, tells the story of Wirz's execution as well as a description of the victim in his death cell prior to the hanging. His wife came on several occasions to see him and on the last visit she was caught attempting to transmit some strychnine to her husband. It was concealed in a "little ball enclosed in oil silk and coated with licorice." From then on, Wirz became stolid, almost stoical regarding his fate. He possessed an attitude of contempt for the government, making the statement: "I'm damned if the Yankee eagle has not turned to what I expected, a damned turkey buzzard." Wirz was a large person, approximately six feet in height. He wore his hair long and possessed a full beard. He went to the gallows bravely and contended that he was innocent of all crimes. As the *Tribune* ended its account: "Wirz's life was not worth much to him or his death worth much to the nation. Many a greater criminal has been pardoned and many better men hanged. The public conscience will probably be satisfied as if a great act of justice had been done."[23]

THE HANGING OF TWENTY MOLLIE MAGUIRES IN PENNSYLVANIA

There is a heavy literature concerning the Mollie Maguires, the terroristic secret society that dominated the political life of several counties in the Pennsylvania coal region during the decades 1860 and 1870. Looking backward, we can afford to be more charitable of his harassing and harassed group of Irish immigrants although, obviously, we cannot condone their evil methods of gaining their

---

[23]See Mencken, *By the Neck,* pp. 114-119.

rights in the labor struggle.[24] No honest critic of labor can excuse the coal barons of the Pennsylvania anthracite region of that era for their exploitive methods nor excuse the dominant earlier settlers of the region—the Welsh and the English—for excluding the later Irish immigrants from earning a living in the mines. The story of the Mollie Maguires is certainly not one-sided.

It was long since stated "where Attila's charger put down his hoof, no grass grew; where Mrs. Mollie Maguire's brogan was put down there was an ugly mark—a corpse." This bastard, or perverted form of fraternalism took the name from, or rather, symbolized, a fictitious old Irish woman who was obsessed with destroying the British in the homeland of these homesick and almost degraded immigrant coal miners. They resented their economic lot which was a hard one and were particularly determined to undermine the power of the coal companies and their bosses.

Like the "Black Hand," or Mafia, the Mollies were highly secret in their organization and ruled the towns and mines of the area through intimidation, terror, mayhem, and murder. They gradually gained political power locally and, to a degree, in judicial and state circles so that they became a serious menace to the economic and political life in Schuylkill, Carbon, Columbia, and Northumberland, the heart of the anthracite coal country.

The coal companies, in order to meet this form of strong-arm methods, called upon the Pinkerton detective agency. It was then that a young Irishman named James McParlan entered the region and, assuming the name of McKenna, posed as a "green goods" man hiding out as a fugitive counterfeiter. His task was to infiltrate the society, to learn their secrets and to bring the perpetrators who were responsible for the murders of coal company executives to book. Through this disguise, aided by his native Irish brogue, he was able in time to gain the confidence of the Mollies and to collect knowledge of their nefarious conspiracy against law and order. This he used against them as they were slowly but inexoribly brought to trial.

---

[24]For an excellent apologia for the group, see Arthur H. Lewis, *Lament for the Mollie Maguires,* New York, Harcourt Brace & World, 1964. For an excellent objective work see Wayne G. Broehl, Jr. *The Mollie Maguires,* Harvard University Press, 1964.

Carrying this law enforcement to its necessary conclusion, which was ultimately done, required great courage on the part of police, jurists, and hundreds of common citizens who were called upon to testify at their trials, because of the terrific pressure and intimidation.

The first group of the Mollies to be hanged consisted of ten men, all executed on June 21, 1877—six at Pottsville, Schuylkill County, and four at Mauch Chunk, in Carbon County. Known locally as "Black Thursday," the mass hanging in the jail yard of the county seat at Pottsville, the affair will never be forgotten. Those hanged in this place were James Boyle, James Carroll, Thomas Duffy, Hugh McGehan, James Roarity, all for the murder of B. F. Yost, a Tamaqua policeman on July 5, 1875, and Thomas Munley, for the murder of two mine employees, Thomas Sanger and William Uren.

The local paper, the *Miner's Journal,* did a fine job in reporting this mass hanging. It stated that the streets outside were packed with a curious but well-behaved crowd and "only 150 who had passes were admitted within the jail yard"; but fully 3,000 were admitted after the executions to view the scaffolds. The six Mollies were hanged in pairs and all evidence indicates that they died gamely and with spiritual counseling.[25]

On the same day, but at Mauch Chunk (now known as Jim Thorp), four more of the secret society were hanged. These were Alexander Campbell, Michael Doyle, and Edward Kelly, all for the murder of John P. Jones, a mine boss, and the fourth, John "Yellow Jack" Donahue, for the killing of Morgan Phillips, another mine boss. A special train brought the bodies of these four Mollies to Pottsville.

This was only the beginning of the retribution. Others who were hanged, with name of county and victims were: Patrick Tully, Patrick Hester and Peter McHugh at Bloomsburg, Columbia County, on March 25, 1878, for the murder of Alexander Rea, a coal mining superintendent, on August 17, 1868; Thomas P. Fisher at Mauch Chunk, on March 28, 1878, for his participation in the murder of Morgan Phillips on December 2, 1871; Dennis

---

[25]August Mencken, *By the Neck,* 1942, pp. 98-108; he reprints the *New York Tribune* story of June 22.

Donnelly at Pottsville, on June 11, 1878, for his participation in the murders of Sanger and Uren; John Kehoe, at Pottsville on December 18, 1878, for the murder of Frank Landon on June 14, 1862 (note: sixteen years earlier); Charles Sharpe and James McDonnell at Mauch Chunk, on January 14, 1879, for the slaying of George K. Smith on November 5, 1863; Martin Bergan at Pottsville on January 16, 1879, for the murder of Patrick Burns a bookkeeper; and last of all, Peter McManus at Sunbury, Northumberland County on October 9, 1879, for the murder of Frederick Hesser, a night watchman at one of the mines.

Law and order were finally established in the region, but it took vast sums of money, courage and a sustained determination on the part of public officials and citizens alike to demonstrate that the forces of outlawry and nihilism have no place in this free country. Aside from the hanging of the thirty-eight Sioux Indians at Mankato, Minnesota, this mass hanging is the largest ever held in this country. It exceeds the witch orgy of New England by one lone victim of the gallows.

CHARLES JULIUS GUITEAU, PRESIDENTIAL ASSASSIN

Four presidents of the United States have been assassinated—Abraham Lincoln, James A. Garfield, William McKinley and John Fitzgerald Kennedy. The assassins of all four met an ignominious death; John Wilkes Booth, shot to death in a Virginia barn by an obscure soldier, member of the searching party; Charles J. Guiteau, killer of Garfield, hanged at Washington, D.C.; Leon F. Czolgosz, *alias* Fred Nieman, assassin of McKinley at Buffalo, N.Y. electrocuted at Auburn State Prison of that state on October 29, 1901; and Lee Harvey Oswald, alleged sniper-killer of President Kennedy, on November 22, 1963, by another sniper named Jack Ruby two days later, on November 24, after Oswald had been arrested for the shooting of the President.

The accompanying sketch is one of Guiteau, self-styled champion of frustrated office-seekers. August Mencken calls him "The Jobholders' Moses".[26]

In the earlier days of the Republic, there was no such thing as civil service. Thus, whenever there was a change of administration

[26]*Op. cit.,* pp. 81-92.

in Washington, those who felt they had contributed to the new regime believed—through the old "spoils system"—they were entitled to a federal job. But there were always many more seekers than jobs.

The head of the party—the newly-elected president—was the fountainhead of the jobs available; so, like locusts, the office-seekers swooped down on the White House, making of themselves a serious nuisance. Guiteau, erstwhile Y.M.C.A. hanger-on, lawyer-swindler, and disgruntled member of the Oneida Community was born at Freeport, Illinois, on September 8, 1841. He became convinced that the Republican Party was beholden to him for some campaigning he had done in New York State during the 1880 election. After Garfield took office, he went to Washington and applied for a consular position either in Austria or Paris. He hounded both the State Department and the White House but with no success.

Focusing the blame for his frustration entirely upon the president, Guiteau decided that success for him could only come by removing the completely innocent President and relying on the incumbent vice-president, Chester A. Arthur.

As Thomas McDade describes Guiteau and his mental state: "Actually Guiteau was by modern medical, if not legal, standards insane. All of his life bears evidence of the crank, the deluded, and the obsessed. As a lawyer (with little or no real training) he collected small debts and kept most of the proceeds for his fee. He wrote tracts on Bible exegisis, gave lectures in halls about the country and was always either being sued or himself threatening to sue for some pretended wrongs."[27] Even his former wife, a Mrs. Dunmire wrote a pamphlet about his "erratic career".

Before killing Garfield, he hounded his goings and comings but apparently could not muster enough courage to kill him. As McDade states: "He bought a revolver, tried it on the trees bordering the Potomac, and followed Garfield's movements through the newspapers. After passing up several chances to do the deed in church and when Garfield was walking on the streets at night, he finally shot him in the railroad station . . . "

---

[27]*Op. cit.*, item 399.

He had learned that the president was about to take a vacation trip, so he hid himself in the Baltimore & Ohio station in Washington. As his innocent victim walked through the train shed to his private car, the obsessed Guiteau shot him. He was immediately seized and jailed. The president hovered between life and death but finally succumbed on September 19, 1881, two and a half months after the fatal shot had been fired. He had been taken to the seashore resort of Long Branch, New Jersey, to escape the oppressive heat of Washington. Shortly thereafter, the assassin was tried, convicted and hanged. The date of his execution was June 30, 1882.

The newspapers made much of the execution. The *New York Tribune* for July 1, in a lengthy story, described the doomed man's movements, moment by moment, up to the final one as he dropped into eternity. The account did not ignore a detail—what his breakfast consisted of, how he was dressed, his last request to have his boots blackened, the visits of his brother and sister to his cell, his fainting spell and his revival before he started the last long walk to the scaffold. The crowd was described "of blacks of all classes, from the gaily-dressed lady of color to the tough boys and wenches who passed their time fooling and giggling."

There was much speculation whether or not Guiteau would carry on without collapsing. He faltered at the gallows but tried desparately to be brave to the end. He read from the Bible: Matthew, 10:28: "And fear not them which kill the body, but are not able to kill the soul; but rather fear him who is able to destroy both soul and body in hell." He closed his eyes and made the following statement: "I tremble for the fate of my murderers . . . This nation will go down in the blood . . . My murderers, from the Executive to the hangman, will go to Hell."

Next he insisted on reading some crude doggerel that he had composed that morning in his cell which, as he said "indicate my feelings at the moment of leaving this world," and "if set to music might be rendered effective." He described them as that "of a child babbling to his mamma and papa." Here they are as delivered by Guiteau on the scaffold:

> I am going to the Lordy,
> I am so glad,

> I am going to the Lordy,
>   I am so glad.
> Glory, hallelujah, Glory, hallelujah!

Then, after repeating the above:

> I saved my party and my land,
>   Glory, hallelujah,
> But they have murdered me for it,
>   And that is the reason,
> I am going to the Lordy,
>   Glory, hallelujah! Glory hallelujah!
> I am going to the Lordy

After the drop fell, a meticulous autopsy was made by the physicians. A careful examination of his brain was made and pictures were taken of it. The news report continues by making the following prediction: "A visit to the jail will no doubt be a regular feature of the sight-seeing of bridal couples hereafter. Several of them have been there and seemed to enjoy their visit . . . Within a year the guards expect to see the gallows hacked to pieces by the relic-hunters."

With Charles Julius Guiteau's death on the gallows the national security of our chief executive was assured until President McKinley's assassination in Buffalo. While officiating at the Pan-American Exposition in that city he was shot by what was termed an "anarchist," one Leon Czolgosz, on September 6, 1901. He died on September 14.

THE HANGING OF THE CHICAGO ANARCHISTS — NOVEMBER 11, 1887

The four men hanged on November 11, 1887, in Chicago, Illinois, were known as anarchists, and were members of the International Workers Association. They were also referred to as the Haymarket Anarchists because of the bombing that occurred on the night of May 4 at Haymarket Square. In that violent but tragically futile act, which was directed at the police, eight officers were killed and several others seriously injured.

This event was the culmination of a series of labor troubles between union and non-union employees of the McCormick Reaper

Company and a strike for an eight-hour-day which affected as many as 50,000 men and their families. Bitterness and unbridled hatred ran rampant during the weeks and days that preceded the dreadful shambles of May 4. The small group of anarchists that agitated the workers during this period maintained that the only way to bring about labor peace and prosperity was to confiscate all property and liquidate its owners.

One of their leaders was George Engel. At a meeting in Bohemian Hall, on May 2, he proposed that all police-stations be seized and prisoners in the jails freed and enlisted in the workers' ranks. The following day, August Spies, another agitator, incited an attack of the Lumber-shover's Union on the McCormick plant.

It was decided among the workers to adopt Engel's proposal so a meeting was called for the evening of May 4. Many police were on hand. A rabble-rouser named Fielde called out "We are peacable" and at the last word of this apparent signal, a bomb was thrown into the ranks of the police. After the first panic, the officers rallied and charged into the crowd. At the time, all of the principals escaped. However, later the following were arrested: August Spies, Albert R. Parsons, Adolph Fisher, George Engel (all of whom were hanged) and Fielde, Lingg, Schwab, and Neebe. Fielde and Schwab received life imprisonment, Neebe, fifteen years, and Lingg committed suicide, in jail, by exploding a dynamite cap in his mouth. The three imprisoned men served seven years and were pardoned by Governor John Peter Altgeld.

There can be little doubt that this was one of the bloodiest cases in the long struggle of labor to secure more of the profits of production. Several pamphlets, representing various versions of the affair, were published following the trial. The titles of some of these were at least vivid, if not frightening. The police version was labeled: "Anarchy and anarchists; a history of the red terror and the social revolution in America and Europe." Another: "Anarchy at an end . . . A history of the most deliberate planned and murderous bomb throwing of ancient or modern times."[28]

The hanging of the quartet was witnessed by nearly 200 persons, fifty of whom were from the press. The affair was carrried out

---

[28]See McDade items, 451-9.

expeditiously and without incident. The victims, one by one, cried out, extolling anarchy with a defiant air. Fischer's voice sounded like a trumpet as he yelled: "Long live Anarchy!" He was followed by Engel who echoed his words. Then Fisher shouted: "This is the happiest moment of my life." Parsons asked to be heard and in a low voice asked: "Oh men of America" then, after a pause, "Shall the voice of the people be heard?" Only Spies seemed unagitated. But he, too, said in a thick muted voice: "Our silence will be more powerful than the voices they are going to strangle today."

The *Chicago Tribune*, for November 12, 1887, presents a detailed and graphic account of the executions as well as the meticulous examination of the bodies by the physicians following the gruesome event.[29]

"HANGING" JUDGE ISAAC C. PARKER, NEMESIS OF THE OUTLAWS OF THE INDIAN COUNTRY

Many schoolboys have vaguely heard of the "Hanging Judge" who sent "bad men" to their doom in some nebulous western part of our country at some equally nebulous time in its history. Aside from those in and "west of Fort Smith" Arkansas, who have absorbed details of their local history, few Americans today know very much about the highly controversial federal judge, Isaac Charles Parker (1838 - 1896) and his twenty-one-year campaign to bring law and order to the Indian country that now comprises several of our southwestern states. At the time, the area was better known as the lands of the Cherokee, Creek, Choctaw, and Chickasaw Nations.

The area was infested by hundreds of roving criminals who wantonly murdered men, women and children, or pillaged and raped, without any show of pity or remorse. These villains were far from being romatic or gallant. Rather they were the dregs of humanity, boasting for years that they could continue their lawless acts with impunity.

This may have been relatively true, prior to the coming of Judge Parker to the region to assume the post of legal representative

---

[29]See August Mencken, *By the Neck*, pp. 72-80; see also, Thomas S. Duke, *Celebrated Criminal Cases of America*, San Francisco, 1910, pp. 395-405.

of the government with headquarters at Fort Smith. This was in 1875. From that year until 1896, when he retired, he meted out justice day after day, with no pause for holidays or vacations. Only on Sundays was his court recessed. It opened early in the morning and did not close until late evening.

The story of Judge Parker and his sustained, fanatical determination to clear the territory of these murderers and thieves is told in detail by Glenn Shirley in his *Law West of Fort Smith,*[30] and by Homer Croy in his *He Hanged Them High.*[31] Much of the following material is from Shirley's work, with occasional references to Croy's more journalistic volume.

Croy has set down the amount of "work" done by Judge Parker in his notorious court from the time he assumed charge in 1871, until he gave up his arduous duties in 1896. Here it is in tabular form:

13,499 cases docketed
 9,454 convictions
   344 cases punishable by death tried
   172 sentenced to be hanged
    88 actually hanged[32]

The reasons why all of those sentenced to death did not meet the gallows are:

  1 killed while trying to escape
  1 judged insane and placed in an asylum
  5 died in prison
  2 pardoned after being sentenced
 23 given new trials and appeal
 43 commuted by the President usually to life imprisonment
  1 released on bond while awaiting trial and neglected to come back[33]

With the work of some 200 deputy marshals, sixty of whom were killed in the line of duty, Judge Parker carried on his relentless

---

[30]New York, Holt, Rinehart & Winston, 1954.

[31]New York, Duell, Sloane & Pearce, 1952.

[32]Shirley lists 79 executed; in Appendix A of his work cited above, in a "Chronology of Hangings' he lists (pp. 210-231) all of these cases by name and date of hanging.

[33]Croy, *op. cit.,* p. 10.

campaign to bring the desperadoes of this dreary endless wasteland to justice. His colorful executioner, George Maledon, was a sharp-shooting officer of the frontier who took great pride in his profession. As Shirley puts it: "his ropes were made of chosen hemp fiber, woven by hand in St. Louis, and treated with a pitchy oil substance to prevent slipping."[34] This bewhiskered "Prince of Hangmen," as he was called by many as he presided over his scaffold, referred to by some journalists as the "Gates of Hell," toured the country for many years after he retired from his gruelling and exacting duties and put on a good show with some of his ropes and other hanging paraphenalia (see Chap. IV, p. 159).

The seventy-nine men who were sent to the gallows by Judge Parker and his wooden-faced executioner met their deaths singly, in pairs, in trios and, in two instances, in sextets. The first infamous sextet, hanged September 3, 1875, consisted of Daniel Evans who had murdered a nineteen-year-old boy named William Seabolt; William Whittington, who killed an elderly man named Turner; James Moore, bad man extraordinary who had killed his eighth victim, Deputy Marshall William Spivey; Snoker Mankiller, an Indian who had treacherously murdered a neighbor, William Short, after borrowing his victim's rifle; Samuel Fooey, another Indian who murdered the "Barefoot School Teacher," John Emmet Neff; and Edmund Campbell, a Negro, who had senselessly killed Lawson Ross and his mistress.[35]

Judge Parker, a devout man, always commented about the criminal's deed and admonished him to prepare to meet his "Maker." Typical is: "Your fate is inevitable. Let me, therefore, beg of you to fly to your Maker for that mercy and pardon which you cannot expect from mortals . . . and endeavor to seize upon the salvation of His Cross."[36]

One must read the roll call of the scoundrels who terrorized the Indian country during these hectic days in order to gain even a modicum of understanding regarding the era of lawlessness that ran rampant during and prior to the Judge Parker incumbency.

---

[34]*Op. cit.*, p. 80.

[35]*Ibid.*, see Chapter 3.

[36]*Ibid.*, p. 37.

There was the notorious Bill Cook (real name William Tuttle) who was given a long prison sentence, the infamous Dalton gang, four of whom were killed at Coffeeville, Kansas October 5, 1892, the extremely unglamorous Belle Starr, female scourge of the area who was killed from ambush.

Then there was the vicious Rufus Buck gang who were taken alive and hanged at Fort Smith on July 1, 1896—five of them. Glenn Shirley says of this vicious quintet whose career lasted but thirteen days: "In that thirteen days they made a criminal record that, considering the time they operated, faded the Starrs, the Daltons, the Rogers and Cook gangs combined. Their acts were heinous and terrifying. They never rose to the level of bandits. They were simply ravishers. Undoubtedly they were the most depraved band of outlaws in America."[37] The five hanged on that fateful day were the gangleader Rufus Buck and Lucky Davis, Lewis Davis, Sam Sampson and Maoma July. Buck was a full-blooded Euchee Indian, Sampson and Maoma July were Creeks and the Davises were mixtures of Creek and Negro. Robbery and rape were their principal crimes. They were tried and hanged for the rape of a farm woman, Rosetta Hassan. As Shirley briefly tells the story of the episode: "They appeared at the home of Henry Hassan . . . and after forcing his wife to prepare dinner for them and gorging themselves like ravenous wolves, they seized and tied her down with a rope, and each took his turn assaulting her while the others held her husband at bay with Winchesters. They then amused themselves by making Hassan and his hired man . . . fight each other and dance, shooting at their heels to make the affair more lively."[38]

Posses from Fort Smith were on the lookout for these desperadoes and subsequently one of them surprised the gang and, after a seven-hour battle, captured them alive. A sigh of relief went up from the settlers near the Creek Nation, as well as from the population of Fort Smith. They were soon convicted and dispatched by hangman George Maledon.

---

[37]*Ibid.*, p. 159.

[38]*Ibid.*, pp. 160-1.

In Rufus Buck's cell was found a picture of his mother with the
following illiterate poem inscribed on the back of it:

My, dreAm, — 1896
i, dremp'T, i, was, in, heAven,
Among, THe, AngeLs, Fair;
i'd, neAr, seen, none, so HAndsome.
THAT, TWine, in golden, HAir,
THey, looked, so, neAT, And; sAng, so, sweeT,
And, PLAY'd THe, golden HArp,
i, wAs, ABout, To, Pick An, ANgel, ouT,
And, TAke, Her, To, mY, HeArT,
BuT, THe, momenT, i, BegAn, To, PLeA,
i, THougHT, oF, You, mY, Love,
THere, wAs, none, i'd, seen, so BeAuTiFuLL,
On, eArTH, or, HeAven, ABove,
gooD, By, My, Dear, Wife, anD, MoTHer
all, so, My, sisTers
RUFUS BUCK
youse Truley
i Day,of, JUly
Tu, THe, Yeore,
off 1896

H
O
L
Y
FATHER   Son
G
H
O
S
T

virue & resurresur.rection,
RememBer, Me, ROCK, OF, Ages:[39]

---

[39]Reproduced as above in Shirley, *op. cit.,* p. 174; also in Olive Woolley Burt, *American Murder Ballads*, p. 211.

Judge Parker's career came to an end in 1896—the year of his death on November 17. Substitutes had taken over his duties with a rather certain knowledge that he would not recover from the illness which proved to be terminal. On hearing the announcement of his death, the prisoners in the jail, who were awaiting trial, shouted with many "whooplas" and ribald rejoicings. One sang out: "The devil's shore got the ole cuss dis time" and another shouted "is he dead? Whoopee!"

Thus ended an era which was a distinct phase of our social history. It, like Parker's grave in the cemetery at Fort Smith, is all but forgotten, except for local people who know them as legend, and a few historians interested in that era.

Judge Isaac Parker is variously remembered but, among those who know only the barest outlines of his career, he is referred to as the "Hanging Judge," cruel, "hardboiled," and perhaps even sadistic and without feeling. But among those who actually knew him, such as journalists who interviewed him, he was the conscientious public servant, kindly, humane, and deeply religious. He realized he had a disagreeable duty to perform and he did it unflinchingly and without personal malice. He has been referred to as the "greatest judge in all the history of the West," a "necessity in the administration of the law of the Indian country."[40]

We do not intend to condone the execution of any of Judge Parker's "victims." His actions were part of a time of violence and they reflected that violence. As one writer puts it: "In one respect Judge Parker's court was unique. The first fourteen years of the twenty-one years during which he presided over it were free of interference by other courts, even the Supreme Court of the United States. His judgments were irrevocable. There was no appeal."[41]

Homer Croy relates the story of the "fanciful bit of journalism" that emerged in the Fort Smith *Weekly Elevator,* which suggested

---

[40]Shirley, *op. cit.,* p. 205.

[41]Paul P. Wellman, *A Dynasty of Western Outlaws,* p. 127, copyright © 1964 by Paul I. Wellman. Reproduced by permission of Doubleday & Co., Inc.

the following be placed on a memorial slab on the site of the gallows so efficiently operated by the hangman, Maledon:

> On this Unhallowed spot stood the Great Pacificator
> Of the Indian Territory.
> Erected 1873, burned 1897.
>   With a Short Shrift
>   And a long rope,
>   Nearly one hundred
>   Of the Worst Outlaws
> Who were a Terror on the Frontier—
>   Were executed
> In a business like manner—
>   In job lots, wholesale and retail
> And with neatness and dispatch,
> To the Great Relief of the citizens of the
>   Indian Country, giving them security of life
>   and a new era of peace, due to the
>   enforcement of the law and to the moral
>   persuasion of the celebrated gallows[42]

BANDITRY IN EARLY CALIFORNIA

Just as law and order came slowly to the section west of Fort Smith, as we have noted above, so did it eventually emerge in the rough-and-tumble state of California. This period in the state's history cannot be told without substantial space being set aside for the analysis and operation of vigilantism but we can no more than mention it here.[43] We have, however, succumbed to the temptation to tell the story of the only female every lynched by vigilantism in California and to touch briefly on the terrorism of the notorious Joaquin Murieta, only by way of actually telling the story of the bandit, Tiburcio Vasquez who was legally hanged at San José, Santa Clara County, on March 19, 1875.

The sad plight of the female, known only as Juanita, a comely Mexican, is well-known to California historians. She lived in a shack on the outskirts of Downieville, sharing her bed with a

---

[42]Croy, *op. cit.*, p. 229. Permission Duell, Sloane & Pearce.

[43]For a good story of this see John W. Caughey, *Their Majesties the Mob: The Vigilante Impulse in America*, Chicago, University of Chicago Press, 1960. ©1960 by the University of Chicago Press.

gambler. On the night of July 4, 1851, after a celebration of the nation's independence, an intoxicated citizen of the town, one Joseph Cannon, stumbled into the woman's abode. Frightened at the intrusion, the woman grabbed a knife and stabbed him to death. It has always been believed that Cannon, on realizing he was in the wrong house, was about to apologize but this gallant gesture was obviously lost on the terror-stricken Mexican woman. She was dragged from her home, subjected to a vigilante court held in the public square and summarily sentenced to death. John Caughey describes the hanging on that fatal day:

> Some one stated that the woman was with child, and the question was raised whether the execution should be delayed. An examination was held, and that statement pronounced false. Then they gave her half an hour to get ready to die. She was finally taken down to the bridge, where there was a scantling tied from one upright to another across the bridge, about four feet high from the bridge, and a rope put up over the cross-beam, with a noose attached to the end of it. A ladder was placed to lead up on to this scantling, and this woman walked up the ladder, unsupported, and stood on the scantling, under the rope, with the hungriest, craziest, wildest mob standing around that I ever saw anywhere.
>
> The woman adjusted the rope around her own neck, pulling out her braid of hair, and at the firing of a pistol, two men with hatchets, at each end, cut the rope which held the scantling, and down everything went, woman and all.[44]

Juanita was the only female ever hanged in California, illegally or legally!

This work cannot possibly be considered a history of the exploits of California bad men. The frontier days of that colorful state have been accurately traced by scholars from within and without its confines. Much has been written about the notorious Murieta (1830-1853) but we propose merely to very briefly sketch the overlying events of his lawless career. It seems not out of place, however, to quote from one of his literary admirers who, in fact,

---

[44]*Ibid.,* p. 49, from statement by David P. Barstow, 1878, for the H. H. Bancroft Collection, pub. in *New Spain and the Anglo-American West* (Los Angeles, 1952) Vol. II, p. 150-152.

took his name as his own. We refer to Joaquin Miller, *nee* Cincinnatus Heine Miller (1841-1913) who wrote of the bandit:

> After the cruel conquest of California from Mexico, we poured in upon the simple and hospitable people from all parts of the United States. Strangers in language and religion, let it be honestly admitted, we were often guilty of gross wrong to the conquered Californians. Out of this wrong suddenly sprang Joaquin Murieta, a mere boy, and yet one of the boldest men in history. But he soon degenerated into a robber and a large reward was offered for his head. The splendid daring and unhappy death of this remarkable youth appeal strongly to me; and, bandit as he was, I am bound to say I have a great respect for his memory.[45]

Born in 1830, in the province of Sonora, Murieta (his real name was Carrilla) came from a respectable family. He fell in love at the age of nineteen with a sweet young girl of sixteen, and they eloped to California, settling in Stanislaus County where the young man obtained work in the mines. Harassed by Americans there, the couple moved on to Calaveras County, where they settled on a small piece of land. Due to a tragic mistake in the matter of a stolen horse which had been sold to Murieta's brother, the vigilantes assembled and Murieta's brother was hanged. The completely innocent Joaquin was himself horsewhipped. Such treatment embittered him beyond any reasonable sense. Rosita, the young man's wife is alleged to have stated many years later that her husband knelt "over the body of his murdered brother and with uplifted dagger he swore that he would devote the remainder of his life to slaughtering Americans, whom he regarded as the foremost enemies of his race."[46]

From that day forth Murieta behaved as if he did, in fact, regard Americans as his mortal enemies. Murder, pillage, mayhem, and frontier gang warfare were to be his stock in trade until he and his Mexican followers became the scourge of the length and breadth of the state. A large reward was placed upon his head, dead or alive, and the active manhunt was stepped up to such a

---

[45] As quoted by Thomas S. Duke, *Celebrated Crimes of America*, San Francisco, The James H. Barry Co., 1910, p. 190.

[46] Duke, *op. cit.*, p. 191.

degree that it seems strange that he eluded the forces of the law for so long. He had several extremely narrow escapes from capture but his charmed life could not go on indefinitely. He was found on July 25, 1853, at a place called Arroyo Cantoova, in the act of washing his horse. Gunfire ensued and Murieta, game to the last, was killed by members of the hunting posse. The leader of the posse, one Capt. Love, in order to submit concrete proof of the bandit's ignominious end, cut off his head and took it to San Francisco where it was placed on display for some time thereafter.

Murieta's followers scattered. Many returned to their homes but a few continued their lawless career. One of his later successors, Tiburcio Vasquez, was almost as notorious, deadly and elusive as his predecessor. He had the bad luck of being hanged for his crimes. A few words follow regarding him and his career. Like Muretta, Vasquez was born in 1835, of respectable Mexican parents, but in California—at Monterey—rather than in Mexico. At an early age, he identified himself with the questionable elements of the town and subsequently ran afoul the law. Some of his cronies became victims of the vigilantes so Vasquez left his native heath and began a maurauding career. Most of his illegal activities, consisted initially of stealing horses around Santa Clara, Merced and Fresno counties. He was in and out of San Quentin prison (escaping from that seemingly impregnable institution at least once) for the next twenty years. On August 26, 1873, he and his gang—notably Abdon Chavez and Clovodea Chavez, among others—decided to rob a general merchandise store and saloon, operated by one Andrew Snyder, located at Tres Pinos, or Paicines, near Hollister. In the confused melee that followed the stick-up, three persons were killed: a sheep-herder named Barney Bihury, an inn-keeper named Leander Davidson, and a teamster named George Redford. All of these victims were innocent bystanders or customers.

The gang made their getaway and continued their criminal mayhem and plunder for some months. Vasquez was finally apprehended not far from Los Angeles on May 14, 1874. He was subsequently tried for the murders of Davidson and Redford and sentenced to death. He was hanged at San Jose, Santa Clara County on March 19, 1875. One by one, the Vasquez marauders were brought to trial for their crimes or killed by other bandits. In time, this period of outlawry came to a natural end and California grew into maturity.[47]

THE GREAT SAN FRANCISCO FIRE AND THE
GASPIPE MURDERS

Certainly the great earthquake and fire that struck the lovely city of San Francisco, in April, 1906, can be recorded as one of the great tragedies in the history of this country. Thomas S. Duke, police captain of the city at the time, refers to it as the "greatest catastrophe in American history."[48] An area of 4.7 square miles of the city were gutted, almost 500 bodies were recovered with an estimated loss of life of well over one thousand, and a property damage of close to $275,000,000.[49]

Whenever a catastrophe of such magnitude strikes a city, an area or a country, crimes of various categories show a sharp increase. The police of the stricken city immediately released petty offenders detained in the jail and transferred all felons to the nearby San Quentin prison. There was, naturally, much lawlessness immediately apparent such as looting, mayhem and even murder. The problem of coping with crime was a serious one which Captain Duke readily admits in his treatise and describes therein. Of special interest are the so-called "gaspipe" murders which terminated in the hanging of two persons convicted of a series of wanton killings during this period of municipal disorganization and upheaval. To testify to this we quote:

> Never since the days of the famous Vigilance Committee in 1852-56 were the citizens of San Francisco more terror-stricken by the criminal element than during the five months following the great earthquake and fire in April, 1906.[50]

Paradoxically, during this crisis, with so much taxable property

---

[47]McDade, *op. cit.*, 1025; also Duke, *op. cit.*, pp. 203-209, from Sawyers *History of Vasquez.*

[48]With the loss of life and property damage this holocaust pales into insignificance when compared to the yellow fever plague of Philadelphia in 1793 when fully 5,000 people died, when the total population of the city was but 40,000.

[49]See Duke, *Celebrated Criminal Careers,* pp. 164-177; figures stated on 165.

[50]*Ibid.,* p. 177.

destroyed, retrenchment of public services in the city hit police protection a crushing blow which the criminal element used to its predatory advantage.

A series of robberies and murders took place during the summer and autumn of the fatal year of 1906 and because of the similarity of the *modus operandi,* the perpetrators became known as the "gaspipe" bandits and murderers. This was obviously because their weapons—at least in some cases—were lengths of ordinary gaspipes covered with wrapping paper. Some of the following robbery-murder cases were associated with two men, both from prominent and wealthy families, although they were tried and convicted on but one murder, that of the Japanese banker, M. Munekato. The first crime to which their names were connected was the murder of one Joseph Pfitzner on August 20, 1906. He was the immigrant son of the chief architect of Emperor William of Germany and operator of a small shoe store. He was clubbed to death and robbed of about $140 and his gold watch. On September 14, two small children entered the clothing store of William Friede, and discovered his badly-battered and bloody body lying on the floor. His cash drawer was empty and his watch gone. On October 3, the Japanese bank, known as "Kimmon Ginko", was robbed of all of its money, in the sum of $2,800 and its president, M. Munekato and his assistant, A. Sasaki, murdered. On November 3, an abortive holdup of the jewelry store of Henry Behrend brought to an end the gruesome murders by these criminals. One, who turned out to be Louis Dabner, was apprehended in the tussle with the proprietor and he subsequently implicated his companion, John Seimson. Seimson was the son of a very wealthy citizen of Honolulu.

The men were tried for the Japanese banker's murder and accordingly convicted and sentenced to death. A fruitless appeal to the higher courts was made, so on July 31, 1908, they were hanged at San Quentin prison "from the same scaffold."[51]

A strange reverberation of this case is set down by Clinton T. Duffy in his book of not-so-pleasant memories which deals with the tragic victims of the gallows in his prison-home, San Quentin.[52]

---

[51]Duke, *op. cit.,* pp. 177-186.
[52]*Eighty-Eight Men and Two Women,* Doubleday, 1962, pp. 36-41.

He tells the story of these two criminals as he remembered them and their crimes when he lived on the prison reservation where his father was a member of the custodial staff. He tells of the games the children played—not cops and robbers but guards and prisoners. He further states that the youngster's sympathies were often with the potential victims of the gallows. He states that in this whole double hanging it was the consensus of the children that a wrong had been done. He explains:

> When they were hanged a deep pall engulfed the village. The kids left home that morning with heavy hearts, and we sat in sullen silence as the witnesses hurried by the front door of the little schoolhouse . . . We all hated and feared the hangman, and we hated him more than ever that day, for he had killed our friend; Seimson, their "beau ideal." As far as we were concerned, he was more beast than man, and we referred to him as "the Killer." There was no place for him in our games. Nobody would play his part.[53]

This is an example of children's reactions to a hanging; that is, of children living hard by a gallows or an execution chamber.

-----

[53]*Ibid.*, p. 37.

Chapter X

THE TREE EMBELLISHED BY BALLAD AND ALLUSION

THE HANGING BALLAD

T HROUGHOUT WE HAVE RELIED on the interesting and unique work of Mrs. Olive Woolley Burt who, as a "folklorist of murder," has diligently sought out and tracked down ballads that are pertinent to our subject and which are definitely an integral part of our American heritage. At what we considered appropriate places in the preceding chapters we reenforced and embroidered our hanging stories with some of Mrs. Burt's ballads. Most of our cases are not, so far as we know, accompanied by ballads. The ingredients or the situation which encourages or prompts the creation of a ballad cannot be more than merely pondered here. Authorities on the ballad can probably supply the answer. Suffice to say that comparatively few of our hangings have merited such a distinction.

In this chapter, we wish further to call on the rich reservoir of Mrs. Burt's collection and then add others which have come to our attention. Later we shall set down allusions gleaned from the literature that are identified with the quaint practice of hanging. As to the ballad, we may well quote from the *Preface* of Mrs. Burt's work: "As such they [the ballads] are the voice of the people, speaking authoritatively upon one of the tragic but very real aspects of our civilization."[1]

THE GREEN-WYATT CASE

Let us take the Henry Green-Mary Ann Wyatt case. Mrs. Burt refers to this as a "family" murder and it is usually referred to as "The Berlin Murder Case." The locale is central New York State.

---

[1]*American Murder Ballads*, New York, Oxford University Press, 1958, p. xiii.

Henry G. Green, twenty-two years old, met Mary Ann Wyatt, eighteen, member of a temperance group playing one-night stand dramas, in 1845. Completely smitten by the feminine charms of this probably chaste trooper, Green forsook his own occupation in the small town of Berlin, Rensselaer County, and joined up with the wandering crusaders. On Sunday, February 10, the two were married. This, Green thought, called for a celebration. He decided on a sleighing party and invited all of his friends in and around his home town to attend. Among these was an old sweetheart, well-endowed with pulchritude and with the world's material goods, Miss Alzina Godfrey. Snuggled up in the bob-sled, Miss Alzina uncautiously but casually mentioned that she had hopes at one time of marrying Henry who had certainly been one of the town's most eligible bachelors. This chance remark, or something else not so apparently innocuous that happened on this wintry outing, changed the mood of the recent bridegroom. It was testi-fied later that he was a "changed man." The day after the ride, Mary Ann complained of being ill. Henry procured some medi-cine and administered it to her in frequent doses. Instead of re-covering, his bride of less than a week grew violently ill, and died all too suddenly. Henry's medicine was arsenic.

As Mrs. Burt so aptly types this case: "It had everything a balladeer could ask for: a rich young man, a beautiful bride, pas-sion, jealousy, married bliss, and tragedy. Practically everyone who could make a rhyme, it seems, composed verses about the crime." There are seven known versions of this case in ballad form, the longest consisting of twenty-four verses. It is much too long to be reproduced here but a few verses will suffice to indicate the rhythm of the century-old folk-tale:

The Murdered Wife

Come young and old attention give and lend a listening ear,
While I relate a case of love that proved a fate severe;
There was a gay and sprightly youth who lived in Berlin Town,
Who saw a damsel, young and fair, that could not on him frown.

'Twas in a brilliant Temperance play on one bright new-year's
    night,
In which she played her part so well she gave him great delight;

He then with rapture gazed on her, and plann'd how he could
  gain
This damsel, beautiful and fair, Mary Ann Wyatt, by name.

The ballad continues by relating the sordid details of Green's
perfidy in negotiating her untimely death after he had married her
and organized the merry sleighing party. The concluding verse
ends as anyone could predict—in remorse:

But now 'tis done, I can't escape a murderer's awful grave!
Oh! pray to God for me, dear sir, that he my soul will save.
Farewell, young mates, I am no more, I pray remember me,
And think how cruel I have been—and shun bad company.[2]

Green was hanged at Troy, N.Y. on September 10, 1845. Mc-
Dade lists several pamphlets (Nos. 384-9) consisting of Green's
confessions, letters from his mother (McDade thinks the reason for
the crime was his mother's disapproval of the girl), the trial, and
other relevant details. The case has also been written up by Dr.
Louis C. Jones, director of the New York Historical Association
of Cooperstown.[3]

This classic case was not without its burlesque ballad, a phenomenon that frequently occurs in sordid, gory, macabre events
in our culture. A kind of parody went the rounds at the time of
the trial. In it the murderer was a cobbler, the victim, "little
Polly Green," whom he poisons with arsenic served up in a sheep's
head broth. The ghost of the sheep appears and says: "A gal
you've poisoned with my head," and carries the murderer off to
hell."[4]

THE ASHLAND, KENTUCKY TRAGEDY

Our second case is the Ashland, Kentucky, murder with its accompanying ballad. On the early evening of December 24, 1881,
Mrs. Gibbons, a mother of three children, left them for a short
time to visit with a neighbor. Near the Gibbons home was a nail
mill that employed several workmen. Three of these men, noticing

---

[2]*Ibid.*, pp. 9-14.
[3]In two articles: "The Berlin Murder Case in Folklore and Ballad," *New York History*,
  XVII, No. 2, N.Y. Hist. Ass'n., and an article in *Bulletin of the Folksong Society of
  the Northeast*, No. 12, 1937. See also, Burt, *op. cit.*, pp. 7-14.
[4]Mentioned by Burt, *op. cit.*, p. 14.

that the children were alone, went to the home intent on attacking the occupants. A boy, Bobbie, seventeen years old, was a cripple. He was attacked and killed. The girls, Fanny, fourteen, and Emma Carico, fifteen, were killed and then raped. The killers' weapons were an axe and a crowbar. In an attempt to hide the results of their hideous crime the murderers set fire to the house. However, they were soon apprehended and two of them, Ellis Craft and William Neal, were subsequently hanged at Grayson, Carter County, the former on October 12, 1884, and the latter on March 27, 1885. The third, George Ellis, received a prison term.[5]

The shocking nature of this crime almost naturally elicited a ballad to cover the details. In fact, there are several versions of the original ballad. It is said that one of these was composed by a twenty-year-old balladeer who later was sent to prison for life for killing a neighbor family.[6] The Ashland ballad consists of thirteen verses which follow here:

> Dear parents, brothers, sisters, come listen while I tell
> About the Ashland tragedy, which you all know full well.
> 'Twas in the town of Ashland, all in the dead of night,
> This horrible crime was committed, but soon it came to light.
>
> The men who did the awful deed were Ellis, Craft, and Neal;
> They thought their crime was hidden, but God the same
>   revealed.
> George Ellis was the weak one; he could not bear his conscience
>   pain,
> And to his friends he trembling revealed the horrid stain.
>
> He blamed Ellis Craft the leader, he had an iron heart;
> 'Twas he caused these lovely children from their mother's arms
>   to part.
> Poor George Neal may be innocent, but from what George Ellis
>   tells
> The crime that he committed will send his soul to hell.
>
> He dragged poor Emma from her bed and threw her on the
>   floor,

---

[5]McDade, *op. cit.,* 284.

[6]Burt, *op. cit.,* pp. 58-9.

He crushed her head with an iron bar till she weltered in her
    gore.
Friends, use your imagination, can't you see those little hands
Upheld, pleading for mercy, murdered by this cruel man.

Those little white hands so tender were upheld in prayer to him,
Now they fall useless at her bleeding side; her dying eyes grow
    dim.
Craft committed the very same offense, then killed the other
    two;
And while their forms laid cold and stiff, Craft said, "What
    shall we do?"

George Neal proposed to burn them up to hide their bloody sin;
Then others might be arrested and they'd not be blamed by any-
    one.
Then, in tones of thunder, Craft sent Ellis to get oil,
To pour upon the children for to hide their bloody toil.

Craft lit a match and held it close to their oil-soaked clothes;
The flame leaped up with searing heat; away the wretches goes.
    [*sic*]
They put themselves far from the scene as fast as they could go;
And thought that no one ever their bloody crime would know.

But the story of the fire spread; the town in mourning wept;
To see the children's burned-up forms, that sight they can't for-
    get.
With screams and bitter weeping all the neighbors gathered
    'round,
Their hearts were torn and bleeding; their tears soaked up the
    ground.

Poor little Bobbie Gibbons, that helpless cripple child
Died defending his sweet sister; he was always sweet and mild.
Now three little forms are buried; they sleep beneath the sod,
Murdered while defending their virtues, and their souls are now
    with God.

Major Allen brought the bloodhounds—their work they did so
    well,
They chased those fiends for days and days, where e'er they
    tried to dwell.

All night long the baying of the hounds sent a death knell
through the town,
Until the fiends were caught at last. For hell their souls are
bound.

They were taken to Mount Sterling—the folks there rate themselves so high!
They say they believe in justice, but they don't want those
fiends to die.
To hear them talk you'd think they have forgot that they have
daughters, too,
For if they don't uphold the law, what will their children do?

May law and justice be dealt out to every wicked man;
And then some day perhaps we can enjoy a moral land.
Now all dear fathers and mothers, a warning from this take,
Stay home with your children and guard them for their sake.

Remember, this is a wicked world, no mortal can you trust;
Trust God, who is all wisdom and doeth all things just.
And let this tragedy be a warning, wherever you may go,
Remember the Gibbons children and Emma Carico.

The Case of Reuben Dunbar, "The Murderer" — New York State — 1851

There are several published pamphlets as well as a mournful
ballad concerning this murder, by Reuben Dunbar, of two children, David L., ten, and Stephen V. Lester, eight, of Westerlo,
Albany County, New York, on September 28, 1850. The children
were nephews of Dunbar's step-father. The killer, fearful that these
children stood in his way of inheriting certain property, killed one
with a powerful blow and the other, by hanging him from a tree.
One of the pamphlets, telling of the crime, used the same language
found so frequently in murder annals—"The most foul and un-
paralleled in the annals of crime."

Dunbar, aged twenty-three, had been entrusted with the children
by their parents. The crime has been likened to one in England
and known to all as "Babes in the Woods" which is said to have
been based on a crime.[7] Mrs. Burt, collector of murder ballads

---

[7] Burt, *op. cit.*, p. 91.

extraordinary, has unearthed a ballad on this atrocious crime, the perpetrator of which was hanged in the Albany jail on January 31, 1851. There are twenty-four verses but seven will suffice to relate the gruesome tale:

> Awake, and muse, awake and sing,
> And softly touch the mournful string;
> In solemn tones, in accents low,
> Tell the sad tale of death and woe.
>
> Oh, brutal man, how can it be
> You'r guilty of such perfidy?
> Two blooming children you have slain,
> A little paltry gold to gain.
>
> The mother dear the lads did send,
> To Dunbar's home, some months to spend,
> But ere they long with him had stayed,
> Silent in death they both were laid.
>
> The mother was distracted quite,
> To think Dunbar would so requite
> The kindness to him always shown,
> Such brutal act scarce e'er was known.
>
> Far from his house he did them send,
> Their precious lives he there did end.
> An awful club his hand did hold,
> To slay these lads but few years old.
>
> Young Stephen deep beneath the ground,
> He put to keep from being found.
> And David high on tree he hung,
> Where the night-bird lonely sung.
>
> This brutal deed was brought to light,
> By beasts that roam abroad at night;
> And now in filthy, loathsome jail,
> Does Dunbar's form grow death-like pale.[8]

---

[8]Burt, *op. cit.*, pp. 91-92; Mrs. Burt states that the ballad was first published in the *Supplement* to the *Ulster County Almanac*, 1855, apparently a composition of the widely famed anonymous balladeer, *Saugerties Bard*. Dr. Louis Jones, Director of the N.Y. Hist. Ass'n., Cooperstown, unearthed the piece.

Charles Birger — Prohibition Era Gangster and His Ballad

It is not new to have ballads about gunmen and all-'round bad men pop up on occasions, especially inareas west of the Alleghenies. It does seem a bit incongruous to be confronted with a dirge about a Prohibition bootlegger, but this is the case.

This rather obscure creature was one Charlie Birger, hanged at Benton, Franklin County, Illinois, on April 19, 1928, for the murder of a "saloon-keeper, crap-game operator" named Joe Adams. Apparently what made Birger's crime so repugnant to the local citizenry was that his victim was also the Mayor of West City. Had Charlie stuck to riddling the bodies of members of his rival gang of bootleggers, the Sheltons, he might have gone the way of other well-disciplined thugs, relatively immune to the local law minions and to bigger and more powerful combines of racketeering.

Birger was spawned in the East Side of Manhattan where, on reaching young adulthood, he took the Greeley injunction seriously and "went West" to southern Illinois and East St. Louis, in particular. Here he joined up with Egan's Rats and fought the Ku Klux Klan in and around Herrin during the early 1920's. Big money was calling and Charlie became a bootlegger in the grand manner. He established himself in Little Egypt in a country estate headquarters known as Shady Rest and fortified it against all comers. Birger made one great mistake. He ordered two of his henchmen to "rub out" Adams and this heedless act brought about his undoing. The local authorities set a trap for him and when he appeared in court by a ruse—totally unarmed—they pounced on him and he was soon convicted and sentenced to death for the murder.

A good account of his last hours is recorded by the reporter of the St. Louis *Post-Dispatch* (April 19, 1928). The account mentions the fact that Birger had tried suicide while awaiting his ordeal with the hangman—he had hanged himself with a strip of blanket but was cut down unconscious and revived. It also refers to his "gameness" and even gentleness as he went up "the thirteen steps" to the gallows and spoke kindly and softly to the professional executioner who, it was said, had officiated at sixty-one previous hangings—Phil Hanna of Epworth, Illinois.[9]

Now to the ballad about Charlie Birger. Mrs. Burt makes it clear that this ballad was not the product of Tin-Pan Alley like so many about the notorious bad-men of that era were—Pretty Boy Floyd, Dillinger, and others of that ilk. No composer is mentioned but she says: "it indicates that even the new-fangled gangster can find a minstrel to recount his story." *The Death of Charlie Burger (sic)* follows:

I'll tell you of a bandit Out in a Western State,
Who never learned his lesson Until it was too late.
This man was bold and careless, The leader of his gang,
But boldness did not save him When the law said, "You must hang."

This bandit's name was Burger, He lived at Shady Rest,
And people learned to fear him Throughout the Middle West.
'Twas out in old West City Joe Adams was shot down,
And then the cry of justice, "These murderers must be found."

Then Thompson was captured And turned state's evidence,
Burger was found guilty, For he had no defense.
He asked for a rehearing, But this he was denied;
In the county jailhouse To take his life he tried.

On the 19th day of April In 1928,
Away out West in Benton Charles Burger met his fate.
Another life was ended, Another chapter done;
Another man who gambled In the game that can't be won.

The Ten Commandments show us The straight and narrow way,
And if we do not heed them Sometime we'll have to pay.
We all must face the Master, Our final trial to stand,
Ane there we'll learn the meaning Of houses built on sand.[10]

Ballad of the Braswell Brothers — Tennessee

We stated above that it is not unusual to find ballads created about the exploits of what we refer to as "criminal gangs," whether they engage in bank robberies, train robberies, cattle rustling, or

---

[9]The news report and other details of the Birger story are incorporated in August Mencken, *By the Neck,* 6-11.
[10]Burt, *op. cit.,* pp. 214-215.

in the more reprehensible crime of kidnaping. Many exciting and well-known crime ballads exist outside our consideration.

One that we include here is probably typical of the lot. It deals with the Braswell brothers, Teke (sometimes referred to in the literature as Leak) and Joe, who, allegedly, began their lawlessness in and around Smithville, DeKalb County, Tennessee, during the 1870's. Their end came at Cookeville, county seat of Putnam County, on the 27th of March, 1878. On that day, they were "strung up" legally for the murder of one Russ Allison, at the "Allison place," a well-known "stand" on the Walton Road, about one mile from Baxter. The murder occurred on November 29, 1875. The unfortunate victim lived some thirty-six hours and, as he died, said to a Mrs. Isbell: "Angie, I'm shot; Joe and Teke Braswell are the ones that shot me."[11]

There are two discrepancies in the Braswell ballad. It may be seen that Nashville seems to have been the locale for the double hanging; also one of the boys was referred to as Leak rather than Teke which seems to have been his factual cognomen. The ballad follows:

> All my friends and near relations come and listen to my song,
> I will sing about the Braswells, The—men that were hung.
> The twenty-ninth of November, Eighteen-hundred seventy-five,
> Was the night they did the murder For which they had to give
>   their lives.
> They said, "Dear father and mother, I hope you'll remember me,
> When we're dead and gone forever, And our faces no more
>   you'll see.
> We have lain so long in prison; In our attempts we never fail,
> God will aid and will assist us, For to break the Nashville jail.
> When they started from that prison, And the guards surrounded
>   them,
> "Leak," said Joe, "We're lost forever, Our escape is very slim."
> Bohannon placed them in a wagon, They were neat and very
>   gay;
> Their coffin was a seat for them, To the place where they hung
>   that day.

---

[11] Walter S. McClain, *A History of Putnam County,* Cookeville, Tenn., Quimby, Dyer & Co. 1925, p. 35.

They had a sister and a brother That did seem so very nigh,
They followed them down to the valley Where they were so soon
to die.

When they climbed upon the scaffold, And the guards surrounded them,
They were joined by McPherrin Who opened up prayers for
them.

The third chapter of Romans, It was read to them that day
there
And after a private conversation They poured out their souls in
prayer.

Then said Joe in a cold voice, "Gentlemen and ladies, too,
If you will give me your attention, I will speak some words to
you."

"I am here upon the scaffold, Here before you all today,
And what it is for is murder," Were the words that he did say.

"What caused me to do this murder, It was whiskey, and money
too,
If you drink a drop of whiskey, Money then might tempt you,
too."

Leak said, "It is a solemn hour, And it tells me I must die;
I am ready and a-waiting; I am prepared and willing to die."

Then, as Abel came on the scaffold, Shaking hands with them
there,
They were delighted at his presence, Seemed very glad to meet
him there.

He said, "Joe, were you at my house, On the night the murder
was done?"
"I was there, and I am guilty," Was the answer that Joe made.

Leak was low and fair complected, Joe was tall and very neat;
They were pale and very silent, Then their lips did seem to
meet.

They listened to the death sentence, Which was there read to
them then,
Then they tied their wrists and ankles and placed caps upon
them.

One said, "Jesus, Lord have mercy; Will you be with me today?"
The other said, "Lord have mercy On them that swore my life
away."

The door fell and left them swinging, There betwixt the earth
  and sky,
It was for a dreadful murder These two men did have to die.

They were cut down and placed in their coffins, Delivered over
  to their friends,
Who were there for the purpose, To receive them at the end.[12]

The Ballad of Thomas Duffy, Mollie Maguire of the Pennsylvania Coal Fields

Thomas Duffy was one of five hanged at Pottsville, Pennsylvania, on June 21, 1877, for the murder of B. F. Yost, a police officer of nearby Tamaqua.[13] According to Arthur H. Lewis, in his *Lament for the Mollie Maguires,* the following verses about Duffy were written by one Manus Coll (or Cull), or as he was better known, "Kelly the Bum" (Daniel Kelly). Plied with a few drinks, he scribbled down the doggerel and it was published in the Shenandoah *Herald* dated September 9, 1876. Perhaps the immortal lament should be just that, rather than a ballad. Here it is as transcribed by Lewis:

My name is Tommy Duffy, I am scarcely twenty-four;
I was born in County Donegal, on Ireland's Emerald Shore.
I left my aging parents, like many of my race,
And now I'm held in durance vile, besmirched in black disgrace.

I was just about eighteen years old when to this land I came,
No sin lay on my conscience, and on my head no shame;
The first place that I earned my pay was in the Jeddo Mine,
And there the men can testify how well I served my time!

The day I left my native land, I swore a solemn oath,
No liquor, grog of any kind would e'er go down my throat.
And now I'm still a-keeping it, and will until I die,
Be it on a bed of roses, or on a gallows high.

I stand accused of murder foul, the same I do deny,
And now my trial will soon come off—the traitors I defy!
But perjury has got its way throughout our happy land,
And like O'Connell,[14] I'll have them swear on every upraised
  hand.

---

[12]Burt, *op. cit.,* pp. 203-206.

[13]A sixth "Mollie" was hanged that same day, at the same place, but for another murder. He was Thomas Munley.

[14]Irish patriot and "Liberator."

May God have mercy on these men, their deeds they can't
    secrete,
When called to face an angry God, before the Judgment Seat.
But such is life for Irishmen, and ever more 'twill be,
For it always was since that bad day, when Paddy's land was
    free.

By all that's holy Up Above, now what I say is true!
I never knew "Powder" Kerrigan,[15] nor any of his crew.
I never kept his company, which he must know right well,
But to save his guilty neck, Alas; he's swear a Saint to Hell.

So here's to all my kindly friends; my enemies also,
And to my foster parents, whom I have brought so low,
As for my loved and pretty wife, to me she is most dear,
I know that she will grieve for me, whilst I am lying here.

But wait, me lads, a little while, and soon you'll see me free,
To face the Bosses, one and all, that tried to bury me,
I'll walk among my fellow-men, with head erect and strong,
To show my vile accusers that they are in the wrong![16]

It is obvious that poor Duffy spoke too quickly and optimistically.

Marine James Bird — "Fighter with Perry" — 1813

One of the most poignant and unjust episodes that has come to
our attention has to do with the plight of Marine James Bird, who,
according to Mrs. Burt, "distinguished himself fighting beside
Oliver Hazard Perry on Lake Erie" during the War of 1812. Due
to a mixup of circumstances involving what was a technical "desertion" from duty, young James Bird was shot sometime in November 1814, and lies buried on "Sand Beach" at Erie, Pennsylvania,
on the shores of Lake Erie. Executed with Bird were two others:
a marine, John Rankin, who was also shot, and John Davis, sailor,
who was "hung to the yardarm" of the *Niagara*.

Shortly after the execution, a ballad was composed by one
Charles Miner and published the same year as Bird's death. It
seems that the unfortunate young man, whose home was in Luzerne
County, Pennsylvania, absented himself to meet a young lady on
shore. Upon his return, he was court martialed and ordered to be
shot. A presidential pardon arrived too late to free him. Regard-

---

[15]Tamaqua (Pa.) bodymaster and informer; turned state's evidence against Mollies.
[16]Lewis, *op. cit.*, pp. 269-270.

ing the ballad, one historian wrote somewhat unfeelingly: "The execution . . . constituted the romance of the war among children and the lower classes. Written in the 'gory' style, rehearsed, or rather screeched by a servant girl with a doleful countenance it made a decided impression on a group of children."[17]

The ballad published by Mrs. Burt in her collection is not authored, so we do not know if it is the same one mentioned above. Her submitted ballad begins with the historical background of the battle of Lake Erie, with an account of the tearful farewells of parents and sweethearts as the soldiers marched away.

> Where is Bird? The battle rages
>   Is he in the strife or no?
> Now the cannons roar tremendous,
>   Dare he meet the furious foe?
>
> Ah! Behold him! See with Perry,
>   In the self-same ship he fights;
> Though his messmates fall around him
>   Nothing can his soul affright.
>
> But behold! A ball his struck him!
>   See the crimson current flow!
> "Leave the deck!" exclaimed brave Perry,
>   "No," cried Bird, "I will not go!"
>
> "Here on deck I've took my station,
>   N'er will Bird his colors fly;
> I'll stand by my gallant captain
>   Till we conquer or we die!"
>
> So he fought, both faint and bleeding,
>   Till our Stars and Stripes arose,
> Victory having crowned our efforts
>   All triumphant o'er our foes.

The author of the ballad then relates some of the story of Bird's desertion and concludes with some sorrowful thoughts on the morning of the execution:

> Oh, he fought so brave at Erie,
>   Nobly bled and nobly dared!
> Let his courage plead for mercy—
>   Let his precious life be spared.

---

[17]Laura G. Sanford, *History of Erie County*, 1894, pp. 248-249.

See him marching! See his fetters!
　Harsh they clank upon the ear.
But his step is firm and manly,
　For his heart ne'er harbored fear.
See, he kneels upon his coffin!
　Sure his death can do no good.
Spare him! Hark! Oh, God they've shot him,
　See his bosom streams with blood!
Farewell, Bird, farewell forever,
　Friends and home you'll see no more.
But his mangled corpse lies buried
　On Lake Erie's distant shore.[18]

Perhaps the most famous hanging song, whether it be labeled a ballad, dirge, or some other musical form, is Rudyard Kipling's *Danny Deever*. In introducing this we turn from factual hangings to legend or pure fiction. The hanging of Danny Deever is usually accepted as fiction, despite its grim reality as a kind of barracks ballad. The story of the hanging, as well as the superb cadence of the author's literary contribution, aid in preserving the ballad. We will allude to it briefly here. We see the hollow square of troops drawn up to witness the hanging of this wretch who killed a soldier buddy while he slept. We hear the *Death March* as well:

"For they're hangin' Danny Deever, you can hear the Dead
　March play,
The Regiment's in 'ollow square—they're hangin' him today."

The final verse adds to the awfulness of the execution:

"What's that so black agin the sun?" said Files-on-Parade.
"It's Danny fightin' 'ard for life," the Colour-Sergeant said.
"What's that that whimpers over head?" said Files-on-Parade.
"It's Danny's soul that's passin' now," the Colour-Sergeant said.
For they've done with Danny Deever, you can 'ear the quick-
　step play,
The Regiment's in column, an' they're marchin' us away;
Ho! the young recruits are shakin', and they'll want their beer
　today,
After hangin' Danny Deever in the mornin'!

---

[18]Burt, *op. cit.*, pp. 183-184.

OTHER QUAINT BALLADS

Another British hanging ballad that competes for fame with
Danny Deever is that which tells the story of Sam Hall who goaded
God into damning nearly everyone about to survive him. Sam's
crime was, of course, murder—so states the ballad. They put him in
jail and "tied him to a log." The "parson came and talked of
Kingdom Come, he can kiss my ruddy Bum," the "sheriff came
with his boys all dressed in blue" and "up went the rope . . with
his friends down below." He saw "Molly in the crowd" and "he
hollored out loud, 'Molly, ain't you bloody proud?' " Finally he
cried out defiantly, "I'll meet you all in hell and hope to sizzle well,
Damn your eyes."[19]

Fact or fiction and confusion in locale complicate the dilemma
of the collector of literary artifacts of hanging. A good example
is Cole Porter's *Miss Otis Regrets,* a plaintive air so exquisitely
rendered by the contemporary sophisticated Nancy Wilson in a
popular album she has assembled for public approval. The story
tells of a young lady—Miss Otis—who is sorry she cannot attend
a luncheon because she is about to be hanged for killing her lover.
The ballad tells the story in a rather unsatisfactory manner. She
laments that she went to lovers' lane the night before and "strayed"
from the narrow path. When she awoke and "found that the dream
of love was gone," she ran to the man in question, "drew a gun from
her velvet gown" and shot down the villain. But, alas, Miss Otis
was not merely hanged; she was dragged from the jail by a mob
and "strung up to an old willow tree." While this story obviously
indicates a lynching, it is too good to be omitted in our story of
hanging. However, it is established fiction.

One periodically hears current hanging folk-ballads, rendered by
popular singing aggregations which, like ships in the night, pass
through the hands of those arbiters of what should be played, the
disc jockeys, and then pass into limbo. Two that come to mind
have the lugubrious titles, *Twenty-Five Minutes to Go* (The
Brothers Four)—more whimsy than tragedy—and *The Wrong*

---

[19]Based on a traditional song by Jessie Cavanaugh and Albert Stanton, copyright by
Hollis Music Co., New York City.

Man. Doubtless there are many more. The words of the former are:

> Well, they're building a gallows outside this jail,
> > I've got twenty-five minutes to go.
> And the whole town's waitin' just to hear me wail,
> > There's twenty-four minutes to go.
> They've given me some beans for my last meal,
> > Twenty-three minutes to go.
> And nobody asks me how I feel,
> > Twenty-two minutes to go.
> So I sent for the governor and the honey darned bunch,
> > Twenty-one minutes to go.
> And I called on the mayor but he's out to lunch,
> > I got twenty minutes to go.
> Then the sheriff said, "Boy, I want to watch you die,"
> > You've got nineteen minutes to go.
> So I laughed in his face, spit in his eye,
> > I got eighteen minutes to go.
> Then I called up the warden to hear my plea,
> > I've got seventeen more minutes to go.
> He said, "Call me back in a week or three."
> > You've got sixteen more minutes to go.
> Now my lawyer says he's sorry that he missed my case,
> > I've got fifteen more minutes to go.
> Well, if you're so sorry come and take my place,
> > I've got fourteen more minutes to go.
> Now here comes the padre for to save my soul,
> > With thirteen more minutes to go.
> And he's talking 'bout burnin' but I'm so cold,
> > I've got twelve more minutes to go.
> Now they're testin' the trap and it chills my spine,
> > Eleven more minutes to go.
> And the trap and the rope, ah they're workin' just fine,
> > I've got ten more minutes to go.
> Now I'm waitin' for a pardon and they'll set me free,
> > With nine more minutes to go.
> But this ain't the movies so forget about me,
> > I've got eight more minutes to go.

Now I'm climbin' up the ladder with the scaffold there,
  With seven more minutes to go.
Now I better watch my step or else I'll break my leg,
  I've got six more minutes to go.
Wuth my feet on the trap, my head in the noose,
  Five more minutes to go.
Won't someone come and cut me down,
  I've got four more minutes to go.
I can see the mountains, see the sky,
  Three more minutes to go.
And it's too darned pretty for a man to die,
  I've got two more minutes to die.
I can hear the buzzards, hear the crows,
  One more minute to go.
And now I'm swingin' and here I go——GO—OHhhhh![20]

Despite the earthiness and crudity of such poignant ballads, one is reminded of at least the title of the musical classic by Hector Berlioz, *Symphony Fantastique,* one part of which refers to "The March to the Scaffold." One may conjure up an absurd contrast between a dignified orchestra on the one hand, with a crooning folk quartet on the other, each describing the painful way to the scaffold.

The collection of ballads assembled by John A. and Alan Lomax* is the source for a few gems that should be incorporated in this chapter. Perhaps the first we should mention is one that has some elements of truth and in a sense can be nailed down. It is the lugubrious story of one Batson which allegedly concerns a murder that took place at Lake Charles, Louisiana. The culprit, a white laborer, was accused and convicted of killing his employer, a Mr. Earle, and his entire family. The bodies were found in a shallow grave with only a sprinkling of red soil over them. As the Lomaxes put it: "Inquiry fails to confirm Stavin' Chain's [the informant] story; but no one who has ever heard him sing the wailing song with his guitar, at times beating a solemn dirge and then shrieking in hopeless despair can ever forget it. You've seen and felt a

---

[20]Words and music by Shel Silverstein, copyright 1962 & 1966, Hollis Music Inc., New York, N.Y. Used by permission.
Our Singing Country.

hanging." We should pause to note that Stavin' Chain is not a person, but, like Paul Bunyan, a balladeer symbol. The dirge is supposed to be sung to the tune of "Frankie and Johnny," a better known American classic.

It takes thirty-eight verses to tell the tearful story of Batson's crime but, actually, there is little detail given; rather it has him moaning and groaning over his fate and fretting at the future of his children and mother. The first verse of the ballad may give us a concrete reason why he may have killed his employer. For six years he worked for Earle and never received any pay. The verses that tell us something of the gallows are these:

> They brought his coffin,
> The day he came to die,
> And he told the sheriff,
> "That's the last time I'm going to lay down."

> Then the priest told Batson,
> "Black box takes you down,"
> Says, "Here comes your black box,
> You'll never rise again."

> They put a black bonnet above his head,
> They put a rope right on his neck,
> They put handcuffs on his hands,
> Balls and chains on his foot.

> The clear blood run out of his eyes,
> Nobody they couldn't see his face,
> Had a tongue stuck out of his mouth
> Six inches long.

> A rubber-tired buggy,
> Decorated horse,
> You know they brought Batson to the graveyard,
> Says, they brought his family back

Another ballad from the Lomax collection is that of *Dupree,* a peripatetic bandit who killed a jeweler to obtain a diamond ring for Betty, his girl friend. He fled to Memphis, then to Chicago where he killed a "cop," and finally he told the judge he committed the murder just to get some of his girl's "jelly roll." The ballad, somewhat like that of Batson's, is a lachrymose lament. The verses surrounding the grim hanging are:

"Give pappy my clothes, give Betty my shoes,
And if anybody asks you, tell 'em I died with the heartbreakin'
    blues."
So they led him to the scaffold with a black cap over his face,
Some lonesome graveyard's poor Dupree's restin' place.
The choir followed behind him singin' "Nearer My Gawd to
    Thee,"
Poor Betty she was cryin' "Have mercy on Dupree."
Betty said to the herse driver, "Buddy, drive yo' dead wagon
    slow,
You got my man, and he can't come back no mo' "
"Sail on, sail on, Dupree, sail on.
Don't mind you sailin' but you'll be gone so dog-gone long."[21]

The time, place and factual authenticity of his piece are all left
to the conjecture of the reader.

The other balads from the same collection are not too interesting
in this connection but there is at least mention of the gallows. One,
entitled *The Reek and the Rambling Blade,* is obscure as to locale
asied from mentioning St. James' Square and "the eastern shore."
The one about to die robbed "old Nelson" of five thousand pounds
which suggests England rather than our own country. He robbed
to keep his Molly "dressed neat and gay" but he had to pay the
penalty of the gallows for his transgressions. So he moans:

> But now I am condemned to die,
> A-many a lady for me to cry;
> Pretty Mollie weeps, tears down her hair,
> A lady alone left in despair.
>
> My father weeps, he maketh moan,
> My mother cries her darling son,
> But all the weeping won't help me
> Or save me from the gallows tree.
>
> Now I am dead, laid in my grave,
> The final joy creeps over my head.
> All around my grave play tunes of joy—
> Away goes a reek and the rambling boy[22]

---

[21]Lomax, *op. cit.,* pp. 328-330; the above Batson quote on p. 340.

[22]*Ibid.,* pp. 314-315.

A ballad that is often cited or quoted that has some bearing on the death penalty is *Brennan on the Moor,* indigenous to Ireland. The words do not take the robbing culprit—for that was what Brennan was—to the gallows, but they leave no doubt that he and his companion, the peddler named Juley Ponds, were doomed to die for "Robbing on the King's Highway." The ballad insists that Brennan, like "Dick Turpin and Sam Bass," and presumably Robin Hood, robbed only the rich and divided their loot "with widows in distress." The highwayman met up with the peddler Ponds and robbed him but, switching the procedure, Ponds robbed Brennan and retrieved his property. In such a fashion the two clubbed together in preying on hapless travelers and in due time came to their untimely end.[23]

One could spend a lifetime collecting items dealing with the practice of hanging alone; and the harvest would undoubtedly run from the noble and heroic to the contemptible and sordid. The allusions to the scaffold, the gallows, the rope, the victim— are prodigious and varied. We submit a sampling.

A widespread ballad that has apparently been current both in this country and abroad has to do with a maid, about to be hanged, who begged her family to pay her fees and save her from her ignominious fate. In this country, this ballad has been known as *The Hangman's Tree* and goes something like the following:

> Slack your rope, Hangman,
> O slack it for a while;
> I think I see my father coming,
> Riding many a mile.
> O father have you brought me gold
> Or have you paid my fee?
> Or have you come to see me hanging
> On the gallows tree?

> *Answer:*
>
> I have not brought you gold,
> I have not paid your fee;
> But I have come to see you hanging
> On the gallows tree.

---

[23]*Ibid.,* pp. 317-319, Macmillan, 1941; copyright John A. Lomax; permission to quote from Alan Lomax.

This continues for some verses, each of which relates the girl's appeal to her mother, brother, and then her sister but to no avail: then finally a reversal: the father repents and says:

> Some of my gold now you shall have,
> And likewise of my fee,
> For I am come to see you saved,
> And saved you shall be.

The Tree in Prose and Poetry

There is something paradoxical inherent in the practice of hanging. Misery, sorrow, grief, as well as the repugnant, ghastly and macabre are all reflected in its operation. Yet one need not look too far to identify a certain grim humor or a ribald bit of doggerel or repartee involving the act. Thus this section will include a kind of *potpourri* of both the tragic and the bizarre from literary and pseudo-literary sources. We may start out by quoting the fictional young man who was about to apply for an insurance policy when he was asked from what his parents died. After stating his mother had succumbed to pneumonia, he volunteered that his father was taking part in a public function when the platform on which he was standing gave way, killing him as a result.

If proof were further necessary to demonstrate or bear testimony to the universal prevalence of hanging humor—we find none whatsoever associated with other methods of legal execution—it could be found also in the drama. One gem comes to mind. The dramatist, Jack Richardson, has written a delightfully jovial skit he aptly entitles *Gallows Humor*.* In one part of the play's progress, we see a doomed man sitting in his cell about to meet his appointment with the hangman when the warden enters, accompanied by a prostitute. It seems a new dispensation makes allowance for the services of a "lady of the street" to render his last minutes as pleasant as she is capable. The fact that he refuses to succumb to her blandishments does not nullify the thesis that a kind of bawdy and earthy humor permeates the American ethos regarding the practice of hanging.

The sporadic but far-flung practice of "hanging in effigy" persons who are disliked locally, for whatever reason, is proof however crude, that the practice of hanging remains smoldering below

---

*Dutton, 1961.

the surface in our American mores. Political leaders who have gained the enmity or ill-will of mob pressure groups may awake some morning in their small towns or metropolitan residential suburbs to see themselves hanged "in effigy" from a stout tree limb. A person awaiting trial for murder or other heinous crime may suffer the same vicarious fate at the hands of irate citizens who have become impatient with the slow-moving legal processes. We mentioned in an earlier connection the case of a man awaiting the death penalty in a small Pennsylvania county seat (Allentown) who was exposed to this fate in the tiny hamlet (Smoketown) where he allegedly committed the crime of murder (see Chapter IV, p. 255). There is also a practice in some sections of the country of holding an annual barbecue, or something similar, at which time a mock hanging of a legendary or historically notorious local horse-thief or outlaw lends color and entertainment to the occasion.

Viscount Templewood (Samuel John Gurney Hoare), throughout his life a strong opponent of capital punishment, is supposed to have stated: "Executions are so much a part of British history that it is almost impossible for many excellent people to think of the future without them."[24]

With this frank statement as the initial quote relative to hanging, we proceed to others—many others—as proof of the popularity of the macabre practice throughout the centuries among Anglo-Saxons. Francis Place is alleged to have been the author of the following doleful piece which has the bellman of Newgate Prison and Tyburn tolling the bells at hanging time, and reciting:

> All ye that in the condemn'd hold doth lie,
> Prepare ye, for tomorrow you shall die,
> Watch and pray; the hour is drawing near,
> That you before th' Almighty must appear.
> Examine well yourselves, in time repent,
> That you may not to eternal flames be sent.
> And when St. Sepulchre's Bell tomorrow tolls,
> The Lord above have mercy on your souls!
> Past twelve o'clock.[25]

---

[24]From his *In the Shadow of the Gallows* (1951), as quoted by Charles Duff, *The New Handbook of Hanging* (frontispiece), 1955.

[25]Quoted by Horace Bleackley, *The Hangmen of England*, London, Chapman & Hall, 1929, 52; he gives credit to Place MSS. and MS. 27, 826, No. 14.

The inured Briton, far from home, and perhaps somewhat home-sick, felt comforted—at least somewhat—when he saw a lifeless form on the gallows. In *Percy's Anecdotes* we find that a writer of a book of travels in the desert makes the following remark:

> After having walked eleven hours without having traced the print of a human foot, to my great comfort and delight, I saw a man hanging upon a gibbet; my pleasure at the cheering pros-pect was inexpressible, for it convinced he that I was in a civi-lized country.[26]

Just the reverse of this joyous panegyric may be adduced from the following lament regarding the institution of hanging:

> God! 'Tis a fearsome thing to see
> That pale wan man's mute agony,
> The glare of that wild despairing eye,
> Now bent on the crowd, now turn'd to the sky,
> As though 'twere scanning, in doubt and fear,
> The path of the Spirit's unknown career . . .
> Oh! 'twas a fearsome sight, ah me!—
> A deed to shudder at, not to see.[27]

The following, however, accepts hanging with all its grimness and lack of humanity. A British prison chaplain is alleged to have made the statement: "A Method originally barbarous . . . has been successfully humanized."[28]

Dr. Samuel Johnson was realistic, if not a crusader, regarding executions. He contended that the "procession to Tyburn" was salutary because it "sustained the criminal." He had the following to add to this thought when hangings were taken from Tyburn to Newgate Prison:

> Tyburn itself is not safe from the fury of innovation. Executions are intended to draw spectators; if they do not, they do not answer their purpose. The old method was most satisfactory to all parties; the public was gratified by a procession, the crimi-nal supported by it. Why is all of this to be swept away?[29]

---

[26]Quoted by Justin Atholl, *Shadow of the Gallows,* London, John Long, 1954, p. 11.
[27]*Ibid.,* p. 76, from *Ingoldsby Legends.*
[28]*Ibid.,* p. 11.
[29]*Ibid.,* p. 52.

Our own Edmund Pearson, master of the art of telling of a murder, quotes this from *The Masque of Anarchy*:

> I met Murder on the way—
> He had a mask like Castlereagh;
> Very smooth he looked, yet grim;
> Seven bloodhounds followed him:
> All were fat; and well they might
> Be in admirable plight,
> For one by one, and two by two,
> He tossed them human hearts to chew.[30]

There are many clever literary allusions to the subject of the hangman or executioner, reverting back to Shakespeare. Somewhere in *Coriolanis* we find: "Some of the best of 'em were hereditary hangmen."[31] In an old ballad, preserved by Horace Bleackley, we note the following about hangmen:

> Ye hangmen of Old England,
> How sturdily you stood,
> A-smoking pipes by Tyburn Tree,
> A-swigging pots in the Old Baliee,
> And strung up all you could.[32]

Here is a verse of a poem composed on the death on the gallows of the notorious and much-hated hangman, John Price, for the murder of Mrs. Elizabeth White, on May 31, 1718:

> Behold a wicked hardened Wretch,
> Whose Neck in justice must be stretched
> Upon the fatal gallows tree;
>   And not a soul to pity me,
>   Not one will my Just Fate bewail,
> Must be hurried from the Gaol.
> It is for Wilful Murder, I
> A Fatal Death am doomed to Die.[33]

---

[30]Pearson, *Studies in Murder*, New York, Macmillan, 1924, title page.

[31]Atholl, *op. cit.*, p. 134.

[32]Bleakley, *op. cit.*, title page.

[33]*Ibid.*, p. 19.

John Milton in *Paradise Lost* speaks his piece about hangmen as follows:

> ——————————Oh! What are these,
> Death's ministers, not men, who thus deal death
> Inhumanity to men, and multiply ten thousand fold the sin of
>   him who slew
> His brother; for of whom such massacre
> Make they but of their brethern, men of men?[34]

Returning to Shakespeare, we find in *Measure for Measure,*— Act IV, Scene 3:

> Master Bernadine, what hoa! your friend, the hangman! you
> must be so good, sir, to rise, and be put to death! pray, Master
> Bernadine, awake, 'till you are executed, and sleep afterward.[35]

Sir Thomas Buxton, eighteenth century prison reformer, allegedly made the following statement: "We rest our hopes on the hangman and in him this vain and deceitful confidence in the ultimate punishment of crime, forget the very first of our duties—its prevention."[36]

Perhaps in justification for cataloging crime and hanging the remark might be made: "Prepare for crime—I'll publish right or wrong; Hanging's my theme, let hangmen be my song."[37] An old Scotch proverb states: "Luck can never come of a half-hanged man."[38] and, as to females Seneca stated long ago: "Because of their vices, women have ceased to deserve the privilege of their sex."[39]

Another ancient sage may also be quoted in this section—we refer to Cicero who smothers both hangman and execution with contempt:

> Away with the executioner and the execution, and the very name
> of its engine! not merely from the lips, but from the very

---

[34]Rev. Charles Spear, *Essay on the Punishment of Death,* Boston, 1844, p. 42.

[35]*Ibid.,* p. 51.

[36]Quoted by Christopher Hibbert, in *Roots of Crime,* Boston, Little, Brown, 1964, in Table of Contents.

[37]Bleackley, op. cit., p. xv.

[38]Atholl, *op. cit.,* p. 187.

[39]*Ibid.,* p. 66.

thoughts, the eyes, the ears, of Roman citizens!—for not alone the occurrence and the endurance of all these things, but also the liability, the apprehension, even the mere mention of them, are unworthy of a Roman citizen and a free man![40]

And the humane and courageous Frenchman, LaFayette, expresses his views on the subject of capital punishment in these words:

> Those who ask for the adjournment of this proposition the question of the abolition of the penalty have not had the misfortune to see their families dragged to the scaffold. I am, for my part, the enemy of the punishment of death and, above all, the enemy of the punishment of death in political matters.[41]

Perhaps the most colorful remarks that sprinkle the literature of hanging have to do with its victims. Dr. Stephen Lushington of London contends:

> Every execution brings an additional candidate for the hangman.[42]

Butler, in his *Hudibras,* makes this contribution to the literature:

> No Indian prince has to his palace
> More followers than a thief to the gallows![43]

And John Gay writes:

> Every man is a hero on his way to the gallows.[43a]

Louis Blake Duff has collected several ballads and literary allusions to hangings, most of them from Great Britain. Following are some that bear reproduction in this collection. First there was Deborah Churchill, born in 1687, hanged in 1708, for shielding her lover as he fought a duel. His opponent was killed because of her intercession. The ingrate male fled to Holland and his sacrificing sweetheart, Deborah, was substituted for him on the gallows —for that was the law at the time. An old reporter of the day pondered "Though she died at peace with God, this malefactor

---

[40]Spear, *op. cit.,* p. 76.

[41]*Ibid.,* p. 88.

[42]Andrew J. Palm, *The Death Penalty,* 1891, p. 127.

[43]Atholl, *op. cit.,* p. 25.

[43a]*Ibid.,* p. 45.

could never understand the justice of her sentence, to the last moment of her life." The English literary luminary, Edith Sitwell, has preserved this episode thus:

> And I forget the moment when I ran
> Between my lover and the sworded man—
> Blinded with terror lest I lose his heart.
>
> The sworded man dropped, and I saw depart
> Love and lover and my life—he fled.
> And I was strung and hung upon a tree.[44]

The noted A. E. Housman has made the scaffold and gallows part of his poem "The Carpenter's Son" from *A Shropshire Lad*. Earlier we referred to the majestic prose of Charles Dickens and William Makepeace Thackeray who described hangings in the London jails. These writers, together with our own Quaker poet, John Greenleaf Whittier, were bitter opponents of capital punishment and all forms of injustice that were the lot of the offender of their day.

We should mention another English reformer, Elizabeth Gurney Fry, the famous prison visitor, affectionately referred to as "Newgate's Angel," who is believed to have made an astute remark that has some meaning at this point: "When thee builds a prison [or a scaffold] thee had better build with the thought ever in thy mind that thee and thy children may occupy [it]."

A gem from Oscar Wilde:

> It is sweet to dance to violins,
>   When Love and Life are fair;
> To dance to flutes, to dance to lutes
>   Is delicate and rare;
> But it is not sweet with nimble feet
>   To dance upon the air.[46]

A Canadian poet, J. E. H. MacDonald puts his contribution this way:

> I saw the gallows lifted high
> And in the cruel rope

---

[44]Reprinted by permission of the publisher, The Vanguard Press, from *The Collected Poems of Edith Sitwell*. Copyright, 1949, 1954 by Edith Sitwell.
[45]*Ibid.*, p. 193.
[46]Duff, *op. cit.*, p. 198.

The twisted law and sin of man
Strangled the Savior's hope.[47]

All of the above come from somewhat venerable sources. Here is one that may be regarded as more callous and more crude, but it is contemporary and worthy of record. It sounds strangely like the ribald talk of the street. It deals with a sensational case in Australia:

Snap goes the trap-door, snap, snap, snap;
Measured is the drop so his backbone cracks;
Cut him down and bury him in Pentridge Prison yard;
Egg and bacon breakfast for the execution guard![48]

---

[47]From *West by East* by J. E. H. Macdonald, published by the Ryerson Press, Toronto.
[48]Introduction, *The Tait Case,* by Creighton Burns, Melbourne Univ. Press, 1962, p. 2.

Chapter XI

THE DRIFT AWAY FROM CAPITAL
PUNISHMENT

ANCIENT AND CLASSICAL METHODS OF INFLICTING
THE DEATH PENALTY

IT HAS NOT BEEN OUR INTENTION to discuss the death penalty, yet, here and there throughout this treatise, there has crept in an occasional overtone suggesting the elimination of social vengeance as personified by the snuffing out of the lives of criminals. Some proof of this rather obvious trend may be adduced by a re-reading of our earlier chapter on Excessive Retribution and Puritanical Zeal in Early Days. Gibbeting, burning at the stake, breaking on the wheel, quartering—all are death-dealing techniques of the not-too-distant past and none such could possibly be revived in our modern era. Even legalized corporal punishment is repugnant to the bulk of Americans with but one state—Delaware—still clinging to the whipping-post. The social historian would find in this metamorphosis a fruitful area of scientific study. The evidence truly indicates more understanding, as well as a compassionate attitude toward the wrong-doer.

The demand for the death of the violator of the taboo, the wilful offender, the transgressor and the sinful, has been universal among primitive people. The painfully slow emergence from the dark night of retributive justice to a more enlightened concept of a reformative and social policy of corrections is only now occupying the attention of the social historian and the criminologist. One sees progress despite lapses in the process. A hundred or more years ago, a prominent cleric and crusader for the abolition of capital punishment, the Rev. Charles Spear, made a list of the Old Testament allusions to the death penalty and deplored the benighted philoso-

440

phy of the times. He equally deplored the reticence of the clergy in not denouncing our gory heritage.[1]

If the use of a pun in a subject as somber or gloomy as this may be excused, it might be stated that with the modern application of electricity to the art of execution, the "death knell" of hanging was sounded in this country. To kill or not to kill a murderer was not considered when the electric chair was developed and propagandized by its exponents; rather the debate centered around whether or not electrocution was quicker and less painful than hanging. The same question was raised some years later, when lethal gas was introduced as a substitute for the electric chair. (How painful is the technique—that has been the question, not necessarily how deterrent or valuable is the practice of legally eliminating the malefactor.)

In truth, the number of offenses against humanity that have elicited the death penalty has decreased throughout the years. One need but examine, and perhaps read, the many works that have been but recently published on the subject of punishment and torture to arrive at this conclusion.[2]

In our own country, at one time, there were many capital crimes such as "murder, manslaughter by stabbing, serious maiming, highway robbery, burglary, arson, sodomy, buggery, rape, concealing the death of a bastard child, advising the killing of such a child, and witchcraft."[3]

Treason has also been generally included in lists of capital crimes. The number varied in colonial times as it varies in the states today. Premeditated murder alone is the one offense that is included on every list throughout the country today. Other crimes high on the lists are rape and kidnaping, with robbery, arson, and train robbery or wrecking. (For analysis of capital crimes by states see *The Death Penalty in America* edited by Hugo Adam Bedau,

---

[1] *Essays on the Punishment of Death,* Boston, 1844 (Fifth Ed.), Essay III, "The Mosaic Code," pp. 156-173; see especially pp. 159-161, which lists the number of capital offenses and Biblical citations concerning them.

[2] We submit the following: George Ryley Scott, *The History of Torture Throughout the Ages,* London, Luxor Press (seventh impression, 1959); John Laurence, *A History of Capital Punishment,* New York, The Citadel Press, 1963, and Eugene B. Block, *And May God Have Mercy,* San Francisco, Fearon Publishers, Inc., 1962.

[3] Thus laid down in "An Act for the Advancement of Justice and More Certain Administration Thereof," passed in Pennsylvania May 31, 1718.

Doubleday & Co., Inc. Anchor Books, 1964, pp· 39 ff.)

Earlier we dealt with the pioneer work of our first abolitionists who called for the riddance of what they considered the scourge of mankind—the death penalty. Their first real victory was to triumph in slowly eradicating the scaffold and gallows from streets and public squares—witness the lag by the last public hanging in the country, at Owensboro, Kentucky as recently as 1936. But public hangings merely gave way to private hangings in county jails away from the ribald throngs.

Rhode Island took initiative to dispose of the death penalty completely at an early date—in 1852. The fear that someone might be hanged although innocent looms constantly as a spectre before most people in all ages. John Gordon was hanged at Providence on February 13, 1845. He had been convicted of waylaying and beating to death a wealthy businessman named Amasa Sprague because the victim had apparently interfered in permitting Gordon from obtaining a liquor license. After he was executed there arose such a feeling that an innocent man had been hanged that the abolition of the death penalty eventually was consummated in 1852. (See Boston *Herald*, May 25, 1890, for details of this episode.)

We, in this country, assay the death penalty in terms only of hanging, electrocution, asphyxiation, and shooting; yet, France uses beheading by the guillotine and Spain by the garrote. The above does not exhaust the various techniques that have been used by mankind to eliminate his enemies. Flaying and impaling was widely practiced in the ancient Orient and came down to medieval Europe. This frightening method of extermination was still used in England during the time of Canute (994-1035). This punishment is described by first skinning the victim alive and then placing the body on a sharp stake where he remained until death intervened. In the meantime, the victim was left exposed to the hot rays of the sun and the depredations of insects and ravenous birds such as vultures and buzzards. We were not too far departed from this disgusting and cruel practice in our own colonial times when persons were gibbeted alive or had their heads or quarters impaled on stakes or on chimney-tops.[4] A variation of this hideous death that was also used in the Orient was the exposure of the doomed wretch to gradual death from insect bites. A classical description of this punishment as applied to the Persian general, Mithridates, follows:

> He was encased in a coffin-like box, from which his head, hands, and feet protruded through holes made for that purpose; he was fed with milk and honey, which he was forced to take, and his face was smeared with the same mixture; he was exposed to the sun, and in this state he remained for seventeen days, until he had been devoured alive by insects and vermin which swarmed about him and bred within him.[5]

Still another widely used method employed in olden times but unknown to modern peoples was to cast the victim from a high rock or precipice to the stones beneath. This was sometimes combined with other punishments. It is said that the Carthaginians frequently flayed the condemned just prior to pitching them from a high rock or precipice. Poisoning was also a form of imposing the death penalty and it has been rendered classic in history through its imposition on the philosopher Socrates, who was obliged to drink the poison hemlock. Beheading has been one of the most universal methods of inflicting the death penalty and has usually been regarded as a relatively noble and even enviable form of dying. In the Middle Ages beheading was considered an honorable method of meeting death, whereas hanging carried with it a definite stigma. The "most magnificent" criminal to be hanged in England, the Earl Ferrers (Laurence Shirley), begged to be beheaded but he was denied this special treatment. He was thus "turned off" in the ordinary manner at Tyburn on May 5, 1760. He did command the most elaborate procession that ever chaperoned a person to the gallows in England or anywhere else.[5]

---

[4]See Chapter II, p. 87 f. Some of the following material has been reproduced in summary from Harry Elmer Barnes & Negley K. Teeters, *New Horizons In Criminology*, ©1943 (1951, 1959), Prentice-Hall, Inc. Englewood Cliffs, N.J. (by permission).

[5]Frederick H. Wines, *Punishment and Reformation*, New York, Crowell, 1895, p. 70.

[5]See Horace Bleackley, *The Hangmen of England*, London, Chapman & Hall, 1929, 100-103.

Methods of beheading have called forth much inventive ingenuity. One of the earliest was the broad-sword. The culprit was usually compelled to stand in a bent posture and a rope was placed about his neck and stretched to prepare him for the death blow. In medieval and early modern times the block and broadax were used for beheading. Beheading of a kneeling victim has been quite widely used in China. Beheading was employed during the Nazi regime where it was carried out with considerable pomp. The executioner wore evening clothes and a high silk hat; the job carried considerable prestige and was much sought after.

Exposure to poisonous serpents was also employed in Oriental and classical times. This type of death was frequently insured by sewing the culprit in a sack in company with a venemous reptile. The infliction of the death penalty by throwing the victim to the lions or other ravenous beasts is well known.

Mass drownings or *noyades* were resorted to during the French Revolution. Jean Baptiste Carrier, the French demagogue and agent of the Committee of Public Safety of Nantes, in 1793, threw thousands into the Loire River. This penalty of drowning was used by Richard the Lion-Hearted who ordained by decree that it should be the doom of any soldier who killed a fellow Crusader during the passage to the Holy Land. The owner of Baynard's Castle in London, during the reign of King John, had the proprietary right to drown anyone convicted of treason in the River Thames. The penalty was used in the British Isles until the beginning of the seventeenth century.[6]

Stoning to death or being crushed to death by the heavy foot of an elephant were found in Oriental cultures. The former was a method used by the Jews and in the New Testament we are familiar with the martyr Stephen being subjected to this penalty.[7] Stoning was retained as a penalty for theft as late as the tenth century in England.

Crucifixion was popular with the Romans although it was used by the Phoenicians, Persians and Carthagenians. It was this method that was used in the execution of Jesus and the two thieves on Golgotha. Extreme debilitation and dehydration resulted from this

---

[6]William Andrews, *Bygone Punishments,* London, 1899, pp. 95-97.
[7]See Leviticus, 20:2.

practice in a slow lingering death on the cross.[8] The Romans sometimes disposed of their enemies by having them pulled apart literally by horses. The painting depicting the third century legendary martyr, St. Hippolytus, being subjected to this torturous death on order of Emperor Valerian, is one of the masterpieces hanging in the Boston Museum.[9]

We mentioned the guillotine or French knife which takes its name from Dr. Joseph Ignace Guillotine (1738-1814) member of the French Revolutionary Assembly and by profession, a physician. He did not invent the instrument. Charles Duff, giving as his source John Murray's *History of the Guillotine* (1853), claims that Guillotine "cribbed" the idea from one Laquainte of Strasbourg and he, in turn, got his notion from a "modest but intelligent and imaginative maker of pianofortes named Schmidt."[10] This device of death is famous in song and story since it has snuffed out the lives of many famous as well as notorious persons, including Louis and Marie Antoinette. It consists of a heavy steel blade held in position by grooves in a wooden frame. The blade gains force for the cutting process through its weight and the long fall.[11]

Garroting has been widely used in Spain and was liberally employed in her colonization and subjugation of the Indians of America during the 1500's. These betrayed people were ruthlessly garroted for expressing opposition to the efforts of the Spanish priests to convert them. This was done in the guise of stamping out heresy. The penalty is still used in Spain as witness the three persons thus subjected to it for "treason" on August 17, 1963. It consists of a process of strangling and is quite painful. The devices used are an iron collar affixed to a post. The victim is fitted in the collar and a screw is slowly tightened until the person's breath has ceased and death ensues.

Shooting by firing squad has been used and still is in some countries. It is still used in our own country, in Utah—as a choice offered the condemned in lieu of hanging. Generally, the victim is strapped to a chair and is blindfolded. The guards making up the

---

[8]See George Ryley Scott, *op. cit.*, pp. 153-154 for discussion of crucifixion.

[9]See *Life Magazine*, October 18, 1963.

[10]*A New Handbook of Hanging*, Chicago, Regnery, pp. 1955, 116.

[11]For a graphic description of the notorious French "Bluebeard," Henri Landru, see Webb Miller, *I Found No Peace*, New York, Simon & Schuster, 1936, pp. 146-55.

squad wear slippers to muffle any sound. None of the squad knows which gun contains a blank cartridge. On signal from the captain the squad fires. In case the live bullets miss the mark, it is generally the unpleasant duty of the captain to give the *coup de grace*. Often a notch is cut in the chair after each victim is disposed of.[12]

Other methods of eliminating convicted criminals, some of them fiendish, which have been employed in the dismal past, and are worthy of mention are suffocation, by one or another technique; burying alive; boiling in oil; pressing to death and burning at the stake. We have discussed the latter two in an earlier connection.

Only the limited ingenuity of mankind in one or another culture or era determines the techniques employed in snuffing out the lives of unwanted members of the group. However, with the painfully slow development of mankind's social conscience the methods became less barbarous and, in time, less painful. Down through the years it can be believed that the still small voice of the minority played a significant role in diminishing the number of human executions.

INTRODUCTION OF ELECTROCUTION

It would be pleasant to believe—and perhaps accurate—that the introduction of electricity to execute criminals had a humanitarian motive. But its original introduction may have been the result of the effort of an electrical company to market its products. At least, this was the belief advanced by the electrical wizard, Nicola Tesla, in the New York *World,* November 17, 1929.

Electricity, by the means of a wired chair, was first introduced in the Auburn state prison of New York on August 6, 1890. Its first victim was William Kemmler, convicted of murder in Erie County. Approximately 700 persons have been electrocuted in that state since that date. In the many states that have used or still use this method, the number would run into the many thousands.

The first electrocution was generally condemned. Typical of the journalistic reaction was that of the Utica, New York *Globe:*

> . . . it is not improbable that the first will prove the last . . .
> Manufactured lightning to take the place of the hangman's rope
> for dispatching of condemned murderers cannot be said to be

---

[12]See Charles P. Larrowe, "Notches on a Chair: Utah Firing Squad," *The Nation,* Vol. 182, No. 15 (April 14, 1956) 291 f.

satisfactory . . . The men who witnessed the horrible scene Wednesday morning in the death chamber of Auburn Prison never wish to be present at another such exhibition. Dr. E. A. Spitzka, the celebrated expert, who was present, unhesitatingly pronounced the experiment a failure and declared it his belief that the law should be repealed and no more experiments made with electricity as a means of execution.[13]

It has generally been believed and accepted that electrocution is painless, or at least less painful than hanging. Here we wish to include some statements by some who are, or were competent to judge. First we have the emphatic contention of a distinguished French electrical scientist, L. G. V. Rota. Labeling this punishment a form of torture, he contends that a condemned victim may be alive for several minutes after the current has passed through his body without a physician being certain whether death has actually occurred. He adds that certain persons have greater physiological resistance to electric current than others, and that no matter how weak the person, death cannot supervene instantly.[14]

Nicola Tesla, mentioned above, whose profound knowledge of electricity made possible the very electric chair which he so violently opposed, writes:

> The alternating current used . . . does not pass in a direct course, despite all of the precautions taken . . . The current flows along a restricted path into the body, and destroys all the tissue confronted in this path. In the meantime the vital organs may be preserved; and pain, too great for us to imagine, is induced. The brain has four parts. The current may touch only one of these parts; so that the individual retains consciousness and a keen sense of agony. For the sufferer, time stands still; and this excruciating torture seems to last for an eternity.[15]

Tesla, in those early days, suggested that if electricity was to be employed to execute, a bolt of artificial lightning should be produced since such could be controlled and would instantly destroy the criminal's consciousness and spare him all agony.

Contrary opinions come from two persons who attended many executions. One was executioner for several eastern states for

---

[13]Quoted by *Correction,* Dept. of Correction, New York, Albany, August, 1940.
[14]London *Daily Mail,* January 14, 1928.
[15]So stated in the New York *World* article, *loc. cit. supra.*

many years—he officiated at 387 legal killings—Robert G. Elliott. He writes in his book, *Agent of Death*: "The first terrific shock of 2,000 volts shatters the person's nervous system instantaneously and beyond recall, and paralyzes the brain before the nerves can register any pain. Medical experts declare that unconsciousness is produced in less than one two-hundredth and fortieth of a second. This, then, is as humane as ordered death can possibly be."[16] The other who vouchsafes its humaneness is Dr. Amos O. Squire, who was for many years the officiating physician at Sing Sing prison's death house. After presenting a grim, yet graphic description of what takes place in "the little green room" he concludes: "In comparing electrocution with hanging . . . I believe that electrocution is more humane and certain and less painful."[17]

We have described the technique of hanging earlier, and later we shall list the stages of gassing a condemned person. Here we quote from the Sing Sing doctor, Amos Squires, since he has graphically described what happens after the signal is given:

> . . . a sound comes from the electrician's niche—not unlike the sound of an x-ray apparatus, a cackle, whine and buzz. The figure in the chair gives one terrific lurch against the straps, every muscle contracting and straining. The face—all that can be seen from mouth to throat—turns crimson. Sometimes a wisp of smoke rises from the top of the head, and with it the smell of burning. . . . After a few seconds the current is cut off . . . the doctor with his stethoscope listens for heartbeats—he listens to them grow fainter and fainter. A brief interval passes. The switch is thrown again—and after contact is broken, again the doctor listens. There is seldom any pulse this time . . . The terrific current causes instantaneous contraction of all muscles in the body, resulting in severe contortions of the limbs, fingers, toes, face, and protrusion of the eyes. If applied for as long as a half a minute, burning rapidly develops at the point of contact, and a post-mortem examination shows eyes in a foggy condition 'with a star fracture of the lens', heart dilated and filled with fluid blood . . . in about five per cent of cases in a contracted or tetanized condition.[18]

---

[16]*Agent of Death*s *Memoirs of an Executioner*, Robert Elliott with Albert Beatty, New York, E. P. Dutton & Co., 1940, p. 149.

[17]*Sing Sing Doctor*, New York, Doubleday, Doran, 1935.

[18]Quoted by Charles Duff, *op. cit.*, p. 118.

In *Scottsboro Boy* Haywood Patterson and Earl Conrad tell of the case of one Will Stokes, an axe-killer from Alabama who was electrocuted. They say: "A guard came along and said 'Stokes died hard. They had to stick a needle through his head to make sure of it.' "[19]

The convicted spies, Julius Rosenberg and his wife Ethel, were electrocuted at Sing Sing prison on June 20, 1953. Julius was given the first shock which lasted three seconds; a second lasting fifty-seven seconds; and a third, also lasting fifty-seven seconds. A doctor duly pronounced him dead. Here is what an eye-witness has to say about the killing of Ethel Rosenberg:

> After the fourth shock, guards removed one of the two straps and the two doctors applied the stethoscopes. But they were not satisfied that she was dead. The executioner came to them from his switchboard in a small room ten feet from the chair. "Want another?" he asked. The doctors nodded. Guards replaced the straps and for the fifth time electricity was applied.[20]

We are unable to offer any conclusive opinion as to the accuracy of those who contend that electrocution is painless and those who maintain that it is a brief but excruciating form of torture. That there is much room for doubt is indicated by the introduction some years ago and the widespread use of lethal gas for execution purposes.

We do know that it often takes several shocks of high voltage to finally convince the attending physician—who often must rely on the executioner himself to give the nod—that the victim is actually dead. The scene within a death house is without question grim and even sickening. As Charles Duff, who bitterly assails electrocution (as well as all forms of capital punishment), states: "Electrocution is unsportsmanlike, and the smell of frying human flesh is sometimes bad enough to nauseate even the press representatives who are present."[21]

In the opinion of these writers, there is little difference between electrocution and hanging in every item connected with the techniques including disgust, efficiency, publicity, and cruelty. In our

---

[19]*Ibid.,* 119 from *Scottsboro Boy,* New York, Doubleday, 1950. Copyright by Earl Conrad. Reprinted by permission of Doubleday & Co., Inc.
[20]Quoted by Duff, 121, from the London *Daily Dispatch,* June 21, 1953.
[21]*Ibid.,* p. 117.

earlier chapters, we described many cases of bungling connected with hanging, both public and private. The same may be said about electrocutions except we have no cases of public spectacles where electric chairs have been used.

There was no impetuous rush among the states to change from hanging to electricity. Introduced in New York, in 1890, as we have noted, it was not until 1915 that Pennsylvania took over the chair from the scaffold. In 1940, the sovereign state of Mississippi changed from the rope to the chair, and made quite a spectacle of the change, as may be gathered from the following *Life* quote:

> This year Mississippi's state legislature voted to abandon the traditional rope and buy an electric chair. Fortnight ago, pleased with their new $4,000 contraption, Mississippi authorities placed it on public exhibition outside the State capitol at Jackson. Crowds saw a big silver truck, a portable generator and a sturdy chair complete with helmet, straps and electrodes. Beside it stood Mississippi's new executioner, Jimmie Thompson, ex-sailor, marine, carnival man and high tension expert. No less proud of his chair than of the black cat, snakes and strawberries tattooed on his velvety skin, he explained that he and his volts would travel from county to county as business required. His fee per job: $100.[22]

How strange it is that Mississippi could obtain a new electric chair at that time when South Dakota was unable to achieve this dubious accomplishment. We note that in 1915, the state abolished the death penalty. But in 1939, the governor asked for its restoration after two murders had been committed within the state by two youthful hitch-hikers from Illinois. The bill to carry out his wishes passed both houses of the legislature and became law. The act did not provide funds for an electric chair. Hence the law was invalid until the appropriation should be made. When the 1942 legislature supplied the funds, war priorities made it impossible for the state to procure the material to construct the death chair. This, of course, has long since been remedied, so South Dakota is listed with the states that operate the death penalty.

------

[22]*Life* Magazine, October 7, 1940, p. 38. ©1940, Time, Inc. Since 1955 Mississippi uses lethal gas in the State prison.

LETHAL GAS

We now turn to the use of lethal gas. It is believed that death by gassing is painless to the victim. If this is debatable, perhaps the claim can be made that it is less painful than electrocution and hanging. However, decisions are more likely to be arrived at by opinions rather than by scientific studies. Here is an opinion advanced by a Catholic priest from California who had seen many hangings:

> Says Father O'Mara, who gave the last rites to the doomed men: "That was the most terrible thing I have ever seen, and I've witnessed fifty-two hangings. I could find nothing humane about it." . . . The prison physician, who had officiated at 15 hangings, comments that "hanging is much simpler and much quicker." A guard, calloused by the gallows, says: "It was pretty awful watching those men stare at you." The prison warden thinks execution by gas should be abolished, declaring it far more ghastly and inhumane than hanging.[23]

The above evidence does not indicate that the process was painful to the condemned but "torture to the spectators." However, it is generally believed, if not demonstrable, that asphyxiation is less brutal than electrocution and far less than hanging. Still, it is quite obvious that the British, who cling to capital punishment, did not accept these statements.* Charles Duff, whose work is mentioned above, strongly maintains that hanging—repugnant though it is—is more advantageous on all counts than the so-called more scientific techniques used in our own country.

We have been considering only the physical torture associated with capital punishment. Far worse than any physical agony that may be claimed is the mental torture experienced for weeks, months, and even years. A condemned person need not give up all hope of reprieve until the last second. The long stay or reprieves tendered the condemned person between time of the imposition of the death sentence and actual execution is paradoxical— a two-edged sword. It may be referred to as mental cruelty on

---

[23]San Diego, California *Sun,* December 3, 1938.

*In November, 1965, Parliament abolished the death penalty, but whether this will have any permanency remains to be seen.

the one hand and the finest expression of justice and compassion on the other.

Persons have languished in the death house in most of our states at one time or another for months, years, and in a few cases over a decade awaiting a final disposition of their cases. Perhaps the most notorious case so far as this tortuous delay is concerned, was that of Caryl Chessman (California) who, after many delays and the expiration of some twelve years, was finally gassed at San Quentin prison on May 2, 1960, on a technical charge of kidnaping. Known as the "Red Light Bandit" this case became a national scandal because of these very delays. The Sacco-Vanzetti case in Massachusetts, in 1927, is another baffling affair even today. These two Italian immigrants—avowed anarchists and draft dodgers—were convicted of killing a paymaster in a robbery at Braintree. They were held under sentence of death for seven years while competent lawyers fought their losing battle in the courts. There is a vast literature on this famous case and already a sizeable bibliography on the Caryl Chessman case.

Another earlier case, involving a woman, elicited a scathing denunciation on our delay with its accompanying tantalizing torture in administering the death penalty, from *The Penal Reformer,* quarterly publication of the Howard League of Penal Reform of London:

> Has anything in the record of brutalities attributed to the American "gangster" equalled in its refinement of cruelty, the fate meted out by the New York State authorities to Mrs. Anna Antonio? The woman was condemned to death for murder in April, 1933, and was prepared for the electric chair on the 28th of June this year [1934]. Less than one hour before the execution, the Governor stayed sentence for twenty-four hours and then subsequently for one month. On July 16th, the death sentence was pronounced again and she was executed on August 11th. She lay in prison under the shadow of execution for fifteen months and three times endured the torments of what she thought was the last day of her life. The savagery of such a penal code is equalled only by the callousness of the people whose conduct was described in a London Sunday newspaper:
>
> "Laughing crowds of men, women and children gathered outside the prison walls in festive mood, singing ribald songs and

telling jokes, and refreshment vendors did a roaring business."
Or is this an example of cause and effect?[24]

Sometimes a person is actually executed while far away, in a
governor's office, frantic efforts are being made to get through a
call to the prison to stave off the hand of the executioner. This
happened in California in connection with the case of Burton
Abbott, convicted of a brutal sex slaying. On March 15, 1957,
this condemned man was actually undergoing execution by gas at
the moment Governor Goodwin Knight was desperately trying to
get a phone call through to stay the execution "for another hour."
The same thing allegedly happened on May 2, 1960, in the Chessman case when, due to a mistake on the part of a jurist's secretary
in dialing the prison phone, the doomed man was asphyxiated.
The judge had agreed to consider some new evidence submitted
by Chessman's lawyer.

Asphyxiation by gas calls for much equipment and skilful hands
to operate it. This is beautifully brought out by Clinton Duffy. He
states that the operation of a gas chamber execution includes:
"funnels, rubber gloves, graduates, acid pumps, gas masks, cheese-
cloth, steel chains, towels, soap, pliers, scissors, fuses and and a
mop; in addition, sodium-cyanide eggs, sulphuric acid, distilled
water and ammonia."[25]

The late Albert Deutsch, noted columnist and critic of modern
penal practice, lists, with tongue in cheek, the twenty-one steps
in negotiating a gas chamber death. These graphically illustrate
the twentieth century refinement of an execution—that is, in our
own country:

> Mix acid and water in mixing bowls A1 and B1.
> Strap prisoner in chair.
> Attach package of sodium cyanide in immersion device.
> Close the seal chamber.
> Test chamber and tightness by using lever 3 and manometer H.
> Release acid to chamber receptacles.

---

[24]October, 1934, 9. For the story of this case, see Wensell Brown, *Women Who Died
in the Chair,* New York, Collier Books, 1958, Chapter 2; the author deals only with
five cases from New York State.

[25]From *The San Quentin Story* by Clinton T. Duffy as told to Dean Jennings. Copyright
1950 by The Curtis Publishing Company. Reprinted by permission of Doubleday &
Company, Inc.

Close supply valves A2 and B2.
Fill mixing bowl with water.
Report "everything ready" to warden.
Immerse sodium cyanide into acid chamber, now in operation.
Warden gives order to clear chamber.
Open exhaust valves by lever E.
Open receptacle drain valves A5 and B6.
Open supply valves A2 and B2.
Open ammonia valves A4 and B4.
Open water valves A4 and B4.
Open air manifold intake valve F.
Open ammonia valve 1, chamber is now being cleared of gas.
Open chamber door; physician's inspection; body removal.
Clean chamber and appurtenances and leave in condition for
the next execution.[26]

In our previous chapters, we described some rather hideous executions when hanging was the vogue throughout the country. It is only fair that we set down here at least one parallel case that is associated with the gas chamber—again in California which has had for the past decade or more some rather unfortunate and notorious cases that went to the gas chamber. On April 7, 1956, one of the most gory—and certainly brutalizing—episodes ever to come from a modern scene involving capital punishment, occurred in the San Quentin prison:

> Husky Robert O. Pierce, twenty-seven, was carried kicking
> and screaming into the lethal gas chamber by five guards after
> his unsuccessful suicide attempt yesterday. Prison officials said
> he slashed his throat in a death cell just outside the gas chamber
> as the prison chaplain . . . was trying to comfort him. He [the
> chaplain] called the guards who grabbed Pierce and wrestled
> him into the lethal chamber as blood spurted from his throat.[27]

Ghastly as the contemplation of this scene undoubtedly is, its direct antithesis is equally revolting. One of the ironies of the death penalty in its pursuance is the case taken of a person condemned to death. Around-the-clock death watch is installed for days, and even weeks before the fatal hour. Letting the victim die a natural death—in case he were seriously ill—would be contrary

---

[26]From PM April 20, 1947.

[27]INS dispatch, The Philadelphia *Inquirer*, April 8, 1956.

to our advanced social thinking as well as cheat the death contraption for a victim.

Throughout we have made a serious effort to be understanding, even sympathetic, of sheriffs and other executioners during the hanging regime. We still tender this feeling toward modern wardens. Many of them are stern opponents of the death penalty. Any solicitation they may direct toward the condemned, such as making their last stay in a prison reasonably comfortable and free from as much anxiety as possible, is to be considered laudatory and praiseworthy. One might wonder, however, to what degree a man will go in obeying orders when he knows he is violating a principle he believes in. Just how the following may be received by our readers will depend on their background and their social understanding of the criminal. In the California prison where reposes the "green capsule" that is the gas chamber, the warden not too long ago suggested that sun lamps be installed in "death row" to militate against prison pallor of the condemned. His recommendation got little support from his superiors.

HOW EFFECTIVE IS THE DEATH PENALTY?

Most of the arguments for and against capital punishment are based on dogma; logic is seldom employed in debate, especially in legislative halls when its abolition is being considered. There are many persons who support their arguments against the death penalty in terms of religion and an equally large number who recoil at its brutality. Conversely, many law-enforcement officers contend that the penalty is necessary as a deterrent and contend that certain types of killers would unleash their murderous compulsions indiscriminately if the penalty was less than death. The literature on the question is prodigious and arguments pro and con continue through the years *ad nauseum*.

The advocates of the death penalty, as well as the general public, focus most of their hatred against the person who murders in connection with a sexual assault, who kidnaps a child and kills it, and the one who kills a police officer. These are persons who are generally given short shrift in the courts or whose pleas for clemency are denied. The public is not so easily aroused emotionally against one who kills in a conventional manner, or in a conventional situation. Little more than casual attention is given a person who kills his spouse, or a citizen in a holdup or the gangland killer who rubs out a competitor. True, if there is a wholesale gangland vendetta underway, there is likely to be incensed editorials in the local press but, in general, the public is seldom aroused regarding a murder unless it is given a big play in the newspapers over a long period of time.

The conclusion seems inevitable that it is not a murder *per se* that whips the public into a frenzy but the *kind* of murder. It seems actually that this phenomenon has been overlooked by advocates and opponents of the death penalty.

Hatred of the criminal, especially of the murderer or rapist, or kidnaper, or arsonist, on the one hand, and sentimentality toward the wrongdoer on the other, will not be of much service to society in attempting to cope with such criminals. The public, as well as our courts and our police, must apply scientific methods when attacking crime. An understanding of human motivation is essential in appraising the behavior of any person, as well as knowledge of the stresses and strains of a culture upon that individual. Responsibility for one's acts is necessary, of course, and strict accountability is of importance. No matter how depraved, no one should be executed unless it can be proved beyond a reasonable doubt that such a policy would rid the world of crime and criminals. The dismal past with its two hundred or more capital crimes and its thousands of victims executed for their commission is adequate proof that no such hope dare be realized. As it is in this country and as it always has been, almost never has a man of wealth or of influence gone to the gallows or electric chair. It is extremely difficult for juries to bring in a verdict of first degree murder and a mandatory death penalty if the defendant has money and thus a good lawyer.

The only argument for or against the death penalty that has any scientific validity is whether or not it deters others from committing repugnant crimes. While it is obvious that a person executed will automatically be deterred from committing another crime, that is not the question. Rather, it is and always has been believed by many that the person executed becomes an example to others not to engage in crime. There is little evidence available that the death penalty really deters those who, by their conditioning, or through compulsions, may commit murder. In those states that do not have the death penalty, we find no more killers than in the states of like social and cultural conditions that maintain capital punishment. By the same token, the facts indicate that there are no more police officers killed in the abolition states than in death penalty states.

While there are many types of murderers we might divide them for convenience into three categories. First there are those who suffer from serious physical, mental, and cultural deficiencies that make it possible for them to contemplate murder as a more or less natural form of conduct and with an amazing casualness. Their point of view is so defective or their sense of social responsibility so blunted, that the compunction against taking human life, which exists in the normal individual, is almost absent; the deterrent effect of a penalty has no meaning to this group. The second type consists of those who are relatively normal physically, mentally, and culturally, but are subjected to intensely difficult or inciting emotional situations which lead them to commit murder, whereas under normal conditions they would lead a law-abiding existence. Again, the deterrent effect of a penalty has little meaning to this group because they do not think of a remote penalty, no matter how severe, when confronted by an overwhelming situation. The third group comprise the professional killers—hired killers—who, in the matter of taking a life, bear a close resemblance in their mental habits to members of a standing army; their job is to kill upon orders. Once again, deterrence of a penalty has little meaning for them.

We might also add a class of murderers who kill to satisfy a deep-seated grudge. Are they deterred by the death penalty? Probably not, for any fear would likely be outweighed by the strong pressure to take a specific life and the mistaken belief that they could escape such a penalty. Triangle murderers and those who kill in a family feud are examples of this type of killer.

It is a strange paradox that murderers, as a class, make the best prisoners and are least likely to commit another murder—or any other crime for that matter—when released from prison. The real enemies of society—aside from professional killers who seldom kill a law-abiding citizen—are those who dabble in crime as a career such as confidence men and women, burglars, robbers, embezzlers, counterfeiters, and forgers, and they are immune to the death penalty. They return from prison to continue preying on society by means of the illicit trade they know so well. In short, then, it is generally accepted that persons convicted of murder and sent to prison "for life" who, of course, have had their sentence commuted, or have been pardoned, make the best readjustment to society after release. We do not intend to condemn those efforts to reform or those who are able to live down a criminal excursion. We do mean to say, however, that capital punishment is and always has been futile.

It has often been advanced by proponents of capital punishment that it is a cheaper way of dealing with murderers than sending them to prison for life. This is a fallacy. It is actually much more expensive to maintain capital punishment, paradoxical though this may be. If we figure the cost of imprisonment at one thousand dollars per year—and if the state had a good system of productive prison labor, this could be reduced by fifty or more per cent—and if we estimate the average lifer's term at ten years(and this is about right the country over), the total would be little more than $10,-000, and even likely to be less. Applied against this are the excessive costs of a court trial in a capital case, the possible cost of a mistrial, second and third trials—the hazards of capital cases in our courts—plus a *pro rated* charge for the construction and maintenance of a death house and apparatus, plus added "round-the-clock" guard service while the condemned is awaiting death, as well as added prison service costs. It is obvious to any fair-minded person and to prudent legislators that the death penalty comes high in monetary costs.

We do not advance any of the sentimental objections to capital punishment; that it is against the spirit of humanity, that it brutalizes the human intellect, that God alone can take a life, and that we must be compassionate in dealing with criminals. We respect persons who have such convictions nonetheless.

The final answer to the person who espouses the cause of capital punishment is that if we desire to get rid of crime and criminals of all kinds we must adopt the same scientific attitude that society has taken about the elimination of physical disease. It is absurd to punish a person who is suffering from cancer or any other malignant disease. It is likewise absurd to punish those who are socially ill to such a degree that they commit socially disapproved acts, especially murder. This may ring as an ideal state of being; yet the citizens of Alaska, Hawaii, Iowa, Maine, Michigan, Minnesota, New York, North Dakota, Oregon, Rhode Island, Vermont, West Virginia, and Wisconsin manage to control murder without the death penalty.* The number of capital crimes has decreased through the years and the number of executions has greatly decreased during the past decade even with a great increase in population. In 1963, there were forty-one but fifteen in 1964. The number fell to seven in 1965; four of these, in Kansas, were hanged.

It is becoming more and more difficult to impanel juries in capital cases. Fewer and fewer are likely to bring in a first degree verdict when they realize they must decide on a question of life or death. We no longer have the mandatory death sentence in this country; there are options of some kind in every jurisdiction.

It is hard to concede that a person of any reasonable cultivation and possessed of even rudimentary knowledge of human behavior can defend this relic of a distant past. The penalty, it can be argued with some degree of cogency, may have some practical significance from one standpoint. Capital crimes, trials, appeals, and executions gather considerable publicity as they progress, and perhaps embody the public's ideals of justice more concretely than any other types of criminal procedure. Thus, to persist in executing the worst offenders is to keep alive a symbol of that ancient injunction, *lex talionis,* where it will be the most telling—to say, in effect, that the state believes in humanity toward offenders where it can afford to be humane, but that vengeance is the sure cure for the "really important" crimes against society. Adopting this form of casuistry, lawmakers can point out to their constituents their own frustration and exasperation concerning certain crimes and offenders and the desperate need of chastising and controlling them by the most heinous penalty that the twentieth century social traffic will bear.

---

*The following states recognize no capital punishment whatsoever: Alaska, Hawaii, Iowa (February 24, 1965), Maine, Minnesota, Oregon (November 3, 1964, by referendum), West Virginia (March 12, 1965), and Wisconsin; Michigan, for treason only; the others with the following qualifications—North Dakota for treason and first degree murder by a prisoner serving a life sentence; Vermont (April 15, 1965) for murder of on-duty police officer or prison guard; New York (June 1, 1965) murder of a police officer or prison guard, or inmate of a prison by a prisoner; and Rhode Island, murder by a life term prisoner. Thus far none of the "qualified" states has executed anyone for the excepted crimes herein mentioned.

But even here there is a flaw in logic. If this kind of philosophy is valid, why not go further and invoke some of the more hideous penalties used so often in earlier days. Revert, for instance, to public executions including burning at the stake. This can never be, as we cannot turn back the clock.

To answer the question we phrased above—"Is Capital Punishment Effective?" it would certainly seem that it is not. While general public opinion polls have tended to indicate a preference for the death penalty, it is of more than passing interest that an Elmo Roper poll taken in 1958 showed that fifty per cent of those asked for their opinion stated they were opposed, forty-two per cent were in favor, and eight per cent expressed no opinion. It was further revealed by the poll that opposition was strongest among lower economic groups with fifty-three per cent expressing that position, whereas, in the upper economic groups, forty-two per cent opposed the penalty.[28]

It is obvious that capital punishment is, in a sense, eliminating itself, ever so slowly. We, the people, when placed on the spot, do not have the courage of our boasts for vengeance. We may be confused concerning our ideas of what to do with our criminals but we are slowly coming to the conviction that legalized death is not the answer. We cannot bury our heads in the sand and exclaim that we change a situation by ignoring it.

We end this chapter—and book—with a few statements from an astute observer of the capital punishment scene in this country, James McCafferty. He notes some trends that are unquestionably diagnostic, regardless of the hue and cry in favor of the sanction's greater use:

1. There is a decided trend toward repealing the death sentence by disuse or by dropping it and substituting life imprisonment or a term of years.

2. Though in the United States there are some thirty-three capital offenses, since 1930, only seven of them have resulted in an execution.

3. Whereas the mandatory death penalty for murder was in effect in several states, today no state can mandatorily carry

---

[28]National Newspaper Syndicate, 1958. A significant index of the trend away from the death penalty by the public was the referendum in Oregon in November, 1964 when the majority of the voters registered opposition.

out the death penalty for first degree murder. (The District of Columbia dropped its mandatory provision in 1962; the State of New York in 1963.)

4. Executions for murder continue downward. During the 1930 decade the average was 151 executions for that offense each year. During the 1950 decade the average dropped to sixty per year.

5. Evidence shows that the death penalty is not final in about half of those sentenced to death. Commutation of sentences to life imprisonment, transfers to mental hospitals for treatment and an occasional death due to natural causes or suicide, account for those who are not executed. Noted too have been the varying time periods between sentence of death and the actual imposition of the death penalty. In 1962 for forty-seven persons executed in the United States, elapsed time from sentence to death to execution averaged twenty and one-half months. The longest elapsed time period on record (1960) occurred in connection with the execution of a convicted California kidnaper, eleven years, ten months, the Caryl Chessman case.

6. The carnival atmosphere of executions in the United States long ago disappeared. The general public has been removed from the death chamber with only a few witnesses present at the time of execution.

7. Finally, in the United States efforts have been made to prevent possible mutilation of the body and to provide a quick and painless expiration for the condemned. Hanging, once the only method for carrying out executions under civil authority, continues in only seven states. Electrocution is used in twenty-four States and lethal gas in eleven States. One State, Utah, continues to permit the condemned prisoner his choice of shooting or hanging. The federal government uses the facilities in the state where the conviction is held.[29]

[29]In *Introduction* to Teeters, *Scaffold & Chair,* Philadelphia, Pennsylvania Prison Society, 1963.

INDEX OF SELECTED NAMES

(Sources in Italics.)

A

Abbott, George, *alias* Almy, 294
Adams, Alan J., 185
Allen, Ethan, 28
Allen, Jack (Abel John), 185
Almy, Frank, *see* Abbott, 293-6
Alwine, Samuel, 363
André, Major John, 368
Andrews, Rev. Eliphalet, 122
Andrews, William, 9, 6, 65, 94-5, 444
Antoine, Abram and Mary, 343
Archer, John Rose, 92
Arnold, Anthony, 91
Arnold, Stephen, 26-7, 73, 237
Asbury, Herbert, 21, 95, 360
Ashmead, Henry, 71, 113
Athol, Justin, 19, 24, 57, 68, 74, 106, 152-7, 171, 182, 232, 434, 436-7
Atzerodt, George, 381 f.
Avery, Rev. Ephraim, 264

B

Bailey, Benjamin, 279-81
Baker, Joseph, 59
Balch, William S., 235
Bancroft, George, 114
Barclay, E. E., 192, 224
Baring-Gould, S., 65
Barker, William, 143, 250
Barnes, Harry Elmer, 443
Barnes, Mary, 135
Barr, Dr. James, 182
Barstow, David S., 405
Bassett, Goody, 133
Bateman, Mary, 74, 306
Batson, 429
Battin, William, 18, 84
Beadle, William, 251
Beard, "Bud," 18
Beatty, Albert, 448
Beauchamp, Jereboam, O., 49, 364
Beck, Henry Charlton, 371

Bedau, Hugo Adam, 441
Bell, Harris, 217
Benders, Kate, 190
Benning, Andrew, 13
Benson, John, 72
Berge, Peter (La Tulipe), 113
Berouse, Joseph, 59
Berry, James, 57, 158, 231
Bethea, Ramsey, 6
Bettinger, J. O., 264
Bevan, Catherine, 105, 346
Bibber, Goodwife, 144
Biddle, Charles, 22, 44, 50, 123-4
Biddle, Edward and John, 241 f.
Bilansky, Ann, 355 f.
Billington, John, 8
Bird, James, 323 f.
Birger, Charles, 418 f.
Bishop, Alice, 120
Bishop, Bridget, 5, 147
Bizel, George T., 195
Blank, Harris, 285
Blay, Ruth, 121
Bleackley, Horace, 19, 55, 57, 190, 246, 433, 435-6, 443
Block, Eugene B., 441
Blundin, Joseph, 75, 344
Bobb, W. P., 168
Bonney, Edward, 273
Boorn, Jesse and Stephen, 234 f.
Booth, John Wilkes, 381 f.
Borchard, Edwin M., 228-9
Borden, Lizzie, 265
Bowman, Ray S., 86
Boyington, Charles N., 24, 103, 195, 313 f.
Bradbury, Mary, 143
Bradford, Isaac, 71
Bradford, William, 8, 111, 152
Brandon, Richard, 57
Brandt, Samuel, 24
Braswell Brothers, 420
Brattle, Thomas, 128
Brimley, George, 133

Bristol, 18
Britton, James, 8
Broehl, Wayne G., 391
Brown, John, 60
Brown, John, 373 f.
Brown, Wensell, 453
Bruelman, John, 258
Brunskill, William, 56
Bryan, Pearl, 337 f.
Buccieri, Pietro, 329
Buchanan, James, 306
Buck, Elizabeth and Solon J., 264
Buck, William J., 60
Buell, Myron A., 162
Bulette, Julia, 322
Bullock, John, 20
Burbey, Louis H., 113
Burke, James, 18
Burnham, Josiah 299
Burns, Creighton, 439
Burr, George Lincoln, 63, 99-100, 128, 130-33, 135-40, 143, 147-8
Burroughs, George, 141
Burt, Olive Woolley, 90, 101, 146, 185, 205, 213, 215, 218-221, 224, 246, 248, 263, 272, 275-7, 283, 285, 289-90, 292, 301, 339-40, 342, 347, 363; 367, 402, 411, 414, 416-7, 422, 425
Burton, Mary, 116 f.
Burton, 233
Butler, Samuel, 437
Butterfield, Roger, 201, 216
Buxton, Thomas F., 436
Byers, Dan, 70

C

Calas, Jean, 89
Calcraft, William, 57
Calif, Robert, 136
Calhoun, Frank, 168, 184
Calkins, Margaret, 122, 299
Cannon, Elizabeth, 361
Cannon, Patty, 225
Carawan, Rev. George W., 65
Carey, Peggy, 115-6
Carlisle, Abraham, 369
Carpenter, David, 218
Carrier, Martin, 140
Carrington, John and Roanna, 133
Carroll, Walter Green, 342
Carson, Ann, 307 f.
Cassady, Peter, 182

Caughy, John W., 404
Cavanaugh, Jesse, 426
Chamberlain, Richard, 22
Chamblitt, Rachel, 84
Champion, 95
Chandler, Peleg W., 10-11, 100, 115, 117-8, 134, 141, 150, 183, 305
Channing, Rev. Henry, 17
Chapman, Gerald, 160-1, 164
Chapman, Lucretia, 352 f.
Cheny, William, 112
Chessman, Caryl, 70, 452
Child, L. Marie, 233, 244
Childs, Frank Lane, 294
Chloe, 12
Christock, Joseph, 217
Churchill, Deborah, 437
Clapp, L. E., 165
Clark, Mrs. E., 310
Clark, Rev. Ephraim, 81
Clark, George, 51
Clark, William John, 360
Clarke, Stephen M., 18, 25
Cleveland, President Grover, 52, 174
Clews, Joanna, 351
Clough, Joel, 39
Coffey, John, 177
Collins, Eddie, 232
Colt, John C., 244, 328
Comings, William Freeman, 238 f.
Conkling, Roscoe, 345
Connor, Catherine, 72, 74
Conrad, Earl, 449
Converse Abigail, 305
Coolidge, Valorous P., 245
Cooper, James Fenimore, 372
Corey, Giles, 98-100, 142-5
Corey, Martha, 144-5
Cornell, Greta, 371
Corrigon, Hugh, 327
Costello, George, 253
Courvoisier, Francois, 32
Coverly, Nathaniel, 224
Cowan, John W., 188
Cowman, John, 135
Cox, Susannah, 54
Craft, Ellis, 414
Crawford, William, 49
Cronin, John, 164
Crowninshield, Richard, 269
Croy, Homer, 160, 287, 399 f.
Cudahy, Eddie, 330
Curley, Thomas, 52
Czolgosz, Leon F., 393

D

Dabner, Louis, 409
Dandy, John, 59
Daston, Sarah, 253
Davenport, Col. George, 272
Davis, E. P., 160
Davis, David Brion, 240
Dawson, David, 22, 369
Dean, Cyrus B., 45
De Fleur, Rose, 314
Delamer, Thomas, 370
Dergan, Bridget, 307
Deutsch, Albert, 453
Diard, Francois Ludgere, 317
Dickens, Charles, 33
Doan, Abraham and Levi, 22, 371
Dole, Esther Mohr, 97
Donnelly, Edward, 64
Douglas, George, 174
Douglass, David, 161
Downe, Capt. Peter, 288
Downie, John, 30
Driver, Robert, 77
Druse, Roxelana, 303-4
Dryer, Jacob, 72
Dudley, Rev. Enos, 226, 264
Duff, Charles, 19, 53, 73, 156, 178, 180, 433, 445, 448-9, 451
Duff, Louis Blake, 21, 44, 56, 74, 91, 158-9, 172, 180, 370, 373, 378, 437-9
Duffy, Clinton T., 73, 169-73, 186, 253, 337, 409, 453
Duffy, Thomas, 422
Duke, Thomas S., 61, 63, 181, 190, 243, 270, 326, 328, 331, 340, 366, 406, 408-9
Dula, Tom (Dooley), 3, 206-9
Dunbar, Reuben, 416
Dunkelberger, George F., 249
Dunton, James, 78
Dupree, 430
Durant, William Thomas, 324 f.
Dyer, Mary, 11

E

Eager, Samuel, 371
Eames, Rebecka, 143
Earls, John, 215, 349
Easty, Mary, 142
Eaton, Gerald, 217
Eckerd, Abram I., 249
Ehrmann, Mrs. Sara, 232, 382

Elliott, Robert G., 448
Emerson, Elizabeth, 121
Engel, George, 397
Erb, Israel, 248
Ettinger, Emanuel, 248
Evans, Charles, 77, 80

F

Falkner, Abigail, 143
Farmer, Daniel, 291
Farnsworth, 237
Fay, Dr. Jonas, 211
Feavor, Nicholas, 77
Ferrers, Earl (Lawrence Shirley), 171, 443
Field, Edward, 96
Fischer, Adolph, 397
Fisher, Lavinia, 35, 54
Fisher, Samuel Rowland, 21, 369
Fisk, James, 365
Fitzpatrick Capt. James ("Sandy Flash"), 64, 71, 285
Fitzroy, Herbert W. K., 108
Flanders, Helen Hartness, 290-1
Fogler, Robert, 177
Folhaber, Jost, 279, 289
Foreman, James, 243
Forrest, Arthur, 243
Foster, Ann, 143
Fowler, Rebecca, 126, 135
Frank, Daniell, 7
Frank, Leo, 257
French, Dr., 212
Freeman, Douglas Southall, 370
Frost, Nathaniel, 24
Fuller, Amasa 361 f.
Funston, John, 284
Furber, Sarah, 214

G

Gabriel, José, 335
Gaines, S. G., 6
Galwin, Peter, 113
Garfield, President James A., 168, 394 f.
Garrett, Catherine, 122
Gay, John, 437
Getter, Charles, 59, 69
Geyer, Frank P., 194
Gibbs, Charles, 61
Ging, Kitty, 189, 217, 273-5
Gipson, Lawrence H., 106-8
Glover, Goody, 136

Goddard, Dr. W. F., 253
Godfrey, Samuel, 45
Goebel, Julius, Jr., 92
Golden, Harry, 258
Gooch, Albert, 332
Good, Sarah, 130-1, 148
Goodell, Abner C., 89
Goodwin, John, 136
Goodwin, Solomon, 81
Gordon, James, 370
Gordon, John, 442
Gordon, Mary Jane, 227
Gordon, Nathaniel, 61
Graunger, Thomas, 111
Graves, Dr. Thomas T., 250
Gray, Roger, 56
Green, Edward W. 287
Green, Henry, 412
Greene, Elizabeth, 121
Greensmith, Nathaniel and Rebecca, 134
Grinder, Martha, 350
Gross, William, 322
Gruening, Martha, 380
Guild, James ("Little Jim"), 15
Guile, Samuel, 112
Guillotine, Dr. Ignace, 445
Guiteau, Charles Julius, 168, 393
Gunness, Belle, 190

H

Halbert, Henry, 259
Hale, Nathan, 368
Hall, Sam, 426
Halzinger Sisters, 224, 342
Haman, 3
Hamilton, Dr., 232
Harden, Rev. Jacob S., 264
Harrington, John, 86
Harris, Alcee, 359
Harris, Mary, 318
Harrison, President William, 181
Harman, S. W., 160
Hartnet, Patrick, 185-6
Hathorne, Judge John, 130
Hayward, Harry, 189, 217, 273-5
Hearsey, Clem, 178-9
Hecht, Ben, 155
Heidt, William, Jr., 51
Heilman, S. P., 86
Heiney, Philip and William, 343
Hellier, Thomas, 91
Hellum, Tony, 359
Hendrickson, Getro, 126

Hendrickson, John, 346
Henning, D. C., 281
Herold, David E., 381 f.
Hibben, Ann, 134
Hibbert, Christopher, 436
Hickey, Thomas, 370
Hickman, Charles, 225
Hickman, William Edward, 333 f.
Hicks, Albert W., 60-1
Hill, Joe, 184-5
Hinks, B. W., 134
Hirshberg, Al, 73
Hoar, Dorcas, 143
Hobbes, Abigail 143
Hoch, Johann, 191
Hoee, William F., 187
Holbrook, Stewart, 190, 195, 199, 275, 294
Holmes, H. H., *see* Mudgett, 192 f., 195
Holmes, Dr. Oliver Wendell, 214, 311
Hopkins, William Seeley, 188
Horn, Tom, 166
Horsemanden, Daniel, 114
Housman, A. E., 438-9
Howard, Andrew, 296
Howe, Elizabeth, 137
Howe, John Lee, 169
Howe, M.A. De Wolfe, 106
Hughes, Langston, 380
Hummel, William, 183
Hunt, Edward, 82
Hunter, Benjamin F., 161
Huntingdon, Rev. Enoch, 82
Huss, John, 102
Hughson, John, 115 f.

I

Illing, Hans A., 184

J

Jackson, John, 228
Jackson, Marilyn M., 305
Jackson, Scott, 338
Jacobs, George, 138
Jacobs, Margaret, 138
Jacobus, Donald Lines, 133-4
James, Robert E., *see* Lisemba, 203
Jefferson, Alexander, 173-4
Jennings, Dean, 453
Jewell, Ellen, 321
Jewett, Jonathan, 250
Joan of Arc, 102

Johnson, Mrs. Catherine, 321
Johnson, Margaret, 133
Johnson, Dr. Samuel, 434
Johnson, Thomas H., 76-7
Johnson, Thomas R., 127
Johnston, Peter, 210
Jones, Joshua, 212
Jones, Louis C., 53, 162, 413, 417
Jones, Margaret, 132
Jonson, Derek, 30
Joyce, John, 286
Juanita, 404
Juban, 218-9
Jubheart, John, 77
Julian, 211, 218 f
Jumpertz, Henry, 327
Jung, Jow, 160

K

Kane, Joseph Nathan, 132
Kantor, MacKinlay, 389
Kassel, Charles, 34
Keck, Charles, 255
Kehoe, Jack, 188-9
Kelley, Levi, 40, 42, 319
Kelly, John, 37-9
Kemmler, William, 446
Kendall, 134
Kennedy, Patrick, 113
Kenney, Penelope, 121
Ketch, Jack, 50, 57, 158
Ketchum, Thomas H., 176
Kidd, Capt., 68
Kinsolving, Rev. Lester, 175
Kipling, Rudyard, 425
Kirby, Archibald, 342
Kirkpatrick, Clifford, 65, 233, 313
Knapp, John Francis and Joseph, Jr.,
    189, 269
Koestler, Arthur, 13, 19, 55, 70, 157
Krakel Dean F., 166

L

Lacy, Mary, 143
Lake, Mrs. Henry, 135
Lambing, A. A., 68
Lamott, Kenneth, 326, 335
Lamphier, David, 53
Langmaid, Josie, 289 f.
La Page, Joseph, 289
Larrowe, Charles P., 446
Latham, Mary, 8

Laurence, John, 441
Lawes, Lewis E., 254
Layton, James, 257
Leadings, Jacob, 25-6
Lechler, John, 34, 40, 47
Le Croix Peter, 59
Leddra, William, 11
Lee, John, 231
Lee, John D., 339 f.
Lee, Pamela, 226
Lee, William, 59
Leisler, Jacob, 183
Leurio, Edward, alias Rulloff, 195 f.
Lewis, Arthur H., 391, 423
Lewis Clarence O., 162
Lewis, Mercy, 129
Lincoln, President Abraham, 62, 381
Lindenmuth, Margaret, 168
Linn, John Blair, 70
Lisemba, Major Raymond, alias James,
    170, 203
"Little Jim," see Guild, 15
Livingston, Edward, 27, 41
Lomax, Alan and John A., 263, 428
Long, Aaron and John, 181, 273
Lough, Glen P., 23
Lushington, Dr. Stephen, 42, 437
Lutherland, Thomas, 9

M

MacDonald, J. E. H., 438
MacKensie, Alexander Slidell, 372
Magowan, James, 55
Maledon, George, 63, 159, 401
Mamachtaga, 66-7
Mark, 89-90, 346
Martin, John, 30
Martin, John Bartlow, 195
Martin, Mary, 9, 66
Martin, Susannah, 137
Marvell, William, 55
Marwood, William, 56, 157
Mather, Rev. Cotton, 9, 78, 131, 136,
    140-1
Mather, Rev. Increase, 77, 79
Mather, Nathaniel, 135
Mathews, Alfred, 70
Mathews, Edward, 246
Matthias, Peter, 286
Mattocks, Peter, 188
Mattson, Margaret, 126
Maxwell, Walter Lennox, 328
Mayberry, David F., 256

McCafferty, James, 460
McCann, Felix, 162
McCarthy, Irene, 143
McCarthy, Justin, 34
McClain, Walter S., 420
McComas, J. Francis, 169, 203, 334
McConaghy, Robert, 199
McDade, Thomas, 9, 15, 17-8, 39-40,
  45, 49, 51, 55, 60-1, 76-7, 81, 84-5,
  89, 92, 121, 161, 187-8, 195, 198-9,
  217, 224-8, 236, 244-5, 251, 256, 259,
  264-5, 270, 279, 282, 287, 290; 292;
  299, 305, 307, 319-24, 326, 328; 333;
  339, 342, 344, 347-8, 354-5, 361-2;
  365, 394, 397, 408, 413-4, 423
McDeirmatt, Michael, 47
McDonald, John, 50
McElwee, Thomas, 344
McFall, John, 5
McFarland, James, 391
McGettigan, Catherine, 122, 299
McKay, Alexander, 337
McKean, Thomas, 67, 119
McNab, John, 214
McQuown, M. L., 349
Meacham, Jeremiah (Mecum), 92
Meeks, Gus, 204
Meeks, Nellie, 205
Mencken, August, 19, 53, 59, 155, 160,
  164, 318, 326, 332, 372, 376, 382,
  390, 392-3, 398, 419
Mencken, Henry L., 155
Miller, Arthur, 100, 129
Miller, Catherine, 360
Miller, Joaquin, 406
Miller, Lena, 349
Miller, Louie, 47
Miller, Perry, 76-7, 127
Millian, John M., 35, 322
Mills, Henry, 227
Mills, Samuel, 296
Milton, John, 436
Mina, Lino Amelio y Epos, 36, 352 f.
Minot, George, 306
Mobley, James, 241
Mock, Kung, 160
Mohawk, Samuel, 200
Monroe, Adolphus F., 256
Moody, Rev. Joshua, 78
Moore, Elizabeth, 122
Moran, James, 34
Moran, Patrick, 243
Mordecai, 3
Morgan, James, 77

Morgan, John F., 21, 202
Morris, James, 216
Moulton, Sherman, 237
Moyer, Jonathan and Uriah, 248
Mudgett, Herman Webster, *alias* H.H.
  Holmes, 192 f.
Muhlenberg, Henry Melchior, 259
Mulliner, Joe 371
Munks, James, 26, 64
Muriata, Joaquin, 406 f.
Murray, John, 445
Musselman, Henry Kobler, 214, 282
Myrick, John, 227

N

Naughton, Frank, 92
Neal, William, 414
Negro Bob (Robert Waldron), 63
Negro Jack, 41, 109
Negro James, 113
Negro Peter, 58, 95
Nettles, Joshua, 361
Nordstrom, Charles, W., 166
Northcott, Gordon Stewart, 335 f.
Noyes, Rev. Nicholas, 140, 147-8
Nurse, Rebecca, 136, 143

O

Occum, Rev. Samuel, 220
Ocuish, Hannah, 16
O'Donnell, Bernard, 19, 346
Offord, Lenore Glenn, 326
O'Neill, Jack, 232
Ormsby, John, 85
Orton, A.R., 224
Osborne, Sarah, 130-1, 148, 253
Oswald, Lee Harvey, 393

P

Palm, Rev. Andrew J., 42, 56, 173,
  178, 185-6, 345, 437
Parker, Alice, 142
Parker, Judge Isaac, 63, 160, 204, 398 f.
Parker, Mary, 143
Parkman, Dr. George, 310
Parris, Elizabeth, 19, 144
Parris, Samuel, 129
Parsons, Albert R., 397
Parsons, Hugh and Mary, 133
Patterson, Haywood, 449

Paul, Moses, 220
Payne, John Howard, 244
Payne, Lewis T., 381 f.
Payne, Zepadiah, 342
Pearson, Edmund, 48, 161, 189, 237, 250, 266, 276, 278, 435
Penn, William, 104, 106
Pepys, Samuel, 33, 153, 171
Perley, Mrs. J. Dudley, 146
Phair, John P., 323
Phillips, Ulrich B., 241
Phillis, 89, 346
Pierrepoint, Albert, 55, 70, 156
Piper, Thomas W., 324
Place, Francis, 433
Plaia, Frank, 254
Pomeroy, Jesse Harding, 13 f.
Poole, William F., 127-8, 132-3, 136
Porter, Cole, 426
Powers, Edwin, 9
Prescott, Abraham, 293
Price, John, 55, 435
Probst, Anton, 201, 217
Proctor, Anne, 100
Proctor, Elizabeth, 129
Proctor, John, 129, 139
Proctor, Thomas, 100
Pudeater, Ann, 142, 146
Purvis, Will, 66, 228, 230
Putnam, Ann, 129, 144

Q

Quelch, John, 82
Quinn, Jimmie, 85

R

Ragan, Elizabeth, 350
Rantoul, Robert, 42
Ravenal, Beatrice St. Julien, 35, 54
Ray, Dr. Cabel, 89
Read, Goodwife (Redd), 143
Read, Wilmott (Redd), 146
Redding, David, 28, 45, 211, 370
Regan, Joseph, 73
Revere, Paul, 89
Reynolds, James, 187
Richardson, Ebenezer, 222
Richardson, Jack, 432
Roberts, John, 369
Roberts, Rev. William, 42
Robinson, Peter, 50
Robinson, Sarah Jane, 348-9

Robinson, William, 11, 26
Rodgers, Esther, 80, 92
Rodriguez, José, 203
Rogers, Rev. John. 80
Rosensweig, Isaac, 285
Ross, Charlie, 330
Ross, Ezra, 306
Ross, Joseph, 112
Ross, William, 277
Rota, L.G.V., 447
Rulloff, Edward H, *alias* Leurio, 195 f.
Runkle, Mary, 226
Rush, Dr. Benjamin, 152

S

Sager, Joseph, 41
Saltonstall, Leverett, 146
Salyard, Charles, 184
Sampson, Patience, 121
Sanford, Laura G., 424
Savonarola, 102
Scans, John, 289
Scharf, J. Thomas, 97
Scheer, Dorothy, 281
Schultz, Herman Paul, 182
Scott, Arthur F., 95, 127
Scott, George Ryley, 99, 102, 441, 445
Scott, Margaret, 143, 146
Sedgwick, Ellery, 348
Seimson, John, 409
Sellin, Thorsten, 87-8, 90 93, 97, 258
Semmes, Raphael, 59, 135
Sender, Ramon, 52
Servitus, 102
Sewell, Samuel, 77, 80, 139
Sexton, Margaret 122
Shakespeare, William, 435
Shannon, William, 5
Sharp, Christian, 69
Sheehan, Bryant, 113
Shelley, Percy B., 94
Sheppard, Muriel Early, 302
Sherman, Lydia, 347
Sherwood, Mrs. Grace, 127
Shirley, Glenn, 63, 159, 204, 399 f.
Shirley, Laurence (Earl Ferrers), 171, 443
Shurtleff, Rev. William, 121
Sickles, Daniel, 362
Silver, Frankie, 300
Simpson, Ann, 355 f., 361
Simpson, Henry, 258
Simpson, Sarah, 100, 111-2, 114, 121

Sims, David G., 49
Sitwell, Edith, 438
Small, Frederick, 48
Smith, A. W., 256
Smith, Claudius, 370
Smith, Edward H., 191, 331
Smith, George, 74
Smith, Harry Hawkins, 371
Smith, J. H., 343
Smith, William G., 169
Smyth, Richard, 308
Sneider, Christopher, 222
Soffel, Kate, 242
Spafard, Abraham, 42
Spangenburg, Rev. Cyriacus, 263
Spargo, John, 29, 211, 370
Spear, Rev., Charles, 25-6, 41, 51-2, 56, 65, 225, 233, 236, 270, 436-7; 440
Spencer, Phillip, 372
Spies, August, 397
Spooner, Bathsheba, 305
Spring, Arthur, 216
Squire, Dr. Amos P., 448
Standish, Miles, 8
Stanton, Albert, 426
Stanton, Edwin M., 382
Starkey, Marion, 5, 130-1, 147, 254
Starkweather, Albert, 167, 217
Starkweather, Charles, 202
Starr, Thomas, 81
Stearns, A. Warren, 15
Stephens, John, 204
Stephenson, Marmaduke, 11, 26
Stone, James M. W., 176
Stokes, Edward S., 365
Stowe, Kesiah, 322
Strang, Daniel, 371
Strang, Jesse, 42, 319
Stupenski, Blaise and Matthias, 188
Surratt, Mrs. Mary E., 381 f.
Sutton, Thomas, 115
Swan, Timothy, 143
Swan, B. L. 134
Sweeting, Whiting, 85

T

Talbert, Albert and Charles, 320
Talby, Dorothy, 8
Taylor, Bayard, 64
Taylor, George and William, 204
Taylor, John, 111
Taylor, John M., 132, 135
Teeters, Negley K., 109, 369, 443, 461

Tesla, Nicola, 446
Thacher, James, 370
Thackeray, William M., 31, 198
Thaxter, Celia, 266
Thayer Brothers 275-7, 342
Thomas, Elisha, 288
Thorpe, Dr., 212
Thurston, Henry W., 15
Tituba, 129
Tomlinson, John, 288
Toppan, Jane, 348
Tracy, Andrew, 178
Trenerry, Walter N., 189, 218, 275, 358, 375
Turner, Edward, 94
Twigg, Mary, 360
Twitchell, George, 249

U

Udderzook, William Eachus, 161, 278
Upham, Charles W., 100, 128-30, 136-40, 142, 146-9
Urie, Rev. John, 117

V

Valentine, 95
Van Valkenburgh, Elizabeth, 354
Van Benthuysen, Robert, 112
Vance, Rev. Abner, 261
Van Duzer, Genevieve, 371
Van Holland, George, 55
Vasquez, Tiburcio, 407
Ver Nooy, Amy, 234
Villon, Francois, 90
Villain, Jean Marie, A., 35, 322
Von Hentig, Hans, 184

W

Wade, Nelson E., 268
Wagner, Louis, 267
Waldron, Robert (Negro Bob), 63
Walker, Gerald, 57
Wall, Rachel, 305
Walling, Alonzo, 338
Wallace, David, 82
Walsh, Thomas, 277
Walters, Ann, 225
Warden, Christie, 294, f.
Wardwell, Mercy and Samuel, 143, 147
Watson, John Fanning, 83, 346

Webster, Daniel, 198, 270
Webster, John W., 310 f.
Weiss, Harry B. and Grace, 103-4, 111
Welch, William, 44
Wellman, Manly Wade, 206, 209, 261, 302, 355, 358
Wellman, Paul I., 114, 160, 181, 273, 403
Wells, Thomas, 6
Werzel, Charles, 183
Wharton, Mrs. Elizabeth, 347
Whatnell, John, 47
Wheeler, George, 327
Whipple, Elmore, 298
Whipple, John, 319
White, J. W. F., 68
White, Capt. Joseph, 269 f.
White, William, 92
Whitla, Billy, 331
Whittier, John Greenleaf, 161
Wigmore, John H., 236
Wild, Sarah, 138
Wilde, Oscar, 438
Wildeman, Henry, 72
Wilkins, Israel, 40
Wilkinson, Thomas, 88
Willard, John, 139
Williams, Abigail, 129, 144
Williams, Gottlieb, 182

Williams, Hiram, 282 f.
Williams, Jack Kenney, 35, 46, 48-9, 58, 74, 109
Williams, T. J. C., 97
Wilson, Amos, 65, 124-5
Wilson Elizabeth, 65, 123
Wilson, Henry, 243
Wines, Frederick H., 443
Winthrop, John, 8-9, 111, 132
Wirz, Capt. Henry, 389 f.
Wisner, Rev. William, 161
Wood, Jesse, 233
Wood, Samuel R., 76
Wood, Warren, 282
Woodbury, George, 40, 122
Wright, David M., 317
Wyatt, Mary Ann, 412

Y

Young, Achsah, 132
Young, Brigham, 340
Young, Granville, 181

Z

Zibulka, Charles, 167, 177
Zimmerman, John, 27, 237

INDEX OF SUBJECTS

A

Abolition; capital punishment, 151, 152, 244, 442, by states, 459 public hangings, 7, 152, 240
Admission; price at hangings, 30
Adultery; hanged for, Mary Latham case, only case in Massachusetts Bay Colony, 8
Alabama; hanged for murder, 24, Boyington case, 313, 314
Allegheny Mts. first hanging west of, 112
Anarchists; activities of, 397, hanging of, 396, list of those hanged, 397
Anger; motivation for murder, 266
Anonymity; of hangmen, 52-3
Arson; capital offense, 4, hanged for in Chester County, Penna., 84
Atkinson; hangman, Penna., 159
Attempt; to escape before execution, 318, from Walnut Street Jail, 309 see escape
Attendance; at hangings, 28, at public hangings, 36-7, see hanging
Atitude; of condemned at gallows, 48, 377, see hanging
Atwater Kent Museum; hanging ropes, etc., 87
Axe; murder, Meeks family, 205-6

B

Backwoods area; murder in, 300
Ballad;
    Abduction & Cruel Murder of Miss Sarah Furber, 214, Almy Case, 296, of Amasa Fuller Case, 362-4, Ashland Ballad, 414-6, Beadle case, 252, Batson case, 429, Bishop Lee, 341, Boston Massacre, 222, Braswell Bros., 419, Bryan case, 338, Charles Borger case, 419, Craft-Neal, 414-6, Daniel Davis Farmer, 292-3, Danny Deever, 425, Dupree, 329-30, of Edward Mathews, 246, the Fisk-Stokes affair, 366-7,
Frankie Silver, 302, by Garfield's assasin, 395-6, Ghost of Joshua Jones Appears, 212, Giles Corey, 101, Goodwyfe Corey, 144-6, Hangman's Tree, The, 431-2, Hymns at the Gallows, 259, James Bird case, 424-5, of John Funston, 284, Josie Longmaid, 290, Ballad of Julian, 218-9, Kitty Ging, 275, lament on hanging, 433, Levi Kelley, 427, Love's case, 276-7, Lydia Sherman, 347, Moses Paul, 220, murder by axe, 205-6, murders in New Hampshire, 288-9, Murdered Pedlar, The, 282-3, Murdered Wife, The, 412, North Dakota hanging, 277, Miss Otis Regrets, 426, Peter Downe, 289, Reek and Rambling Blade, The, 430, Reuben Dunbar, 417, Salem Conspiracy, The, 271-2, of Sam Hall, 426, Thomas Duffy, 422-3, of Tom Dula, 208-9, of Reverend A. Vance, 262-3, written by condemned, 402
Balloon ascension; at Walnut St. Jail, 30
Banishment, Quakers, 11
Bank theft, greed, 286
Bank robbery, 287-8
Barbadoes; Quakers, 10
Barrel murders; strange case of, 327
Bells; use of at hangings, 21
Benefit of clergy; 10, see Neck Verse,
Behavior; of condemned at gallows, 301, 339, of condemned's parents at gallows, 326, of crowd at hanging, 309, 323, see hanging
Beheaading; dismemberment, 93, 95-6, 443, Negroes, 96
Betrayal; Elizabeth Wilson, 123
Biblical justification; drawing & quartering, 94
Bier; custom of, use to prove guilt, 9, law of, 9
Bilboes; gibbeting, 89
Bleak House; by Charles Dickens, 33
Blood; custom of bier, 9
Body; disposal of, 210, sale of, 211,

snatching of by medical men, 212, *see* medical men

Bones; of hanged, superstitions, 65

Boston; hanging of William Leddra, 12

Boston Evening Post, hanging & gibbeting of slaves, description, 89

Boston Massacre; 222

Boston; piracy, hanged for, 92

Boston Post; hanging of innocent person, 232

Brain; of murderer examined at Cornell Univ., 198, *see* hanging, *see also,* medical men

Branding; benefit of clergy, 10, used as a substitute for death penalty, 109

Breaking neck; hanging, 156

Breaking on the wheel; gibbet, 89, torture, 440

British; supplying re: treason, 28

Broadside; ballad, Beadle case, 251, hanging, Julian case, 219, pardons, Boston Massacre, 222

Brothers; hanged together, 342, *see* hanging, *see also,* multiple hangings

Buckshot scaffolds; 164, *see* gallows

Bungling at gallows, 57, 69, 122, 166, 169, 173-177, 199, 202, 229, 231, 269

Burglary; capital offense, 4

Burning; as punishment, 103, cost of, 109, to death, 115, gibbet, 91, last legal, 109, legal, 104, Negroes, 104; at stake, 29, 102, in Penna., 104, 106, not witches, 126, wizzardry, 126, women, 105

C

Calcraft; hangman, 32

California; banditry in, 404, last person hanged in, 335, only female hanged, 405, Sacramento-a strange case, 169, wife killer, 203

Capital crimes; USA early history, 441

Capital punishment;
abolition of, 151, 152, 244, by states, 459 argument against, 460-1 beheading, 443, British Royal Commission on, 70, 157, by snakes, animals, drowning, stoning crucifiction, pulled apart by horses, devoured by ants, shooting, garroting, 443-4, casting from a height, 443, cost of, 458, denouncement of, 452, 459 drift away from, 440-461, as a deterant, 459,

effect of delay in application, 452, effectiveness of, 455-7, halt of, 151, lethal gas, use for, 451, murders as the result of, 41, opponents of, 235

Captain Sandy Flash, 288

Cart; drawn to gallows, 21-2, 122, 149, 207, allowed to walk, 353

Carolina, North; only female hanged, 300, Anne Simpson—Belansky Case, 355

Castration; 106

Cattle war; story and result, 166

Chesapeake Bay; place of execution, 59

Chicago; Haymarket riots, anarchists, 4

Children; cursing parents, capital offense, 15, hanged for, 15

Chinese, hanging of, Tong Wars, 160

Church belfries; murder in, 324

Civil War; Andersonville, commandant hanged, 389-90, murder in, 317

Claiming bodies; by medical men, 216

Clan, Doan; of Penna., 22

Clergy, benefit of; 10

Coal miners; struggles, 390, *see* Mollie Maguires

Colonial times; women, Susanna Cox Cox case, 54

Colorado; state prison hanging, 165, Lisemba case, 203

Commutations; death sentence, 71, 342

Condemned; behavior at gallows, 184, 248-250, 337, last requests, 184, suicide of, 249-50

Confessions at gallows, 82

Connecticut; youngest child hanged in, 16, witches, 126

Conspiracy; Negro, 114, 116

Cost of hanging, 183

Counterfeiting; as a capital offense, 4, 77, 82

County jails; hanged in Penna., 5

Court charge; sentence, 117

Crowds;
at hanging, 23, 27, 232, attitude at mass hanging, 60, 94, 149, 184, 229, 304, 229, 299, 306, 309, 325, 370, 376, 452, attitude toward hangman, 52, behavior at, holiday mood & size, 28, 41, 45, behavior at private execution, 358, description of hanging, 395, Mollie Maguires hanging, 392, size at anarchist's hanging, 397

Crucible, The; by Arthur Miller, 129

Cruelty; 27
Cumberland county; crowd at hanging, 184

D

Dancing on air; 156, Oscar Wilde, 458-9, *see* hanging
Death, by fright before hanging, 254-5
Death cart; drawn to gallows, 122, *see* cart
Death penalty; technique, 154, 157, *see* capital punishment
Delaware; capital punishment, 152, flogging, 152
Deportation; England to USA, 72, pardon, 73
Dickens, Charles; attended hanging, 33
Dismemberment; 96, *see* beheading
Disposal of hanged body; 210-1
Dissection; 222, by medical men, 216, 219, public protest, 216, *see* medical men
Doan Clan; 22, 64, 371, *see* Tories, *see also,* Penna.
Double hanging; 30, *see* multiple hanging
Drawing; 98, to gallows, 207, quartering, 23, 97, hurdle sled, 22, 94, 176 quarter, 93-4, biblical justification, 94
Dress of condemned at gallows; 187, 189, 315
Drop; length of, 156, 169, 170, long drop, 157, *see* height-weight ratio
Drums; at hangings, 26
Duel; female hanged for, 437, refusing as a cause of murder, 364
Dying speeches; 82

E

Early days; newspaper accounts of hanging, 20
East Jersey; condemned for beastiality, 111
Effigy; hanged in, 183
Electrocution;
19, introduced in Miss., 450, description of, 450, introduction of and debate 441, report of New York World, 446-448, inventor of, 446-448, first victim, 446-448
England; escaped from gallows in, 231, executioner James Berry, 182, execu-
tion of children in, 13, hanging in, 66, hanging deterrent in, 42, hanging knot, 157, hangmen are traditional in, 55, last public hanging in, 6, Newgate Prison, 6, public debaucheries in 31, transported felons in, 119, witchcraft executions in, 127
Escape;
attempt, 318, to avoid gallows, 242, gallows escapes, 228, 231, 237-9, 241, slave escapes, 18, from Walnut St. Jail, 399
Exclusion; sheriff's right, in private hanging, 153
Executioners; 52, 54, attacked, 54, bungling, 180, James Berry, England, 182, 231, Jack Ketch, euphemism, 57, 158-9, Joe the Hangman, 180, status, 54, suicidal problems, 56, "Young man Be an Executioner," 57
Executions;
of children, 13, electrocution, 19, *see* electrocution, gas chamber, 19, of the Mollie Maguires, 188, multiple by shooting, 114, public, 32, 53, public number of, sermons at, 76, by shooting, 114, types of, 7, *see* capital punishment, *see also* hanging
Exhibit; of skeleton 211
Experiment; with body, 217, *see* medical men

F

Family group hanging; 343, *see* multiple hangings
Famous hanging ropes; 168
Fear; at gallows, 24
Females;
burned at stake, 89, first hanging of, 8, gallows sermon, 80, gibbetted, 80, hanged in early days, 87, hanged in Mass. Colony, 120, 122, multiple hanging, fictional, 342
Fetters; use of, 148
Fictional hanging cases, 224-226
First;
bank robbery in USA 287-8, female hanged, 8, Jew hanged, 285, juvenile court 12, hanging in USA, 7, hanging in prison, 6, hanging for counterfeiting, 82, hanging west of Allegheny mountains, 68, Negro hanged, 107,

person hanged, San Quentin, 335, person recorded as hanged, 3, state to abolish public hanging, 7, state to legislate against public hanging, 152

Flax ropes; used in hanging, 168

Flogging; 152

France; witchcraft executions, 127

Friends, Society of, 10

Fright, at gallows, 174-5

G

Galloping-gallows; type of scaffold, 159

Gallows ballads; 208-9, Ebenezer Richardson, 221, Furber case, 218, *Ghost of Joshua Jones Appears*, 212, Ballad of Julian, 219, Meeks Story, 206, Tom Dula, 214, *see* ballads

Gallows;
behavior of condemned, 301, behavior of parents of condemned, 326, blundering at, 177, *see* bungling, bungling at, 173-177, cheating the, 248-250, cheating by death, 241, 254-5, cheating by suicide, 244, 260, by confusion, 82, descriptions, 162-3, description of hanging, 39, destruction of, 170, Charles Dickens present, 33, dress at, 187, 189, Druse case, 304, escape from, 315, fear at, 24, female hanged, 80, "Gallows Hill", 86, Humor by Jack Richardson, 132, improved, 159, music at, 49, painted red, 365, pardons at, 228, 274, public demand for release of condemned, 125, reprieves at, 228, 274, 257, 304, room, 170, sermon at, 76, 221, spanking of children; 65, speech, 118, suicide, 248-250, superstition, 149, trap, strange type, 163, 46-7, 67, 207, 257, 298, unusual comments, 177, used for other victims, 162, victim's dress at, 188, water used as a means of trap-release, 165, case of Will Purvis, 228

Garfield, James A.; assassin hanged, 393-395, story of his assassin, 393

Garroting; for treason, 445

Gas; description of use, 454
lethal, pain involved, 156, use of lethal gas, opinion, 451, steps in utilization and preparation, 19, 453

Gas Pipe Murders; San Francisco Fire, 408-9

Germany; witchcraft executions, 127

Ghosts; hanging, near gallows, 63-4

Gibbet;
"bilboes", 87-8, breaking on the wheel, 89, burned at the stake, 91 as, a deterrent, 91, of females, 80, 87, hanged in chains, 88, 92, in Massachusetts, 115, Negroes, 89, Paul Revere, 90, piracy, 88-9, as a practice, 440, preservation of body, 89, superstitions, 88, use of tar, 90, in USA, 88

Gravestone; peddler memorialized, 281

Great Britain; condemned played to the crowd, 50, unable to hang one man, 232

Greed; bank theft, 286, murder for, 266, strange case, 285

Gubernatorial grace; 75

Guillotine; history of invention, 445

H

Hanging;
admission price, 30
admission tickets, 245
for adultery, 8
aftermath, suggestibility of witnesses, 43
Alabama, 24
for arson, 4
attendance at, 45
attitude of condemned, 48, 51
ballad, *see* ballads
behavior of victim, 337, 387-389, of crowd, 59, 323
at Boston, 12
breaking neck, 156
broadsides, 219
bungling; 57; 68-9; 166, 174-6, 188, 199, 208, 231, 269, 378
burglary, 4
not burned (witches), 126
in chains, gibbet, 88, 92-3, 115, 161, *see* gibbet
in chair, 76
of Chicago anarchists, 396
of children, 15
Chinese Tong Wars, 160
Civil War, John Brown, 373, cases, 368
of commandant of Andersonville, 368, 389, 390
of condemned, kidnaper, 334, of nun

murderer, 329
cost of, 58, 93, 176
for counterfeiting, 4, 22, 82
in county jails, 6
crimes related to, 42
crowd at, attitude toward, 376, behavior & size, 41, 45, 94 184, 229, 238, 281, 291, 299, 309, 325, 358, 370, 376
death by fright, 254-5
description of, 38-9
for desertion, Revolutionary War, 372
disposal of body, 210-1
drama, 21
dress at gallows, 190
in effigy, 183, 432
in England, 66
famous persons associated with, 170
father and son, 343
females, 120, females first hanged, 120, *see* females hanged, Mass. Colony, 305
fictional, 224, 226
of first Negroes, 107
at gallows, 274, *see* gallows
of Gas Pipe Murderers, 429
handbook on, 19
for highway robbery, 4
for horse stealing, 4
of Indians, 66-7
of Indians at Mankato, Minn., 375
of Indians, 401
individual reaction to, 45
for infanticide, 4
of the innocent, 232-3, 442
inside state prisons, 57, 323
interrupted, 254
on islands, 59
in jails, 6
jerked downwards, 161, upwards, 160
of Jews, 285
of Joe Mulliner, the Robin Hood of Mordecai Swamp, 371
for kidnaping, 62, 332, 337
type of knot, 156
land leased for, 59
large crowds at, 304
last public, in England, 6, in USA, 6, 442
laws pertaining to, 153
of Lincoln conspirators, 368, 381-9
long drop for, 57
lynchings, 3
medical men's role in, 210, 212
method of, 171

military, 26
of Mollie Maguires, 390, 392
Most magnificient in England, 172, 443
multiple, 30, 370, 379, of anarchists, 396, of brothers, 420-1, sentenced by hanging judge 400, classic cases, 342
of NAZI war criminals, 380-1
of Negroes, 379, *see* slaves, 117, 380, for poisoning, 346
Newspaper acct. of last hrs, of condemned, 418, coverage, 43-4
number estimated, 3
pain involved, 153-155, 158
pamphlets, pertaining to 77, 286, Bridget Dergan case 307, McCarty case, 324, Robert McConaghy case, 199
pardons, 71-73, identified with Boston Massacre, 222
in Pennsylvania, 5, Bellefonte county, 24, no. of persons, 26
physician present 210, 212
of pickpockets, 41
for piracy, 59, 60-1, 68, 81, 372
Poetry by condemned, 316-7
popularity of, 433
pregnancy, 74, *see* pleading the belly
premature, 51
preparation for, 37
prison, first hanging in, 6
private, 6, 151, 153
public 6, 19, abolished, 7, description of all, 25, oulawed, 151
by Puritans, 11
of Quakers, 10-1, 369
for rape, 4, 112
reprieves, 237
restraining board, 170
Revolutionary War cases, 368
rope, breaking, 68, *see* bungling, slipping, 230, types used by George Maledon, 400, used as cure for physical ails, 46
at Salem, 25
at San Quentin, 325
second rope, use at, 66
for sex crimes, 110
sheriff's role—personal experience, 175
sheriff's role in, 60
ship's, on board, 60
in slavery, 6, 62, 105, 116
and souvenirs, 183
special devices, 167

state prisoners, 6
strange cases of, 195 232
in streets and squares, 19
suicide before, 63
for treason, 369
from "trees", 371
"tree", 411, euphemism for gallows in
prose & poetry, 432, in interest of
National Security, 368, *see* "Turned
Off," 122
for trunk & barrel murder, 327
types of scaffolds, 164, *see* gallows,
164-5
as a type of suicide, 258
USA first, 7
US Army manual, 173
upwards, jerked, 165-6
use of carts, irons and bells, 21, *see*
cart drawn, irons, bells gibbets and
hanged in irons
in Vermont, 28, 45-6
victim freed, 66
and viewing of body, 183
views on, 437
    Butler, 437
    Cicero, 437
    Gay, 437
    LaFayette, 437
    Lushington, 437
vigilante, 3
Virginia, in colony of, 7
in Washington, 5
Weight-height ratio, 158
wheelbarrow men, 118-9
for witchcraft, 132-134, 139-149,
witnessed, 43
women, 121, *see* female
youngest child, 16
Hangman;
    Atkinson, Penna., 159
    attacked, 56
    attitude toward condemned, 335,
    people's attitude toward, 54-5
    James Berry, England, 231
    breast beating by, 66
    British, 157
    Bungling; 66, *see* bungling
    Calcroft, 32
    competence, 155, *see* bungling
    Cratwell, 55
    disguise, 53
    employment of outsiders, 53
    of England, 190
    euphemism, "Jack Ketch," 57

Great Britain, 232
held in contempt, 56
inexperienced, 175
knot, placed to right side, 156
Maledon, George, 400, memorial slab,
404
money per hanging 56
ropes, 167, carried to place of execution, 178
sheriff, 158
status of, 51
traditional in England, 55
Haymarket anarchists; 4
Height & weight ratio; figured length of
rope, 158, 169
Hemp rope; used for hanging, 171-2
Highway robbery; capital offense, 4
Holmes—Mudgett; mass murder, 192-195
"Holy Experiment" of William Penn;
107
Horse stealing; capital offense, 4
Horsemonger Lane Jail; double hanging
at, 33
Hospital; murder in, 329
"Hurdle;" 23 *see* cart
Hysteria; historical importance, 4

I

Indian country; law enforcement, 159,
lawlessness, 398
Indian wars; 272
Indians;
    attitude of crowd at hanging of 38
    Sioux at Mankato, 376, female hanged,
    halfbreed ambushed, 343, hanged,
    66-7, 400-1, hanging of 38 Sioux at
    Mankato, Minn., 114, multiple hang-
    ing, 375, hanging of, 222, murdered,
    392-3 murdered by 218-220
Infamous cases; 192-195
Infanticide; 80, capital offense, 4, case
of Elizabeth Wilson, 122, 124
Innocent person hanged; 232-3
Inside prison; hanging 323, *see* hanging,
private
"Iron fist," Doan gang, 23, *see* Penna..
Irons; use of at public hangings, 21

J

"Jack Ketch;" hangmen euphemism, 57,
158-9
Jerked upward, 166, *see* hanging

Jews; hanging of, 285
Judges comments; at pirate-slaver hanging, 62
Jury; dismissal—double jeopardy, 351
general, 28, secluded without food & drink, 351

K

Kentucky;
last person publicly hanged, Owensboro, 6, persons hanged from trees, 6
Kidnaping;
16, 330, hanging, 62, *see* hanging, as capital offense 337, identification of public with, 330, and murder, execution for 176, 332
Knot; hanging, England, type, 156-7, loops, legends about 172-3

L

Last;
legal burning, 109, pirate hanged, 60, person hanged in California, 335, public hanging 34, public hanging in England, 6, public hanging in New Hampshire 297-8, public hanging in New York, 40, requests of condemned, 184
Law of the bier, 9
Legal burning, 104
Lincoln, Abraham; 62, conspirators in assassination, 4, hanging of assassins, 381-389, intercession in multiple Indian hangings, 376
Lindbergh law, 332
London; bungling, 68, *see* hanging, bungling, Tyburn, place of execution, 171
Long drop; 57, *see* height-weight ratio, 157, type of hanging, 159
Loops; knot, legends about, 172
Lore of hanging; 183
Louisiana; Harris Hellum case, 359
Lust; murder, 266
Lynchings; 3, before legally hanged, 256-7, female in California, 404, of Italians, 180-1

M

Maine; last hanging, 268
Maguires, Mollie; multiple hanging, 184
Maledon, George; hangman for Judge Issac Parker, 401
Mankato, Minn.; multiple hanging, 4
Maryland; females hanged, 120, *see* females, hanging for treason in Revolutionary War, 96, place of hanging, 59
Massachusetts Bay Colony;
gibbeting in, 89, hanging in, 114, 123, hanged for beastiality in, 111, innocent person hanged in, 232, mass execution, murder of Indians in, 114, Plymouth first person hanged for murder in, 8, Salem, 99, 128, 129
medical men; body snatching 215, claiming bodies, 216, dissection, 216, examination of own victim, 246, phrenology, 216, purchase of bodies, 215, role of, 210, 212
Middle Ages; burn at stake, 102, witches, 127
Military; 41, hangings, 26, presence at hanging, 35, trial, 29
Ministers; hanging of, 261, 264, murder, 259-61
Minnesota; Mankato, multiple hanging of 38 Sioux Indians, 375, only female hanged, 357, Simpson-Belansky case, 355, Hayward-Ging case, 273
Minors; executed, 13, 18, hanging of, 26
Mississippi; Will Purmo case, 66, 228-30
Missouri; Burton case, hanging innocent person, 233, Talbert case, 320
Mob; interfere with sheriff's duty, 18
Mollie Maguires; ballad for one who was executed, 422-3, hanging of, 184, 390-393, *see* multiple
Mudgett-Holmes, 192-5, multiple hanging; classic cases, 342, double hanging, 33, hanging, Spooner case, 306, Indians, 381, Mollie Maguires, 184
Murder;
by axe, 55, 205-6, in backwoods community, 300, in church belfries, 324, conviction without a body 234, first person hanged for, 8, for greed, 266, hanging for, 290, and kidnaping, 176, and lust, 266, and ministers, 259-261, of nun, persons convicted of, 329, propagated by hanging, 152, for revenge and spite, 203-4, at "Smutty Nose," 189, by slaves, 18, *see* Negroes, women, and propensity for, 346
Music; at gallows, 26, 49

N

Narrative of the witchcraft cases, 130
National Security; hanging in defense of, 368

Navy; executions, 5

"Neck verse;" re: clergy, form of pardon, 10

Negroes;
burning of, 103-4, conspiracy, New York City, 92, 114, 116, decapitated, 95, discrimination in trials, 112-3, female hanged, 123, gibbeting, 87, hanged-head displayed, 96, hanged for poisoning, 346, hanged, 117, 400, multiple hanging of, 379, murder committed by, 359, murderer's actions at hanging 173, murder, hanged for, 256, plots to riot, 118, Queens, L.I. riots, 115, 118, 379-80, slaves, 106, trials of, 107, witches, Salem, 129

Newcastle Code; 106-7, repeal, 108

Newgate Prison, 31, scaffold, 6

New Hampshire;
abolished public hanging, 7, Amherst murder, 291, ballads, 288, comments on training for hanging, 175, Concord, 48, famous case from, 293, last public hanging, 297, Portsmouth 124, public hanging abolished, 240, strange case, escaped gallows, 238

New Jersey;
abolished public hanging, 7, child hanged in, 15, hanging of Peter Robinson, 50, hangman James Van Hise, 159

New York;
abolish public hanging 7, Cooperstown, hanging at, 26, 42, electrocution introduced, 450, execution, 174, Grover Cleveland, sheriff in, 52, hanging of Jack Allen, 185, hanging of John Kelly, 37, Jessie Strang case, 42, 319, last public hanging, 40, Negro conspiracy, 92, pirates hanged, 59, riot of slaves, 114-5, Rulloff case, 196-8, triple hanging in, 275

Noose; number of loops in, 172

North Carolina; Ballad of Tom Dula, 206, Rev. George Washington Carowan, 65, 260, Frankie Silver case, 302

Nun; murder in a hospital, 329

O

Ohio; crimes related to hanging, 42, hanging of John W. Cowan, 188, Pearl Bryan tragedy, 337

Old Baily; hanging at, 32

Old Stone Prison, Philadelphia; 21

Old Testament; allusions to death penalty, 3, 440

Opponents; capital punishment, 235

P

Pain; in electrocution, 447, in hanging, 153-155, in lethal gas 156

Pardon; arriving too late, 73, Boston Massacre, 224, commutation to imprisonment 71, deportation, 73, at gallows, 72-3, 228, for pregnancy, 73-4

Parents; behavior, condemned's, 326

Parker, Isaac; the hanging judge, 399, death of, comment on, 403

Peddlers, early plight, 279, murdered, 280, perils of, 282-3, postboy murder, 284

Peine forte et dure; Giles Corey, 98, *see* pressing to death

Pennsylvania;
Atwater Kent museum, 87
bungling at the gallows in, 178, *see* bungling
burned at the stake in, 106
Elizabeth Wilson's betrayal, 123-4
escape to avoid gallows, 242-3
females present at hanging in, 36
fictional hanging cases in, 227
first state, to abolish public hanging, 7, to legislate against public hanging, 152
gallows, ghost, 65, victim, mode of dress, 188
gibbeting, iron, 88-9, *see* gibbet
hanging, 5, 26, in effigy as social practice, 433, interrupted by illness, 254
hangman, Atkinson, 159
lore of hanging, 183
Mollie Maquires, hanging of, 390
Newcastle Code, 106
number of persons hanged in county jails, 5
peddler murdered, 280
Penna. Prison Society, founded, 119
perils of peddlers, 279
persons hanged in, 287
pirates, 107
Ross kidnaping, 330
sex crime, 112
suicide of condemned, 248-250
triangle murders, 360
wheelbarrow men, 118

Whitla abduction, 331

wife poison husband, 346

William Udderzook case, 278

Philadelphia, 83-4, 123, cost of public hanging, 58, Doan gang, 64, last public hanging, 34, Moyamensing prison, no. of persons hanged, 172, no. of loops in knot, 172, new account of trial in Revolutionary War, 96, Walnut St. Jail, 309

Phrenology, 217, medical men, 216

Physician, role in execution, 210, 212

Pickpockets, 41

Pillories, public punishment, 19

Piracy;
81, Boston, 92, capital offense, 4, Captain Kid, 69, definition of, inclusion of slavers, 61, dying speeches, 82, fifth section, U.S. statutes for slavers, 62, gibbeting, 88, hanging, 60, 68, hanged in NYC, 59, hanged for, put in irons, 372, penalty of quartering, 94, In Penna., 107

"Pleading the belly"; 74, execution stay, 306, pregnancy and hanging, 405

Plymouth colony; 120

Poem; on hanging, *The Masque of Anarchy*, 435, *Measure for Measure*, 436, *Paradise Lost*, 436, on horror of hanging, 162

Poetry; by condemned, 316-7, relating to hanging, 438-9

Poison; perpetrated by slaves, 346, murder cases involving, 344

Postboy; murder, Ohio, 284

Pottsville, Penna.; Mollie Maguires, hanging of, 184

Presidential assassins; fate of, 393

Pressing; only case in USA, 100, Salem, 98, *see peine forte et dure*

Prison; Colorado State, 165, Moyamensing 172, Old Stone 21, San Quentin, 31, 44, 167, 170, 325, Sing Sing, 254, Tyburn, 171

Prohibition; the gangster era, 418

Prostitution; & murder, Ellen Jewett, 321

Psychiatric examinations; 13

Public;
demand gallows release of condemned, 228, execution, 32, 53, 151, hanging cost, 58, hanging, 19, 176, hanging attendance, 36, hanging, description of, 25, 34, hanging dress of women, 36, hanging outlawed, 151, Philadelphia, 34, protest, dissection 216

Punishments; other, 93, public, 19

Purchase bodies; medical men, 215, *see* medical men

Puritans; 87 Quakers hanged by, 11

Q

Quakers;
banished, 11-2, Barbadoes, 10, hanging of, 10 losing influence, 108, pamphlets, 77, persecution of, 26, role in creation of penal code, 105, sheriff abusing, 30, whipped, 12

Quartering; 440, cutting body into parts, 95, 440, drawing and, 93-4, 97, pirate, first in England, 94

Queens, Long Island; Negroes riot, 118

R

Rabbitt apparatus; scaffold, 165

Rape; capital offense, 4, hanging, 112, West Jersey, 113

Release of condemned; at public demand, 229

Remarks; at gallows, by condemned, 185

Reprieve; capital punishment, 237, gallows cheated, 71, 228, 253, 304, too late, 73, 122, 125

Restore life; attempts by medical men, 212, 217

Restraining board; hanging, 170

Retribution; 87

Revenge; murder, type of motive, 203

Revolutionary War; 44, hanging for desertion, 372, of Tories, 370, traitor hanged, 369-70

Rhode Island; hanging innocent person, 232, preacher tried for murder, 264-5

Riots; 27-8, slaves, 115

Rope breaking; 69-71, *see* bungling

Rope;
description, 168, drop 171, *see* height-weight ratio, famous, 168, flax, 168, gallows, 187, *see* gallows, hangmen, 178, hemp used in hanging, 168, length of, 171, loops, legends about no., 172, manufacture of, 167, preparation, 171, type of knot, 168, 172, type used by hangman Maledon, 400, slipped, 230, *see* bungling, strange story, 169, thickness, 168, type used for Lincoln conspirators, 386, type of and length, 170, weight of victim, 171, types of hemp, 171

Royal Commission; capital punishment, 70, 157

S

Sale; of hanged body, 212, *see* hanging, medical men
Salem; hanged at, 25, hanging of witches, 5, 136-46, Massachusetts, 122, 129, murder for money, 269-70, pressed to death, 99, witchcraft at, 130, witch, cleared of charges, 254, *see* witches
San Francisco fire; Gas Pipe murders, 408
San Quentin; hanging in, 170, 325
Scaffold; buckshot as means of tripping, 164, crowds at, 184, description of 162-3, preserved, 173, Rabbitt apparatus, 165, types of, 46-7, 207, water trap, 164-5, *see* gallows
Scattering; decapitating & dismemberment, 95
Schoolmaster; convicted of murder, 27
Sermon; at Execution, 17, 76, 92
Set free; double jeopardy, 351
Sex crimes; hanging, 110, Penna., 112
Side speeches; at gallows, 82
Sheriff;
fright at gallows, 174, at hangings, 60, interview on experiences, 175, professional hangman, 158, right to exclude from hanging, 153, role in hanging, 27, training for hanging, 175
Ships; hanging on, 60
Skeleton, of hanged man for exhibit, 211-2, of John Earls, 349, use of, 218
Smutty Nose; murder at 189
Slaves;
6, 14, abolitionists, John Brown, 373, beheading of, 96, conspiracy to rebel, 373, hanged and dismembered, 96, hanged, 18, 62, 104-5, 116, murdering by poison, 346, Negro, 106, 116, not allowed to testify, 317, see Negro, riots, 115, opinions on conditions of, 117, testimony of, 64
"Sled;" drawing to gallows, 22, 176, *see* cart
Society of Friends; 10
Sold; bodies of hanged persons, 214, *see* medical men
Sioux Indians, multiple hanging, 4
South Carolina;
actions of condemned, 48, Charleston, 54, children executed, 13, cost of hanging, 58, crowds at hanging, 35, double hanging, 48, early statutes permitting burning, 109, witches 126

Souvenirs; hanging ropes, pieces of scaffold, 183
States; capital punishment abolished in, 459
Suicide;
aftermath of hanging, 42, beating the hangman by, 63, before trial 251, cheated gallows, 200, 244, 248-50, in the courtroom, 65, forced by gallows type, 164, by hanging, 258, pre-execution, 76,
Superstitions; gallows, 149, gibbeting, 88, hands of hanged, 65, hanging, 74
Speech; Ethan Allen, 29, gallows, 118
Spies; description of, 449, electrocution of, 449, *see* treason
Spirits; near gallows, 63, *see* superstitions
Spite; murder, a type of motive, 203-4
Stake; burned at, 89
"Star chamber," 151
States; using capital punishment, 151
Stocks; public punishment, 19
Strange cases;
Almy-Abbot Christie Worden case, 294, Ann Simpson, Ann Belansky, 356, Bridget Dergan case, 307, Bowen case, 250, Boyington Tragedy, 313-4, Chessman case, 452, Classical poison cases, 347 Durant affair, 326, Edward H. Rulloff case, 195, escape gallows, 237-9, Frankie Silver case, 300-1, Henry G. Green case, 412, Joanna Clew case, 351, Joaquin Murieta, 406-7, Josie Langmaid, 289, Knapp-Crownin-shield case, 269, Mary Harris case, 319, Murder for insurance, 273, Nelson E. Wade case, 268, poisoning, 347, Postboy murder case, 285, Prof. Webster-Harvard, 310-1, Rosensweig-Blank case, 225, Roxalana Druse case, 303-4, Smutty Nose murder case, 266, Spooner case, 305, Sacco-Venzetti, 452, Talberts of Missouri, 320, Thomas Walsh case, 277, Trunk and barrel murders, 327

T

Tar; use to preserve gibbeted body, 90
Tong; hanging of members of, 160
Torturing; breaking at wheel, 440
Tories; 22, 29, hanging of, 370, Doan gang, 371
Transported; felons from England, 119
Trap door; stuck, 231, *see* bungling
Trap; gallows, jerked upwards, 163

"Tree"
Attitudes at, 48-51, bungling at, 66, *see* bungling, crowd at 37, fear and bravery, 25, gets name, 46, hanging, 5, 6, 60, 160, reprieves at, 27; *see* reprieves, Salem victim, 136, sermons at, 76, speeches at 82, victim of 8, youngest victims of, 12
Treason; during Revolutionary War, 22, 82, 368-71, convicted of, 24, supplying British, 28
Trial; military, 29, Negroes, 107
Triangle murder case, 352
Trunk murders, 327
"Turned off," 122, *see* hanging
Tyburn; crowds, 30, doggerel about hanging, 172, location of, 171, procession to, effect on public, 434
Types of gallows; 207, *see* gallows

U

U.S. Army manual; hanging, 173
United States Navy; executions, 5

V

Vermont;
hanging of David Redding, 28, hanging of Cyrus Dean, 45, Anne Freeze case, 323, Stephen Boorn case, 234
Victims; attitudes at the "tree," 48-51, lot made easy by hangman, 54, gravestone, 281, remarks of, 184, "tree", 8, *see* hanging of "tree", Salem, 136, youngest of "tree," 12
Vigilante hangings; 404
Virginia;
case of David Wright, 317-8, in colony of, 7, display of parts of condemned body, 96, hanged & quarters displayed, 95, hanging & dismemberment, 96, Vance case, 261, witches, 127
Voodoo; Tituba, Salem, Mass., 130

W

Walnut Street Jail; hanging in, 30, Ann Carson case, 309
Wardens; last requests of condemned from, 186
Washington;
type of rope, 168, Charles W. Nordstrom hanging, 166,
Water trap; scaffolds, 164-5, *see* gallows
West Jersey; rape in, 113
Wheelbarrow men; 120, hanging of, 118-9
Whipping-post; in Delaware, 440, public punishments, 19
Whiskey; hangmen, use before executions, 179
Witchcraft;
belief in, 128, disbelief in, 128, general comment, 100, hanged for, 120, indictment for, 132
Witches;
Connecticut 126, hanged not burned, 126, Massachusetts, 126, Middle Ages, 127, persons executed as, 127, Salem, general statement, 5, South Carolina, 126, treatment of, 126, Virginia 127
Witch Hill; Salem, Mass., 149
Witch hunt; Salem, story of, 150
Wizzardry; burned for, 126
Women; Colonial times, 54, dangerous sex of species, 344, hanged, 121, more prone to murder than men, 346, of the streets, 321,